THE RANDALL HOUSE BIBLE COMMENTARY

THE RANDALL HOUSE BIBLE COMMENTARY

ROMANS

by
F. LEROY FORLINES

FIRST EDITION

RANDALL HOUSE PUBLICATIONS
NASHVILLE, TENNESSEE 37217

RANDALL HOUSE BIBLE COMMENTARY, ROMANS

RANDALL HOUSE PUBLICATIONS
NASHVILLE, TN 37217
ISBN 0-89265-949-1

LIBRARY OF CONGRESS CATALOG CARD NUMBER:
86-62606

General Editor:
ROBERT E. PICIRILLI
Academic Dean, Free Will Baptist Bible College
Nashville, Tennessee

Associate Editor:
Harrold D. Harrison
Editor-in-Chief, Randall House Publications
Nashville, Tennessee

Acknowledgements

The author expresses thanks to these publishers for permission to quote from the following works:

Buswell, James Oliver, *A Systematic Theology of the Christian Religion*. Copyright© 1962, by Zondervan Publishing House. Used by permission.
Earle, Ralph, *Word Meanings In The New Testament*, Vol. III, Romans (Beacon Hill Press, 1974), used by permission.
Harrison, Everett F. *Romans In The Expositor's Bible Commentary,* Vol. X, Ed. by Frank E. Gaebelein, Romans—Galatians (Zondervan Publishing House, Copyright © 1976), used by permission.
Hendriksen, William, *Exposition of Paul's Epistle To The Romans* (Baker Book House 1980), Copyright owner William Hendriksen 1980, 81.
Lenski, R. C. H. *The Interpretation of St. Paul's Epistle To The Romans* (Copyright 1961, Augsburg Publishing House). Excerpts are reproduced by permission. 1974, by the Zondervan Corporation. Used by permission.
Murray, John, *The Epistle of Paul To The Romans,* Vols. I & II (Eerdman's Publishing Co., © Copyright 1982), used by permission.
The New International Dictionary of the Christian Church. Copyright © 1974, by the Zondervan Corporation. Used by permission.
Piper, John, *The Justification of God, An Exegetical and Theological Study of Romans 9:1-23* (Baker Book House 1983).
Yeager, Randolf O. *The Renaissance New Testament* Vol. II (Copyright 1983 by Randolf O. Yeager), used by permission of the publisher, Pelican Publishing Company, Inc.

Dedication

This commentary is dedicated to the memory of our grandson:

Stephen Parker Forlines
B. October 2, 1985 D. July 5, 1986
Parents: Jonathan and Susan Forlines

We were blessed with the presence of Stephen during a part of the time of writing this commentary. Soon after he was born, a problem presented itself which was later diagnosed as a very rare muscular disorder. Though his stay with us was short, through Stephen God touched and blessed many lives.

GENERAL EDITOR'S PREFACE

This volume on Romans, together with another on 1 and 2 Corinthians scheduled for publication at the same time, introduces a new series of Bible commentaries to be called The Randall House Bible Commentary. Several volumes covering the rest of the New Testament are in various stages of preparation and planning as these first volumes go to press. After the New Testament commentaries have been completed—a project that will occupy several years—attention will be turned to the Old Testament.

The entire project is being carried out by Randall House Publications, the publishing arm of the Department of Sunday School and Church Training of the National Association of Free Will Baptists. All the commentaries will be written by Free Will Baptists, but the publisher's aim is to produce works that will be of interest and help not only within the denomination but also for the Christian public at large.

I am pleased to serve as a general editor for the New Testament commentaries. Nothing interests me more than gaining and sharing understanding of what the Bible says. Those of us who are working on these volumes share an unclouded commitment to the fact that the Bible is the inerrant Word of God. That means that the Bible is God speaking. It means that the Bible has the authority to speak with the voice of God in governing our lives. How important, then, that we respect Him enough to determine exactly what He has said and how that is to be applied in Christian living. If any reader doubts that God can speak in human language in such a way that we can know truth about Him and about how we are to live, I recommend that section of the Introduction to Romans (in this volume) that is entitled "Approach to Interpreting the Bible."

These commentaries are not intended to be highly technical. Nor are they meant to be merely devotional. Our aim is to steer a course between these two kinds of commentaries, producing volumes that can be understood by the general Christian public and yet that seriously expound the text. Every writer is expected to comment with the Greek text before him, but to do so in a way that the reader who has not had formal instruction in Greek can understand what he says. Inasmuch as possible, technical comments about Greek words or syntax are put in parenthesis so that the reader may read around those comments if he wishes. Greek words are transliterated in English italics. (The commentaries are not meant to provide for detailed treatment of problems of textual criticism. In most cases, where significant manuscript differences exist, the variations are given enough attention that the reader will be able to understand what is involved.)

It is also our aim to be practical; above all, the Bible is to be lived. This concern for the practical should be manifested in the exposition of the text. It is also seen in the fact that each unit of material is followed by a section entitled "Application: Teaching and Preaching the Passage." These sections not only deal with practical application but also provide help for teachers and preachers of the Bible. Each unit of material also closes with a "Summary" that is intended to give an overview of what the text has been interpreted to mean.

We have tried not to clutter the exposition any more than necessary. For that reason, we have adopted the simplest possible method of identifying sources quoted. Only the last name of the author and the appropriate page number in his work are given. Complete lists of all the works thus cited are given in the bibliographies at the end of the commentaries.

As general editor it is my privilege, here, to describe for our readers the theological position that will be represented in all the volumes in this series. I welcome that opportunity, all the more because I know that various aspects of our position will be unfamiliar to many Christians outside our fellowship. Not as far as the "fundamentals" of the Christian faith are concerned. Free Will Baptists are firmly committed to the cardinal Christian doctrines: the classical Trinitarian doctrine; the virgin birth, deity, vicarious atonement, bodily resurrection, and literal second coming of Christ; salvation by grace involving the necessity of the new birth; permanent personal existence in Heaven or Hell; and so on. We are in the mainstream of the traditional Christian faith. We also share with many other groups the heritage of Baptists.

The part that some will find unfamiliar comes to light when I say that we are "Arminian," and then I hasten to qualify that. "Arminian" means many things to many people, and Free Will Baptists are not Arminian according to the meaning that many give the word. We are Arminians in the sense that Arminius himself was Arminian, in the sense that the original Remonstrance was Arminian. We are not Arminian as that movement developed in many circles.

Most Arminians espouse the "governmental" view of the atonement, for example. The article on Arminianism in Baker's *Evangelical Dictionary of Theology*, written by an Arminian, assumes that any who do not are inconsistent. Consistent or not, Free Will Baptists believe in the "divine satisfaction" view.

Arminians are at least accused of believing in salvation by works; we emphatically affirm that salvation is not by works but by grace alone, by faith alone, by the work of Christ alone—as did the Reformers.

Many Arminians believe in "entire sanctification." Free Will Baptists do not follow this Wesleyan addition to the original teachings of Arminius.

Some Arminians have "solved" the hard problems, for example, by denying the eternal election of individuals, or by denying that God foreknows the free acts of men, or by weakening depravity in a Pelagian or semi-Pelagian manner. We disavow such "solutions"; they do not help our cause at all.

If there were such a phrase, I would say that Free Will Baptists are "Reformed Arminian." I would immediately be accused of contradiction, of course. If I reminded my accuser that Arminius himself was Reformed, he would probably remind me in turn that Arminius' followers (after his death) were turned out of the Reformed Church. Even so, I think that many Christians will be at least a little surprised to learn that there are "Arminians" who believe in total depravity, in the eternal (conditional) election of individuals to salvation, in Christ's death as penal, substitutionary (universal) atonement that fully satisfied the just demands of a holy God for the infinite punishment of sin, in salvation (including perseverance in salvation) that is conditioned on faith and not on works or merit. Such is the position of the writers of the volumes in this series. Space does not allow elucidation here; I trust that the commentaries will provide, here and there, some elucidation—even though they are not intended to present "systematic theology."

There are disputed theological points that Free Will Baptists have no "official" position on. Prominent among these, for example, is eschatological detail. While we are all committed to a personal return of Christ to this earth, and to the attitude that all believers now should live with the consciousness that the Second Coming may be very near, a Free Will Baptist may be pre- or amillennial. On such points the writers are free to express whatever viewpoints they prefer.

In conclusion, I speak for myself, for the writers of these and subsequent volumes, and for the publishers when I say that the commentaries are published with prayerful desire that they will help believers—whether preachers or laymen—understand better what the Bible says and how to live under its authority. For these times, as for any times, that is the need for Christ's Church.

Robert E. Picirilli
Nashville, Tennessee 1986

AUTHOR'S PREFACE

It has been my privilege to teach Romans for about 30 years. It is my favorite book of the Bible. I count it a privilege to have had the opportunity to write this commentary.

When I read a commentary I like to know the theological view of the writer. If the reader shares my same concern, I invite him to read the "Preface" by the general editor, which is included in this volume. Further clarification of my personal theological views are given in the comments below and in the commentary itself.

In writing this commentary, I became even more impressed at Paul's burden for the Jews. I believe the main burden of Paul in 1:18—3:20 was to get the Jew to see that he was lost. Paul gave considerably more attention to the case against the Jew in 2:1—3:8 than he did the Gentile in 1:18-32.

Paul's burden in chapters 9, 10, and 11 was to get the unbelieving Jew to see that he was lost. He wanted him to see that salvation was not guaranteed to him simply because he was a Jew. He wanted the Jew to see that God was deeply interested in his salvation.

As distinguished from the dispensationalist who sees a disjunctive relationship between Israel and the church, I see a conjunctive relationship between Israel and the church. In fact, I see the church as a continuation of Israel. I think this viewpoint is clearly established by Paul in chapter 11. I think this view is also supported by the way Paul anchors salvation both for Jews and Gentiles in the Abrahamic Covenant in chapter 4.

It was my policy as near as was reasonably possible, where difference of opinion exists, to present the different viewpoints and to list some of the commentators who subscribed to each view. I have done this more consistently than any other commentary of my acquaintance on Romans. I believe that this feature of my commentary should make it of special value to students and to those who want to extend their study of Romans to other commentaries.

I have not failed to make clear what my position is where differences exist. I have not failed to criticize others where I thought such criticism was justifiable. I expect to be criticized by others. I have tried to be fair and accurate in what I have said about the views of others. If I have failed in this, I express my deepest regrets.

I deeply appreciate the untiring efforts of those who have written commentaries on Romans. I have benefited from their labors. I am in their debt. I trust God will use this commentary to help others understand this great treasury of truth which God gave to us through the Apostle Paul.

F. Leroy Forlines
Nashville, Tennessee 1986

CONTENTS

THE EPISTLE OF PAUL TO THE ROMANS

INTRODUCTION

While as Christians we hold every book in both the Old and New Testaments to be important, many have considered one particular book to be of special value to them. With many in the history of the church, Romans has been given this place of special value. Godet (1) in the "Introduction" to his *Commentary On The Epistle To The Romans* gives a brief summary of the esteem given to Romans in the history of the church:

> Coleridge calls the Epistle to the Romans 'the profoundest book in existence.' Chrysostom had it read to him twice a week. Luther, in his famous preface, says: 'This Epistle is the chief book of the New Testament, the purest gospel. It deserves not only to be known word for word by every Christian, but to be the subject of his meditation day by day, the daily bread of his soul... The more time one spends on it, the more precious it becomes and the better it appears.' Melanchthon, in order to make it perfectly his own, copied it twice with his own hand. It is the book which he expounded most frequently in his lectures. The Reformation was undoubtedly the work of the Epistle to the Romans, as well as that to the Galatians; and the probability is that every great spiritual revival in the church will be connected as effect and cause with a deeper understanding of this book.

Philip Schaff in the preface of the American edition of Lange's Commentary (v) says:

> The Epistle to the Romans is the Epistle of the Epistles, as the Gospel of John is the Gospel of the Gospels. It is the heart of the doctrinal portion of the New Testament. It presents in systematic order the fundamental truths of Christianity in their primitive purity, inexhaustible depth, all conquering force, and never failing comfort. It is the bulwark of the evangelical doctrines of sin and grace against the obscuration of the gospel, whether by judaizing bigotry or paganizing licentiousness.

While pointing out the high esteem given to Romans, Schaff (v) goes on to say:

> But it is certainly also the most difficult book in the New Testament, unless we except the Gospel of John and the Revelation... If St. Peter did not hesitate to state that there are 'some things hard to be understood' in the Epistles of his 'beloved brother Paul,' we need not be surprised that even such divines as occupy the same general platform widely differ in their interpretations. The Epistle to the Romans, more than any other, is a battlefield; and every chapter, especially the third, the fifth, the seventh, and the ninth, is contested ground.

Meyer (V:xii) with reference to the diligent effort required for a careful exegesis of Romans commented, "But on what portion of the New Testament could the labour and trouble...be less spared than on this, the grandest and richest in contents of all the Apostle's letters?"

INTRODUCTION

It should be obvious that a study of Romans deserves our most careful attention. Before beginning our exegesis of the text, let us now turn our attention to matters of introduction to the epistle.

The Author

While all of Paul's epistles have not fared so well in the hands of critics, the Pauline authorship of Romans has been almost uncontested in the history of the church. I will reserve further observations about Paul and make them as occasion calls for such in the exegesis of the book.

The Place and Date of the Writing

Our information concerning the place where Paul was located when he wrote Romans is based on the reference in 16:1 where he commends Phebe, whom we conclude was the bearer of the epistle. Paul pointed out that she was "a servant of the church which is at Cenchrea." Cenchrea was a port of Corinth. Therefore, we conclude that Paul wrote Romans while in Corinth.

It was during his third missionary journey while at Corinth that Paul wrote Romans. Paul did not go to Corinth until his second missionary journey (Acts 18). Between this visit and his next visit, which occurred on his third missionary journey (Acts 20:23), Paul wrote 1 Corinthians and 2 Corinthians. In 1 Cor. 16:1, 2, Paul asked the church at Corinth to lay aside an offering for the saints in Jerusalem. In 2 Cor. 8 and 9, he reminded them that he would be coming soon for this offering. In Rom. 15:26-28, Paul makes mention of the fact that he had the offering and would be taking it to Jerusalem. This information makes it clear that Romans was written during Paul's third missionary journey.

Having established that Romans was written on Paul's third missionary journey, our next concern is to determine the approximate year in which it was written. Dates usually range from A.D. 54 to A.D. 59.

In Acts 18:12-17 Paul appears before Gallio, the proconsul of Achaia. Based on an inscription with reference to Gallio found at Delphi and published early in this century, it is usually thought that Gallio was proconsul of Achaia about A.D. 52. There are some difficulties about fixing the exact year with absolute certainty. But we can have certainty within a year or two. Based on the date of Gallio and allowing for the time from Acts 18:7-12 to Acts 20:2,3, it is concluded that the date of the writing of Romans was probably as early as A.D. 56 or as late as A.D. 58. (See Cranfield 1:12, 13.)

The Occasion and Purpose

It is clear that one of the main contributing factors which led to Paul's writing of Romans was to prepare the way for his intended visit to Rome. He had desired for many years to go to Rome, but had been hindered by an unfinished task. He had finished planting churches in the major cities in the area covered by his missionary journeys, and felt that he was now free to move to greater horizons (Rom.1:13; 15:19-24). This epistle would prepare the Christians at Rome for his visit and hopefully create an interest in supporting his intended work in Spain.

There does not appear to have been any particular crisis in the church at Rome that Paul was addressing. However, there were problems that churches in those days would have confronted. Romans is a universal epistle. It would have been appropriate for almost any church. It is obvious that Paul had a compelling desire to write a developed and somewhat systematic treatment of the Christian faith. It is obvious that he wanted to give a developed treatment of the problems that plagued the church, particularly as these problems related to the Jewish-Gentile problems. What better place could he have sent such an epistle than to the capital city of the

Roman Empire from which its influence could spread?

The Origin of the Church

Nothing is known with absolute certainty about the beginning of the church at Rome. However, it is implied by Paul that there had been a church in Rome for several years prior to the writing of this epistle (Rom. 1:13; 15:23). It would have taken some time for the knowledge of the faith of the Christians at Rome to have made its way throughout the Roman Empire (Rom. 1:8; 16:19).

There have been basically three views set forth on the founding of the church at Rome. (1) That it was founded by the Apostle Peter and that he served as the first bishop for 25 years. (2) That the church at Rome was founded by the "strangers of Rome, Jews and proselytes" (Acts 2:10) who were in Jerusalem on the day of Pentecost. (3) That it was founded by various converts of Paul who had moved to Rome.

There is no evidence to support the view that Peter had been to Rome by the time of the writing of Romans. It appears from Acts 15 that he was still residing in Jerusalem at the time of the Jerusalem Council which was about A.D. 50. Further difficulty presents itself against this view. It was out of keeping with Paul's approach for him to build upon another man's foundation (Rom. 15:20). We can also rest assured that in greeting so many by name in chapter 16, Paul would surely have made reference to Peter if he were residing in Rome as bishop of the church at that time.

I think it can be assumed with reasonable certainty that no apostle or otherwise outstanding Christian leader went to Rome and founded the church in the same way it can be said that Paul founded churches on his missionary journeys. Rather, it would appear that converts as they returned to Rome found each other and would have met informally. In the course of time, they would have become organized with officers like other churches. Granting the history of the church and the organizational progress made in other places by this time, I think we can assume that the church at Rome was an organized church with officers by the time Paul wrote Romans.

Some may object to the position that the church at Rome was organized with officers at this time by saying that if so Paul would have given recognition to the bishop or pastor. However, it must be remembered that it was Paul's practice in his epistles to address the church as a group rather than address the church through its pastor. Philippians is the only epistle in which the bishops and deacons are included in the greeting (Phil. 1:1).

If the church at Rome developed from Christians returning to Rome and finding one another, and if the formal organization was a development which occurred in due time, it appears to me that the origin and development of the church at Rome could have drawn from a variety of sources. If we consider the arrival of the first Christians in Rome to be the date of the origin of the church in Rome, then we would most likely attribute the origin of the church to the "strangers of Rome, Jews and proselytes" (Acts 2:10) who would have been converted at Pentecost and would have returned to Rome. If on the other hand, we consider the time of the origin of the church to be the time when it was strong enough to be a viable group and would have taken on formal organization, by that time Paul's converts who went to Rome as well as other converts could have contributed to the founding of the church at Rome. It appears to me that this is the most likely explanation for the origin of the church at Rome.

The Composition of the Church

A reading of Romans makes it obvious that the church was made up of both

Jewish and Gentile converts. Opinions vary concerning which group was in the majority. Most have been of the opinion that the majority were Gentile converts. Based on the growth rate of converts among Gentiles as compared to Jews in other areas where the population was predominately Gentile, I think we can fairly assume that by the writing of Romans there would have been more Gentiles than Jews in the church. Many are of the opinion that when Paul expresses his desire to "have some fruit among you also, even as among other Gentiles" (Rom. 1:13) that he was implying that the church was largely made up of Gentiles.

I think that we can safely conclude by the attention given to the Jewish-Gentile problem that there was a significant number of Jews in the church. It is doubtful that Paul would have given so much attention to the Jewish-Gentile problem if there had been only a sprinkling of Jews in the congregation.

The Text

There has been some debate among scholars over whether the Romans' letter originally consisted of all 16 chapters. This problem grows out of the view that there were two shorter versions of Romans which were circulated. One of these, it is thought, ended at 14:23 while the other, is thought to have ended at 15:33.

There is strong support for the position that the original letter included all 16 chapters. There still needs to be an explanation of why shorter versions might have circulated.

Let us first address the reason for circulating a version that ended at 15:33 (if such were the case). As I have observed earlier, Romans by its very nature is a universal epistle. It is very likely that Paul might have desired that his most extensive treatment of the Christian faith be widely read. If this be the case, it can be easily seen that chapter 16, which for the most part consisted of greeting several of the Roman Christians by name, would not have been included in this wider circulation.

The wider circulation of Romans is made more plausible when we keep in mind that it was Paul's desire that at least some of his epistles should receive a wider readership than the church or churches to which the epistle was addressed. He directed the Colossians, "And when this epistle is read among you, cause that it be read also in the church of the Laodiceans; and that ye likewise read the epistle from Laodicea" (Col. 4:16). Also, it must be kept in mind that it has been widely accepted that Ephesians was a letter that was to be widely circulated, not just a letter to the church at Ephesus.

Concerning the possibility that a shorter version ended at 14:23, the opinion finds some support that Marcion in the second century shortened the text to suit his heterodox aims. This seems to be the opinion of Origen.

While critics have challenged the view that the original text included chapters 15 and 16, able scholars have defended the position that they were included in the original letter. I subscribe to this view. There is no existing Greek manuscript of Romans that would represent either of these shorter rescensions.

Approach to Interpreting the Bible

It does not fall within my purposes to become deeply involved in the controversies about what the Bible is, or how it is to be interpreted. However, in view of the conflict and confusion that exists, I do feel compelled to make a few observations.

Almost without fail, the average Christian of whatever persuasion believes that human language is capable of communicating knowledge about God and God's will for human beings. He is totally unaware of the fact that contemporary theology, as distinguished from conservative or orthodox theology, is generally agreed on the conclusion that human language is not capable of communicating truth about God.

Contemporary theology, as that term is used by theologians, does not simply refer to contemporary writings on theology. It refers to a modern or recent version of theology. Contemporary theology is either neo-orthodox theology or a shading up from neo-orthodox theology. There can be no real grasp of the difference between contemporary theology and orthodox theology without a grasp of these basic ideas that I am presenting.

Contemporary theology proceeds on the basis that God is "Wholly other" or so totally different from man that God is on an entirely different frequency from the frequency of man. The human quest for knowledge which falls within the framework of scientific investigation is viewed as the limit of rational knowledge. Scientific knowledge is rational reflection upon sense data aided by instruments of precision. That which does not fall within the sphere of scientific investigation (or empiricism) is considered to be in the realm of the irrational.

When it is said that that which is beyond empiricism is in the realm of the irrational, two things are involved: (1) Reason cannot discover such knowledge and (2) the law of non-contradiction cannot be applied to such knowledge. The law of non-contradiction means that two contradictory statements cannot both be true. One can be true, or both can be false, but two contradictory statements cannot both be true.

Certain things should be becoming obvious now. Knowledge of God is viewed by contemporary theologians as being outside the empirical or scientific realm, which for them means that it is in the realm of the irrational. Knowledge of God is not considered to be discoverable by reason, nor can the law of noncontradiction be applied to it. The human mind is thus forced into the intolerable position of believing that the contradictory can be true.

If knowledge of God is in the realm of the irrational, it is obvious that human language is inadequate as a vehicle to convey truth or information about God. Since the Bible comes to us in human language, the question arises: What is the Bible? In contemporary theology the Bible is not revelation. It is a witness to revelation. As a witness to revelation, God uses it to speak to man, but it never conveys information about God or a message from God to man.

This would mean that God's revelation is a personal revelation. That revelation comes as a personal encounter with Jesus Christ, but there is never a disclosure of information in that personal encounter. The writers of the N.T. bear witness to having had a personal encounter with Jesus Christ which was a personal revelation of God. This is a witness to us that God will reveal Himself to us through Jesus Christ. The writings of the N.T. also include reflections upon this encounter with God. These reflections are helpful in developing theological beliefs. However, these reflections of the N.T. writers never become an objective authority as a source of truth or a test of truth. The N.T. in contemporary theology is important; but remember, it is a *witness to* revelation, not revelation.

Contemporary theologians tend to look at the conservative or orthodox view of the Bible as a relic of the past. They are of the opinion that evolutionary views of the origin of the universe, earth, and man have been well enough established by scientific research to invalidate the view set forth in Genesis 1 and 2. They are also of the opinion that higher criticism has devastated the orthodox view of the authorship of certain books in the Bible.

For example, they reject the Mosaic authorship of the Pentateuch. They reject the single authorship of Isaiah. They accept a date for Daniel that will make it deal more with history than prophecy. None of this disturbs the contemporary theologian because the complete truthfulness of Scripture is not in any way essential to his view. In fact, to accept the complete truthfulness of Scripture would totally devastate his whole approach.

Contemporary theology can be handled in such a way as to be far more illusive than the liberalism of the early part of this century. Liberalism at that time denied the miraculous in Scripture which put it in conflict with the virgin birth, the miracles of Christ, and the bodily resurrection. The contemporary theologian is obligated by his approach neither to accept nor reject these. Opinions differ on these matters from one theologian to another. Where the illusiveness comes in is when a Biblical scholar is trying to maintain acceptance in a movement that is basically conservative or evangelical. He can answer questions in such a way that he can convince the masses that he is upholding the Bible and has not departed from the time-honored views of his denomination.

It should not be surprising that a person who does not believe that God has communicated information about Himself in the Bible would not believe that God has given us an inerrant account of matters relating to science, history, and geography. According to them, God has given us no information at all. Such people confuse many by claiming to believe the infallibility of the Bible. They speak of its adequacy. Basically what they believe is in the instrumental value of the Bible to be used in the salvation encounter with God. But at no point does the Bible impart content revelation.

Contemporary theology will never be communicated to the masses. It is on a different wave length from the way the masses think. Only the highly trained who spend an unusual amount of time will ever know exactly what these theologians are trying to communicate. What comes down to the masses will tend to be a watered down or corrupted version of the Christian message, but it will not be an understanding of what the contemporary theologian has in mind. Contemporary theology has many varying shades, but I believe that what I say is generally characteristic of it.

I believe that we can have a rational knowledge of God and that human language can convey truth from God about God, about man, and the universe. God is a personal God who can speak and act. He has acted in creating the universe and man. He has created man in His own image (Gen. 1:26). The image of God in man means that man is rational (Col. 3:10) and moral (Eph. 4:24). The fact that man is rational and moral means that he is a personal being.

Both God and man are rational and moral, or personal beings. My difference with contemporary theology does not come at the point of the inability of scientific or empirical reasoning to unveil the mind of God and discover the plan of God. Paul confirms such a limitation in 1 Cor. 2:9. God is not perceivable by the five senses. The fact that God is a personal being means that He cannot be known unless He chooses to make Himself known. At the same time God, as a personal being, can speak. By the design of man as created he is able to receive and understand God's revelation. According to Paul, what man could not know by empirical reasoning, nor by philosophical reasoning based on empirical data, God has revealed to us (1 Cor. 2:9).

I will wait until the question of general revelation presents itself in Romans 1 before I deal with that subject. My concern here is with special revelation. That revelation has come to us through the Bible and Jesus Christ. Jesus Christ is presented to us in the Bible. God's revelation has come to us in human language.

A rational God has created the universe. He has created man. He has spoken to man. He has made it possible for man to have a rational comprehension of God, himself, and the created order. All of this means that we can have a systematic theology and a Christian world view.

I am not at this point trying to avoid the fact that man has suffered from the fall, but I do want to say that man did not cease to be a rational creature in the fall. I do not deny the necessity of regeneration and the indwelling Holy Spirit for man to develop a thoroughly Christian world view and a systematic theology. This brief treatment will suffice here.

Some declare the human mind and language inadequate to understand and communicate truth about God. Based on the Bible's own statement, they refer to:

For my thoughts are not your thoughts, neither are your ways my ways, saith the LORD. For as the heavens are higher than the earth, so are my ways higher than your ways, and my thoughts than your thoughts (Is. 55:8, 9).

To claim to know truth about God is not the same as claiming to have exhaustive knowledge of God. We do not have an exhaustive knowledge of God. We do not have an exhaustive knowledge of human beings, but that is not the same as saying that we do not have any true knowledge of human beings. Also, it might be pointed out that if human language cannot convey information about God, Is. 55:8,9 did not say anything about God.

Having set forth my conviction that God's revelation (or God's Word) has come to us in human language, let us now turn our attention to the significance of this observation for our approach to interpreting the Word of God. It is a very simple observation, but an exceedingly important one to observe that the Bible uses language the same way we do in ordinary speech and writing. This means that a noun is a noun, a verb is a verb, an adjective is an adjective, etc. It means we must know the meaning of the words used just like we do in human communications. In other communications, background and context are important. The same is true of Scripture. If it is not immediately obvious what the meaning is in other communications, we give careful examination to the words used and how the thought is developed. The same is true with Scripture. In other words, *we use the normal approach to interpreting language when we interpret the Bible.*

The approach has been called the grammatico-historical method of interpretation. This means that we interpret the Bible in keeping with the laws of grammar and the historical context.

The most common designation for the approach that I have set forth is literal interpretation. When people say that they believe in the literal interpretation of the Bible, they simply mean that what it says is true. They do not mean to deny that the Bible makes use of figurative language. The proponents of literal interpretation recognize that the Bible has both literal and figurative language. While I agree with what is intended by literal interpretation, I admit that it is a bit awkward to talk about the literal interpretation of figurative language. Another problem is that the critics have been able to confuse some people by trying to make it look like those who believe in the literal interpretation do not recognize the place of figures of speech. This is usually done by the opponents of inerrancy. They talk about the absurdity of thinking of Jesus as a literal door. The advocates of literal interpretation are well aware of the fact that to refer to Jesus as a door is a metaphorical expression.

INTRODUCTION

The questions that we need to answer for ourselves and the questions we need to pose to others to find out where they stand on Scripture are: (1) Is human language capable of conveying truth about God? (2) Do we have rational knowledge of God and His will for us, i.e., is this knowledge subject to the law of non-contradiction? (3) Is the Bible the Word of God in human language? (4) Do we arrive at the meaning of the Bible by applying the normal laws of interpretation?

The interpreter of the Bible must at all times keep in mind that the main theme of the Bible is the redemption that God has provided through Jesus Christ. This redemption is designed not only to give forgiveness of sins, but also to aid man in developing a meaningful experience (Jn. 10:10; 8:32; 1 Tim. 4:8). God's revelation is aimed at ministering to human need. When we study the Bible, we must be concerned about how its message relates to human need. It is necessary to know the meaning of words and the Biblical context, but we must also keep in mind the context of the commonality of human experiences from one time to another and from one culture to another. The interpreter of the Bible must be acquainted with life as well as word meanings and the logical development of thought. The Bible must be studied in the arena of life. There must be an interaction of the Bible and life. Our aim must go beyond the level of winning a debate over the meaning of controversial passages or helping in the understanding of difficult passages. Our aim must be to minister to people's needs through the discovery and presentation of truth.

OUTLINE OF ROMANS

PART ONE

GOD'S PROVISION OF RIGHTEOUSNESS: ITS NEED, MEANING, AND IMPLICATIONS (1:1-8:39)

I. Paul's Introduction (1:1-17)
II. Man's Failure to Be Righteous Before God (1:18-3:20)
III. God's Provision of Righteousness for Those Who Have Failed (3:21-5:21)
IV. God's Provision of a New Life for Those Who Receive the God-Provided Righteousness (6:1-7:6)
V. A Rejection of the Idea That Deliverance From the Law Through a God-Provided Righteousness Implies That the Law Is Sinful (7:7-25)
VI. The Glorious Blessings of the Person Who Has Received the God-Provided Righteousness (8:1-39)

PART TWO

ISRAEL AND THE GENTILES IN GOD'S PLAN OF REDEMPTION (9:1-11:36)

I. God's Sovereign Right in Rejecting the Unbelieving Israelites (9:1-29)
II. Human Responsibility in Acceptance and Rejection by God (9:30-10:21)
III. The Present and Future of Israel and the Gentiles in the Program of God (11:1-36)

PART THREE

PRACTICAL INSTRUCTIONS AND PERSONAL REMARKS (12:1-16:27)

I. Instructions in the Practical Aspects of the Christian Life (12:1-15:13)
II. Personal Remarks (15:14—16:27)

The Epistle Of Paul To The Romans

Commentary

Part One

God's Provision of Righteousness: Its Need, Meaning, and Implications (1:1—8:39).

I. PAUL'S INTRODUCTION (1:1-17).

A. Paul Greets The Christians at Rome (1:1-7).

1. Paul introduces himself (v. 1).

1 Paul, a servant of Jesus Christ, called *to be* an apostle, separated unto the gospel of God,

As was the custom in those days, Paul identified himself by name at the outset of the letter rather than at the end as our custom is today. The first mark of identification after giving his name was to refer to himself as **a servant of Jesus Christ**. The word "servant" is translated from the word (Greek *doulos*) which means a slave. By referring to himself as a slave of Jesus Christ, Paul did not intend to imply any negative connotations that went with the term slave. It was simply an expressive way of recognizing that he belonged to Jesus Christ and was submitted to Him. It was not an undesirable relationship, rather a desirable one. Paul gladly submitted himself to Jesus Christ and announced this relationship to others.

Called to be an apostle. The words *to be* are italicized. In the translation of the King James, the translators chose to use italics to show when there were no Greek words from which the words are translated. In translating from one language to another, it is frequently necessary to supply words that are not in the other language to make the meaning clear. However, if we know words are supplied not based on Greek words, an approach to translation without the italicized words may be preferred. This in no way reflects on the inspiration of Scriptures (whether to use or not use the supplied words in a given case). There is agreement on this among all who work with the Greek N.T. and the Hebrew O.T.

The translation—**called to be an apostle** focuses on the idea that the object or aim of this calling was for Paul to become an apostle. Another way of translating it is "a called apostle." This would mean an apostle by calling. If we take this approach, Paul is stressing the fact that the idea of his being an apostle did not originate with him. He was not so presumptuous as to intrude into the office of apostleship. He was called by Jesus Christ. This seems to be the true meaning. Paul stresses the idea that his apostleship was "not of men, neither by man, but by Jesus Christ, and God the Father" in Gal. 1:1.

The word *apostle* (Greek *apostolos*) means "sent one." An apostle is authorized or commissioned for his work. He is sent with a message.

The word *apostolos* is used in both a general and a special sense in the N.T. In the general sense, it could refer to people who were sent by churches as messengers (2 Cor. 8:23; Phil. 2:25). In the general sense of the word, those who were sent by the early church as itinerate missionaries were apostles sent by the churches.

In the special sense of the word it was applied to the twelve apostles, Paul, and a few more. There is no general agreement concerning who should be added to this list other than The Twelve and Paul. We need not concern ourselves here with an exact list of those who were considered apostles in the special sense. It is clear that Paul, when he referred to himself as an apostle, was referring to himself as an apostle in the special sense of the word.

There were certain qualifications that were required of one to be an apostle in the special sense. (1) It was necessary for him to have seen the risen Christ so he could be a witness of the resurrection (Acts 1:21, 22; 1 Cor. 9:1). Paul met this requirement (1 Cor. 15:8). (2) It was necessary for the claim of apostleship to be authenticated by miraculous signs from God. Paul passed the test at this point (2 Cor. 12:12). (3) It was necessary for him to be called of God to the office of apostleship. Paul claimed to have had such a call. If he had made a false claim, such could have been shown. While not every one whose ministry was accompanied by miraculous signs was an apostle, it is evident that God would not have borne witness to a false claim to be an apostle with miraculous signs.

In the special sense, an apostle was able to speak with authority directly from God. In the special sense, the office of apostleship ceased to exist when the N.T. apostles died. Our authority is not directly from God, but from God through the Bible. A hearer has a right to test the truth of our message by the Word of God as it has come to us in Scripture.

Separated unto the gospel of God. The gospel is good news or glad tidings from God to man. While the major stress on Paul's separation to the gospel is on the proclamation of the gospel, it probably includes a more complete identification of Paul with the gospel. Paul's life, his thought, and his message were so thoroughly identified with the gospel of God that a person could not think about Paul without thinking about the gospel.

2. He identifies the gospel (vv.2, 3).

2 (Which he had promised afore by his prophets in the holy scriptures,)
3 Concerning his Son Jesus Christ our Lord, which was made of the seed of David according to the flesh.

Which he had promised afore by his prophets in the holy scriptures. Paul makes it clear that the gospel of God which he preached had not suddenly appeared on the scene without any prior preparation. It had been promised by the O.T. prophets and was a fulfillment of that promise.

It is unthinkable that an event as important as the birth, life, death, and resurrection of Christ would suddenly be thrust upon the world without any prior preparation. While it is certain that Paul's reference to the O.T. promise of the gospel was important for Jews, it was also important for Gentiles. The Gentiles needed to know that the gospel was fulfillment of a redemptive movement of God that had already been at work in history.

We find it hard sometimes to understand why God waited as long as He did before sending Christ, but we can accept the fact that it was that way. We could not have believed in Christ if there had been no prior preparation. Even a limited knowledge that God prepared the way for the coming of Christ, as revealed in the O.T., contributes to the possibility of our having a rationally consistent faith.

Concerning his Son. Verse 3 is grammatically tied in with v.1."Concerning his Son" is a further development of what was involved in the gospel of God.

It was good news from God about His Son.

Jesus Christ our Lord. Recent translations place these words at the end of v. 4 rather than in v. 3 as it appears in the King James. This makes no change in the meaning of the passage. The only question is whether these words appeared in the original manuscript in v. 3 or at the end of v. 4. Studies in Greek manuscripts have led the majority of Greek scholars to believe that it was originally at the end of v. 4. Either place we put it, the Lordship of Jesus Christ is clearly declared. It was out of his recognition of Jesus Christ as Lord that Paul referred to himself as a slave of Jesus Christ.

3. He identifies Jesus Christ (vv. 3, 4).

3 Concerning his Son Jesus Christ our Lord, which was made of the seed of David according to the flesh;
4 And declared *to be* the Son of God with power, according to the spirit of holiness, by the resurrection from the dead.

Which was made of the seed of David according to the flesh. The reference here is to the human nature of Christ. The recognition of Jesus as the seed of David is very important. The time of David marked an important point in the history of Messianic prophecy. Prior to the time of David, there were only six references made to a personal Redeemer or Messiah (Job 19:25; Gen. 49:10; Num. 24:19; Dt. 18:15, 18; 1 Sam. 2:10; 2:35). The Covenant God made with David was the first in the history of redemption which brought into clear focus and created a popular awareness of a coming Messiah. He was to be King forever on David's throne (2 Sam. 7:12-16; 1 Chr. 17:11-14). Jesus could not have been recognized as the promised Messiah if He had not been of the seed of David. Linking Jesus Christ and the gospel with the O.T., wherever it is found, aids not only the Jew, but also the Gentile in experiencing faith in Jesus Christ.

And declared to be the Son of God with power. Grammatically, the words "with power" could be related either to "declared" to or the "Son of God." If it is related to *declared*, it would mean that He was declared with power "...by the resurrection from the dead." In other words, the resurrection of Christ served as a powerful declaration of the fact that He is the Son of God.

If *with power* modifies "the Son of God," He would be the Son of God with power. Either interpretation would be theologically correct, but we cannot take "with power" to modify both "declared" and "the Son of God." It seems to me that the most likely interpretation is to understand "with power" to modify "the Son of God."

The word for power used here is Greek *dunamis*. In Mt. 28:18 Jesus said, "All power is given unto me...." The word used there (Greek *exousia*) means authority. *Dunamis* means inherent power or ability. It is frequently translated "miracle" in the N.T. Jesus has both authority and power. By His *dunamis* (power) Jesus worked miracles. By His *exousia* (authority) He drove the moneychangers out of the Temple.

According to the spirit of holiness. The expression "the spirit of holiness" has been interpreted in different ways. The problem centers around the fact that the expression is found nowhere else in the N.T. Apart from a careful study, almost anyone would assume the "spirit of holiness" refers to the Holy Spirit. Once commentators have made a thorough study, a division of opinions results. There are able defenders of the view that the expression means the Holy Spirit. For those interested in a defense of this position, I recommend the treatments given by Bruce (73) and Cranfield (62-64).

Others, upon careful study, have interpreted "the spirit of holiness" to refer to the Divine nature of Christ. This is the view which I accept. It is obvious both in Greek and English that a parallel construction is seen between "according to the flesh" of v. 3 and "according to the spirit of holiness" in v. 4. **According to the flesh** clearly refers to the human nature of Christ. Flesh is used to refer to the whole nature of Christ. It is obvious that flesh refers to the whole human nature, not just his physical body. That does not mean that the human nature of Christ was restricted to flesh. Flesh is used here as a synechodoche. A synechdoche is a figure of speech in which the part is given for the whole or the whole is given for the part. In this case the part is given for the whole. Flesh is intended, then, to represent the whole human nature—flesh and spirit, or body, soul, and spirit.

If we follow through on the implication of the parallel construction between "according to the flesh" and "according to the spirit of holiness," we would conclude that the first refers to the human nature of Christ, and the second refers to the Divine nature of Christ. Both the words "spirit" and "holiness" are clearly applicable to the Divine nature of Christ. For a defense of this view, see Hodge (20), Lange (62), Liddon (4), and Olshausen (66, 67).

A few commentators have understood "the spirit of holiness" to refer to holiness of the human nature of Christ which transcended the holiness of other human beings. Among the advocates of this view are Earle 16, Sanday and Headlam 9.

By the resurrection from the dead. It was by Christ's resurrection from the dead that He was declared to be the Son of God with power. Miracles in the N.T. had a sign value; i.e., they had theological significance. The miracles of Christ were a sign of the fact that God stamped His approval on Jesus Christ. His claims and teachings were thereby confirmed as being true (Acts 2:22; Jn. 20:30, 31). The miracle of the resurrection of Christ is the miracle of miracles. By the resurrection of Christ, God gave Him the clearest possible stamp of approval. If Jesus had remained in the tomb, all of His claims would have been voided. When God raised Him from the dead, He declared in no uncertain terms that He is the Son of God.

4. He states the purpose of his apostleship (v. 5).

5 By whom we have received grace and apostleship, for obedience to the faith among all nations, for his name.

By whom we have received grace and apostleship. "By whom" refers to Jesus Christ. Jesus Christ was both the source of the grace (or unmerited favor) of Paul's redemption as well as the source of his apostleship.

For obedience to the faith. One of the most difficult matters in translation from one language to another is the use or nonuse of articles. The Greeks used articles when we do not. This problem is of such great proportion that while the King James translators italicized other words where there was no Greek word from which they are translated, they did not italicize articles when there was no article in the Greek. For this reason the only way we can know whether an article was in the Greek is to check it ourselves, or have someone check it for us. The same holds true for all other translations.

Our translation reads "obedience to the faith." However, there is no article in the Greek. A literal translation would be "obedience of faith." There is a debate over whether, in this case, it should be translated with or without the article. I am of the opinion that with very few exceptions in the N.T. we should translate the article before faith, and if it has no article we should not insert one before faith in the English translation.

The presence of the article in the Greek means that "the faith" is the body of truth we believe. For example, "contend for the faith" (Jude 3) means to contend for the truth revealed in the N.T.

The absence of the article before faith refers to the experience of believing. For example, when we speak of having faith in Christ, we are referring to the experience of faith. Attention will be called to the presence or absence of the article with faith in Romans as the study progresses.

The most likely meaning of "obedience of faith" is obedience which is faith. Faith in the Greek is in the genitive case. To understand the meaning to be obedience which is faith would be understanding the genitive to be the genitive of apposition. Faith in this case would be obedience. This is not equating faith with good works. It simply views faith as obedience to the gospel when it calls on us to believe in Jesus Christ. For a listing and discussion of other possible interpretations see Cranfield (66, 67), Godet (82), Hodge (21, 22), and Lange (63).

The meaning of the preposition "for" (Greek *eis*) as translated here denotes purpose. The purpose of Paul's apostleship was to get people to obey or believe the gospel.

Among all nations. The word "nations" (Greek *ethnos*) is in the plural form. If an American citizen refers to "the nation" without further qualification, he is referring to the United States. If he refers to the nations, he will most likely be referring to the nations other than the United States.

A similar development took place in Israel. After they became a nation, a reference to "the nation" by an Israelite was a reference to the nation of Israel. A reference to "the nations" was a reference to all who were not Israelites. Since Israel was the only nation which was in a covenant relationship to Yahweh (Jehovah), other nations worshiped other gods and were thus pagan or heathen. The expression "the nations" in the Biblical context usually carries with it a religious connotation. The plural is translated frequently "Gentiles" and a few times "heathen."

It is significant to observe that when the Great Commission commanded making disciples of all nations (Matt. 28:19), it was a commission to Jewish apostles to become involved in aggressive evangelism among the Gentiles. This marked a new phase in God's program of redemption.

In the O.T. the nation of Israel had as its major responsibility the maintaining of its distinction as the covenant people of Yahweh. They were to be a witness to other nations, but they were not commanded to become involved in an aggressive program of converting the Gentiles. Jesus, Himself, said that He was "not sent but unto the lost sheep of the house of Israel" (Mt. 15:24). He expressed reluctance in the few contacts He had with those who were not Jews. This was not because He did not love them, but the preparation and timing had not come for the aggressive move among the Gentiles.

The Great Commission was the first aggressive move for a large scale work to be done among the Gentiles. This command to aggressively evangelize the Gentiles was not immediately implemented. This was not set in motion until Peter preached to Cornelius (Acts 10:34-48). It was a difficult decision for Peter to make. He required clearcut evidence that God was actually asking him to preach the gospel to the Gentiles (Acts 10:1-33). A period of seven or eight years passed between the Great Commission and the beginning of its implementation by the preaching of Peter to Cornelius.

This strikes us as hard to understand. Why was there such a delay? It is hard for us to grasp the impact that had been made upon the Jews about their separateness from the Gentiles. Some of this was based on Divine instruction and some on Jewish bias and misunderstanding. That justification was by faith in Jesus Christ had to be clearly established among Jewish Christians. The transition of thought from the O.T. way to the N.T. way was hard for Jewish believers to make. The aggressive involvement of Jews with Gentile evangelism was hard for them to grasp based on their background experiences.

Keep these things in mind as we study the Jewish-Gentile problems raised by Paul. Paul gives much attention to the Jewish-Gentile problem because only 15 years passed between the preaching of Peter to Cornelius and the writing of Romans by Paul. Also, it had been only 6-8 years since the Jerusalem Council (Acts 15) dealt with the question of Gentile circumcision.

Paul, as the apostle to the Gentiles (or the nations), played the major role in setting in motion God's program of aggressive evangelism of the Gentiles. At the same time he maintained a deep interest in the conversion of the Jews. This thrust him into a deep involvement of what it meant for Jews and Gentiles to become N.T. Christians. He was also deeply involved in the practical problems of how Jewish and Gentile Christians related to one another.

For his name. Paul's primary motivation in winning converts among the Gentiles was "for his name" or that God's name might be honored, exalted, and glorified. The aim of God's program is "*that* every tongue should confess that Jesus Christ *is* Lord, to the glory of God the Father" (Phil. 2:11). That should also be our aim.

5. He identifies and greets the recipients of the epistle (vv. 6, 7).

6 Among whom are ye also the called of Jesus Christ:
7 To all that be in Rome, beloved of God, called *to be* saints: Grace to you and peace from God our Father, and the Lord Jesus Christ.

Among whom are ye also. This is a recognition of the fact that a large number of the church at Rome were Gentiles. They were among the believers from all nations.

The called of Jesus Christ. They were Jesus Christ's called ones. They belonged to Him. For the last almost 2,000 years the Gentiles have far outnumbered Jewish converts. We have become so accustomed to this that it does not amaze us anymore. However, Paul was amazed that there was an aggressive program of evangelism among the Gentiles. He was amazed and they were too that they could be referred to as Jesus Christ's called ones.

To all that be in Rome. Paul at last identifies the recipients of the epistle to be the Christians at Rome. It is *all* the Christians at Rome who are being addressed. This includes both Jews and Gentiles. The epistle was not just to the leaders. It was not just to Paul's acquaintances. It was to all in Rome who knew Jesus Christ.

Beloved of God. They were all objects of God's love.

Called to be saints. The same observations can be made here about the italicized words "to be" that were made in v.1. They were saints by calling. They had not intruded as uninvited guests. They were saints by Divine right. They had been called. "Saints" is a translation of the word (Greek *hagios*) which means holy.

They were God's holy ones. All believers are saints. We are set apart for God's use. This we are positionally. It is expected that we will be experientially separated from sin, conformed to righteousness, and dedicated to God. The primary thrust of holiness is dedication to God, but there can be no movement toward God without a movement away from sin. The very nature of God makes it so that to move in His direction is to move away from sin.

"Grace" was the greeting used in the Western world, while "peace" was the greeting used in the Eastern world. Paul combines the two greetings. Grace is the objective source of blessings from God. Peace is the subjective experience of blessings from God.

When Paul connects "from God our Father, and the Lord Jesus Christ" as the source of grace and peace, it is obvious that he is stressing the equality of the Father and His Son, thus recognizing the deity of Christ.

B. Paul Expresses His Personal Concern for the Christians at Rome (1:8-16).

1. He expresses thankfulness for their testimony (v.8).

8 First, I thank my God through Jesus Christ for you all, that your faith is spoken of throughout the whole world.

First, I thank my God through Jesus Christ for you all. At this point, Paul becomes more personal in his comments. He expressed his gratitude to God for the saints at Rome. Telling them of his gratitude to God conveyed how deeply he appreciated them.

Paul's expression of gratitude to God for the saints at Rome was the natural application of Christian principles and values to the situation. Paul had many negative concerns, but he did not allow negative concerns to keep him from acknowledging and appreciating the positive. He was able to count his blessings.

The practice of thanksgiving contributed to Paul's happiness and mental wellbeing as he faced the stresses of life. The expression of this gratitude also contributed to the wellbeing of others. It also served to help establish a good working relationship between Paul and the people.

Anyone who has given attention to a study of human personality and human relationships knows the importance of thanksgiving for the person himself and for interpersonal relationships. It is important that we, as Christians, not simply express gratitude because it works and because it helps in getting along with others. We must practice thanksgiving because it is the Christian thing to do. The rewards will follow.

That your faith is spoken of throughout the whole world. The same observation is made in Rom. 16:19a where Paul said, "For your obedience is come abroad unto all *men*." Paul was thankful that knowledge of believers in Rome had spread throughout the world. The world, as it was known to him, would have been the Roman Empire. This news would have traveled as it did for two reasons. (1) People would have been interested in what was taking place in the capital city of the empire. (2) It was said that all roads lead to Rome. It was natural that significant news events would travel more broadly from Rome than other less important cities.

2. He expresses his desire to visit the Christians at Rome (vv. 9, 10).

9 For God is my witness, whom I serve with my spirit in the gospel of his Son, that without ceasing I

make mention of you always in my prayers;
10 Making request, if by any means now at length I might have a prosperous journey by the will of God to come unto you.

For God is my witness. This is a way of saying, "God will back me up in what I am about to say."

Whom I serve with my spirit in the gospel of his Son. Of the word (Greek *latreuo*) translated "serve," Picirilli (11) says:

> The word for 'serve' here is not the usual one which means bond-service. This word means priestly service. And this is the reason for the phrase 'with my spirit.' Paul does not minister as did the Old Testament priests in physical ordinances and sacrifices of flesh. But he offers spiritual sacrifices; he performs a spiritual service in the realm of the gospel of Christ. The New Testament pictures all believers as priests and everything they do for God as spiritual sacrifices (see Phil. 4:8 and Heb. 13:15, 16, for example).

That without ceasing I make mention of you always in my prayers. In 1 Th. 5:17 Paul said, "Pray without ceasing." Many people have been bothered about the meaning of "without ceasing" and "always." They have felt an obligation to understand *without ceasing* and *always* in an absolute sense. It is obvious that nobody prays 24 hours a day. Even if he did, he would not be praying for the same thing all the time. Some, in order to hold on to an absolute meaning, have said that the meaning of praying without ceasing means to be always in an attitude of prayer where praying would be the natural thing to do when the occasion calls for it.

I think the answer is much simpler. We need not interpret "without ceasing" and "always" in the absolute sense. The Bible uses language the same way we do in ordinary speech and writing. When we say of someone, "He is always sticking his foot in his mouth," we mean that he does it frequently or he has a habit of doing it. In such an expression no one would even consider interpreting always in the absolute sense.

Paul made mention of the Roman Christians frequently or regularly in his prayers. Frequently or regularly is what is meant for us in the matter of praying without ceasing. Vine (179) in his *Expository Dictionary of New Testament* Words, says concerning "without ceasing," (Greek *adialeiptos*): "used...not of what is not interrupted, but of that which is constantly recurring."

Making request, if by any means now at length I might have a prosperous journey by the will of God to come unto you. With reference to "a prosperous journey by the will of God to come unto you," a more common understanding of the Greek would be "prospered by the will of God to come unto you." The difference in interpretation would be: (1) "A prosperous journey by the will of God" would refer to Paul's safety and wellbeing as he makes the trip to Rome. (2) "Prospered by the will of God to come unto you" would be a prayer that it would soon be God's will for Paul to go to Rome.

"Prospered by the will of God" is preferred and suits the context better. It seems clear at this point that Paul desired that it would soon be the will of God for him to go to Rome. This fits the idea of "making request, if by any means now at length" or "at last." Paul's urgency as expressed in his prayers was that God would soon make it so his trip to Rome would take place.

3. He tells why he wishes to visit them (vv.11, 12).

11 For I long to see you, that I may impart unto you some spiritual gift, to the end ye may be established;
12 That is, that I may be comforted together with you by the mutual faith both of you and me.

For I long to see you, that I may impart unto you some spiritual gift. The word for "gift" (Greek *charisma*) is modified by the word "spiritual." It is used in Rom. 12:6 to refer to those gifts which equip believers for service. It is used in 1 Cor. 12 to refer to both miraculous (sign) and nonmiraculous (nonsign) gifts.

The question before us is: Does Paul have in mind either the nonsign gifts for service or the signgifts where the miraculous was involved? Some automatically conclude that either or both are involved simply because the word "gift" (Greek *charisma)* is modified by "spiritual."

It will be helpful to examine the various uses of the word *charisma* in the N.T. The other occurrences of this word in Romans are 5:15, 16; 6:23; 11:29; and 12:6. In 5:15, 16 the reference is to the gift of justification. In 6:23 it refers to the gift of eternal life. What is meant by gift in 11:29 is not made specifically clear. In 1 Cor. 1:7 it seems to have a broad meaning. First Cor. 7:7 refers to the gift of God in enabling the person who has the gift to remain unmarried without burning with lust. In 2 Cor. 1:11, the word means gift in a general sense. The word refers to spiritual gifts in the limited sense in Rom. 12:6; 1 Cor. 12:4, 9, 28, 31; 1 Tim. 4:14; 2 Tim. 1:6; and 1 Pet. 4:10.

Thus far it has been established that "gift" (Greek *charisma*) does not always have a specialized meaning. It sometimes has the same general meaning that our word "gift" has. We should also point out that where spiritual gifts in the specialized sense are referred to, other Greek words are sometimes used. In Eph. 3:7 a different word (Greek *dorea*) is used to refer to spiritual gifts. In Eph. 4:8 another word (Greek *doma*) refers to spiritual gifts. It is evident that Paul had essentially the same meaning in mind in those verses that he did in other places by using *charisma*. In Heb. 2:4 the word translated gift (Greek *merismos*) means distributions.

We can conclude from this evidence that the simple occurrence of the word "gift" (Greek *charisma*) modified by spiritual does not mean that it must have a specialized meaning. The meaning is much the same if Paul had said that he wanted to be a spiritual blessing to the people when he visited them.

To the end ye may be established. Paul's desire was to impart to them some spiritual gift. This does not imply any special need of the Roman Christians. It is a desire that Paul would have had any time he visited a church. As Hodge (26) explains:

> This includes not only an increase of confidence in their belief of the gospel, but an increase of strength in their religious feelings, and in their purpose and power of obedience. Comp. 1 Thessalonians iii.2; I sent Timothy 'to establish you, and to comfort you concerning your faith.' And 2 Thessalonians ii. 17, 'Now our Lord Jesus Christ comfort your hearts, and stablish you in every good word and work.'

That is, that I may be comforted together with you by the mutual faith both of you and me. Paul wanted his visit to be a benefit or blessing to the saints at Rome, and also expected to be blessed by their faith. It is important for those in leadership roles to let other Christians know that they are a blessing. The blessing is a two-way street.

4. He explains why he had not been sooner (v. 13).

13 Now I would not have you ignorant, brethren, that oftentimes I purposed to come unto you, (but was let hitherto,) that I might have some fruit among you also, even as among other Gentiles.

I would not have you ignorant, brethen, that oftentimes I purposed to come unto you, (but was let hitherto,). The word "let" means hindered. The word "let" which means to permit or allow is a different word altogether. The word "let" as used in this verse is no longer in use in our language (see *The Oxford English Dictionary*).

We learn from Rom. 15:19-24 what had hindered Paul from visiting the people earlier. It was not a Satanic hindrance. Rather, it was the hindrance of an unfinished task (vv. 20-22). In 15:23 he said, "But now having no more place in these parts." By "these" Paul meant from Jerusalem to Illyricum (v. 19). He felt that he had completed his assignment of planting churches in these areas and was now ready to move on to other places. The work which had hindered his ministry was now completed. Paul was only waiting for the will of God as it related to the time of his visit to Rome.

That I might have some fruit among you also, even as among other Gentiles. The same Greek word appears here for Gentiles that is translated *nations* in v. 5. (See the discussion on the word in v. 5.)

The word translated *fruit* is from the Greek *karpos*. Discussions on the meaning of fruit are frequently limited to soul winning. While that is a part of what is meant by the word (Jn. 4:36), fruit also applies to other things. In Mt. 3:8 John the Baptist called upon his hearers to "bring forth therefore fruits meet for repentance." Fruit refers to a change of behavior that was called for by repentance. In Rom. 6:23 holiness is referred to as fruit. In Rom. 15:28 the offering for the saints at Jerusalem was referred to as fruit. Giving thanks to God is referred to as fruit in Heb. 13:15. New Testament usage of the word *fruit* makes it evident that Paul meant that which would strengthen them as Christians through his labor among them as well as his hope to gain new converts. A study of the use of the word *fruit* in the N.T. makes it obvious that its scope is comprehensive rather than restricted to soul winning.

5. He expresses his eagerness to preach in Rome based on his debt to all people and his confidence in the gospel (vv. 14-16).

14 I am debtor both to the Greeks, and to the Barbarians; both to the wise, and to the unwise.
15 So, as much as in me is, I am ready to preach the gospel to you that are at Rome also.
16 For I am not ashamed of the gospel of Christ: for it is the power of God unto salvation to every one that believeth; to the Jew first, and also to the Greek.

I am debtor both to the Greeks, and to the Barbarians. There is some difference of opinion on whether by "Greeks" Paul restricted it to those who spoke the Greek language, or whether it referred to those who had been brought under the influence of Greek culture and influence—or we could say the Greek and Roman culture. Alexander the Great extended the influence of Greek culture and influence throughout his empire. When the Roman Empire was established, the influence of Greek culture, thought, and language remained strong. "Greek" is probably used here in the broad sense to include Greek and Roman culture, rather than the limited sense of those who spoke Greek. "Barbarians" would refer to those who were outside Greek and Roman culture. By Greeks and Barbarians, Paul meant to embrace all Gentiles.

Both to the wise, and to the unwise. It appears that the wise and unwise refer to the same people as Greeks and Barbarians. "Wise" referred to the educated. "Unwise" referred to the uneducated. For a presentation of different ways of looking at the groupings in this verse, see Cranfield (83, 84).

There may be some doubt about the exact meaning of the terms in this verse, but one thing is clear. Paul meant that he was debtor to all people including every stratum of society.

So, as much as in me is, I am ready to preach the gospel to you that are at Rome also. "So" indicates that the readiness that follows grows out of the debtorship that was acknowledged in v. 14. "As much as in me is" means all that is resting or depending upon Paul. So far as Paul is concerned, he is ready to preach the gospel in Rome. He is only waiting upon the will of God. This word "ready" (Greek *prothumos*) is not referring to a reluctant readiness, but to an eagerness.

For I am not ashamed of the gospel of Christ. Those who are interested in figures of speech will find it interesting that Bruce and Lenski consider the words "I am not ashamed of the gospel of Christ" to be a figure of speech called "litotes." This figure of speech is an understatement, used for effect in this case. In some cases it is used to avoid censure. Paul is actually meaning that he glories in the gospel. He is proud of the gospel and counts it an honor to proclaim it.

For it is the power of God unto salvation. This is why Paul was not ashamed of the gospel of Christ. He was confident that the gospel of Christ is effective. It will accomplish all that it claims. Salvation is salvation from the penalty of sin, the power of sin, and ultimately the presence of sin.

To every one that believeth. Paul was confident that the gospel offer was to everybody. He never feared that he might preach the gospel to some to whom the gospel was not offered and for whom the gospel would not be effective in delivering them from their sins.

To the Jew first, and also to the Greek. This point will be further elaborated in other places in this commentary, especially chapters 4, 9, and 11 where it will be an essential part of the interpretation. However, brief attention will be given here. Our understanding of the development of redemptive history is greatly lacking if we do not understand the place of the Jew in the program of God.

From the Abrahamic Covenant onward, all covenants of God were made with Israel. God has never made a redemptive covenant with the Gentiles. Gentiles become the seed of Abraham and thus partake of the redemptive blessings of God.

Through Abraham, God called into existence the nation of Israel. It was to Abraham and his seed that salvation was promised. It was to Israel that the Messiah was promised and to Israel that He came. It was to Israel that the gospel was preached for about 7 or 8 years before it was preached to the Gentiles.

It was Paul's practice, though he was the apostle to the Gentiles, when he went into an area to go first to the synagogue and preach there until they ran him off. This was because he went to the Jews and let them know that their long awaited Messiah had come.

That referred to above is what is meant by "to the Jew first." While we should have a concern about evangelizing unsaved Jews, this does not mean that each one of us is now obligated first to witness to the Jews about us before we witness to Gentiles.

The meaning of "Greek" in "also to the Greek" is the non-Jewish world. It is not because all were Greek, but as Hodge points out the Greeks were the ones with whom the Jews were more familiar.

By the time of the writing of Romans, the preaching to the Gentiles was in full swing. They had already become the majority in Christendom. See Hendriksen (61) on "the Jew first and also to the Greek."

C. Paul Introduces A "God-Provided Righteousness by Faith" as the Theme of the Epistle (1:17).

17 For therein is the righteousness of God revealed from faith to faith: as it is written, The just shall live by faith.

For therein is the righteousness of God revealed. The words that are translated "therein" are literally translated "in it." "It" refers to the gospel. The gospel reveals a God-provided righteousness. Since this will receive considerable development beginning with 3:21, its meaning will not be elaborated here. It is simply a God-provided righteousness to meet the needs of sinful man.

From faith to faith. A number of different interpretations are given to this expression: (1) From the faith of the O.T. to the faith of the N.T. (2) From the faith of the preacher to the faith of the hearer. (3) From one degree of faith to another degree of faith. (4) By faith from the beginning to the end. (5) By faith and given to the response of faith (or by means of faith and given to the ones who believe). (6) By faith to beget faith (offered by means of faith or on the condition of faith in order to secure the response of faith). For discussion on different interpretations see Cranfield (99, 100) and Murray (31, 32).

I take the sixth view to be correct. "By" is the preferred translation (of Greek *ek*) rather than "from." The preposition (Greek *ek* in *ek pisteos)* occurs several times in the N.T. with faith and consistently means "by faith" (Rom. 4:16; 5:1; 9:32; Gal. 3:11, 22, 24; 5:5). It would certainly seem that in keeping with the meaning of this in other places we would understand it to mean "by faith or on the condition of faith."

Our next concern is with the meaning "to faith" (in Greek *ek pisteos eis pistin*). The question centers around the meaning of the preposition *eis*. This is the same preposition that is translated "for" in v. 5 in "for obedience of faith." It appears to me that it (Greek *eis*) has the same meaning in the expression before us that it did in v. 5. The meaning there denoted purpose. (See notes on v. 5.) "For obedience of faith" means for the purpose of or in order to get people to obey and believe the gospel. In the verse before us, it appears to me that the God-provided righteousness is preached by (available on the condition of) faith to beget (in order to secure the response of) faith from the hearer.

There is some difference of opinion among commentators over whether "by faith" is connected with the verb "revealed" or with "righteousness." It appears to be connected with righteousness. The meaning is that in the gospel, a God-provided righteousness offered on the condition of faith is revealed.

As it is written, The just shall live by faith. This is a quotation from Hab. 2:4. The word for "just" (Greek *dikaios*) means righteous or the one who is in right standing with God. The source of living is faith. If righteousness is required for us to have spiritual lives (which Paul will show in 1:18—3:20), and one lives spiritually by faith (as shown by Hab. 2:4), it follows that one must receive righteousness by means of faith.

We are not to understand that in Habakkuk's day the idea of a God-provided righteousness would have been understood with the same clarity that it took on in the N.T. revelation. We are to understand that what Paul was teaching was in complete accord with what God had revealed through Habakkuk.

Summary 1:1-17

Paul introduced himself as a slave of Jesus Christ and a called apostle. His primary responsibility was to proclaim the good news from God about Jesus Christ to the Gentiles. He greets the Christians at Rome and expresses his appreciation for them and his eager desire to visit them. He had had this desire for a long time, but had been hindered by his church planting responsibility. He was only waiting for God's timing for his visit to Rome. He was eagerly awaiting the time when he could preach the gospel in Rome because he considered it an honor to preach the gospel of Christ. He was convinced of its efficacy. The gospel he preached revealed a righteousness which was from God for sinful man. This righteousness was available to all men everywhere on the condition of faith. The gospel which he proclaimed had been promised in the O.T. and was fully consistent with it.

Application: Teaching and Preaching the Passage

1. It was an honor to be an apostle. It was the highest office in the church. Paul was not bragging about being an apostle. He stated that he was an apostle so the people would know that he spoke with Divine authority. He had the necessary credentials for what he was saying and doing.

Sometimes we tend to operate on the assumption that humility requires us to hide or downplay the credentials which qualify us for our work. Yet, without knowing our qualifications, people do not know what confidence to place in what we say. We do not want to boast or brag, but we can at the appropriate time and in the proper way declare what our qualifications are.

If we, like Paul, keep ourselves reminded and acknowledge to others that we are servants (or slaves) of Jesus Christ, it will form the basis for a proper Christian humility. The servant attitude will be a corrective to a sinful pride about our qualifications or our accomplishments (v. 1).

2. In Christian apologetics there is not complete agreement on the exact contribution the place the resurrection of Christ has in convincing unbelievers about the truth of Christianity. Some take it to be the single truth that validates all other Christian truth. Others, while granting special significance to the resurrection of Christ, take a more comprehensive approach to validating the claims of Christianity. It is not my purpose to resolve this problem, but I do want to stress the fact that the resurrection is the miracle of miracles. By it Jesus Christ is declared to be the Son of God. It is well worth our time to prepare ourselves well on the Biblical teaching and evidence of the resurrection of Christ (v. 4).

3. A number of things that Paul spoke of in vv. 8-16 contributed to his healthy mental state and helped him establish a good relationship with the believers at Rome. We might say that Paul was practicing good public relations.

(1) He expressed his thanksgiving to God for the faith of the Roman Christians (v. 8).

(2) This expression of thanksgiving to God for the people implied an appreciation for the people (v. 8).

(3) Paul was guided by a sense of debtorship to all people and sought to

fulfill this responsibility (v. 14).

(4) Paul went about his work with a sense of eagerness and enthusiasm (vv. 9-15).

(5) Paul was able to have a deep desire to go to Rome while on the other hand not feel guilty about not having been sooner. He recognized that it was an unfinished task that had hindered him (v. 13).

(6) Paul wanted to be a blessing to the people (v. 11).

(7) Paul recognized that the people could also be a blessing to him (v. 12).

If we take a broad look at Christian values and principles and practice them, we will automatically do those things that help us have a good healthy state of mind. It will also help others have a good state of mind and will help in having good interpersonal relationships. We should appreciate the work of those who have sought to be true to the Word of God, in the study of human behavior and experience. However, when valid principles and values are found, it will be discovered that they have been a part of Christian truth all the time. The more fully we understand and practice Christianity, the more balanced and well-adjusted we will be.

4. It is our responsibility just as it was Paul's to reach all classes of people (v. 14). While it is the same gospel for all people, there is some difference in the way we approach different people. Some people can be won more easily than others, but it is our responsibility to reach both those who are easier and those who are harder to reach. For example, there is quite a bit of difference in reaching people in a foreign culture and reaching people in our home area. There are differences in how to reach those who have been brought up under the influence of Christianity and those who have been saturated with the influence of humanism. We must recognize these differences and prepare accordingly.

5. The God-provided righteousness about which Paul speaks is God's greatest gift to us as individuals. It is what makes it possible for us to escape the wrath of God. We should accept the responsibility of getting an in-depth understanding of this God-provided righteousness by an in-depth study of Romans (v. 17).

II. MAN'S FAILURE TO BE RIGHTEOUS BEFORE GOD (1:18—3:20).

Paul now begins to develop a doctrinal treatment of the subject of justification (or the God-provided righteousness). His first step is to show that all men, whether Jew or Gentile, have failed to measure up to what God requires of men. This will form the basis for understanding that the only hope man has, to be delivered from the wrath of God, is the God-provided righteousness he had referred to in 1:17.

A. The Gentiles Have Failed Before God (1:18-32).

It is clear that this passage addresses the condition of the Gentiles since it deals with those who have encountered only the general revelation of God as distinguished from special revelation. General revelation refers to God's revelation in the created order, history, and the nature of man. While this passage addresses the condition of the Gentiles, it is applicable to Jews, too: the principles are universal.

1. The wrath of God is revealed (v. 18).

18 For the wrath of God is revealed from heaven against all ungodliness and unrighteousness of men, who hold the truth in unrighteousness.

For the wrath of God is

revealed. "For" connects v. 18 with v. 17. Verse 17 spoke of the revealing of a God-provided righteousness offered on the condition of faith. Verse 18 speaks of the revealing of the wrath of God.

As I see it, "for" tells us that a reason follows for what precedes. The reason God has revealed a God-provided righteousness by faith is that the "wrath of God is revealed from heaven." The only escape from this wrath is to receive this God-provided righteousness which gives a person the only right standing with God that is possible for fallen man. (For a discussion of other views of the connection, see Cranfield 106-108.)

On the meaning of "wrath" (Greek *orge*), there is a conflict of opinion. Some reject the idea that wrath involves a personal or emotional response on the part of God (Dodd 20-24; Kasemann 37). Some of this seems to grow out of an attempt to make a distinction between the wrath of God and the wrath or anger of men. Men's anger is frequently unjust and sometimes irrational. Obviously such cannot be said of God's wrath. God is always just and always rational.

We need not eliminate the personal or the emotional from God's wrath in order to eliminate the unjust and the irrational. A person is one who thinks, feels, and acts. God *feels* His wrath toward sin just as He *feels* His love toward us. His feeling of wrath toward sins is a necessary consequence of His determination to remain holy. God cannot be holy and not be angry with sin. At the same time God's wrath is always under the control of His holiness. This eliminates any possible association of injustice with God's wrath.

There is some discussion over whether the wrath referred to is revealed by special revelation or general revelation, and whether it is the wrath of God observed in history or the wrath of God to be manifested at the final judgment. There is no question that special revelation reveals the wrath of God. In this verse, however, Paul's focus is on the revelation of God observed in human experience. Paul will make clear that knowledge of the wrath of God does not depend on special revelation. If that were the case, he could not say of those who have not received special revelation, "Who knowing the judgment of God, that they which commit such things are worthy of death" (v. 32).

If "the wrath of God" points out the need for a God-provided righteousness (to escape this wrath), then it must include the way that wrath will be revealed at the final judgment. But Paul also appears to have the judgment of God in human experience in mind. The wrath of God in human experience points to the wrath of God at the final judgment. (For different shades of thought on the wrath of God—including neoorthodox or contemporary theology, as well as conservative thought—see Barrett 33; Bruce 83, 84; Cranfield 108, 109; Dodd 20-24; Hendriksen 62-68; Hodge 35; Kasemann 27; Knox 397; and Shedd 18, 19).

From heaven. That the wrath of God is being revealed "from heaven" indicates that the ultimate source of the revelation of God's wrath is God Himself.

Against all ungodliness and unrighteousness of men. The popular interpretation of ungodliness seems to be that it refers to extreme wickedness. However, this is not what is meant by the word (Greek *asebeia*). The basic idea is lack of reverence for God. It may refer to active irreverence, or it may refer simply to the lack of reverence. It is the failure to recognize God for who He is and what He is. It is a failure to let one's life be guided by a proper recognition of God. (See Earle 31, 32.)

Unrighteousness (Greek *adikia*) refers to the failure to measure up to God's moral standard. Ungodliness refers to disobedience to the first Table of the Law, the first four commandments (Ex. 20:3-11). Unrighteousness refers to disobedience to the second Table of the Law, the last six commandments (Ex. 20:12-17).

Stated positively, obedience to the first Table of the Law would be godliness (Greek *eusebeia*); obedience to the second Table of the Law is righteousness (Greek *dikaiosune*). The term that combines obedience to both Tables of the Law is *holiness*. Jesus summed up obedience to the first table as loving God, and to the second table as loving one's neighbor (Mt. 22:37-39).

Most commentators are in basic agreement concerning the meaning of ungodliness and unrighteousness, with some minor differences. Some consider ungodliness to be sin against God while unrighteousness is sin against men (Barnes 40). This is an oversimplification. True, unrighteousness involves sin against other people. At the same time, sin against people also involves sin against God because it violates God's moral teachings. Therefore, unrighteousness also involves ungodliness (Vine *Romans* 17, 18).

Some caution against considering ungodliness and unrighteousness as two kinds of sin (Cranfield 111, 112; Hendrikson 68; Lenski 92). There may be some justification for this concern. Perhaps it is better to look at ungodliness and unrighteousness as two categories. However, there are some sins in which ungodliness is more in focus.

Who hold the truth in unrighteousness. The question here centers around the meaning of "hold" (Greek *katecho*). Depending upon the context, it may mean:

(1) To possess or hold to the truth, or

(2) To suppress or hinder the truth.

A few commentators understand the meaning, here, to having the truth in their *possession*: that is, they acknowledge the truth but fail to live by it (Lightfoot 251; Murray 36, 37).

The vast majority take the position that the meaning here is to *suppress* or hinder the truth (Bruce 84; Cranfield 112; Godet 100; Hendriksen 69; Hodge 36; Lenski 92, 93; Meyer 56; Moule 42; Olshausen 81, 82; Picirilli 19; Sanday and Headlam 41, 42).

In this verse, Paul calls attention to the three ways in which sin manifests itself: ungodliness, unrighteousness, and the suppression of the truth. God's wrath is against every expression of sin in all men. The outreach of God's wrath is coextensive with the human race. Paul starts a journey in 1:18 that he concludes in 3:19, 20, where he concludes that all men, apart from Jesus Christ, stand under condemnation.

While the principles of 1:18 are universal, what follows is an application of these principles to the Gentiles, who have never received the special revelation. Their only message from God is general revelation. In 1:19-32 there are three lines of thought. The ungodliness of the heathen is exposed in 1:21-23 and 25. Their unrighteousness is exposed in 1:24-32. Their suppression of the truth is exposed in 1:19-23, 25, and 28. This suppression of the truth refers to the attempt to hinder the truth from being expressed both to and by others.

2. The Gentile is inexcusable (vv. 19-23).

a. God's general revelation is adequate (vv. 19, 20).

19 Because that which may be known of God is manifest in them; for God hath shewed *it* unto them. 20 For the invisible things of him from the creation of the world are clearly seen, being understood by the things that are made, *even* his eternal power and Godhead; so that they are without excuse.

Because. This conjunction connects

what follows with what precedes, giving a reason that God's wrath is against all ungodliness, unrighteousness, and the suppression of the truth.

That which may be known of God is manifest in them. Commentators are divided over the meaning of the word translated "may be known" (Greek *gnostos*). In all other places where it is used in the N.T., the meaning is "known" (Lk. 2:44; 23:49; Jn. 18:15, 16; Acts 1:19; 2:14; 4:10, 16; 9:42; 13:38; 15:18; 19:17; 28:22, 28). But Greek authorities tell us that in classical Greek *gnostos* also has the meaning "knowable." Many interpreters take the position that it should be understood as "knowable" here. (For a defense of this position, see Cranfield 113.) Others are strongly committed to the view that "known" is the correct meaning here. (For a defense of this position, see Lange 82; Meyer 56.)

If we accept the meaning "knowable," there are three different approaches we can take. (1) We can understand Paul to teach that God could be known through general revelation, but because of depravity no person actually knows Him that way. (2) We can take him to mean that the masses have failed to know God through general revelation, but a few along the way—like Plato and Aristotle—did know God. (3) We can interpret Paul to mean that God *can* be known by general revelation, and then understand him to develop his thought from "can know" to "do know" in the verses that follow.

If a person takes this third position, his difference with those who say that the passage means that God is known as a result of general revelation would be only a technical point. Both would agree that men who have only general revelation possess knowledge of God.

Since the word *gnostos* refers to the actual possession of knowledge (and not mere "knowability") in all other occurrences in the N.T., it appears to me that it should be understood that way here, at least if this can be justified by the context. It appears that Paul does affirm the possession of knowledge of God through general revelation in v. 20.

The reference to "manifest in them," I take to refer to general revelation of God in the created order. Human beings are part of that created order. Therefore, our own rational and moral constitution is involved in the possession of this knowledge of God by general revelation.

What I have said raises the question about what can be known about God through general revelation. It raises a question concerning the validity of natural theology. I will delay further discussion of this until v. 20 has been examined.

For God hath shewed it unto them. "That which is known of God is manifest (Greek *phaneron*); for God has manifested (Greek *ephanerosen*) it." This statement stands as a clear testimony to the fact that all knowledge of God is the result of God's initiative toward man. There is no knowledge of God apart from God's selfinitiative and selfdisclosure. (This is a note that has been sounded loud and clear by Carl F. H. Henry in *God, Revelation and Authority*, II:17-29.)

For. By this connection, v. 20 explains how God has manifested this knowledge to man. It is a commentary which expounds upon what is simply stated as a fact in v. 19.

The invisible things of him. God is not perceivable by the five senses.

From the creation of the world are clearly seen, being understood by the things that are made. "From the beginning of the world" means *since* the beginning of the world. This marked the beginning of general revelation.

"Are clearly seen" is translated from *kathorao*. The word for *invisible* in the first part of the verse is *aoratos*. There is a play on words here, which can be caught if we translate: "the invisible things of Him are made clearly visible." Paul is using the figure of speech known as oxymoron. It is a startling statement because on the surface to speak about *invisible* things being clearly visible sounds like a contradiction. Of course, the visibility occurs in the mind's eye as the result of God's revelation rather than through the five senses. Only on the surface is there a contradiction to call attention to the real truth where there is no contradiction.

"Being understood" (Greek *noeo*) tells us that what is clearly seen is perceived or understood by the mind. The means which God used in bringing about this perception is "by means of the things that are made." This refers to the entire created order, including the rational and moral nature of human beings.

Even his eternal power and Godhead. These words tell us what knowledge is possessed (v. 19). It tells us what the invisible things are which are made visible to the mind's eye by means of the created order.

The word translated "eternal" (Greek *aidios*) occurs only twice in the N.T. (The other place is Jude 6.) It means eternal or everlasting and modifies both "power" (Greek *dunamis*) and "Godhead" (Greek *theiotes*).

There is widespread doubt that "Godhead" is the best translation of this word. Actually, there are two nearly identical Greek words in the N.T., each one occurring but once: *theiotes* here and *theotes* in Col. 2:9, the one correctly translated "Godhead." The latter is the one always used by the Greek fathers "as alone adequately expressing the essential Godhead of the three separate persons of the Holy Trinity"; while the one used here in Romans means a "manifestation of the divine, of some attributes...but never absolute essential Deity" (Trench, *Synonyms of the New Testament* 10).

Trench was of the opinion that Paul followed this distinction in the words, and that seems correct. If the full essence of the "Godhead" were meant here, that knowledge would require *special* revelation. But what Paul is speaking of is knowledge of God's existence as a being with the nature and attributes of God. He is saying that the eternal power and the attributes of God have been made visible to the mind's eye by God's initiative in revealing Himself in the things He has made.

At this point two questions are raised: (1) Is Paul saying that man can construct proofs for God's existence by reflecting upon the created order? (2) Does Paul furnish legitimate grounds for natural theology?

A full discussion of this subject belongs to systematic theology, apologetics, epistemology, and philosophy of religion. However, the Christian in studying these areas of thought must be instructed by Scripture. The passage before us is the most basic of all passages of Scripture on this subject.

In answering the first question, I would say that Paul is not discussing proofs for God's existence. He is assuming that men have a knowledge of God's existence. The question is not how people learn that God exists. He is talking about how people know what God is like and that they do possess a basic knowledge of what God is like.

Since Paul is not addressing the subject of how people come to believe in God, we cannot say that this passage either speaks against proofs for God's existence or justifies constructing such proofs. I might add that no other passage can be found to support the view that the Bible teaches that we can prove the existence of God. Of course, it does not say that we cannot prove God's existence.

The Bible assumes that people believe in a deity of some kind and then proceeds to present a case for deciding in favor of the true and living God. The futility of believing in idols is shown in the O.T. to help the person believe in Yahweh, the true and living God, the God of Abraham, Isaac, and Jacob, the covenant-God of Israel. Note this kind of reasoning in Is. 44. Also, observe the challenge of the people to decide between Yahweh (the LORD) and Baal in 1 Kgs. 18:21-39.

It is also important to observe the sign-value of the miracles of Jesus Christ and the resurrection of Jesus Christ. While I am not denying that the miracles of Christ and His resurrection could have some value in confronting a naturalist, I am saying that the context in which the miracles and resurrection of Christ occurred was not a context of naturalistic or humanistic unbelief. The context was first Jewish. The sign-value of the miracles and resurrection was to help those who already believe in the God of Israel to understand and believe that Jesus was His Son and the long awaited Messiah.

Later on when the preaching of the gospel was extended to the Gentiles, it was addressed to those who "did service unto them which by nature are no gods" (Gal. 4:8). The miracles that occurred during the transition period and the message of the resurrection of Christ were to help those who believed in false gods to come to believe in Jesus Christ. It enabled them to believe in the God of Israel and Jesus Christ His Son.

Any contribution that Paul makes, in this passage, to the question how people believe in God can be developed only by implication. Paul tells us that God confronts man through His revelation in the created order and man's own rational and moral constitution as a result of this confrontation. A person is pictured as believing that God exists. We would gather that it is a rational decision. The activity which is translated "being understood" (Greek *noeo*) is the perception of the "mind" (Greek *nous*), as functioning rationally. These observations seem implied, but there is no explanation either stated or implied that would elaborate from this passage the process by which a person comes to believe in God. (A developed case cannot be given here on the value of arguments about how people come to believe in God. For those interested in my approach to this subject, see *Systematics* 67-80.)

Now we turn our attention to the second question: Does Paul furnish grounds for natural theology? When we think of "natural theology," the Roman Catholic theologian, Thomas Aquinas (1224-1274) comes to mind and Bishop Joseph Butler of the Church of England (1692-1752). An introductory acquaintance with natural theology and the conflicting opinions regarding it can be gained by reading C. A. Beckwith, "Natural Theology" in *The New Schaff-Herzog Encyclopedia of Religious Knowledge*, VIII:85; David Cairns, "Natural Theology," in *A Handbook of Christian Theology*, 249-255; Carl F. H. Henry, *God, Revelation and Authority*, Vol. II, 104-123; Robert C. Newman, "Natural Theology," in *The New International Dictionary of the Christian Church*, 695; Anders Nygren, *Commentary on Romans*, 102-109; and T. H. L. Parker, "Natural Theology," *Baker's Dictionary of Theology*, 372.

The question whether Paul furnishes the grounds for a "natural theology" is not the same as whether man can know the existence of God and something about God through general revelation. Natural theology implies a development of thought that includes a convincing case for God's existence and a rather clear picture of what God is like. In some cases it even anticipates redemption. However, those who believe in natural theology would agree that the redemptive message could come only by special revelation. It is as if there is some neutral platform from which the unbeliever can construct a case for God's existence, a clear view of what God is like, and an expectancy for a redemptive revelation that could make a person a ready recipient of the gospel once it was presented unto him.

Once natural theology was strong in the Protestant church world, but this century marks a decline in it among Protestants. Some neo-orthodox theologians have almost or altogether denied the validity of any general revelation from God. Conservatives have continued to hold to general revelation, but either deny altogether or give a restricted meaning to natural theology.

Natural theology would imply a developed and organized body of knowledge. Paul pictures fallen man as abusing and suppressing the knowledge of God that he possesses rather than developing and organizing it.

This is not to say that the knowledge of God possessed by fallen man is of no value. "General revelation sets the stage for special revelation. The stage is set for man to receive a clearer message of sin and judgment. A feeling of need is present that can be clarified by special revelation to be the need of redemption" (*Systematics* 15).

So that they are without excuse. "So that" expresses *result*, and that is one of the possible meanings of the Greek phrase (*eis to einai*). Another possible meaning is *purpose*: "in order that they might be." Both interpretations of the expression are found among those commenting on this passage. (For purpose, see Godet 104 and Meyer 59, 60; for result, see Cranfield 116, Lange 183, and Lenski 99, 100.)

While I would accept the fact that God so designed creation that if man should sin he would be without defense, I do not believe that is the point that Paul was addressing. The "without defense" is not based on the design of creation to make God knowable. Rather, it is based on the fact that the invisible things of God (His eternal power and Divine attributes) are clearly seen. It is the possessed knowledge that renders the pagan without defense. Therefore, the "without defense" is set forth here as a result of the fact that God has so revealed Himself even by general revelation.

Without defense. This word (Greek *anapologetos*) means without legal defense. The case is so well established against anyone who is guilty of ungodliness, unrighteousness, or the suppression of the truth that no defense attorney could build an acceptable case before God as Judge. General revelation is so effective that knowledge of God is possessed. Ignorance cannot be entered as a plea and successfully defended.

Whatever may be the truth about the statement, "If the heathen would live up to the light that they do have, God would see to it that they would somehow get in touch with the gospel," this is not the point that Paul is making here. He is not in any way addressing their not having received the gospel. Rather, he is saying that there cannot be a defense made for ungodliness, unrighteousness, and the suppression of the truth.

b. They Have Sinned Against Knowledge (vv. 21-23).

21 Because that, when they knew God, they glorified *him* not as God, neither were thankful; but became vain in their imaginations, and their foolish heart was darkened.

Because that. The "so that" before "they are without defense" shows that a reason precedes which explains why they are without defense. They are without defense because as a result of God's revelation in the created order, they are in possession of knowledge of God's eternal power and Divine attributes. "Because that" introduces a second reason they are without defense.

When they knew God. "When they knew" is a translation of the Greek *gnontes*, the aorist participle of *ginosko*. A literal translation would be "knowing." An important question is: What is the *time* period referred to by "knowing?"In reading the translation "when they knew God," there is a natural tendency to understand it to mean that at sometime in the past the heathen knew God, but now they do not. This is the opinion of the average reader before he investigates the passage. A few commentators present this view: "Here he is only speaking historically of that true knowledge of God which existed in men originally, and which they gradually lost" (Olshausen, 87). According to this interpretation, the Gentile world was not ignorant of God at first, but "Its ignorance is the result and punishment of its great sin of neglect. They lost even their imperfect knowledge (*gnosis*), because they did not raise it to full knowledge (*epignosis*) through the labor of the heart" (Lange 83, 84).

Based on this interpretation, the pagan would be without defense because at one time his ancestors knew God. But they departed from God. It is grammatically possible to treat *gnontes* as a past time participle and give it the meaning "when they knew." There is another possibility which I think fits the context better.

It is possible to view the "knowing God" as descriptive of the present as well as the past. This would make the "knowing God" contemporaneous with the failure to glorify God, to be unthankful, and so on. It seems that most commentators take this position, but they do not say much to help the reader weigh the matter and make his own decision.

Hodge explains, "Thus in the present instance, in vv. 19, 20 he proved that the heathen had a knowledge of God which rendered him inexcusable, and then the fact that they were without excuse is proved by showing that they did not act in accordance with the truth" (38). Lenski comments, "In spite of the fact that they knew, knew at the very time, they did not let this knowledge control or even check them" (102).

Hendriksen explains:

> It confirms the statement that by their unrighteousness these wicked people are constantly attempting to suppress the truth that has been and is continually being revealed to them, and that they are accordingly without excuse.
>
> For although they knew God from his works in creation, they did not glorify him: did not acknowledge him as their God and did not bestow upon him the honor and praise they owed him (71).

I think most anyone would be more at ease with the thought that the heathen are without defense because of their own failure than because their ancestors did not properly respond to knowledge of God at a time in the distant past. However, we must justify our interpretation from the text.

Our first step is to observe that participles get their time from the context. The word "knowing" by itself does not tell us whether it is past, present, or future. "Knowing" has the same time reference as "they glorified him not as God." The verb "glorifed" is aorist indicative. The most frequent use of the aorist indicative is a reference to that which is past and over. However, the aorist indicative is frequently understood as a culminative aorist, usually translated with the helping verb "have" (cf. Rom. 2:12 and 3:23).

When we say "all have sinned," we mean all in the past and continuing into the present. The same general idea applies to "as many as have sinned" in 2:12. There is no thought of restricting the application to that which is past and over.

I would suggest that each aorist indicative in this passage (1:21-32) be treated the same way it is in Rom. 2:12 and 3:23. It would read as follows: "Because knowing God, they have not glorified him as God, neither have been thankful." This approach to translating the passage is found in Cranfield; *The James Moffatt Translation*; *The New English Bible*; and *Weymouth's New Testament*. The meaning would still cover the past, but would also include the present. A further support for a present application of the truth of the passage is seen in the fact that 1:32 has an unquestionable present application while it is clearly in the same time frame as the rest of the passage.

Now that the case has been given for believing that "knowing God" is contemporaneous with the behavior that follows, we need to give more attention to what is meant by "knowing God." It is important to observe that the meaning is not: It is possible for them to know God. Rather, the meaning is: They know God. Since we must confront the meaning of knowing God, I will at this point refer to "who knowing the judgment of God, that they which commit such things are worthy of death" (1:32). On the one hand we have Paul claiming that all men by general revelation know the eternal power of God, His divine attributes, and that because of God's judgment men are worthy of death. On the other hand we have those who deny God's existence, those who take an agnostic approach to God, and those while believing in God either deny or take a weak view of the judgment of God.

It appears to me that one of the most important tasks of theology is to recognize and explain the contradiction experienced by those who both *know* and *deny* that they know God. To me, the key is found in the recognition that suppressed knowledge is still knowledge. We experience knowledge on both the conscious and subconscious levels.

Only a small part of our knowledge is in the conscious mind at a given time. A great body of knowledge is stored for recall as needed. There are some things we would rather not recall. What is stored in the subconscious mind is knowledge whether we want to recall it or not. One of the main points that Paul is stressing is that fallen man is guilty of suppressing the truth, but such suppression can never be rightly called ignorance.

It is important to observe that the attempt to suppress the knowledge of God into the subconscious never totally succeeds. If it totally succeeded, there would be large segments of the world who would avoid religious knowledge and concern. Seldom, if ever, do we encounter a person who denies the existence of God without some indication that he is experiencing contradiction. He is suffering from a divided self. The atheist or naturalist already knows what we mean when we speak of God. People may argue against guilt before God, but the idea of guilt is already there before they make their protest.

When man fell into sin, he not only revolted against God; he also revolted against himself. Sin introduced a foreign element into man's being. Man was created in God's image. He was designed for holiness. It is a contradiction of man's humanity for him to sin. Our humanity and sin can never be brought together in full harmony; yet, in spite of this, man goes on and lives in this contradiction.

For a person to deny God's existence or His judgment is to contradict not only a system of truth but also himself. Atheism, naturalism, secular humanism, agnosticism, and paganism put man in conflict with himself. I am not saying that through general revelation man has a well-developed understanding of God which he is suppressing. I am saying that he knows there is a Divine being. He has some basic idea of what God is like. He knows that his actions are incompatible with God. The message of special revelation does not create these basic ideas of what God is like. Rather, it clarifies, develops, and puts them in proper focus.

We do not make a human being moral by teaching him moral truth. Rather, we can teach him moral truth because he is morally constituted. We do not make a person rational by giving him an education. Rather, we can educate him because he is rationally constituted. We do not make people religious when we proclaim the truth of special revelation to them. Rather, they are capable of responding to special revelation because they are religious by their very design.

I understand that it is necessary for the Holy Spirit to work before we can get a positive response from the preached Word. At the same time such a response would be impossible if man were not moral, rational, and religious by the design of his very being. No amount of preaching to a herd of cattle will get a response. The Holy Spirit will never make a Christian out of a cow.

I believe it is this failure to recognize that suppressed knowledge is still knowledge that accounts for the view that in vv. 19-21 Paul is talking only about the *possibility* of knowledge of God rather than the actual *possession* of such knowledge. Those who deny that all men possess this knowledge of God will certainly take the position that the passage teaches that the pagan are without defense because they *could* know if they would. However, an examination of the passage in its entirety fails to support such a conclusion.

Even if we conceded, which I do not, that v. 19 says "knowable" rather than "known" (see above), the case would still not be established against the possession of knowledge of God. We must still face up to the meaning of "clearly seen" (v. 20), "being understood" (v. 21), "knowing" (v. 32). To me, these support the conclusion that the pagan does possess knowledge of God through general revelation. It is this knowledge, not the possibility of knowledge, that renders the pagan without defense.

They glorified him not as God. The beginning of a right relationship with God is a proper recognition of who He is and bestowing upon Him the respect, honor, and glory that is due Him. In spite of the fact that pagans of all ages have had adequate knowledge to do so, they have not glorified Him as God. This makes them guilty of ungodliness.

Neither were thankful. The dependence that goes with being created by God means that we should recognize God as the giver of "every good gift and every perfect gift" (Jas. 1:17). Gratitude moves us in the right direction. Ingratitude renders a person incapable of pleasing God—it sets in motion a number of other sins.

But became vain in their imaginations. Concerning the word imaginations (Greek *dialogismos*), Shedd explains: "The word denotes the rational and not the imaginative faculty....The term 'speculations' is nearer the meaning. The writer has in mind the great and perverse ingenuity with which the human intellect is employed, in inventing the various schemes of pagan idolatry" (23).

When we think of the pagan or heathen, our tendency is to think of very backward people who yet live in crude or primitive conditions. Certainly, what Paul says applies to such people. However, this was not the kind of pagan world which Paul had encountered. It was the kind of world that before Paul's time had produced the classical literature of Homer, Cicero, and Virgil. It had given the world the great minds of people like Socrates, Plato, and Aristotle. It was the Roman world which is still considered famous for its knowledge of government, architecture, and engineering. The pagan world which Paul knew, at least among the wealthy, showed a high degree of refinement.

Yet it was this otherwise advanced culture that was vain in its reasonings or speculations. Its religious thoughts had become vain or worthless.

And their foolish heart was darkened. The word foolish (Greek *asunetos*) means without understanding. Further comment on this word is reserved until v. 31.

I believe there is a consensus among people in general that our English word "heart" refers to the seat of the emotions. There is, also, a consensus among Biblical scholars that the Greek word for heart (*kardia*) refers to the seat of the emotions. But those who have made a thorough study of this word have also concluded that heart in the N.T. also refers to the seat of the intellect and the will as well as the emotions.

It is easy, upon an examination of the 160 occurrences of the word in the N.T., to see why many scholars have reached this conclusion. However, I want to challenge this conclusion. First, I want to show why anyone would think that the evidence supports the conclusion. (1) In support of the heart being the seat of the intellectual life the following is given: People reason in their hearts (Mk. 2:6, 8; Lk. 1:17; 5:22). They understand with their hearts (Jn. 12:40). Thoughts are in the heart (Mt. 15:19; Mk. 7:21; Lk. 2:35; 9:47; 24:38; Acts 8:22; Heb. 4:12). (2) That the heart is the seat of the emotions is supported by the following: Trouble is related to the heart (Jn. 14:1, 27). Sorrow is experienced in the heart (Jn. 16:6). Rejoicing occurs in the heart (Jn. 16:22; Acts 2:26). Anguish is experienced in the heart (2 Cor. 2:4). The heart experiences comfort (Col. 2:2; 4:8; 2 Th. 2:17). (3) In support of the heart's being the seat of the will, attention is called to the "counsels of the hearts" (1 Cor. 4:5); "decreed in his heart" (1 Cor. 7:37); and "he purposeth in his heart" (2 Cor. 9:7).

There appears to be a consensus today that there are cognitive, affective, and volitional experiences in the personal life. It is commmon to associate the cognitive experiences with the mind, the affective experiences with the heart, and the volitional experiences with the will. Frequently, the mind is referred to as the faculty of our being with which we think, the heart the faculty in which we experience emotions, and the will the faculty of choice. Others reject the idea that mind, heart, and will each refer to a faculty of our being. They prefer to think of the person as experiencing thinking, feeling, and acting.

I think we can avoid the problem of speaking about mind or heart or will as being a faculty of our being. We can say that the mind refers to our capacity to think, the heart to our capacity to experience emotions, and the will to our capacity to make choices. Certainly, we can all agree that such capacities exist.

The question before us is: Does the heart refer to our capacity to think, feel, and act, or does the heart refer just to our capacity to experience emotions? I am going to choose the latter position and will state my case.

There is agreement that the heart is the seat of the emotions and that it refers to the deep inner self. Men are capable of actions that reflect the inner self, and they are capable of actions that do not reflect the inner self. Jesus said, "*Ye hypocrites, well did Esaias prophesy of you, saying, This people draweth nigh unto me with their mouth, and honoureth me with their lips; but their heart is far from me" (Mt. 15:7, 8)*. This makes it clear that there can be a surface type of behavior which is merely acting. It does not involve or reflect the heart or the inner self. The converse of that would be an action that does reflect the heart or the inner self. In the latter case, that does not mean that the whole idea had its origin in the heart.

Rather, it means that in the process the heart has become involved and is reflected in the action.

Reason, per se, is an activity of the mind. However, ideas in the mind are reflected in attitudes or feeling in the heart. To speak of reasoning in the heart does not mean that the heart is doing the reasoning. Rather, it means that the heart has become involved. The ideas or thoughts take place in the mind and a corresponding attitude or feeling occurs in the heart. It is then and only then that we can speak of reasoning in the heart.

The same line of reasoning applies to the will. A choice is made by the will. The choice can be said to be a choice of the heart when it reflects the inner self. The inner self is involved in the choice, but the act of choosing is made by the will.

I believe that the explanation I have given fits the use of the word for the heart in the N.T. When this approach is used, it will also help show the important place the N.T. gives to emotions. When the heart is understood to refer sometimes to the intellect, sometimes to the emotions, and at other times to the will, the stress given to emotions or feelings in the N.T. is undercut.

The mind is the gateway to the personality. Cognitive ideas are expressed to the mind and grasped and understood by the mind. When the proper development takes place, truth is presented to and grasped by the mind. These ideas develop attitudes in the emotions. The truth becomes real. Value (importance) is felt. Truth has become internalized. Out of a prepared mind and heart appropriate actions (decisions of the will) can take place. Genuine Christian behavior takes place only when the truth has entered and resides in the inner chambers of the heart. (See notes on "mind" on v. 28.)

"Their foolish heart was darkened." How tragic! That which was designed to honor God has been informed by error. Their deep inner self was guided by and agreed with error. In the innermost chambers of their inner self, they experienced darkness.

22 Professing themselves to be wise, they became fools.

As a result of their vain speculations and darkened heart, they claimed to be wise in the direction they were taking. In fact they became fools (Greek *moraino*: the noun form of this is *moros* from which we get our word *moron*). By God's standard, they were the opposite of what they claimed to be. They had traded for worthless error. All men who depart from God claim that such a move is wise. But the truth is that such action manifests a gross lack of wisdom.

23 And changed the glory of the uncorruptible God into an image made like to corruptible man, and to birds, and fourfooted beasts, and creeping things.

It is usually agreed that "changed" (Greek *allasso*) means "exchanged." The pagan had exchanged the glory of the incorruptible God for an image made like to corruptible man and to birds and beasts. The glory (Greek *doxa*) of God refers to the majesty and splendor of God:

> In extra-biblical Greek the primary meaning of *doxa* is 'opinion,' its secondary meaning 'the opinion which others have of one,' so 'repute,' 'good repute,' 'glory.' But in the Bible the meaning 'opinion' has almost completely disappeared, and *doxa* has acquired a new meaning as a result of its being used to translate the Hebrew *kabod*, namely, 'glory,' 'splendor,' 'majesty,' with reference to external appearance (Cranfield 119, 120).

Concerning the various forms of idolatry, Vincent (671) explains:

> Deities of human form prevailed in Greece; those of bestial form in Egypt; and both methods of worship were practiced in Rome. . . Serpent-worship was common in Chaldaea, and also in Egypt. The asp was sacred throughout the latter country. The worship of Isis was domesticated at Rome, and Juvenal relates how the priests of Isis contrived that the silver images of serpents kept in her temple should move their heads to a supplicant (*Satire* 6:537) (671).

Albert Barnes comments regarding birds:

> The *ibis* was adored with particular reverence among the Egyptians, on account of the great benefits resulting from its destroying the *serpents* which, but for this, would have overrun the country. The *hawk* was adored in Egypt, and the *eagle* at Rome. As one great principle of pagan idolatry was to adore all objects from which important benefits were derived, it is probable that all *birds* would come in for a share of pagan worship, that rendered service in the destruction of noxious animals (46).

3. God has delivered the pagan over to the insistence of his depraved nature (vv. 24-32).

a. God has given them over to sexual uncleanness (vv. 24, 25).

24 Wherefore God also gave them up to uncleanness through the lusts of their own hearts, to dishonour their own bodies between themselves:
25 Who changed the truth of God into a lie, and worshipped and served the creature more than the Creator, who is blessed for ever. Amen.

The "wherefore" shows the connection of what follows with what precedes. The suppression of the truth and the practice of the folly of idolatry in spite of their knowing God is the reason for the judgment which follows.

God also gave them up to uncleanness through the lusts of their own hearts. There has been some misunderstanding concerning the meaning of "God also gave them up." Some think the people had committed the unpardonable sin. They think Paul is saying that God has given up on the people mentioned. Such an interpretation is to be rejected for two reasons: (1) An examination of the uses of the word translated "give up" (Greek *paradidomi*) does not support the idea that it refers to a giving up from which there is no hope. This word is used in Rom. 8:32 where Paul says that God "delivered up" Jesus for us all. It is the same word which is used in 1 Cor. 5:5: Paul instructs the church with regard to the person guilty of incest to "deliver" him to Satan for the destruction of the flesh. Such a state was not intended to be without remedy as is seen in Paul's words, "That the spirit may be saved in the day of the Lord Jesus." It is clear that Paul hoped this disciplinary action would bring repentance and salvation. (2) Many people, in the history of the church have been saved from the sins Paul enumerates here in Romans.

God gave them *over* to the sins that their heart was already intent on doing. Yet, this was an act of judgment on God's part: "It is impossible to stop short at the idea of simple *permission*: 'God *let* them give themselves over to evil.' God was not purely passive in the terrible development of Gentile corruption. Wherein did His action consist? He positively withdrew His hand; He ceased to hold the boat as it was dragged by the current of the river" (Godet 107).

Some are of the opinion that uncleanness (Greek *akatharsia*) in this verse includes homosexuality. However, I agree with Lange: "The Apostle evidently distinguishes two degrees of this abandonment; v. 24 and v. 26. As the unnatural sins of lust are not mentioned before v. 26, so may we understand v. 24 as referring to the natural forms of sensuality" (85).

The practice of sexual immorality had the effect of dishonoring their bodies between themselves. "Body" is a figure of speech (called a synechdoche) where the part is given for the whole. The body represents the total person. One is reminded here of what Paul says in 1 Cor. 6:18, "Every sin that a man doeth is without the body; but he that committeth fornication sinneth against his own body."

Based on what I have learned about people, it is my conclusion that no other sin that is widely committed has such devastating effects on the personality as sexual experiences outside of marriage. This devastation not only extends to those who are the perpetrators of these experiences, but also to those who are innocent victims. Most people have not the slightest idea of the suffering and detriment experienced by those who are the victims of rape or incest. If for no other reason, sexual purity should be practiced and promoted for the mental well-being of people.

Who changed the truth of God into a lie. This verse is a restatement of the reason for the delivering over to sexual uncleanness of v. 24. It is a concise statement of what had been elaborated in vv. 21-23. The truth (Greek *aletheia*) had been exchanged for the lie (Greek *psuedos*). The truth of God conforms to reality. God is the true and living God. The lie refers to idolatry. An idol is a lie because it claims to be a god when in fact it is not. It represents no reality beyond itself.

And worshipped and served the creature more than the Creator, who is blessed for ever. Amen. "More than" (Greek *para*) is used here in the sense of "rather than." They worshiped the creature rather than the Creator.

Paul found this worship of images made in the likeness of created beings revolting. The mention of the Creator brought forth an outburst of praise "who is blessed for ever." "Amen" is a transliterated Hebrew word meaning truth. According to *Vine's Expository Dictionary of New Testament Words*, when Amen is said by God, it means "it is and shall be so." When it is said by men, it means "so let it be" (55).

b. God has given them over to homosexuality (vv. 26, 27).

26 For this cause God gave them up unto vile affections: for even their women did change the natural use into that which is against nature:
27 And likewise also the men, leaving the natural use of the woman, burned in their lust one toward another; men with men working that which is unseemly, and receiving in themselves that recompence of their error which was meet.

For this cause God gave them up unto vile affections. "For this cause" connects v. 26 with v. 25. Because of the pagans' worship of the creature rather than the Creator, God has given them over to vile affections.

In v. 24 Paul refers to lust (Greek *epithumia*). In v. 26 he refers to affection (Greek *pathos*):

> An *epithumia* is a single evil desire, a *pathos* is a constant burning passion. The former may be checked like a fire that is just starting; the latter is a conflagration

that overwhelms all constraint and controls a man completely (Lenski 112).

The word "vile" is from the Greek *atimia*, a noun. The verb form (*atimazo*) is translated "to dishonour" in v. 24. These passions were dishonoring or degrading because they were unnatural. The degrading of the sexual relationships in v. 24 grew out of the fact that they occurred outside wedlock.

For even their women did change the natural use into that which is against nature. The reference is to the fact that these women had become lesbians: "That he should have mentioned the women first is undoubtedly for the purpose of accentuating the grossness of the evil. It is the delicacy which belongs to the woman that makes more apparent the degeneracy of homosexual indulgence in their case" (Murray 47).

And likewise also the men, leaving the natural use of the woman, burned in their lust one toward another. The word burned (Greek *ekkauo)* refers to the intensity of their lust. This particular word for lust appears only here in the N.T.: "It is a reaching out after something with the purpose of appropriating it" (Vincent 672).

Men with men working that which is unseemly. Unseemly (Greek *aschemosune*) refers to the shamefulness of their deed.

And receiving in themselves that recompence of their error which was meet. Recompence (Greek *antimisthia*) refers to wages. In the negative sense, as used here, it refers to a penalty. "Meet" (Greek *dei*) carries with it the idea of necessity. It was necessary for God to judge their error.

There are two opinions concerning the "error" that received the penalty which was necessary. (1) The "error" refers back to the departure from God into idolatry. Being delivered over to homosexualty was a part of the punishment that was meted out to them for their departure from the true God (Cranfield 127). (2) The "error" refers to the sexual perversion of homosexuality. The penalty for this "error" is considered to be the problems suffered by those who are homosexual. (See Hendriksen 79.)

It appears to me that the second interpretation is the correct one.

While Paul's comments in 1:18-32 were intended to refer to the whole world of paganism, the pagan world with which he was most acquainted was the Greek and Roman world. This otherwise highly advanced world, for the time, was deeply contaminated with gross immorality.

> The prevalence of this horrible vice is abundantly illustrated in the classics . . . .Dollinger remarks that in the whole of the literature of the ante-Christian period, hardly a writer has decisively condemned it. In the Doric states, Crete and Sparta, the practice was favored as a means of education and was acknowledged by law. Even Socrates could not forbear feeling like a Greek on this point (see Plato's *Charmides*). In Rome, in the earlier centuries of the republic, it was of rare occurrence; but at the close of the sixth century it had become general. Even the best of the emperors, Antoninus and Trajan, were guilty (Vincent, 672).

In recent years there have been those who have advocated homosexuality as an alternate lifestyle. There have even been those who propose to be evangelicals who have claimed that the Bible does not condemn homosexual experience as long as there is love and a permanent commitment between the parties involved. They consider their condition to be "natural" and not condemned by Paul. (See Richard Quebedeaux, *The Worldly Evangelicals*, 128-131.)

Such interpretation will not stand. It is clear that in vv. 26, 27 the "natural" refers to a sexual relationship between male and female. It is necessarily implied that homosexuality is not natural, that is, not in harmony with God's design for men and women. Also, 1 Cor. 6:9, 10 is clear in condemning homosexuality.

While there can be no doubt that Scripture condemns homosexuality, it is incorrect to say that such people cannot find forgiveness and deliverance. "God also gave them up" in v. 24 does not mean that there is no hope for them. (See comments on v.24.) Also, it is clear in 1 Cor. 6:9-11 that some people at Corinth had been forgiven and delivered from homosexuality.

c. God has given them over to all kinds of unrighteousness (vv. 28-32).

28 And even as they did not like to retain God in *their* knowledge, God gave them over to a reprobate mind, to do those things which are not convenient;
29 Being filled with all unrighteousness, fornication, wickedness, covetousness, maliciousness; full of envy, murder, debate, deceit, malignity; whisperers,
30 Backbiters, haters of God, despiteful, proud, boasters, inventors of evil things, disobedient to parents,
31 Without understanding, covenant breakers, without natural affection, implacable, unmerciful:
32 Who knowing the judgment of God, that they which commit such things are worthy of death, not only do the same, but have pleasure in them that do them.

And even as they did not like to retain God in their knowledge. The word "like" (Greek *dokimazo*) needs explanation:

> Actually, the verb *dokimazo* has two main meanings: (1) 'Test' or 'prove'; (2) 'approve' as the result of the testing. It was used of testing metals or coins, to see if they were genuine. This gives a startling connotation to the passage under consideration. Humanity had tested Deity and disapproved Him. Consequently man had rejected God (Earle 39).

The people under study tested God. He failed their test. They did not approve to retain (or to have) God in their knowledge (Greek *epignosis*). This word refers to *full* knowledge. They chose to suppress into the subconscious mind (as much as possible) the knowledge which they possessed of God. (See comments on v. 21.) They did not approve to allow this knowledge of God to advance to full knowledge and be acknowledged by the conscious mind. Rather, they chose to reject God and move in the pathway of idolatry (vv. 21-23, 25).

God gave them over to a reprobate mind. The first part of v. 28 begins with "And even as": Even as (or just as) they disapproved of God, so God gave them over to a reprobate mind.

The word for "reprobate" (Greek *adokimos*) means disapproved. There is a play on words. They did not *approve* to have God in their knowledge; therefore, God gave them over to a *disapproved* mind.

To do those things which are not convenient. Convenient (Greek *katheko*) is that which is normally proper. This they were failing to do. Shedd (30) says that the phrase "things which are not convenient" is a figure of speech (called a litotes) for *detestable*. The kind of mind which God disapproved was that which was bent on doing what is morally detestable. Because of their refusal to acknowledge and follow God, He gave them over to a mind that would contrive all kinds of evil things to do.

The mind (Greek *nous*) is the capacity for thinking. With the mind we reason, comprehend, and understand. It is true that it is used sometimes with a moral or spiritual connotation, but it always involves thinking.

Sometimes the word involves the mind, the heart, and the will. According to *Thayer's Greek-English Lexicon of the New Testament*, one of the meanings of *nous* is, "The mind, comprising alike the faculties of perceiving and understanding and those of feeling, judging, determining. . ." (429). This is the use of mind in repentance (Greek *metanoia*) which means to change one's mind. When a person says, "I have made up my mind to serve the Lord," he means, "I have decided with my mind, heart, and will to serve the Lord." However, it is important to observe that whenever the "mind" does embrace emotions and will, thinking is always involved. It never refers simply to emotions as such, nor to will as such. It is thinking that embraces the heart and will. Where the *mind* is involved, there is always thinking. Where the *heart* is involved, there is always a measure of feeling of inner reality. (See comments on v. 21.)

In the verse before us, the mind gave rise to wrong ideas. These ideas were accompanied by inner agreement, and that led to improper behavior.

Being filled with all unrighteousness. Unrighteousness (Greek *adikia*) is a general term which includes all of the sins listed in vv. 29-31.

Fornication (Greek *porneia*) is a broad term to cover all forms of sexual sin. There is no basis for limiting the Greek word to sexual intercourse between unmarried people. (In view of the fact that *porneia* is not in the oldest Greek manuscripts here, many scholars are of the opinion that it was not in the original manuscript. Whether or not, the Scriptures make abundantly clear that it is sinful, so it will do no damage to the message of God if it is included here.)

Wickedness (Greek *poneria*) refers to active wickedness or mischief.

Covetousness (Greek *pleonexia*) is greed: "the sinful desire which goes out after things of time and sense of every form and kind. Hence it is defined by Paul (Col. 3:5) as *idolatry*, the worship of another object other than God, and is so often associated with fleshly sins, as 1 Cor. 5:11; Eph. 5:3, 5; Col. 3:5" (Vincent 673).

The covetous person is controlled by an insatiable desire for having more. He is never satisfied regardless how much he has. His desire for more may create a pressure that can cause him to resort to wrong means to fulfill his desires.

Maliciousness (Greek *kakia*) is considered by some to refer to a bad inward disposition while wickedness (*poneria*) refers to the outward manifestation of the inward disposition. Others point out that it is difficult to support this difference.

Envy (Greek *phthonos*) "is the feeling of displeasure produced by witnessing or hearing of the advantage or prosperity of others; this evil sense always attaches to this word" (*Vine's Dictionary* 377).

Murder (Greek *phonos*): some suggest that the placing together of envy and murder is because of the similarity of the sound of the two words in Greek. Bible writers, too, at times enjoyed making a play on words.

Debate (Greek *eris*) refers to strife. It does not condemn the exchange of differences of opinion when such is properly conducted.

Deceit (Greek *dolos*) refers to bait. It is the intention to mislead another for one's advantage.

Malignity (Greek *kakoetheia*) refers to "an evil disposition that tends to put the worst construction on everything" (*Vine's Dictionary* 714).

Whisperers (Greek *psithuristes*)

refers to those involved in secret slander.

Backbiters (Greek *katalalos*) refers to those involved in open slander.

Haters of God (Greek *theostuges*) is thought by some to be understood in the passive sense—hated by God. The majority accept the active—haters of God. This view best suits the context: "In classical Greek *[theostuges]* seems always to have a passive sense, 'hated by God,' and the Vulgate understands it here as 'hateful to God'; but an active sense fits the present context much better and should be accepted" (Cranfield 131).

Despiteful (Greek *hubristes*) refers to an insolent person. "It is best understood here as signifying the man who, in his confidence in his own superior power, wealth, social status, physical strength, intellectual or other ability, treats his fellow men with insolent contemptuousness and thereby affronts the majesty of God" (Cranfield 131).

Proud (Greek *huperephanos*) is "From *huper* and *phainomai*, to appear above others, arrogant in thought and conduct, 'stuck up'" (Robertson 332).

Boasters (Greek *aladzon*) "denotes the man who tries to impress others by making big claims. It was used of the braggart, the charlatan, the quack, the impostor" (Cranfield 132).

Inventors of evil things (Greek *epheuretas kakon*) refers to those who look for new ways to commit sin: "So intent were they on practicing evil, so resolved to gratify their passions, that the mind was excited to discover new modes of gratification" (Barnes 52).

Disobedient to parents (Greek *goneusin apeitheis*) is not simply disobedience to a command. It is the disobedience that grows out of the refusal to be persuaded. It is the same as we would mean by saying that children will not listen to their parents. They refuse instruction.

Without understanding (Greek *asunetos*) is also used in 1:21. It describes the effect of the fall on the intellect. (See Shedd 32.) "*Asunetos* is a verbal adjective from *suniemi*, to put together, and *a* privative, unintelligent, not able to put together the manifest evidence about God (v. 20)" (Robertson 329). In commenting on the use of *asunetos* in 1:21, Vincent observes, "They did not combine the facts which were patent to their observation" (670).

When fallen man is viewed as being thus "without understanding" this appears to me to mean unable to put things together to form a correct world-view. He is unable to get a true grasp of meaning and purpose.

Apart from the redemptive revelation of God in Scripture, and apart from the experience of saving grace, man's knowledge is fragmentary. Man as created in the image of God, though fallen, is still capable of outstanding achievements. The accomplishments of our own generation in such things as medicine, electronics, and space travel attest to the fact that men are able to go a long way in intellectual achievements as it relates to parts of the whole. At the same time our generation with its secular bent is painfully aware of its inability to adequately deal with problems like drugs, alcohol, and crime. Man is made for meaning and purpose and will malfunction without having a view that puts things together.

Why is fallen man unable to put things together? Many are of the opinion that if man had not fallen, general revelation would have been adequate for him to construct a proper world-view and chart his course before God. In my opinion this is incorrect. The need for special revelation grows out of the fact that God is personal and man is personal. It was special revelation that told Adam that he would die if he ate of the tree of the knowledge of good and evil (Gen. 2:17).

For man to understand God, the universe, and himself, would have required special revelation in addition to general revelation. A personal knowledge and acquaintance with God would have required that God speak even if sin had never entered the picture. We can learn a great deal about a material object by investigation; but if we are going to learn much about a *person*, it is necessary for him to communicate with us. This is true because of the nature of personality, and not because of the limitations suffered by the mind of man through the fall.

It is important that we recognize that man not only fell into sin, but he also fell from God. When he fell from God, he was placed in an awful predicament. His design called for a relationship with God, yet he was shut off from God. He was made for purpose and meaning, but he was unable to discover it or put it together. He was afloat on the sea of life with unmet needs and unanswered questions.

No amount of intelligence before the fall or after the fall could possibly put together a world-view that would give purpose and meaning to life except by the speaking of the personal God. When man fell from God, he fell from a relationship where personal communication existed between him and God. Thus he closed the door, so far as he was concerned within himself, to any possibility of putting things together to form a meaningful picture of the whole of reality. This alienation and the lostness that goes with it will remain until man heeds the redemptive revelation of God, experiences the saving grace of God, and is restored to a functional relationship with God.

The fact that fallen man cannot discover meaning and purpose means that he will have the painful experience of contradiction. The only morality that his deep, inner self will accept is the morality of the Ten Commandments, written in his own moral constitution (Rom. 2:15). Yet his inability to put things together, plus the power of sin in his fallen nature, will at times pull him into sin regardless of what he acknowledges. At other times, he will call that right which is wrong. His conscious mind may be deceived into thinking that abortion, euthanasia, homosexuality, and similar sins are right. But his subconscious mind cannot escape that which is written in his moral constitution. Our being will never accept the gross violation of the morality of the Ten Commandments.

There is another side of the contradiction in man's experience that must not be overlooked. While fallen man cannot put things together, he is able to have fragmentary knowledge of ethical matters which show that all traces of nobility are not gone. Compassion and kindness surface at times. Voices for decency may be heard here and there. The moral constitution is not completely silenced because fallen man is still in the image of God. But all signs of nobility are isolated fragments, never put together in a meaningful whole. Contradiction manifests itself, as is plain in our day. The same people who promote abortion and support homosexuality as an alternate lifestyle are at times seen promoting care for the less fortunate.

Covenant breakers (Greek *asunthetos*) refers to: "men who treat covenants as 'a scrap of paper'" (Robertson 333). "Even their strongest promises, their sworn word, cannot be trusted" (Lenski 122).

Without natural affection (Greek *astorgos*). "Among the various words for 'love' in Greek *storge* was the one which particularly denoted family affection" (Cranfield 132). The word used here means the absence of this family affection. It "denotes the destruction even of the feelings of natural tenderness, as is seen in a mother who exposes or kills her child, a father who abandons his family, or children who neglect their aged parents" (Godet 111). "It was not unusual for pagans to drown or in some other way to destroy unwanted off-spring. In this connection think of the present-day *abortion*, for which all kinds of excuses are being invented" (Hendriksen 82).

"Never was the life of the child so precarious as at this time. Children were considered a misfortune. When a child was born, it was taken and laid at the father's feet. If the father lifted it up that meant he acknowledged it. If he turned away and left it, the child was literally thrown out. There was never a night when there were not thirty or forty abandoned children left in the Roman forum" (Barclay 39).

Implacable (Greek *aspondos*). As with the word for fornication (v. 29), there is a question whether this word was in the original manuscript. See comments on v. 29. The word refers to "one who cannot be persuaded to enter into a covenant" (*Vine's Dictionary* 590).

Unmerciful (Greek *aneleemon*) means pitiless. This is a fitting description of the others referred to in this verse, especially those who were without natural affection.

Who knowing the judgment of God, that they which commit such things are worthy of death. For those who deny that pagans have some knowledge of God this verse presents a problem in saying that they know the judgment of God and that "they which commit such things are worthy of death." This problem has been dealt with in the comments about "knowing" (v. 21). In many this knowledge is suppressed into the sub-conscious mind, but suppressed knowledge is still knowledge.

Paul did not say that they had a well-developed doctrine of judgment and Hell. He said they knew that people who did such things (as are listed in vv. 29-31) were "worthy of death." Whenever the message of judgment and Hell as set forth in special revelation is presented to a person, it is not addressing a completely blank area of his knowledge.

When special revelation is allowed to work in a person's heart and mind, it does not introduce knowledge where total ignorance has existed. Rather, special revelation enlarges and clarifies that which is already there by general revelation.

Not only do the same, but have pleasure in them that do them. The word translated "have pleasure in" (Greek *suneudokeo*) means literally "to think well with." In Acts 8:1 it is translated "consenting." Paul was "consenting" to the stoning of Stephen. In Luke 11:48 it is translated "allow." Jesus accused the Pharisees of approving or "concurring with" their forefathers when they killed the prophets.

Paul accused the pagans of not only committing the sins enumerated, but also concurring, approving, or delighting in the same actions when practiced by others. There are two possible interpretations of this. Some commentators understand Paul to mean that the people under discussion not only practice the sins enumerated; they also approve or delight in seeing other people do the same. The addition of delighting in seeing others commit these sins is thought to add to the seriousness of their guilt.

Other interpreters think Paul is referring to two classes of people: (1) those who practice these sins and (2) those who delight in seeing others commit these sins. (For this view see Barrett 41.)

The most natural meaning is the first view. (See Cranfield 134, 135.) The reason some have opposed the first view is that they think it would say that delighting in an evil deed is worse than performing the deed. It does not seem to me that Paul is making a blanket statement that it is worse to delight in an evil deed than to perform the evil deed. Rather, he is saying that a deeper degree of sinfulness is represented when a person delights in seeing others sin than would be if he simply committed the sin.

There is hypocrisy in condemning in others what one does; but as long as a person condemns sin in others, there is some hope he will yet come under conviction about his own sin. However, when people not only fail to see the sinfulness of other people's actions but also delight in their sins, our hope for their repentance is greatly lessened.

Most people who are involved in gross sin, while they may have moments of pleasure in their sin, are not exactly at peace with themselves in what they are doing. It represents a lower degree of depravity when a person begins to delight in seeing others dragged into the same pit with him.

Another point to be considered is that in a moment of passion, pressure, or weakness a person may do something that is out of character for him. That person is not under the same pressure to delight in the sinful practices of others. (See Calvin 83; Cranfield 135; Hendriksen 82.)

Summary
1:18-32

In 1:17 Paul had pointed out that the gospel tells us about a God-provided righteousness which is available to us on the condition of faith. A reason needed to be given for this provision of righteousness on the part of God. This reason is given in v. 18.

This God-provided righteousness is needed because the wrath of God is revealed from Heaven against all lack of reverence for God, all unrighteousness, and the suppression of the truth.

Why is God's wrath revealed even against pagans? Because that which is known is manifest in them. God has taken the initiative in revealing Himself. Through the created universe and through the man's own make-up as designed by the Creator, the eternal power and the basic nature of God are clearly seen. For this reason even those who have only general revelation are without defense for their sin. No defense attorney can successfully claim ignorance for the pagan based on his lack of special revelation.

Another reason that the pagans are without defense is the fact that even though they know God, they have not treated God with due respect and appreciation. They have become vain in their reasoning. Their deep inner self has been darkened. They have exchanged the worship of God for the worship of idols. These idols are made in the likeness of man, birds, fourfooted beasts, and even creeping things.

Since they have not treated God with due respect, and since they have suppressed the knowledge of God into their sub-conscious minds so they can act as if they do not know God, He has given them over to the practice of adultery. God ceased to restrain them and lets them do that which is dishonoring to them. This action was taken against those who had exchanged the truth of God for a lie. Idols are a lie because they represent a god who does not exist.

The fact that they have exchanged the truth of God for a lie is also the basis for further punishment from God. God has given them over to the practice of homosexuality, which in turn has its own penalty.

These people had put God to a test and did not approve to have Him in their minds. God, then, gave them over to a mind which He disapproved. This mind led them into all kinds of unrighteousness.

They continued in these wicked acts in spite of the fact that in their deep inner being they knew that the judgment of God was against such actions. They knew that they were worthy of death. To make matters worse, in addition to their practice of these sins they delighted in seeing others do the same things.

Application: Teaching and Preaching the Passage

1. There can be no adequate preaching of the gospel by preaching its positive side without its negative side. Paul made it unquestionably clear that it was the wrath of God which made the God-provided righteousness necessary (v. 18).

2. The passage has the three failures of v. 18 running through it. Ungodliness (the lack of reverence) is treated in vv. 21-23, 25. Unrighteousness (the failure to do right) is treated in vv. 24, 26-32. The suppression of the truth is treated in vv. 21-23, 25, 28.

These are three ways sin expresses itself. All sin is placed in one of three categories. God's wrath is against all three. The person whom we call "the good moral man" is guilty of *ungodliness*. He is not living a reverential life before God. This is evidenced by the fact that he has not submitted his life to God through Jesus Christ. He is also guilty of *unrighteousness* and the *suppression of the truth*, but it may be easier to get him to see his need by pointing out how he is guilty of ungodliness. (See comments on v. 18.)

3. Paul, unquestionably, considered the heathen to be without defense for their sins. There were two reasons given for this: (1) God's revelation of Himself to them through general revelation (vv. 19, 20) was of such a nature that they could not plead ignorance. (2) They are responsible for the way they have treated God in light of the fact that the knowledge of God exists within them (vv. 21-23, 25).

4. It is very serious for a person to fail to glorify God and to fail to be thankful to God. This was the first step made by the pagan world in its departure from God into the lowest levels of idolatry. If a person does not repent of his failure to treat God properly, he is leaving himself open to the worst kind of error (vv. 21-23).

5. A study of this passage convinces us of the fact that God has so designed man that as a result of general revelation all people know of God (vv. 19-21). This is true whether they admit it or not. It is still knowledge even if it is suppressed into the sub-conscious mind and denied entrance to the conscious mind. The same can be said about a knowledge of God's judgment (v. 32). We can rest assurred that when we address a person with the redemptive message of special revelation, we are not addressing one who deep-down knows nothing about God, sin, and judgment. We are giving a further clarification of and a development of what is already there. (See comments on v. 21.)

6. In his revolt against God, fallen man turns out to be the great loser. God delivers him over to the sinful urges of his own heart. In the practice of sexual immorality, a person places himself in a state of contradiction of the very design that God placed in his deep inner self. This violation of the moral constitution of man results in an unavoidable inner conflict. Sexual sin is dishonoring to the body, which stands for the whole personality (v. 24). The fact that people do suffer from their sins turns out to be for their own good. It is this suffering which forms a point of contact for the message of redemption which is man's only answer for his needs (v. 24).

7. In recent years an effort has been made to make homosexuality an acceptable, "alternate" life-style. A few have claimed that the Bible does not condemn homosexual acts between persons who love one another. Such a conclusion will not stand in the light of vv. 26, 27 and 1 Cor. 6:9-20.

While we deplore attempts to make homosexuality an acceptable life-style, God has been able to work good out of these attempts. Along with setting forth the Biblical condemnation of homosexuality, some have also felt an obligation to minister to homosexuals, and with some degree of success.

Christ died for homosexuals. There is hope for homosexuals. On the one hand, we must insist that homosexual behavior is sin; on the other hand, we must try to help them. It is not easy to help people overcome homosexuality, but we must try. (For those who want to be more informed on how to work with homosexuals, I would recommend the book edited by Charles W. Keyser, *What You Should Know About Homosexuality*. Another helpful book is *The Returns of Love* by Alex Davidson. This book deals with the struggles of a person who controlled his homosexual tendencies; it should be of value to a person who is trying to overcome homosexuality. Both of these books take the position that homosexuality is a sin. On some other points mentioned in these books there may be room for a difference of opinion.)

8. A profitable study can be made of the list of sins given in vv. 29-31. (See comments on these verses.) It would be of further value to compare the lists in 1 Cor. 6:9, 10; Gal. 5:19-21; and Eph. 5:3-5.

9. A valuable lesson is learned from the words, "not only do the same, but have pleasure in them that do them" in v. 32. Paul is telling us that it is wrong for us to enjoy it when others commit sin. This principle should guide us in our pursuit of pleasure. It will help us decide what we should watch and listen to.

10. If God holds the heathen accountable for their sins as this passage (vv. 18-32) teaches, how much more accountable to God are we who have become acquainted with the special revelation of God in the Bible!

B. The Jews Have Failed Before God (2:1—3:8)

There is a difference of opinion whether Paul has the Jews in mind at the beginning of chapter 2 or whether he begins to deal with the Jews in 2:17. The *Scofield Bible* outline suggests that Paul is addressing Gentile moralizers in vv.1-16. In v. 17 he begins to address the Jew.

Very few agree that Paul does not address the Jew until verse 17. There is a general consensus that Paul has the Jew in mind from the beginning of the chapter. Some take the position that Paul also had in mind those Gentiles who promoted high moral ideals. I am of the opinion that Paul had Jews in mind when he started chapter 2. To whatever extent his comments fitted Gentile moralizers, it would grow out of the fact that Paul was dealing with universal principles (for discussion on who Paul had in mind see Bruce 86-89; Cranfield 137-140; Godet 113, 114; Haldane 72, 73; Hodge 46, 47; Lenski 28-30; Murray 54-56; and Olshausen 93, 94).

When it came to a matter of establishing guilt before God, the Jews presented a unique problem. It was easier to establish the guilt of the pagan who only had general revelation than it was of the Jew, who had received special revelation.

If we wanted to establish the guilt of the whole human race, we would take the easier step first. We would establish the guilt of those who have been confronted by special revelation. Then, we would attempt to establish the guilt of those who have not been confronted by special revelation.

The easier step for Paul was to establish the guilt of those who only had general revelation. Therefore, he took that step first (1:18-32). Then, the more difficult step followed. In 2:1—3:8 he seeks to establish the guilt and condemnation of the Jew.

While Paul's aim in 1:18—3:20 was to establish the guilt of the whole human race before God, it appears that the predominate concern of his mind was to establish the guilt of the Jew. This concern shaped his approach. Since it would not be difficult to convince the Jew of the guilt and condemnation of the Gentile, he dealt with that first. Then, in 2:1—3:8, he proceeds to show there are no grounds for the Jew to expect to escape God's wrath when he is guilty of the same sins which he condemns in the Gentile. The fact that it was more difficult to convince the Jew of his guilt before God is manifested by the fact that only 15 verses were taken up with establishing the guilt of the Gentiles (1:18-32). Thirty-seven verses (2:1—3:8) were given to establishing the guilt of the Jew.

The main difficulty of the Jew grew out of a misunderstanding of the Abrahamic Covenant. God promised to Abraham and his seed the land of Palestine for an eternal inheritance (Gen. 13:14, 15 and 17:8). This was an eschatological promise to Abraham and his seed. Later developments show that the Covenant seed were the descendants of Abraham through Jacob (Rom. 9:6-12). (Attention will be given to the significance of the Abrahamic Covenant in chapters 4, 9, and 11.)

Since the covenant seed of Abraham were given the eschatological promise of the eternal inheritance of the land of Palestine, the Jews were prone to think that being the seed of Abraham guaranteed their redemption. It was this kind of thinking that caused John the Baptist to say to the Pharisees and Sadducees, "Bring forth therefore fruits meet for repentance: And think not to say within yourselves, We have Abraham to *our* father: for I say unto you, that God is able of these stones to raise up children unto Abraham" (Mt. 3:8, 9, see also Jn. 8:33-40).

That there was a line of thought among the Jews in which they assumed they would receive preferred treatment from God is seen in some of the apocryphal books. The writer of *Wisdom of Solomon* says, "For thou didst test them [Israel] as a father does in warnings but thou didst examine the ungodly [the Gentiles] as a stern king does in condemnation" (11:10). "So while chastening us thou scourgest our enemies [the Gentiles] ten thousand times more, so that we may meditate upon thy goodness when we judge, and when we are judged we may expect mercy" (12:22).

There was also some sense in which the Jews were depending upon their own righteousness. It was this false reliance upon their own righteousness which caused Paul to say, "But Israel, which followed after the law of righteousness, hath not attained to the law of righteousness. Wherefore? Because they sought it not by faith, but as it were by the works of the law" (Rom. 9:31, 32a).

Hodge combines both their hope based on the covenant and their hope based on works in his comments:

> In order to appreciate the apostle's reasoning...it should be remembered that the principal ground on which the Jews expected acceptance with God, was the covenant which he had made with their father Abraham, in which he promised to be a God to him and his seed after him. They understood this promise to secure salvation for all who retained their connection with Abraham by the observance of the law and the rite of circumcision. They expected, therefore, to be regarded and treated not so much as individuals, each being dealt with according to his personal

character, but as a community to whom salvation was secured by the promise made to Abraham (46, 47).

It was as if, because of the nature of the Abrahamic Covenant, Israel expected to experience corporate salvation. Because the Jew was a descendant of Abraham, his individual redemption was guaranteed along with the group (Israel) by birth and circumcision.

One would gather that in the prevailing Jewish thought the only way a Jew could be left out of the eschatological promise of the eternal inheritance of the land would be through becoming an apostate. This seems to be what Hodge is referring to in the quotation above when he said, "They understood this promise to secure salvation for all who retained their connection with Abraham by the observance of the law and rite of circumcision."

Philip Birnbaum in *A Book of Jewish Concepts* says, "Rabbi Israel Baal Shem Tov, founder of the Hasidim, is reported to have said: Every Jew is an organ of the *Shekkinah* [the Divine Presence]. As long as the organ is joined to the body, however tenuously, there is hope; once it is cut off, all hope is lost" (609, 610). This quotation comes from his treatment of "apostasy."

(The Hasidim to which he referred were not the Hasidim who were the forerunners of the Pharisees. Rather, they were a sect of Polish Jews in the eighteenth century. While this reference did not come from the N.T., it would seem that such thinking probably existed in N.T. times.)

It is apparent that the Jews prior to and during N.T. times had a difficulty in reconciling their beliefs that they were the especially favored of God with some of their experiences. The writer of the apocryphal book 2 Esdras is puzzled at what appears to him to be the preferred treatment given Gentiles. He is puzzled because of the covenant relationship of God with Israel and what appears to him to be the superior obedience of Israel. He says:

> *28 Then I said in my heart, Are the deeds of those who inhabit Babylon any better? Is that why she has gained dominion over Zion? 29 For when I came here I saw ungodly deeds without number, and my soul has seen many sinners during these thirty years. And my heart failed me. 30 For I have seen how thou dost endure those who sin, and hast preserved thy enemies, 31 and hast not shown to anyone how thy way may be comprehended. Are the deeds of Babylon better than those of Zion? 32 Or has another nation known thee besides Israel? Or what tribes have so believed the covenants as the tribes of Jacob? 33 Yet their reward has not appeared and their labor has borne no fruit. For I have traveled widely among the nations and have seen that they abound in wealth, though they are unmindful of thy commandments. 34 Now therefore weigh in a balance our iniquities and those of the inhabitants of the world; and so it will be found which way the turn of scale will incline. 35 When have the inhabitants of the earth not sinned in thy sight? Or what nation has kept thy commandments so well? 36 Thou mayest indeed find individual men who have kept thy commandments, but nations thou wilt not find* (2 Esdras 3:28-36).

The covenant relationship is referred to, and the concept of corporate righteousness is seen in this quotation from 2 Esdras (see also in this book 4:22-32; and 6:55-59).

While on the one hand there seemed to be the view among the Jews that almost all of them would be saved, on the other hand there was the note that only a few might be saved. Again we quote from 2 Esdras:

> *47 And now I see that the world to come will bring delight to few, but torments to many. 48 For an evil heart has grown up in us, which has alienated us from God, and has brought us into corruption and the ways of death, and has shown us the paths of perdition and removed us far from life—and that not just a few of us but almost all who have been created* (7:47, 48; See also 7:59-61, and 8:13).

The prevailing opinion among the Jews seemed to be that the Abrahamic Covenant put them in special relationship with God as far as salvation is concerned. It was in the context of this covenant relationship that their righteousness would have been evaluated. It appears that a concept of corporate salvation prevailed that would have come out of their understanding of the Abrahamic Covenant and the concept of corporate righteousness.

Since the Jew was misled by his view of corporate salvation, it would be of value if he could see the guilt of the nation as well as his individual guilt. He needed to reach the same conclusion as Isaiah when he said, "Woe *is* me! for I am undone; because I *am* a man of unclean lips, and I dwell in the midst of a people of unclean lips" (Is. 6:5).

1. The Jew is found wanting because he is guilty of the same sins as committed by the Gentiles (v.1).

1 Therefore thou art inexcusable, O man, whosoever thou art that judgest: for wherein thou judgest another, thou condemnest thyself; for thou that judgest doest the same things.

Therefore (Greek *dio*). Some believe that "therefore" reaches back only to 1:32 (Godet and Olshausen). Others believe that it includes 1:18-32 (Cranfield, Lenski, and Meyer). It appears to me that the reference is to 1:18-32. This conclusion seems necessary in light of the meaning of "the same things" at the end of v. 1.

Thou art inexcusable, O man, whosoever thou art that judgest. "Inexcusable" (Greek *anapologetos*) is translated "without excuse" in 1:20. The meaning is "without defense." "Whosoever" points out that the principle Paul is elaborating is universal. While it applies to anyone it fits, as Paul develops his thought he is primarily developing his case against the Jews who readily pass judgment on the Gentiles.

For wherein thou judgest another, thou condemnest thyself; for thou that judgest doest the same things. In 1:32 Paul had pointed out that the judgment of God is against: (1) those who commit the sins mentioned in chapter 1 and (2) those who concur in their hearts when other people commit these sins. It should be more obvious that God judges those who judge others for what they, themselves, are doing.

"The same things" obviously refers to the sins mentioned in 1:18-32. It is not necessary to conclude that Paul meant that the manisfestation of sin among Jews was identical to that among Gentiles. The only thing required by "the same things" is that the Jew would at some point be guilty of the sins mentioned. As Meyer says, ". . . not indeed according to all their several concrete manifestations, as previously described, but according to their essential moral categories; see vv. 17-24" (82).

The development of this thought is presented in this chapter: If a person were able to stand before God on his own merits, he would have to produce absolute righteousness. To violate at any point means to fail. No man can declare himself innocent of every sin mentioned in chapter 1. When the Jew judged the Gentile for his sin, he acknowledged that kind of knowledge that would render him responsible for the same actions in himself.

2. The Jew cannot escape God's judgment because its principles are universal (vv. 2-16).

a. It is according to truth (2:2-4).

2 But we are sure that the judgment of God is according to truth against them which commit such things.

We are sure. The meaning is "we know" (Greek *oida*). While "we" would obviously include Paul and the Jews under consideration, it goes beyond that to include mankind in general. As Hodge explains, "*We* does not refer to the Jews, as peculiarly instructed, but to all men" (47).

Paul builds his case with the Jew by stating a common ground that no one who takes God seriously could deny. Murray commenting on "we know" explains, "He means by this that it is incontestable truth with respect to which he will not allow any hesitation. He states it as an axiom of thought apart from which we cannot speak of *God's* judgment" (57).

That the judgment of God is according to truth. By "according to truth," Paul means that God's judgment will be accurate. A guilty person will be judged guilty. If he is innocent, he will be judged innocent.

In our courts a verdict could be wrong. The prosecuting attorney is trying to get the jury to believe the defendant is guilty. The defense attorney is trying to get the jury to believe the defendant is innocent. Under these circumstances it is possible for the jury to render an incorrect verdict. There is no such risk in the Divine judgment. The verdict given by God will always be true. Briscoe observes:

> Even the best legal systems in the world ask for nothing more than a verdict 'beyond reasonable doubt.' In a court of law everyone knows that the evidence is open to question, the witnesses are prone to error, the jury can be misled, and the judge is quite capable of making a mistake. But in the Court of God there will be no misunderstanding, no misrepresentation, no miscarriage of justice, no misdemeanor, and no mistakes—all will be according to truth (58).

Against them which commit such things. "Such things" refers back to "the same things" of v. 1.

Paul is driving home to the Jew the fact that no matter who a person is if he fails to meet God's requirement he will be judged guilty. The fact that the Jews are Abraham's seed will not change this principle (see Haldane 76 and Hodge 48).

3 And thinkest thou this, O man, that judgest them which do such things, and doest the same, that thou shalt escape the judgment of God?

Paul puts this verse in the form of a question. He seeks to get the Jew to see that this thinking is absurd. Such would suggest that a person could judge another while being guilty of the same sins. Certainly, no thinking person would expect to go free while condemning another for what he, himself, is doing. Yet, the unbelieving Jews were guilty of this very kind of thinking.

4 Or despisest thou the riches of his goodness and forbearance and longsuffering; not knowing that the goodness of God leadeth thee to repentance?

Paul is pressing his case further against the unbelieving Jew. He raises a question intended to help the Jew recognize that he has grossly misinterpreted the goodness of God. The first occurrence of the word "goodness" (Greek *chrestos*) and the second occurrence (Greek *chrestotes*) mean kindness or generosity. Forbearance (Greek *anoche*) refers to a temporary suspension of wrath (Vincent 675 and Trench 186, 187). Longsuffering (Greek *makrothumia*) is the opposite of being short-tempered. Vine explains, "If forbearance denotes delay in executing judgment, longsuffering denotes the particular disposition which delays it" (*Romans* 29). "Despise" (Greek *kataphroneo*) means "to think down." Paul is suggesting that the unbelieving Jew had grossly misunderstood the goodness of God toward them. They thought that God's goodness toward them indicated a right standing with Him.

The Jew was guilty of "not knowing that the goodness of God leadeth thee to repentance." "Not knowing" (Greek *agnoeo*), according to Cranfield, "denotes here a thoroughly blameworthy not-knowing" (144). Such ignorance was inexcusable. They were guilty of thinking down toward (or holding in contempt) the goodness of God.

The word "repentance" (Greek *metanoia)* occurs only here in Romans. The other occurrences of this word in Paul's writings are 2 Cor. 7:9, 10 and 2 Tim. 2:25. The verb form "repent" (Greek *metanoeo*) occurs only in 2 Cor. 12:21.

The scarce use of "repentance" seems to puzzle some people since it is involved in becoming a Christian. This problem will be solved by a correct understanding of the relationship between repentance and saving faith.

Repentance involves both a turning *from* and a turning *to*. While both elements are in the word, the major thrust is on the "turning to." The "to" on which repentance terminates is identical with saving faith. The exercise of repentance terminates in faith. To have faith of necessity involves repentance.

The close relationship of repentance and faith could be illustrated thus. If we were to say to a man in Atlanta, "Leave Atlanta and go to New York," it would involve a "from" and a "to." This would illustrate repentance.

If we simply say to the man in Atlanta, "Go to New York," that would illustrate faith. Though you do not stress the fact that he must leave Atlanta, it is obvious that if he would go to New York he would have to leave Atlanta.

In salvation there is no repentance if it does not terminate in believing in Jesus Christ as Lord and Savior. If a person does exercise faith in Jesus Christ as Lord and Savior, it is obvious that he must turn away from unbelief. (For a more complete discussion of repentance and faith, see Forlines, *Systematics* 199-205.)

Concerning the words for repentance, Cranfield explains:

> The fact that these words are so seldom used by Paul certainly does not mean that repentance is not important for him. The explanation of it is rather that repentance is for him an integral element of *pistis,* [faith] (144, 145, note 2).

b. It is a righteous judgment (vv. 5-16).

(1) God's judgment will be according to one's deeds (vv. 5-10).

5 But after thy hardness and impenitent heart treasurest up unto thyself wrath against the day of wrath and revelation of the righteous judgment of God.

Up to v. 5 Paul had raised some questions which were designed to get the unbelieving Jew to understand the fallacy of the case which he had built for himself. In v. 5 Paul describes in no uncertain terms the tragic state of affairs of the Jew who thought he would get by simply because he was of the seed of Abraham.

But after thy hardness and impenitent (Greek *ametanoetos)* **heart.** This refers to the refusal to repent which grows out of the hardness or stubbornness of the heart.

In a very pointed way, Paul said to the Jew that by this path of action **thou treasurest up unto thyself wrath.** The refusal to let the goodness of God lead him to repentance would turn out to be very costly. There is irony in Paul's statement. The treasure which the Jew was laying up was the very opposite of what he was expecting. It was an accumulation of wrath.

Against (Greek *en)* is better understood as "in" or "on." The Jew was storing up wrath "in" **the day of wrath and revelation of the righteous judgment of God.** This is the "day when God shall judge the secrets of men" in v. 16. The judgment of God will be a righteous judgment. The holy nature of God requires that it be such.

6 Who will render to every man according to his deeds.

The point of this verse is clear and simple. When we appear before God, the thing that counts is not going to be whether we are Jew or Gentile. It will make no difference what our station in life was. The thing that will matter is what kind of deeds we have performed.

While reading vv. 6-16, a person may wonder: how is what Paul is saying consistent with the doctrine of grace which he so ably presents in his writings? It will be better to see how Paul develops his thought in this passage before dealing with how this fits in with his doctrine of grace (see comments on v. 13).

7 To them who by patient continuance in well doing seek for glory and honour and immortality, eternal life.

Paul is describing those whose deeds are such that they will be blessed of God when He judges men.

To them who by patient continuance (Greek *hupomone*) **in well doing.** Earle gives a rather extensive treatment of the word (Greek *hupomone*) which is here rendered "patient continuance." He concludes by saying, "It is clear that in this passage *hupomone* means more than passive endurance. It obviously has the sense of active perseverance or steadfastness. For the Greek literally reads 'steadfastness' of [or *in*] good work" (Earle 50, 51; brackets his).

Seek for glory and honour and immortality (Greek *aphtharsia)*, **eternal life.** It is only in this verse that this word is translated "immortality." In 1 Cor. 15:42, 50, 53, 54, it is translated "incorruption." Incorruption is the preferred translation here. Immortality is a necessary inference from incorruption. Godet says, "[It refers to] the absolute impossibility of any wound or interruption or end to this state of being" (118, 119).

The way this verse is usually translated the object of the seeking is glory, honor, and incorruption. The reward which is "rendered" (v. 6) is eternal life. Some hold the opinion that the object of the seeking is eternal life and the reward which is rendered is glory, honor, and incorruption. The last view is held by Lenski (151). Most commentators hold the first view and do not make reference to the second view. Godet (118, 119); Lange (97, 98); Meyer (86); and Olshausen (101) mention the last view, but favor the first.

It is usually agreed that either would be grammatically possible. I agree with Lenski for the following reasons: (1) It is beyond dispute that the object of render in v. 10 is "glory, honour, and peace." (2) The basis for receiving glory, honor, and peace is working good. It seems that Paul is saying essentially the same thing in vv. 7 and 10.

8 But unto them that are contentious, and do not obey the truth, but obey unrighteousness, indignation and wrath.

But unto them that are contentious (Greek *eritheia*). The word occurs 7 times in the N.T. In 2 Cor. 12:20; Gal. 3:20; Phil. 2:3; Jas. 3:14 and 16, it is translated "strife." In Phil. 1:16 it is "contention."

The exact meaning of this word is uncertain. Some understand the meaning to be "factious." Others understand it to mean self-seeking. Discussions on the meaning of the word can be found in Barrett 47; Cranfield 148; Earle 51, 52; Lenski 152; and Murray 65.

While there can be no dogmatic case built for which meaning was intended by Paul, it appears that self-seeking may be the meaning. The self-seeking person has rejected the theocentric view of life. Instead he has chosen a self-centered outlook. The self-centered outlook causes him to be ruled by immediacy. He looks for pleasure today without considering the consequences for eternity. This blinds him to the eternal consequences of his actions.

And do not obey (Greek *apeitheo*) **the truth, but obey** (Greek *peitho*) **unrighteousness.** Failure to obey refers to disobedience that grows out of a refusal to believe or be persuaded of the truth. As Hodge says, "This clause therefore means, *who refuse assent and obedience to the truth*" (51).

Instead of believing and obeying the truth, they believe and obey (Greek *peitho)* unrighteousness.

Indignation (Greek *thumos*) **and wrath** (Greek *orge*). Hendriksen explains, "If when these two words are used in connection with *God*, there is a difference in meaning, it would probably be that [*orge*] stresses the *presence* or *feeling* of keen divine displeasure or indignation, while [*thumos*] places the emphasis on its *effusion*" (93).

9 Tribulation and anguish, upon every soul of man that doeth evil, of the Jew first, and also of the Gentile.

Tribulation (Greek *thlipsis*) **and anguish** (Greek *stenochoria*). In v. 8 "indignation and wrath" are what God expresses toward those who obey not the truth. "Tribulation and anguish" refer to the sinner's experience of God's wrath and indignation.

Vine says, "*Thlipsis* is the suffering which results from what presses hard on the soul." He continues to say, "*Stenochoria*, literally, signifies the condition of one who is shut up without the possibility of escape, and hence it comes to denote a condition of distress. The four words [wrath, indignation, tribulation, and anguish] suggest a series of causes and effects. The first indicates God's attitude, the second the expression of that attitude, the third the results therefrom, the fourth the realization of entire helplessness" (*Romans* 33).

Upon every soul (Greek *psuche*) **of man that doeth evil.** The word refers to the person, not a part of the person. (See Forlines, *Systematics* 114-117 for a discussion of the meaning of soul.) Those who do evil will experience tribulation and distress in the eschatological future when God brings them to judgment.

Of the Jew first, and also of the Gentile (or Greek since the word is *Hellen*). This is the first time in chapter 2 that Paul mentions the Jew by name. The "Jew first" involved both a privilege and an accountability. This verse deals with the accountability. See comments on 1:16 for a discussion of the privilege.

10 But glory, honour, and peace, to every man that worketh good, to the Jew first, and also to the Gentile.

Paul again turns his attention to those who are working good. This verse says essentially the same thing that v. 7 does. As in v. 9 "Gentiles" is from *Hellen* which is the word for "Greek." See comments on 1:16 with reference to "the Jew first and also to the Gentiles."

(2) God's judgment will be without respect of persons (vv. 11-16).

11 For there is no respect of persons with God.

"Respect of persons" (Greek *prosopolempsia)* is derived from words (Greek *prosopon* and *lambano*) which mean face or person and receive. The meaning is to receive a face. The idea would be to judge a person based on his appearance without regard for his basic character. This would be to show partiality or favoritism. This God will never do. Family or race will mean nothing when we stand before God.

12 For as many as have sinned without law shall also perish without law: and as many as have sinned in the law shall be judged by the law.

In this verse Paul divides human beings into two classes—those without law (Greek *anomos*), and those in the law (Greek *nomos*). Those without law refers to all people who have not been a recipient of the law of God as given by special revelation. With regard to those "in the law," the Mosaic Law is that which immediately comes to mind. It could also refer to the revealed moral will of God as it is given in the N.T. Those without law are those who have neither the Mosaic Law, nor the moral will of God as found in the N.T.

Those "in the law" are those who have received the moral revelation of God in either the O.T., the N.T., or both. While the principles would apply to anybody who had received the revealed law of God, Paul is primarily concerned with the Jew who had the Mosaic Law.

Paul points out that those who sin without law will perish. This refers to the Gentiles who had not been confronted by the moral will of God as it has been given by special revelation.

The Jew who had sinned against the revealed moral will of God would be judged by the revealed law of God. While those who have not received the written law of God will not escape judgment, it is inferred that those who sinned with a knowledge of written law will be judged more severely.

13 For not the hearers of the law

are just before God, but the doers of the law shall be justified.

For not the hearers of the law are just before God. Paul wanted to drive home to the unbelieving Jew that while there were advantages in having the law, the simple possession of the law would not make anybody just in the sight of God.

But the doers of the law shall be just before God. "The doers of the law" are the same as those who continue in "well doing" in v. 7 and those who "work good" in v. 10.

Paul's reference to the reward of those who "continue in well doing" in vv. 7 and 10, and his statement "the doers of the law shall be justified" in v. 13 has raised some questions: (1) Is Paul consistent here with what he says elsewhere about justification by faith? (2) Assuming that it is consistent, how do we explain the consistency?

The question of consistency is tied in with the inspiration and authority of the Bible. Those who hold to Biblical inerrancy work on the assumption that there can be no contradiction with the rest of what Paul teaches. Several different views are held of how what Paul says here harmonizes with his doctrine of justification by faith.

The view that has more adherents than any other is that the "good works" and the "doers of the law" are the good works of a Christian. If a person's works do not attest to his salvation, he is not saved. The works referred to would be the essential evidence of being a Christian (Black 55; Cranfield 151, 152; Lenski 147, 148, 159, 160; Mills 56, 57, 61; and Sanday and Headlam, 57).

That works are an essential evidence of salvation is true, but that is not what Paul is speaking of in vv. 6-13. It is clear that in this passage the aim of Paul is to convince the unbelieving Jew that he is guilty and condemned. It does not fit Paul's purpose in this passage to deal with the evidence of salvation. He deals with that in chapters 6-8.

Another view, which has fewer adherents, is that "faith" is the good works in vv. 6-13. John 6:29 is given in support of this view. Jesus said, "This is the work of God, that ye believe on him whom he hath sent." This view has been set forth by Olshausen (99). Lange's view (96) does not seem to be significantly different from Olshausen's though Lange does list his view as being different.

Regardless of how appropriate it may be to speak of faith as a work, that cannot be the meaning here. This view must be rejected on the same basis as the one above. It is contrary to the purpose of the passage to understand Paul to be describing Christians.

A third view is that Paul is speaking hypothetically. It is said that perfect law-keeping would be required if a person would be justified by the law. Paul's hope was that in the light of this demand of the law for perfect obedience, the Jew would see that he is condemned rather than justified by the law. If the Jew could see that he was condemned by the law, it would improve his chances of becoming a Christian. (Adherents of this view are Barnes 61, 62; Haldane 81-85; Hodge 49, 50, 53, 54; Shedd 44, 45; and Steele and Thomas 21). A few combine some elements of the first view with this view. Verse 6 is viewed as teaching that works are the evidence of saving faith. Their notes on v. 13 will more clearly spell out the hypothetical view (see Hodge).

The hypothetical view is a move in the right direction, but it falls short of a complete understanding of what Paul is communicating in vv. 6-13. When Paul speaks of "patient continuance in well doing" (v. 7); "every man that worketh good" (v. 10); and "the doers of the law"

(v. 13), he is speaking of absolute obedience or absolute righteousness. That absolute righteousness is what Paul is speaking of is made clear by v. 12. "As many as have sinned" is the opposite of "the doers of the law." Wherever there is sin, the person is disqualified as a doer of the law.

In a different context, it could be legitimate to think of doers of the law in a relative sense, but such cannot be the case here. No person could, in this context, qualify as a "doer of the law" and at the same time belong to "as many as have sinned." That being true, only absolute righteousness will stand the test of the judgment as spoken of in v. 13.

I agree with those who hold the hypothetical view in saying that Paul's aim is to get the unbelieving Jew to see that as a law violator he is under condemnation. Where I differ is that I do not see it as hypothetical. *Paul is not simply telling the law violator that he is condemned; he is telling him what is required of anybody who will ever be justified in God's sight.*

The only way that any person can ever be justified before God is to have absolute righteousness (or to say it another way to be considered a doer of the law). Briefly put, in 2:6-13 Paul is saying that a person must have absolute righteousness. In 3:10 he points out, "There is none righteous." In 3:20 he points out that "by the deeds of the law shall no flesh be justified in his sight."

We must have absolute righteousness (2:6-13). We do not have righteousness (3:10). We cannot produce absolute righteousness (3:20). The only hope of justification for either Jew or Gentile is to have absolute righteousness provided for us. Just as surely as Paul, up through 3:20, sets forth our need, in 3:21-26 he proclaims a provision of absolute righteousness by Christ to meet our need.

As human beings we must be "doers of the law." In Christ we have His righteousness which, so far as our justification is concerned, makes us "doers of the law." Christ's obedience becomes our obedience. It can be seen that to be doers of the law (or to have absolute righteousness) is not a requirement that is set aside by grace. Rather, the requirement, which we could not meet, was met for us by Jesus Christ.

Having examined about 50 commentaries on this passage, I find John Gill's to be the view nearest to mine:

> These words must be understood either hypothetically, thus, not the hearers of the law, but if there were any perfect doers of it, they would be justified before God; or else of such persons who are considered in Christ by whom the whole perfect righteousness of the law is fulfilled in them, and who may be reckoned as perfect doers of it in him, their Substitute, Surety, and representative (12).

14 For when the Gentiles, which have not the law, do by nature the things contained in the law, these, having not the law, are a law unto themselves.

In the KJV vv. 13-15 are in parentheses. In the NIV vv. 14, 15 are placed in parentheses. If we follow the KJV we would understand vv. 12 and 16 to be connected since vv. 13-15 are considered parenthetical. According to the NIV vv. 13 and 16 would be connected since vv. 14 and 15 are parenthetical. Another view is to reject the idea that any of the verses are parenthetical and to consider v. 16 as connected with v. 15 (NASB).

I believe v. 16 is connected with v. 13, and vv. 14, 15 would be considered parenthetical. Verse 13 explains why those who have sinned will be condemned as is set forth in v. 12. They will be condemned because only "the doers of the law will be justified" (v. 13). A person who has sinned is not a doer of the law. Therefore, he is condemned.

Verses 13 and 16 would fit together in this way: "The doers of the law shall be justified. . .in the day when God shall judge the secrets of men." The time of the action spoken of in v. 13 will be the time mentioned in v. 16. It will be,"In the day when God shall judge the secrets of men by Jesus Christ. . . ."

The purpose of vv. 14 and 15 is to explain why and how the principle set forth in v. 13 is universal. These verses illustrate, in principle, how the Gentiles could theoretically be doers of the law though they have never received a direct moral revelation from God. There is no intended suggestion that anyone among the Gentiles was ever justified in this manner.

For when the Gentiles, which have not the law. Cranfield believes that "by nature" (Greek *phusis*) is connected with "law" which would read, "which have not the law by nature." The meaning would be, "They did not possess it by virtue of birth (as did the Jews)" (157). That which they did not possess by nature was the written law of God. "Do" would not be connected with "nature." Though they did not possess the written law by birth, they "do the things contained in the law."

Cranfield's interpretation is influenced by the fact that he believes that in vv. 6-16 the works referred to are the works of a Christian. Therefore, he interprets vv. 14, 15 to refer to Gentile Christians who "do the things contained in the law." He understands "the work of the law written in their hearts" in v. 15 to refer to a fulfillment of Jer. 31:33 which speaks about the New Covenant when God would write His law in the hearts of believers (158, 159).

Most commentaries, without comment, accept the connection of "nature" (*phusis*) with "do" in, "which have not the law, do by nature the things contained in the law." To connect "by nature" with "law" as Cranfield does has had only a few adherents. Hodge and Lange point out that Bengel, Ruckert, and Usteri support this view, but both Hodge (55) and Lange (101) reject it.

Harrison mentions the view that interprets "which shew the work of the law written in their hearts" as being a fulfillment of Jer. 31:33 (31). However, he joins Nygren in rejecting this interpretation.

Cranfield has been more consistent than most who consider the reference to "working good" in vv. 6-13 to refer to the good works which attest to saving faith. He has been consistent by continuing in vv. 14 and 15 to interpret them as referring to Gentile Christians.

It does not appear to fit in with Paul's purpose at this point to be discussing the evidence of being a Christian. Paul's aim is to show that all men are under condemnation and cannot merit their own justification.

In v. 14 Paul is showing how, in principle, it is "law doing," not "law hearing," that would justify a person. If the Gentile who had not received the written law would **"do by nature the things contained in the law, these having not the law, are a law unto themselves."** By nature (Greek *phusis*) refers to that which is designed by God into the moral constitution of a human being. It is that which he knows in his own rational and moral constitution apart from having received the written revelation of God.

"The things contained in the law" refer to those aspects of behavior prescribed in the written law which the Gentiles perform without being acquainted with them.

"These having not the law, are a law unto themselves" does not mean that each person is a law unto himself to do as he pleases. Rather, it means that, though he does not have the written law, his own moral constitution informs him. Hodge explains:

> The Gentiles, then, are law unto themselves; they have in their own nature a rule of duty; a knowledge of what is right, and a sense of obligation. As the absence of all moral acts among the lower animals shows that they have no sense of right and wrong, that they are not under a moral law, so the performance of such acts by the Gentiles, shows that they have a law written on their hearts (55).

15 Which shew the work of the law written in their hearts, their conscience also bearing witness, and *their* thoughts the mean while accusing or else excusing one another;)

Which shew the work of the law written in their hearts. These words are an explanation of how the Gentiles are able to have the kind of knowledge which could lead to performing "the things contained in the law" in v. 14.

The foundation for the truth of vv. 14, 15 is the fact that human beings are created in the image of God. The image of God involves a rational (Col. 3:10) and a moral likeness (Eph. 4:24). Even in his fallen state, man still has the categories of right and wrong. Though he may give some things the wrong label, he cannot eradicate the categories of right and wrong which he has by the design of creation.

The law of the heart does not speak with the clarity of written law. But it does speak with a force that cannot be totally silenced. Men need the clarification that the written law gives, but whenever the written law is presented, to those who have never heard it, it will never be addressed to a moral blank.

The main source of general revelation is the moral and rational constitution of man. "General revelation sets the stage for special revelation. The stage is set for man to receive a clearer message of sin and judgment. A feeling of need is present that can be clarified by special revelation to be the need of redemption. A longing is present that can be clarified to be a longing for redemption" (Forlines *Systematics* 15).

Their conscience (Greek *suneidesis)* **also bearing witness, and *their* thoughts** (Greek *logismos*) **the mean while accusing or else excusing** (Greek *apologeomai*) **one another.** The word for conscience refers to knowing with oneself (or telling oneself) that an action is either right or wrong. The conscience does not create its own standard. Rather, it serves as a monitor to judge a person's decisions in the light of his values (or standard).

Concerning the meaning of conscience, Cranfield explains:

> The basic idea conveyed is that of knowledge shared with oneself—so, in particular, these expressions denote a painful knowledge shared with oneself of having done wrong or (less frequently) a knowledge—not painful—of one's innocence, or, in other words, what is signified by such English expressions as a 'bad conscience,' 'a good conscience,' 'a clear conscience' (159, 160).

Thoughts (Greek *logismos*) refers to the reasoning process. The activity of the conscience is manifested in the inner self when the conscience, serving as judge, either accuses or defends (Greek *apologeomai*) a person's thoughts and actions.

Two different interpretations are given for "one another": (1) The accusing and defending are done by persons one to another. (2) "One another" refers to the reasoning process within the individual when the conscience, as judge, accuses some actions while other actions are approved.

I agree with Vincent in accepting the second view. He explains:

> As the other parts of the description refer to the individual soul in itself and not to relations to others, the explanation expressed in Rev. [the Revised Version]—the mutual relations and interchanges of the individual thoughts—seems preferable (676).

The conscience is an unquenchable testimony of the fact that man is inescapably concerned about right and wrong. The "bearing witness" is the witness of the conscience of the fact that the law is written in the heart of man.

Murray (76) is of the opinion that either view on the interpretation of "one another" makes good sense in the context. Therefore, he would say that we cannot be certain which Paul intended. (Among those who interpret the accusing and defending to refer to persons with one another are: Haldane 91; Lange 102; Liddon 48; Meyer 94; and Vine, *Romans* 37. Among those who take the accusing and defending to be within the individual are: Cranfield 162; Godet 125; Hodge 56; Lenski 170; Shedd 48; and Vincent 676.)

16 In the day when God shall judge the secrets of men by Jesus Christ according to my gospel.

As pointed out above, the thought of v. 13 is connected with that of v. 16. It would read, "For not the hearers of the law are just before God, but the doers of the law shall be justified. . . . In the day when God shall judge the secrets of men by Jesus Christ according to my gospel."

"According to my gospel" means that the gospel is the source of (or concurs with) the information regarding the judgment in which Jesus Christ will be judge. It will be a true judgment and a thorough judgment. The secrets which have escaped the attention of others on earth will be brought to light. *The only thing that will stand in this judgment will be absolute righteousness.* Paul waits until 3:21 before he takes up the discussion about this God-provided righteousness. At this point, in the development of his thought, his aim is to get all to see that man must have absolute righteousness if he is to be justified before God. He is building a strong case for this conclusion that by his own efforts no person has this absolute righteousness.

3. He is guilty because he fails to live up to his own teachings (vv. 17-24).

In vv. 5-16 Paul made it clear that the principles of God's judgment were universal. God's requirement is absolute righteousness whether the person be Jew or Gentile.

Having established his point that absolute righteousness (doers of the law) is God's requirement, Paul proceeds with some very pointed questions. These are designed to get the Jew to see that his works do not add up to absolute righteousness. *The moment the Jew concedes that he has failed in one point in keeping the law, he will see that he has failed to produce absolute righteousness.* It is Paul's desire that the Jew see that he has failed to be an absolute keeper of the law. Once he has seen this, it will be easier for him to see his need of Jesus Christ.

17 Behold, thou art called a Jew,

and restest in the law, and makest thy boast of God.

There is a manuscript difference here. Some have "Behold" (Greek *ide*); others have "But if" (Greek *ei de*). Most are of the opinion that the latter is the preferred reading. The substance of the passage is not altered significantly by whichever reading is accepted.

If the reading "behold" is used, it would imply that Paul has been talking about the Jew prior to this point. At this point, he would be naming the person (the Jew) whom he was already addressing.

If the other (*ei de*) is chosen, a common way to translate would be, "But if thou art called a Jew." It would be possible to understand Paul to be addressing someone else in 2:1-16, and understand "but if" to signal a change in whom Paul is addressing. But such need not be the case. The meaning could be,"Since thou art called a Jew." This I take to be the correct understanding.

If "but if" or an equivalent is used, it will require some other form of punctuation at the end of v. 20 since vv. 17-20 would no longer constitute a sentence. This is usually done with a dash or a semicolon.

Thou art called a Jew. Concerning the word Jew (Greek *Ioudaios*) Trench says, "This name was for the Jew his special badge and title of honor" (133). Also, Earle (59, 60) has a good treatment of the word "Jew."

And restest in the law, and makest thy boast of God. Paul is working his way with the Jew from the advantages which he believed he had to a corresponding responsibility that goes with these advantages.

Earle remarks, "This verse mentions three sources of Jewish pride. The people were proud to be named Jews; they rested on the law; they boasted of a special relationship to God" (60).

Concerning their "boast of God," Hodge explains: "The Jews regarded themselves in such a sense the people of God, as to be secure of his favour, let their personal character be what it might. They boasted that he was their God, that they monopolized his favour, all other nations being his enemies" (60).

18 And knowest *his* will, and approvest the things that are more excellent, being instructed out of the law.

And knowest *his* will. They knew God's will through the revealed Scripture.

And approvest (Greek *dokimazo*) **the things that are more excellent** (Greek *diaphero*). Approve can mean either "to test" or "to approve as the result of testing." *Diaphero* is also capable of having two different meanings: (1) the ability to distinguish the superior from the inferior, or (2) to approve rather than to make a distinction that which is superior or excellent. Either interpretation would fit the context. It appears that to approve that which is morally better is what Paul had in mind (for discussion of these words, see Cranfield 165, 166; Earle 60, 61; Lange 108; and Wuest 46).

Being instructed (Greek *katecheo)* **out of the law.** Concerning *katecheo*, Vine explains, ". . .to instruct, whence our words 'catechize,' etc., primarily denotes oral instruction" (*Romans* 39). The instruction from the law formed the basis for their knowing God's will and their approval of that which is morally better.

19 And art confident that thou thyself art a guide of the blind, a light of them which are in darkness.

Verses 17, 18 show the privileges which were enjoyed by the Jew. Verse

19 marks the transition from the privileges to the role for which these privileges qualified him as perceived by the Jew.

And art confident that thou thyself art a guide (Greek *hodegos*) **of the blind.** The word means literally "a way leader." The Jew was persuaded that he was qualified to show others the right way. While they viewed themselves as guides of the blind, Jesus called the Pharisees "blind leaders of the blind" (Mt. 15:14) and "blind guides" (Mt. 23:16).

A light to them which are in darkness. To the Jew, the Gentiles were in darkness. They considered themselves to be a light unto the Gentiles.

20 An instructor of the foolish, a teacher of babes, which hast the form of knowledge and of the truth in the law.

An instructor (Greek *paideutes*) **of the foolish** (Greek *aphron*). The word for instructor (Greek *paideutes*) in this verse and instructed (Greek *katecheo*) in v. 18 are two different words. Concerning *paideutes*, Sanday and Headlam comment, "'A schoolmaster,' with the idea of discipline, correction, as well as teaching; cf. Heb. 12:9" (65). Some give the translation "corrector." Foolish (Greek *aphron)* is defined by Wuest as, "without reason, senseless, stupid, foolish, without reflection of intelligence" (47).

A teacher of babes (Greek *nepios*). It literally means one who cannot talk. Metaphorically it refers to one who needs to be taught on the elementary level.

Which hast the form (Greek *morphosis*) **of knowledge and of the truth in the law.** Vine explains: "*Morphosis*, form, is that by which the inward character of a thing is made known to our senses" (39). It refers to the form as an expression of the inner substance. The law which the Jews possessed was an expression of the moral and spiritual truth given them by special revelation from God. It was this "form of knowledge and of the truth in the law" which, as he viewed it, gave the Jew the qualifications to be an instructor and a teacher to the Gentiles.

In commenting on vv. 19 and 20, Godet explains:

> At first, he takes the poor Gentile by the hand as one does *a blind* man, offering to *guide* him; then he opens his *eyes*, dissipating his *darkness* by the *light* of revelation; then he *rears* him, as one would bring up a being yet *without reason*; finally, when through all this care he has come to the stage of the *little child, nepios* . . . he initiates him into the full knowledge of the truth, by becoming his *teacher* (128).

Harrison's comments on vv. 19 and 20 are also helpful:

> We can paraphrase here: 'You come to the Gentile and propose yourself as a guide for his blindness (when, as a matter of fact, as I have already shown, he has a light and a law as well as you). You come to the Gentile as though he were dumb and childish, giving you the whip hand, which you thoroughly relish. To you they are mere infants, knowing next to nothing.' By employing terms actually used by the Jews for Gentiles, one after the other not once suggesting that the Gentile has anything to his credit, but invariably magnifying the Jew, Paul has succeeded in exposing Jewish pride and boasting as utterly ridiculous (33).

21 Thou therefore which teachest another, teachest thou not

thyself? thou that preachest a man should not steal, dost thou steal?

Thou therefore which teachest another, teachest thou not thyself? The negative particle (Greek *ou*) in the question implies an affirmative answer on the part of the Jew. It is similar to saying, "You teach yourself, don't you?" While it is expected that the Jew would answer, "yes," it is obvious that Paul is planning to attack the validity of this claim.

The first part of v. 21 is general. The questions which follow deal with specifics. If it is really true that the Jew is teaching himself, it will be borne out in the answers to the specific questions.

Thou that preachest a man should not steal, dost thou steal? While this question does not contain the negative particle (Greek *ou*), as the first question does, it is obvious that Paul is suggesting that some would be forced to plead guilty.

Hendriksen observes: "It is interesting to note how precisely Jewish sources agree with the implied charges made here by Paul. The question: 'you who teach others, don't you teach yourself?' is found again and again in rabbinical writings."

He then gives a quotation to support his observation: "You have many a man who teaches himself but does not teach others, many a man who teaches others but does not teach himself, many a man who teaches himself and others, and many a one who teaches neither himself nor others" (Hendriksen 105, quoted from Strack and Billerbeck, *Kommentar Zum Neuen Testament aus Talmud Und Midrash* 107).

Hendriksen then (105) points to other pages in Strack and Billerbeck which deal with the conduct of Jewish leaders, "For instances of stealing that occurred among the 'learned ones' see the same source, again p. 107; for adultery, pp. 109-11—sometimes of a very scandalous nature among the rabbis!—and for the robbing of temples, pp. 113-115."

22 Thou that sayest a man should not commit adultery, dost thou commit adultery? thou that abhorrest idols, dost thou commit sacrilege?

The question is posed to the Jew about whether his teaching and his practice are consistent with one another as it relates to adultery. It is implied that some would have to admit that they, themselves, do what they forbid others to do.

Thou that abhorrest idols, dost thou commit sacrilege (Greek *hierosuleo*)? The literal meaning of sacrilege is "to rob temples." In Deuteronomy 7:25, 26 the Israelites were forbidden to take idols into their possession. Yeager gives the meaning: "...to rob a temple of idols which were then offered for sale to idol worshippers. To traffic in idols" (II:313).

23 Thou that makest thy boast of the law, through breaking the law dishonourest thou God?

Is this verse a statement or a question? A few, among whom is Olshausen, are of the opinion that beginning with v. 21 Paul is to be understood as making statements rather than raising questions (113). The majority take v. 23 to be a question. However, there are several who understand it to be a statement of fact rather than a question (Cranfield 170; Earle 63; Meyer 97; and Sanday and Headlam 66).

It is better to take v. 23 to be a statement rather than a question since v. 24 assumes the Jews were dishonoring God by their failure to obey God's law.

There is a question regarding whether these verses are referring to literal thievery, adultery, and robbing of idol temples on the part of Jews. Barrett says, "It is certainly possible to address instances of all three, but such instances are beside the point. Paul's argument is lost if he is compelled to rely on comparatively unusual events, and it is simply not true that the average Jewish missionary acted in this way."

He goes on to say, "The fact that the actual crimes were occasionally committed adds of course some vividness to the argument, and the criminals in some sense involved the nation in their guilt; but the nation was inwardly guilty already. When theft, adultery, and sacrilege are strictly and radically understood, there is no man who is not guilty of all three. Compare Matt. 5:21-48, and the Old Testament quoted below [Mal. 3:8; Hos. 1-3; and Jer. 3:8]" (56, 57).

Since Paul's aim in this passage is to help the unbelieving Jew recognize his guilt and condemnation before God, we must interpret what Paul is driving at in that context. This purpose would have taken into account the Jewish pattern of thought. This being true, this purpose would have been served better by taking these sins in the more obvious sense. The context has not been developed adequately for the Jew to have recognized his guilt based on committing these sins inwardly.

While it is probably true that adultery and thievery were not practiced by a majority, that would not be necessary for Paul's purpose to be accomplished. It would have been effective for any Jew who was guilty of such acts.

We must also interpret Paul's implied charges in the light of the Jewish concept of corporate righteousness and corporate salvation. (See the discussion of these ideas in the introduction to chapter 2.) As long as the Jew recognized the prevalence of these sins among his people, it would help strike a blow to his confidence in their corporate righteousness. This would aid Paul's goal of getting the Jew to see that *he will stand before God as an individual rather than with the group.* Once the Jew discarded his confidence in salvation based on being the seed of Abraham and corporate righteousness, it would not be so hard for him to see his failure before God as an individual.

Separate attention needs to be given to the robbing of temples (Greek *hierosuleo)* referred to in v. 22. Yeager understands Paul to be referring to the literal theft and sale of idols. (See also Godet 129; Lenski 188, 189; Liddon 54; Meyer 100; Murray 84; Sanday and Headlam 66; *Theological Dictionary of the New Testament* III:256.)

Others take the meaning to refer to a mistreatment of the Jewish temple by either the desecration of the temple (see Mt. 21:12-14), or the failure to pay tithes for the support of the temple ministry (see Mal. 3:8-10). In a more general sense it is applied to disrespect for God and sacred things (see Barnes 68; Cranfield 169, 70; Hodge 62; Plumer 100, 101; and Shedd 55).

Olshausen understands the reference to be to covetousness viewed as idolatry. He quotes Paul as saying, "Thou abhorrest idols, and yet, in thy covetousness, thou practicest idolatry" (114).

The evidence seems to point to robbing temples as the most likely interpretation. In Acts 19:37 "robbers of churches" is the noun form of the Greek word found in Rom. 2:22 which refers to robbing temples. This reference, in which the town clerk clears Paul and his companions of being guilty of robbing temples, implies that some Jews on occasion were guilty of such (see also Josephus, *Antiquities*, Book IV, 8:10). While claiming to abhor idols, they were profiting by trafficking in idols. This was done in violation of Dt. 7:25, 26.

24 For the name of God is blasphemed among the Gentiles through you, as it is written.

The main thrust of this verse is that because the Jews' lawbreaking brought God's judgment upon them, the Gentiles profaned God's name. When God used other nations to chastise Israel, these nations concluded that it was because God could not protect His people (see Ezek. 36:20).

Hendriksen explains: "The Old Testament passage takes into consideration the assumption on the part of the Gentiles that when a nation is conquered and deported, its God has also been conquered. So the conquered nation is blasphemed along with its god. Cf. Ezek. 36:20. Here in Rom. 2:24 the Gentiles are represented as reasoning: the people (Israel) behave wickedly; therefore their god must be wicked also, for people resemble their god (106)."

4. He is guilty because his circumcision is not backed up by inward righteousness (2:25-29).

25 For circumcision verily profiteth, if thou keep the law: but if thou be a breaker of the law, thy circumcision is made uncircumcision.

For circumcision verily profiteth, if thou keep the law. This is the first mention of circumcision in Romans. There were three things that were of utmost importance in Jewish thought regarding salvation: (1) the Abrahamic Covenant; (2) circumcision; and (3) submission to Mosaic Law. Only by considerable study and thought can we begin to grasp the significance of these three. Paul's thinking in 2:1—3:8 can only be grasped by giving careful study to the whole passage. Each part must be studied in the light of the whole.

Hodge shows the extreme value the Jews placed on circumcision. He says:

> It is obvious that the Jews regarded circumcision as in some way securing salvation. That they did so regard it, may be proved not only from such passages of the New Testament, but also by the direct assertion of their own writers. Such assertions have been gathered in abundance from their works by Eisenmenger, Schoettgen, and others. For example, the Rabbi Menachem, in his commentary on the Books of Moses, fol. 43, col. 3, says, 'Our Rabbins have said, that no circumcised man will see hell.' In the Medrasch Tillim, fol. 7, col. 2, it is said, 'God swore to Abraham, that no one who was circumcised should be sent to hell.' In the book Akedath Jizehak, fol. 54, col. 2, it is taught that 'Abraham sits before the gate of hell, and does not allow that any circumcised Israelite should enter there' (63).

But if thou be a breaker of the law, thy circumcision is made uncircumcision. In deciding what is involved in "lawbreaking," it will be helpful to consider the word of James, "For whosoever shall keep the whole law, and yet offend in one *point*, he is guilty of all" (Jas. 2:10). We must also keep in mind that the aim of God is to get the Jew to see that he is guilty and condemned (Rom. 3:8, 19, 20).

It was Paul's aim that he be able to help the individual Jew see that he has failed to measure up to what God requires. As a lawbreaker he has failed to meet God's standard of absolute righteousness. This failure means that he would be dealt with by God as if he were an uncircumcised lawbreaker.

26 Therefore if the uncircumcision keep the righteousness of the law, shall not his uncircumcision be counted for circumcision?

Therefore (Greek *oun*) tells us that the idea expressed in this verse is a logical inference from v. 25. To **keep the righteousness of the law** would mean to produce absolute righteousness (see comments on v. 13). If the Gentile could produce this, he would meet God's requirement for justification (see comments on vv. 14, 15).

Paul is suggesting this line of reasoning, not because such happens, but to show how the universal application of the principles would fit. Absolute righteousness, if it could be produced by an uncircumcised person, would mean he would have the standing with God that circumcision should signify for the Jew.

27 And shall not uncircumcision which is by nature, if it fulfil the law, judge thee, who by the letter and circumcision dost transgress the law?

The fulfilling of the law, in light of the context, would involve absolute obedience of God's law. If such should ever occur, the logical result would be that the uncircumcised person's obedience would pass a negative judgment upon the Jew who failed to render such obedience. This would be true in spite of the Jew's advantage of having the letter (the written law) and circumcision (the sign of the covenant).

28 For he is not a Jew, which is one outwardly; neither *is that* circumcision, which is outward in the flesh.

Paul is pointing out the fact that being a Jew by birth and being circumcised as a sign of the covenant is not adequate. The person who is a Jew in this respect only is not a Jew. When it is said that he is not a Jew, the meaning is that he is not a Jew in the full sense of the word. To be a Jew in the full sense of the word means that he would have that relationship with God which results in receiving the promises made to Abraham's seed.

29 But he *is* a Jew, which is one inwardly; and circumcision *is that* of the heart, in the spirit, *and* not in the letter; whose praise *is* not of men, but of God.

But he *is* a Jew, which is one inwardly (Greek *kruptos*). *Kruptos* means "in secret." It is in secret in the sense that it speaks of an inward reality that is not seen by the eyes.

And circumcision is that of the heart, in the spirit, and not in the letter. I am in agreement with Haldane when he says:

> It is essential to keep in view that here, and in all that precedes, from the beginning of the 18th verse of the first chapter, Paul is referring not to the Gospel, but exclusively to the law, and clearing the ground for the establishment of his conclusion in the following chapter, verse 19th and 20th, concerning the universal guilt of mankind, and the consequent impossibility of their being justified by the law. The whole is intended to prepare the way for the demonstration of the grand truth announced, ch. 1:17, and resumed ch. 3:21, of the revelation of a righteousness adequate to the demands of the law, and provided for all who

believe (104).

While the language of vv. 28, 29 would be suitable if the intent was to show a Jew who professed faith in Christ how to distinguish a false, empty profession, the context is against such an interpretation. Paul is striving to show the unbelieving Jew the inadequacy of his circumcision and law observance to measure up to God's requirements for justification.

The "circumcision of the heart" explains the meaning of "inwardly." The inward must correspond completely with that which is signified outwardly.

Some have understood "spirit" to refer to the Holy Spirit (see Cranfield 175). This interpretation requires the verse to be referring to the sanctification that accompanies justification. It is obvious that Paul has not yet advanced to the subject of sanctification in Romans. This will come later.

Others understand "in spirit" (no article before spirit in the Greek) to be joined with the word "heart" which precedes. It serves to further explain heart. In this case the spirit would be the human spirit (see Lenski 205 and Vine, *Romans* 43).

Not in the letter. The point here is that it takes more than following outwardly. If it were possible for the Jew to produce absolute righteousness, such obedience would have to go beyond the observance of the details of the law. Obedience would have to be an expression of inner reality.

Whose praise is not of men, but of God. If the Jew should be able to produce absolute righteousness, he would receive the approval and praise of God. However, no one will be justified this way. If the Jew can see his failure to have what God requires, then he will be more likely to listen when Paul speaks about the God-provided righteousness in 3:21 and following.

5. The failure of the Jews does not alter the fact that they had a position of advantage (3:1-4).

1 What advantage then hath the Jew? or what profit *is there* of circumcision?

For a good understanding of Romans, it is necessary to have a basic grasp of the Abrahamic Covenant. As a result of this covenant, the Jews (the descendants of Abraham through Jacob) are the covenant people of God. As was observed in the introductory comments to chapter 2, the Jews were prone to think that this covenant secured salvation for them. Yet Paul, himself a Jew, argued in chapter 2 that God's principles of judgment are universal. Absolute righteousness is required of anyone who stands justified before God. The Jew, in spite of the Abrahamic Covenant, must have this absolute righteousness or suffer the wrath of God. The Gentile, if he could produce absolute righteousness, would stand justified before God.

It might begin to appear to the Jew that Paul was saying that being the covenant people of God had no advantage at all. In fact, they were probably wondering if Paul either viewed the Abrahamic Covenant as being worthless, or thought that God had terminated His covenant relationship with Israel.

One of Paul's tactics in Romans is the use he frequently makes of rhetorical questions. David Brown in commenting on Rom. 6:1 points out: "This, it will be observed, is a marked characteristic of our apostle's style in this Epistle—to mark sudden transitions to a new branch of his subject as a mode of putting and answering questions, or a way of calling attention to some important statement" (VI:224).

A study of these questions (3:1, 31; 6:1, 15; 7:7; 9:14; and 11:1) in Romans suggests that these were questions Paul had probably encountered from some who had heard his teachings. Before he raises each of these questions, it might appear that Paul has developed his case in such a way that it puts him in conflict with an incontestable truth. The incontestable truth here is that there were some advantages and benefits from being a Jew (one of the covenant people).

By foreseeing these questions, Paul himself raises the questions that would have been in the mind of the Jewish reader. **What advantage then hath the Jew?** Or another way of saying this is, What advantage is it to be one of the Covenant People of God?

What profit is there of circumcision? By noting the value that Jews have placed on circumcision (see comments on 2:25), one can see that Paul's comments in vv. 25-29 touched a very sensitive nerve with the Jews. If Paul wished to keep their attention, he must deal with the problems he had raised.

2 Much every way: chiefly, because that unto them were committed the oracles of God.

Much in every way. If anyone had decided that Paul was denying any advantage or profit to the Jew, he wanted to clear up the misunderstanding. There were several advantages that the Jew had.

Chiefly (or first). While Paul could have given several advantages, he felt it necessary to list only one.

Because that unto them were committed the oracles (Greek *logion)* **of God.** This word occurs four times in the N.T. The other occurrences are Acts 7:38; Heb. 5:12; and 1 Pet. 4:11. In all places it is plural and is translated in the KJV as "oracles."

Concerning this word, Vincent explains, "*Strictly*, brief *utterances. Both* in classical and *Biblical Greek* of divine utterances" (678). Here the word (*logion*) means the Old Testament as an embodiment of Divine utterances. It is quite obvious that the God of Abraham, Isaac, and Jacob had spoken and in so doing conveyed information about Himself, His plans, His purposes, and His promises. This is in sharp contrast to the view of contemporary theology which denies propositional or content revelation. (See the introductory article on this subject on page 1.)

The word "committed" (Greek *pisteuo*) is a translation of the passive form. This word is used in 1 Cor. 9:17; Gal. 2:7; and 1 Tim. 1:11. In these passages Paul speaks of the gospel as having been committed or entrusted to him.

Harrison's comments are helpful. He explains:

> To be 'entrusted' with the divine oracles obviously means more than to be the recipient of them. Actually it means more even than to be the custodian and transmitter of them. What is called for, in the light of the meaning of [oracles] is faith and obedience. Just at this point the Jew failed (v.3). Paul has already dealt sufficiently with Jewish failure in terms of the law, but here he deals with it in terms of God's revealed purpose (35, 36).

Israel had the privilege of being the unique people of God. They were in a covenant relationship with God. The everlasting possession of the land of Canaan was promised to them as the seed of Abraham (Gen. 13:14; 17:8). They were the recipients of God's redemptive revelation. Their need was simply to believe the redemptive revelation that was theirs from God. No other nation has had this advantage. Regardless of how much may be known of God through general revelation, redemptive knowledge comes only by special revelation. Redemptive revelation had been committed or "entrusted" to the Jews as the seed of Abraham.

3 For what if some did not believe? shall their unbelief make the faith of God without effect?

For what if some did not believe (Greek *apisteo*)? In vv. 2, 3 there are four Greek words which come from the same root: committed or entrusted (*pistueo*) in v. 2; did not believe or were unfaithful (*apisteo*), unbelief or unfaithfulness (*apistia*), and faith or faithfulness (*pistis*) in v. 3. Our question is: Which of the meanings is correct?

Lenski insists that with the words occurring together "...the first [*pisteuo*, entrusted]...fixes the sense of the rest: 'They were entrusted—They proved unworthy of the trust (unfaithful)—unfaithfulness—faithfulness'" (214). Hodge agrees with the meaning "unfaithfulness" (70).

The majority take the meaning to be "unbelief" rather than "unfaithfulness" (Cranfield 180; Godet 133; Meyer 112; Sanday and Headlam 71). Cranfield does not rule out the possibility that the meaning is "unfaithfulness." However, he decides in favor of "unbelief" as the meaning. This is based on the meaning given to these words in other places.

Most who take the meaning here to be unbelief think the reference is to the Jewish unbelief of the Messianic claims of Christ. I agree with Hodge when he says:

> To understand the passage as referring to Christ, seems inconsistent with the whole context. The apostle has not come to the exposition of the gospel; he is still engaged in the preliminary discussion designed to show that the Jews and Gentiles are under sin, and exposed to condemnation; an exposure from which no peculiar privileges of the former, and no promise of God to their nation could protect them (71).

I agree that in this verse the word (*pistis*) refers to the "faithfulness" of God. If we take the meaning in the first part of the verse to refer to Israel's "unfaithfulness," we will have a consistent translation of these words from the same word group. It appears that the words (*pistueo, apisteo, apistia,* and *pistis*) were deliberately chosen. This would seem to point to the conclusion that all would either refer to "belief and unbelief" or "faithfulness and unfaithfulness."

All things considered it seems that the best reading of vv. 2, 3 is: "God's oracles were *entrusted* to them. What if some were untrustworthy? shall their untrustworthiness make the trustworthiness of God without effect?"

In the context of Jewish concern, the disturbing question would be: Has the unfaithfulness of the Jews to the oracles (Greek *ta logia*) of God rendered the Abrahamic and other covenants worthless? Paul's answer (in the next verse) is, "Emphatically No."

Paul's main aim is to get the Jew to see that there is no redemption apart from Jesus Christ. As a means of moving toward this goal, he needed to get across three points: (1) For justification, God will accept nothing less than absolute righteousness, not even from a descendant of Abraham. (2) The Jew must rid himself of any such idea as corporate salvation based on being the covenant seed of Abraham. (3) Any dependence, whether for the individual Jew, or the nation as a whole, on circumcision or lawkeeping is bound to fail.

Hodge gives evidence for the concept

of corporate salvation among the Jews. He explains:

> Traces of this opinion abound in the New Testament, and it is openly avowed by the Jewish writers. 'Think not,' says the Baptist, 'to say within yourselves, We have Abraham to our father: Matt. 3:9. 'We be Abraham's seed,' John 8:33. Comp. Rom. 2:17; 9:6; and other passages, in which Paul argues to prove that being the natural descendants of Abraham is not enough to secure the favour of God. That such was the doctrine of the Jews is shown by numerous passages from their writings. 'If a Jew commit all manner of sins,' says Abarbanel, 'he is indeed of the number of sinning Israelites, and will be punished according to his sins; but he has, notwithstanding, a portion in eternal life.' The same sentiment is expressed in the book Torath Adam, fol. 100, in nearly the same words, and the reasons assigned for it, 'That all Israel has a portion in eternal life....' Justin Martyr, as quoted by Grotius on chap. 2:13, attributes this doctrine to the Jews of his day: 'They suppose that to them universally, who are of the seed of Abraham, no matter how sinful and disobedient to God they may be, the eternal kingdom shall be given.' This interpretation, therefore, makes the verse in question present the objection which the Jew would most likely urge (70, 71).

The picture that was developing in the Jew's mind at this point would have been quite confusing. He knew that Paul, himself a Jew, would have certainly known that salvation was promised to the seed of Abraham. There was certainly no debate between the Jew and Paul over whether there was such a thing as redemption for the Jews. But it was becoming unquestionably clear that at least "some" of the Jews, according to Paul's thinking, were not going to inherit the promise of eternal life as set forth in the Abrahamic Covenant (Gen. 13:14; 17:8). In fact, it sounds as if Paul is painting the whole world into a corner with no way out. But this cannot be since he has already spoken of salvation in 1:17.

4 God forbid: yea, let God be true, but every man a liar; as it is written, That thou mightest be justified in thy sayings, and mightest overcome when thou art judged.

God forbid (Greek *me genoito*) literally means "May it not be." The word *God* is not found in the expression. The choice of "God forbid" as a translation appears to be a strong way of saying "*No*" in the Greek translated by a strong way of saying "No" in the English.

Paul emphatically denies that unfaithfulness on the part of Jews would in any way render ineffective the faithfulness of God in fulfilling His covenant promises to them. The possibility of anything rendering ineffective the covenant promises of God to Israel is to be ruled out. In fact, as Paul develops his case in chapters 4 and 9-11 it is this faithfulness of God to His covenant promises which forms the basis for hope of salvation among both Jews and Gentiles.

Yea, let God be true, but every man a liar. It is absolutely unthinkable that anything could ever reflect on the integrity of God.

As it is written. The remainder of this verse is a quotation of Ps. 51:4b. It is taken from the Septuagint rather than the Hebrew. In Ps. 51:4a David had said, "Against thee and thee only have I sinned, and done *this* evil in thy sight." In this confession David was acknowledging that the fault was all his. When David acknowledged his guilt, it was clear that God's verdict against him was just and fair.

Paul referred to David's statements as a true expression of his own sentiments. God's faithfulness to all of His promises will never waver. Men may hurl accusations against God, but when all facts are brought to the bar of justice God will be declared true in all of His statements and promises.

Paul wanted it to be perfectly clear that his views did not at any point go counter to the promises of God. He could never consider such.

6. The fact that the Jew's unrighteousness caused God's righteousness to stand out in a greater way does not furnish grounds for escape from God's wrath (3:5-8).

5 But if our unrighteousness commend the righteousness of God, what shall we say? *Is* God unrighteous who taketh vengeance? (I speak as a man)

Paul raises yet another question which a Jewish reader might pose. The question implies that the Jew's unrighteousness sets forth God's righteousness in a brighter, clearer way. This would mean that God would derive a benefit from the Jew's unrighteousness. This seems to arise out of the thought of vv. 3, 4. God was faithful in spite of the Jew's unfaithfulness. Unrighteousness would include unfaithfulness, but would be broader. Just as white appears whiter in contrast to black, so God's righteousness is seen as being even brighter and greater in contrast to the Jew's sin.

Paul does not challenge the observation about the contrast between the Jew's unrighteousness and God's righteousness. However, he sharply disagrees with any suggestion that the benefit of having His righteousness to shine brighter denies God the right to punish sin. In fact, Paul found such an idea so repulsive that he disclaimed any connection with the idea. "I speak as a man" made it clear that such thinking was not his.

6 God forbid: for then how shall God judge the world?

God forbid. Paul quickly negates any such thought as accusing God of unrighteousness. If the thinking of the Jewish objector to v. 5 were valid it would undercut God's right to judge the world. Anyone could lay claim to the idea that compared with his sin God's righteousness is seen brighter and clearer.

7 For if the truth of God hath more abounded through my lie unto his glory; why yet am I also judged as a sinner?

Various interpretations have been given to this verse. Many take it to be a restatement and expansion of what is said in v. 5. In that case the "I" would represent the Jew (Barnes 76, 77, Cranfield 185, Sanday and Headlam 73, 74, and Shedd 66).

Godet and Hodge take the position that v. 7 is not limited to either the Jew or the Gentile in this verse. Verse 7 is viewed as an amplification of the thought already expressed in v. 6. Godet understands "I also" to mean, "I who, as well as the rest, have contributed to thy glory" (137). Hodge states, "I, therefore, stands for any one: 'Any one may say, Why am I also judged as a sinner'" (74)?

Haldane understands Paul to be speaking of himself. Paul is asking the

Jew why he was condemend by the Jew since they viewed his teaching to be a lie. Could he not also ask why the Jews judged him as a sinner since his lie (as they would call it) would cause God's truth, by contrast, to shine even brighter? (113).

I agree with Olshausen (124). Paul is showing how the pagan could use the same argument on his behalf that the Jew had set forth in v. 5. The word for lie (Greek *pseusma*) is from the same root as *pseudos* which is used in 1:25 to denote the "lie" of paganism in contrast to the truth of God.

Hodge (73, 74) and Godet (137, 138) show an interest in this view but reject it since they think it suggests too restricted a use of "world" in v. 6. They take "world" to include both Jews and Gentiles, rather than restricted to Gentiles. I fail to see a problem. It would have been very easy for a Jew to think of world, when used in a negative way, to refer to the rest of the world, which would refer to the Gentiles.

The pagan could say, "Why am I also judged as a sinner?" His case would be as valid as that of the Jew in v. 5. Such reasoning would undercut God's right to judge anyone.

8 And not *rather*, (as we be slanderously reported, and as some affirm that we say,) Let us do evil, that good may come? whose damnation is just.

It helps in seeing what Paul is saying if we insert, as many translations do, "why" before "not." Also, we need to read together that which precedes and that which follows the parenthetical material. (A presentation of several punctuation problems related to this verse is in Cranfield 185-187.)

And [why] not *rather*...Let us do evil that good may come? If, as the Jew seemed to think, God could not judge their unrighteousness since it caused His righteousness to be seen in a brighter way, the logic of this verse would follow. The best guarantee of receiving good from God would be to practice evil. Thus Paul shows the absurdity of the reasoning of the Jew in v. 5. Whatever problems the unbelieving Jew might have had, he certainly would not want to accept the end to which this reasoning would take him.

In the parenthetical material, Paul points out that some were saying that Paul, himself, was actually teaching, "Let us do good that evil may come." It is likely that Paul had encountered this accusation from some Jews. To those Jews who would so accuse Paul, he is saying, "You, not I, are the ones whose reasoning would lead to such an absurd conclusion."

Whose damnation is just. The majority of commentators understand the reference here to be to those who accused Paul of teaching, "Let us do evil that good may come." Paul, according to this view, would be saying that those who made such an accusation are justly condemned (Barrett 65; Cranfield 187; Godet 138; and Yeager 187).

Hodge (75) and Lange (119) set forth the view that the teaching, "Let us do evil that good may come" is what is condemned. The translation in the *Amplified Bible* would support this view.

It appears to me that "whose" (Greek *hon*) is referring to those who falsely accused Paul. The concept "Let us do evil that good may come" was not introduced because some were teaching it (even if some were). Rather, it was because it was the logical end to which Jewish reasoning (v. 5) would lead. Then Paul pointed out that there were those who falsely accused him of such teaching. If Paul had been dealing with the actual case of teachers of antinomianism, as suggested by Hodge and Lange, it would fit for the emphasis to have dealt with a judgment against such teaching. Since he was dealing with a false charge, it seems better to deal with the judgment of the false accusers.

At this point Paul simply denounces any charge of antinomianism. He will give a developed answer to such a charge in 6:1—7:6.

(Barclay 51-54 gives an interesting treatment of the basic ideas of 3:1-8. It takes the form of a discussion between Paul and an imaginary objector.)

C. Paul's Conclusion With Regard To The Guilt Of The Human Race (3:9-20).

1. The Jew has no moral advantage over the Gentile (v.9).

9 What then? are we better *than they?* No, in no wise: for we have before proved both Jews and Gentiles, that they are all under sin.

The basic thrust of this verse is clear. Both Jews and Gentiles are under sin. For those who would become involved in detailed exegesis there are numerous problems to be dealt with. None of these would alter the basic meaning of the verse.

What then? are we better *than they?* The main problem in this verse centers around the word (Greek *proecho*) which is translated, "are we better than they?"

There are basically three possible meanings of this word, which means literally "to hold before." The form which appears in the text is the middle or passive form. The possible meanings are: (1) To understand the middle voice to have an active voice meaning. The meaning would be "to excel" or "to have an advantage." (2) To understand the use here to have the middle force. The meaning would be "to make or have a defense of oneself" or "to give or have an excuse for oneself." (3) To understand the meaning to be passive. The meaning would be "to be excelled," "to be surpassed," or "to have a disadvantage."

Those who take the first meaning are Cranfield (188, 189); Harrison (38); Hodge (77); and Shedd (67). The meaning would be, "are we Jews better ?" or "do we have an advantage?" Since Paul had said in 3:1, 2 that the Jews did have an advantage, a clarification needs to be made. As a means of harmonizing this verse with 3:1, 2, some have understood the words which in the KJV are translated "no, in no wise" (*ou pantos)* to mean "not altogether" (Cranfield 190). The meaning would be that though the Jews did have some advantages (3:1, 2), they did not have a moral advantage. For that reason they are as condemned as the Gentiles.

Most would understand Paul to be giving a strong negation (Denny 606; Godet 140; Haldane 114; and Hodge 77). They would harmonize this denial of advantage of the Jew with 3:1, 2 by saying that in this verse Paul is only dealing with the moral issue. The Jew is just as guilty as the Gentile.

The second view given above as an interpretation of the word (*proecho*) is supported by Godet and Meyer. Godet (139, 140) understands the meaning to be, "Are we sheltered?" The meaning is, "Have we a shelter under which we can regard ourselves as delivered from wrath?" The answer is a strong negation, "Certainly not."

Meyer gives the meaning, "*Do we put forward (anything) in our defence?* Is it the case with us, that something serves as a defence, that can secure us against the punitive righteousness of God?" (120).

The third interpretation is held by Denny and Sanday and Headlam.

Denny takes the question to be, "Are we [Jews] excelled [by the Gentiles]?" (605). Another way of saying it would be, "Are we worse than the Gentiles?" The meaning subscribed to by Sanday and Headlam is, "Are we excelled?" "Are we Jews worse off than the Gentiles?" (76). According to this view after Paul finished his case against the Jew, the Jew was made to wonder if he was not, according to Paul's teaching, worse off than the Gentiles.

The first meaning is the most widely held and, in my opinion, is a proper interpretation of Paul's thought. Paul raises the question of whether the Jews, so far as sin and guilt are concerned, were better off than the Gentiles. His burden was to get the Jew to see that the Abrahamic Covenant, circumcision, and lawkeeping would not justify him if he did not have absolute righteousness.

Commenting on this verse Sanford Mills, a Jewish Christian, says:

> They were the recipients of the law, the oracles of God, but their possession did not make them any better. Rabbis have taught Israel differently. They have taught Israel that they have a choice place or a choice position. They say that 'all Israel has a share in the world to come. . . .' This Rabbinical wishful thinking of the Jew is contrary to the testimony of the Scriptures (86,87).

For we have before proved (reference being to 1:18—3:8) **both Jews and Gentiles** (*Hellen*, the word for Greek—see notes on 1:14), **that they are all under sin.** There are two aspects of sin: (1) guilt and (2) depravity. Sin as guilt is that which places us under condemnation. Sin as depravity is that power within us that draws us into the path of sin. Haldane takes the position that Paul deals with sin as placing man under condemnation rather than as bringing him under the dominion of sin (115). Cranfield (191) and Murray (102) take the position that the reference here is restricted to that which brings a person under its dominion. It is probably best to understand both guilt and depravity as being involved in Paul's charge in this verse. There does not appear to be an adequate reason for choosing one and rejecting the other (see Godet 140; Hodge 78; Lange 120; and Picirilli 51).

2. Every human being is under sin (vv.10-12).

Verses 10-12 are a somewhat free rendering of Ps. 14:1-3 and 53:1-3. Picirilli points out, "The evidence given in 1:18-3:8 has been based mostly on the actual circumstances within the pagan and Jewish world. But now Paul turns to the infallible Scriptures to see what God himself has to say" (51).

10 As it is written, There is none righteous, no, not one.

As it is written. This expression tells us that Paul considers what he has said about the Jews and Gentiles being under sin to have the full support of the O.T. What follows is a collection of verses from different places in the O.T. to support this claim. We must keep reminding ourselves that Paul has a deep concern for Jews. He has far greater trouble convincing the Jew that he is condemned before God than is the case with the Gentiles. These references to the O.T. represent another serious attempt to get the Jews to see their lack of righteousness. They claim allegiance to the same Scriptures that Paul does.

There is none righteous, no, not one. In 2:6-16 Paul made it clear that no man could be justified before God without absolute righteousness. In this verse he emphatically states that not one human being by his own action has produced absolute righteousness. This failure included every Jew as well as every Gentile.

11 There is none that understandeth, there is none that seeketh after God.

There is none that understandeth (Greek *suniemi*). The meaning of this word is to "send together" or to "put together." Those who are in revolt against God are capable of great intellectual feats. However, as long as they rule God out of the picture or keep Him removed from the center, they can have only fragments of knowledge. They cannot put things together to form an adequate worldview. When God is left out, an essential ingredient is omitted. When a person seeks to develop a worldview without God, it is a case of "the bed is too long and the cover is too short."

The only source which I have found that gets to the heart of the meaning of the word (Greek *suniemi*) is Yeager. He explains:

> To understand in this sense is to 'put it all together.' Such a thinker sees and finds maximum concrescence. Truth is consistent, coherent and correspondent to reality. There are no parts of truth that oppose each other. Each part coheres with all other parts and all parts correspond to the real world (338).

See also my comments on *asunetos* (1:31).

No one can put together an adequate view of life and thought if he leaves God out. For this reason we need to be alert to what we hear, see, and read from the secular world. We should also promote Christian education.

There is none that seeketh after God. Fallen man does not seek after God. The searching that goes on in pagan religions is a resistance of God rather than a seeking after God. For those who live in a "Christian" context, that which has any resemblance to seeking after God is in response to being sought by God. In salvation God takes the initiative toward man. Jesus said, "No man can come to me, except the Father which hath sent me draw him" (Jn. 6:44b).

12 They are all gone out of the way, they are together become unprofitable; there is none that doeth good, no, not one.

They are all gone out of the way. As Hodge explains: "Blinded by sin to the perfections and loveliness of God and truth, they have turned from the way which he has prescribed and which leads to himself, and have made choice of another way and of another portion" (79).

Yeager says, "They saw that they were on a collision course with God (Romans 1:18-32), and they turned aside to avoid Him" (339).

They are together become unprofitable. The Greek word (*achreioo*) means useless. Earle points out that the Hebrew word in Ps. 14:3 "literally means 'go bad, become sour.' The picture is that of milk turning sour until it is not only useless but repulsive" (73).

There is none that doeth good. The statement is absolute. There is not one person who has succeeded in practicing the good. As Shedd says, "No man does good spiritually, perfectly, and without a single slip or failure from first to last" (69).

3. The depraved nature of man expresses itself in corrupt deeds (vv. 13-18).

Every human being is guilty of failing in the matters referred to in vv. 10-12. When reference is made to specific sins in vv. 13-18, not everyone has performed all of the sins listed. However, the prevalence of such sins in the human race is such that everyone is familiar with them.

With regard to vv. 13-18 Harrison observes:

> So far as relationship with God is concerned, the rupturing power of sin has been noted (vv.11, 12). But what effect does sin have on the sinner? The effect is total, because his entire being is vitiated. Observe at this point the various members of the body referred to: The throat, the tongue, and the lips (v.13); the mouth (v. 14); the feet (v. 15); and the eyes (v. 18). This list serves to affirm what theologians speak of as total depravity, i.e., not that man in his natural state is as bad as he can possibly be, but rather that his entire being is adversely affected by sin (39).

13 Their throat *is* an open sepulchre; with their tongues they have used deceit; the poison of asps *is* under their lips.

Their throat is an open sepulchre. This part of the verse is taken from Ps. 5:9. Shedd observes: "The description is applicable to written as well as spoken words. Little is known of Jewish literature other than the Old Testament Scriptures; but some portions of Greek and Roman literature stink like a newly-opened grave" (69).

With their tongues they have used deceit (Greek *dolioo*). Psalm 5:9 reads, "They flatter with their tongue. The Hebrew refers to speaking with a smooth tongue. The Greek word (*dolioo*) is in the imperfect tense, thus denoting a habit of using deceit. Haldane explains: "They have flattered with the tongue, and this flattery is joined with the intention to deceive. This also characterizes in a striking manner the way in which men employ speech to deceive each other, in bargains, and in everything in which their interest is concerned" (119).

The poison of asps is under their lips (from Ps. 140:3). There is no way of determining, with certainty, which venomous snake Paul had in mind. This does not hinder us from getting the basic thrust of what he is saying. Haldane explains: "This denotes the mortal poison, such as that of vipers or asps, that lies concealed under the lips, and is emitted in poisoned words. As these venomous creatures kill with their poisonous sting, so slanderers and evil-minded persons destroy the character of their neighbors" (119, 120).

14 Whose mouth *is* full of cursing and bitterness.

Whose mouth is full (Greek *gemo*) **of cursing** (Greek *ara*) **and bitterness** (Greek *pikria*) (from Ps. 10:7). Vine in giving the meaning of full explains, "To be full, to be heavily laden with, was primarily used of a ship; it is chiefly used in the N.T. of evil contents, such as extortion and excess...." (Vine, *Dictionary* 477). Concerning cursing (Greek *ara*), Vine says, "In its usual form, a malediction, cursing (its other meaning is 'a prayer')" (264).

Haldane comments:

> Paul describes in this and the foregoing verse the four principal vices of the tongue,—filthy and infected discourse; deceitful flatteries; subtle and piercing evil speaking; finally, outrageous and open malediction. This last relates to the extraordinary propensity of men to utter imprecations against one another (120).

Concerning bitterness Shedd says, "Denotes intense hatred" (70). Concerning "cursing" and "bitterness" Plumer observes: "The two words embrace the most odious forms of ill will and malignity, describing a character selfish and impious" (117).

15 Their feet *are* swift to shed blood.

This verse is from Is. 59:7. The reference here is to murder. From the murder of Abel by Cain to the present, the pages of history have been filled with murder.

16 Destruction and misery *are* in their ways.

Destruction (Greek *suntrimma*) **and misery** (Greek *talaiporia*) ***are* in their ways** (from Isa. 59:7). Concerning the meaning of destruction Shedd observes, "An utter destruction which bruises and grinds down to the very substance and fibre, is the result of such murderous hatred" (70). Yeager gives the meaning, "Physical destruction, calamity, ruin, devastation, a laying waste, scorched earth policy" (345).

With regard to misery Yeager gives the meaning, "hardship, trouble, misery, calamity" (345).

The "misery" is caused by the "destruction." Violence and suffering are in all of their ways.

17 And the way of peace have they not known.

This is taken from Isa. 59:8. In all of their ways (plural) there is not a way (singular) that leads to peace. I agree with Cranfield when he says "that they do not know how to go about to establish true peace among themselves, though some commentators take the reference of [peace] to be rather to the peace of salvation (cf. Lk. 1:7-9)" (195). Up to this point Paul has been working to establish the fact that no man can produce the kind of righteousness God requires rather than showing their ignorance of the gospel.

18 There is no fear of God before their eyes.

This quotation comes from Ps. 36:1. This lack of reverential fear of God characterizes the heart of those guilty of the sins in vv. 13-17. Cranfield explains: "It is by his eyes that a man directs his steps. So to say that there is no fear of God before his eyes is a figurative way of saying that the fear of God has no part in directing his life, that God is left out of his reckoning, that he is a practical, whether or not he is a theoretical atheist" (195).

4. The whole race is under condemnation (vv. 19, 20).

19 Now we know that what things soever the law saith, it saith to them who are under the law: that every mouth may be stopped, and all the world may become guilty before God.

That this verse speaks of universal guilt and condemnation is quite clear. There are basically three questions which need to be answered: (1) What is the meaning of "law"? (2) Who are those under the law? (3) On what basis are all, both Jews and Gentiles, under condemnation?

There are a number of ways people have dealt with this verse: I will list five views.

(1) The law embraces the whole O. T., not just the Ten Commandments. This is based on the opinion that the law of v. 19 refers back to vv. 10-18 which were from Ps. and Is. That law

was addressed to the Jews. The reference to the law was made for the sake of convincing the Jews of their own guilt and condemnation. It is felt that Paul did not need, at this point, to develop his case against the Gentiles. The universal condemnation of v. 19 did not depend upon the universal intent of the law in that verse. The case against the Gentiles had been stated in 1:18-32 (Cranfield 196, 197; Denny 607, 608; and Harrison 39, 40).

(2) This is like (1) in that only the Jews were under (or "in") the law. The Jews were a test case for all the world. Yeager explains: "The Jews who broke the law were no different genetically than the Gentiles who never saw the tablets of stone. . . . The entire race is guilty. If Israel could not keep the law, neither could the Gentile" (350).

Yeager also adds that the law of the conscience furnishes another reason for the condemnation of the Gentiles.

(3) This agrees with (1) and (2) in that the law is considered to be the O.T. moral revelation which was given to the Jews. The Gentiles as well as the Jews are condemned by the teaching of the O.T. Murray says:

> This establishes an all important consideration that although the Gentiles did not have the Old Testament law and in that sense were without the law, yet they were not outside the sphere of judgment which the Old Testament pronounced. This is saying that the descriptions given in those passages quoted were characteristic of the Gentiles as well as the Jews and the corresponding judgment rested upon them to the end that they all might be without excuse and be condemned in the sight of God (106, 107).

(4) This view has much in common with (3). It uses a different approach on how the Gentile is included among the condemned. Haldane states:

> The first clause of this verse, though specially applicable to the Jews, proves that since they, who enjoyed such peculiar privileges, were chargeable with those things of which the law accused them, the rest of mankind, whom the apostle here includes under the term 'all the world,' must also be under the same condemnation. The law of nature, written on their consciences, sufficiently convicts the Gentiles; and as to the Jews, who try to stifle the conviction of their consciences by abusing the advantages, of the law, that law itself, while it accuses, convicts also of sin. This expression, then, must include the whole human race (122, 123).

It should be observed that though Haldane refers to the law of conscience in these observations, he does not think law in v. 19 includes the law of conscience. This he bases on the presence of the article with law in v. 19.

(5) Views (1)-(4) all tend to restrict the meaning of "law" in v. 19 to the O.T. revelation of law. This view (5) understands "the law" in v. 19 to be broader than the O.T. revelation. Commenting on "the law" in this verse Shedd says: "Paul has been speaking, last, of the Jews; yet not the written law exclusively, because the Gentiles are included in [every mouth] and [all the world]. The written law contains the unwritten, by implication and hence may be put for all law, or law generally" (71).

Barnes (82, 83) and Hodge (80) are in essential agreement with the view presented by Shedd.

If this view (5) can be substantiated, it is to be preferred because it makes all people, whether viewed individually or collectively, declared guilty of violating the law mentioned in the verse.

The case for this view is strong. The extension from the O.T. revelation of law to the inclusion of any other revelation of law (whether by special revelation or the law of the heart), is done by the figure of speech known as synechdoche. In a synechdoche the part is given for the whole, or the whole is given for the part. In v. 19 "the law" is the part given for the whole. Part of the law is the O.T. revelation of the law of God. The whole includes all other revelations of God's law. This view avoids the awkwardness involved in the other views in their attempt to move from a limited "law" to an unlimited application of the guilty verdict of that law. A synechdoche is a valid use of language. The context demands that "the law" and "the guilt" of this verse be coextensive (for a discussion of the use of "law" in Romans, see Bruce 52-58).

Every mouth may be stopped. Stuart observes, "The phraseology is borrowed from the custom of gagging criminals, i.e., stopping their mouths in order to prevent apology or outcry from them, when they were led out to execution" (101).

All the world may become guilty (Greek *hupodikos*). Concerning the meaning of this word, Yeager explains, ". . . under condemnation; the legal position of the defendant who has lost his case; legally guilty. Romans 3:19" (349).

After discussing the difficulties regarding the use of "guilty" Cranfield explains that its meaning ". . . in this context is probably that of men standing at God's bar, their guilt proved beyond all possibility of doubt, awaiting God's sentence of condemnation" (197).

20 Therefore by the deeds of the law there shall no flesh be justified in his sight: for by the law *is* the knowledge of sin.

Therefore (Greek *dioti*). In the KJV this word is translated "because" 8 times; "for" 8 times; "because that" 3 times; and "therefore" only in this verse. The English conjunctions "because," "for," and "because that" have the same basic meaning—what follows the word is a reason for what precedes. "Therefore" has the reverse meaning. A conclusion follows based on the reason that preceded. In this verse it is better to translate by "because" or an equivalent. Most translations do this. The meaning would be: The failure to achieve justification by the "deeds of the law" is the *reason* every mouth may be stopped and all the world may become guilty before God.

By the deeds of the law. The obedience referred to here would be obedience to God's revelation whether it be the revealed law of the Bible or to that which is written in the moral constitution of man.

There shall no flesh be justified in his sight (from Ps. 143:2). Flesh refers to the total person. Vine explains, "by synechdoche, of mankind, in the totality of all that is essential to manhood" (*Dictionary* 447). Paul emphatically denies that there is such a thing as absolute obedience to God's requirements. Not one person in the whole human race has or can measure up to God's law.

For by the law *is* the knowledge of sin. The law serves as a standard of measurement. When fallen man stands beside the law, he becomes painfully aware of his sin. At that point it will become clear to him that his "mouth has been stopped and he is guilty before God."

The picture of 1:18—3:20 is dark and dismal. It is a mistake some have made to see Paul addressing saved people in some of these verses. It tends to obscure Paul's development of thought as he shows man's total failure before

God. The way has been prepared for us to have an interest in God's provision for our need of absolute righteousness.

Summary 2:1—3:20

The Jew would have had no problem in agreeing with Paul's treatment of the Gentiles in 1:18-32. The tendency, however, was for the Jew to overlook the implications that the case against the Gentiles had for him as a Jew. The same sins, more or less, that were found among the Gentiles were also found among the Jews. Paul begins to hammer home to the Jews that God had the same reason for condemning them that He had for condemning the Gentiles.

The Jews felt that they would be granted immunity from punishment because they were the seed of Abraham. Paul addresses this fallacy, not directly, but from necessary implication. God's principles of judgment are universal. He does not have one set of principles for the Gentiles and another set for the Jews.

God's requirements call for absolute righteousness or absolute obedience. To stand before God would require absolute righteousness no matter who the person is. A Jew cannot get by without absolute righteousness. If a Gentile could produce absolute righteousness by living by the law written in his heart, he would be acceptable to God. It is not that Paul thought a Gentile could produce absolute righteousness. He was showing how the universal principles would work if absolute obedience were possible.

Paul in v. 17 moves in to shatter the false hope of the Jews. This false hope came from a false understanding of: (1) the Abrahamic Covenant, (2) circumcision, and (3) lawkeeping.

The Jew prided himself in his covenant relationship with God and his possession of the law. Paul moved in to get them to see that the gap between their teachings and their living, of necessity, results in condemnation in the light of God's absolute standard. This was designed for the Jews to see that they failed both as individuals and as a group. Neither the Abrahamic Covenant, circumcision, nor lawkeeping could suffice to prepare the way to eternal life apart from having met God's requirement of absolute righteousness.

By the time he reached 3:1, Paul had planted question marks in the mind of a Jewish reader. It sounded as if Paul had counted their covenant relationship with God as either not existing or as being worthless. Paul made it clear that he had not intended to deny that Jews had an advantage. Their chief advantage was that they had received special revelation (the oracles of God, v. 2). God would be true to His promises to Israel regardless of the unfaithfulness of many.

Paul moves to another defense tactic in his "argument" with the Jews. They were wanting to suggest that God's righteousness benefited by appearing brighter and clearer by contrast with their unrighteousness. In fact, after receiving this benefit, would God not be unrighteous to take vengeance on them? Paul immediately shows the fallacy of such an argument. The heathen could use such an argument to escape God's wrath. In fact, if that reasoning were valid the best thing to do would be to do evil in order to get good from God. Paul disowns any such thought and says concerning those who implied that he taught such, that their condemnation is just (v. 8).

At this point the case had been conclusively established against both Jews and Gentiles. "They are all under sin" (v. 9).

Paul now turns his attention to several references to the Psalms and one from Isaiah. The O.T. had been very clear in showing the depth of the depravity of man. Experience, observation, and Scripture all pointed to the conclusion that all were under sin.

Paul concluded by pointing out that God's law, regardless of how a person encounters it, stops his mouth and shows him to be guilty before God. He is guilty because no person can furnish the perfect obedience required by the law. The law, far from pointing to justification, shows a person his sins and makes him aware of his guilt before God.

Application: Teaching and Preaching the Passage

1. This is a very important passage on establishing the necessity of atonement. An understanding of the necessity of atonement will help us understand the nature of atonement. In 2:5-13 Paul makes it clear that God requires absolute righteousness if man is to be justified. In 3:10 Paul makes it clear that no one has absolute righteousness. In 3:20 Paul makes it clear that no human being can produce the righteousness required to be justified. The only possibility for man's justification is for God to provide absolute righteousness for man (3:21). (See discussion in connection with 2:13 and the discussion about atonement in connection with 3:25, 26.)

2. While Paul's main concern in 2:1—3:8 is with the Jew, the principles apply wherever they fit because the principles are universal:

(1) We cannot do the same things we judge another for and not expect to be judged ourselves (2:1, 3).

(2) In God's judgment the real truth will come out (2:2).

(3) God's judgment will require absolute righteousness (2:5-13).

(4) It is not *who* you are, but *what* you are that will count before God. If a Gentile could produce absolute righteousness he would be justified though he did not descend from Abraham (2:14-16).

(5) If a person does not have absolute righteousness, regardless of the fact that he may be a teacher of the law to others, he will be dealt with as a lawbreaker. His only hope will be the provision of righteousness Paul will mention in 3:21-26.

(6) The Jews were the Covenant People of God. Yet neither this mere fact nor the mere fact that they were circumcised could guarantee their justification before God (2:25-29). If this be the case, we can rest assured that Gentiles, who are not the Covenant People of God, cannot count on family relationships, church membership, or baptism for their justification.

(7) The Jew went to great lenghts to try to defend his own justification. He went so far as to suggest that if his unrighteousness in contrast with God's righteousness made God's righteousness look better, it would be wrong for God to condemn him. Paul explained that if we follow that line of thought God could judge nobody (3:5-8). It is futile for us to try to rationalize our way into a right relationship with God. We must come to God on His terms. He will accept nothing less than the death and righteousness of Christ which can be ours by faith.

(8) Fallen man is capable of developing good insights into many things. This is because he is rational as one who is created in God's image. However, his knowledge is always fragmented. He can never put together a meaningful view of the whole of reality. (See comments on the word for "understand" in the notes on 3:10.) Man is hungering for a worldview that will put things together with meaning. It is our responsibility to

present to people a meaningful view of the whole of reality—one that puts things together.

(9) The behavior of fallen man as depicted in 3:13-18 not only means that man needs a God-provided righteousness, but also that he needs a new birth. His experience with sin and God needs to be changed not only for the sake of his relationship to God, but also for his own good. Fallen man is in trouble with himself, and each with one another.

(10) In 3:19, 20 Paul sums up the matter. The whole race stands condemned before God. Fallen man is in a predicament that he cannot get out of by his own works. His only answer is through a way which God has provided. Paul will discuss this way in 3:21-31.

III. GOD'S PROVISION OF RIGHTEOUSNESS FOR THOSE WHO HAVE FAILED (3:21—5:21).

A. The Description, Condition, And Ground Of This Righteousness Are Given (3:21-31).

If God's revelation had only included 1:18—3:20, we would be in absolute despair. The history of man would be nothing but sin, ruin, and judgment. But such is not the case. Man is *helpless* but not *hopeless*.

1. It is provided by God (v. 21a).

21 But now the righteousness of God without the law is manifested, being witnessed by the law and the prophets.

But (Greek *de*). Frequently "but" introduces a new and more desirable line of thought than that which precedes "but." Such is the case here. Yeager observes that this little conjunction, here, "is one of the most fortunate adversatives in the New Testament, equal in importance to the one in Eph. 2:4, and for the same reason. They stand between the damnation of mankind and the salvation which only God can provide" (353).

Now. Some take the position that "now" is a logical now marking a transition from sin and guilt to salvation from sin. Others take "now" to be temporal. At this point in redemptive history the righteousness of God has been revealed. The temporal view is correct. "Now" has the same meaning as "at this time" in v. 26.

The righteousness of God. A more thorough treatment will be given to "the righteousness of God" in v. 26 after completing the study of propitiation in v. 25. It is sufficient for now to say that it is a righteousness from God, or a "God-provided righteousness."

2. It is apart from personal law-keeping (v. 21b).

Without the law. The meaning is "apart from law." Some understand "apart from law" to modify "the righteousness of God"; others take it to modify "is manifested." If it modifies "is manifested," the meaning would be that the law is not the instrument of revelation by which this righteousness from God is made known.

I am of the opinion that "apart from law" modifies "the righteousness of God." It is a righteousness that does not depend on personal law-keeping. By the test of 100% obedience to the law the whole human race failed (1:18—3:20). God as Judge required absolute righteousness. Man failed. God, through the atoning work of Jesus Christ, provided a righteousness that would meet His approval. This righteousness would do for man what personal law-keeping (actually law-failure) could not do. This God-provided righteousness makes it so a person can be justified in His sight.

3. It is witnessed by the Old Testament (v. 21c).

Is manifested. Justification before God for anyone would have to be through this God-provided righteousness. However, this was not clearly seen prior to Christ. This truth has now been openly made known.

Being witnessed by the law and the prophets. The law and the prophets stand for the entire O.T. By covenants, prophecies, and types, the O.T. bears witness to the truth of this God-provided righteousness. *There is a continuity and a harmony between the Old and New Testaments.*

4. It is by faith in Christ (v. 22a).

22 Even the righteousness of God *which is* by faith of Jesus Christ unto all and upon all them that believe: for there is no difference.

As a further step in describing and clarifying this God-provided righteousness, Paul says it is "**by faith of Jesus Christ**." It is generally agreed that the meaning is "faith in Jesus Christ." Grammatically, it could be either Christ's faith or our faith in Him as the object of our faith. It should be too obvious to require proof that it is our faith in Christ which is spoken of here.

5. It is offered to everybody (vv. 22b, 23).

Unto all and upon all them that believe. Most are of the opinion that "upon all" was not a part of the original text. The meaning is not materially affected whether it is kept or omitted. If we retain it, the meaning is that the God-provided righteousness is offered to everybody, but is only bestowed upon those who believe.

If "upon all" is omitted, the meaning is that this God-provided righteousness is offered to everybody on the condition of faith in Jesus Christ.

For there is no difference. This part of the verse is usually taken along with "for all have sinned" in the next verse to mean that this God-provided righteousness is offered to all because all have the same need. While it is true that all have the same need, that is not the point Paul is addressing here.

This expression tells why this God-provided righteousness is offered to all instead of a select few. Since the Jewish-Gentile problem was a consuming concern of Paul's in this book, the thought that occupied his mind was that this provision of righteousness was offered to the Gentiles, not just to the Jews.

Why was this provision of righteousness offered to the Gentiles, not just the Jews? It was because there was no difference or distinction that could be found between Jews and Gentiles which could justify such a limitation of the offer.

This is precisely what Paul says in 10:11-13: "For the scripture saith, Whosoever believeth on him shall not be ashamed. For there is no difference between the Jew and the Greek: for the same Lord over all is rich unto all that call upon him. For whosoever shall call upon the name of the Lord shall be saved" (Rom. 10:11-13).

The same reasoning that prohibits God from offering salvation to Jews only, without offering it to Gentiles, also means that there is no basis for God to restrict, in any other way, His offer of salvation.

An illustration will help us see the point. Let's suppose that a fifth grade teacher had to be out of the room. As an incentive for good behavior, she promised every child a piece of candy upon her return if he would not talk while she was gone. Upon her return, she found that every child in the room had talked.

She would have two choices consistent with fairness: (1) She could close the door completely on the candy offer. That would be her just right. (2) If she wanted to be merciful, she could make a new offer on a new condition to all of the class.

She could, consistent with fairness, make a new offer to none. Or she could make a new offer to all. She could not make a new offer to some because there would be no difference, in that all talked and violated the condition of her offer. *Is not this the very same principle that Paul is setting forth in 3:22, 23, and 10:11-13?*

The particulars with which Paul dealt (in the case of the Jewish-Gentile problem) were determined by his context. However, the principles were universal. It was the universality of the principles of judgment that Paul used so effectively in 2:1—3:8 in showing the guilt of the Jews.

Is it not a universal principle that God cannot offer this God-provided righteousness to a select few? In the light of universal guilt, God could have justly closed the books on the human race and offered no salvation. He could, instead, offer salvation to all, as He did on the condition of faith. He could not have offered it to only a select few.

I am sure some would answer that God can do anything. No, God cannot do anything. He cannot violate His own righteous nature (Tit. 1:2). He cannot make a square circle.

23 For all have sinned, and come short of the glory of God.

For all have sinned(Greek *hamartano).* This form of the word which appears here is aorist indicative. It can be translated "have sinned" and be interpreted to refer to the fact that all people have sinned in their own experience. Some understand the meaning to be that all sinned in Adam. This is the view taken by Shedd. He says, "The apostle has in mind a particular historical event: the same, namely, with that alluded to in [all have sinned] of 5:12, the sin in Adam" (76). The translation would be "all sinned" or "all did sin."

It is true that "all have sinned" (Greek *pantes hemarton*) in 5:12 refers to the fact that all sinned in Adam. However, that is in a different context. Dana and Mantey are correct when they say concerning 3:23:

> Paul had been discussing the fact of sin as universal in the human race, and would here stress the fact that past experience stands as evidence that all are condemned under the law, and that all, therefore, fall short of the glory of God. The idea emphasizes the reality of a fact which has taken place, hence should be construed as a culminative aorist and best rendered, *all have sinned* (*A Manual Grammar of the Greek New Testament* 98).

As a result of their sin all **come short** (Greek *hustereo*) **of the glory** (Greek *doxa*) **of God**. Concerning the words "come short" Wuest explains, "to be left behind in a race and so fail to reach the goal, to fall short of the end, to lack" (59). After pointing out that the present tense calls for the meaning "keep coming short" Picirilli explains, "This expression pictures the frustrating failure that is repeated over and over by man as he vainly keeps trying to achieve righteousness by his own efforts" (60).

There are several different opinions on the interpretation of "the glory of God." Here are five views. (1) It is the same as the eschatological glory of God in 5:2. This view has considerable popular support, but does not receive much support in the commentaries. Harrison points out, "This glory cannot be eschatological, as in 5:2, since even believers, for whom the sin problem has been solved, lack the future glory now" (41).

(2) The share of Divine glory which Adam had before he sinned. Barrett considers the reference to be to: "the glory with which Adam was created and which he (and all mankind with him) lost through sin. The glorious state of Adam in the Garden of Eden is a common conception in the Rabbinic literature, and in the Apocalypses" (74).

Cranfield sets forth the same view and points out that the glory which was lost "will be restored in the eschatological future" (204). Murray (113) and Harrison (41) have essentially the same view.

Taking the context in which it appears, it seems that a current problem and cause are more likely. If a clear reference to all having sinned in Adam were in this verse, as some think, this view would be more plausible.

(3) The glory of God is the Divine ideal or requirement for man. Bruce explains, "Through sin man falls short of the ideal which God had in view when He brought him into being" (102). See also Hamilton (61), Moule, *Cambridge* Bible (84), and Thomas (112, 113). If this had been the meaning here, it would appear, in the light of his emphasis on righteousness, that Paul would have said, "They have failed to attain righteousness" rather than to use the word (Greek *doxa*) glory.

(4) The glory of God refers to glorying before God as in 4:2. Luther says, "Men are altogether without any virtue in which they may glory (*before God)*.... the real glory before God is righteousness, wisdom, and spiritual strength, and all these come from God and with respect to God (*He being the donor*)" (77, 78).

If this had been the meaning, Paul would have used boasting (Greek *kauchesis*). See Rom. 3:27; 4:2; and 1 Cor. 5:6. See also the word (*kauchaomai*) in 1 Cor. 1:29; 2 Cor. 10:17; and Gal. 6:14.

(5) The glory of God refers to Divine approval or approbation. This use of the Greek word (*doxa*) is demonstrated in Jn. 12:43. "The praise of men" and "the praise of God" are synonomous with "the approval of men" and "the approval of God." "Come short of Divine approval" fits the context and is to be accepted. David Brown (208); Hendriksen (128, 129, note 94); Hodge (90); Shedd (77); and Vincent (683) support this view. See Vincent's treatment of the word; Hendriksen for a critical evaluation of the different views on "the glory of God"; and Murray (112, 113) for a less detailed treatment of the different views.

6. It is bestowed without cost as an unmerited favor (v.24).

24 Being justified freely by his grace through the redemption that is in Christ Jesus.

It is better to understand the last part of vv. 22 and 23 to be parenthetical. Paul wanted to head off any thinking that suggested this God-provided righteousness was offered to only a select few. Verse 24 is connected with "believe" in v. 22. All those who believe are *being justified*.

The word "believe" in v. 22 and the "being justified" in v. 24 are (Greek) present tense participles which refer to linear or continued action. This is not to suggest that justification is progressive or unfinished. Justification is always complete. You either have it or you do not. (More will be said about the nature of justification in v. 26.)

The continuous action of believing in v. 22 refers to the continuous flow of people coming to God believing in Jesus Christ. The continuous action of justification in v. 24 refers to the continuous activity of God in justifying those who are coming to Him by faith in Jesus Christ. (This regards the linear participles as "iterative.")

Freely (Greek *dorean*). The word "freely" in English can be "an unhindered flow" or "without cost." The Greek word means without cost. This is the same word that is translated "freely" in Rev. 21:6 and 22:17. There is no price tag on the water of life!

By his grace. This justification is bestowed as an unmerited favor upon us who justly deserved to go to Hell for eternity.

Through the redemption (Greek *apolutrosis*) **that is in Christ Jesus**. "In Christ Jesus" refers to the union of Christ and the believer. Chapter 6 furnishes a better opportunity to develop this thought.

Redemption refers to redemption by the payment of a ransom (Greek *lutron*). In Mt. 20:28 Jesus spoke of His having come "to minister, and to give his life a ransom [*lutron*] for many."

Since the illustration of paying a ransom price to a kidnapper is frequently given to illustrate Christ's payment of the ransom price, it is easy for misunderstanding to develop. There is a tendency to think of the kidnapper as illustrating Satan. Some think of Christ as paying the ransom price to Satan. This is not the case. Deliverance from Satan is not dependent upon his faithfulness to a promise to let us go free upon a ransom payment, by Christ. Redemption from Satan is by *power* not by *price*.

The ransom is paid to God. As Paul said in Gal. 3:13, "Christ hath redeemed us from the curse of the law, being made a curse for us." The ransom was paid to God as Lawgiver whose law had been violated.

It is good to remember that an illustration does not always furnish an exact parallel. The payment of a ransom to a kidnapper illustrates deliverance by the payment of a ransom. When details are overworked, we risk going into error. This also applies to the interpretation of types and parables in the Bible.

7. It is grounded in the atoning work of Christ (vv. 25, 26).

25 Whom God hath set forth *to be* a propitiation through faith in his blood, to declare his righteousness for the remission of sins that are past, through the forbearance of God.

Whom God hath set forth (Greek *protithemi*). The meaning of this word is "to set before." Two meanings are suggested: (1) To set forth beforehand, to foreordain, to purpose, or to design. The reference would be to the eternal plan of God in which He purposed to send Christ to be a propitiation (see Cranfield 208, 209; Godet 150, 151; and Hendriksen 131, note 99). Black (68) also shows an interest in this view.

(2) To set forth publicly. An overwhelming majority of commentators take this view (see Denny 610, 611; Harrison 43; Hodge 92; Liddon 74, 75; Meyer 133, 134; Murray 117, 118; Sanday and Headlam 87; Shedd 79; and Vincent 684).

Though either meaning would make sense, the second one is to be preferred by the context. "Declare" which occurs here and in v. 26 fits the idea of setting forth publicly. Concerning the use of this Greek word Shedd observes, "Plato

(Phaedo, 115) employs this word to describe the laying out of the corpse of Socrates; Herodotus, to denote the display of gold and silver untensils (III., 148)" (79).

***To be* a propitiation** (*hilasterion*). A number of problems need to be dealt with regarding the translation of this word. The first is one raised by C. H. Dodd. He explains:

> The Greek word (*hilasterion*) is derived from a verb which in pagan writings and inscriptions has two meanings: (a) 'to placate' a man or a god; (b) 'to expiate' a sin, i.e. to perform an act (such as the payment of a fine or the offering of a sacrifice) by which its guilt is annulled. The former meaning is overwhelmingly the more common. In the Septuagint, on the other hand, the meaning (a) is practically unknown where God is the object, and the meaning (b) is found in scores of passages. (54).

Dodd prefers "expiation," which is a good term, but since it is more general than "propitiation" it is possible (though not necessary) to give it a much weaker meaning. The meaning, according to Dodd, is "a means whereby guilt is annulled" (55). The problem here is not as much with the words Dodd uses as it is with the weakened meaning.

The heart of the problem is seen in this statement by Dodd: "The rendering **propitiation** is therefore misleading, for it suggests the placating of an angry God, and although this would be in accord with pagan usage, it is foreign to biblical usage" (55).

Leon Morris who is well known for his answer to Dodd's argument remarks: "The idea of the wrath of God is stubbornly rooted in the OT where it is referred to 585 times. The words of the *hilaskomai* group do not denote simple forgiveness or cancellation of sin, but that forgiveness or cancellation of sin which includes the turning away of God's wrath (e.g., Lam. 3:42, 43)" (888).

See also Cranfield (215, 216) and Bruce (105) for a response to Dodd's view.

Wuest in commenting on the word *hilasterion* says: "This is a far cry from the pagan idea of propitiation which appeased the anger of the god and purchased his love. The words, 'an expiatory satisfaction' seem to be the words rather than 'propitiation' to adequately translate *hilasterion*" (61).

It is important to recognize that Dodd and Wuest are not in total agreement. Wuest has a serious view about the penal death of Christ. The problem Wuest has is with the type anger demonstrated by pagan gods and the idea of paying off the god to get him to remove his anger.

Certainly, it is important to recognize the difference in the anger of a pagan god that may be based on whim and fancy and that of the God of Scripture whose wrath does not violate His holiness. Rather, it grows out of His holiness. It is certainly important that we not look at atonement as a bribe. However, we need not forsake the word "propitiation" to do this. Words have a denotation and a connotation. In both pagan and Christian usage, propitiation denotes that which diverts wrath. When it comes to connotation, the meaning of propitiation differs drastically depending on whether it is used in a pagan context or a Christian context.

It must be remembered that very few Greek words were coined in order to present Christian truth. Instead, existing vocabulary was used. The shades of meaning changed drastically, in many cases, as they were changed from a pagan context to a Christian one. This very principle makes it possible to translate the Scriptures into the language of pagan cultures, or for that matter our own. The Biblical context will do all that is necessary with the word "propitiation" to remove any pagan connotations.

This is not the only question about the meaning of the word (*hilasterion*) in this verse. The next question is whether it should be translated "mercy seat" or some form of the word propitiation. This problem arises from the fact that the only other time this exact word is used in the N.T. is in Heb. 9:5 where it definitely refers to the mercy seat and is so translated.

The mercy seat was the lid of the Ark of the Covenant which was in the Holy of Holies or the Most Holy Place in the tabernacle. It was here that once a year the high priest took the blood of the goat that was slain and sprinkled it on and before the mercy seat. The mercy seat was the place of propitiation. Bruce (104-107), Harrison (43), Lenski (255-258), and Nygren (156-159) take the position that "mercy seat" is the preferred translation.

The basic reason for this view is that the word in the Septuagint (the Greek translation of the O.T.) referred to the mercy seat. Also, the only other reference, as has been pointed out, in the N.T. (Heb. 9:5) in which it appears has the meaning mercy seat.

Those who reject this view point out that in Heb. 9:5 the article (Greek *to*) precedes the word. It is argued that the absence of the article makes another translation more likely. Cranfield points out another problem with this view:

> While it is an understandable paradox to refer to Christ as being at the same time both priest and victim, to represent Him as being the place of sprinkling as well as the victim is surely excessively harsh and confusing. Moreover, there seems to be something essentially improbable in the thought of Paul's likening Christ, for whom, personally, man's redemption was so infinitely costly, and to whom he felt so tremendous a personal indebtedness (cf., e.g., Gal. 2:20) to something which was only an inanimate piece of temple furniture (215).

Before proceeding with more evaluation of the use of "mercy seat" as a translation, let us look at other suggestions for translating *hilasterion*. Cranfield gives an excellent summary and evaluation of the other views:

> The remaining possibilities are: (i) 'propitiatory' or 'propitiating' (a masculine adjective agreeing with *hon*; (ii) 'a propitiator'; (iii) 'a propitiation' or 'a means of propitiation'; (iv) 'a propitiatory sacrifice.' Of these (ii) should probably be rejected, in spite of the considerable support it has had. . .on the grounds that there does not seem to be any independent attestation of such use of *hilasterios* in ancient times (had this been Paul's meaning, he would probably have used the word *hilastes*). Between the other three possibilities there would seem to be little substantial difference, since, even if the word is explained as having one of the more general senses (i) and (iii), the presence of [in his blood] would still indicate that a propitiatory sacrifice is in mind. On the whole it seems best to accept (iv) (216, 217).

Since "a propitiatory sacrifice" is a possible translation, and since it fits easily in the passage, it would appear to be the preferred translation. With regard to the use of "mercy seat," while it is not the translation I take, it need not be rejected on the basis that it makes Christ "the place of propitiation" rather than the sacrifice. If "mercy seat" is chosen, it could be understood as a metonymy. "A metonymy is a figure of speech in which one word is given for another which it suggests. For example, the cause may be given for the effect or the effect for the cause. Another example of this is, "for he [Christ] is our peace. . ." (Eph. 2:14). The meaning is that Christ is the cause or source of our peace. The container may be given for that which is contained. An example of this is referring to the contents of the cup as the cup in the Lord's Supper (1 Cor. 11:25)" (Forlines 157).

Still another example of metonymy is found in 3:21. There "law and the prophets" is given for the O.T. Literally prophets were authors of the prophetic writings, but by metonymy, the word "prophets" refers to prophetic writings. That in v. 21 "prophets" refers to their writings, not to the prophets themselves, is obvious.

If "mercy seat" were the required translation, it would be understood as a metonymy and, in that case, the actual reference to Christ would be the propitiatory sacrifice, which was presented at the mercy seat (the place of propitiation). He would not be the place of propitiation.

We use metonymies with ease in our own language. This happens without actually knowing what a metonymy is. It sometimes seems a bit awkward when we see them in Scripture. We get hung up on the literal meaning when understanding it as a metonymy removes the difficulty. Remember, the Bible uses language the same way it is used in everyday speech and writing.

The case for "propitiatory sacrifice" is good, and since it is much easier to grasp, it is preferred. As shown above, even with the "mercy seat" translation, the meaning would still be "a propitiatory sacrifice."

Still further clarification is needed in understanding "propitiation." The *nature* of propitiation is better understood in the light of the *purpose*. Since this purpose is set forth in the remaining part of vv. 25 and 26, the discussion of propitiation will be completed in v. 26.

Through faith in his blood. Many are of the opinion that "in [by] his blood" is connected with propitiation rather than being the object of faith (see Cranfield 210, Murray 120, 121, and Sanday and Headlam 89). "Propitiation by his blood" seems to be more likely, in this verse, than "faith in his blood." The emphasis would be upon the blood sacrifice. The object of faith would be Jesus Christ (v. 22).

There is an interesting observation to be made if, as some texts read, an article precedes "faith" in the Greek. Most do not think there is any significant difference in the presence or absence of the article before faith. I am of the opinion that it does make a difference. Without the article, faith refers to the experience of believing. Faith in Christ refers to the experience of believing. "The faith" refers to that which is believed. I am of the opinion that "the faith" in the N.T. is a synonym for "The New Covenant." (See further commentary on v. 30.) If this be the case, the meaning is propitiation by His blood through the New Covenant.

Some comment needs to be made about the use of the word blood. The significance of blood in the propitiatory sacrifice of Christ goes beyond the mere shedding of blood. The shed blood of Christ stands for the death of Christ and all that is meant by that death. It represents the fact that in His death Jesus Christ paid the full penalty for sin. Tholuck says that the blood "stands, by metonomy [sic] for *bloody death*" (110, 111).

To declare (Greek *endeixis*) **his righteousness for the remission of** (Greek *paresis*) **sins that are past, through the forbearance of God.**

Very few agree with Barnes in taking "sins that are past" to refer to the past sins of the individual (89). There is a general consensus that the reference is to the time before the cross.

Barnes (89), Lenski (260), and Stuart (113) take "his righteousness" to be the same as in 1:17 and 3:21, 22. This would put the righteousness in the context of justification. The exact way it is related to justification depends on the interpretation given in 3:21, 22.

Cranfield (211), Denny (612), Hodge (95, 96), and Murray (118) consider righteousness to be an attribute of God. This fits the context better. In this context, the reference is to God's judicial righteousness, which is referred to as justice.

This is the only time this word translated remission occurs in the Bible. There are two conflicting views concerning its use here. (1) Some think that it refers to the way God forgave the sins of believers before the cross. They distinguish this word from the one usually translated forgiveness or remission (Greek *aphesis*). According to Lightfoot *aphesis* refers to the "revocation of punishment" while *paresis* refers to "the suspension of punishment" (273). According to this view, Rom. 3:25 means that God "passed over" the sins of believers before the cross since He knew Christ would later make atonement for them. At that time they would actually be remitted.

An illustration will help. When we buy a car by having it financed by a bank, we actually experience owning the car immediately. However, it is ours in a different sense when we make the last payment. The O.T. believers experienced forgiveness before the cross, but forgiveness was theirs in a different sense when Christ actually made atonement.

A person may take this view concerning the difference between the forgiveness of O.T. saints before the Cross and at the time of the Cross without taking it to be the subject under discussion in this verse. But some who take the meaning here to be the forgiveness of the sins of O.T. saints consider the word used here (*paresis*) to be a term especially chosen to set forth that difference (Lenski 261; Olshausen 155, 156). Hodge (96, 97) and Stuart (114) take the reference to be forgiveness of sins before the cross, but see no essential difference between the two Greek words (*paresis*) and (*aphesis*).

(2) Another interpretation (of *paresis*) is to make the reference to the withholding of God's *judgment* (not *forgiveness*) on the sins of *all* people before the Cross (Lange 134; and Meyer 138, 139). The "passing over" of sins, according to this view, includes sins of both saints and sinners. This is not however, to be understood as saying that there was no difference in God's treatment of saints and sinners before the Cross.

The point of this view is this: The justice of God calls for infinite wrath (the equivalent of eternal punishment) to be poured out on sin. If this is the requirement of God's holy nature, why did He not immediately inflict His penal wrath on Adam and Eve and destroy the human race? The fact that this was not done could have caused some to question whether God would actually inflict penal wrath on fallen man.

Lange observes: "The judicial government of God was not administered in the ante-Christian period, either by the sacrificial fire of the Israelitish theocracy, or by the manifestations of wrath to the old world, both Jews and Gentiles, as a perfect and general judgment" (134).

Either interpretation (of *paresis*) would make good sense in the context. For a long time I held the view that the meaning was restricted to the "passing over" (forgiveness) of the sins of O.T. saints. It now appears to me that this refers to the withholding of God's wrath from all people prior to the cross.

The key to understanding who is referred to by the word seems to be the word forbearance (Greek *anoche*). This word does not occur at all in the Septuagint. It occurs in only one other place in the N.T., Rom. 2:4.

In Rom. 2:4, the reference is clearly to the unsaved. The forbearance in this case was the withholding of God's penal wrath. There does not seem to be an adequate reason for understanding 2:4 to refer to the unsaved and to understand the use in 3:25 to be restricted to the saints.

The point seems to be that God had withheld His wrath from all: (1) from the unsaved because there had been no execution of penal wrath upon them; (2) from the saved because there had been no actual atonement (only symbolic atonement) which paid the penalty by a substitute. Thus, it can be seen that forbearance can be applied to God's dealings with both the saved and the unsaved before the Cross.

It must be remembered that the judgment of God on sin in the present life is not an execution of God's penal wrath. Even Christians are not delivered completely from some of the temporal judgments of God against sin. They are delivered from penal punishment. If this were not the case, there would be no forgiveness. God's judgment against sin in this life has basically a teaching value. Others are warned when someone is judged. For the Christian judgment is essentially a form of chastisement.

We have yet to decide the meaning of the phrase which is translated "to declare" (Greek *eis endeixin*). The word can mean either "to demonstrate" or "to prove." These meanings tend to blend together. Sanday and Headlam give the meaning as "proof by an appeal to fact" (89).

Having examined the parts of the verse, let us now put the meaning together. The purpose of the propitiatory sacrifice is to prove that God did not compromise His judicial justice in holding back His penal wrath from men prior to the Cross. (This does not mean that God would never judge them. It only means that God did not immediately send them all to Hell and end the history of the human race on earth.)

How was this purpose of the propitiatory sacrifice accomplished? (1) The penalty was paid for the sins of all mankind including those of O.T. saints. This made it clear that the question was settled. The wrath that God withheld from the O.T. saints did not represent a compromise of His justice. At the cross their sins were paid for and justice was satisfied.

(2) As it relates to withholding His penal wrath from the unsaved (during their life on earth) the cross sent a message loud and clear. The withholding of God's penal wrath from the unsaved refers only to this life. If God's justice required the execution of His wrath on His own Son before He would forgive anybody's sins, surely He will execute His wrath on those who refuse His Son.

The Cross of Christ gives out two emphatic messages: (1) Based on Christ's death, God will forgive all who come to Him by faith in Christ. (2) There is no hope of avoiding God's wrath apart from Christ. Judgment is sure to come.

26 To declare, *I say*, at this time his righteousness: that he might be just, and the justifier of him which believeth in Jesus.

In v. 25 we see proof that God's justice was vindicated in connection with the withholding of His penal wrath prior to the Cross. (The reason for not referring to Acts 17:30 and other such passages is that it is not certain they are referring to the same thing as that referred to in v. 25.)

Verse 26 deals with proof that God, at the *present time*, does not compromise His justice when He justifies the one who believes in Jesus. God is now bestowing absolute righteousness as a gift upon those who had failed to achieve this requirement by their own effort. This is done when, and only when, the person believes in Jesus Christ.

Doctrinal Discussion: The Necessity of Atonement

It is time to elaborate on "the righteousness of God" as set forth in vv. 21, 22: the "propitiatory sacrifice" and "justification." The way we interpret these terms will be determined by our concept of the necessity of atonement. Our concept of the *nature* of atonement is determined by our concept of the *necessity* of atonement. These observations will also direct our understanding of justification.

The most important chapter in the Bible in helping us see *the necessity* and *requirements* for atonement and justification is chapter 2 of Romans. The way we interpret chapter 2 will determine the way we interpret 3:21-26.

There are basically two views of atonement which compete for acceptance by conservative Christians. These are the satisfaction view and the governmental view.

The Satisfaction View of Aonement

Since most conservative Christians have subscribed to the satisfaction view, it will be described first. According to this view it is absolutely necessary for sin to be punished. The love of God could not forgive sin apart from paying the penalty required by justice. If there was to be atonement, it must include the payment of the penalty of sin. Also, absolute righteousness must be provided.

The Governmental View of Atonement

The governmental view was first set forth by Hugo Grotius (1583-1645). According to this view, there is no absolute necessity that sin be punished. Sin requires punishment only as it is necessary to secure the end of God's government. This being true, the penalty can be set aside and never be paid either by the person or a substitute. This can be done if another means can be provided which will protect the interests of government, which is the happiness of man. It is concluded that atonement is necessary to protect the interests of government since forgiveness too easily granted would present problems.

According to this view, the punishment in Hell is a penal punishment. The purpose of a penalty is to be a moral force that will discourage sinning. If there can be another force to discourage sin, the penalty can be set aside and never paid.

Christ's death is not that of a substitute paying a penalty. Rather, His death is a *substitute* for a penalty. His death is not a penal death in any strict sense of the word. His death, for those who believe, is a moral force that will discourage them from sinning and will encourage them to do right.

In this view, there is no imputation to the believer of either the death or the righteousness of Christ. The faith of the one who believes in Christ gets the same acceptance before God that absolute righteousness would. In the light of the person's faith in Christ, God sets aside the requirement of both absolute righteousness and the penalty for sin.

The Satisfaction View of Justifiation

In the satisfaction view, God, as Judge, justifies the one who believes in Christ. This He does because the believer receives from Christ both His righteousness and His death.

The Governmental View of Jusification

In the governmental view, God acts as a governor does when he grants a pardon. The governor can set the penalty aside. A judge must give the penalty prescribed by law. God, as Sovereign, pardons the sinner who believes in Christ. This He does by setting aside the requirements of the law, both for absolute righteousness and for a penalty.

Value of Propitiation: Inherent or Revelational?

Another important distinction is that according to the satisfaction view the propitiatory sacrifice of Christ has *inherent* value. He actually paid the penalty for our sins. He actually met the requirements of the law. According to the governmental view, the value is only *revelational*. The value of the death of Christ is in the message it conveys. It reveals God's attitude toward sin. The message of the cross is that if a person does not repent and believe in Christ he will suffer eternal punishment. The cross tells the sinner that he will be pardoned if he believes in Christ.

Some who have held to the governmental view since Grotius include John Miley, Charles Finney, James H. Fairchild, and H. Orton Wiley. For a presentation and evaluation of these views see Forlines *Systematics* 149-174.

Most commentaries do not give a complete development, but what they say tends to comply with the satisfaction view. Among those commentators on Romans who are in essential agreement with the governmental view are John Brown (37), Godet (160-162), and Stuart (116).

Views Tested by Scripture

Now the question is: How do these views fare in the light of Romans 2 and 3? The burden of Paul in chapter 2 was to get the Jews to see that the only righteousness that God would accept is an absolute righteousness. Any person who has sinned has failed to produce what God requires. *The point is this: God did not relinquish His requirement of absolute righteousness after man fell. It is still required of anyone before he can be received into a positive relationship with God.*

In Romans 2 the only people, according to Paul, who will be justified are *the doers of the law*. The "doing" here is a complete or absolute doing of the law. This is another way of saying absolute righteousness (see comments on chapter 2. The comments on 2:13 give different views and defend the requirement of absolute righteousness).

Paul makes it unquestionably clear that none have absolute righteousness (3:10). It is also clear that none can by their own works produce absolute righteousness (3:20).

Nothing that Paul says in 3:21-26 is to be taken as in any way altering the Divine requirement of absolute righteousness. Rather, the message is that God has provided for us the absolute righteousness which His holy nature required. This is the righteousness which is spoken of in 3:21, 22.

The Nature of Christ's Propitiatory Sacrifice

A full understanding of this God-provided righteousness involves an understanding of the propitiatory sacrifice.

While I do not believe "mercy seat" is a proper translation of *hilasterion* (see v. 25), since the mercy seat was the place of propitiation in the tabernacle, it is important to see what took place at the mercy seat (see Heb. 9:5).

The Ark of the Covenant was located in the Holy of Holies where the High Priest went only once a year on the day of atonement. The Ark of the Covenant had within it the tables of the law. The law represented the demands of the law which were (1) righteousness and (2) a penalty against sin in case of disobedience. When the High Priest slew the goat that was slain on the day of atonement and took his blood into the Holy of Holies and sprinkled it on the mercy seat, it was as if he were saying to the law, 'This symbolizes the meeting of the demands you have made from sinners.'

The fact that the animal was without spot and blemish symbolized righteousness. The fact that the animal was slain symbolized the payment of a penalty through a substitute. The satisfaction of the law was symbolized. This satisfaction included both the payment of the penalty and the provision of righteousness.

From the above discussion, we would observe that at the place of propitiation the law is satisfied. This, of course, tells us what the design of propitiation was. It was designed to satisfy the penal demands of the law, thus making it so that God can turn away His wrath from the sinner who believes in Christ, and at the same time maintain His justice. It was designed to satisfy the demand for righteousness, thus giving positive grounds for God to view favorably the sinner who believes in Jesus and at the same time maintain His justice.

What the Old Testament sacrifice did in symbol on the day of atonement, Jesus Christ did in reality. He lived a completely holy life, thus fulfilling the demand for righteousness. He paid the full penalty for sin, thus fulfilling the demand for a penalty. Propitiation, to sum it up, is the full satisfaction of the demands of the law, for righteousness and the payment of a penalty, by Jesus Christ, thus making it possible for God to turn His wrath from the sinner who believes in Jesus, and to view him with favor, and at the same time remain a God of justice (Forlines *Systematics* 154, 155).

The purpose of propitiation is clearly stated in vv. 25, 26. That purpose is to prove that there was no compromise of God's justice in connection with His withholding penal punishment prior to the death of Christ. Punishment could be delayed because God had planned a way in which He could forgive sin without justice suffering loss. Once the propitiatory work of Christ was accomplished, it was clear that in passing over the sins committed before the Cross, there had been no compromise of His justice.

The purpose of propitiation also makes it clear that, at the present time, God can justify the person who believes in Christ without doing violence to His justice. Christianity stands unique in this regard. No other religion confronts and deals with the problem of maintaining a consistency between the justice of their god and the forgiveness of sin. Because of the propitiatory sacrifice of Christ, God can be both a God of justice and a God of mercy to those who come to Him believing in Jesus Christ.

God-provided Righteousness

We have reached the point now that we give a more detailed explanation of the "righteousness of God" in 3:21, 22.

There are three Greek words from the same root which require our attention: (1) the adjective which is usually translated "righteous" or "just" (Greek *dikaios*; (2) the noun which is translated "righteousness" (Greek *dikaiosune*); and (3) the verb which in most instances is translated "justify" (Greek *dikaioo*).

According to Vine, the adjective (*dikaios*):

> ...was first used of persons observant of *dike*, custom, rule, right, especially in the fulfillment of duties towards gods, and men, and of things that were in accordance with right. The Eng. word 'righteous' was formerly spelt 'rightwise,' i.e., (in a) straight way. In the N.T. it denotes righteous, a state of being right, or right conduct, judged whether by the Divine standard, or according to human standards, of what is right. Said of God, it designates the perfect agreement between His nature and His acts (in which He is the standard for all men)" (623).

This word occurs 7 times in Romans. In 3:10; 5:7, 19 it is translated "righteous." In 1:17; 2:13; 3:26; and 7:12 it is rendered "just." With reference to God it may refer to the fact that in His general dealings with His creature He always does right. When used in a judicial setting as in Rom. 3:26, it refers to His attribute of justice.

It is helpful to observe that in English we speak of God as being "righteous" and as being "just." In the Greek, the word may refer to God as righteous, in a general sense, or it may, in a more specific sense, refer to His judicial righteousness. In the restricted sense, we translate by the word "just" as observed in 3:26. The context must decide whether we should translate as "righteous" or "just."

Concerning the noun (*dikaiosune*), Liddon explains:

> *Dikaiosune* is that relationship to *dike* or Right which fulfills its claims; which makes a moral being what he should be. . . .*Dike* is in pagan language Right (as apprehended by established usage, —The best available criterion), and so personified as the daughter of Zeus and Themis; this abstract divinity is mentioned in Acts 28:4. . . .
>
> The principle of *dikaiosune* then is always the same, viz. conformity to right, but the actual moral attainments which it represents vary with varying conceptions of and the subjects to which it is attributed. . . . The Biblical sense of *dikaiosune*, therefore, is that conformity to Right which God enjoins and of which He is the standard (15, 16).

With reference to God righteousness is an attribute of God which means that all that He does is in conformity to His holy nature. This is the meaning in vv. 25, 26.

Our present concern is with the expression "righteousness of God" as it occurs in 1:17 and 3:21, 22. Before we get to the more basic consideration, let us examine the views on the relationship between God and righteousness in the usage under investigation. There are essentially two views: (1) A righteousness which will stand before God. (2) A righteousness which is from God.

I think it should be obvious that the righteousness in 1:17 and 3:21, 22 is the same of which Paul speaks in Phil. 3:9. "And be found in him, not having mine own righteousness, which is of the law, but that which is through the faith of Christ, the righteousness which is of God by faith." In "of God" the preposition "of " (Greek *ek*) means "from." The righteousness which is under consideration is from God. Surely, the righteousness that is from God will stand before God. The standing, however, before God is an inference from the nature of the righteousness rather than from the meaning of the expression "righteousness of God." Olshausen says: "The translation of *dikaiosune*, by 'the righteousness which avails before God,' is not false but only derived; [the righteousness of God] means in the first place the righteousness which is wrought by God, but that which God produces answers to its idea, and must therefore avail before Him" (144).

Righteousness is that which conforms to the moral nature of God, or another way of saying it is that which conforms to the requirement of God's law. It is a righteousness which is from God which He has provided for us.

What were the requirements of the law? In chapter 2 Paul made it unquestionably clear that God required absolute obedience or absolute righteousness. The word *righteousness*, without qualification, means absolute righteousness. For the sake of emphasis and clarity, it is frequently put "absolute righteousness." In the light of chapter 2 any righteousness which is not absolute is unrighteousness. When we discuss the subject of sanctification, we will be able to talk about relative righteousness.

It is obvious in justification that the only righteousness God will accept is absolute righteousness. If Jesus was going to make righteousness available for us, it was necessary for Him to become incarnate and live a life of perfect conformity to God's holy nature.

There is yet another requirement that must be met. Righteousness is what the law requires for justification. If man had never sinned, the only need would have been a continued absolute obedience. However, sin introduced a new chapter. God's holy nature will not tolerate the nonpayment of the penalty. The law requires the payment of a penalty. This penalty as experienced by man is eternal punishment. The "righteousness of God" provided for us includes: (1) Christ's righteous life and (2) Christ's death. His death involved infinite suffering which is the equivalent of eternal death. Jesus, on the Cross, suffered the wrath of God. It is important to remember that the sufferings of Christ went far beyond the sufferings which were inflicted upon Him by men. "Yet it pleased the LORD to bruise him; he hath put *him* to grief." (Is. 53:10a).

For years I have tended to believe that the God-provided righteousness included both the active obedience of Christ (His righteous life) and His passive obedience (His death). It was not until reading Haldane's treatment of the "righteousness of God" that I saw where anybody had addressed the problem. As Haldane remarks:

> No explanation of the expression, 'The righteousness of God,' will at once suit the phrase and the situation in which it is found in the passage before us, but that which makes it that righteousness, or obedience to the law, both in its penalty and requirements, which has been yielded to it by our Lord Jesus Christ. This is indeed the righteousness of God, for it has been provided by God, and from first to last has been effected by His Son Jesus Christ, who is the Mighty God and the Father of eternity (131, 32).

The reading of Haldane's treatment of the "righteousness of God" (126-138) is highly recommended.

We need to examine two more ways some have interpreted the righteousness of God: (1) God's method of justifying sinners. The exact wording may differ, but the essential wording is found in Barnes (29-31); John Brown (24-30); and Harrison (41). (2) The status of righteousness that the believer has as a result of God's justifying act (Cranfield 97-99; Godet 146; and Lenski 79, 80).

If these statements were to appear apart from the words "the righteousness of God" they would be true statements. However, put into the context of Rom. 1:17 and 3:21, 22, they are not a correct interpretation of the righteousness of God. The first view confuses the righteousness that justifies with the method of justification. The second view confuses the status of one who is righteous with what gives him that status, namely, righteousness.

Another problem with these views is that a person could take either of them and fit them in with any view of atonement he may choose. This could also include the governmental view or an even weaker view. Or the person could accept the satisfaction view. Along with not being technically correct, they are too vague.

To the best of my knowledge of those listed above who adhere to the interpretation of "God's method of justifying sinners" or "the status of righteousness bestowed by God's act of justification," only three adhere to the governmental view of atonement—Barnes, John Brown, and Godet.

Haldane has well said:

> 'The righteousness of God' cannot mean *God's method of justification, nor the justification which God bestows,* because the word translated *righteousness* does not signify *justification.* Righteousness and justification are two things quite different. God's righteousness is revealed in the Gospel, just as God Himself is said to be revealed. To reveal God is not to reveal a method of God's acting, and to reveal God's righteousness is not to reveal a method of God's making sinners righteous, but to reveal the righteousness itself (127).

Justification

Now, let us turn our attention to justify (Greek *dikaioo*). The meaning is to declare or pronounce just or righteous, or to declare in right standing. Since God cannot declare something to be what it is not, and since fallen man is not righteous, in order for God to be able to pronounce a human being righteous, He had to make the provision for man.

It should be quite clear that God makes an uncompromising demand of man for absolute righteousness (chapter 2). Just as surely as God required absolute righteousness, He has provided it (3:21-26).

By His active obedience, Jesus Christ produced absolute obedience. By His passive obedience, He paid the penalty for our sins. He suffered the full wrath of God for our sins. When a person believes in Christ as His Lord and Savior, the active and passive obedience is placed on his account.

The Believer's Account	
Debits	Credits
Perfect obedience	Christ's life of obedience
Eternal Death	Christ's Death
Paid in full or Justified	

It should be observed that the nature of the God-provided righteousness is determined by the nature of the requirements of God's holy nature. Those requirements are: (1) perfect obedience (or obedience without exception) and (2) eternal death. Haldane correctly states that these two constitute God's righteous requirement. The meeting of these requirements by

Jesus Christ constitutes righteousness. When this righteousness is made available, it is called a God-provided righteousness. The moment a person receives this righteousness, on the condition of faith, he is justified.

The view of justification given above is the view that corresponds with the satisfaction view of atonement. This is the view which, in my opinion, is set forth in the Bible. It will be more convenient to set forth the view which corresponds with the governmental view in comments on 4:3-5.

8. It leaves no room for boasting (v. 27).

27 Where *is* boasting then? It is excluded. By what law? of works? Nay: but by the law of faith.

Having conclusively shown that not one person will receive right standing with God based on his own righteousness, and having set forth the way of justification based on a God-provided righteousness, Paul felt obligated to say, **"Where *is* boasting? It is excluded."** There is a lot to be thankful for, but there are no personal grounds for bragging about the fact that we are justified.

To refer to the chart above, on the payment side, *not one thing that we have ever done or ever will do will ever appear as a part of the price for our* justification. As the song says, "Jesus paid it all, All to Him I owe."

By what law? The meaning of law here is "a guiding principle." **Of works? Nay: but by the law of faith.** The "works way," if it could succeed, would furnish grounds for boasting, but it had been proved to be an utter failure. The "faith way" does work, but since it grounds justification solely in the work of Christ, it eliminates all personal boasting.

9. It is received on the sole condition of faith (v. 28).

28 Therefore we conclude that a man is justified by faith without the deeds of the law.

Therefore. What follows is a conclusion established by what precedes.

A man. The reference is to any member of the race, male or female, Jew or Gentile.

Is justified by faith without the deeds of the law. The subject here is justification, not sanctification. The exclusion of "the deeds [or works] of the law" is from justification. In the believer's life, there will be some "law-keeping" or "obedience to God," but that will be related to his sanctification, not his justification.

10. It is offered to Jew and Gentile alike on the same condition (vv. 29, 30).

29 *Is he* the God of the Jews only? *is he* not also of the Gentiles? Yes, of the Gentiles also.

The King James Version does not translate a particle (Greek *e*) which occurs at the beginning of the verse. Out of 357 occurrences of this particle, 20 are left untranslated. The more frequent translation is "or" which occurs 259 times (J. B. Smith, *Greek-English Concordance* 165).

It should be translated "or." This is done in several other translations. The reading would be, "Or is he the God of the Jews only?" With this reading let us go back to the word "man" in v. 28. The meaning is "any person." Paul is saying, "Any person, Jew or Gentile, will be justified on the condition of faith. Or is he the God of the Jews only?"

Paul then proceeds to ask, ***"Is he* not also of the Gentiles?** The answer is: **"Yes, of the Gentiles also."** When Paul argued for the guilt of the Jew, he started with the guilt of the Gentile and moved toward the guilt of the Jew. This was because it was harder to convince the Jew of his plight before God. In establishing the universality of the gospel offer, he moved from the Jew to the Gentile. In view of their misunderstanding of their covenant relationship with God, it would have been easier for the Jews to have believed, if the offer had been limited to them.

30 Seeing *it is* one God, which shall justify the circumcision by faith, and uncircumcision through faith.

Seeing *it is* one God. Paul's argument in this verse centers around the fact that there is only one God. The so-called gods of the Gentiles did not exist. Therefore, God was the God of the Gentiles as well as the Jews.

Which shall justify the circumcision by faith (Greek *ek pisteos*), **and uncircumcision through faith** (Greek *dia tes pisteos*). Most do not recognize any difference between "by faith" and "through the faith." It will be observed that in the first expression, there is no article; while in the second expression, there is an article. It would be translated "through the faith."

Liddon was on the right track when he made this distinction between these: "It was a development of the subjective belief of the Jews which would lead to their justification: it was the objective faith of Christendom, of which as yet they knew nothing, which would be the means of justifying the Gentiles" (80).

Galatians 3:23 offers a good opportunity to see the significance of having the article before faith. If we translate the article where it appears in the Greek before faith, it will read, "But before [the] faith came, we were kept under the law, shut up unto the faith which should afterwards be revealed" (Gal. 3:23).

Concerning Gal. 3:23, John Brown understands "the faith" to mean "the revelation believed." He goes on to explain: "The phraseology adopted by the apostle, the revelation of faith [the last part of v. 23], makes it evident that faith refers to doctrine. He speaks of it as 'afterwards to be revealed'" (173). Lightfoot understands 'the faith' to mean "the Gospel, the objective teaching, the system of which 'faith' is the leading feature" (148) (see my "Legalism in Galatians" in *Dimension*, Winter quarter 1984-85).

A place where the presence of the article clearly makes a difference is Jude where he says, "Contend for the faith" (v. 3). It clearly refers to what is believed rather than the act of believing as would be the case without the article (see also Acts 6:7).

In almost every case where "faith" is preceded by the article in the Greek New Testament (except in constructions denoting possession) the reference is to what is believed. Further, just as "the law" had come to mean "the Mosaic Law" or "the Covenant of Law" where the context supports this interpretation, "the faith" had come to be a synonym for "the New Covenant" or "the faith way." (This is an area where more research should be done.)

Taking Liddon's comments above, along with the rest of what has been said about "the faith," it appears that a modern day parallel to v. 30 would be: With reference to those who have heard the gospel, we say, "You must believe to be saved." With regard to the heathen, we say, "We must take the gospel to them."

31 Do we then make void the law

through faith? God forbid: yea, we establish the law.

Do we then make void the [no article in the Greek] **law through** [the] **faith? God forbid** (Greek *me genoito*)**: yea** (Greek *alla*)**, we establish the** [no article] **law.** This question arises naturally, especially for Jews, after Paul denied that lawkeeping was in any way involved in our justification. Paul emphatically negates (see explanation of "God forbid" in comments on 3:4) any idea that law has been voided. The absence of the article before "law" indicates that the reference is to law as law. Another way of saying it is the essence of law without reference to a particular form through which it is expressed. The Jew, of course, would think of the Mosaic Law.

Paul goes beyond denial. He proceeds to say, "Rather (a better translation of *alla*), we establish law." This is done through the New Covenant.

The highest honor ever paid to the law was made by Christ when He established the New Covenant. He met every requirement of the law. He was in perfect harmony with the law (not the oral law of the Jews, but God's law in its every expression). When Jesus Christ suffered the full penalty of the law, He showed the highest possible regard and respect for the law. It is a serious mistake to suggest that through grace God discarded the requirements of the law.

The Nature of Grace

To be technical, grace is not an attribute of God as such. Grace is a provision of God made possible through atonement. God could not save sinners simply by exercising an attribute of grace. This would be incompatible with His holiness. He can exercise grace only in accord with the provision of atonement and the application of that atonement on the condition of faith.

It is also of interest to note that grace gets its characteristic not only from love, but from holiness. The fact that grace is offered is owed to the love of God. The fact that it is free is owed to the holiness of God. The same holiness which demanded that the full penalty of sin be paid before man could be forgiven also demanded that no more be collected. Holiness will not tolerate an underpayment nor an overcharge. To charge more than what Christ paid through atonement for our forgiveness would have been an overcharge. Holiness would not tolerate this. Therefore, the characteristic of grace that describes it as an unmerited gift owes its origin to holiness (Forlines *Systematics* 47).

Some connect v. 31 with chapter 4 rather than with what precedes. This is unnecessary. It seems to be obvious that Paul is again anticipating a question which a reader might have. He raised the question in order to answer it (see comments on Paul's use of questions in Romans in the comments on 3:1).

Summary 3:21-31

Paul had in 1:18—3:20 painted a dark picture of the world. God requires absolute righteousness. No man has absolute righteousness. No man can, by his own efforts, produce absolute righteousness.

Man was helpless, but he was not hopeless. After making it look as if there was no answer, Paul speaks of a God-provided righteousness. This righteousness will meet God's requirement for absolute righteousness.

This God-provided righteousness is offered to everybody, Jew or Gentile, on the condition of faith. It is offered to everybody rather than "some" because there is no basis for offering it to some and not all. *All* have sinned and keep falling short of Divine approval.

Upon believing in Christ, a person is justified without charge. Jesus paid our ransom price and became our propitiatory sacrifice by His blood. This propitiatory sacrifice proved beyond doubt that God's delaying His penal punishment for sin in no way compromised His justice as the Supreme Judge of the universe.

The propitiatory sacrifice met all the requirements of the law on our behalf: (1) the perfect obedience required by the law and (2) the penalty for our sins as required by the law. This made it so there is no conflict with God's justice when He justifies the person who believes in Jesus.

This method of justification rules out all boasting on our part. We have much to be thankful to God for, but we have done nothing that would serve as grounds for bragging about being justified.

In his case, Paul had made it unquestionably clear that this justification was apart from personal law-keeping and it was for both Jew and Gentile.

Since there is only one God, it should be obvious that Jews and Gentiles have the same God. It should also be obvious that He would have only one plan of justification for both Jew and Gentile. The New Covenant works for the Gentiles, too.

Though a person can be justified apart from personal law-keeping, that in no way voids the law. Christ paid the highest honor ever paid to the law when by His life and death He met all of the requirements of God's law for us.

Application: Teaching and Preaching the Passage

1. In 1:18—3:20 Paul spoke about the need for an absolute righteousness. In 3:21-31 he speaks about God's provision of the righteousness that man needs.

2. Concerning this God-provided righteousness:

(1) It is apart from one's own personal law keeping (without the deeds of the law) (v. 21).

(2) The O.T. by its types and prophecies bears witness to the truth of the righteousness that has been provided through Jesus Christ (v. 21).

(3) It is ours on the condition of faith in Jesus Christ (v. 22).

(4) It is offered to all on the condition of faith because there was no distinction found in the human race that would justify offering it to some without offering it to all (vv. 22, 23).

(5) We are justified (declared as being righteous or in right standing with God) without cost as an unmerited favor (v. 24).

(6) The redemption that gives us this God-provided righteousness is ours by being in union with Christ (v. 24; see a development of this thought in 6:3-5).

(7) God provided us this righteousness in such a way that it satisfied the justice of God. The righteous life of Christ satisfied the demand for absolute righteousness. The death of Christ satisfied the penalty of eternal death required by the law (vv. 25, 26). It is Christ's law obedience in life and in death which justifies us, not any law obedience of our own.

3. Since we are justified by faith and not by works, we cannot boast about how good we are (v. 27).

4. This God-provided righteousness is available not only to the Jews (the Covenant People of God), but also to the Gentiles (vv.29, 30).

5. Grace does not make the law void. When Jesus Christ satisfied the demands of the law on our behalf, He paid the highest honor to the law that was ever paid. Grace establishes the law (v. 31).

B. The Fact that Faith is the Sole Condition of Receiving this Righteousness is Defended (4:1-25).

1. Righteousness is by faith apart from works (4:1-8).

1 What shall we say then that Abraham our father, as pertaining to the flesh, hath found?

Most of the Greek manuscripts have the word for "father" (*pater*), although some very important ones have "forefather" (*propator*). The essential meaning is the same either way.

The biggest point of concern in translating this verse is: With what do we relate "according to the flesh" (Greek *kata sarka*)? The KJV translates this "as pertaining to the flesh" and connects it with "father." The meaning is "Abraham our father according to the flesh." Most would connect it with "found." Thus, it would read, "What shall we say then that Abraham our forefather hath found according to the flesh?"

Either way, Abraham is injected into the picture, and this will serve to be an important part in Paul's presentation of the gospel and of the relationship of Jews and Gentiles in the context of the gospel.

Why does Paul introduce Abraham into the picture? To whatever extent it is related to the occurrence of the word "boasting" in 3:27 and 4:2, I will take up in v. 2. At this point, I would say that Paul had the same reason that led him in Gal. 3 to bring Abraham into the picture.

Anyone who studies ch. 4 of Romans and ch. 3 of Galatians must admit that, in God's program of redemption, Abraham and the Abrahamic Covenant are considered by Paul to be exceedingly important. Regardless what else is seen in the Abrahamic Covenant, it has something to do with a proper understanding of justification, whether we are thinking about Jew or Gentile. There is something about the Abrahamic Covenant which means that a Gentile must become "the seed of Abraham" if he is to receive God's verdict—"justified." It is also clear that for the Jew, it takes more than being a descendant of Abraham if he is to be declared justified by God.

It is impossible to overestimate the importance of the Abrahamic Covenant in the understanding of the program of redemption. While Gen. 3:15 is the first promise of redemption, it is not very explicit. It served for a time in the progress of redemptive revelation. The time came for a more explicit revelation of God's program of redemption. (Progressive revelation, as used here, means that God gave a starting point for redemptive revelation in Gen. 3:15. At various times along the way, He introduced more information about redemption until His revelation reached its climax in the birth, life, death, and resurrection of Jesus Christ.) A major step was made in the revelation of the program of redemption when God made His covenant with Abraham. *The Abrahamic Covenant is the basic redemptive covenant. To abrogate it would be to abrogate the plan of redemption. It will forever be in force.*

In the light of these observations, it is of utmost importance to go back and take a look at what Paul is saying in the light of the Abrahamic Covenant. This will be important for both Jew and Gentile. Also, the harmony between the

Abrahamic Covenant and the New Testament teaching on justification serves as an apologetic to establish the faith of Christians and to reach unbelievers.

2 For if Abraham were justified by works, he hath *whereof* to glory; but not before God.

For if Abraham were justified by works. Paul is saying, "Let us assume that Abraham was justified by works and see where such thinking would take us."

He hath whereof to glory. There would be a grounds for boasting. "Whereof to glory" (Greek *kauchema)* and "boasting" in 3:27 (Greek *kauchesis)* have the same root. According to Vine (494, 495), the word used here refers to a "ground of glorying," a ground for boasting. The word in 3:27 denotes "the act of boasting."

But not before God. Paul denies that Abraham had any grounds for boasting. "We may paraphrase: 'But as a fact he had no ground of boasting; for, in view of the holiness of God, that could not be, even for him. And (v. 3) Scripture bears out this in direct terms; for it records that he was accepted as believing" (Moule, *Cambridge Bible* 89).

In denying that Abraham was justified by works, Paul was running counter to Jewish thought.

> That Abraham was justified by works was indeed what Paul's Jewish contemporaries were accustomed to assume. According to Jer. 23:10, 'Abraham was perfect in all his deeds with the Lord, and well-pleasing in righteousness all the days of his life;' and in *Kidd.* 4:14 it is stated that we find Abraham our father had performed the whole law before it was given, for it is written, Because that Abraham obeyed my voice and kept my charge, my commandments, my statutes, and my laws [Gen. 26:5]. He was one of the righteous ones not needing repentance—'Thou therefore, O Lord, That art the God of the just, hast not appointed repentance unto the just, to Abraham, and Isaac, and Jacob, which have not sinned against thee; but thou hast appointed repentance unto me a sinner' (Prayer of Manasses (8)). On such view Abraham clearly has ground for glorying (Cranfield, 227).

3 For what saith the scripture? Abraham believed God, and it was counted unto him for righteousness.

For what saith the scripture. In presenting his case to a Jew, this is a very crucial moment for Paul and for the Jew. If the Jew can be convinced, the gospel will have scored a major victory. If the Jew will accept the fact that Abraham was justified by faith rather than works, he will begin to be ready to hear the gospel.

Abraham believed God, and it was counted unto him for righteousness. There was an emphasis given to Gen. 15:6 in Jewish thought that requires our attention. Lightfoot in his *Commentary on Galatians* (158-164) discusses this emphasis in Jewish thought prior to and during the time of Paul. He explains:

> As early as the First Book of Macabees attention is directed to this lesson. 'Was not Abraham found faithful in temptation, and it was imputed unto him for righteousness?' (I Mac. 2:52). Here however it is touched upon very lightly. But there is, I think, sufficient evidence to show that at

the time of the Christian era the passage in Genesis relating to Abraham's faith had become a standard text in the Jewish schools, variously discussed and commented upon, and that the interest thus concentrated on it prepared the way for the fuller and more spiritual teaching of the Apostles of Christ (159). Further on he observes:

> If a full record had been preserved of the Rabbinical Schools of Palestine and Babylonia during the Apostolic age, we should probably have found that an equally prominent place was assigned to the faith of Abraham in their teaching also. The interpretation put upon the passage, and the lessons deduced from it, would indeed be widely different; but the importance of the text itself must have been felt even more strongly where the national feeling was more intense. The promise to Abraham, the charter of their existence as a people, was all more important to them, and its conditions would be minutely and carefully scanned (161).

After referring to 1 Maccabees 2:52, Cranfield says:

> More explicit are the words attributed to Rabbi Shemaiah (about 50 B.C.) in *Mekilta* on Ex. 14:15 (35b): 'The faith with which your father Abraham believed in Me [it is God who is represented as speaking] merits that I should divide the sea for you, as it is written: 'And he believed in the LORD, and He counted it to him for righteousness.' Subsequently this understanding of the verse was generally accepted in Rabbinic Judaism. Typical is the statement in *Mekilta* 40b (Ex. 14:31): 'So you find that our father Abraham became heir of this and of the coming world simply by the merit of faith' (229). Cranfield goes on to say:

> Thus it is apparent that, in appealing to Gen. 15:6 in support of his contention that Abraham was not justified on the ground of works and has no right to glory before God, Paul was deliberately appealing to a verse of Scripture which his fellow Jews generally assumed to be clear support for the diametrically opposite view (229).

From the quotations from Lightfoot and Cranfield given above (see also Hendriksen 145, 146, and Sanday and Headlam 100, 101), the following conclusions should be obvious: (1) The Jews did stress the faith of Abraham. (2) Their concept of Abraham's faith was in accord with their view that Abraham was justified by works. (3) Paul made reference to the faith of Abraham with a full awareness of their teaching about Abraham's faith. (4) Paul intends to show that faith cannot be considered a work or merit.

Attention needs to be given to the difference between the interpretations of "It was counted to him for righteousness" as given by those who believe in the satisfaction view and those who believe in the governmental view of atonement. However, at present it would be better not to interrupt the flow of thought in Paul's answer to the Jewish interpretation of Abraham's righteousness. The expression, "It was counted to him for righteousness" will be discussed in the comments on v. 5.

4 Now to him that worketh is the reward not reckoned of grace, but of debt.

In light of the Jewish thought on Abraham's faith, it must be observed that Paul is not simply talking about "works as works," but also "faith as works." Paul will not let the Jew get away by using the term "faith" while considering it to be "work" or "merit."

The word for "reward" (Greek *misthos*) means "pay" or "wages." The word for "debt" (Greek *opheilema*) means "what is owed" or as Vine puts it, "that which is legally due" (279).

The point is simply this: If you work for it (whether works in general or whether faith is confused with works) the wages received are legally due to the person who receives the wages. It would be an insult to a person who had worked all week for the employer, at the end of the week, to say, when he hands the employee his check, "This is a gift which I give you by grace."

Paul is saying to the Jew, "It cannot be by works and by grace at the same time." Paul's words in Rom. 11:6 are appropriate here: "And if by grace, then *is it* no more of works: otherwise grace is no more grace: But if *it be* of works, then is it no more grace: otherwise work is no more work."

Paul is, in essence, saying to the Jew, "Let's base our case on Scripture." The Scripture says, *Abraham believed God, and it was counted to him for righteousness* (Gen. 15:6). Not one word is said about works. What did Abraham believe? He believed that God would give him a son, who would actually be *his* son, and that there would be a great host of people who would descend from him (Gen. 15:4, 5). This promise was an important step in the direction of the implementation of God's redemptive plan. It was far more than a simple promise that Abraham would have a son and a large number of descendants. It was believing in the redemptive promises of God. This was the faith that was imputed to him for righteousness. There is not one thing in that that sounds like being justified by works.

5 But to him that worketh not, but believeth on him that justifieth the ungodly, his faith is counted for righteousness.

But to him that worketh not. Paul had shown in v. 4 what justification by grace was *not*. Here he proceeds to gives a *positive* description of justification by grace. The first step is for a person to cease depending on works. It is important to observe that it is not the *fact* of works that Paul is discussing, but the *purpose* of such works. Paul is not saying that a person must take the path of disobedience in order to be justified. He is saying that a person must totally abandon any thought of depending on his obedience for justification.

But believeth on him that justifieth (Greek *dikaioo*) **the ungodly** (Greek *asebes*), **his faith is counted** (Greek *logizomai*) **for** (Greek *eis*) **righteouseness.**

Before getting involved in the main thrust of this verse, let us observe that justification is for the ungodly. The only kind of human beings who are justified are those who are ungodly. With the name of Abraham having been mentioned three times already in this chapter, the Jews would have been painfully aware that Paul was including Abraham among the "ungodly." Though he had not been named in 2:1—3:20, it was clear that the verdict "guilty" would have been passed upon Abraham.

If Paul's line of thought had been sinking into the Jewish reader's heart, he would begin to realize that Paul was not just being negative toward the Jew. He was telling the real truth about justification as it was experienced by Abraham. Paul's teaching about justification was in complete harmony with the Abrahamic Covenant. He was expounding, "Abraham believed God and it was counted unto him for righteousness" in the light of the birth, life, death, and resurrection of the Jewish Messiah. Don't forget, every Jewish reader knew full well that the Greek for Christ (*Christos*) was the same word in Greek that "Messiah" was in the Hebrew.

The Governmental View of Justification

Let us now turn our attention to the governmental view of justification. (See also the treatment of this view under "Doctrinal Discussion" following the comments on 3:26.) We will look at the view of justification that develops out of the governmental view.

For those who subscribe to this view of atonement, vv. 3 and 5 would be foundational so far as Scripture is concerned. Concerning the person who is declared or pronounced righteous (or justified), his faith is counted for (or as) righteousness. God's original requirement had been "absolute righteousness," but all men failed to meet this requirement. As the governmentalist sees it, that ended any possibility for a human being to ever be pronounced righteous by God in His capacity as Judge (or based on judicial justice).

Adherents to the governmental view are not agreed upon the best way to express it, but when they get through the essence is: Though faith is not righteousness, it gets the same consideration as righteousness would. Upon the exercise of faith in Jesus Christ, the penalty for their sin is dismissed. There is no imputation of the death of Christ to the believer. According to this view, Jesus did not pay the penalty for our sins.

There is no imputation of Christ's righteousness. God simply treats the believer, in the light of his faith in Christ, as if he were in fact righteous. The chart at the bottom of this page will illustrate this view.

This view is confusing "condition" and "ground." (See chart that sets forth the satisfaction view of justification following comments on 3:26.) In the satisfaction view, the death and righteousness of Christ are entered on the believer's account and become the *ground* of his justification. Faith is but the *condition* that must be met before these are entered on the believer's account. The only way the governmentalist can escape the charge that in his view "faith is the ground" is for all practical purposes to eliminate a "ground" and say that faith is only a condition, not a ground. If he will call something else the "ground," it cannot be a *causal* ground (as the work of Christ is, in the satisfaction view).

It is impossible to give a full treatment of the views of atonement and justification. Commentaries which support the concepts of the governmental view are: Barnes (see the "Publisher's Preface" and also note the editor's comments which support the satisfaction view as distinguished from the view set forth by Barnes 29-31 and 95-98); John Brown, the denial of Christ's penal death (37), and the denial of imputation of Christ's righteousness (42); Denney (615, 616); Godet (160-62, 170); Sandy in *Ellicot's Commentary* (220, 277, 278); Sanday and Headlam (100, 101); Stuart 122-127); and Vincent (689). In *Meyer's Commentary* in the "Supplementary Notes" by Timothy Dwight (174, 175) the concepts of the governmental view are supported.

The Believer	
Debits	Credits
Absolute Righteousness	Faith in Christ
Justified or Counted as Righteousness	

Among the commentaries which support the satisfaction concepts are: Haldane (162, 163); Hamilton (68, 69); Hendriksen (146); Hodge (108-110); Lenski (290, 291); Picirilli (68-72); Plumer (157-160); and Shedd (92, 93).

Now, let us return our attention to "**His faith is counted** (Greek *logizomai*) **for** (Greek *eis*) **righteousness**." It must be admitted that, so far as this expression is concerned, the governmental view is grammatically possible. (See 2:26 where uncircumcision is counted "for" circumcision.) The big question is: Does it fit the context of Scripture as it relates to atonement and justification? Of immediate concern is: How does such an interpretation fit what Paul has already said in Romans? To answer this question, we must go back to what Paul said about the necessity of atonement.

There are three very important truths set forth in Rom. 2:1—3:20. (1) God's requirement for justification is absolute righteousness (2:1-16: see notes on 2:13). (2) No human being has produced absolute righteousness (3:10). (3) No human being by his own activity can produce absolute righteousness.

The big question before us now is: Is it universally and unchangeably true that "God requires absolute righteousness for justification?" If it is true, the governmental view and all similar views cannot be considered valid interpretations of atonement and justification. *The same principle that eliminates the governmental view establishes the satisfaction view.* What God requires has been provided by Christ. He provided for us and offers to us nothing less than absolute righteousness (see notes on 3:25, 26).

If the satisfaction view is true, how do we understand "his faith is counted for righteousness"? There are two possibilities. The first is to keep the translation as it is and understand it to mean "faith, embracing its object which is Christ," is counted as righteousness (Lenski 290). The meaning would be similar to Jesus' statement to the woman in Lk. 7 when He said, "Thy faith hath saved thee" (Lk. 7:50). It is quite obvious that it was Christ who saved the woman. This being true, it was faith embracing its object. The One embraced by faith saved her. In this instance, faith would be a metonymy.

There is another view that seems more likely. A distinction is made between "the imputation [or counting] of faith" (v. 5) and "the imputation of righteousness" (v. 5). A further point of clarification comes from the meaning of "for" (Greek *eis*). While "for" is a proper translation, there are other possibilities. A very common translation in "unto." It is also translated "toward."

By translating it as "toward," it would read, "his faith is counted toward righteousness." Faith, then, is counted (or imputed) toward the receiving (or imputation) of righteousness (see Alford 347, 348; Black 76; Haldane 162, 163; Hodge 110; and Plumer 160).

We need to give attention to the word translated "count," "reckon," and "impute" in ch. 4 (Greek *logizomai*). This word occurs 11 times in ch. 4. In 4:3 and 5 it is translated "count"; in 4:4, 9, 10 "reckon"; and in 4:6, 8, 11, 22, 23, and 24 it is translated "impute." Concerning this word Moule points out: "Its plain meaning is (like that of the Latin *imputare*) to *put down on an account* (whether as a debt or credit the context decides). The *reason why* of the imputation does not lie in the word itself, which may equally be used where merit and grace, wages and gift, are in question (*Cambridge Bible*, 89).

Plumer has some penetrating insights on this subject. He observes:

> It is impossible that any righteousness imperfect in God's esteem should justify any creature

in his sight. If it could, it would be an acknowledgment either that the precept of the law was too strict or that the penalty was too rigorous, and so God had consented to some abatement or relaxation of his requirements. And this would be denying and contradicting himself. This consideration alone shows that God cannot accept the act of faith itself as a meritorious ground of justification . . . . The only way, in which faith can justify a sinner before God, is by laying hold of the righteousness of Christ, receiving it, and appropriating it according to the free and gracious offer of God to reckon it to all who heartily accept it (158).

There is one more point that needs to be cleared up. It is said by some on both the governmentalist and the satisfactionist sides that in justification, God declares us to be something we are not. We cannot be both declared righteous and not be righteous in the same sense at the same time. It is a fact that by our own achievements we are not righteous, but that is not what is addressed in our justification. The basis of our justification is Christ's righteousness. When, according to justification, we are said to be righteous, the meaning is that we possess righteousness—the righteousness of Christ.

I am in agreement with Hodge when he says: "When, therefore, God justifies the ungodly, he does not regard him as being other than he really is. He only declares that justice is satisfied, and in that sense that man is just; he has a *dikaiosune* [righteousness] which satisfies the demands of the law" (112).

(There will be further clarification about imputation in the comments on 5:12-19 and 6:1-11.)

6 Even as David also describeth the blessedness of the man, unto whom God imputeth righteousness without works.

David is another very important person in the redemptive history of Israel. In The Davidic Covenant (2 Sam. 7:1-17 and 1 Chr. 17:1-15), the foundation is laid for the fact that the Messiah would be born as a descendant of David and would be heir to David's throne. Paul had already said that Christ "was made of the seed of David according to the flesh" (1:3). The significance of David in Jewish history would make his observations very important.

Even as David also describeth (Greek *lego*) **the blessedness** (Greek *makarismos*) **of the man unto whom God imputeth righteousness without works.** The word translated "describeth" means "to say" or "to speak." The word translated "blessedness" means "blessing." David speaks about the blessing of the man who has righteousness placed on his account apart from any dependence on his own works. See comments above where a distinction is made between "the imputation of faith" and "the imputation of righteousness."

7 *Saying,* blessed *are* they whose iniquities are forgiven, and whose sins are covered.
8 Blessed *is* the man to whom the Lord will not impute sin.

These verses are from Ps. 32:1, 2. In v. 7 the words which require our attention are "iniquities" (Greek *anomia*), "forgiven" (Greek *aphiemi*), and "covered" (Greek *epikalupto*).

The first (*anomia*) means "lawlessness." Wuest refers to it as "contempt" and "violation of the law" (68). The second (*aphiemi*) means "to send away," "to put away," or "to remove."

The third (*epikalupto*), according to Robertson, means "to cover over [upon, *epi*] as a shroud" (351).

"To put sin away" and "to cover sin" are figures of speech designed to help us know that as believers in Christ our sins are forgiven. If we take a strictly literal look at the words, there would be a conflict. The concept of having our sins taken away suggests that they are not on the scene. The concept of covering sin, if taken in a technically literal sense, would mean that the sins are there, but they are covered. We need not get bogged down in such technicalities.

To take away and to cover are terms which tell us that we are no longer, as believers, held accountable for the penalty of our sins. When God sees us in Christ, He does not see our sins. Rather, He sees the righteousness of Christ.

God uses a variety of ways to describe our forgiveness. For some to think of their sins as taken away seems to be more meaningful. To others, to think of their sins as covered seems to be more meaningful.

In v. 8 that which requires our attention is the meaning of "The Lord will not impute sin." We cannot have the death and righteousness of Christ placed on our account and at the same time have our sins placed there too. If a person has saving faith in Christ, he is justified. If he is justified, he is not being held penally responsible for his sins. This is not to say that he cannot be dealt with and chastised for his sins.

Paul now has two of the most important men in the history of Israel on his side. What happened to Abraham (faith counted for righteousness) is corroborated by the words of David. To have sins "forgiven," "covered" and "not imputed" necessarily implies "the imputation of righteousness." It implies "apart from works" because the removal of "demerit" is seen in vv. 7 and 8, but nothing is said about "merit."

Calvinists frequently charge Arminians with making faith a work. It can be seen why they would say this about the Arminians who believe in the governmental theory of atonement and justification (see above in connection with v. 5). However, there is no way they can make the same charge about those Arminians who have the satisfaction view of atonement. I am not saying that Arminians who believe in the governmental view believe faith is a work. I can see why the Calvinist would think that is the case, however.

Faith is a *condition* for justification, but it is never imputed to the believer to serve in the place of righteousness. Neither is it ever regarded as a part of the righteousness which justifies. The death and righteousness of Christ, and that alone, is placed on the believer's account as the ground for his justification.

By the way, if faith can be a condition for becoming saved, without being considered a "work," it can be a condition for continued salvation without being a work. To deny that this can be so is to deny the very fact that Paul has labored so hard to prove in the first eight verses of this chapter. (For those who would like to read a view of the possibility of loss of salvation consistent with the satisfaction view of atonement and justification, see Forlines, *Systematics* 199-230.)

2. Righteousness is by faith apart from circumcision (4:9-12).

9 *Cometh* this blessedness then upon the circumcision *only,* or upon the circumcision also? for we say that faith was reckoned to Abraham for righteousness.

Cometh this blessedness then upon the circumcision *only*, or upon the uncircumcision also? Circumcision is a metonymy referring to the Jews as a whole. Uncircumcision is a metonymy referring to the Gentiles as a whole.

This verse is connected with v. 8. The "blessedness" is that spoken of by David. Paul is now dealing with a problem of utmost importance to both Jew and Gentile.

Cranfield observes: "We may assume that it would be generally taken for granted by the Rabbis of Paul's day that the blessing pronounced in Ps. 32:1f applied exclusively to the Jews" (234).

To substantiate this point he says, in footnote 4:

> Cf., e.g. (the of course later): *Pesikta* R. 45 (185b): 'On the Day of Atonement God cleanses Israel and atones for its guilt, as it is written, "For on this day shall atonement be made for you, to cleanse you," Lev. 16:30. And, if thou wouldst say, "Another nation too he cleanses" [know that] it is not so, but it is only Israel; for so spake the prophet Micah (7:18): "Who is a God like unto thee, that pardoneth iniquity, and passeth by the transgression of the remnant of his heritage?" It is only Israel that he forgives. When David saw how God forgives the sins of the Israelites and has mercy upon them, he began to pronounce them blessed and to glorify them: "Blessed is he whose transgression is forgiven, etc.," Ps. 32:1' (234, 235).

At this point in Romans, it is not a shock to the Jewish reader for Paul to speak about the God-provided righteousness being available to the Gentiles. He is simply offering further proof for what he had already said. This is the first time that he has explicitly addressed the question of whether circumcision was required of Gentiles.

For we say that faith was reckoned (or imputed) **to Abraham for righteousness.** This is mentioned by Paul as step 1 in showing that circumcision is not required for this righteousness. Step 2 follows.

10 How was it then reckoned? when he was in circumcision, or in uncircumcision? Not in circumcision, but in uncircumcision.

Paul's point is simply this: Abraham had "faith imputed for righteousness" (v. 5) before he was circumcised. Cranfield points out that according to Jewish chronology there was a period of 29 years between Gen. 15:6 (the imputation of faith for righteousness) and the time of Abraham's circumcision in Gen. 17:24 (235).

It is certainly obvious that Abraham's justification in no way was conditioned on his being circumcised. The time difference between his justification and his circumcision proves that point. This observation is of utmost importance. Remember, the basic redemptive covenant was made with Abraham. Also, remember the "uncircumcised Abraham" was justified by faith.

11 And he received the sign of circumcision, a seal of the righteousness of the faith which *he had yet* being uncircumcised: that he might be the father of all them that believe, though they be not circumcised; that righteousness might be imputed unto them also.

Circumcision as a "sign" was a tangible or external reminder that Abraham was in a covenant relationship with God and that in that covenant relationship his faith was counted for righteousness.

Circumcision as a seal (Greek *sphragis)* according to Moule is "a formal, legal attestation that He who prescribed the rite held to His grant already made" (*Cambridge Bible* 92). Vine comments: "The Rabbis spoke of circumcision as the seal of Abraham. A seal was primarily used to authenticate and ratify a covenant" (*Romans* 65).

That he might be the father of all them that believe, though they be not circumcised. This of course is a reference to Gentile believers. To refer to Abraham as the father of Gentile believers grows out of the fact that he was declared righteous by faith before he was circumcised.

A very important fact is now beginning to be seen. Gentile believers are also involved in the Abrahamic Covenant. It is clear both in Rom. 4 and Gal. 3 that to receive this God-provided righteousness and the promises that go with it, a Gentile must become the seed of Abraham. This involves more than simply viewing Abraham's faith as an example to follow. The involvement of Gentiles in the Abrahamic Covenant will be receiving more attention in this chapter and in chapter 11.

That righteousness might be imputed unto them also. Since he is the father of "all them that believe," the Gentiles as well as the Jews, righteousness can be imputed to both who believe.

12 And the father of circumcision to them who are not of the circumcision only, but who also walk in the steps of that faith of our father Abraham, which *he had* being *yet* uncircumcised.

And the father of circumcision. The understanding of this part of the verse is a key to understanding the last part. We have just seen that circumcision was a sign and a seal of the righteousness which was by faith. A major point with Paul is that Gentiles may have the righteousness that comes by faith without having this sign or seal. To speak of Abraham as the father of circumcision is to speak of him as the father of those who have what circumcision stands for (Phil. 3:3). This includes those who do not have the sign or seal (circumcision) as well as those who have the sign or seal. (For a parallel, see "his uncircumcision be counted for circumcision" (2:26). Is he not saying that if there would be such a case as one who totally kept the law he would have what circumcision stands for? The blessing of circumcision would be his without circumcision.)

I am in essential agreement with David Brown, who comments:

> Here the same sentiment [as expressed in the latter part of v. 11] is expressed, but in a somewhat unexpected form—namely, that Abraham is the father of circumcision to all uncircumcised believers.This cannot refer to the distinctive peculiarities of the circumcised, in which uncircumcised Gentiles could of course have no share: it simply means that all that was of essential and permanent value in the standing before God of the circumcised—all that circumcision chiefly set its seal on—is shared in by the believing children of Abraham who are the strangers to the circumcision of the flesh (211).

To them who are not of the circumcision only, but who also walk (Greek *tois stoichousin)* **in the steps of that faith of our father Abraham, which *he had* being *yet* uncircumcised.** The article *(tois)* with walk (*stoichousin*) has baffled commentators. The reason for this is that they have assumed that "the father of circumcision" in the first part of the verse was restricted to Jews. This being their conclusion, the rest of the verse must apply to Jews only. The last part would add the condition of faith in addition to being a Jew. In my opinion this is not the case. The last part of the verse is dealing with Gentiles.

In order to make the point simple, we could say that circumcision according to v. 11 stands for a blessing (righteousness). If this is the case, the essence of the first part of the verse is that Abraham is the father of circumcision. This is another way of saying that he is the father of the blessed. There is no problem with seeing Abraham as the father of the blessed and understanding the reference to be to both Jewish and Gentile believers.

Now, to the problem connected with "them who walk" (*tois stoichousin*). The normal way to translate this is "to those who walk" (see Lightfoot 279, 280). To treat it this way suggests that another group (Gentile believers) is being added to Jewish believers mentioned in the first part of the verse. Once we understand "the father of circumcision" (in the first part of the verse) to include both Jews and Gentiles, there is no problem in understanding the last part to refer to Gentiles. Verse 12 simply amplifies the meaning of "the father of them that believe" in v. 11.

It is almost unanimous among commentators to either ignore the article (*tois*) or to figure out some strained reason for saying it should not be translated. Lenski made a noble effort to find a way to translate the article, but still considered the reference to be to Jews (306).

3. Righteousness is by faith apart from law (4:13-25).

13 For the promise, that he should be the heir of the world, *was* not to Abraham, or to his seed, through the law, but through the righteousness of faith.

This verse introduces an important thought. It refers to Abraham and his seed as promised heirs of the world. This must be very important because he continues to speak of the "heirs" in v. 14 and the "promise" in vv. 14-16.

The question is, What is the "world"? There are a variety of answers. Black says: "The words have also for Paul Messianic overtones: the promise was, that through one of his descendants the whole earth would be blessed, and through him Abraham's true seed would enjoy world-wide dominion" (78).

Lenski comments: "'Heir' of the world does not mean 'ruler' of the world but future possessor of it by means of inheritance. It is at present not a fit possession, being filthy with sin; it will be fit when God makes it 'a new earth' as John saw it in Rev. 21:1. After it has been cleansed, Abraham will enter upon his inheritance, as will all his seed through him as their father" (310).

Hamilton explains: "The best interpretation seems to be the future eternal kingdom of God which will be established with its earthly phase in a regenerated world where all the redeemed will possess an inheritance" (72).

Bruce comments:

> When Abraham's heritage is delimited in geographical terms it lies between Egypt and the Euphrates (Gen. 15:18; cf. 13:14f.), but in the spiritual and permanent sense in which the promises made to him are interpreted in the New Testament, his inheritance cannot be confined within such earthly frontiers (cf. Heb. 11:10, R.V: 'he

looked for the city which hath the foundations, whose builder and maker is God') (116).

David Brown takes yet another approach. He explains:

> Abraham is 'the heir of the world' *religiously* rather than locally. *By his Religion he may be said to rule the world.* As the parent of that race from whom the world has received 'the lively oracles, '. . .and 'of whom as concerning the flesh Christ came, who is over all, God blessed for ever'—in this sublime sense is Abraham 'the heir of the world' (211).

The Abrahamic Covenant and the Inheritance of Abraham and His Seed

It can be seen that there is quite a variety of answers given concerning the meaning of "heirs of the world." This promise to Abraham is of utmost importance for an understanding of how God progressively revealed His plan of redemption. For that reason, we must see if we can discover what the true meaning is, whether one of those given above or yet another.

It is admitted that there is no precise statement in the Abrahamic Covenant which says that Abraham and his seed will inherit the world. However, I believe we can see that this concept is rooted and grounded in the Abrahamic Covenant.

Before going to the Abrahamic Covenant, let me give some evidence that the concept of inheriting the earth was a commonly recognized fact. Jesus said, "Blessed are the meek: for they shall inherit the earth" (Mt. 5:5). This is taken from Ps. 37:11.

This Psalm makes several references to this inheritance. Verse 9 says, "Those that wait upon the LORD, they shall inherit the earth." Verse 18 reads, "The LORD knoweth the days of the upright: and their inheritance shall be for ever." Verse 22 says, "For *such as be* blessed of him shall inherit the earth." Verse 29 reads, "The righteous shall inherit the land, and dwell therein for ever." Verse 34 says, "Wait on the LORD, and keep his way, and he shall exalt thee to inherit the land."

Taken at face value certain observation can be made: (1) The righteous will inherit the earth. (2) They have not as yet inherited the land. (3) When the inheritance is received it will be forever.

Where did this idea come from? When did it originate? What is it based on? I believe the answer is found in the Abrahamic Covenant.

In Gen. 13:15 God says to Abraham, "For all the land which thou *seest,* to thee will I give it, and to thy seed for ever." Again in 17:8 God says to Abraham, "And I will give unto thee, and to thy seed after thee, the land wherein thou art a stranger, all the land of Canaan, for an everlasting possession; and I will be their God."

It can be shown that this is a promise that Abraham and his seed will receive in the eschatological future. I disagree with Leupold when he says:

> True, Abram becomes possessor only in his seed—'to thy seed I will give it.' But such a possession is none the less real. Such possession is guaranteed by God as extending *ahh olam,* 'for a long time.' We have preferred to render this expression thus, because it actually implies nothing more than for an indefinitely long season whose end cannot yet be determined, being derived from *olam,* 'to be hidden' (441).

There are two problems which must be addressed: (1) Was the promise made to Abraham as a personal possession as well as to his seed? (2) Is "a long time" an adequate translation of the Hebrew (*olam*)?

Let us address question (1). I believe it can be established that the promise was made to Abraham as something that he, himself, would possess. This is clearly and unquestionably established by Stephen when he said, "And he [God] gave him [Abraham] none inheritance in it, no, not *so much as* to set his foot on: yet he promised that he would give it to him for a possession, and to his seed after him, when *as yet* he had no child" (Acts 7:5).

If the reading of Gen. 13:14 leaves any doubt that Abraham was promised he would some day possess the land, Acts 7:5 should remove that doubt.

Now let us look at the Hebrew word translated "for ever" (*olam*). It is true that this word without a proper context does not mean eternal. I believe this word is close in meaning to our word "always." "Always" means the longest time made possible in the context. When a groom sings to his bride, "I'll be loving you always," how long does he mean? He means until either he dies or she dies. Anything less than that is less than "always." This time may be short or it may be long. The length of time is determined by how long both would live. It would not go over well with the bride if he only promised to love her for a long time.

If the meaning of *olam* is the longest possible time permitted by the circumstances, how long would it be? It would be forever because God is eternal and Abraham will live for eternity.

Having given the case for saying that Abraham was promised the eternal possession of the land, what are the implications? The implication is that the possession will be Abraham's after his resurrection. He will then live in it for eternity. Some years ago I was discussing the promise of the everlasting possession of the land with a Rabbi. I asked him what he thought it referred to. He gave exactly the same interpretation that I have set forth.

Now let us turn to Heb. 11 and see what light is shed on the subject. It is said that Abraham "was called to go out into a place which he should after receive for an inheritance" (v. 8). "He sojourned in the land of promise" (v. 9). After mentioning Isaac, Jacob, and Sarah, it is said, "These all died in faith, not having received the promises, but having seen them afar off, and were persuaded of *them* and embraced *them,* and confessed that they were strangers and pilgrims on the earth" (v. 13).

What is said here fits exactly with what is said in Gen. 13:14; 17:8; and Acts 7:4. God promised Abraham the possession of the land of Canaan. He did not receive it as a possession, not even a little bit, during his lifetime. This did not hinder his faith because he saw his possession "afar off." The reference here is to time, not space.

In v. 16 the writer of Hebrews says, "But now they desire a better *country,* that is, an heavenly." In this case "heavenly" is a reference to the quality of the inheritance, not the location.

Now, let us turn our attention to the "new earth" referred to in Rev. 21:1. Some say the reference here is to an annihilation of the earth as we know it, and the creation of a totally new earth in no way related to this earth. Others say the reference is to a renovation of this earth. Some say it is impossible to decide which view is correct.

When our thinking is rooted and grounded in the Abrahamic Covenant, the answer must be the renovation of this earth. Let us return to Genesis. God showed Abraham the land around him and told him that would be the land he would possess forever. In 17:8 the land that is promised to Abraham was, "the land wherein thou art a stranger, all the land of Canaan, for an everlasting possession."

The solution is simple. If God promised the land of Canaan for an everlasting possession, it follows that the "new earth" referred to in Rev. 21:1 must be a renovated earth. Otherwise, it would not happen as promised.

An illustration will help. Suppose a father promised his son an old car (in this case a specific one) for his birthday. He could have the car so renovated that it hardly looked like the same car. That would be consistent with his promise. If he should instead, of giving the old car, give him a new car, the son would not object, but it would not be consistent with the promise. We, when human beings are involved, could easily make the necessary adjustments in such a case. However, we believe God will do exactly what He said He would. That being true, the new earth will be this earth made new.

There is yet another problem we must deal with. How do we get from the land of Canaan, as the inheritance in Gen., to the *whole* world as an inheritance as set forth in Rom. 4:13? It appears that the answer is found in the fact that while the land of Canaan was promised to the Jews, Abraham was also the father of many nations. As a necesarry inference then, the whole earth is promised to Abraham and his seed.

Abrahamic Covenant As The Basic Redemptive Covenant

It seems that the focal point in the Abrahamic Covenant has tended to deal with whether there will be a 1,000-year reign of Christ on earth with the Jews returned to Palestine. The Abrahamic Covenant has some bearing on the subject, but such is not the focus of the covenant. The covenant deals with an everlasting possession of the land, not a 1,000-year possession.

In relating the Abrahamic Covenant to redemption, two parts of the Covenant are usually referred to: (1) Abraham believed God and "he counted it to him for righteousness" (Gen. 15:6). (2) The other part is the reference to "in thee shall all the families of the earth be blessed" (12:3) and "thou shalt be a father of many nations" (17:4).

We have already seen the fact that Abraham's faith was counted for righteousness is very important in establishing justification by faith. The concept of justification by faith, as set forth in the Abrahamic Covenant, was important. It would, however, speak far more clearly about justification to us than it did to the faithful before Christ.

In light of the N.T. we can see the significance of "in thee shall all the families of the earth be blessed" and how that ties in with the fact that Christ as the seed of Abraham has blessed all nations. However, that required N.T. fulfillment before anyone could have developed a great deal of redemptive thought from it.

The real heart of redemptive promise in the Abrahamic Covenant with Abraham and to his seed is the promise of the everlasting possession of the land of Canaan and, by extension as explained above, the whole earth (Gen. 13:14 and 17:8). That promise is one for the eschatological future. It is a promise which necessarily involves the resurrection of the body. It is a promise of eternal life. That is the eschatological future of the redeemed. No wonder Paul has given so much attention to Abraham!

Now we can turn our attention to Rom. 4:13. As has been pointed out, the world will be the inheritance of the seed of Abraham in the eschatological future. Now we are to understand that the seed of Abraham refers both to Jewish and Gentile believers. More will be said about this at appropriate points in Romans.

This future inheritance of the redeemed (or seed of Abraham) is not "through the law, but through the righteousness of faith." It is not by law-keeping; it is received on the condition of faith.

Cranfield explains:

> Paul's statement stands in striking contrast to the Rabbis' assumption that all the promises were made to Abraham on the basis of his fulfillment of the law (which according to them was already known by him and performed in its completeness although it had not yet been promulgated) and to their understanding of his faith as itself a meritorious work (239).

14 For if they which are of the law *be* heirs, faith is made void, and the promise made of none effect.

Paul is saying that if "law-keepers" (that is, those who keep the law for their justification) inherit, the faith or the "faith-way" is void or empty. In the Greek, faith is preceded by an article (see comments on 3:30 where reasons are given for believing that "the faith" is somewhat synonymous with "the New Covenant").

Paul is stating that if law-keeping were the basis for receiving the inheritance mentioned in v. 13, that would render the faith way (or the New Covenant) void or meaningless. And if the New Covenant were rendered useless, that would spell absolute tragedy because the promise would be nullified.

Paul's point is simple and clear. If the faith way is true, then redemption is ours if we will believe. If it is not the way, there is no way. Law-keeping cannot do it.

This verse reminds me of an event during my childhood. I had a record for crying a lot. One summer my father said, "Son, if you won't cry until the fall, I will give you a pony." The fall was the time set because it was then he would sell his crop. That was quite a promise to a young boy during the depression years. However, the case was dismissed that very day. My sister, next to me, had me crying before the day was over.

To a young boy with a track record like mine for crying, it was worthless to receive such an offer. With the track record that we human beings have for sinning, it would be worthless for us to be offered an inheritance conditioned on law-keeping. (See Gal. 3:13-18 for Paul's case in saying that the law could not change what had already been established in the Abrahamic Covenant.)

15 Because the law worketh wrath: for where no law is, *there is* no transgression.

Because the law worketh wrath. This verse tells why the promise would be worthless if it should be conditioned on law-keeping. Not only does law fail as a means of receiving the inheritance, it has severely negative consequences. It works wrath.

For where no law is, *there is* no transgression (Greek *parabasis*). This word refers to the overstepping of a stated boundary. Sin is sin without a written law, but the presence of a stated law makes sin take on the character of transgression. If a land owner did not want you to hunt or fish on his land, it would incur his displeasure if you went fishing on his land. However, if he put signs up saying, "No Trespassing" or "No Hunting and Fishing," violations would cause the case to take on a new level of seriousness.

The Mosaic Law put up "the signs." Sin was sin before, but after the signs, including the Ten Commandments and other moral teachings, sin then took on the form of transgression. To follow the law way is to incur the wrath of God.

16 Therefore *it is* of faith, that *it might be* by grace; to the end the promise might be sure to all the seed; not to that only which is of the law, but to that also which is of the faith of Abraham; who is the father of us all.

Therefore *it is* of (or by) **faith, that *it might* be by grace.** "Therefore" connects this verse with the preceding verses. Since "the law way" is utterly hopeless God has offered, on the condition of faith, the receiving of His God-provided righteousness in this life followed by eternal life on this earth made new in the next life. To condition this on faith makes it so that God can show His grace. This God-provided righteousness comes to us as an outright gift.

To the end the promise might be sure (Greek *bebaios*). This word is translated "sure" in 2 Pet. 1:10, 19; "stedfast" in 2 Cor. 1:7; Heb. 2:2; 3:14; 6:19; and "firm" in Heb. 3:6. The inheritance (eternal life on this earth made new. See comments on v. 13.) is made available on the condition of faith so we can have assurance. This is the opposite of the "none effect" in v. 14.

To all the seed; not to that only which is of the law. The context makes it clear that "they which are of the law" in v. 14 is used differently than "that only which is of the law" in this verse. In v. 14 "they which are of the law" would represent those who were trying to receive their inheritance by law-keeping. For the reasons given in v. 14, this would be absolutely unworkable.

In v. 16 "that which is of the law" represents those who are Jews. This is similar to saying "those who are of the circumcision." The reference is clearly to Jews who, from a background of law, come to God through faith in Jesus the Messiah.

But to that also which is of the faith of Abraham. These are Gentile believers as distinguished from the Jewish believers.

Who is the father of us all. The "all" here includes both Jewish and Gentile believers. It seems so easy for us to accept the fact that both Jewish and Gentile believers can be called the seed of Abraham, and thus share in the future inheritance with him. But remember the Jew of Paul's day had to "unlearn" much of what he had previously been taught before he could accept this truth. For the Gentile, it was a blessing almost too good to be true.

17 (As it is written, I have made thee a father of many nations,) before him whom he believed, *even* God, who quickeneth the dead, and calleth those things which be not as though they were.

The first part of this verse is from Gen. 17:5. The words *who quickeneth the dead* in the context refer to the ability of God to make good His promise to Abraham and Sarah in spite of the fact that Abraham and Sarah were "dead" reproductively (v. 19).

The words "*calleth those things which be not as though they were*" refer to the first part of the verse. The reading is not, "I *will* make you a father of many nations." Rather, it is "I *have* made you a father of many nations." Though, at the time, Abraham was not even the father of one nation, yet the fact that he would be, in time, the father of many nations was so fixed in the mind of God that He said, "I have made thee a father of many nations." Some have called the Hebrew in Gen. 17:5 for "I have made" the prophetic perfect. (For a more thorough presentation and defense of this view see Murray 146, 147. For presentations and evaluations of the different views see Cranfield 244, 245; Hodge 124; and Sanday and Headlam 113.)

18 Who against hope believed in hope, that he might become the father of many nations, according to that which was spoken, So shall thy seed be.

This verse is telling us that though all known natural circumstances were against Abraham and Sarah having a son, Abraham believed. The difference was, "*according to that which was spoken, So shall thy seed be.*" God had promised. That was the only reason Abraham had for believing.

19 And being not weak in faith, he considered not his own body now dead, when he was about an hundred years old, neither yet the deadness of Sarah's womb.

There is a problem with the Greek text of this verse. Some important texts have "not" (Greek *ou*) before the Greek word for "considered." Others omit the word. Strangely enough, the essential meaning of the verse is not altered whether "not" is kept in or omitted.

If we leave "not" in, the meaning is that even though Abraham knew that he and Sarah were dead, so far as reproduction was concerned, that was not considered. He did not allow this knowledge to cause him to weaken in his faith. This is the thought in the KJV.

Most other translations omit the "not" before considered. The meaning is: Because of his faith Abraham refused to believe that God would fail in His promise. This he did in spite of the fact that from a natural viewpoint he knew that he and Sarah were dead so far as reproduction was concerned.

20 He staggered not at the promise of God through unbelief; but was strong in faith, giving glory to God.

He staggered (Greek *diakrino*) **not at the promise of God through unbelief.** This Greek word is translated "doubt" in Mt. 21:21; Mk. 11:23; Acts 10:20; 11:12; Rom. 14:23; and "waver" in Jas. 1:6. The one who "wavers" in Jas. 1:6 is the "double minded" person in Jas. 1:8.

Wuest gives the meaning "to vacillate between two opinions or decisions" (72). Vincent says, "The word implies mental struggle" (691).

Abraham was not double-minded; he did not waver between belief and unbelief.

But was strong in faith, giving glory to God. Out of his faith he gave glory to God. There was no boasting on Abraham's part. God's promise had come to Abraham out of God's grace and goodness. Abraham responded appropriately.

21 And being fully persuaded that, what he had promised, he was able also to perform.

This verse is exceedingly important. If we do not get the message of this verse, we may tend to be confused and discouraged when we think of the strength of Abraham's faith.

Abraham's faith did not begin within himself. Rather, it began with God. He was believing what God had *promised. If there had been no promise, there would have been no faith.*

Abraham's faith illustrates what I call "specific faith." Based on a promise from God, he believed that a specific thing would happen: he and Sarah would have a son.

Another kind of faith is what I call "general faith." If we have no specific promise from God about a matter, we pray with general faith. General faith believes in the power of God, the love of God, the wisdom of God, etc. Having this kind of faith, we take our concerns to God and let our desires be known. Since we have no specific promise in such cases, we cannot have specific faith.

When we try to have specific faith in all matters, we set ourselves up for false guilt, discouragement, and frustration. More will be said about this in the section on practical application.

22 And therefore it was imputed to him for righteousness.

It is important to keep in mind that Abraham was believing in redemptive revelation. It had a lot of personal meaning to Abraham and Sarah to have a son. However, Abraham knew that the promise of Isaac went far beyond a blessing to him and Sarah. He did not know the details that we know through further revelation. He did know that he was becoming involved in something that would be far-reaching in its effects. He knew also that it was all a part of a plan that would culminate in eternal life on this earth for him and his seed. That is the kind of faith that *was imputed to him for righteousness* (see comments on v. 5).

23 Now it was not written for his sake alone, that it was imputed to him;
24 But for us also, to whom it shall be imputed, if we believe on him that raised up Jesus our Lord from the dead.

Justification has always been by faith. That is the point that Paul has effectively dealt with in this chapter. Paul built his case in vv. 1-22. In these verses he makes application of what he has said up to this point. It is important to observe that the case Paul built for justification could have been written a thousand years before. The most recent person mentioned was David. Only a small amount of the material in the chapter (vv. 7, 8) was related to David. The rest of 1-22 predated David's time.

In saving faith, there are two elements: (1) trust and (2) acceptance of redemptive truth. The element of trust is the same at any point in redemptive history. The *content* of redemptive truth that is believed depends upon what point in the progressive revelation of redemptive truth the person lived. For example, more was revealed to Abraham than to Adam; more to Moses than to Abraham; more to David than to Moses, etc.

No one in the O. T. could have had available to him the clear knowledge that we have of Jesus Christ. Saving faith would have involved believing that part of redemptive truth with which they were confronted. For us, we are confronted with the truth of the birth, life, death, and resurrection of Christ; we must believe the revelation of Jesus Christ in the N. T. Or, to state it negatively, a person cannot reject the Biblical revelation of Jesus Christ and at the same time exercise saving faith. We may not have a good understanding, but we must believe.

When we believe in Jesus Christ as our Lord and Savior, we receive the death and righteousness of Christ. We become the seed of Abraham (see vv. 13, 16, 18 and Gal. 3:29). Having become the seed of Abraham we can look forward in the eschatological future to an inheritance of eternal life on this earth made new (see comments on v. 13).

25 Who was delivered for our offences, and was raised again for our justification.

Who was delivered for our offences. There are two ways this can be considered: (1) our offences are what caused Him to die or (2) His death was for the purpose of atoning for our offences.

And was raised again for our justification. This, also, is capable of two interpretations: (1) He was raised because He had accomplished our justification or (2) He was raised in order to make our justification become a reality.

I think the second interpretation in both instances is the correct one. The death of Jesus Christ is what made atonement for our sins. (It is not suggested that those who take the other view do not believe that Christ's death atoned for our sins. It is only a matter of what we understand Paul to say in this verse.) However, if Christ had not been raised from the dead, there would be no justification. Only a living Savior can bestow justification upon those who believe. (For a discussion of the different views see Cranfield 252; Hendriksen 161, 162; Hodge 129, 130; Moule *Cambridge Bible* 98; Murray 154-157; Sanday and Headlam 116; and Yeager 413.)

Summary
4:1-25

Abraham is an exceedingly important person in Jewish thought. It was with him that God made the basic redemptive covenant. This makes him very important in the development of Jewish and Christian thought.

The place of importance which Abraham occupied demanded that Paul refer to him as he sought to give proof for his view of justification by faith. An examination of the way Abraham was justified shows that he believed God and it was counted to him toward receiving righteousness. This was exactly what Paul was teaching.

Contrary to Jewish thought, Abraham was not justified by works. It is not simply that he was not justified by "work as works." He was not justified by "faith as works."

If Abraham had been justified either by "works as works" or "faith as works," there would have been a debt owed to him by God. This would have been grounds for boasting on Abraham's part. But this is not the way Scripture says it was.

Real justifying righteousness comes to those who quit depending on their own works to meet God's requirement. God gives righteousness to the ungodly when they exercise saving faith. This is the only way anybody ever receives righteousness. This means that, contrary to Jewish thought, before his justification Abraham was an ungodly man just like the rest of us. The righteousness that he had was by faith. This is a plain statement of Scripture.

Paul now refers to David who is another very important person in the history of Jewish and Christian thought. In Ps. 32:1, 2, David spoke about God forgiving and covering sin and not imputing sin. There is no mention of merit. What David says fits in with what happened to Abraham.

The Jews tended to think that God forgave their sins, but not those of the Gentiles. Paul shows that Abraham was justified long before he was circumcised. This meant that it was his faith without circumcision that was the condition for his righteousness. This means that

Gentiles can receive this God-provided righteousness, without being circumcised, just like Abraham did. The result of all this is that Abraham is the father of Gentile believers just as he is the father of Jewish believers.

It also means that Gentile believers are Abraham's seed and partake with him of the same righteousness. They also share with Abraham in the eschatological promise of eternal life on this earth made new.

If the condition for receiving God's inheritance depended on law-keeping, the promise would be worthless. But God wanted to make the eternal promise something that both Jews and Gentiles could receive. For that reason, He made it available on the condition of faith. This made it so people could have assurance about receiving the promise.

The idea of God being the Father of both Jewish and Gentile believers fits in with what God told Abraham when He said, "I have made thee a father of many nations."

Abraham believed that he would be a father of many nations even though he did not have a son at the time. He had confidence that God would give him a son even though all other circumstances, except the promise of God, would have said that he would never have a son.

The promise of a son was much more than a personal blessing to Abraham and Sarah. It was tied in with God's redemptive plan. That is what made Abraham's faith justifying faith. He believed in God's redemptive revelation and God imputed it to him for righteousness.

God had the fact recorded that faith was imputed to Abraham. When the whole picture was put together, it revealed that we could believe and our faith would be imputed to us for righteousness (or faith imputed toward the receiving of the God-provided righteousness).

Now that Jesus has come, we place our faith in Him to receive the God-provided righteousness. He paid the penalty for our sins by His death. His resurrection makes Him a living Savior who can bestow justification upon those who believe in Him as Lord and Savior.

Application: Teaching and Preaching the Passage

1. This passage divides itself into a three point outline:

(1) Justification is by faith apart from works (vv. 1-8).

(2) Justification is by faith apart from circumcision (vv. 9-12).

(3) Justification is by faith apart from law keeping (vv. 13-25).

2. It is important to get a good grasp of the importance of Abraham and the Abrahamic Covenant in understanding this chapter. (See comments on v. 1 and "The Abrahamic Covenant and the Inheritance of Abraham and His Seed" in the comments on v. 13.)

3. According to the Abrahamic Covenant, Abraham was righteous on the condition of faith (v. 3; see also Gen. 15:6). Justification by faith did not originate in the N.T. It is rooted and grounded in the Abrahamic Covenant.

4. When a person ceases to depend on his own works as a way of becoming righteous, and places his faith in Jesus Christ, his faith will be recognized as the only condition required for receiving the God-provided righteousness (v. 5).

5. David also gives testimony of the fact that God places righteousness on our account on a basis other than our works (vv. 6-8).

6. It is quite clear in vv. 1-8 that Paul contrasts works and faith. Faith is not works. If faith can be required as a condition for receiving justification and it not be considered as being by works, it can be required as a condition for

continuing in salvation and it not be by works.

7. While N.T. baptism is not an exact counterpart of O.T. circumcision, I think we could conclude that what Paul says in vv. 9-12 illustrates the fact that baptism, though very important, is not a condition for justification.

8. Abraham was offered eternal life in the eschatological future in the land of Palestine. This was offered on the condition of faith. The righteousness that was required of him and his seed is on the condition of faith (v. 13).

9. If law keeping had been made the condition of receiving God's promise, faith as a condition, as stated in the Abrahamic Covenant, would have been made void. The promise would have been made of no effect because no one could have produced the absolute law keeping which would have been required. (v. 14).

10. When God made salvation conditioned on faith, He made it sure to all who come to Him to receive it. We could not produce the kind of law-keeping that would have been required. By God's help, we can believe. This gives us a "sure promise" (v. 16).

11. God honored Abraham's faith. It was a faith that believed even though circumstances did not favor believing. What favored believing was the fact that God had promised (vv. 17-21).

Many Christians get confused about Abraham's faith. They decide that they would like to have a particular thing. Then, they try to have enough faith to get it. Often times, it does not work. They blame themselves for not being able to have enough faith. They wonder why Abraham could have enough faith and they cannot.

What we frequently miss is the fact that God had *promised* Abraham and Sarah that they would have a son. Therefore, they could have specific faith. The reason we are not able to have faith to get what we would like to have is frequently related to the fact that we do not have a specific promise from God. Since we do not have a specific promise, we cannot have specific faith. In such cases we must have general faith and leave the matter in God's hands. General faith tells us that God cares and will deal with us in the light of our best interests and His purposes, but it does not assure us that God will grant our specific request (see discussion on general faith and specific faith in comments on v. 21).

12. There are two aspects of saving faith. One is trust. The other has to do with the content of what is believed. The element of trust has been the same at all times in redemptive history. People have always needed to trust in God. However, the content of saving faith has not always been the same. In the O.T., each person was to believe the redemptive revelation that had been given up to his own time. Now, redemptive revelation involves the fact that Jesus Christ is Lord and Savior. That must be believed now for salvation (vv. 23-25).

C. The Rejoicing and Assurance of Those Who Have Received the God-provided Righteousness Are Set Forth (5:1-11).

1. We have peace with God (v. 1).

1 Therefore being justified by faith, we have peace with God through our Lord Jesus Christ.

Therefore being justified by faith. Paul considers that he has established his case for justification with God. He now turns attention to the practical results.

We have peace with God

through our Lord Jesus Christ. Yeager says, "Peace can be defined both as absence of war and absence of worry" (414). The absence of war would mean the cessation of hostility. We are at peace with God (no longer at enmity with God), and God is at peace with us (we are no longer objects of His wrath). Another way of saying it is that reconciliation has taken place between God and us. This is most likely the meaning here. It is the foundation of what follows.

The peace referred to as "the absence of worry" is the inner peace we experience. This peace is based on the fact that between us and God there is "the absence of war." Both viewpoints of peace are taught in Scripture, but the "absence of war" seems to be the concept Paul has in mind here.

2. We rejoice in hope of the glory of God (v. 2).

2 By whom also we have access by faith into this grace wherein we stand, and rejoice in hope of the glory of God.

By whom we have access (Greek *prosago*) **by** [the] **faith into this grace wherein we stand.** Bruce comments on access: "Access denotes the privilege of approaching or being introduced into the presence of someone in high station, especially a royal or divine personage. Here Christ is viewed as ushering believers into their new state of grace and acceptance before God (cf. Eph. 3:12)" (123).

A person is either under law or he is under grace. Under law he is guilty, judged, and condemned. Under grace he stands protected from judgment and condemnation because through Christ he has a God-provided righteousness.

In the Greek there is an article before faith. Based on observations given in the comments on 3:30, there is a good possibility that the meaning is "the faith way" or "the New Covenant."

Through Jesus Christ, we have access by the New Covenant into this grace wherein we stand. Stand indicates steadfastness, firmness, and assurance.

And rejoice (Greek *kauchaomai)* **in hope of the glory of God.** This word is translated "glory" in v. 3 and "joy" in v. 11. Denny says that this word "always implies the *expression* of feeling" (623). The meaning is to rejoice, to exult, or to be in a state of jubilation.

The word "hope" as used in the N.T. refers to joyful, confident expectation. In Heb. 6:18, 19 "hope" is referred to as "the anchor of the soul both sure and stedfast."

The "glory of God" is referring to the glory of the eschatological future. It is that of which Paul speaks when he says, "that we may be also glorified together" (8:17) and "the glory which shall be revealed in us" (8:18).

Paul is saying, "We are rejoicing in joyful, confident expectation of the glory of God which shall be ours in the next life." It is much like saying that we are now rejoicing in what we know will be ours in the next life.

3 And not only *so,* but we glory in tribulations also: knowing that tribulation worketh patience.

And not only so, but we glory (Greek *kauchaomai*, same word as rejoice in v. 2) **in tribulations also.** When we realize the tribulations that Paul experienced as described in 2 Cor. 11:23-27, we know that Paul was well qualified to speak about tribulations. That is what makes this statement so meaningful. It was certainly not that Paul enjoyed tribulations. Rather, it was because he knew that God worked through these difficulties to help him grow in the likeness of Christ.

Knowing that tribulation worketh patience (Greek *hupomone*). This explains what Paul meant when he said he rejoiced in tribulation. The word refers to the quality of a seasoned character. It is translated "endurance" or "perseverance." Denny says that it "has more of a sense of bravery and effort than the English 'patience': it is not so passive" (624). Barclay says: "*Hupomone* is not a spirit which lies down and lets the floods go over it; it is the spirit which meets things breast forward and overcomes them" (74; see there for illustrations from the lives of those who have demonstrated *hupomone*).

In discussing how tribulation works perseverance, Hodge remarks, "It calls into existence that strength and firmness evinced in patient endurance of suffering, and in perseverance in fidelity to truth and duty, under the severest trials" (134).

The thrust of "worketh" in "worketh patience (endurance)" is telling us what tribulations are designed by God to do. It is what will take place when we allow God to use them in our training and development. Some do not face tribulations with the right attitude. In such cases, patience or endurance is not a guaranteed result.

4 And patience, experience; and experience, hope.

And patience experience (Greek *dokime*). With reference to this word, Wuest explains: "The word means either *the process* of trial, *proving*, as 2 Cor. 8:2, or *the results* of trial, *approvedness*, Phil. 2:22" (79).

With reference to the translation "experience" Vincent used only one word, "*wrong*" (692). That is probably true so far as the use of the word at the time Vincent made the statement. However, at the time of the KJV (1611) the case was different. *The New Century Dictionary* gives as obsolete meanings of experience: "trial or testing; an experiment; proof derived from trial." These observations are also confirmed by *The Oxford English Dictionary*.

It can be seen that in 1611 the translation "experience" had the same possible meaning as the Greek word. That does not help us decide which of the meanings is used here, but it does help us understand the occurrence of "experience" in the KJV.

Many understand the meaning to be "tested," "tried," or "approved" character (Black 78; Earle 99; Vincent 692; and Wuest 79). This view focuses on the results as seen in the believer. It is how he comes through the test.

Hodge takes a little different approach. He comments, "'*Hupomone*,' the endurance of trial, therefore, makes a man *dokimos* [approved]; in other words, it worketh *dokime*. It produces a strong, *tested faith" (135)*.

The approval is still referring to the person, or what is taking place within him.

According to Barnes, "The meaning is, that long afflictions borne patiently show a Christian what he is; they test his religion, and prove that it is genuine" (110). Here again, we see that the believer himself is what is tested.

Another way of looking at the result of testing or trial is to see it as "proof." This is the meaning in 2 Cor. 13:3, "Since ye seek a proof of Christ speaking in me." The word "evidence" would give us the same meaning.

Haldane comments: "Here it means proof; for a trial may detect a hypocrite as well as a manifest saint. But proof implies that the trial has proved the genuineness of the tried person, and also the faithfulness and support of God, which will enable us to overcome every difficulty" (189).

It will be observed that Haldane views "proof" as applying to (1) "the genuineness of the tried person," and (2) "the faithfulness and support of God." Both may be true statements, but according to the laws of hermeneutics, a choice will have to be made. In this single occurrence of the word, it cannot have both meanings. Both could be wrong, but only one could be right.

My reason for referring to Haldane is because out of several commentaries consulted he is the only one who thought the proof had any reference to God. Under the possibility of understanding the meaning to be "evidence" or proof, Hodge says, "This would give a good sense here: 'constancy produces evidence' of the fidelity of God, or of our fidelity" (135). This was the only other reference to God other than that of Haldane. As we saw above, this was not the view Hodge took.

I believe the meaning in the context is proof of the presence of God with us to help us and to work out His purposes in our lives. When God works in our lives through times of difficulty and uses that difficulty to season our character with steadfast endurance, this is *a proof of His presence in our lives.*

All of the views set forth speak of a truth. The only question is what is taught in this context by the word (*dokime*). My conclusion was reached because it is by far the clearest, the easiest, and the most convincing interpretation to make the transition to "hope."

And experience (*dokime*) **hope.** When God uses tribulations to help us develop the quality of steadfast endurance, it proves to us that God is truly at work in our lives. That proof of the presence of God in our lives gives us another reason for our hope. The "hope" here is the same as in 5:2. It is the joyful, confident expectation of the blessings of God in the next life.

The "hope of the glory of God" in v. 2 is based on our confidence that comes to us when we believe the gospel. The "hope of the glory of God" is a hope that grows out of our experience with God in the troubles and trials of life. We can sing with the children, "Jesus loves me this I know for the Bible tells me so." We can also sing, "Jesus loves me this I know for my experience tells me so." I know that the foundation of our hope must be in the Word of God. But a strong healthy hope needs the assurance that comes from the experience of the presence of God at work in our lives.

I essentially agree with the following from David Brown:

> Thus have we hope in two distinct ways, and at two successive stages of the Christian life—*First*, Immediately on believing, along with the sense of 'peace with God' (v. 1); *Next*, After the reality of this faith has been 'proved,' particularly by the patient endurance of trials sent to test it. We first get it by looking *away from ourselves* to the Lamb of God; next, by looking *into* or upon ourselves as transformed by that 'looking unto Jesus.' In the one case, the mind acts (as they say) *objectively*; in the other, *subjectively*. The one is (in the language of some divines) the *assurance of faith*; the other, the *assurance of sense* (214).

5 And hope maketh not ashamed; because the love of God is shed abroad in our hearts by the Holy Ghost which is given unto us.

And hope maketh not ashamed. "The shame of disappointment never follows this hope" (Moule, 101).

Because the love of God is

shed abroad (Greek *ekcheo*) **in our hearts by the Holy Ghost which is given unto us.** Since "the love of God" can mean either "God's love for us" or "our love for God," some have chosen the last meaning. It seems too obvious that it is God's love for us. There is no reason for saying more than that a difference of opinion exists.

The word (*ekcheo*) literally means "to pour out." Sanday and Headlam observe, "The idea of spiritual refreshment and encouragement is usually conveyed in the East through the metaphor of *watering*. St. Paul seems to have had in his mind Is. 44:3, 'I will pour water upon him that is thirsty, and streams upon the dry ground: I will *pour My Spirit* upon thy seed" (125).

In their expanded translation, they say, "That Holy Spirit which we received when we became Christians, floods our hearts with the consciousness of the love of God for us" (118, 119). What follows in vv. 6-11 is an elaboration of this love. When through the aid of the Holy Spirit we get an understanding of God's love, *fear* is replaced with *confidence*. We know that our "hope of the glory of God" (v. 2) will never fail us or disappoint us.

Paul assumes that the Holy Spirit is given to all Christians. Also, there is no suggestion of a special work that some have experienced and others have not.

6 For when we were yet without strength, in due time Christ died for the ungodly.

For "time" (Greek *kairos*), Vine gives the meaning: "Literally, 'according to season,' that is to say, a time Divinely appointed as opportune for the manifestation of God's love in Christ" (75). Some translate, "the right time."

The death of Christ was not that of a defenseless, helpless person carried to His death in spite of what He or His friends could do. It was on God's calendar at a fixed time. At the right time He became incarnate and headed for the cross. As the song says, "He could have called ten thousand angels," but He did not. His death was a part of God's eternal plan. He came to die for those who were "ungodly." Not only were we ungodly; we were also helpless (without strength). In the desert of man's experience, Christ came and by His atonement made an oasis and invited all to come.

7 For scarcely for a righteous man will one die: yet peradventure for a good man some would even dare to die.

For scarcely for a righteous (Greek *dikaios*) **man will one die.** A righteous person does what the law requires. He tells the truth. He pays his bills. He is dependable, etc. Few, if any, would die for such a person.

Yet peradventure (perhaps) **for a good** (Greek *agathos*) **man some would even dare to die.** The good man is the person who goes beyond the call of duty. He is the generous, free-hearted person. For such a person it is possible that a few people would actually die.

Some have failed to see any distinction between the righteous person and the good person. However, Lightfoot (286, 287) builds a strong case for making a difference. He concludes by saying as it relates to Romans 5:7:

> And for the matter at hand, there is all the difference in the world between the [good man] and the [righteous man]. The [good person], as such, is full of sympathy and consideration for others. The well-being of others is his first concern. He is beneficent and kind. This is the idea of *agathotes* [goodness]. On the

other hand the [righteous person], as such, puts out of sight the feelings of others. He is absolutely without sympathy. Now sympathy elicits sympathy. Consequently, the [good person] will be met with sympathy; others will be ready to do and to suffer for him in their turn: but the [righteous person] will evoke no such love, no willingness to make sacrifice in return (287).

Paul did not give this verse just to teach us the difference between a righteous person and a good person. Rather, it is setting forth human love at its highest so it can be contrasted with God's love in the next verse.

8 But God commendeth his love toward us, in that, while we were yet sinners, Christ died for us.

Having set forth human love at its highest, Paul turns his attention to the love of God. Concerning the word commendeth (Greek *sunistemi*), Earle explains, "The verb literally means 'place together.' It has two distinct uses in the N.T.: (1) commend; (2) show, prove, establish" (70). (For a more detailed presentation of the use of this word see Hendriksen 173, note 146.) The word "demonstrate" seems to be a good translation here.

God commendeth (demonstrates) **his love toward us, in that while we were** (not good as mentioned in v. 7; not even righteous, but) **yet sinners, Christ died for us.**

Human love at its highest would die for one who is a generous benefactor, but God's love was demonstrated when we had nothing to commend us to God—no merit at all. Yet He loved us enough to send Jesus Christ to demonstrate His love for us by making atonement for our sins. No wonder the song writer said, "The love of God is greater far than tongue or pen can ever tell."

9 Much more then, being now justified by his blood, we shall be saved from wrath through him.

Much more then. What follows is something that has great certainty: *being justified* (having right standing with God because the death and righteousness of Christ have been placed on our record) *by his blood.*

We were sinners which, so far as God is concerned, is the worst circumstance we could have been in. He abhors and hates sin. When our sins were placed on Jesus on the cross, the holiness of God required Him to turn His back on the Savior. In that darkest moment, in either Divine or human history, Jesus cried out, "My God, my God, why has thou forsaken me?" (Mt. 27:46, also Mk. 15:34). Sin is so opposite of what God is that when Jesus took our sins upon Him, our sins broke the perfect fellowship that had always existed between the Father and the Son and made Him the object of God's wrath. (See comments on atonement in connection with the study of propitiation in 3:25, 26.)

With that which God abhors with a holy hatred in our hearts and on our record, God's love motivated Him to send Christ to pay the full penalty for our sins. The cross is the highest demonstration of God's love. It will forever remain the highest point in the revelation of God's love. What made it the highest demonstration of God's love is that the cross was also the highest demonstration of the holiness of God. It was the inflexibility of God's holiness that made it necessary for Jesus to suffer the full release of God's penal wrath before He could forgive our sins.

We shall be saved from wrath through him. The wrath of God here is the eschatological wrath of God. At that moment when God releases His wrath on Christ-rejecting sinners, Jesus Christ will protect us from the wrath of God. As long as we have Christ's death and righteousness on our account, we are as safe from the penal wrath of God as Christ is. (It is important for us to remember the distinction between remedial punishment—chastisement—and penal punishment. The Christian is delivered from penal punishment, but he is not delivered from remedial punishment.)

Jesus Christ did the hardest thing He will ever do for us, and that under extremely adverse circumstances (the fact that we were sinners). Once we accept that truth, to believe the rest should be easier than to believe that He died for us under these circumstances. The reason it should be easier is "we are now justified" and that "by his blood." For Him to buy us at such an awful cost (1 Cor. 6:19 and 1 Pet. 1:18, 19), surely we are important to Him now. We are in much better condition and that because of Him. Surely, He will stand for us in the future. The rest of what He will do for us will be much easier than what He has already done.

10 For if, when we were enemies, we were reconciled to God by the death of his Son, much more, being reconciled, we shall be saved by his life.

For if, when we were enemies we were reconciled (Greek *katallaso*) **to God by the death of his Son.** There are two ways the word *enemies* can be understood: (1) The hostility growing out of man's depravity. In this sense, man is viewed as being hostile toward God. This is called the active use of the word. (2) In the second use of the word, we are considered enemies by God. This is the passive use of the word "enemy."

According to Vincent, the Greek word (*katallaso*): "...means primarily *to exchange*; and hence to change the relation of hostile parties into a relation of peace; *to reconcile*. It is used of both mutual and one-sided enmity. In the former case, the context must show on which side is the active enmity (693).

The reconciliation called for by the active use of the word refers to that change which takes place in us when we are regenerated. The hostility within us is changed. The reconciliation called for in the passive use is the change of attitude of God toward us when we, on the condition of faith, have the benefits of Christ's propitiatory sacrifice applied to our account, i.e., the death and righteousness of Christ. The justice of God is satisfied and God is reconciled to us, and in so doing we also become reconciled to God. Judicially, we are no longer enemies in God's eyes.

When redemption is viewed in its entirety (justification and sanctification), we become reconciled to God in that we are no longer considered enemies by God. This part of our reconciliation is closely related to our justification.

We also become reconciled in that our hostility toward God is changed. This part of our reconciliation is involved in our sanctification. Liddon is speaking along the same line when he says, "Christ's death removed God's enmity against man, and man's enmity against God only ceased, as a moral consequence of faith" (100, 101).

Since it is quite clear from v. 9 that the satisfaction of God is in focus, in view of the fact that Paul dealt with justification, I conclude that the enmity in focus in v. 10 is passive. The reconcilation, then, focuses on the fact that God no longer views us as enemies. He no longer views us as enemies because the propitiatory sacrifice of Christ has been applied to our account.

Thus *God is satisfied and we are justified and thereby reconciled to God.*

Lightfoot takes the position that "The New Testament speaks of mankind as reconciled to God, not God as reconciled to man" (288). Sanday and Headlam take issue with Lightfoot and present a defense of the view "that the natural explanation of the passages which speak of enmity and reconciliation between God and man is that they are not on one side only, but are mutual" (129, 130).

For some good treatments of the view that, in this context, the emphasis is on the fact that God no longer views us as enemies, see Harrison (60); Hodge (138, 139); Meyer (191); Murray (172-174); and Shedd (117, 118).

Much more, being reconciled, we shall be saved by his life. If Christ would die for us under the most adverse circumstance, now that we are justified and reconciled by His death, surely He will live for us. A part of this is His work of intercession (Heb. 7:25). We need not fear the future because He who conquered death and came forth in a triumphant resurrection is available to carry out in the future what He died in the past to accomplish. (For a good summary of the development of Paul's thought in vv. 9, 10 see David Brown 216.)

11 And not only *so,* but we also joy in God through our Lord Jesus Christ, by whom we have now received the atonement.

And not only *so,* but we also joy (Greek *kauchaomai*) **in God through our Lord Jesus Christ.** The word translated "we rejoice" in v. 2 and "we glory" in v. 3 is translated "we joy" in this verse. Whether looking at a glorious future (v. 2), whether experiencing sustaining grace during difficult times (v. 3), or accessing what he now has through Christ (v. 11) Paul says, "I rejoice with jubilation."

By whom we have now received the atonement (Greek *katallage*). The word translated "atonement" is the noun form of the verb "reconcile" used in v. 10. Thus, "atonement" is actually the experience of reconciliation which results from *the act of reconciliation* in v. 10.

In the KJV this word *katallage* is translated "atonement." Leon Morris says: "This is one of the few theological terms of Anglo-Saxon origin. It means 'at-one-ment' and signifies the process of making God and man one after the tragedy of man's sin had separated them (Isa. 59:2) and made them enemies (Col. 1:21)" (83).

It is generally agreed today that "reconciliation" is preferred to translate the word rather than "atonement." The term "atonement" is usually used as an overall term to refer to the work of Christ which makes our justification possible.

Trench observes:

> When our translation was made, it signified, as innumerable examples prove, reconciliation, or the making up of a foregoing enmity; all its uses in our early literature justifying the etymology now sometimes called into question that 'atonement' is 'at-one-ment,' and therefore = 'reconciliation': and that consequently it was then, although not now, the proper rendering of *katallage* (292, 293).

The word *"now"* is a very important word in this verse. Up to this point in chapter 5, Paul was stressing our assurance and our joyful expectancy that when God's wrath falls on sinners, it will not fall on us. In this verse Paul is stressing what we already possess. Christianity promises more than "pie in the sky by and by." At this very moment we have rejoicing with jubilation because we have already been reconciled to God through Jesus Christ.

Summary 5:1-11

Having established that justification is by faith, Paul turns his attention to those things which strengthen our assurance and form the basis for rejoicing. Since we are justified, we are at peace with God and God is at peace with us.

Through Jesus Christ we have access to that sphere of life where grace reigns. Since our salvation is by grace, we can stand with assurance about our relationship with God. This assurance leads us into a joyful, confident expectation of the time when the glory of God will be revealed in us (8:18).

Once we understand our relationship with God we can rejoice when we experience tribulation. This is because we experience the sustaining grace of God during these times. God uses tribulation to help us develop steadfast endurance. Through this experience we develop assurance that God is with us in our daily experiences. This assurance of His presence in our lives strengthens the confidence we have concerning His blessings in the eschatological future.

The Holy Spirit works in our heart to help us understand the love God has for us. It is almost too good to be true that when we were helpless and ungodly, Jesus came and died for us—yet we know that it is true.

As it relates to human love, we would not likely find anyone who would die for a person who did only what was required of him. Human love at its highest might die for a generous person who always goes beyond what duty requires.

The amazing thing about Divine love is that Christ died for us when we were not going beyond what is required. In fact, we were not even doing what is required. The truth is that Jesus died for us when we were sinners.

If Jesus died for us when we had nothing good going for us, we should certainly not have any trouble believing that He will protect us from the eschatological wrath of God. Or to put it another way, if Jesus died for us when we were enemies, surely He will live for us now that we have been reconciled to God by the death of God's Son. The hardest part for Jesus is behind Him. Surely, now that He has saved us by His death, He will do the easier and as living Lord and Savior give us that kind of assistance that we need.

While the Christian can rejoice about a great future with Christ, that is not all there is to the Christian life. It is more than "pie in the sky by and by." We are already enjoying the fact that we are presently reconciled to God.

Application: Teaching and Preaching the Passage

1. This passage is devotional in tone. It is as if Paul, in the midst of this important doctrinal study of how we receive the God-provided righteousness, takes out time to rejoice in the implications of these great truths.

2. The fact that we are justified by faith means that we are now at peace with God. All of the obstacles between us and God have been removed (v. 1).

3. Through Jesus Christ we have access to the grace of God. Another way of saying this is that Jesus Christ is the doorway to grace (v. 2).

4. Because of the assurance that grace gives us, we are rejoicing in the joyful, confident expectation of having the glory of God showered upon us in the eschatological future (v. 2).

5. We also glory (or rejoice) in tribulations. This is because God uses tribulation to help develop in us a seasoned character. We develop steadfast endurance. This development of steadfast endurance helps us know that God is at work in our lives. When we know that God is at work in our lives, it gives us experiential proof that we are saved. This experiential proof makes our hope stronger. As believers we can now say we know we belong to God because the Bible tells us so and also because our experience with God in times of difficulty tells us that we belong to Him (vv. 3,4).

6. This joyful, confident, expectation that we have through Christ will not let us down (v. 5).

7. Sinners have no strength within themselves to make them presentable to God. But that is not the end of the story. In due time God opened up a sure way to salvation by sending Christ to die for us (v. 6).

8. Verse 7 serves as a background for v. 8. In v. 7 we see human love at its highest. We would hardly find anyone who would die for a person who lived up only to what is expected or required. However, we might find someone who would die for a generous, free-hearted person who was always going beyond the call of duty.

God's love transcends human love at its highest. God loved us so much that He sent Christ to die for us when we were neither righteous nor good, but sinners (vv. 7,8). These verses furnish one of the greatest texts in the Bible to preach or teach about the unparalleled love of God.

9. The "much mores" of vv. 9 and 10 are intended to strengthen our assurance. According to v. 9, if Jesus would die for us when we were sinners (unfavorable circumstances) it is far more reasonable to believe that when the wrath of God falls in the eschatological future he will save us from that wrath. That will be easy for Him. Dying for us was hard. If Jesus did the hardest thing He could ever do when the circumstances were unfavorable (we were sinners), surely under favorable circumstances (we are now justified by His blood) He will do that which will be easy for Him to do (v. 9).

10. The same basic reasoning of v. 9 applies in v. 10. Jesus died for us under unfavorable circumstances (we were enemies). Now the circumstances are favorable (we have been reconciled to God by the death of His Son). Surely under these favorable circumstances, He will live for us which is far easier than dying for us. The living for us appears to be His work as our intercessor.

11. We are not only rejoicing about what will take place in the eschatological future, we have something to rejoice or joy about now. We have already been reconciled to God and are presently enjoying the benefits of that reconciliation (v. 11).

12. It should be observed that "rejoice" (v. 2), "glory" (v. 3), and "joy" (v. 11) are translations of the same Greek word. One can organize a message about the three things over which Paul was rejoicing.

13. While this passage presents the idea of a rejoicing Christian, it does not present the idea of a problem-free life. Such a view has no basis in Scripture.

D. The Fact That One Person, Jesus Christ, Is the Source of Righteousness For Many Is Defended (5:12-21).

Preliminary Observations
Righteousness
The Context

Why does Paul want to discuss the relationship of Adam to the race at this point? It is because in Romans he has made one Person the sole basis for our right standing with God. This is something that could be applied to thousands, yea, millions! For those who hear it favorably, it may sound too good to be true. For those who were antagonistic, it might be used as a point of attack. "Surely," they might have said, "one person could not possibly furnish all the righteousness that is needed for multitudes of people."

When the occasion calls for it, Paul makes use of the *a fortiori* argument. This argument seeks to move from something that is harder to believe to the easier to believe. This is the kind of argument used in 5:8-10. In vv. 12-19, Paul shows that it is easier to believe that Christ, one Person, can be the cause of the justification for many than it is to believe that Adam could be the cause of condemnation for many.

A Punctuation Problem in Verses 15 and 16

It is commonly recognized that Paul shows a comparison between Adam and Christ, but the picture is confused by making the major thrust of vv. 15-17 to deal with contrasts rather than comparison.

This confusion exists because it is almost unanimously agreed that vv. 15-17 begin with statements of fact rather than raising a question. Out of more than 40 commentaries examined, only four manifest any awareness that some have considered these verses to be introduced by questions.

Godet calls attention to such an idea but dismisses it by saying: "But the construction of the sentence does not lead naturally to the idea of interrogation. And what is still more strongly opposed to this explanation is, that the sentence so understood would express the development of an analogy, while the rest of the verse states a difference" (214, 215).

Lange takes the same position and calls attention to Meyer's argument against considering them to be questions. He says: "Rosemuller, and others, would neutralize the negation by regarding *ouk* as interrogative; but this, as Meyer remarks is forbidden by the contrasting character of the contents" (182).

Meyer places his comments in a footnote, "This contrast forbids the taking *all' ouk* [but, not]...*charisma* [free gift] *interrogatively (Mehring and earlier expositors) and so getting rid of the negation" (209, note 2).*

Only Griffith Thomas decides in favor of these statements as questions among those commentaries consulted. He remarks:

> Usually it is thought that as in verses 12-14 the Apostle states the fact of the analogy, so here in verses 15-17 he proceeds to point out the contrasts, or the aspects in which the analogy does not hold good, but it seems far more natural to read the first clause of verse 15, and also the first clause of verse 16 as questions in each case. The 'but' does not introduce the contrast, but the details of the analogy. Does it not seem improbable that after introducing the analogy between Adam and Christ the Apostle should develop the contrasts rather than the correspondences? And the thought of a contrast does not give any force whatever to the 'also' of verse 15. Then again we see, the 'so then' of verse 18 introduces the summing up of the preceding arguments, summarizing correspondences rather than contrasts. Of course there are remarkable contrasts between the sin of Adam and the work of

Christ, but the very contrasts strengthen the argument for the analogy which is the point St. Paul wishes to emphasize (157,158).

In a footnote Thomas calls attention to others who understand the interrogative form to be correct, He says:

> I am greatly indebted, on vers. 14-19, to some ms. notes by my friend the late Canon Jones, Moore College, Sydney, Australia, who died after these lines were written. A similar view is taken of the interrogative form of vers. 15, 16 by Mr. J. Fort, in *God's Salvation* and by *The Englishman's Greek Testament* (158).

The quotation from Thomas referred to by Chafer, in his *Systematic Theology*, does not discuss the problem, but since he quoted Thomas approvingly, it is assumed he was in agreement (II:306).

I first saw these treated as questions in *Berry's Interlinear Greek-English New Testament*. After treating them as questions in his translation, he points out in a footnote, *"The various Editors do not mark this as a question"* (italics his). This was a welcomed suggestion. The wording had always seemed awkward. Reading them as questions seemed to be more natural. Also, the passage has a more natural flow of thought. The meaning became clearer.

As a statement, the first part of v. 15 reads, "But not as the offence, so also is the gift." As a question, it reads, "But as the offence, shall not the free gift also be so?"

In v. 16 as a statement it reads, "But not as it was by one that sinned, so is the gift." As a question, it reads, "But as by the offence of one, shall not the free gift be?"

The Difference in Interpretation

The use of questions to introduce vv. 15, 16 will not change any fundamental thought of the passage. It will, however, change the emphasis in vv. 15-17. That change will take out the awkwardness of trying to make the emphasis on contrasts. In so doing it will make it easier to see the major thrust of the passage.

Romans 5:12-19 could be outlined as follows: (1) Verses 12-14 state the relationship between the race and Adam. (2) Verses 15-17 argue that it is much more reasonable to believe that one could be the grounds of justification for many than that one could be the grounds for the condemnation of many. (3) Verses 18, 19 give the conclusion of the argument: Just as the race was condemned because of what Adam did, so the many who are redeemed are justified because of what Christ did.

Godet argued that the construction does not lead naturally to the idea of interrogation (214, 215). I am not aware of any special construction used in Greek for questions except the use of one particle (*ou*) to give the implied answer of "yes" and another (*me*) to give the implied answer of "no." The constructions under consideration use the one which implies "yes." This is exactly what you would expect if an analogy is intended.

Not only does the purpose of the passage call for analogy, but there are also some other constructions which favor it. Verse 15 has "as" (Greek *hos*) . . ."so" (Greek *houtos*). Verse 16 has "as," with "so" implied but not stated. Verse 18 has "as. . .so"; v. 19 has "just as" (Greek *hosper*). . .so." In none of these references other than vv. 15 and 16 would a person even question that comparison is what Paul is emphasizing. Does it not seem that in this context "as...so" in vv. 15 and 16 would stress comparison rather than contrast?

Another point of consideration is the use of "also" (Greek *kai*) in v. 15. As

Thomas points out, a contrast does not give any force to "also" (157, 158). In fact it is very awkward when it is translated as a statement. However, if it is translated as a question, the "also" fits. In fact, "also" emphasizes agreement.

Paul's use of "much more" (Greek *pollo mallon*) in vv. 15 and 17 also favors the idea of analogy. The idea in each case is that if we grant what happened to the race as a result of Adam, it is even more reasonable to believe what is said about the relationship of the redeemed to Christ. In other words, it is more reasonable to believe in justification from one than condemnation from one; thus, he is arguing for analogy. The conclusion in vv. 18, 19 confirms that Paul's basic thrust is comparison, not contrast.

It would certainly seem strange for a person to present an argument for contrast in order that he might draw a conclusion which presents a comparison. "So then" (Greek *ara oun*) in v. 18 would certainly indicate that vv. 18 and 19 give a conclusion based on the preceding argument.

No one denies that the *results* from Adam to the race and from Christ to the redeemed are different. However, that is not the point of Paul's argument. *He is not arguing about results, but the principle involved in how these results came to be.* The difference in the results is too clear to require an argument.

Now let me give a brief summary of vv. 12-19 according as each view would present it. If these clauses are considered as *statements,* the line of thought would be: In vv. 12-14, Paul points out that the race is condemned because of an involvement in what Adam did. He closes this section by pointing out that Adam is a type of Him who was to come, who was Christ. Having pointed out that there is an analogy between Adam and Christ, Paul hastens to point out that there are contrasts. The contrast is found in the results coming from the two (vv. 15-17). This is followed by a conclusion consequent upon what he has just said. That conclusion is that just as the race was condemned for what Adam did, so the redeemed receive righteousness because of what Christ did.

If these are considered as *questions,* Paul points out in vv. 12-14 that the race is condemned because of their involvement in what Adam did. At the end of v. 14, Paul points out that Adam was a type of Christ. In vv. 15-17, he presents the comparison that would explain in what sense Christ is a fulfillment of that which Adam symbolized. In these verses he argues that it is more reasonable to believe that one could be the source of righteousness for many than to believe that one could be the source of condemnation for many. This leads to the conclusion that just as the race was condemned for what Adam did, so the redeemed receive righteousness because of what Christ did (vv. 18, 19).

Views About the Effect of Adam's Sin on the Race

In spite of the fact that Paul's main concern in this passage is on the reasonableness of justification of "many" by "one," the history of interpretation has become more involved on the relationship of the race to Adam's sin. For that reason, attention must be given to this subject since the passage does deal with it.

Immediate Imputation

There are two basic approaches which accept the immediate imputation of Adam's sin to the race. One is based on the fact that Adam is the natural head of the race. The other view suggests that Adam is the federal head of the race and as such the representative of the race.

Natural Headship

This view has commonly been referred to as the Augustinian view (among adherents there may be some differences on details, but the basic principle is the same). This view states that guilt, condemnation, and depravity were passed on to the race from Adam.

> The race was in Adam and has descended body and spirit from him. [This involves the traducian view of the origin of the immaterial part of man. As a result of natural propagation the immaterial part (spirit, or soul and spirit) is passed on to Adam's descendants along with the physical body.] The fact that we were in Adam means that we were identified with him in his sin [when he sinned, the race sinned]. This necessitates our being a partaker with him in his guilt and condemnation. To say otherwise would say that not all of Adam was condemned because that which was in Adam's loins, which is the race potentially, was as much a part of Adam as any other part. No matter how many subdivisions there may be, the parts never lose their real identification as being a part of the original whole. [There is an unbroken continuity between every human being and Adam.] We have never lost our identification with him in his sin (Forlines *Systematics*, 127).

Some speak of the solidarity of the race with Adam in describing the relationship of the race to Adam, as set forth in the natural headship view. This is a good term, but those who believe in other views use it also. For that reason we need to be careful to determine how each person is using it. Another name that is sometimes used is "realism." Barclay says, "The passage ought to be given what is called the realistic interpretation, namely that, because of solidarity of the human race, all mankind actually sinned in Adam" (80). (On natural headship see Bruce 124-130; Lenski 358-362; and Shedd 120-142.)

Federal Headship

> According to the federal headship view, Adam became the representative of the race by Divine appointment. The reason for Adam's being chosen was his natural headship, but natural headship did not of itself involve the race in Adam's sin. God entered into a covenant with Adam promising to bestow eternal life upon him and his posterity if he should obey God and corruption and death would pass on to his posterity if he should disobey God. It is the covenant relationship...that involves the race in the consequences of his sin. Instead of saying the race sinned in Adam, this view would say, 'All are accounted sinners' (Forlines *Systematics*, 125).

They may say that all sinned in Adam when referring to Rom. 5:12, but when they explain what this means it will be "all are accounted sinners."

An illustration will help. Suppose a teacher chose one member of the class to represent the class in taking an examination. The grade that this student made would be the grade that all members would receive. That would be true whether the grade was a passing grade or a failing grade. All of the other members would receive this grade and the corresponding treatment that went with this grade. (See Hodge 144-176 and Hamilton 83-85.)

Mediate Imputation

According to this view, imputation would be indirect rather than direct. The race would receive depravity from Adam, *but not the guilt for his act of sin.* However, *he would be guilty because depravity apart from acts forms the basis of guilt.* Sometimes people confuse this view with the natural headship view of immediate imputation. The natural headship view of immediate imputation holds that Adam's guilt is directly imputed to the race. The theory of mediate imputation is indirect imputation. Guilt is imputed because of depravity received from Adam, but Adam's guilt is not imputed to the race. (Some say that this was Calvin's view. See Lange 192, 193; Shedd 124; and Calvin 111, 112.)

No Imputation

In distinction from all the other views mentioned, this view denies that there is any imputation to the race of the guilt of Adam whether immediate or mediate. Infants are born with a depraved nature, but they share no part in Adam's guilt and condemnation. There is no individual guilt and condemnation until the individual becomes morally accountable and commits sin. Depravity will, of course, inevitably lead to sinning. (See Cranfield 271-283 and Barnes 117-138.)

Murray has an excellent treatment of the imputation of Adam's sin to the race. It is evident that he believes in the immediate imputation of Adam's sin to the race (182-206). He says:

> We must conclude that the 'all sinned' of verse 12 and the one trespass of the one man of verses 15-19 must refer to the same fact or event, that the one fact can be expressed in terms of both singularity and plurality, as the sin of one and the sin of all. And the only solution is that there must be some kind of solidarity existing between the 'one' and 'the all' with the result that the sin of the one may at the same time and with equal relevance be regarded as the sin of all (186).

All that I read of Murray's comments sounded like the natural headship view; however, the next sentence that follows the above quotation is, "What this solidarity is it is not our purpose at the present to determine." It is assumed that he meant by this that he was not, in the commentary, trying to decide between the natural headship, federal headship, or some other possible alternative.

Infant Salvation

In writing a commentary, one must not only address the concepts that are taught in the book; but it is also necessary, at least, to mention those questions that are unavoidably raised in connection with what is said in the book. Any time that Rom. 5:12-19 is discussed the question of infant salvation arises. I believe in infant salvation. Some believe infants are "safe" rather than "saved." They are considered safe by those who reject the concept of the imputation of Adam's sin to the race. In my view there is "racial sin" and "individual sin." There is "racial guilt" and "individual guilt."

If we can have racial guilt and individual guilt, it is conceivable that we can also have justification from racial guilt as distinguished from individual guilt. The incarnation created that kind of solidarity with the race which would make the application of atonement to remove racial guilt automatic. The solidarity with Christ which brings justification from personal or individual guilt requires a personal faith which results in a personal union with Christ.

In this view Christ has already delivered the whole race from the penalty of racial guilt. That means that, as it now stands, no one will go to eternal punishment apart from personal sin. However, if Christ had not come, there would have been no forgiveness for racial guilt.

I do not believe it is possible to avoid sin upon reaching what we call the age of accountability. In fact, when the person makes the transition to personal accountability, he becomes accountable for the attitudes and dispositions that are already there. (For further thoughts on infant salvation, see Forlines *Systematics* 171-173.)

These observations have been presented prior to dealing with the passage because reading what is set forth in "Preliminary Observations" will make it easier to grasp these views. To interweave them bit by bit in the exegesis of the passage could have been confusing.

1. It parallels our relationship to Adam from whom all received guilt, depravity, and condemnation (vv. 12-14).

12 Wherefore, as by one man sin entered into the world, and death by sin; and so death passed upon all men, for that all have sinned.

Wherefore (Greek *dia touto*). The literal reading is "on this account." In this verse, it is much easier to know what Paul is saying than it is to know how he is saying it. By looking at the context it is reasonably certain that Paul has realized that justification by "One" for "many" may need some defense for his readers. So he introduces a parallel between Christ and Adam. The Jewish readers would have no problem in recognizing the negative results which came from Adam (one person) to the whole race. This being true Paul introduces the thought that if we can accept the fact that Adam (one person) by his sin introduced sin and death to the whole race, surely we should be able to accept the truth that Christ (one person) could by His atoning work introduce righteousness and life to all who believe in Him.

As by one man sin entered into the world. The "as" compares the fact that Christ as "one" brings justification and reconciliation. The justification by One is as (or like) it was with one person being the cause of the entrance of sin and death into the world. The one man, of course, is Adam.

The saddest words ever written are "sin entered into the world." They mark a drastic change in human history.

And death by sin. Some understand the meaning here to be limited to physical death. Others understand the meaning to be physical, spiritual, and eternal death. Perhaps the answer is found in understanding the reference to be to physical death, but to understand physical death to be a synechdoche where a part is given for the whole. If so, the end result would be physical, spiritual, and eternal death.

And so death passed upon all men. The reference is to the universality of death in the human race.

For that (Greek *eph' ho*) **all have sinned** (Greek *pantes hemarton*). There is broad agreement that the first of these means "since" or "because." This would be consistent with the KJV "for that." Some have thought that it should be translated "in whom." The "in whom" would refer back to the one man. Though the meaning would be consistent with what is being taught in the passage, this translation is usually rejected.

The big problem is, What is meant by "all have sinned" (*pantes hemarton*)? It can be understood, grammatically speaking, to mean that every human being sins in his own experience. In this case it would have the same meaning here that is does in Rom. 3:23.

Some have argued that it must mean the same thing here that it does in 3:23 since the same words occur in both places. There is no reason, however, that the words must mean the same in all places. What makes the difference is the context. We have already observed that "the righteousness of God" can mean either an attribute of God or the God-provided righteousness. In 3:21-26 the meaning is seen to change when the use is close together. With the space between 3:23 and 5:12, and a different context, there is nothing to say that the meaning must be the same. It could be the same, but it is not necessary.

Another way is to translate "all sinned." This is the way it would be translated unless the context would indicate otherwise.

These words have been the occasion of a great deal of controversy. There are other problems that need to be dealt with, but the first one is whether the meaning is "every one in his own experience has sinned," or "in the distant past the whole race sinned."

While either view is possible grammatically, the context requires that we make a choice.

I think the chart below will help us see how the context decides the question.

On the 'effect' side of the chart, it is obvious that the effect in 5:15-18 is the same as the effect in 5:12. If it is clear what the cause of the effect is in 5:15-18, that should help clarify what the cause is in 5:12. The cause in 5:15-18 is 'one person,' 'one man's offence,' and 'one offence.' Putting that together, it is clear that the cause is one offense committed by Adam when he ate the forbidden fruit. If 5:12, 15-18 all give the same effect, it is to be expected that 5:12, 15-18 will all give the same cause. The cause is clear in 5:15-19. This interprets the cause in 5:12. While Greek grammar may allow the statement in 5:12 to refer to each individual's sin, the context decides against it and in favor of the other grammatical possibility. It is clear in the total context that 5:12 is to be interpreted, 'all sinned in Adam' (Forlines *Systematics*, 124).

Many people find this hard to accept, whether it be from the natural headship view, or the federal headship view. They say, "It doesn't seem fair." To deny the imputation of Adam's guilt will not relieve the problem. If a person takes the Biblical account of Adam and Eve seriously at all, then physical infirmity, depravity, and death are ours as the

CAUSE	EFFECT
5:12 'All sin' or 'all sinned'	'Death passed upon all men'
5:15 'The offence of one'	'Many be dead'
5:16 'By one [person']	'Condemnation'
5:17 'One man's offence'	'Death reigned'
5:18 'The offence of one' (The Greek means 'one offence')	'Judgment came upon all men to condemnation'

consequence of sin. Saying that it is unfair will not change that. So there is no interpretation whether true or false that escapes all of the difficulty.

It seems to me that the case is quite strong for the immediate imputation of Adam's sin. There are two possibilities: The natural and the federal headship views which advocate immediate imputation. While those who hold the federal headship view may use the words "all sinned in Adam," when they interpret it, it comes out to be "all are accounted as sinners." This calls for the passive voice, but the Greek *(hemarton)* is active rather than passive. Shedd gives a rather lengthy refutation of the passive interpretation (124-128). It is too lengthy to include here, but I will give his first objection. "If this interpretation be correct, it is the only instance in Scripture in which this active verb, in the active voice, has a passive signification" (124).

The view of mediate imputation suffers a like fate. It would require the meaning "became sinful." Shedd considers the same arguments that are opposed to the federal headship view to stand against this view since it too requires the passive voice.

While there is not a direct statement in which the actual words "all sinned *in Adam*" are given, it appears to me that "all sinned in Adam" is a necessary implication from the passage. The words "For as in Adam all die, even so in Christ shall all be made alive" (1 Cor. 15:22) also lend support for natural headship.

As we complete this chapter and go through the first 11 verses of chapter 6, we will gain more insight into the principle of imputation.

> The principle involved in the imputation of something from one person to another is identification by union with the person. This is true whether it be sin or righteousness. The Scripture knows of no other way that the action of one person can be imputed to another. This is the principle involved in the imputation of the death and righteousness of Christ to the believer (Forlines *Systematics*, 127).

Support for and criticisms of the various views can be found in the sources mentioned above. Since there is not a consistent use of terms, it is sometimes difficult to decide what view a commentator holds. The reason for that may be that many who write commentaries have not given a great deal of time to the study of systematic theology. For that reason, terms which are used in commentaries may not be used as precisely as they would in a treatment of systematic theology. This same observation applies to other subjects as well.

13 (For until the law sin was in the world: but sin is not imputed when there is no law.
14 Nevertheless death reigned from Adam to Moses, even over them that had not sinned after the similitude of Adam's transgression, who is the figure of him that was to come.

My approach will be to present different views and then present my view at the end rather than trying to weave my thoughts with those of others.

For until the law sin was in the world. The time period is that of the time before the Mosaic Law.

But sin is not imputed when there is no law. Commentaries present several different views on the meaning of this part of the verse. (1) Most would agree that these words imply that there was law prior to the Mosaic Law. This conclusion is based on the fact that physical death was universal before the Mosaic Law. Also, the flood, the judgment against Sodom and Gomorrah, and other incidents show that *God did impute* (place on peoples' account thus holding them responsible) *sin prior to the Mosaic Law.* It is usually agreed that the law implied is the law of the heart (or conscience) which is spoken of in Rom. 2:14, 15 (Fairbairn 417-420; Haldane 209, 210; and Murray 188, 189).

(2) Others take the view that the only sin in view in vv. 13,14 is Adam's sin. The period from Adam to Moses, according to this view, was without stated laws such as that given to Adam and those found in the Mosaic Law. For this reason the sins that occurred in this period did not take on the character of "transgressions." This thinking is based on, "For where no law is, *there* is no transgression" (Rom. 4:15b). Since personal sins did not take on the character of transgression, it is said that they were not imputed. According to this view, there is *only one possible explanation for the reign of death during this period, i.e., the imputation of Adam's sin accompanied by the penalty of death* (see David Brown 219, 220; Godet 209-212; Vine *Dictionary* 592, 593, and *Romans* 80).

An observation should be made concerning a distinctive feature of Godet's view. While he insists that all sinned in Adam, he considers the death that is inflicted on mankind as a result of that sin to be restricted to physical death (205 and 212). He goes on to say: "We should add, however, that death, even when taken simply as physical death, always implies an abnormal state in relation to God, a state which, if it continues and develops, cannot fail to draw after it fatal consequences to man" (205).

Godet goes on further to say:

> This imputation of Adam's sin, as the cause of death to every individual man, would be absolutely incomprehensible and incompatible with the justice of God, if it passed beyond the individual domain of life marked off by the mysterious relation between the individual and the species [the race]. The sequel will show that as soon as we rise to the domain of spiritual life, the individual is no longer dependent on this solidarity of the species, but he holds his eternal destiny in his own hands (212).

In commenting on v. 12, he says: "Adam received the unique mission to represent the whole species concentrated in a single individual" (209).

Because of its uniqueness, comment on this part of Godet's view is given here rather than later. He has a very awkward situation. He has developed two kinds of sins: (1) one that only brings physical death, and (2) one that brings eternal death. While some sins may be more serious than others, the Scripture knows of no kind of sin that will not result in eternal death apart from being covered by the atoning work of Christ.

One can appreciate the problem Godet is grappling with. He desires (as the quotation indicates) to develop a view that ultimately sends no one to eternal punishment apart from his own personal sins. A more tenable approach to this problem is one that anchors the safety of the infants' eternal destiny in the atoning work of Christ rather than one that denies the need of salvation. (See discussion on infant salvation in the "Preliminary Observations" preceding the comments on v. 12 above.)

(3) This view has some things in common with the second view. The difference is that, according to view (2) no one's personal sins were imputed from Adam to the Mosaic Law. In this

view the vast majority did not sin against a stated Divine command. Since they did not, their personal sins were not imputed. The fact that these people died was evidence that their death was based on the imputation of Adam's sin to them.

This view also considers that the punishment of Cain, the flood, Sodom and Gomorrah, etc. were evidence that some peoples' personal sins were imputed to them during the period from Adam to Mt. Sinai. This indicates that some peoples' sins were violations of Divine commands and took on the character of transgressions (Meyer 203-205).

Alford's view fits into view (3), but it is not exactly like Meyer's view. Alford says:

> In the case of those who had not the written law, *hamartia* [sin] is not fully formally reckoned as *parabasis* [transgression] set over against the command: but in a certain sense, as distinctly proved in 2:9-16, it is *reckoned* and they are condemned for it. . . .The revelation of law *exaggerated*, brought into prominent and formal manifestation, the sinfulness of sin, which *was before culpable and punishable* but in a less degree.

He goes on to say: "Although the full *ellogismos* [imputation] of sin did not take place between Adam and Moses, the *universality of death is a proof that all sinned*,—for death is the consequence of sin:—in confirmation of ver. 12" (361).

Alford, it can be seen, considers the universality of death (especially as it relates to those whose sin had not taken on the character of "transgression") to be a proof of the interpretation that all sinned in Adam.

(4) This view takes a different approach to the word "imputed." Instead of viewing it as an act of God in charging those under consideration with guilt, it is the act of man himself. Calvin recognizes that there is evidence that God did hold people responsible for their sins. This is evidenced by the punishment of Cain, the flood, the downfall of Sodom, etc. This being true he looks for an application in the area of men's own recognition of sin, he explains: "The apostle, therefore, notes the perversity of men, when not aroused by the law, in having laid aside to a great degree the distinction between good and evil, and indulged their lusts without care or disturbance, as if there were no judgment of God" (112).

The reference then, as Calvin sees it, is to the dulling of moral sensitivities in the absence of written laws.

Stuart also subscribes to this view. He considers the meaning of impute (Greek *ellogeo*) to be "regard, account, or esteem." Men did not properly recognize sin for what it was (173-175).

Nevertheless death reigned from Adam to Moses, even over them that had not sinned after the similitude of Adam's transgression. How the various views given above relate to this has already been observed. It is usually agreed that the "similitude" or the "likeness" of Adam's transgression refers to sinning in the face of a direct command of prohibition from God.

Those who adhere to views (1) and (3) would likely think that *most* did not sin in the face of a stated law during this time, although some did. Those who adhere to view (2) would say that *no* one from Adam to Moses sinned in the face of a direct command. The qualification "had not sinned after the similitude of Adam" referred to all from Adam to Moses.

The nature of view (4) would be such that an adherent could say that none sinned after the likeness of Adam's transgression in this period. Or he could say that some did, but most did not.

One interpretation of "them that had not sinned after the similitude of Adam's transgression" is that the reference is to infants. The death of infants is taken as a proof that Adam's sin was imputed since that would be viewed by them as the only explanation for the death of infants since death is a judgment of God (see Haldane 210). The reason for applying this to infants is that the law of the heart was a sufficient reason for the imputation of personal sins on the part of others. It will be observed that Haldane advocated view (1) above. This does not suggest that all who hold to view (1) would agree with Haldane on this point.

A Suggested Interpretation

Anyone who has read several commentaries on this passage knows that it does not submit to easy interpretation. The problem is twofold: (1) knowing exactly what Paul's purpose in the passage is, and (2) being able to show how the parts of the passage are used by Paul to accomplish his purpose.

Part of Paul's strategy in Romans, as has been seen, is to anticipate the problems that some of his readers may have. This is particularly true with reference to his Jewish readers. Most are of the opinion, as can be seen from the various views given above, that Paul is building a case for what he meant by "all have sinned," or "all sinned." However, there is no evidence that Jews would have had any difficulty in accepting the concept that all sinned in Adam.

If Paul had found it necessary to have put up a strong proof for the relationship of Adam's sin and the race, it would have defeated his purpose. Paul is here using an *a fortiori* argument. This argument moves from that which is more difficult to believe to that which is easier to believe. In this case the more difficult truth to believe is that Adam (one person) is the cause of sin and death for the whole human race. The easier truth to believe is that One (Jesus Christ) is the cause of justification and life for all who believe in Him. *Although believing that Adam's sin is imputed to all may be harder, Paul assumes that there would be agreement on that.* Otherwise to have introduced the relationship of Adam's sin to the race would have made Paul's purpose harder to achieve rather than easier.

Those of us who are far removed from the Jewish experience with the law do not run the same risk of misunderstanding what Paul said about the law that a first century Jew would have. Let us review what Paul has said about the law up to this point. The law pronounces the whole world guilty (3:19). "By the law is the knowledge of sin" (3:20). The God-provided righteousness is apart from personal law-keeping (3:21, 28). The promise that God made to Abraham and his seed is not received by law-keeping (4:13-15). "The law works wrath" (4:15).

It is obvious that Jewish audiences tended to misunderstand and distort what Paul said about law. They had been schooled (especially the Pharisees) into believing that "law" was supreme. It was as central in their thinking as Jesus Christ is in ours.

Their tendency toward misunderstanding could have led to a false view of "by one man sin entered into the world" (v.12). In light of what Paul had said about law, his "downgrading" of the law (as they would see it) might have caused them to think that the "one man" he meant was Moses.

If this was the case, it is easy to see why Paul would introduce observations about the time period from Adam to

Moses. It was his aim to show that there was both law and sin in the world long before God gave the law through Moses.

Taking this approach, the necessary inference of v. 13 is that law was in the world before the Mosaic Law. That is evidenced by the fact that God did impute sin (or view persons as guilty) prior to the Mosaic Law. The case of Cain, the flood, the Tower of Babel, etc., give every reason to know that God did hold people responsible for their sins.

In this view "them that sinned after the similitude of Adam's transgression" would refer to those who were not confronted with a direct command from God. This would be most but not all during this time period.

This view would be in keeping with the stress that Paul gives in chap. 2. The moral law is written in the moral constitution of every human being (2:14, 15). This moral revelation makes it so all people "know the judgment of God that they which commit such things are worthy of death" (1:32). If Rom. 1:18—3:20 tells us anything, it lets us know that there is no such thing as people who have reached the age of accountability whose sins are not imputed.

It is clear that "as many as have sinned without law shall also perish without law" (2:12).

The "one man through whom sin entered into the world" was Adam, not Moses. The advent of the Mosaic Law did not mark the beginning of the imputation of sin.

The nearest to my view that I have found is a quotation from Jonathan Edwards, "For *before* the law of Moses was given, mankind were all looked upon by the great Judge as sinners, by corruption, and guilt derived from Adam's violation of the original law of works; which shows that the original universal rule of righteousness is not the law of Moses; for if so, there would have been no sin imputed before that was given, because sin is not imputed where there is no law" (Jonathan Edwards, *Original Sin* 275. Wores. edit. quoted in Stuart 176).

Stuart was not in agreement with Edwards, but he did explain the implication of Edwards' view, as follows: "Thus the main design of the apostle is to show, that the Jews could not claim their law as the only criterion of right and wrong; and in order to do this, Paul shows that men were condemned on account of *imputed* sin, before the giving of the law" (176).

Who is the figure (Greek *tupos*) **of him** (Christ) **that was to come.** The word for figure is the Greek word from which we get our word "type." Paul is telling us that Adam was a type of Christ. Adam is the head of a fallen race. Christ is the head of a redeemed race.

It will be observed that in the KJV vv. 13-17 are in parentheses. This means that v. 12 and v. 18 go together as the translators saw it. The parentheses should only apply to vv. 13, 14. Paul took time to clear up a possible misunderstanding. Having finished, he now gets back on the subject introduced in v. 12.

We must keep in mind that v. 12 is the beginning of an attempt to show that it is easier to believe that Christ is the head of a redeemed race than it is to believe that Adam is the head of a fallen race. Paul has set forth the headship of Adam as it relates to sin and death. Now, as would be expected by the use of the word (*typos*) "type," Paul will develop the analogy between Adam and Christ.

2. That One could be the source of righteousness for many is more reasonable than that

one could be the source of condemnation for many (vv. 15-17).

15 But not as the offence, so also *is* the free gift. For if through the offence of one many be dead, much more the grace of God, and the gift by grace, *which is* by one man, Jesus Christ, hath abounded unto many.

But not as the offence, so also *is* the free gift. In the "Preliminary Observations" preceding v. 12, a case was built for taking this to be a question (see notes above). It would read: "But as the offence of one shall not the free gift also be so?" As a question, this leads naturally, as would be expected, to a comparison between Adam and Christ.

For if through the offence (Greek *paraptoma*) **of one many be dead.** "The Greek word means a 'falling beside' or deviation from the path, whether due to carelessness or willfulness. *Trespass* appears to be the nearest equivalent in modern English" (Earle 108).

It is quite clear that Paul is placing the blame for "many be dead" on the trespass or sin of one person—Adam.

Much more. These words indicate that Paul is going to present something that should be easier to believe than what he has just said.

The grace of God, and the gift by grace, *which is* by one man, Jesus Christ, hath abounded unto many. If a person can believe that one person could cause sin and death to be charged to the whole human race, it should certainly be easier to believe that One could be the Savior of many.

We have different problems in our day. We have more difficulty believing one could be the cause of sin and death for many than we do in believing that One could save many. That is because we have 2,000 years of church history behind us. We sing about the "Old, Old Story." It would be different if it were the "New, New Story."

16 And not as *it was* by one that sinned, so *is* the gift: for the judgment *was* by one to condemnation, but the free gift *is* of many offences unto justification.

And not as *it was* by one that sinned, so *is* the gift. Again, we treat this as a question, "But as by the offence of one, shall not the free gift be?" Again the stress is on analogy.

For the judgment *was* by one to condemnation. The "one" in light of the next part of the verse is "one offence."

But the free gift *is* of many offences unto justification. It took only one sin to condemn the whole race. However, since our own sins have been added, we need forgiveness for more than Adam's sin. Therefore, the justification that Christ provides covers not only Adam's sin, but ours also. As Hodge says, "Christ has done far more than remove the curse pronounced on us for the *one* sin of Adam; he procures our justification from our own innumerable offences" (167).

17 For if by one man's offence death reigned by one; much more they which receive abundance of grace and of the gift of righteousness shall reign in life by one, Jesus Christ.)

This verse picks up with the comparison that is suggested by the introductory question in v. 16.

It stresses more than the likeness between Adam and Christ as being the head of two races: (1) a fallen race and (2) a redeemed race. Stress is given to the generosity of God. There is an 'abundance of grace."

Concerning "shall reign in life by one," Vine comments: "The precise contrast to 'death reigned' would have been 'life shall reign,' but the contrast is far greater than this. It is not that life reigns instead of death, but that those who receive grace will themselves reign in life. That we are to reign in life involves much more than participation in eternal life; it indicates the activity of life in fellowship with Christ in his kingdom" *Romans* (82).

3. The conclusion stated (vv. 18, 19).

18 Therefore as by the offence of one *judgment came* upon all men to condemnation; even so by the righteousness of one *the free gift came* upon all men unto justification of life.

Therefore. What has preceded has formed the basis for a conclusion. It is evident that the conclusion stresses analogy between Christ and Adam. By taking verses 15 and 16 to be introduced by questions, the way is prepared for a conclusion that will deal with comparison rather than contrasts. It is obvious that there is a contrast in results, but that is too obvious to require proof.

As by the offence of one (Greek *henos paraptomatos*). This is understood by most to be "one offense" or "one trespass."

***Judgment came* upon all men to condemnation.** The "one trespass" is the cause of the fact that condemnation came upon all men. The one offense was the first sin of Adam.

Even so. These words stress the fact that there is a parallel between what precedes and what follows.

By the righteousness of one (Greek *henos dikaomatos*). Harrison explains:

> Over against Adam's act, Paul put another of an entirely different character—an act of righteousness. The same Greek word occurs at the end of v. 16, where it is rendered 'justification.' Perhaps 'act' is a bit narrow for this context. 'Work of righteousness' might be better. In fact, the whole scope of the ministry of our Lord could be in view (64).

It appears that what we have here is all that Jesus did to accomplish our justification. What the law requires is righteousness. The requirement of the law from us was: (1) absolute righteousness or obedience (2) or else eternal death. Since the law required this, the fulfillment of both on the part of Christ is called "righteousness." Or, to use the word in this verse, "a righteous act," or "a righteous work."

This "righteous work" is available for all men. When received it results in "justification of life."

The words "upon all men unto justification of life" must be understood as "all who are identified with Christ." The righteousness of Christ is effective for all who trust in Him.

19 For as by one man's disobedience many were made sinners, so by the obedience of one shall many be made righteous.

For as by one man's disobedience many were made sinners. This verse represents the final step in Paul's development of the analogy between Adam and Christ. Adam's disobedience was the disobedience of the race. The act of "one" was the act of "all." The use of the word "many" as distinguished from "all men" in v. 18 stresses the fact that "all" consisted of a very large number.

So. This word shows that there is a parallel in what Adam did and what Christ is doing for those who are properly related to Him.

By the obedience of one shall many be made righteous. If a person has carefully followed Paul's thought beginning in v. 12, he should no longer find it hard to believe that One could be the cause of salvation for such a great host of people. The details of our relationship to Christ differ drastically from our relationship to Adam. However, there is a common principle that is involved in the imputation of Adam's sin and the imputation of Christ's obedience.

We were in Adam when he sinned. Each of us is, now, a separate individual, but an unbroken continuity exists between us and Adam. We were not "in Christ" at that point in time when He died, but as believers we are now in union with Him. This union is what makes the imputation of His death and righteousness possible. In chap. 6 attention will be given to a development of our understanding of the union of Christ and the believer.

4. Grace has abounded more than sin (vv. 20, 21).

20 Moreover the law entered, that the offence might abound. But where sin abounded, grace did much more abound.

Moreover the law entered (Greek *pareiserchomai*) **that the offence might abound** (Greek *pleonazo*). In vv. 13, 14 Paul spoke about the time prior to law to make it clear that sin predated the law and that Adam, not Moses, was the one through whom sin entered into the world. Having completed the parallel between Christ and Adam, Paul now brings the subject of law into the picture again. This time he wanted to address the purpose of the law.

The meaning of the word translated "entered" is "enter along beside." The law came in along beside the offense. Vine gives the meaning of the word translated "abound" as "to superabound" (*Dictionary* 20). The law came into the picture so that sin could be seen for the monster that it is. The law brought the character of sin to light. (And as 7:5, 8 point out in some measure it actually increased the activity of sin. That will be discussed more when we come to chapter 7.)

But where sin abounded, grace did much more abound (Greek *huperperisseuo*). The Greek word for "more abound," according to Vine, means, "to abound exceedingly" *Dictionary* (20). Though the law showed sin for the ugly monster that it is, the grace of God was more than equal to the task. It is on this verse that the words, "Grace that is greater than all our sins" are based.

21 That as sin hath reigned unto death, even so might grace reign through righteousness unto eternal life by Jesus Christ our Lord.

That as sin hath reigned unto death. Sin will reign until it brings forth death. We need to keep this verse in mind as we deal with the believer's death to sin in the next chapter.

Even so might grace reign through righteousness unto eternal life by Jesus Christ our Lord. The foundation of grace is the God-provided righteousness. There are two spheres of life: (1) the sphere where sin reigns unto death, and (2) the sphere where righteousness reigns unto eternal life.

Summary 5:12-21

Paul had made it clear that the only way to be saved is through Jesus Christ. This, of course, meant that One person—Jesus Christ—is the sole basis for salvation. That meant that One person was the Savior of many. This, for some, would be a little hard to grasp.

In order to deal with the difficulty of believing that One could be the Savior of many, Paul decided to use an analogy. He showed that there is an interesting parallel between Adam and Christ. His readers would not likely have any trouble believing that the one sin of Adam plunged the whole race into sin and death.

To make it clear that sin and death did not originate with the Law of Moses, Paul called special attention to the period from Adam to Moses. The law of the heart was sufficient for God to hold people responsible for their sins.

Having finished the parenthetical material in vv. 13 and 14, Paul re-introduced the subject of the analogy between Adam and Christ. This he did by referring to Adam as a type of Christ.

Since there was common agreement about the relationship of the race to Adam's sin, Paul deals with that thought first. If we have no difficulty in believing that Adam, as one person, could be the cause of sin and death for the whole human race, surely it should be easier to believe that the atoning work of Christ, as one person, could avail for a large host of people who trust in Him. This being true, Paul drives home this truth that just as Adam was the cause of sin and death for the whole race, even so Christ is the cause of justification for all who believe in Him.

Having finished the analogy between Adam and Christ, Paul picks up the subject of law again. The purpose of the law was to bring sin out for what it really is. This would help people see more clearly their need of redemption.

Paul ends on the note that there are two spheres of life. The first is the one where sin reigns unto death. The other is the one in which, through Jesus Christ, righteousness reigns unto eternal life.

Application: Teaching and Preaching the Passage

1. The main point in this passage is not usually perceived. While Paul deals with our relationship with Adam's sin, that is not the main point here. Paul simply presents the fact that all sinned in Adam as an uncontested truth. What he is driving at is this: It is far more reasonable to believe that God would save many based on what one person (Christ) did than it was for Him to condemn many on the basis of what one person (Adam) did. That is the thrust of the "much mores" in vv. 15 and 17.

2. Though this passage has as its main thrust the reasonableness of the fact that Christ as one person can justify many, it is a fact that it is the most important passage in Scripture for helping us to understand our relationship to Adam's sin. A brief treatment of the main views on Adam's sin and the race has been given in the introductory comments on the passage.

Comments on the passage direct attention to the correct view and tell why. It is important to come to grips with these views and determine which is correct. Considerable time and effort are required to do so, but are necessary to be well-grounded in the faith.

3. A punctuation problem relating to vv. 15 and 16 is dealt with in the introductory comments on this passage. An understanding of this problem will

give a smoother flow to the passage, and will help to see what Paul is showing. That is: it is more reasonable to believe that God would save many by Christ than to condemn many by Adam (which He did).

4. In v. 20 Paul discussed one of the purposes of the Mosaic law. It entered that the offence might abound. The entrance of the law brought sin into a fuller manifestation of what it already was. This made it clearer just how bad sin was (see also 7:5, 8).

5. The unparallelled blessing is that sin was not outdone by God's grace (v. 20).

6. There are two spheres mentioned in v. 21, the sphere of sin and the sphere of grace. Death reigns in the sphere of sin. Those who remain in that sphere will experience eternal death. In the sphere of grace, because of the righteousness of Christ, the reigning is "unto eternal life by Jesus Christ our Lord." It is our opportunity and our responsibility to help lead people from the sphere of sin into the sphere of grace.

IV. GOD'S PROVISION OF A NEW LIFE FOR THOSE WHO RECEIVE THE GOD-PROVIDED RIGHTEOUSNESS (6:1—7:6).

A. The Person Who Has Received This God-provided Righteousness Died To Sin With Christ (6:1-14).

1. Paul denies that grace encourages sin (vv. 1, 2).

1 What shall we say then? Shall we continue in sin, that grace may abound?

What shall we say then? Paul has established the fact that when we believe in Jesus Christ as our Lord and Savior, we receive a God-provided righteousness. This righteousness is the only grounds for our justification—no more and no less.

Paul is saying, "Now that we have established the doctrine of justification by faith, what are the practical consequences of this view?"

Shall we continue (Greek *epimeno*) **in sin, that grace may abound?** The word suggests more than just continuing; it refers to "persisting" in sin. We have encountered this corruption of Paul's teaching earlier in Romans. Paul said that some slanderously reported that he taught, "Let us do evil, that good may come" (3:8).

The very presence of this question is an inference that some thought that grace encouraged sin. Why would anyone make such an inference? The answer is found in 5:20, in the immediate context, and, in the greater context, in Paul's teaching on justification. It is not difficult to see how from Paul's words, "Where sin abounded, grace did much more abound" (5:20) a person could gather (by distortion) that the way to receive an increase of grace would be to sin more.

The reason for Paul's raising this question was based on more than a distortion of 5:20 by some. A lot of careless statements have been made as a result of a shallow look at Paul's teaching on justification. Let us look at some of the statements Paul has made up to this point. "Being justified freely [without cost] by his grace" (3:24). "A man is justified by faith without the deeds of the law" (3:28). Chapter 4 teaches that justification is by faith apart from works (vv.1-8); apart from circumcision (vv. 9-12); and apart from law (vv. 13-25). The only basis for justification is the imputed death and righteousness of Christ.

Paul's teaching is very clear in support of the view that justification is apart from merit. If justification is absolutely apart from human merit, then some may wonder about just how strong a footing sanctification has.

The question raised in this verse could come from a number of sources. A sincere believer may think that it looks like grace could lead some people to be lax in their moral lives. Some may think that if we have both the death and the righteousness of Christ, we could get by with anything. The possibility of such erroneous thinking has led some to accept the governmental theory of atonement rather than the satisfaction theory (see notes on 3:26 and 4:5).

At the time Paul wrote Romans, the Pharisees would have had serious trouble with the teaching of grace. Some may have found it hard to really grasp the doctrine of grace. But others were vicious about the way they attacked the doctrine of grace. In writing this chapter Paul was preparing believers to be able to answer the questions that were hurled at them by the Jews.

> It was essential for the apostle to vindicate his doctrine not only from such objections as he knew would be made by the enemies of the cross of Christ, for whom he has an eye throughout the whole epistle, but also to Christians themselves, whom he was directly addressing (Haldane 238).

No doubt Haldane is correct in including both the enemies of the cross and Christians among those Paul had in mind rather than limiting it to Judaizers as Tholuck does (175), or to Christians as Lenski does (387). (Much of what I will say on this subject is adapted from my own unpublished thesis, *A Study Of Paul's Teaching On The Believer's Death To Sin And Its Relationship To A New Life*, submitted in partial fulfillment of the requirements for the Master of Arts degree, Winona Lake School of Theology, 1959.)

2 God forbid. How shall we, that are dead to sin, live any longer therein?

God forbid. (See comments on "God forbid" in the notes on 3:4.) Paul emphatically denies that his teachings on grace encourage sinning. Paul will show that the relationship between justification and sanctification is such that the antinomian (the teaching that grace delivers the Christian from moral concern) charge cannot possibly be true.

In trying to avoid antinomianism, it is easy to be tempted to change the teaching about justification. Another temptation is to so define saving faith that it disallows antinomianism. Surely, we must avoid that which gives license to sin, but we must not corrupt the doctrine of grace to do so.

How shall we, that are dead (Greek *apethanomen*) **to sin, live any longer therein?** The words "are dead" translate an aorist indicative. We have had occasion before to look at the use of the aorist indicative (1:21-32; 2:12; 3:23; and 5:12).

The KJV in translating "dead to sin" is treating the aorist as a culminative aorist. More often the culminative aorist is translated with "have." Whether it be translated "dead to sin" or "have died to sin" the stress of the culminative aorist is on results. The present experience of "dead to sin" would be based on the fact that the believer "died to sin." The aorist is more frequently treated as a simple past tense when it is translated into English. A careful examination of the passage reveals that "died to sin" is the proper meaning in this context.

There is no question that Paul is dealing with sanctification in chapter 6. The question is: How does he approach sanctification? It is obvious that "died to sin" has some relationship to sanctification.

Is Paul saying that the believer died "ethically" to sin, or "penally" to sin? The majority understand the believer's death to sin to be an ethical death. There are several variations of the ethical view. The fact that they all have in common is that the believer has in some way died to sinning. Or it could be said that he experiences a deadness to sin.

Another way the death to sin has been understood is that the believer has died penally to sin with Christ. This is the view being set forth. At the end of the comments on v. 11, the ethical views will then be presented. It will be easier to follow this way.

It should be obvious that those who hold the governmental view of atonement would reject the penal view. This is true because they do not believe that the death of Christ was a penal death (see the presentation of the governmental view in connection with the comments on 3:26 and 4:5).

It is obvious that to reject the penal view of the death of Christ will mean to reject the penal view of "died to sin" in Rom. 6. On the other hand, a person may believe in the penal death of Christ and not believe that the penal death is in view in Rom. 6.

A few more observations need to be made about the governmental view of atonement. While some Calvinists have believed in the governmental view, it has had more acceptance among Arminians. The reason for the acceptance of the governmental view by some Arminians grew out of the fact that they did not know how to develop a sound emphasis on sanctification consistent with the satisfaction view. (In the following discussion, as the different problems arise, it will be shown that *no point of Calvinism is an essential corollary of the satisfaction view of atonement.)*

Let us now return to the meaning of "died to sin." It must be the same kind of death which Jesus experienced. It is Christ's death which we are baptized into (v. 3). "We have been planted together in the likeness of his death" (v. 5). Our death is like His death (vv. 10,11).

I agree with Moule:

> It appears then that *our* 'death to sin' (in Christ) must be explained by what *His* death to it was. And His was a death such as to free Him not from its *impulses* (for He was essentially free from them) but from its *claim,* its *penalty,* endured for us by Him. His death *once over,* the claim of sin was cancelled. Therefore, for those who 'died in Him,' it was cancelled likewise. The phrase thus has, in the strict sense of it, not a moral, but a legal reference (*Cambridge Bible,* 112).

It is quite clear that no matter what "died to sin" means, it has something to do with not living any longer in sin. As we move through the passage, this connection will be seen.

2. Identification with Christ in His death opens the way for the entrance of God's sanctifying grace (vv. 3-10).

3 Know ye not, that so many of us as were baptized into Jesus Christ were baptized into his death?

Paul will explain in this verse *how* the believer died to sin. He is reminding his readers that when they were baptized into Jesus Christ, they were baptized into *His death.*

The question which comes to mind is, "What kind of baptism does Paul have in mind?" Is the reference to water baptism? Or is it the baptism by the Holy Spirit into the body of Christ (1 Cor. 12:13)?

I think all would agree that when we think of baptism, water baptism comes to mind, even if a decision is made against it. Unless there is a strong reason to think otherwise, we should conclude that Paul has water baptism in mind.

To understand what Paul is saying, we must look at baptism as a metonymy. In this case baptism is spoken of as if it actually placed us into Jesus Christ. I doubt anybody seriously believes that water baptism, itself, places a person "into Jesus Christ" in the technical sense. It baptizes a person into Jesus Christ figuratively. No matter what a person's view is of baptism, he cannot fully explain his view without making reference to the symbolism of baptism.

> In saying that baptism is a metonymy in this passage, we are saying that the wording credits baptism with what actually belongs to the thing symbolized. Water baptism does not baptize a person into Christ. It only symbolizes baptism into Christ. It is baptism by the Holy Spirit (1 Cor. 12:13) that baptizes into Christ. In this baptism we are united to Christ. In this union, His death becomes our death (Forlines, *Systematics*, 157).

While the passage does not actually use the words "the imputation of the death of Christ," it is probably the most important passage in the N.T. in developing an understanding of what is involved in imputing something from one person to another.

The substitutionary work of Christ is not substitution pure and simple. If that were the case, if Christ died for everybody, everybody would be saved. It takes more than saying Christ died *for* me. I must be able to say, "I died with Christ." Or God must be able to say for me, "He died in Christ."

The following line of reasoning has been used against the satisfaction view.

> There are two types of punishments meted out by the judicial system—pecuniary punishment and penal punishment. Pecuniary punishment is the punishment that takes the form of a fine. It is possible for a substitute to pay a fine for a person. Penal punishment involves a punishment of the person. The person goes to jail, to prison, or is put to death. In our judicial system there is no substitution in the area of penal punishment. The punishment of sin is not pecuniary, but penal. Therefore, it is argued that there can be no substitutions for us.
>
> This objection does bring up a valid point. Substitution pure and simple whereby one person does something for or in the place of another would be invalid in atonement.
>
> The answer to this objection is found in the union with Christ and the believer. . . .By indentification with Christ the believer can say, 'I died with Christ.' *The action can be considered to be his, not simply an action that was performed for him.*
>
> In our judicial system, we cannot have penal substitution because there is no way it can be said that a person went to jail without actually going. In Christ, we can say we died with Him without actually going through this experience. Therefore, penal substitution is possible (Forlines,

Systematics, 169).

Identification by union makes that which was not actually a part of a person's experience his by identification. For example, prior to the time that Hawaii became a part of the United States, a citizen of Hawaii could not have said, 'We celebrate our day of Independence on July 4.' Immediately upon their becoming a state, the same person who formerly could not make the statement could say, 'We celebrate our day of Independence on July 4.' What happened on July 4, 1776, became a part of their history. The history of the United States became the history of Hawaii, and the history of Hawaii became the history of the United States.

Prior to the union with Christ on the condition of faith, a person could not say, 'I died with Christ.' Immediately, upon union with Christ a person can say, 'I died with Christ.' The history of the cross become his history, not in the actual sense, but by identification so that he received full credit for that death. At the same time, the history of our sins became Jesus' history, not in the same sense that His character was affected, but so that they would come in contact with the penalty He had already paid for them. He took the responsibility for them, but it was a responsibility that He had already assumed on the cross (Forlines, *Systematics*, 159, 160).

In speaking about the union between Christ and the believer, Shedd explains:

> Upon this spirited union, rests the federal and legal union between Christ and his people. Because they are spiritually, vitally, eternally, and mystically one with him, his merit is imputable to them, and their demerit is imputable to him. The imputation of Christ's righteousness supposes a union with him. It could not be imputed to an unbeliever, because he is not united with Christ by faith (*Dogmatics*, II:534).

In commenting on the expression "baptized into Jesus Christ," Morrison explains:

> The phrase is a Pauline idiom, but it simply denotes inward union with Christ, effected through inward baptism. That is the Apostle's idea. He is thinking of such union as qualifies believers of the gospel for affirming, *we died to sin; we died, namely, in Christ, in order that we might die to sin* (4).

Chalmers also has some helpful comments. He observes:

> We get into this condition, not by actually suffering the death; but, as it is expressed in the third verse by being baptized unto the death of Christ, and so in the fourth verse by being buried with Him in this baptism, and in the fifth verse planted together with him in the likeness of His death—all indicative of our being forensically dealt with on account of Christ's death just as if we ourselves had undergone the sufferings which for us He endured (154).

It should be made clear that a number of commentators believe that Jesus' death was a penal death without believing that Paul is speaking of a penal death here. If a person takes the "death to sin" to be an ethical death that does not mean that he does not necessarily believe in the satisfaction view of atonement.

Having studied the imputation of Adam's sin to the race in 5:12-19, and having looked at the imputation of the death of Christ to the believer, we can see a bottom line principle as it relates to imputation. *There is no imputation of either merit or demerit from one person to another unless it can in some valid sense be said to be the action of that person.*

This was accomplished in the sin of Adam because the race was in him. So it can be said that the race sinned in Adam.

We were not in Christ when He died on the Cross. However, as believers, we are now in Christ because we have been baptized into Christ by the Holy Spirit (1 Cor. 12:13). Being in Christ indentifies us with the history of the Cross. It is for this reason that Paul could say, "I am [or I have been] crucified with Christ" (Gal. 2:20). As we move through Rom. 6 we will see this same thought in vv. 6 and 8.

The principle of identification by union does more than make imputation possible. *It makes it necessary.* The nature of the case made it necessary for Adam's sin to be imputed to the race because when Adam sinned the race sinned.

Once a person is in union with Christ, the nature of the case makes it so the death of Christ is his death. We could also say the same thing about Christ's righteousness. *We cannot be in union with Christ without having the death and righteousness of Christ placed on our account.* This is true because the union with Christ makes it so we can say, "I died with Christ. I fulfilled the requirements of the law in Christ." *As long as a person is "in Christ" the nature of the case means that he is justified.*

4 Therefore we are buried with him by baptism into death: that like as Christ was raised up from the dead by the glory of the Father, even so we also should walk in newness of life.

Therefore. By *therefore,* Paul is saying that what follows in v. 4 is a logical result of what he had said in v. 3. **We are** [were] **buried with him by baptism into death.** There seems to be wide agreement that we are not to understand Paul to say, "We were buried into his death." Rather, the meaning is "By baptism into death, we were buried with him." (See David Brown 225; Cranfield 304; Hodge 194; Murray 215, 216; and Vine, *Romans,* 88.)

In this verse Paul develops the symbolic meaning of baptism. It symbolizes: (1) the death, burial, and resurrection of Christ, (2) our baptism into Christ by the Holy Spirit, and (3) our identification with the death, burial, and resurrection of Christ. It should be obvious that immersion symbolizes these truths better than any other mode of baptism.

The inclusion of burial is to emphasize the concept of death. Also, it sets the stage in our thinking for resurrection to enter the picture.

That like as Christ was raised up from the dead by the glory (Greek *doxa*) **of the Father.** On the use of the word "glory" Vincent says, "The glorious collective perfection of God. . . . Here the element of power is emphasized, which is closely related to the idea of divine glory" (696).

Even so we also should walk in newness (Greek *kainotes*) **of life.** The word refers to the newness of quality.

Jesus Christ was raised from the dead in triumphant power over sin. The power of sin and Satan could not keep Him in the Tomb. Paul is saying that just as Christ was raised in triumphant power over sin, we also should live in truimphant power over sin. Or, to put it another way, we should manifest a new life-style in our walk.

5 For if we have been planted together in the likeness of his death, we shall be also *in the likeness* of *his* resurrection.

For if we have been planted together (Greek *sumphutos*) **in the likeness of his death.** "Planted together" is a horticultural term. Morrison explains, "The expression *sumphutoi gegonamen* in v. 5, *we have become grown together,* makes it evident that the apostle is thinking of the vital union that subsists between Christians and Christ" (7).

Conybeare and Howson give the translation, "For if *we have been grafted* into the likeness of his death." In a footnote they explain, "Literally, *have become partakers of a vital union* [as that of a graft with the tree into which it is grafted] *of the representation of his death [in baptism]" (511, note 5).*

If there was a question in anyone's mind about whether v. 3 speaks of a union between Christ and the believer, the use of this word "planted together" should settle the question. Also, it should be clear that this union forms the basis for the believer to have "the likeness of Christ's death."

When Paul speaks of the likeness of Christ's death, he is making a distinction between actually dying with Christ by experiencing the agonies and sufferings of the Cross, and dying with Him by identification. The believer did not experience the wrath of God for his sins with Christ at the time of the crucifixion. Yet, by identification with Christ the believer can own the death of Christ as his very own.

The believer's death with Christ by identification is the *likeness* of Christ's death because it has all the power to free the believer from condemnation of sin that it did for Christ when He uttered the words, "It is finished" (Jn. 19:30). It is different because the believer did not experience that death in any sense of actuality.

We shall be also *in the likeness of his* resurrection. When put into practice, the likeness of Christ's resurrection is manifest by walking in the newness of life referred to in v. 4.

The relationship between justification and sanctification is now taking shape. The "likeness of Christ's death" is *justification.* The likeness of His resurrection is *sanctification.*

It is important for us to observe that Paul is saying *"If we have been justified, we will also be sanctified."* Just as Christ's death makes our justification possible, His resurrection makes our sanctification possible.

Why does Paul (in essence) say, "If we have been justified, we shall be sanctified?" A few observations need to be made: (1) Sanctification is dependent upon justification, not the reverse. (2) While justification and sanctification are distinct, they cannot be separated. It is impossible to have one without the other. (3) It is inconceivable that God would make holiness an optional accessory in salvation. If His holiness would accept nothing less from Christ than paying the full penalty of the law for our justification, surely He will pursue His interest in holiness with us after we are justified. (4) Justification opens the way for the entrance of God's sanctifying grace.

A person cannot partake of the likeness of Christ's resurrection if he does not partake of the likeness of His death. This is true because unresolved guilt blocks the entrance of God's sanctifying grace. As Haldane states:

> So long as the sinner is under the guilt of sin God can have no friendly intercourse with him; for what communion hath light with darkness? But Christ having

cancelled his people's guilt, having redeemed them from the curse of the law, and invested them with the robe of his righteousness, there is no longer any obstacle to their communion with God, or any barrier to the free ingress of sanctifying grace (248, 249).

6 Knowing this, that our old man is crucified with *him,* that the body of sin might be destroyed, that henceforth we should not serve sin.

Knowing this. This verse will explain why being united in the likeness of Christ's death will contribute to newness of life. Or another way of putting it is that v. 6 explains why what Paul said about newness of life in v. 5 is true.

That our old man is [was] **crucified with *him.*** It is easy to misinterpret this verse by failing to keep the context in mind. The crucifixion of "the old man" with Christ must refer to the penal crucifixion of the old man. This is true not only based on the preceding verses, but also v. 7. As we shall see when we look at verse 7, the word "freed" should be "justified." This being true the crucifixion of the old man with Christ results in justification.

What makes it easy to misunderstand is that Paul is talking about sanctification along with justification. If we do not properly distinguish justification from sanctification, in this passage, it is easy to conclude that "the old man" is "the sinful nature." When this is done in one way or another, it is said that the sinful nature was crucified with Christ. Further discussion about the view that the old man is the sinful nature will be delayed until views different from mine are treated.

"The old man" is the pre-salvation self or person. Paul is saying that when we were baptized into Christ, His penal death became our death. In Christ the person we were, was crucified. The penal death was inflicted upon us.

When one becomes a Christian, he is a new person. That being true what he was prior to conversion is now viewed as "the old man." We do not exist as two concurrent people—the old and the new. Rather, we are now new persons. The conflict we have going on within us is not properly termed as a conflict between the old man and the new man (see Murray 219, 220).

That the body of sin might be destroyed (Greek *katargeo*).

Concerning the "body of sin" Vincent explains: "The phrase *body of sin* denotes the body belonging to, or ruled by, the power of sin, in which the members are instruments of unrighteousness (ver. 13). Not the body as containing the principle of evil in our humanity, since Paul does not regard sin as inherent in, and inseparable from the body. . ." (697).

Harrison says that the body of sin "seems to mean body insofar as it may become the vehicle of sin" (70).

The word "destroyed" according to Alford means "annulled as far as regards activity and energy is concerned" (368). Perhaps a good way to say it is, "That the body may be put out of commission so far as being a vehicle for sin is concerned."

That henceforth we should not serve (Greek *douleuo*) **sin.** The word translated "henceforth...not" (Greek *meketi*) means "no longer." Since this part of the verse tells us what we are "no longer" to be, it is obvious that what we are "no longer" to be is what we "once were." "Serve" refers to being under dominion of or in slavery to sin.

The meaning is this. Prior to our union with Christ our bodies were instruments of sin. We were in bondage to sin. When we were united with Christ

His penal death, which He suffered for our sins, became our death. In this our old man (the pre-salvation self) was crucified with Christ so that His death became for us our penal death. The purpose in all of this is that our bodies would cease serving as slaves to sin.

7 For he that is dead is freed from sin.

For he that is dead [died] **is freed** (Greek *dikaioo*) **from sin.** Out of 39 other N.T. occurrences of the verb translated "is freed," it is translated "justify" 37 times, once as "be righteous," and once as "justifier."

Unless there is a very strong reason for doing otherwise, the translation in v. 7 should be "has been justified (perfect passive in Greek)." In the view I am presenting we need not look for another way to translate it. In fact, it fits beautifully into Paul's line of thought to translate, "has been justified."

The only reason for choosing "freed" as is done in the KJV, NASB, NIV, and others would be that justified would not fit the context. In my judgment, the only reason that anyone feels that "justified" does not fit the context is that he has not carefully followed the way Paul reveals the relationship between justification and sanctification. Such an interpreter does this because he considers the "death to sin" in this passage to be an ethical death rather than a penal death. In other words he considers "death to sin" to deal directly with sanctification. Instead, he should consider the death to sin to form the basis for justification, and then show its relationship to sanctification.

The movement of thought beginning with v. 5 is: If we have been justified (united together in the likeness of Christ's death), we will also be sanctified (in the likeness of his resurrection).

The reason for justification contributing to sanctification is that our pre-salvation self was crucified with Christ. The crucifixion with Christ was designed not just to form the basis of our justification. It was designed to help put the body out of commission as an instrument of sin so we would quit being slaves to sin.

The reason that it worked that way was that our old man (the pre-salvation self) was crucified with Christ. Having died penally with Christ he has been justified from sin.

Now the question is how could dying penally to sin with Christ make it so that the body as an instrument of sin would be put out of commission so we would no longer live under sin's dominion?

In 5:21 Paul said "sin reigned unto death." The ultimate end of the reign of sin is death. Until death there is nothing to check the power of sin over the individual; but after a person by faith becomes united with Christ in His death, he is released from the area of sin's dominion. When sin brings death, it has done all it can do. Its power and claims are broken. The believer is delivered into a new sphere "that as sin reigned unto death, even so might grace reign through righteousness unto eternal life by Jesus Christ our Lord" (5:21)

Since the believer is delivered into the sphere of grace where the power of sin is broken, the latter part of v. 6, which says that "we should not serve sin," is possible.

No doubt Paul had vv. 6 and 7 in mind when he said, "For sin shall not have dominion over you: for ye are not under the law but under grace" (6:14).

8 Now if we be dead with Christ, we believe that we shall also live with him.

The meaning of this verse can easily be seen in the light of the previous verses. "If we died with Christ [justification], we believe that we will also live with Him [sanctification]." Also, in the light of the next verse, to live with Christ means to live forever.

9 Knowing that Christ being raised from the dead dieth no more; death hath no more dominion over him.

Knowing. The meaning is "because we know." What follows in this verse will tell why we will live with Christ forever. We will live with Him forever because He will live forever. In His first coming, death exercised dominion over Christ. It is true that Christ entered voluntarily into death. On the other hand, once our sins were laid on Him, He was obligated to die. Death did have dominion over Him.

Once Jesus died and thus completed paying the penalty for sin, He can never again be called on to die. For that reason, to live with Christ is to live eternally. It follows, then, that as long as we are in Christ the second death (Rev. 21:8) will have no dominion over us.

A word of explanation is needed here to show why it is possible, in the light of all this, for a person to make shipwreck of his faith, or to put it another way, commit apostasy. Since the death of Christ was an actual death, there is nothing that can ever change that fact. So He cannot possibly be made to die again.

Our death, however, is ours by identification with Christ. It will remain ours as long as we are in union with Christ. We will remain in union with Christ as long as we have saving faith. If a Christian should cease to be a believer and become an unbeliever, he will no longer be meeting the condition of faith. In that case he will be taken out of Christ (Jn. 15:2). This being true he will no longer have the death of Christ as his because he will no longer be in union with Christ. More could be said about this, but space will not permit it. (For a development of this view on perseverance, see my *Systematics* 199-230.)

10 For in that he died, he died unto sin once: but in that he liveth, he liveth unto God.

For in that he died, he died unto sin once. I can see no possibility that Christ's death can be viewed, in its essential nature, as being other than a penal death. In fact, it is for this reason that it cannot be repeated again. Once the penalty is paid, He cannot be required to pay it again. The fact that He cannot be called on to die again is made clear both in v. 9 and in this verse. Commenting on the word for "once" (Greek *ephapax*), Cranfield says, "Once for all, an altogether decisive and unrepeatable event" (314).

The believer's death to sin has been clearly identified with the penal death that Christ paid. It will be seen in v. 11 that the believer's death to sin is the same kind as the death that Christ died. If this is true, the believer's death to sin is a penal death.

But in that he liveth, he liveth unto God. The life that Jesus now lives is a "Godward" life. Therefore, the life which we live with Him is to be a Godward life.

3. The believer is called upon to keep in mind the fact that he is dead to sin and alive unto God in Christ (v. 11).

11 Likewise reckon ye also yourselves to be dead indeed unto sin, but alive unto God

through Jesus Christ our Lord.

Likewise (Greek *houtos*). The meaning is "in the same way." **Reckon** (Greek *logizomai*) **ye also yourselves to be dead** (Greek *nekros*) **indeed unto sin.** Concerning "reckon," Moule says, "This word, just as in 3:28 (E.V., 'conclude'), marks a solid inference from facts" (116).

In the other references to the believer's death to sin, it was suggested that it should be translated "died." The case is different in this verse. Here we have an adjective meaning "dead."

We are to consider ourselves to be dead to sin in the same way Christ died to sin. His death was a penal death. We are dead to sin because we paid the penal death in Christ.

But alive unto God through (Greek *en*) **Jesus Christ our Lord.** "Through" should be translated "in." Paul is saying that the foundation of the believer's death to sin and being alive unto God is the union we have with Christ. (See comments on vv. 3 and 5.)

The word in the Greek for "reckon" or "conclude" is a present infinitive. This means that the action is linear. Linear action will come out if we give the meaning as follows: "Keep reckoning on the fact that you are penally dead to sin and that you are alive to God."

Paul is saying, "Keep on thinking about these matters." If we keep thinking about what Christ has done for us, that will contribute to our living a life of victory over sin.

To this point in the passage, we have seen two ways in which the believer's penal death to sin with Christ contributes to a new life: (1) The penal death applied in justification opens the way for the entrance of God's sanctifying grace (see v. 5). (2) The penal death to sin breaks the power of sin (see v. 7).

A third way it contributes to living a new life is by its contribution toward assurance of salvation. A person struggling with lack of assurance may use so much energy dealing with that problem that he does not have strength left to fight with sin. Few things contribute as much to assurance of salvation as thinking about the fact that our union with Christ means that His penal death is ours. We can see that what God demanded from us, Christ paid for us and that in Him it is ours.

A fourth way that it helps us is this: when we understand better what God has done for us, the love of God constrains us. Paul confirms this fact when he says, "For the love of Christ constraineth us" (2 Cor. 5:14). For the believer to take account of the love of Christ will have a continuous constraining and transforming effect on his life.

Other Views on 6:2-11

These views have one thing in common: They all consider the believer's death to sin to be an ethical death as distinguished from the penal view which has been presented. There are 5 varieties of interpretation among those who believe the ethical view.

(1) *This view could be called "death by profession."* Stuart (207) says,"How shall we who have renounced sin, and profess to be insensible to its influence any more continue to practice it or be influenced by it?"

Such a view does not adequately deal with dying with Christ to sin in the various verses from 6:2-11. See the discussion above.

(2) *This view understands the meaning to be dead to sin by identification with Christ in His death "unto" sin.*

The key word is "unto." Death *"for* sins" is understood to refer to the aspect of Christ's death upon which our justification is based. The death of Christ *"unto* sin" has to do with the death to the sin principle.

Newell explains, "Let us distinguish at once between being justified from *sins*—from the guilt thereof—by the blood of Christ, and being justified from *sin*—the thing itself" (216).

Coltman supports the same view when he says, "Faith takes Christ for sinfulness as well as for sins" (122).

It will be observed that Newell and Coltman make a difference in "sin" as singular and "sins" as plural. Sins (plural) are paid for by the atoning (or penal) death of Christ. *Sin* in the singular is considered to be a reference to the sin *principle.*

Newell does not say that the believer is thus dead to sin in *experience* but in his position by identification with Christ. Just as we exercise faith in Christ for the forgiveness of our sins, we are to also exercise faith to believe that we died to the sin principle by being identified with Christ in His death "unto sin" (meaning the sin principle).

An examination of Paul's use of the singular and the plural of "sin" will not support the distinction made by Newell. The only place in Romans where the plural for sin occurs (other than in a quotation from the O.T.) is 7:5. The reference there is to motions (or passions) of sin. It is obvious that to fit Newell's thinking the use in 7:5 should have been singular rather than plural.

The view held by Wuest is similar to that of Newell. He takes the meaning to be that Jesus died with respect to our sinful nature. This death becomes ours by identification with Christ. (See "Victory Over Indwelling Sin," *Bibliotheca Sacra*, CXVI January, 1959, and *Word Studies (Romans)* 90-108.)

(3) *Death as a result of the realization of Christ's Death on the Cross.*

Godet explains, "He could not appropriate Christ to himself as dead *for* his sin without finding himself die, through this death undergone for him *to* sin itself" (237).

Godet's position seems to be summed up thus: In view of man's sin and Christ's love in dying on the cross, the believer cannot help but die to sin.

While it is agreed that such a realization of Christ's death on the cross would certainly have a bearing on one's relationship to sin, yet such cannot properly be considered as an interpretation of the believer's death to sin in Rom. 6. This view overlooks the fact that the believer's death to sin is a death *with Christ.*

(4) *Death as a matter of reckoning one's self to be dead to sin.*

Erdman says concerning reckoning ourselves dead to sin, "So we regard ourselves. We are not to imagine, however, for a moment that in reality such a death has taken place. Our evil passions and dispositions are still active and powerful. We must, however, disown their rule" (72).

The essence of this view is that the believer is not dead to sin, but if he regards himself to be so, he may reap the practical results as if he were dead.

Shedd's comments size the situation up well. He says:

> The notion of reckoning, or imputing, is congruous with dying for sin and justification, but incongruous with dying to sin and sanctification. Believers can 'reckon' or 'account' themselves to have died fully and completely *for* sin, in and with Christ; but they cannot 'reckon' or 'account' themselves to have died fully and completely *to* sin. They may regard themselves to be completely justified, but not completely sanctified (157).

The point of the whole matter is: Would God expect me to think that something is true which is in fact not true?

(5) *Death by a sanctifying act of God subsequent to conversion.*

This is the view set forth by Hills when he says, "But we *experimentally* die to sin as an actual act when sanctifying grace destroys the abnormal proclivity to sin, and we become dead to the enticements of sin" (30).

One of the first rules of hermeneutics is that a passage of Scripture must be interpreted in the light of its context. When the context in which the believer's death to sin is studied, we find it denying the charge that justification by faith apart from human merit encourages sin (vv. 1 and 2). In order for Paul to accomplish his purpose it would be necessary for him to deal with that which is true of all justified persons. Should he deal with a select group of Christians only, he would actually forsake the purpose of the passage.

The only way that Paul could successfully deny the charge that grace encourages sin would be for the words, "We who died to sin" (v. 2) to refer to all justified people. In view of Paul's purpose, the view of death by a sanctifying act of God subsequent to conversion cannot be what Paul is teaching in Rom. 6.

Each view examined would have other points of difference on how the passage is to be interpreted. Probably, the most significant difference is what is meant by "dying with Christ"?

Newell and Wuest believe that the death to sin is ours by being identified with Christ. Where they differ with my view is in saying that the death to sin is an ethical one rather than penal.

However, some others deny that there is anything taught here about death by identification with Christ whether ethical or penal. The concept of "dying with Christ" is simply dying to sin "like" Christ died to sin. It is only a matter of analogy. Godet says, "Jesus does not communicate to us His death itself; we possess only its likeness in our death to sin" (243).

It is clear that the relationship between Christ and the believer as it relates to sin is only an analogy in Stuart's view. He comments: "The simple sentiment is as before, viz. that 'as Christ died and rose again, so the Christian (in a moral sense) dies and rises again; as Christ lives a new life, so does he...'Christ died once and for all, and so the Christian must die once and for all to sin, i.e., he can no more resume the practice of it (217).

One of the reasons Godet and Stuart take the approach they do is that they subscribe to the governmental view of atonement. This would account for their not interpreting the passage as referring to a death to sin by identification with Christ (see 3:26 and 4:5 for a discussion on the governmental view of atonement).

4. The believer is challenged to be separated from sin and dedicated to God (vv. 12-14).

12 Let not sin therefore reign in your mortal body, that ye should obey it in the lusts thereof.

Paul has shown that not only does his view of grace not encourage sin; it actually forms the basis for living a changed life. Paul is challenging them to refuse to allow sin to reign in their body which is subject to death. This is something that is possible. One of the greatest sources of help in this victorious march is to keep in mind and reflect upon the truth that we are dead to sin and alive unto God in union with Christ.

13 Neither yield ye your members as instruments of

unrighteousness unto sin: but yield yourselves unto God, as those that are alive from the dead, and your members as instruments of righteousness unto God.

Neither yield ye your members [hands, feet, eyes, ears, etc.] ***as* instruments** (Greek *hoplon)* **of unrighteousness unto sin.** This is an extension of what Paul was speaking about in v. 12. The word "instruments" is also translated "tools" or "weapons."

Some are of the opinion that since the Greek word for "yield" is a present imperative that the meaning is "stop yielding." Such is not the case here, however. If the words were spoken to someone who was yielding himself to sin, that would be the case. However, we have no reason to believe that the Roman Christians were in the habit of yielding themselves to sin. The meaning is, "Do not be yielding your members as tools, etc."

But yield yourselves unto God, as those that are alive from the dead. The appeal is made on the basis of the fact that through Christ they have been made alive. The appreciation of this fact is the basis of Paul's appeal to them. In this part of the verse, Paul is moving from the negative challenge as we see in v. 12 and the first part of v. 13.

And your members *as* instruments of righteousness unto God. Paul did not stop at challenging the people to forsake sin. He told them what they should do.

14 For sin shall not have dominion over you: for ye are not under the law, but under grace.

For sin shall not have dominion over you. The reference here is to the believer that the power of sin is broken. It is not said that a Christian will not commit some acts of sin. It is saying that he will not be under the domination of sin.

For ye are not under the law, but under grace. Paul is suggesting that it is a gross misunderstanding of grace to say that it encourages sin. The fact is that the reverse is true. Grace contributes to holy living. The power of sin is broken by grace. Under grace the believer has already died penally to sin—thus breaking its power (see v. 7).

B. The Person Who Has Received This God-provided Righteousness Has Been Changed From a Servant of Sin to a Servant of Righteousness (6:15-23).

1. Grace is not an encouragement to sin because one's obedience determines to whom he belongs (vv. 15,16).

15 What then? shall we sin, because we are not under the law, but under grace? God forbid.

The question here is similar to the question raised in v. 1. By this time the reader should have been able to see through the false charge that Paul's teaching on grace encourages sin. However, Paul raised the question again so he could repudiate such a charge from another angle.

16 Know ye not, that to whom ye yield yourselves servants to obey, his servants ye are to whom ye obey; whether of sin unto death, or of obedience unto righteousness?

This is a very important verse as it relates to putting down the charge that grace encourages sin. There are some essential fruits of sanctification. In the life of a Christian, sanctification may not always be in good health, but it cannot be non-existent.

The question is, "Whom do you obey, sin or righteousness?" You are the servant (or slave) of the one whom you obey. If you obey sin, you belong to sin and sin leads to death. If you obey righteousness, you belong to the sphere of righteousness and can expect the benefits that come from being in the sphere of righteousness.

What Paul says here is in no way in contradiction to the doctrine of grace. The manifestation of the fruits of sanctification in no way contributes to justification. However, we are not to suppose that God will give justification without giving sanctification. If a person is sanctified, there will be at least some indication of that in the way he deals with sin.

2. The believer has become a servant of righteousness (vv. 17,18).

17 But God be thanked, that ye were the servants of sin, but ye have obeyed from the heart that form of doctrine which was delivered you.

Having pointed out that the servants of sin belong to sin and the servants of righteousness belong to righteousness, Paul then calls attention to the fact that there was a time when the readers were servants of sin. He is thankful that, though at one time they were servants of sin, such is not the case now. The change came when they obeyed from the heart the gospel which was presented to them (on the word "heart" see comments on 1:21).

In the light of the words, "Ye have obeyed from the heart that form of doctrine which was delivered you," Paul would have thought it quite strange if someone had said, "I don't believe in a set of doctrines. I believe in a person." I do not think it ever dawned on Paul that a person could have believed in Christ without believing the truth about Christ as it is revealed in the N.T.

18 Being then made free from sin, ye became the servants of righteousness.

Being then made free (Greek *eleutheroo*) **from sin.** Commenting on "freed" in 6:7, it was pointed out that the proper meaning of the Greek word used there was "justified." The word which is here translated "made free" properly means "to set free." The believer has been set free from being a servant (or slave) of sin.

Ye became the servants of righteousness. Paul is saying that at the moment they were freed from being slaves of sin, they became slaves to righteousness.

3. The believer is challenged to serve the new master as diligently as he served the old master (vv. 19-23).

19 I speak after the manner of men because of the infirmity of your flesh: for as ye have yielded your members servants to uncleanness and to iniquity unto iniquity; even so now yield your members servants to righteousness unto holiness.

I speak after the manner of men because of the infirmity of your flesh.

Moule comments: "He apologizes so to speak, for using the peculiarly earthly image of the slave-market to enforce a truth of the most exalted spiritual dignity; namely, the necessary conformity of the will of the justified to the will of God" (120).

The reason for Paul having to speak as he did was "because of the infirmity of your flesh." This made it necessary for Paul to resort to a clear, but crude illustration.

For as ye yielded your members servants to uncleanness and to iniquity unto iniquity. Paul is telling the people that when they were servants (or slaves) to sin they went all out for sin. They served well.

Even so now yield your members servants to righteousness unto holiness. Paul is saying to them, "Just as you used to diligently serve the old master (sin), even so, now give all diligence to serving the new master (righteousness)."

20 For when ye were the servants of sin, ye were free from righteousness.

Paul reminds the people that they so fully and effectively served sin that they were in fact "free from righteousness."

21 What fruit had ye then in those things whereof ye are now ashamed? for the end of those things *is* death.

Taking a further look at their former service to sin, Paul is asking, "What did you get out of it?" or "What pay did it offer?" The pay was "death." They served well that which had nothing to offer in the long run but death.

22 But now being made free from sin, and become servants to God, ye have your fruit unto holiness, and the end everlasting life.

Paul now points out how different it is to serve God. The fruit leads to holiness and the end will be everlasting life. What a contrast between the fruit for serving sin and the fruit for serving God!

23 For the wages of sin *is* death, but the gift of God *is* eternal life through Jesus Christ our Lord.

Paul now puts it all together. Sin pays the horrible wage of death. God gives eternal life through (or in union with) Jesus Christ our Lord. The death referred to here must embrace the "second death" referred to in Rev. 21:8.

Paul's point is that by all reasoning we should serve God and righteousness well. We served sin well with only death to look forward to. Surely with the gift of eternal life to look forward to we should certainly serve God with no less zeal than we did sin.

C. The Person Who Has Received This God-provided Righteousness Has Been Delivered From Subjection To The Law To Subjection To Christ (7:1-6).

1. Paul illustrates the fact that the dominion of the law is ended by death (vv. 1-3).

1 Know ye not, brethren, (for I speak to them that know the law,) how that the law hath dominion over a man as long as he liveth?

Know ye not, brethren, (for I speak to them that know the law). In the Greek a particle (*e*) occurs before "know." On occasions translators leave it untranslated. If we translate the particle, it would read "Or know ye not." In this case "or" would connect the thought of this verse with that which precedes it.

Conybeare and Howson translate it and show its connection with the preceding passage thus: "[I say that you are not under the law]; or are you ignorant, brethren. . .?" (513). "Or" connects this passage with the fact that Paul taught that Christians are not under law in 6:14,15.

There seems to be little doubt that Paul has the Mosaic Law in mind. Both the Jewish and Gentile elements in the church at Rome would have had an adequate acquaintance with the Mosaic Law to have understood what Paul was saying. It is true that up to a point a person could understand Paul's observation by comparing it with civil law. But when Paul becomes more specific in vv. 2 and 3, the focus is on the Mosaic Law.

How that the law hath dominion over a man (Greek *anthropos*) **as long as he liveth?** The word translated "man" refers to a member of the human race whether male or female. The words for "male" and "female" will be seen in vv. 2 and 3. Paul's point is that the Mosaic Law was binding during a person's lifetime.

2 For the woman which hath an husband is bound by the law to *her* husband so long as he liveth; but if the husband be dead, she is loosed from the law of *her* husband.

For the woman (Greek *gune*) **which hath an husband is bound by the law to *her* husband** (Greek *aner*) **so long as he liveth.**

"Woman" can refer to a female whether married or unmarried. Where the context indicates that the woman in view is married, it is translated "wife."

The word translated "husband" can refer to a male whether married or unmarried. The context decides whether it is translated "man" or "husband."

The word translated "which hath an husband" (Greek *hupandros*) is a compound (*hupo* plus *aner*) that literally means "under a husband." The words, "The woman which hath an husband" are, literally, "the under (or subject to) a man woman."

The reason we need to get this clear is because we need to understand this in order to see the application Paul is making in vv. 3-6.

But if the husband be dead, she is loosed from the law of *her* husband. When her husband dies she is legally free from her husband.

3 So then if, while *her* husband liveth, she be married to another man, she shall be called an adulteress: but if her husband be dead, she is free from that law; so that she is no adulteress, though she be married to another man.

So then if, while *her* husband liveth, she be married to another man, she shall be called (Greek *chrematizo*) **an adulteress.** This is a strong, deliberate word. A modern equivalent would be, "She will be labeled as an adulteress."

The words, "she be married to another man" is literally, "she be to another man." The concept of the word used in v. 2 is the thought implied here. As we just saw, it means to be under or subject to a man. Paul is saying that if a woman, while her husband is living, submits to another man, she will be labeled an adulteress.

But if her husband be dead, she is free from that law; so that she is no adulteress, though she be married [or subject] **to another man.** Once her husband dies she is no longer subject by the law to him. She can now be subject to another man and not be an adulteress.

Paul used vv. 1-3 to develop an illustration to help us understand vv. 4-6. These verses also illustrate an important rule of interpretation. That rule is: "It is possible to state a rule that may have a rare exception without stating that exception." In this case, the rule was that under the Mosaic Law if a woman married another man before the death of her former husband she would be labeled an adulteress.

Without getting involved in why this was possible, and what is now possible, it is apparent that Dt. 24:1, 2 would imply that there were some cases where divorce and remarriage were permitted under the Mosaic Law. In such cases the woman would not be labeled an adulteress. Paul is not denying the possibility, under the Mosaic Law, for divorce and remarriage without the wife being guilty of adultery. He is simply stating the rule without stating the exception. It should be obvious in the light of Dt. 24:1, 2 that Paul would not deny that an exception existed.

If we will remember that in Scripture sometimes a general rule that has an exception may be stated without the exception, we can deal with some problems without having to resort to a forced harmony.

2. The believer died to the law through the body of Christ (v. 4a).

4 Wherefore, my brethren, ye also are become dead to the law by the body of Christ....

Wherefore. What preceded was developed as an illustration. What follows in vv. 4-6 will be an application of the illustration.

My brethren, ye also are become dead to the law by the body of Christ. In chapter 6 this death is referred to as "death to sin." It was a penal death paying the penalty for sin. In this verse the same penal death viewed from a different angle is viewed as "death to the law." The death which we died in Christ paid the penalty required by the law.

The word "become dead" (Greek *thanatoo*) refers (in the Greek passive form, as here) to being put to death. Hodge says:

> The form of expression is probably used because the death of Christ, in which we died, was an act of violence. He was put to death, and we in him. To be slain to the law, means to be freed from the law by death. Death, indeed, not our own, but ours vicariously, as we were crucified in Christ, who died on the cross in our behalf, and in our stead (216).

Concerning put to death "by the body of Christ," there are different viewpoints, but most views can be put in two categories: (1) those who think the reference is to "the body of Christ" being put to death for us on the cross and (2) those who take the reference to be to the mystical union with the body of Christ. (For presentations of the different views see Lange 220, 221 and Plumer 312, 313.)

Yeager says:

> Paul is applying the analogy of the marriage code. The believer in his unregenerate days was married to the law and thus bound by it. But we died when Christ died (Gal. 2:20) because we had been 'baptized by the Holy Spirit into the body of Christ' (1 Cor. 12:13) and thus we were associated with Him (2 Peter 2:24). We are thus free from any further obligation to the law, because in Christ, we paid the penalty (483).

Some of what Yeager says sounds like he is saying that the believer had already been baptized into Christ so that he was in Christ when Christ died (see above quotation and p. 450). Instead of being in Christ when He was crucified, I believe we were placed into a union with Christ when we first believed. Thus we became identified with Him, and the history of His crucifixion became our history.

3. The believer is now subject to Christ, not the law (v. 4b).

4 ...that ye should be married to another, *even* to him who is raised from the dead, that we should bring forth fruit unto God.

That ye should be married. The word "married" in this case is implied, but not stated, in the Greek. The Greek would be translated literally "That ye should be to another." For the meaning of this, we go back to v. 2. The key word (*hupandros*) means "subject to a husband." With this in mind, the words "that ye should be to another" mean that ye should be subject to another.

Verse 4 is not referring to marriage as a *union* between husband and wife. There is no denying that this union exists, but it is not what Paul has in mind here. He views marriage here as a relationship in which the wife is *subject* to her husband.

Paul is saying that there was a time when we were subject to the law. When we died with Christ, we were put to death so far as the law is concerned. That death ended our subjection to the law.

To be subject to the law meant to be under the condemnation of the law. Depravity being what it is meant we could not meet the requirements of the law. This meant that we were under the dominion of sin. We were under the penalty of the law.

When we died to the law through the body of Christ, we were no longer under the dominion of the law. This made it possible to be subject to someone else.

***Even* to him who is raised from the dead.** Our new "husband" (by the analogy) is Christ. We are now subject to Him.

That we should bring forth fruit unto God. When we were under subjection to the law, that relationship as we have seen was not conducive to bearing fruit for God. Now that we are subject to Christ, as we saw in chapter 6, there are a number of things that we have going for us which will help us bear fruit for God.

To think that grace would encourage sin is to grossly misunderstand it. The fact is that grace makes possible a new life in which we are aided and encouraged to bear fruit for God.

4. Deliverance from subjection to the law contributes to a new life (vv. 5, 6).

5 For when we were in the flesh, the motions of sins, which were by the law, did work in our members to bring forth fruit unto death.

For when we were in the flesh (Greek *sarx*). Concerning this word, Harrison's observations are helpful:

> Paul has used 'flesh' in several senses thus far: (1) the humanity of Jesus Christ (1:3); (2) the physical body (2:28); (3) mankind—'all flesh' (3:20); and (4) moral, or possibly intellectual weakness (6:19). Now he adds a fifth: The so-called 'ethical' meaning of flesh, which is the most common use of the word in his writings and denotes the old sinful nature (77).

Murray's thoughts are also helpful.

He explains:

> 'Flesh' in this ethically depreciatory sense means 'human nature as controlled and directed by sin.' It is not because the word 'flesh' itself denotes what is bad or connotes badness. It is often used without any evil reflection or association. . . .The frequency with which the word is used of our Lord is sufficient to show that 'flesh' is not intrinsically evil. . . .It is when 'flesh' is used in an ethical sense that it takes on this sinful quality. 'Flesh' when used in this sense has no good or even neutral associations; it is unqualifiedly evil. Hence when Paul speaks of having been 'in the flesh' he is referring to that period when sin exercised the dominion and is equivalent to saying 'When we were in sin' (244, 245).

The question arises, How did the word "flesh" come to be synonymous with that within us which causes us to be prone toward sin? It is obvious from what Harrison and Murray say that flesh *as flesh* is not sinful.

Here is a possible explanation. While they are not sinful, in and of themselves, the desires that come from the physical body can be fulfilled in a way that would involve sin. The means that we use to fulfill them may be sinful. Or the *time* that we fulfill them may be sinful.

Christian ethics, both in deciding what is right and in doing what is right, requires the context of eternity and, for this life, the long-range. Battling against the eternal and the long-range is the principle of immediacy. When we are engaged in a struggle between the eternal and the immediate, we are involved in an ethical conflict. Sin will be on the side of immediacy.

One of the strongest powers that sin has over us is the power of immediacy. For example, the fulfillment of the sexual desire in marriage is proper (Heb. 13:4). But the power of immediacy frequently draws people into a sexual experience outside of marriage.

If we reflect on the fact that a lot of sins involve the fulfillment of physical desires, we can see why flesh is used as a synonym for the sinful nature. When this is put in the context of the eternal or long-range versus the immediate, we can see that physical desires out of control give rise to moral defeats.

When ethics is deeply rooted in the eternal and the long-range, the body will be an instrument of righteousness. When ethics is rooted and grounded in the principle of immediacy, the body will be an instrument of sin.

It is quite clear that, by "when we were in the flesh" Paul was referring to the time before conversion (see also 8:8, 9).

The motions (Greek *pathemata*) **of sins, which were by the law, did work in our members to bring forth fruit unto death.** The word translated "motions" means passions. The law instead of helping the person under it to live right tended to aggravate or stir up the sinful passions. In such cases, instead of curbing sin, the law stirred some into more sinning (see v. 8). In so doing the law made a negative contribution. Indirectly, it made a contribution to our bringing forth fruit for death.

6 But now we are delivered from the law, that being dead wherein we were held; that we should serve in newness of spirit, and not *in* the oldness of the letter.

But now we are delivered (*katargeo*) **from the law.** The word for delivered is the same as was used in v. 2, translated "loosed." In v. 2 it speaks of the woman's freedom from the law, as it relates to her husband, after the death of the husband. In this verse the reference is to the deliverance from the law as experienced by believers.

There are two ways in which we, as believers, are delivered from the law: (1) We are delivered from the law as a slave-guardian (Greek *paidagogos*). (2) We are delivered from the penalty of the law.

In Gal. 3:19—4:7 Paul points out that O.T. believers were under the law as a slave-guardian (*paidagogos*). In wealthy Greek and Roman homes, the young boy from the age of 5 or 6 to the age of 16 or 17 was placed under such a person. He (the *paidagogos*) was a trusted slave who would go with the young boy to protect him and to help instill in him the family values. When the young boy reached the appropriate level of maturity at about 16 or 17, he was released from subjection to the slave-guardian.

O.T. believers were under the law as a slave-guardian. The word (*paidagogos*) by its etymology means "a child-leader." This meant that those under it were viewed as children. When Paul spoke in Gal. 3:24 of the O. T. believers as being under the law as a "child leader" (*paidagogos*), he meant that those under the law were viewed as children. This was the experience of O.T. believers.

When Paul said of N.T. believers, in Gal. 3:25b, "We are no longer under a schoolmaster [Greek *paidagogos*]," he meant that we have been delivered from the law as a child-leader. This means that O.T. believers were viewed as children. We are viewed as adults. (For a more thorough study see "Legalism In The Book of Galatians" by F. Leroy Forlines in *Dimension* winter Quarter 1984, 85, Vol. 1, No. 3.)

The second way we are delivered from the law views the law as that which sets forth a moral standard and pronounces a penalty upon those who violate this standard. In this sense all unbelievers are under the law. All believers have been delivered from the law as that which pronounces a penalty upon disobedience. By God's grace we have been delivered from the penalty of the law because in Christ we have already paid this penalty.

The deliverance from the law of which Paul speaks in the verse before us is the deliverance from the law as that which pronounces a penalty upon disobedience. A proper grasp of this deliverance from the law delivers us from *soteriological* legalism (the concept which bases salvation on works).

The deliverance from the law as the child-leader (*paidagogos*) is not dealt with in chap. 7. This kind of deliverance from the law is dealt with in Gal. 3:19—4:7. This delivers us from *ethical* legalism. This kind of legalism in its thorough form seeks to explain every ethical decision in terms of a law.

The most thorough form of ethical legalism is that which was practiced by the Pharisees. Through their oral law (or the tradition of the elders) they far exceeded the ethical legalism of the Mosaic Law.

That being dead wherein we were held. In this translation, it is the law which is said to have died. Hodge explains:

> If *apothanontos* [being dead], found in the common text [*Textus Receptus*], is the true reading, (*that having died*,) then it is by the death. . .of the law that we are thus freed, even as the woman is freed by the death of her husband. But if, as all modern editors agree, *apothanontes* (*we having died*) is the true reading, then it is by our own vicarious death in Christ, our having died with him whose death is a satisfaction of the law, that we are thus delivered. This is in

accordance with ver. 4, where it is said *we* died to the law (219).

There seems to be very broad acceptance of "we having died" (*apothanontes*) as the proper reading. The death which delivered us from the law, as that which pronounces a penalty on sin, is the death which *we* died in Christ to the penalty of the law (v. 4). This view does raise a question. In the illustration (vv. 2, 3), it was the husband who died. It was his death that freed the wife to marry someone else. What we have here in the application is that *we died rather than the law.* This need not bother us. The point of the illustration is that death ends the jurisdiction of a relationship. Our death to the law freed us from the law and introduced us to a new relationship. This new relationship to Christ prepares the way for a life which will be pleasing to God.

That we should serve in newness of spirit, and not *in* the oldness of the letter. "Newness" (Greek *kainotes,* from *kainos)* means new in quality. "Oldness (Greek *palaiotes*, from *palaios*) refers to "'that which is old in point of use, worn out, useless'" (Wuest 117).

Many are of the opinion that we should understand the word "spirit" to be a reference to the Holy Spirit (Cranfield 339, 340; Harrison 77; Hendriksen 218; and Murray 246). Others are of the opinion that the human spirit is in focus (Godet 269; Lenski 455; Shedd 177; and Vine, *Dictionary* 793).

It is my opinion that the "newness of spirit" refers to the renewed human spirit. The only other occurrence of the word "newness" is in 6:4 where the reference is to "newness of life." While this does not mean that it must refer to the newness of the human spirit, it does suggest that it would be appropriate to regard "newness of the spirit" as meaning the human spirit. Shedd says that it "denotes, here, not the Holy Spirit, which is never a 'new' spirit, but the human spirit enlightened, enlivened, and actuated by the divine: a new spirit in man, compared with the previous one" (177).

It seems that the reference is to the renewed spirit of the believer. The renewal would, of course, have been accomplished through regeneration by the Holy Spirit.

Summary
6:1—7:6

Up to this point the basic thrust of what Paul has said has been to establish the fact that God had met our needs which grew out of our failure to be able to fully keep the law. God met these needs by the death and righteousness of Jesus Christ. Nothing less could meet our needs. Nothing else could bring justification. This justification is ours on the sole condition of faith.

Many people, in the days of the early church, misunderstood Paul's teaching. They claimed that it encouraged sinning. Some of these people were probably, for a time, honestly confused. This would have cleared up as they gained a better understanding. Others were hardened in their hearts and vicious in their attacks.

Paul realized that regardless of why some people misunderstood, it was necessary for him to make it unquestionably clear that grace did not encourage sinning. In answering the charge that grace encourages sin Paul developed three lines of thought.

In the first line of thought (6:1-17) he pointed out that the believer died to sin in Christ. This death to sin broke the power of sin (6:6, 7, and 14). Also, this death to sin in Christ opened the way for the entrance of God's sanctifying grace. Paul insists that if we are justified, we will also be sanctified.

As the believer meditates on the fact that he has died with Christ, he will see these things that God has done for him in his death to sin with Christ. It will take on more meaning as time passes on. One of the benefits will be that he will have a strong assurance of his own personal salvation. This will release his energies to be engaged in a victorious battle over sin.

The second line of thought is, though there was a time when the believer was a servant of sin, he is now a servant of righteousness (6:15-23). By the very nature of the case, grace cannot possibly encourage sinning. The fact is that if you serve sin, you belong to sin and the end will be death. Those who serve righteousness belong to God and righteousness.

Paul pointed out to the Roman Christians that when they were servants of sin, they went all out for sin. They served sin well for a poor paycheck—death. They should now serve God with the same diligence that they once served sin. Surely, they should see the reason for this. They served sin well when it was leading them down the pathway of death and destruction. Surely, that which offered them the fruit of holiness and the end everlasting life, deserved their full commitment.

The third line of thought is that at one time, the believer (before he became a believer) was subject to the law as his master. When the law was his master, it gave no assistance to live by its standard; now that Christ is the believer's master things are different. He has been renewed by the Holy Spirit. God is working in the heart of the believer to help him internalize truth. He need not be bogged down with needless emphasis on details. The more truth is written in the heart, the more natural it will be for the life to be fruitful unto God.

Application: Teaching and Preaching the Passage

1. It is important to see that Paul is dealing with three lines of thought in building his case for the fact that those who have received the God-provided righteousness will live a new life:

(1) The fact that the believer died to sin with Christ contributes to a new life (6:1-14).

(2) The believer is no longer a servant of sin; he is a servant of righteousness (6:15-23).

(3) The believer no longer has the law as his master. Christ is his master (7:1-6).

2. The believer died to sin (death as the penalty to sin) in Jesus Christ (6:3-8). The way the union of Christ makes the death of Christ ours is one of the most blessed truths of the Bible. This truth should be studied until it becomes clear and takes on meaning (see comments on these verses).

3. Dying to sin with Chist forms the basis of our justification. We are told in v. 5 that if we are justified we will be sanctified (note also v. 8). Dying to sin with Christ removes the obstacle of guilt. It opened the way for the entrance of God's sanctifying grace which is working in us to transform us into the likeness of Jesus Christ. It is very important that we not fall prey to the idea which is prevalent among many that a person can be justified without being sanctified. The terminology that is frequently used to express this thought is that a person can receive Jesus as Savior without receiving Him as Lord. Such is not the case as I have shown in comments on this passage. (See also the following observations.)

4. The old man, which is the pre-salvation self, has paid the penalty to sin in Christ. The aim of this is that we should not serve sin (v. 6).

5. Jesus Christ has already paid the

penalty for sin once. He can never be placed on the cross again for our sins (vv. 9, 10). As long as we are in union with Christ we are as safe from the wrath of God as He is. His paid penalty is our paid penalty. We remain in Christ as long as we continue in saving faith.

6. If we keep thinking about the fact that we have paid the penalty to sin in Christ and that we are alive unto God in Christ it will have a transforming effect on our lives.

7. There is a guarantee that salvation changes a person (2 Cor. 5:17 and Eph. 2:10). However, this change is not absolute. Therefore, it leaves room for a challenge to move and conquer sin in our lives (vv. 12, 13).

8. Paul makes clear that "sin shall not have dominion" over those who are under grace (v. 14).

9. Paul makes it unquestionably clear that if a person serves sin he belongs to "sin unto death." If a person belongs to God and righteusness, he will serve God and righteousness (v. 16).

10. Paul reminds the people that when they were servants of sin they served sin well. He appeals to them to serve righteousness now with the same zeal that they once served sin (vv. 19, 20).

11. Paul makes a value appeal to the people. The payoff of sin was death—something of negative value. The rewards of being on God's side and serving God are holiness and everlasting life—things of positive value (vv. 21-23).

We must keep reminding people that true value is on the side of Christian values. Righteousness is not only right, but good. "Godliness is profitable unto all things, having promise of the life that now is, and of that which is to come" (1 Tim. 4:8). Living by Christian values contributes to self-respect and a deep sense of personal satisfaction. It fits in with what God has designed us to be.

12. The basic thrust of 7:1-6 is that when we died with Christ to sin we also died to the law. Being dead to the law freed us from being subject to the law as our master, so we could be subject to Christ as our master. The design of this change of masters from the law to Christ is "that we should bring forth fruit unto God" (v. 4). The law held up an ideal, but did not offer help in reaching that ideal. With Christ as our master, we are renewed and we receive help in meeting this ideal.

V. A REJECTION OF THE IDEA THAT DELIVERANCE FROM THE LAW THROUGH A GOD-PROVIDED RIGHTEOUSNESS IMPLIES THAT THE LAW IS SINFUL (7:7-25).

Preliminary Observations

It could be safely said that this passage has been the occasion of more controversy than any other in Romans. The major points of concern are: (1) Is the passage autobiographical? (2) Is Paul speaking about an unregenerate person, or a regenerate person? Or does he speak of the unregenerate in vv. 7-13, and the regenerate in vv. 14-25? (For reviews of the history of the interpretation of this passage, see Hodge 239, 240; Lange 227, 228; Meyer 266, 267; Olshausen 237; and Tholuck 211.)

As it relates to whether the passage is autobiographical, many people never consider whether it could be otherwise since it is written in the first person. However, most who face the question recognize a problem.

Why would anyone question whether it is autobiographical? Many question whether the account in 7:7-25 can be harmonized with what Paul says about himself elsewhere. For example, in Acts 23:1b he says, "I have lived in all good conscience before God until this day." Again he says, "And herein do I exercise myself, to have always a conscience void of offence toward God, and *toward* men" (Acts 24:16). In describing his life before his conversion, he says, "Concerning zeal, persecuting the church; touching the righteousness which is in the law, blameless" (Phil. 3:6). Looking back on his days when he was a persecutor of the church, he says, "Who was before a blasphemer, and a persecutor, and injurious: but I obtained mercy, because I did it ignorantly in unbelief" (1 Tim. 1:13). This was not the way he viewed it when he did it. He viewed it, at that time, as right and proper. Now he understands that he could view it that way, then, only because of his ignorance in unbelief.

It can be pointed out that he says in 1 Tim. 1:15b, "That Christ Jesus came into the world to save sinners: of whom I am chief." This is Paul's estimate looking back. It was not his estimate at the time. While Phil. 3:6 and 1 Tim. 1:13 deal with Paul's life before he was converted, Acts 23:1 and 24:16 cover his whole life up to the time he made the statements.

The use of the first person suggests that the passage should be interpreted as autobiographical if other factors permit it. However, we do not have to assume that in every instance the first person is used, it automatically means the person is speaking about himself. In Rom. 3:7 Paul uses the first person. The vast majority of commentators do not believe that he was speaking about himself.

Harrison observes:

> It is difficult to decide. The first person ('I') was occasionally used in antiquity as a rhetorical device for expressing something applicable to others. It was so used somewhat by Rabbis (W. G. Kummel, *Romer 7 und die Bekehrung des Paulus* [Leipzig: J. C. Hinrich, 1929], pp. 128-131). That Paul could think and write in this fashion is apparent from Romans 3:7 (83).

When application is made of the truth learned from the law in vv. 14-24, the description is of one who is defeated. The person in these verses is not one who is living "in good conscience before God" as was the case with Paul in Acts 23:1. (See also Acts 24:16.)

I am not suggesting that Paul knew nothing of conflict. Every Christian, and at least to some extent every sinner, knows something about a gap between what he is and what he knows he ought to be. The question before us is not the mere fact of a conflict created by this gap. It is a question of the degree of guilt and defeat the person is or has been experiencing.

There are basically three approaches that are taken on whether the passage is autobiographical: (1) That it is autobiographical in a more or less strict sense of the word. (2) That it is autobiographical only in the sense that it is depicting things that Paul would have in common with others. (3) That Paul in establishing rapport with the person so described. In these passages he feels that identification which he manifests by saying "I."

Godet, whose work on Romans first appeared in 1879, lists Hofman and Pearsall Smith as the only ones which he knew that "restrict the application of the passage to the apostle's own person" (271). Bruce takes the passage to be autobiographical. Then he says, "Paul, of course, did not think of his own experience as being unique; he describes it here because it is true in a greater or lesser degree of the human race" (148). See also Lenski (475).

Olhausen is an example of the second view. He says, "Hence it can only be said that the Apostle is certainly speaking of himself, but simply according to the experience he had in common with mankind, not acccording to his own individually" (236). There would be several variations of this view. Is Paul talking about the human race generally? Is he refering to the Jews under the law? Or is it someone else?

The principle involved in the third view was involved in the view held by the Greek fathers according to Tholuck (214) and Lange (226). Tholuck in describing their view says, "Paul transfers to himself the state of others" (214). He states that this is similar to the word (Greek *metaschematismos*) which is translated "I have in a figure transfered to myself and Apollos" (1 Cor. 4:6).

This is the view which I accept. For reasons already given, I see no way that this passage could be given as an account of Paul's experience. Paul, by rapport, felt a very strong identification with what he was saying. But not all the details could be documented as occurring in his experience.

There is not a great deal of difference between my view and the second. It may be more of a difference in the way each is said, than an essential difference.

We are still left with the question, with whom does Paul identify himself in this passage? In view of the purpose of the passage, it would be a person under the law being led by the law to Christ. The particular interest in the context would apply to a Jew though the principles would apply wherever they fit.

The account is given in an ideal form and order. For that reason Paul begins with the time he was without law. The commandment came. He saw that he was under the sentence of death. He saw that he was in bondage to sin. He cried out for deliverance.

The question always arises: When was Paul without the law (v. 9)? If Paul is giving an autobiographical account, that is a valid question. Most would admit that it is hard to answer.

If the account is not autobiographical, it is not necessary that an answer be given. In giving a logical development of the ministry of the law, a person would illustrate how it would be without law. This would be necessary to show the difference that the law made once it had come. If an answer has to be given, the tendency in a Jewish context would be to say before the giving of the Mosaic Law.

It is not a matter of crucial importance what position a person takes on whether or not the passage is autobiographical. (For those who would like to investigate this question further, see Bruce 148; Cranfield 342-347; Godet 271; Harrison 83, 84; Lange 226; Olshausen 236; and Sanday and Headlam 186.)

There are basically four views concerning the question of whether this passage deals with the regenerate or unregenerate.

Prior to the controversy between Augustine and Pelagius, the prevailing view was that the passage referred to the unregenerate. This was the view of Augustine before the controversy with Pelagius began. At some point along the way, Augustine changed his view. He then took the whole passage to refer to the regenerate (*A Treatise Against Two Letters of The Pelagians*, Book I, Chapters 14-24).

In the commentaries checked, only three others were found who take the position that the entire passage refers to the regenerate. These are Luther, Calvin, and Newell. Some may question whether this is the position of Calvin. Lange lists Calvin among those who believe the whole passage deals with the regenerate. Calvin is more explicit about it being the regenerate when he gets to vv. 14, 15. It seems to me too that this is Calvin's view, but it is not made as obvious that vv. 7-13 refer to the regenerate as it is in vv. 14, 15.

Among the adherents of the view that the whole passage deals with the unregenerate are: Arminius, Black, Clarke, Coneybeare and Howson, Denny, Timothy Dwight (Supplementary notes in *Meyer's Commentary*) Godet, Greathouse, Meyer, Robertson, Sanday and Headlam, Stuart, Tholuck, and Williams.

A person's view of this passage does not determine whether he is an Arminian or a Calvinist. It is of interest that the first point of conflict that later separated Arminius from Calvinism was his study of this passage. Regardless of what a person thinks about the conclusion of Arminius, anyone reading the treatment by him would have to agree that he had a sharp and penetrating mind (see *The Writings of James Arminius*, II:221-452).

The third view is a modification of the second. According to this view, the reference is to an unregenerate but awakened person. This would be a person who has allowed himself to be informed by the law. The Holy Spirit would be working in his life through the law bringing him under conviction and preparing his heart and mind for a readiness to receive Christ as Lord and Savior.

It would be this type person in particular that Paul has in mind. The distinctive feature about this view is that there is the feeling that since Paul uses the present tense, he understands that this same type of conflict would continue to occur in the believer (Lange 227, 228; Philip Schaff 228, and Olshausen 238, 239).

The fourth view understands vv. 7-13 to refer to the unregenerate, and vv. 14-25 to refer to the regenerate. Among the adherents to this view are: Alford, Barnes, David Brown, Bruce, Cranfield, Haldane, Hendriksen, Hodge, Lenski, Murray, Picirilli, Plumer, Shedd, and Yeager. Some of these may differ concerning the exact point at which the passage divides.

I view the passage from the standpoint that Paul is defending the fact that the law is good. He does that by illustrating how the law, when it succeeds, works in the heart and mind of one who is unregenerate to lead him to see his need of Jesus Christ. I understand that this illustrates the way the Holy Spirit uses the law to help a person see his need of Christ. That should go without saying, but Paul did not mention the ministry of the Holy Spirit in the passage.

The passage is not addressing the experience of every unregenerate person at all times. Paul is telling what could apply to every unregenerate person if he should let the Holy Spirit use the law to show him his need of Christ. It is assumed that what has been set forth would refer to the unregenerate person who has been awakened.

I am in essential agreement with what Arminius said about the person under consideration. He explains: "But we are not, in this place, treating about all the unregenerate in general, but only about those in whom the law has exerted all its efficacy, and who are, on this account, reciprocally said to be under the law" (II:229).

I agree with Lange, Olshausen, and Schaff in saying that the believer can and does experience *conflict*. I do not believe, however, that it is the common experience of believers to experience the degree of *defeat* set forth in the passage.

In the sense that wherever a principle fits it can apply I could agree that a believer can in some measure identify with the principle of conflict in the passage. That, however, grows out of the universality of principles rather than that Paul meant to address believers as well as unbelievers.

I am of the opinion that the words unregenerate and regenerate are not well-chosen for studying this passage. The reason is that the traditional view of Calvinism is that regeneration precedes faith. Packer says, "Many seventeenth century Reformed Theologians equated regeneration with effectual calling and conversion with regeneration. . .later Reformed Theology has defined regeneration more narrowly, as the implanting of the 'seed' from which faith and repentance spring (1 John 3:9) in the course of effectual calling" ("Regeneration" in *Evangelical Dictionary of Theology* 925).

The order in salvation in the Calvinistic viewpoint is as follows: regeneration, saving faith, and justification. So we can ask the question, Does the Calvinist (or Reformed) theologian, when referring to Rom. 7:7-25, mean the regenerate person before he becomes a believer or after he becomes a believer? He could mean either or both. Probably he means after he becomes a believer, but it can be seen that the Calvinist should make it clear what he means. It is somewhat ambiguous.

The terms "believer" and "unbeliever" would probably be more accurate terms than "regenerate" and "unregenerate." However, the terms "regenerate" and "unregenerate" have become so embedded in the discussions of this passage that it would be hopeless to try to change the terminology now.

A brief observation follows on the Calvinistic view of regeneration. All agree that regeneration is an act of sanctification. If this is granted, they have a person who has at least some degree of sanctification before he is justified. It seems that this puts a Calvinist in an awkward position. I think that a Calvinist would agree with my position that God cannot move in with His sanctifying grace until our guilt problem is solved by justifying grace. Maybe they do not agree.

I appreciate the diligent labor of those who understand 7:7-25 differently than I do. Differences of opinion, on this passage, so far as I am concerned, are not a reason for a break of fellowship. I will be forthright in my criticism of differing views. I expect others to do the same with my view.

A. The Law Reveals the Nature of Sin (7:7-13).

1. A problem is raised with regard to the law (v. 7).

7 What shall we say then? *Is* the law sin? God forbid. Nay, I had not known sin, but by the law: for I had not known lust, except the law had said, Thou shalt not covet.

What shall we say then? *Is* the law sin? We have already observed that Paul makes a special use of questions in Romans. Paul is aware that people can misunderstand what he is saying. Whether Paul is aware of the possible misunderstanding of what he says because he can anticipate the questions that his readers would have, or whether it is because he has faced such questions in the past, is not important. What we need to understand is the logic behind the question.

Why would Paul raise the question, "Is the law sin?" Because the emphasis up to this point is on what the law cannot do. The law cannot justify (3:20). The law works wrath (4:15). The law tended to make sin abound (5:20). To be out from under the law was supposed to be a plus factor so far as righteous living is concerned (6:14 and 7:6). The law stirred the passions of sins in us into activity (7:5).

We need to keep reminding ourselves how important the law was to the Jewish people of that day, especially in Phariseeism. Law to them was supreme. Even a converted Jew would have difficulty understanding the removal of law from the center of the picture. It is not hard at all to see why a Jew would raise the question, and why he would need an answer.

God forbid. [See notes on 3:4]. **Nay, I had not known sin but by the law.** It should be obvious that what follows is to be a defense of the good of the law. The statements about the law being good in vv. 12, 13, and 16 stress the fact that the law is good.

We can rightly expect that what follows will be giving a positive treatment of the law. *Instead of telling us what the law cannot do, we would expect the passage to tell us what it can do.*

With regard to what law Paul has in mind, it would fit wherever it applies. However, at that point in Jewish and Christian history, it would have been impossible to have avoided taking the primary reference to the Mosaic Law.

Another point that needs to be made is that, *at that time, it would have been nigh unto impossible that the concern would have been understood as arising out of any other context than that of a Jewish concern.* Even Gentiles would have wondered how all of this squared with Jewish thought.

If what has been said is true, Paul would be expected to defend the good of the law to those whose concern came from a Jewish context. What they are really wanting to know is, "Has the ministry of the Mosaic Law been a mistake?"

Paul emphatically denies that the law is sin. He then proceeds to show the positive ministry of the law. He said, "I would not have had an adequate knowledge of sin had it not been for the law." There can be no adequate understanding of the gospel unless a person has been informed by law of the nature of sin.

For I had not known lust (Greek *epithumia*), **except the law had said, "Thou shalt not covet** (Greek *epithumeo*)." Paul's reference here is to the last of the Ten Commandments. The question arises: Does Paul mean to restrict his discussion to this one commandment, or does this one commandment stand for the whole? Without question, "Thou shalt not covet" here is a synechdoche where the part is given for the whole. However, in a case like this "Thou shalt not covet," though standing for the whole law, is to receive special emphasis.

The only difference in the Greek words for "lust" and "covet" is that the one for "lust" is a noun while the one for "covet" is a verb. Hodge explains: "The word *epithumia* [lust] means simply *earnest desire*, and the verb *epithumeo* [covet] is to desire earnestly. It depends on the context whether it is directed towards what is lawful or what is forbidden" (222).

In the Ten Commandments, lust or covetousness refers to a misdirected desire that has gotten out of control. It is assumed that Paul's choice of this commandment as his illustration grew out of the fact that *it is the most obvious stress on attitude that is found in the O.T. Law.*

2. The power of sin is revealed (v. 8).

8 But sin, taking occasion by the commandment, wrought in me all manner of concupiscence. For without the law sin *was* dead.

But sin taking occasion by the commandment, wrought in me all manner of concupiscence. Concerning "occasion" (Greek *aphorme),* Yeager explains: "Properly, a place from which a military movement or attack is made; a base of operations; beach-head. Metaphorically, whatever stimulates an endeavor and by which it is made; incentive; opportunity, stimulation, suggestion, supposed justification for some thought or action" (489).

The meaning of this verse is much the same as 7:5 where the law stirred the passions of sin into activity. There is some truth to the statement, "If you tell me not to, it makes me want to do it." When sin stimulates a person to violate the law, the fault is not with the law. The problem lies with sin. In such a case sin is taking occasion by the law to stimulate a person into sinning. Sin used the commandment, "Thou shalt not covet" as a means of stirring the person into more covetousness. Note that the word for concupiscence (Greek *epithumia*) is the same as for "lust" in v. 8. The verb form of this word was translated "covet" in v. 8. Variety makes for better reading, but it is good to know when you have the same word translated different ways.

It is important that law could never be the *cause* of a person's sinning. It is that within us that causes us to sin, not the law against it. The law is used by sin as the *occasion* to get us to sin. But sin is always the *cause.*

For without the law sin *was* dead. The idea is that sin is somewhat dormant when the law is not openly known. It is still seen, but it is not seen for what it really is.

3. The result of sin is revealed (v. 9).

9 For I was alive without the law once: but when the commandment came, sin revived, and I died.

For I was alive without the law once. There are a number of different interpretations of this part of the verse. Interpretation is determined by whether one thinks the passage is autobiographical, and whether the person under consideration is viewed as unregenerate or regenerate. Calvin views the time to be before Paul became a Christian. He explains, "He refers, therefore, to the law absent because, although it was before his eyes, it did not impress on him a serious sense of the judgment of the Lord" (144).

Others take the reference to be to the period, as we would call it, before he reached the age of accountability. Those who take the autobiographical view find it hard to be convincing about the time Paul was without law.

Cranfield says:

> Paul is using the first person in a general sense, and refers to man's situation before the giving of the law, along with which Paul probably has in mind the state of man pictured in Gen. 1:28ff. . . . In the primal state described in Genesis 1 man 'was alive,' and in the time before the law was given through Moses, while man certainly could not be said to be alive in the full sense which [live] has for example in 1:17 or 8:13, he may be said to have been alive in the sense that his condition then was life, in comparison with his condition after the law had been received (this seems a more natural interpretation than to take the point to be that, not yet knowing himself to be a sinner, he seemed to himself to be possessed of life)" (351, 352).

If we must decide a time when

"without the law" man was alive, it seems Cranfield is on the right track. However, the approach followed in discussing this subject in the "Preliminary observations" above is a more likely interpretation.

We can see by now, in the light of v. 7, that Paul is making a case for the fact that the law is good. This is of special importance to his Jewish readers.

In developing his case for the good of the law, Paul projected himself into the position of a person who had gone through the various stages necessary for a good working knowledge of the law.

In order to build his case, Paul apparently felt that he should project himself into the role of a person without the law and then work from there. If this be the case it is not necessary that there be an actual time in mind when either Paul, himself, or someone else was actually in such a state. At least one thing is clear. If Paul did have a special time and a special person or group in mind, we do not have enough information with which to build a dogmatic case.

It appears that the condition when he was "without law" is simply pictured as a background to enter the stage of being taught by law. Being taught by the law was the reality which he wanted to address for his readers. We can get the thought of the rest of what Paul wanted to say without being sure of all the details in this verse.

But when the commandment came, sin revived, and I died. There can be as many views on the time when the commandment came as there are on the time referred to by "without law." Most of those can be logically developed from the different views given above on the time referred to by "without law."

One point is clear. When the light of law was shined on sin, it became clear that when he was "without law" he had been deceived about what his relationship to sin was.

Many are of the opinion that "I died" in this verse refers to a state or misery as compared with the former state. Or it could be said to be the end of self-assurance (see Hendriksen 221; Hodge 224; Moule 128; and Murray 251).

The first clue to the meaning of "died" is that it has a negative connotation. "Death to sin" and "death to law," as we viewed them, in chap. 6 and 7:4 have a positive connotation.

The next clue to the meaning of "died" comes from the fact that it is in a context where the law meets sin. In such a case the preference should be given to considering "I died" as meaning coming under the sentence of death for sin as prescribed by the law (see Cranfield 352 and Lange 231). This is the meaning of "I died." This meaning will be backed up as we go through the next few verses.

4. The deceitfulness of sin is revealed (vv. 10, 11).

10 And the commandment, which *was ordained* to life, I found *to be* unto death.

There is nothing in the nature of the law, as law, which means that it must inflict death. The law is an expression of the holy nature of God. The holy nature of God existed before the sentence of death was ever inflicted.

The holy nature of God has been in fatal conflict with sin because sin is an assault on the holiness of God. The law of God which is an expression of the holy nature of God must, because of the nature of sin, inflict the sentence of death.

The law is not a foe which unjustly

sentences us to death. It is a friend which tells us about our sins and the sentence of death we are under. It is a friend to let us know about our plight because we must know what the problem is before we will avail ourselves of the remedy.

11 For sin, taking occasion by the commandment, deceived me, and by it slew *me.*

For sin taking occasion (same Greek word as in v. 8) **by the commandment deceived me.** The similarity between vv. 8 and 11 is obvious. Sin is viewed in v. 8 as taking occasion by the law to stir up lustful or covetous desires.

In this verse sin takes occasion by the law to deceive those who are confronted by it. The children of Israel were deceived when the law was presented to them. When they were confronted with the demands of the law, they answered, "All that the LORD hath spoken we will do" (Ex. 19:8). It appears that they naively thought they could keep the law. But their history records quite another story.

And by it slew *me.* The "it" refers back to "the commandment" which stands for the law. The fact that the death is inflicted by the law means that the reference is to death as the penalty of the law.

5. In light of the goodness of the law, sin is seen as being exceedingly sinful (vv. 12, 13).

12 Wherefore the law *is* holy, and the commandment holy, and just, and good.

Wherefore (Greek *hoste*). This conjunction tells us that what follows in the verse is the result (or conclusion) in Paul's thinking of the observations that have been made about the law in vv. 7-11. We need to keep ourselves reminded that Paul is defending his position that the law is not sinful.

The law *is* holy, and the commandment holy, and just, and good. Paul considered that what he had said in vv. 7-11 formed a basis for declaring that in no way can it be said that the law is sinful. When sin misuses the law to stimulate covetous desires, the problem is with sin, not the law. When the person under the law discovers that he is guilty and condemned, the problem is with sin, not the law. The law is serving a useful purpose when it helps us to see what we really are. The law is friend, not foe.

13 Was then that which is good made death unto me? God forbid. But sin, that it might appear sin, working death in me by that which is good; that sin by the commandment might become exceeding sinful.

Was then that which is good made death unto me? Is the law to be blamed for the fact that I am under the sentence of death?

God forbid (see notes on 3:4). Paul emphatically denies that the law is to be faulted in any way for the fact that we are under the sentence of death.

But sin, that it might appear sin, working death in me by that which is good. That which is "good" in this verse is the law. When sin brings us under its sway and forces the law (that which is good) to pronounce the death sentence upon us, it shows sin to be what it really is.

That sin by the commandment might become exceeding sinful. "Exceeding" translates a two-word Greek phrase (*kath' huperbolen*, whence our English word "hyperbole"). According to Vine (395, 396) the latter word means "a throwing beyond, hence, a surpassing. . . . It always betokens pre-eminence"; and the whole phrase signifies "beyond measure, exceedingly."

An illustration will help us get the picture. Suppose you knew a man who was noted for his good character and his ability to keep his cool under the most adverse circumstances. One day you heard that some person had provoked this man to the point that he lost his cool and beat him up. What would it tell you about the person who provoked him to that point? You would have a very negative opinion about a person who could provoke such a good person to take such action. The same is true with the law and sin. For anything as good, and holy, and just as the law, to be forced to pronounce the death penalty on sin tells us that sin must be *exceedingly* sinful.

Since the vast majority take vv. 7-13 to refer to the unregenerate, it is not necessary to spend a lot of time defending that conclusion. It should be obvious in these verses that the law pronounces the penalty of death on the sinner. If this sentence of death has not been removed by dying to the law through union with Christ (see 7:4), the person is under the sentence of death and is therefore unregenerate.

B. The Law Reveals Man's Relationship to Sin (vv. 14-23).

This is where the differences of interpretation begin to show up. In many respects, it can be said that two opposite interpretations are given for the passage. On the one side, it is said that the picture is that of an unregenerate person in a state of utter defeat and misery. On the other side, it is said that this illustrates the normal nature of Christian experience.

It is known that the tendency is for Arminians to take these verses to refer to an unregenerate person. The tendency is that the Calvinist takes the passage to refer to a regenerate person. However, though that is the tendency, the list of supporters above of the different views will indicate that, as it relates to vv. 14-25, neither list is made up exclusively of Arminians or Calvinists.

There is absolutely no question about whether a Christian experiences a conflict between what he is and what he knows that he ought to be. There is such a conflict. The question simply put is: Does Paul treat that conflict in these verses?

There is not the slightest doubt in my mind about the fact that fallen man is depraved. This means that there is not the slightest possibility that any human being would be able to live without sinning. There is no merit of any kind that he could produce that would earn justification before God.

It is utterly impossible for a person to come to Christ apart from the drawing power of the Holy Spirit (Jn. 6:44). This work of the Holy Spirit, in which He leads and draws a person to Christ, cannot be called regeneration. Regeneration follows faith rather than preceding it. A regenerate person is a saved person.

I believe in total depravity, by which I mean that every part of fallen man is touched by depravity. Thus I believe in original sin.

Let me also say that I am not the least bit inclined to believe in sinless perfection. I believe that I have a healthy dissatisfaction with myself. I do not have a totally negative view of myself. I dare not downgrade the handiwork of God. I am His both by creation and by redemption. It is not honoring to God for me to dwell on and to exaggerate how sinful and sorry I am.

Let me also say that I could never for one minute stand justified apart from the death and righteousness of Jesus Christ.

I hope that, having made these observations, I will not be misunderstood concerning what I say either in describing or in defending my view.

The main problems to be dealt with in deciding whether these verses deal with the regenerate or the unregenerate are: (1) Why did Paul shift from past tense to present tense? (2) Is it possible to consider a Christian to be "carnal sold under sin" (v. 14)? (3) Is it possible for an unregenerate man to "delight in the law after the inward man" (v. 22)? (4) What bearing does "O wretched man that I am!" (v. 24) have on deciding whether the person is regenerate, or unregenerate (v. 24)? (5) What is meant by death in the expression "the body of this death" (v.24)? (6) How do we explain, "So then with the mind I myself serve the law of God; but with the flesh the law of sin" (v. 25)?

Many feel that any view on this passage other than their own would be incompatible with their system of theology. This need not be the case. In many cases, those who have different interpretations of this passage may be in essential agreement on their views of depravity, regeneration, internal conflict, and victorious living. Of course, differences can be so described that the interpretation of the passage may be in conflict with a particular system of theology.

1. He is sold under sin (v. 14).

14 For we know that the law is spiritual: but I am carnal, sold under sin.

For we know that the law is spiritual. Keep in mind that Paul is still making his case against the idea that the law is sinful (see v. 7). In vv. 7-13 he defended the law as not being at fault. The fact that sin used the law as an occasion to stimulate covetous desires, did not mean that blame rested with the law. Rather, the blame rested with sin.

The fact that he was deceived into thinking at first that he could keep the law was not the fault of the law. It was the fault of sin.

The fact that that which is holy, just, and good (the law) found it necessary to give the sentence of death on the law violator did not mean that the law was at fault. Rather, sin was at fault. This puts sin in its proper light. It is "exceeding sinful."

Having looked at the law and sin from different angles, sin has been seen to be the real culprit, not the law. Sin is exceedingly sinful. The law is holy, just, good, and spiritual.

But I am carnal. There are manuscript differences for the word translated "carnal." Some have one word (Greek *sarkikos*); some have another (*sarkinos*). Most who have studied the problem consider the second one to be the true reading.

Explaining the difference between these two words, Cranfield (357) says that the second one (*sarkinos)* means "composed of flesh" and the first one (*sarkikos*) means "determined by flesh" (357). On these two words Williams comments, "I am made of flesh that is frail (*sarkinos*). This is the meaning of this adjective, while *sarkikos* means fleshly, pertaining to flesh. Paul feels that his very moral constitution is frail and impotent" (268).

Sold (Greek *piprasko*) **under sin.**

The meaning of "carnal" (regardless which of the two nearly identical words is original) in this context is basically determined by: (1) It is in contrast with "spiritual." (2) It is explained by "sold under sin." The "carnal man" is in slavery to sin.

Concerning "sold," Lightfoot explains, "'*Sold,'* and therefore its bond-slave (comp. 6:16). 'Sin is my task-master, compelling me to do what I would not do of myself'" (303).

There are a number of questions that we need to face at this point. The majority of those who believe that the passage is divided between the unregenerate and the regenerate understand this to be the turning point in the passage. At this point Paul introduces the regenerate person. The main reason given for this is the change from the past tense to the present tense. There is a better explanation of the tense change.

It will be observed that the first part of this verse is in the present tense. "The law is spiritual." Paul started in v. 7 by raising the question: "Is the law sinful?" Having shown that the problem is with sin rather than the law, he says, "The law is spiritual."

There is no way that the statement "The law is spiritual" can be separated from vv. 7-13. If we base our case on the change from the past to the present tense "The law is spiritual" must be separated from vv. 7-13. It can hardly be denied that it is a wrap-up of the case in vv. 7-13. The "I" of the last part of the verse is a part of the "we" in the first part. The "I" is contemporaneous with the "we." There is not the slightest reason to believe that a conversion has taken place between the two statements.

As I see it, here is what happened. It was as if, when Paul concluded with v. 13, he said, "What is the meaning of all this?" (1) There is no blame at all to be placed on the law when it comes to the predicament in which we find ourselves as it relates to the death sentence we received from the law. (2) "The law is spiritual," but, as for me, I am carnal sold under sin. Sin has really done me in. Sin is the culprit, not the law. I am the victim.

It is quite natural that a change of tense from past to present could mark a change in the progress of the presentation. Paul is saying, "I have told you that the problem is with sin, not the law. Now, let me share with you what the message is for me. I am carnal sold under sin."

An additional fact that could account for the tense change is that in establishing the feeling of identification with the person being depicted, the present tense enhances that. It also helps the reader establish rapport with the person in the passage.

The change in the passage to personal application and to enhance identification are adequate reasons for the use of the present tense. In fact it is the natural, normal thing to do. In vv. 7-13 Paul discusses the nature of sin and the law. In vv. 14-25, he discusses the relationship of the person to sin and the law. He is in bondage to sin. When the law is allowed to fulfill its intended purpose, the sinner is led to a point of desperation and cries out for help (v. 24).

Now, back to the question of whether vv. 14-25 are dealing with the regenerate or the unregenerate. *If Paul is actually introducing the regenerate* at this point, it is the strangest introduction of a regenerate person ever heard. Out of the clear blue sky he says, "I am carnal sold under sin." But, if Paul is speaking of an *unregenerate* person all the way through, it is to be expected that he would deal with the hard negative truth that the law shows the unregenerate about his bondage to sin. The time was ready to introduce this painful truth.

There is one important observation that requires our attention at this point. *It is not that the same kind of person is seen by one group to be regenerate and by another group as being unregenerate.* That may be true up to a point. But the fact is that those who believe the person is regenerate, do not see the person described by Paul in the same state of sin, guilt, and misery that I do. To me, the picture is that of a miserable person in utter defeat. The examination of the next few verses will support this observation.

The following quotations from those who believe that 7:14-25 is speaking of the regenerate illustrate the fact that these commentators are viewing the person as a different kind of person than I do.

Cranfield explains:

> Understood in isolation from the teaching of chapters 6 and 8 and 12ff., these words would certainly give a thoroughly wrong impression of the Christian life; but, taken closely together with it, they bring out forcefully an aspect of the Christian life which we gloss over to our undoing.... The more seriously a Christian strives to live from grace and to submit to the discipline of the gospel, the more sensitive he becomes to the fact of his continuing sinfulness, the fact that even his very best acts and activities are disfigured by the egotism which is still powerful within him—and no less evil because it is often more subtly distinguished than formerly (357, 358).

Hendriksen comments:

> Paul has not sold himself. Someone else has sold him. He, Paul deplores this situation. It is as if we hear him utter a sigh of agony when he complains, 'I am...sold as a slave under sin!' Can one who so intensely laments his remaining sinfulness be anything but a believer...?
>
> ...that one who in verse 14 deplores his sinful condition is the same person who in the chapter's closing verses exercises his delight in the law of God, looks forward with impassioned and irresistible longing to the day of his deliverance from the present momentous inner struggles and is filled with the blessed assurance that victory is bound to come; in fact, that 'in principle' it is here already! (231, 232).

Hodge explains:

> A man may be subject to a power which of himself, he cannot effectually resist; against which he may and does struggle, and from which he earnestly desires to be free; but which, notwithstanding all his efforts, still asserts its authority. This is precisely the bondage to sin of which every believer is conscious. He feels that there is a law in his members bringing him into subjection to the law of sin; that his distrust of God, his hardness of heart, his love of the world and of self, his pride, in short his indwelling sin, is a real power from which he longs to be free, against which he struggles, but from which he cannot emancipate himself (230).

These are not adequate descriptions of the person referred to in this passage. This should become obvious as we look at the next few verses.

Attention should be given now to how those who take the person to be regenerated justify the use of the word "carnal" to refer to the regenerate. Reference is made to 1 Cor. 3:1-3 where Paul rebuked the Corinthians because he "could not speak unto you as unto spiritual, but as unto carnal, even as unto babes in Christ" (v. 1). "For ye are yet carnal" (v.3).

My first observation is that the addition of the words "sold under sin" in Rom. 7:14 are against giving the word a weakened interpretation. In 1 Cor. 3:1-3 two points of information tell why the word carnal is used: (1) They were "as carnal" because they were babes who could not handle the meat of the Word. (2) They were referred to as "being carnal" because "there is among you envying, and strife, and divisions. Are ye not carnal and walk as men?" These problems are to be taken seriously, but that is not the same as giving a right to an unrestricted use of the word carnal as it is found in Rom. 7:14.

While there are degrees of difference among those who take 7:14-25 to refer to the regenerate, there are basically two shades of difference: (1) The person presented in these verses is a normal or mature Christian. (2) The person is one who is a defeated Christian. He is living below his privileges. He has not come to really understand the delivering power of the Holy Spirit.

Cranfield is an example of the first interpretation. These comments are taken from his discussion of v. 24. He says, "The one who speaks in verse 24 is a Christian (and a mature Christian—not merely one who is still on the same specially low level of Christian existence)" (369). The majority of commentators who understand these verses to refer to the regenerate would be in essential agreement with Cranfield.

In discussing the use of the word "carnal" in 1 Cor. 3:1-3 and the use here in v. 14, Arminius says:

> But in whatever sense or manner the word is used, in this passage, it brings no advantage to the cause of those who declare that the apostle calls himself *a carnal man* in Romans 7:14. For if the same word is not used in I Cor. 3:1, in a sense similar to that which it bears in Romans 7:14, then it is adduced in an unlearned and useless manner in elucidation of this question; for equivocation is the fruitful parent of error. If the word is to be received in the same sense in both passages, then I am at liberty firmly to conclude from this, in favor of my opinion, that the apostle cannot be called *carnal* in Romans 7:14; for under that appellation he severely reprehends the Corinthians because he 'was not able to speak unto them as unto *spiritual* persons,' since they were such as were still carnal; which he would have done without any just cause, if he were himself also comprehended under the same title when understood in the same signification (II:250).

The point that Arminius is making would create the same problem whether the passage is considered autobiographical or not as long as the passage is understood to depict the normal Christian experience. This would be true because Paul would be included in the category of normal Christians.

The view that takes the passage to be the defeated Christian who is living below his privileges is found more in popular preaching and writing than in commentaries. A form of this view is presented by Ironside. He says:

> If I am addressing any believer who is even now in the agonizing throes of this terrific struggle, endeavoring to subject the flesh to the holy law of God, let me urge you to accept God's own verdict on the flesh and acknowledge the impossibility of ever making it behave itself. Do not fight with it. It will overthrow you every time. Turn away from it; cease from it altogether; and look away from self and law to the risen Christ (92, 93).

It appears that Lloyd-Jones advocates a view that will fit in this general category. From what he says, it sounds like it is a state of conviction which a believer may be in, "But for a time they are in a position, as it were, of being . . .neither unregenerate nor regenerate" (256) yet, he says, "At the same time I have given abundant proof of the fact that the man is not unregenerate" (256). Yet he says later, "Thank God, this is not the picture of the regenerate man!" (257).

I take it that he is saying that there are some regenerate people who are involved in the experience of defeat and conviction, but this is not the "normal picture" of a regenerate person.

I do not believe that the word *carnal* in its unrestricted sense is used to describe Christians in the N.T.—much less with the added words "I am sold under sin!" The words of A. T. Robertson need to be carefully weighed. He says, "There is a great deal of controversy as to whether Paul is describing his struggle with sin before conversion or after it. The words 'sold under sin' in verse 14 seem to turn the scale for the pre-conversion period" (369).

As we progress through the passage, further reasons will be given for believing that the extent of involvement in sin and defeat in this passage is incompatible with the regenerate state. In these verses Paul elaborates on what it means to be "carnal sold under sin."

15 For that which I do I allow not: for what I would, that do I not; but what I hate, that do I.

For that which I do (Greek *katergazomai*) **I allow not: for what I would that do I** (Greek *prasso*) **not; but what I hate, that do I** (Greek *poieo*). One sees immediately that three different Greek words are translated "do" in this verse, and these three are used throughout the passage. The first word (*katergazomai*) in addition to this verse in this passage (vv. 14-23) is translated "do" in v. 17, "perform" in v. 18, and "do" in v. 20. In v. 19 the second word (*prasso*) is translated "do." The third word (*poieo*) is translated "do" in every occurrence in this passage. The other verses are vv. 16, 19, 20, and 21.

Concerning these words Denny (641) explains, the first word (*katergazomai*) "is to effect, to bring about by one's own work"; the second one *(prasso)* "is to work at, to busy oneself with, a thing with or without success, but with purpose"; the third *(poieo)* "is simply to make or produce" (641).

The word which is translated "allow" (*ginosko*) means "to know." It appears to me that the best translation here is "to understand."

We need to look at the word "would" (Greek *thelo*) before we put the meaning of the verse together. In vv. 15, 16, 19, 20, and 21, it is translated "would." In v. 18 it is translated "will." It appears that in these verses the meaning is to wish or desire rather than to will or make a choice.

Paul is saying, "I do not understand it. I wish to do one thing, but I end up doing another. I hate and deplore what I do." It appears that what we see here is utter defeat. This point will be elaborated more when we come to v. 23.

16 If then I do that which I would not, I consent unto the law that *it is* good.

If then I do (Greek *poieo*) **that which I would** (Greek *thelo, wish*) **not, I consent unto the law that *it is* good**. One word for "good" (Greek *agathos*) appears in vv. 12, 13, 18a, and 19. Another word for good

(Greek *kalos*) appears in vv. 16, 18b, and 21. Denney explains, "*Kalos* suggests the moral beauty or nobility of the law, not like *agathos* (ver. 12) its beneficial purpose" (641).

The word in vv. 12, 13, 18a, 19 (*agathos*) refers to the law as "good to me" or "for me." The word in vv. 16, 18b, 21 (*kalos*) refers to the beauty or excellence of the law.

The word translated "consent" (Greek *sumphemi*, made up of *sun* "with" and *phemi* "to say or speak") means "to speak with." Thus it comes to mean "to consent" or "to concur." Paul is saying that since he wishes to obey the law rather than disobey (as he does), that means that he recognizes and concurs with the beauty and excellence of the law.

17 Now then it is no more I that do it, but sin that dwelleth in me.

Now then it is no more I that do (Greek *katergazomai* [see v. 15]) **it, but sin that dwelleth in me.**

"Dwelleth" translates a Greek verb (*oikeo*) that has the same root as the noun for house (*oikos*). Thus it means "being housed." Sin is "housed" or has taken up residence in him.

In the Greek verb translated "do," "I" is already included since it is a first person form. The addition of the written pronoun "I" (Greek *ego*) makes it emphatic. Denny explains, "*Ego* is the true I, and emphatic. As things are, in view of the facts just explained, it is not the true self which is responsible for this line of conduct, but the sin which has its abode in the man" (641).

Paul is not meaning that a person in such a condition is not responsible for what he does. Rather, he is pointing out that the power of sin is so great that he cannot control his actions: He is "being controlled" rather than "being in control."

A word of explanation needs to be made with regard to the use of "I" (Greek *ego*) for the true self. Some might question whether the true and genuine side of the unregenerate person would be on the side of the law, the right, and the good.

Any adequate understanding of human personality, whether saved or unsaved, must take into account the principle of contradiction. When man sinned, he not only revolted against God he also revolted against himself. This means that an unsaved person experiences internal conflict. Certainly, there is a difference in the conflict experienced by the saved and the unsaved. That difference is not, however, that the unregenerate person experiences no conflicts, while the regenerate does.

Man was created in the image of God. He was designed for righteousness. He was not designed for sin. Sin introduced a foreign element into man's being. It is a foreign element whether the person is saved or unsaved.

It is impossible for a human being to have harmony by trying to harmonize his inner being around the experience of sin. It is for this reason that we can know that certain experiences are devastating for human beings. Regardless of what a person may try to say in his conscious mind, his sub-conscious mind will never accept sexual immorality, dishonesty, etc. The evidence of this is found in the experience of guilt, lack of self-respect, and personality maladjustment among those who are in gross violation of the Ten Commandments. This is true whether the person has heard of the Ten Commandments or not.

The only answer to the sinner's guilt problem is to receive the death and righteousness of Christ by faith. The only answer for his internal problems is internal conformity to the image of

Christ which involves the experience of moral and spiritual truth.

How does all of this relate to the *ego* or the "I" as being the "true self"? The "true self" is what a person is by the design of creation. He cannot escape from his true self. He can reckon with the problem and find an answer through redemption. Or he can refuse to face up to the situation and suffer the consequences. Man is made for righteousness as truly as a fish is for water.

It must be remembered that the categories of right and wrong have not been removed by the fall. Fallen man tries to change the label on things. He tries to call sins by the name of right. He cannot totally succeed in this. The widespread use of illegal drugs and alcohol is a testimony of the fact that people cannot ignore moral and spiritual truth and at the same time be happy, well-adjusted people. The use of illegal drugs and alcohol is to a large extent an emotional pain killer.

Sin forces man into the experience of a divided self. This division is painful because it was never intended to be, and it can never totally succeed.

It is important to observe that we are not talking about "two selves." We are talking about a divided self. We may speak about our "better self" or our "worst self." We should not, in so doing, understand the reference to be to "two selves" within one person. It is a division within the *one* self which tries to destroy the deepest and truest self. It is an attempt to deny and repudiate that which has been inescapably designed into every human being.

It is this very experience which demonstrates the fact that fallen man is still in the image of God. We cannot by practice and determination totally destroy that which is designed into the very essence of our being. It will not be totally silenced.

The "I" or "ego" is that true self which is in keeping with what a human being is supposed to be. In v. 17 it is painfully present. It is painful because it is under the control of sin which it can never fully accept.

18 For I know that in me (that is, in my flesh,) dwelleth no good thing: for to will is present with me; but *how* to perform that which is good I find not.

For I know that in me (that is, in my flesh,) dwelleth (Greek *oikeo*, see v. 17) **no good** (Greek *agathos*, see v. 16) **thing.** The "flesh" as used here refers to what a fallen man is apart from God. *The flesh is motivated by immediate concerns rather than eternal values.* The flesh is that in a person which revolts against the "true self" which belongs inescapably to a person by the design of Creation. It is that which puts a person who sins in a state of contradiction. He both wants and does not want to do the same thing.

In the flesh, Paul says, "dwells no good thing." The "good" Paul refers to (Greek *agathos*) is that which is "good for a person." That which has residence in the flesh is not good for his welfare. It results in malfunction of his personality.

For to will (Greek *thelo*) **is present with me.** This would come from the true self which a person has by the design of creation and informed by the law of God. There is both a desire to do the right and good and a desire to do otherwise. The true self recognizes the law as good and in some measure desires to live by it.

But *how* to perform (Greek *katergazomai*) **that which is good** (Greek *kalos*) **I find not.** The good in this part of the verse refers to moral excellence. Though he recognizes what moral excellence is when confronted by the law, and though he desires to live by it, he cannot. He is not in control. He is being controlled by sin.

The picture here is that of a person who is in utter defeat. He is not a person who has a few such experiences of defeat along the way. I insist that this kind of defeat to the degree which is set forth here is inconsistent with what the N.T. says about a saved person.

19 For the good that I would I do not: but the evil which I would not, that I do.

For the good (Greek *agathos*) **that I would** (Greek *thelo*) **I do** (Greek *poieo*) **not: but the evil** (Greek *kakos*) **which I would** (Greek *thelo*) **not, that I do** (Greek *prasso*). Concerning the word "evil" (*kakos*), Vine explains, "*Kakos* is antithetic to *kalos*, fair, advisable, good in character, and to *agathos* beneficial, useful, good in act; hence it denotes what is useless, incapable, bad" *Dictionary* (390).

His better judgment tells him that the law is both good (*kalos*) and "*good*" (*agathos*). Sin is challenging the high value placed on that which is good as set forth in the law. As the serpent told Eve, "Ye shall not surely die" (Gen. 3:4), sin is trying to convince a person that sin is not bad (Greek *kakos*). Sin uses this to lead people into sin, but such an opinion is short-lived. The better judgment that cannot be totally silenced in a person bounces back and recognizes sin as being bad or evil. But even then he finds himself unable to live in accord with his recognition of the moral excellence set forth in the law.

20 Now if I do that I would not, it is no more I that do it, but sin that dwelleth in me.

Now if I do (Greek *poieo*) **that I would** (Greek *thelo*) **not, it is no more I that do** (Greek *katergazomai*) **it, but sin that dwelleth** (Greek *oikeo*) **in me.** This is a clear picture of bondage to sin. There is no denial of responsibility for sin. This recognition of bondage to sin prepares a person to desire deliverance by outside help. That is his only hope. The truest "I" or "self" is not in control. It is being controlled.

21 I find then a law, that, when I would do good, evil is present with me.

I find then a law, that, when I would (Greek *thelo*) **do** (Greek *poieo*) **good** (Greek *kalos*), **evil** (Greek-*kakos*) **is present with me.** The word "law" as used here is a *principle* which describes his behavior. That principle of truth is that when he wishes to do that which is morally excellent (Greek *kalos*), evil (Greek *kakos*) is present to run interference with that which is morally excellent. (For the meaning of *kalos* and *kakos* see vv. 16, 19, and 21.)

22 For I delight in the law of God after the inward man.

For I delight (Greek *sunedomai*) **in the law of God after the inward** (Greek *eso*) **man** (Greek *anthropos*).

This verse is the focal point of the hottest contention in this passage. Those who take vv. 14-24 to refer to the regenerate insist that it cannot be said by the unregenerate, "I delight in the law of God after the inward man." It goes without saying that those who believe it refers to the unregenerate would disagree.

In 2 Cor. 4:16 the inward man is contrasted with the outward man. The inward man is not the regenerate nature of a Christian. Rather, it is the inward man which, in the case of a Christian, is regenerated.

The words "inner man" or the equivalent occur in only two other places, 2 Cor. 4:16 and Eph. 3:16. In each of the other occurrences, the reference would be to a regenerate person. That does not mean that it cannot be used to refer to an unregenerate person in another context. It would, however, suggest that strong consideration should be given to that interpretation.

In this passage we are faced with the following dilemma: Will we consider a person who sees himself to be "carnal sold under sin" a Christian? Or will we consider a person who "delights in the law of God after the inward man" an unregenerate person? To call the person who is carnal sold under sin a Christian seems to undercut what it means to be a Christian. To speak of an unregenerate person as one who delights in the law of God after the inward man seems to say too much for the unregenerate person. Yet, it seems that we must settle for one or the other.

It is the facing of such dilemmas that warns us against over-simplification. These dilemmas force us to do deeper thinking than we otherwise would. We will, as a result of this dilemma, find ourselves explaining why a regenerate person can say, "I am carnal sold under sin." Or we will find ourselves explaining why an unregenerate person can say, "I delight in the law of God after the inward man."

The "inward man" of this verse is essentially the same as the "I" of vv. 15-20. The "I" of v. 17 is that which he was in the deepest and truest sense. The "I" was able to hate sin (v. 15). It was able to "consent unto the law that it is good" (v. 16). The "I" was able to wish to perform the good (v. 18). In spite of hating sin, consenting that the law is good, and wishing to obey the law he was unable to perform that which his best and truest self wished to do.

The question before us is: Is it possible for a person short of regeneration to have such an experience as is described in this verse? Let us see if ascribing such language to an unregenerate person is justifiable in the light of Scripture.

Before moving further, let us see what Paul is actually saying in "I delight in the law of God." "I delight" (Greek *sunedomai*) means to rejoice with the law. It would involve a recognition of the good of the law and an appreciation of the law. This rejoicing would take place in the inner being, or that which is a person's deepest and truest self.

Let it be said that the deepest and truest self may not be the strongest. In fact that is the case here. It is called the deepest and truest not because of the strength of its desire, but rather, because it is that which more truly manifests the design of God in the person. In the light of v. 23 we can see that "the law of sin" defeats the truest self which delights in the law of God.

Arminius explains:

> The apostle wished only to ascribe this 'delighting' to the man *according to one part of him*, and to take it away according to *the other part of him*. But since the apostle not only takes this 'delighting' from *the other part of him*, but likewise attributes it to the power of *warring against that inward man and overcoming him*, it is evident that the restriction has been added on this account—to shew that, in the man who is now the subject of discussion, 'the inward man' has not the dominion, but is in fact, the inferior (II:308).

If we stay strictly with the context, Paul is talking about a person who is so instructed by the law that he sees his desperate circumstances. He comes, in v. 25, to recognize Christ as his only way of deliverance. This being true the fullest application of what Paul says belongs only to those who have, in the light of God's law, recognized their own guilt and utter failure. When confronted by Christ they are ready to recognize Him as the only answer to their guilt and bondage.

The question before us is: Is it possible for a person to delight in the law of God before he is regenerated? The answer is "yes." In Is. 58:2 God's message to the wicked is, "Yet they seek me daily, and delight to know my ways. . .they ask of me the ordinances of justice; they take delight in approaching to God." Note also what Paul said of the unbelieving Jew, "Behold, thou art called a Jew, and restest in the law, and makest thy boast of God, And knowest *his* will, and approvest the things that are more excellent, being instructed out of the law" (Rom. 2:17, 18). If Paul could say that of one who is, at the time, showing no conviction as it relates to his sin and circumstances, surely there should be no problem in believing that in the process of being prepared to receive Christ a person could "delight in the law of God after the inward man."

In a measure any unsaved person can, if confronted by God's written law, give at least some degree of approval. If he does not have the written law, his own moral constitution will to some extent inform him of what is right and good. He can have at least some appreciation for the right and the good.

Except in the case of those who were saved so early in life that they cannot remember, all of us can remember a conflict between what we knew was right and our own actions. We can also remember approving deeds which we were not able to perform. This was the case because, even though we were sinners, the design of God in us refused to be silent.

It is a mistake to assume that depravity introduced a complete reversal of moral values into a person's experience. One must resist his own experience and observation to believe that an unsaved person either is or can be living in internal harmony while being completely devoted to evil. God's moral design cannot be totally silenced.

> The sinner is so constituted that he has the categories of right and wrong. Right is considered a plus factor, and wrong is considered a minus factor. No human being does what he knows to be wrong without to some extent considering it to be a minus factor. This fact cannot be obliterated. Sin has introduced a foreign element in man's being. Man was made for righteousness. He was not made for sin. A human being can never live in sin and have self-acceptance and full harmony of being. Sin has placed man in conflict, contradiction, and confusion. To whatever extent a person has forfeited the morality of the Ten Commandments, to that extent he is in trouble not only with God but with himself. No person who lives in gross violation of the morality of the Ten Commandments is happy (Forlines, *Systematics*, 120).

Godet calls attention to statements made by those of the pagan world who give evidence of a conflict similar to what is seen in this passage. He says, "This is the passage in all Paul's Epistles which presents the most points of contact with profane literature" (293). In a footnote he gives some short quotations to back up his observation. Ovid said, "*Desire counsels me in one direction, reason in another.*" Again he said, "*I see the better part, and approve it; but I follow the worse.*" Plautus explained, "*I knew what I ought to be, but unhappy that I am, I could not do it.*" Seneca raised the question,"*What then is it that, when we would go in one direction, drags us in the other?*" Epictetus said, "*He who sins does not what he would and does what he would not.*"

Godet adds: "We need scarcely add the well-known comparison of Plato, which represents the human soul as like a chariot drawn by two horses, the one of which draws it upward, the other downward" (Godet 293, note 1).

What has been said is based on the fact that God created man in His own image. The design of God in man was not totally obliterated in man by the fall. The image of God in man consists of a rational likeness (Col. 3:10) and a moral likeness (Eph. 4:24). To put it simply, the image of God in man is seen in the fact that man is a personal being. God is personal. Man is personal.

Depravity has put man in conflict not only with God, but with himself.

Man did not cease to be a personal being in the fall. Man is designed to have the categories of right and wrong. He was made to believe in God. He will be affected adversely when he tries to go contrary to his design.

On the one hand man is designed for that kind of experience which is based on values that arise out of the context of eternal concerns as it relates to the next life and the long range as it relates to this life. On the other hand the flesh with its strong orientation for the immediate, wars against the eternal and the long range. The sinner ends up doing like Esau did when he sold his birthright for a mess of pottage. Sin offers quick thrills and excitement. When it is followed it throws the person in conflict both with God and with himself.

Paul has made it quite clear up to this point in Romans that there is a design of God in man that at least to some extent affects his experience. Rom. 2:14, 15 makes clear that moral law has been written or designed into the heart of man. In 1:32 the design of God in man is such that even those without special revelation know "that they which commit such things [the sins listed in 1:29-31] are worthy of death." See comments on 1:21 for a discussion of the fact that even the pagan knows that there is a God.

When we put it all together, there is no reason to question the fact that an unregenerate person can have the experience referred to in 7:22. This is especially true when the context makes it clear that this delight is defeated. This delight in the law does not lead to obedience to the law, but it is a part of that experience which the Holy Spirit can use to help that person realize his need of Christ.

An unregenerate person cannot develop a single mind in which his undivided being is committed to delighting in the law of God. He is capable of being double-minded. He can, so to speak, have one mind that delights in the law of God, and yet another mind that is set in opposition to that which is represented by the law of God. Remember that James said, "A double minded man *is* unstable in all his ways" (1:8).

23 But I see another law in my members, warring against the law of my mind, and bringing me into captivity to the law of sin which is in my members.

But I see another law in my members, warring against the law of my mind (Greek *nous*). The "members" referred to here are the members of the body such as hands, feet, eyes, ears, etc. "Another law" seems to be the same as "the law of sin" found in the last part of the verse. The mind (*nous*) would be a part of the inward man of v. 23. In this case it is the mind as it sides with the law. It is the mind in its deepest and truest sense. This does not mean that the mind in its entirety delights in the law of God. Rather, it is the mind in its best sense. The sad fact is that the mind is divided.

The law of sin is in a state of declared war against the mind as representing the deepest and truest side of the person. It is locked in fierce conflict against that for which the law of God stands.

And bringing me into captivity to the law of sin which is in my members. Concerning the words "bringing me into captivity" Barnes comments, "Making me a prisoner, or a captive. This is the completion of the figure respecting the warfare. A captive taken in war was at the disposal of the victor" (167, 168).

In v. 14 Paul said, "I am carnal sold under sin." In vv. 15-23 he describes what it means to be "carnal sold under sin." It is a state in which the better judgment or the better self is brought to a crushing defeat. He is a captive to sin.

C. The Law Reveals to Man That He Must Look Outside Himself for Deliverance (7:24,25).

24 O wretched man that I am! who shall deliver me from the body of this death?

O wretched (Greek *talaiporos*) **man that I am.** Olshausen points out that the word translated "wretched" is from two words that mean "to suffer" and "a rock, a heavy stone," and therefore "is very suitable for describing the hard pressure under which the man is suffering during the dominion of sin" (257). Vincent says it means, **"Originally,** wretched through the exhaustion of hard labor" (705). It is the expression of one who is tired and weary from defeat. He is miserable. He is in desperate need of deliverance.

Who shall deliver me from the body of this death? The use of "who" suggests that the need is for a personal deliverer.

"The body of this death" could also be translated "this body of death." As the KJV translates, "this" modifies death rather than body. It seems to me that the meaning of "death" in this verse is what demands most of our attention.

There can be no doubt about the fact that the predominant meaning of "death" in Romans is "death as the penalty of sin." See 1:32; 5:12, 14, 17, 21; 6:16, 21, 23; 7:5, 10, 13; and 8:2, 6.

The "death to sin" which the believer died to in Christ (6:2-8, 11) refers to the payment of the penalty for sin. In 7:4 the reference to the believer's death "to the law by the body of Christ" is the death penalty as prescribed by the law.

It is obvious that the death referred to in 7:24, and the other occurrences in 7:7-25, is not the death believers died in Christ either to sin or to the law. To have died to sin with Christ or to the law is good. The death in 7:7-25 is bad.

No one could question that the death referred to in 7:7-25 is bad. It is granted that Paul *could* use "death" in v. 24 in a different way than anywhere else in Romans. However, first consideration should be to death as the penalty for sin. If it makes sense in the context, it should require a very strong reason for taking death to have some other meaning.

If death in v. 24 is a reference to the penalty for sin, the case is settled on the side of understanding Paul to be talking about an unregenerate person. The cry for deliverance would be a cry for deliverance from sin and its penalty. If we conclude that "this" modifies "death," "this death" would be the same death that is in the picture in vv. 9-13. That death is inflicted by the law (v. 13).

It is usually agreed that the "body" in this verse is the physical body. That being true, we should understand body to be a synechdoche in which the part is given for the whole. The reference would be to our total being, not just the physical body. It is the whole person who is under the sentence of death.

Godet makes an interesting observation on behalf of taking the reference here to be to the unregenerate. "Who" (Greek *tis*) is an indefinite pronoun. This means that the cry for help was from one who at the time could not name his deliverer. Godet says, "A Christian may find himself in distress: but he knows at least the name of his deliverer" (290). The law can show the need of a deliverer, but it cannot name the deliverer.

25 I thank God through Jesus Christ our Lord. So then with the mind I myself serve the law of God; but with the flesh the law of sin.

The KJV translates, "I thank God." Most other translations read, "Thank God" or the equivalent. The difference in translation is based on a difference of opinion on how the Greek text should read.

There is no essential difference in the meaning whether it reads, "I thank God" or "Thank God." Those interested in a discussion of the textual problems can find treatments in Cranfield 367, note 1; Godet 290, 291; Murray 269, note 37; and Sanday and Headlam 184.

Thanks is given to God for the fact that through Jesus Christ there is deliverance from the penalty (the sentence of death) and the power of sin. The answer for the one who has seen his miserable state of affairs through his encounter with the law is Jesus Christ. In this answer Paul did not go into detail. It was not necessary because it had already received adequate treatment earlier in the book. Also, it would be given further treatment in chap. 8.

The kind of deliverance referred to and the time of the deliverance will be understood by a person in the light of his interpretation of the preceding verses. My own interpretation reflects belief that Paul has presented the experience of the unregenerate in 7:7-24. In that light the deliverance would involve the initial experience of salvation.

There are basically two views among those who believe that Paul has been presenting the experience of the regenerate: (1) That the deliverance looks forward to the eschatological future. (2) That the deliverance refers to a victory to be experienced by the believer in the present life.

Some commentators are vague about whether the deliverance refers to this life or the life to come. Among those who take Paul to be referring to the regenerate, and who set forth a clear position, most take the reference to be to the eschatological future when our bodies will be resurrected. (Among those who take this view are Cranfield 369, 370; Hendriksen 238; and Murray 269, 270.)

Lenski also belongs to this group. This would be a necessary inference from his statement, "When and how this will take place is reserved for later statement in 8:11, 17, 21, 23" (490). These verses all relate to the resurrection of the body and the eschatological future.

Haldane agrees that the deliverance does not take place in this life. However, he gives death as the time when the believer will be "entirely freed from the evil nature" (299).

Among those who believe the deliverance to refer to victory to be experienced by the believer in this life are Bruce (156, 157); McQuilkin (83); and Moule. Moule paraphrases, "who giveth that deliverance, in covenant and in measure now, fully and in eternal actuality hereafter **through Jesus Christ our Lord**" (*Romans,* 201).

After summing up the teaching of Rom. 7, McQuilkin says: "If that were the end of the story, then the Christian indeed would be wretched. But that is not the end of the story. Paul goes on in chapter 8 to explain the wonderful working of God the Holy Spirit in every believer" (83).

There is an important difference in these two views. Those who view the deliverance as occurring at the time of the resurrection take 7:14-24 to refer to the *normal* state of a mature Christian in this life. There is no deliverance in this life from the state described in 7:14-24.

Those who understand the deliverance to take place in this life do not understand the description in 7:14-24 to be the condition of the mature Christian. It is either the picture of a *defeated* Christian, or it is the way a Christian would be if he did not have the delivering power of the Holy Spirit.

As set forth in earlier comments on 7:14-24, I have concluded that Paul presented a picture of one who was unregenerate. The full force of what Paul said would apply only to one who had been properly taught by the law. He recognized the fact that the law is good. This would certainly imply that the Holy Spirit had been working in the person's heart through the law. He recognized that though he saw the good of the law, he was an utter failure before it. He was miserable and wretched. Being taught by the law, he could cry out for deliverance. But the law could not name the deliverer.

The law paved the way, so far as realizing the need is concerned, but only the gospel could name the redeemer. In v. 25 he recognizes Christ as the deliverer. At that moment he experienced salvation.

Since further defense of my view requires a treatment of the last part of this verse, additional comment will be reserved until then.

So then with the mind (Greek *nous*) **I myself serve** (Greek *douleuo*) **the law of God; but with the flesh the law of sin.** Cranfield remarks:

> It is hardly surprising that many of those who have seen in v. 24 the cry of an unconverted man (or of a Christian on a low level of Christian life) and in v. 25a an indication that the longed for deliverance has actually been accomplished, have felt this sentence to be an embarrassment, since, coming after thanksgiving, it appears (on this understanding of vv. 24-25a) to imply that the condition of the speaker after his deliverance is exactly the same as it was before it (368).

Certainly, the fact that the reference to serving sin in the verse follows the recognition that Christ is the deliverer does raise questions. However, it is even more of a problem to take the position that the deliverance spoken of has no application to the here and now. It is unthinkable that Paul would have described such a distressing experience and then say that the situation would in this life remain unchanged. Is Paul really saying that there will be no deliverance until the resurrection?

Murray, who puts the deliverance into the eschatological future, says "That it parallels 1 Cor. 15:57, where the hope of the resurrection is beyond question, is not by any means an unreasonable supposition" (269). First Cor. 15:57 does refer to the resurrection. There Paul says, "But thanks be to God, which giveth us the victory through our Lord Jesus Christ." But is he talking about the same thing here in Rom. 7:25?

In 1 Cor. 15 the victory is from our corruptible and mortal body. The wording of v. 57 could apply to any victory, but the context shows that it deals with the fact that our present bodies are corruptible and mortal. We could also add that the hope of the resurrection gives us patience to wait for it. Murray says concerning the person referred to in 7:25, "The warfare continues, but he is upheld in the conflict by the assurance that finally there will be complete deliverance" (270).

Two observations are worthy of note: The first is that if the last part of 7:25 simply indicates a continuation of what has already been set forth in vv. 14-24, there is no sign that he is being upheld by a hope of the resurrection. He is defeated, not upheld.

The second observation is that the contexts of Rom. 7:25 and 1 Cor. 15:57 are very different. The context of 1 Cor. 15 deals with the condition of the physical body. The context of Rom. 7:25 is failure before God's moral law. First Cor. 15:57 deals with a deliverance from the corruption and mortality of the physical body. Romans 7:25 deals with deliverance from the penalty and the power of sin.

How do we deal with the problem of the word order? We may be puzzled about why immediately after Paul said, "I thank God through Jesus Christ our Lord" he said, "So then with the mind I serve the law of God, but with the flesh the law of sin." However, there seems to be no real difficulty in what he meant.

It is quite clear that v. 25b is a brief summation of what is said in vv. 14-24. On the basis of reasons already given it is insisted that vv. 14-24 speak of an unregenerate person. He is concerned about his condition. It has become more than he can bear. He cries out, "O wretched man that I am! who shall deliver me from the body of this death?" Then, he says, "I thank God through Jesus Christ our Lord." It is on the basis of this that in 8:1 he says, "There is therefore now no condemnation to them which are in Christ Jesus."

It is quite clear that the deliverance referred to in v. 25a is the deliverance from the penalty and power of sin. If so, regardless of the fact that the next words read, "So then with the mind I myself serve the law of God; but with the flesh the law of sin," they must be understood as referring to that which is chronologically prior to the recognition of Christ as the deliverer, not a state remaining after the recognition of Christ as Lord and Savior.

We may not know why Paul said it that way, but he did. The meaning is not obscured by it.

We may compare the puzzle of the bumble bee. It is said that according to the law of aerodynamics bumble bees should not be able to fly. But nobody argues that they cannot fly. We may not know *why* Paul used the order that he did in v. 25, but that should not keep us from knowing *what* he said.

In discussing the various views and the pros and cons of each, it is easy to lose sight of the *purpose* of the passage. It is clearly seen in v. 7 that *the purpose of vv. 7-25 is a defense of the good of the law. Whatever the passage says about the unregenerate or the regenerate is secondary to the defense of the good of the law.*

Hodge says: "The main idea of the whole passage, the subject which the apostle laboured to have understood, is the impotence of the law—the impossibility of obtaining deliverance from sin through its influence or agency" (239).

Up to 7:7 Paul had made it quite clear that the law was impotent so far as justification from sin is concerned. It is also clearly implied that deliverance from the law is supposed to be beneficial insofar as our sanctification is concerned. It should not be necessary to restate the reasons for believing these conclusions.

While Paul has pointed out the impotence of the law for justification and sanctification, that is not the purpose of vv. 7-25. The purpose of these verses is to show what the law could do. In spite of the fact that the law could neither justify nor sanctify, the law was not sinful (7:7). It was not devoid of value. As this passage plainly tells us, in spite of the law's failure to bring salvation, it was good.

What does this passage tell us that the law has done and can do which is good? We must see this or we miss the point of the passage. There are basically three things the law *can* do which are pointed out in this passage. (1) In vv. 7-13 we see that the law tells us what the nature of sin is like. Sin is powerful (v. 8). It is deceitful (vv. 10, 11). It is exceeding sinful (v. 13). Sin is such that the law which is good must impose the penalty of death on the sinner (vv. 9-11, and 13).

(2) In vv. 14-23 the law reveals man's relationship to sin. He is enslaved by sin in spite of the fact that he hates sin (v. 15) and recognizes the good of the law and delights in the law (vv. 16-23).

(3) The law can help prepare the way for the gospel. A person so instructed by the law knows how bad sin is. He also knows that in spite of his noblest efforts to do otherwise, his slavery to sin shows him to be a miserable violator of the law. The law helps him see the need of a deliverer, although it cannot name the deliverer. The gospel names the deliverer. If he has allowed the Holy Spirit to use the law to properly instruct him, he has been prepared to respond to the gospel by recognizing Christ to be his Savior and Lord. If this is the positive ministry of the law, it is obvious that vv. 14-24 are referring to one who is unregenerate.

To sum it up, the person under consideration is said to serve with his mind the law of God, but with the flesh the law of sin. The serving of the law of God consisted of "hating sin" (v. 15); "consenting that the law is good" (v. 16); "wishing to perform what the law required" (v. 18); and "delighting in the law of God" (v. 22).

The serving of the law of sin consists of "sinning even though he hated it" (v. 15). This includes "the inability to perform the good required by the law" (v. 18) in spite of the fact that one recognizes the law as good (v. 16) and in spite of the fact that he delights in the law (vv. 22, 23).

The word "serve" in v. 25 (Greek *douleuo*) means "to be a slave to sin." If this is taken to be a reference to a believer, it is in contradiction with 6:6 where it is said "that henceforth we should not serve [*douleuo*] sin." In 6:16 the word for "servant" (Greek *doulos*) means slave. To obey sin means to be a slave to sin. To be freed from sin in 6:18 (freedom from slavery to sin) means that the believer has become a slave to righteousness. It is quite clear in the light of chap. 6 that the person in 7:7-24 cannot be considered a believer. He is not a slave to righteousness. So far as any good action is concerned, His "serving" goes no further than his mind.

Plumer who takes 7:7-25 to be Paul speaking of himself as a believer says concerning v. 25, "Sin had not dominion over him, though it had power against him. He did highly and prevailingly please Christ, and did not willingly or habitually serve sin" (359).

There is no trouble seeing how Plumer's comments fit Paul. But how do those comments fit the person in vv.

14-25? What would it take to indicate that sin has dominion over a person? If to be "carnal sold under sin" (v. 14), to be defeated on every hand in spite of his desires (vv. 15-22) does not mean to be under the dominion of sin, what would mean that?

It seems that there are basically two reasons that many have chosen to believe that Paul is dealing with the regenerate in vv. 14-25: (1) They are afraid that to take the reference to be to an unregenerate person would weaken the doctrine of depravity. (2) They feel a sense of rapport or identification with what they are reading.

Let us consider the first reason. A concern that we have an adequate view of depravity is to be appreciated. Some who believe that the reference is to the unregenerate have had a weak view of depravity. However, it is difficult to see on what basis one can say that the doctrine of depravity is weakened by understanding the passage to deal with an unregenerate person.

What is so weak about a doctrine of depravity that sees fallen man in the agony of contradiction? The power of depravity thwarts the strongest desires and efforts of a person to break loose from the power of sin. Depravity sets out to tear the person apart. As depraved, man is bent on breaking loose from all traces of being in the moral image of God. This cannot be done. When he fails in this, the depraved man makes a strong attempt to suppress the truth regarding God and righteousness. He is a person made in the image of God but in the grip of the enslaving power of sin.

The alternative to the view of the depraved person as having a divided self is to see him as an undivided self. What would such a person be like? He would be a person who is singly devoted to sin with no internal conflict produced from his moral constitution. That would mean that he would have internal harmony organized around the principle of evil. Such a view of depravity is too simplistic. It is grossly inadequate. It does not square either with the teaching of Scripture or with the facts of human experience.

Let me repeat again that the exact picture in vv. 14-24 is that of one who has allowed the Holy Spirit to use the law as a means of getting him to see the need of deliverance and to respond to the gospel. However, the concept of a divided self can to some extent be seen in all those who are unregenerate. A knowledge of these facts and how to discern their presence in people will be an invaluable tool in reaching people with the gospel.

Many will object to the reference to the ministry of the Holy Spirit in vv. 7-25. They will point out that He is not mentioned. The ministry of the Holy Spirit is not limited to the places where He is named. His ministry is also found where we can see the evidence of His work.

Let us now deal with the second reason, given above, why many people understand the reference to be to the regenerate person. Any person who is experiencing internal conflict likes to know that someone else has been down the same road. He finds it reassuring to find that some other believer has had an experience similar to his own. He sees himself in vv. 14-24.

I find no fault with the believer who has a sense of identification with these verses. Both saint and sinner know what tension, conflict, and contradiction are. The difference comes in *the degree* of the conflict. If the words in vv. 14-24 mean anything at all, they mean that the person is practicing sin. That Paul is talking about practicing sin is made clear by his use of the words "that which I do" (Greek *katergazomai*) (v. 15); "I that do it" (vv. 17 and 20); "that

I do" (Greek *poieo*) (vv. 15 and 19); "I do" (vv. 16 and 20); and "that I do" (Greek *prasso*) (v. 19). These words are in the present tense. Both the tense and the meaning of these words support the conclusion that Paul is speaking about practicing sin.

Arminius says concerning Augustine's view of this passage: "He interprets the evil which the apostle says he did by the word *to lust* or *to indulge in concupiscence*; and the good which he says he omitted, by the word *not to lust*—a most absurd and distorted application of these terms!" (II:440). Arminius goes on to discuss at length the fact that the three words translated "do" (*katergazomai, poieo,* and *prasso*) refer to actions rather that lust (II:440ff).

It is not at all necessary to find the inner conflict of the believer in this passage in order to believe in such a conflict. From the day I was saved until the present moment I have been aware of the principle of conflict. Such conflict can be seen in Gal. 5:17. Every admonition to a believer assumes at least some level of conflict.

In a time of weakness a Christian could experience an intense inner conflict, but his general condition will not be as is described in vv. 14-24. John tells us, "Whosoever is born of God doth not commit [does not practice] sin; for his seed remaineth in him: and he cannot sin [practice sin], because he is born of God" (1 Jn. 3:9). John also says, "For whatsoever is born of God overcometh the world: and this is the victory that overcometh the world, *even* our faith" (1 Jn. 5:4).

I find no fault with anyone who finds some application of the principle of inner conflict from vv. 14-24 to the conflict within a believer. However, in the light of 1 Jn. 3:9 and 5:4 (and several other passages that could be cited) the extent of the defeat set forth in this passage cannot apply to the regenerate person.

As we go on into chap. 8, we will see more reasons for understanding this passage to refer to the unregenerate. Anyone analyzing this passage should bear in mind: (1) Those who take this passage to refer to the regenerate do not see the level of defeat and misery as would be seen by those who understand it to refer to an unregenerate person. (2) Those who take this to refer to the unregenerate understand the level of defeat and misery to be greater than those who take the reference to be to the regenerate. The responsibility of the exegete is to decide which view is correct. While I think it is important to arrive at the truth set forth in the passage, I do not believe the matter of whether a person takes the passage to be unregenerate or regenerate in and of itself should be a test of fellowship.

Summary 7:7-25

Up to this point, Paul has shown the inadequacy of the law to provide justification (3:20; 4:14, 15; and 7:5). He has also shown that the law is inadequate to produce sanctification (6:14—7:6). In fact, deliverance from the law is seen as contributing to our sanctification (7:6).

In view of the fact that Paul had given such stress to the inadequacy of the law in justification and sanctification, it is understandable that in 7:7 he would raise the question, "Is the law sin?" His answer involved a quick denial. This meant that what follows would take on the form of a defense of the good of the law.

In setting forth the case in behalf of the good of the law, Paul points out that it was the law which gave him a true picture of sin. It was as if sin was dormant until the law came. The law stirred sin into activity. It stirred up all kinds of lust. The cause of the spread of lust was sin, not the law.

When sin was stirred into activity by the law, sin was seen for what it is. It is clear that the violation of the law put him under the sentence of death. When it came to light that sin had caused the law to find it necessary to inflict the death penalty, the picture for a while was confused. Is the law the culprit? Is it really the cause of the sentence of death? No. The culprit is sin. The fact that the law which is holy, just, and good found it necessary to inflict the death penalty upon sin makes it clear that sin is exceeding sinful. It would surely take something very bad for something as good as the law to find it necessary to inflict the death penalty.

In addition to showing the nature and the penalty of sin, the law helps the person see his own relationship to sin. It is one of being carnal, sold under sin. He finds that no matter how good he sees the law to be and no matter how bad he finds sin to be, he still remains a slave to the bondage of sin. His better self is unable to perform what he learns from the law to be good. He is in conflict and contradiction within himself.

This experience of conflict, contradiction, and despair led him to cry out, "O wretched man that I am! who shall deliver me from the body of this death?" (v. 24).

Within himself he can wish the good but he cannot bring it to pass. It is clear that he is a slave to sin. He is under the sentence of death. His only hope is in Jesus Christ.

Application: Teaching and Preaching the Passage

1. What Paul had said about the law up to this point could raise questions in people's minds about whether he had a negative image of the law (see comments on v. 7). At this point Paul deemed it wise to defend the good of the law. This he did in the remainder of the chapter.

2. There are three basic reasons given for the fact that the law is good:

(1) The law reveals the nature of sin (vv. 7-13).

Sin is powerful (v. 8). Sin is the cause of death (vv. 9-11). Sin is deceitful (vv. 10, 11). Sin is exceedingly sinful (v. 13).

(2) The law reveals man's relationship to sin (vv. 14-23).

Fallen man is sold under sin (v. 14). Though he admits that the law is good and wishes to live by it, because of sin he is unable to do so. Though he delights in the law of God, he is still brought into captivity to sin (vv. 21-23).

(3) The law reveals man's guilt and bondage to sin and thus prepares the way for the gospel (vv. 24, 25).

3. This passage illustrates how depravity puts a person in conflict with and in contradiction to his design. Man both wants to and does not want to do the same thing. He is a victim of a divided self (see comments on v. 25). Much attention needs to be given on how we can effectively confront fallen man with his experience of internal conflict, contradiction, and a divided self. This is the source of many of the problems that lead to alcohol and drugs.

4. This is the most controversial passage in the Book of Romans. The different views relating to the passage are set forth in the introduction to the passage. These should be carefully studied and evaluated in the study of the text.

VI. THE GLORIOUS BLESSINGS OF THE PERSON WHO HAS RECEIVED THE GOD-PROVIDED RIGHTEOUSNESS (8:1-39).

A. There Is No Condemnation (8:1-3).

1 *There is* therefore now no condemnation to them which are in Christ Jesus, who walk not after the flesh, but after the Spirit.

***There is* therefore now no condemnation to them which are in Christ Jesus.** Our first concern is to decide what "therefore" reaches back to in the preceding context. Hodge comments:

> The word *therefore* indicates that what follows is an inference; but from what? From the conclusion of the seventh chapter, or from the whole previous discussion? The latter seems to be the only correct view of the context because the fact that there is no condemnation to believers is no fair inference from what is said at the close of the preceding chapter (248).

Cranfield would be in essential agreement with Hodge but would make a more precise statement concerning the reference. He denies any reference back to 7:25 by "therefore." He connects it with 7:6 (373).

Cranfield and Hodge are rejecting the reference back to 7:25 because of their interpretations of 7:25a. The reason is that since vv. 7-24 are viewed by them as referring to one who is already saved, they do not view 7:25a as dealing with justification. This being the case, "no condemnation" could not be an inference from 7:25a.

Those who take 7:7-25 or 7:14-25 to refer to the regenerate have a problem relating 8:1 to the context. That is the reason Cranfield and Hodge go back beyond 7:7 to find the basis for the inference "no condemnation."

Others who take 7:7-25 or 7:14-25 to refer to one who is already regenerate take yet another approach. Hendriksen and Murray in distinction from Cranfield and Hodge recognize a relationship between the immediately preceding context and 8:1.

Hendriksen says: "There is a close connection between 'Thanks be to God through Christ Jesus our Lord' (7:25a) and 'There is therefore now no condemnation', etc. (8:1) . . . .For Paul 'no condemnation' means freedom not only from sin's *guilt*, but also its *enslaving power*" (245).

Murray and Hendriksen are in agreement in the inclusion of both justification (freedom from guilt) and sanctification (freedom from the enslaving power of sin). They seem to think that this inclusion of both justification and sanctification in "no condemnation" is required by the context. Murray explains:

"If, however, this view of condemnation is adopted, then this verse, as inference, can be connected with what immediately precedes, either restrictedly (7:25) or more inclusively (6:1-7:25). The latter alternative is preferable . . ." (275).

Lenski takes yet another view. He says: "Since Paul serves God's law with his mind and inward being although his flesh still serves the sin's law (7:25), neither he nor those like him are under condemnation from God" (494).

All of the above (from Cranfield, Hodge, Hendriksen, Murray, and Lenski) reflect an attempt to cope with the meaning of 8:1 in keeping with the fact that they understand 7:14-25 to be a reference to the regenerate.

Cranfield and Hodge reject any connection between "There is therefore now no condemnation" and 7:25 because they see nothing in it to form the basis of the inference of no condemnation in 8:1.

Hendriksen and Murray seek to

establish a connection between 7:25 and 8:1, but they do so at the expense of tampering with the meaning of "no condemnation." When they make the meaning of "no condemnation" to include both "freedom from guilt" and "freedom from the enslaving power of sin," they make "no condemnation" include both justification and sanctification. There is no warrant for making "no condemnation" include sanctification, nor is it necessitated by the context.

Lenski's view is an attempt to reason from the evidence of salvation to the assurance of justification. In an appropriate context such would be possible. However, I can see no basis for giving it such a meaning in this context. Later on in the chapter Paul will reason from the evidence of salvation to the presence of salvation (8:13), but that is not the case here. Even if we take the words, "So then with the mind I myself serve the law of God; but with the flesh the law of sin" (7:25), to refer to a regenerate person, it would not likely be the basis for inferring "no condemnation." We would think that any reference to assurance of "no condemnation" would be *in spite of* the description in 7:25, not an inference from it as would be required by "therefore."

If my interpretation of 7:14-25 is correct, there is no problem at all in connecting "therefore" of 8:1 with 7:25. The person who was so painfully aware of his guilt, condemnation, and bondage to sin realized his need and recognized Jesus Christ to be his deliverer. The words "There is therefore now no condemnation" follows clearly and logically from "I thank God through Jesus Christ."

I am aware of the fact that the need of the person in 7:14-24 is not only deliverance from guilt, but also deliverance from the bondage of sin. However, deliverance from the guilt of sin is necessary as the grounds for being delivered from the power of sin. Chapter 8 begins with "no condemnation" and will move toward sanctification.

I want to give another reason for connecting "therefore" with 7:25. The tone of 7:14-25 is one of deep personal involvement. The subjective feeling is strong. That being the case, it is highly unlikely that with a mere stroke of the pen that line of thought could be dropped and suddenly refer back to 7:6.

In the words, "There is therefore now no condemnation," there is a note of rejoicing and a deep sigh of relief. In the KJV the negative Greek particle (*ouden*) is translated "no." Shedd says, "*Ouden* is highly emphatic, by its position: 'none at all, of any kind'" (226). Wuest translates this verse, "Therefore, now, there is not even one bit of condemnation to those who are in Christ Jesus" (127).

We see here one who has moved from a state of deep despair to confidence that in Jesus Christ all condemnation has been taken away. This position of no condemnation is "in Christ Jesus," i.e., "in union with Christ Jesus." (For a discussion of how the union with Christ makes "no condemnation possible, see comments on 6:3-8.)

Who walk not after the flesh, but after the Spirit. It is usually agreed that these words were not likely in the original autograph. This does not alter the meaning of the passage since these words are found in v. 4. The *Majority Text* includes these words. They are omitted in the *United Bible Society Text*.

2 For the law of the Spirit of life in Christ Jesus hath made me free from the law of sin and death.

"For" suggests that what follows is a reason that there is no condemnation as stated in v. 1. If that be the case, v. 2 is speaking of justification rather than sanctification.

It is clear that v. 4 does deal with sanctification. This fact has caused many to conclude that v. 2 must deal with sanctification. As we saw in v. 1, some feel compelled to find sanctification in "There is. . .no condemnation."

As I see it, Paul is doing the same thing here that he did in chap. 6. In 6:2-11 he showed how justification contributed to sanctification. In chap. 8, Paul begins with justification in v. 1 (no condemnation), and moves toward sanctification in v. 4 ("who walk not after the flesh, but after the Spirit"). In vv. 2, 3, Paul is still dealing with justification where he gives a brief treatment of how it is accomplished.

Most would agree, if v. 1 speaks of justification and is connected with v. 2 by "for," that we would likely expect v. 2 to be a part of the reason (or basis) for justification. This is especially true if we see how this prepares the way for the transition to sanctification in v. 4.

In v. 2 Paul speaks about a deliverance *from the law of sin and death.* Many are of the opinion that "the law of sin and death" is the same as "the law of sin" in 7:23. (See Cranfield 375; and Plumer 369, 370.) If this be the case, v. 2 deals with sanctification because it refers to deliverance from the dominion of sin.

The more likely interpretation of "the law of sin and death" is "the law which says that sin brings death." This is exactly what the moral law of God says. As Ezekiel says, "The soul that sinneth, it shall die" (18:4b).

When we were under the law of God (as distinguished from being under grace), the law pronounced the death penalty upon us because we had sinned. Under grace we have been delivered from the curse (or penalty) of the law. Denny says, "It is subjection to the law of sin and death which involves condemnation; emancipation from it leaves no place for condemnation" (644).

Calvin remarks, "I would not dare, with some interpreters, take *the law of sin and death* to mean the law of God. This seems too harsh an expression" (157). Haldane answers those who would agree with Calvin: "Since, then, the law of God, which though it commands holiness, gives the knowledge of sin, and the breach of it is death, it may, without arguing the smallest disrespect or disparagement to the holy law, be called *the law of sin and death*" (318). (See also Hodge 251.)

If we take the above interpretation of "the law of sin and death" to be correct, it follows that this verse deals with justification. This is true because it is justification that frees us from the death penalty inflicted by the law.

Notice the first part of the verse: **the law of the Spirit of life in Christ Jesus.** If we take this to refer to the way justification is accomplished, then it will follow that "in Christ Jesus" refers to the union of Christ and the beliver. In this union the death and righteousness of Christ become the death and righteousness of the believer. This means that in Christ we have all that God requires of us. We have His death which pays for our sins and His righteousness which meets God's requirement of absolute obedience. (See the discussion on the union of Christ and the believer in comments on 6:3-8.)

Now look at **the law of the Spirit of life.** I agree with Hodge when he says, "*The law of the Spirit* is here opposed to *the law of sin and death*, mentioned in the other clause of the verse. The interpretation of the one phrase, therefore, must decide that of the other" (250).

"The law of the Spirit of life" is the source of the deliverance from "the law of sin and death" (the death sentence inflicted upon sin by the law). That being true we would expect "the law of the Spirit of life" to deal with the application of the benefits of atonement.

If "the law of sin and death" means the law which says that sin brings death, it should follow that "the law of the Spirit of life" would mean "the law which says that the Holy Spirit gives life (deliverance from death)." This life would be given in union with Christ. The Holy Spirit by baptizing the believer into Christ formed the union between Christ and the believer.

The meaning of the verse is, "The law which says that the Holy Spirit gives life in union with Christ has made me free from the law which inflicts death on the sinner."

3 For what the law could not do, in that it was weak through the flesh, God sending his own Son in the likeness of sinful flesh, and for sin, condemned sin in the flesh.

For. "For" connects this verse with v. 2. It will explain why union with Christ delivers us from the death sentence of the law.

What the law could not do, in that it was weak through the flesh. If we understand v. 2 to be dealing with justification, it follows that what the law could not do was to provide justification. (See Hodge 252; and Haldane 320.) If we take v. 2 to be dealing with sanctification, it follows that what the law could not do is to deliver from the power of sin. (See David Brown 237; and Murray 277.)

It should be obvious that the law can neither justify nor sanctify. Our concern is to decide which of these impossibilities for the law Paul is dealing with here. Since I have decided that v. 2 deals with justification, I conclude that Paul is speaking of the impossibility of the law to justify.

The reason the law could not justify was not a fault of the law. Rather, it was *our* fault "through the weakness of the flesh." Our depraved nature made it utterly unthinkable and impossible for the law ever to render the verdict "justified" upon us as it relates to our own actions.

God sending his own Son in the likeness of sinful flesh. Bruce explains:

> The words are carefully chosen. 'In the likeness of flesh' by itself would be docetic [a denial of the humanity of Christ]; the essence of the apostolic message is that the Son of God came 'in flesh' and not merely 'in likeness of flesh.' Paul might have said simply 'in flesh,' but he wished to emphasize that human flesh was the realm in which sin gained a foothold and dominated the situation until the grace of God drew near. Hence, he says not simply 'flesh,' but 'sinful flesh' ('flesh of sin'). But to say that the Son of God came 'in sinful flesh' would imply that there was sin in Him, whereas (as Paul puts it elsewhere) He 'knew no sin' (2 Cor. 5:21). Hence He is described as being sent 'in the likeness of sinful flesh'" (161).

In order for Christ to be our Redeemer, it was necessary for Him to be both fully human and fully Divine. In typology we see that it was necessary for a redeemer to be a kinsman (Lev. 25:47-55). Only a kinsman had the right to be a redeemer. Christ fulfilled this requirement by His incarnation. He was truly human.

The price for our redemption was such that it could not be paid by one who was only human. By being fully God, as well as fully human, Christ was able to pay the full price for our redemption (Forlines, *Systematics* 132,133).

And for sin (Greek *peri hamartias*). This is understood by many to mean "sin-offering" or "sacrifice for sin." The case for believing the reference to refer to a sin-offering is well stated by David Brown:

> Since this very phrase is profusely employed in the LXX to denote the Levitical 'offerings for sin' (nearly sixty times in the one book of Leviticus), and since in that sense it is twice used in the Epistle to the Hebrews (10:6, 8)—in quotation from Ps. 40 [verse 6]—we cannot reasonably doubt that this (which is the marginal reading in our own version [KJV]) was the sense intended by the apostle, and that it would be so understood by all his readers who were familiar with the Greek Old Testament" (238).

Additional references in the O.T. where the word (Greek *hamartias*) meant sin-offering are Lev. 4:32; 5:6-9; 6:25; Num. 8:8; and 2 Chron. 29:24.

No one denies that its use in the Greek O.T. to mean sin-offering could suggest the same meaning here in Romans. However, some insist that the context here rules out that meaning (Alford 387; Cranfield 382; Godet 299; Lenski 500; and Murray 280). The reason given for rejecting the translation "sin-offering" is that the context does not support such a conclusion. It is said that the context is dealing with deliverance from the power of sin, not the penalty of sin. Some would admit that the concept of deliverance from the penalty of sin is in the verse, but the predominant thought is dealing with deliverance from the power of sin.

Others recognize the validity of considering the meaning to refer to a sin-offering, but consider the reference not to be restricted to deliverance from the penalty of sin. Deliverance from the power of sin is also thought to be included (Barnes 172; Plumer 371, 372; and Sanday and Headlam 193. Plumer also includes a discussion of the different views and their advocates).

David Brown considers the reference to be to sin-offering, but denies that justification is in view here. The deliverance is from the power of sin. (See quotation below on "condemned sin.")

I agree with those who take the meaning of "for" sin (Greek *peri hamartias*) to refer to sin-offering. When we think of a sin-offering, we think of it as paying the penalty of our sin. That is its most natural meaning. It should require strong evidence to think otherwise. I agree with Hodge (253) in limiting the focus in the meaning to expiation for sin.

Condemned (Greek *katakrino*) **sin in the flesh.** The way a person approaches these words depends on whether he thinks vv. 2, 3 are dealing with deliverance from the penalty of sin (justification) or whether they deal with deliverance from the power of sin (sanctification). The most natural meaning of "condemned sin" is to inflict the penalty upon sin. However, those who take the verse to be dealing with deliverance from the power of sin feel obligated to give it another meaning.

On the meaning of "condemned sin in the flesh" Brown says:

> Not in order to the *pardon* of it (as *Calvin, Hodge,* etc.); for justification, as we have seen, is not the thing here intended, but 'inflicted on it judicial vengeance in the flesh of Christ,' and *so condemned it to lose its hold over men*—at once to let go its iron grasp, and ultimately to be driven clean away from the domain of

human nature in the redeemed" (238).

Hodge strongly disagrees with those whose views agree with Brown. He gives three reasons for disagreeing:

> 1. Because *katakrino* never means to destroy, but always means to condemn.... 2. The sacrifice of Christ was the condemnation of sin. . . .His sufferings were penal, as they were judicially inflicted in satisfaction of justice. The proximate design and effect of a sacrifice is expiation, and not reformation or inward purification. . . . 3. The context requires this interpretation. The argument of the apostle is, that there is no *katakrina* (condemnation) to us, because God *katekrine (condemned) sin in Christ. The other interpretation supposes him to say, that there is no condemnation to us, because sin is destroyed in us. That is, we are justified on the ground of our own inherent goodness or freedom from sin. But this is contrary to the Scriptures, and to the faith of the Church (253).*

Some would agree that deliverance from sin is the essential evidence that a person is saved and thus justified. As a principle, it is true that the evidence of salvation helps us know that a person is justified. However, that is not the most natural way to interpret vv. 1-3. The language of these verses fits the idea that the condemnation of sin refers to the penal death of Christ which forms the grounds for our justification.

In the flesh. The NIV translates, "And so he condemned in sinful man." "In the flesh" is understood as "in sinful man." This would be equivalent to saying that God condemned the sin that was in the human race.

Plumer, with some modification, holds this view. He says:

> "Two explanations are offered. One is that God condemned sin in the flesh of Christ. . . . The other is that he condemned it in human nature. But it is better to unite the two and say that God condemned sin in human nature, of which Christ is a partaker" (372, 373).

Almost all commentaries take the reference to be to Christ's human nature. Hodge explains:

> *He thus condemned sin in the flesh;* that is he condemned it in the flesh or nature, which his Son assumed. Christ took upon himself our nature, in order to expiate the guilt of that nature which had sinned. As Christ, the apostle tells us, Heb. 2:14-18, did not undertake the redemption of angels, he did not assume their nature, but took part in flesh and blood (253).

The important truth of Christ as the Kinsman Redeemer is involved here. It was man that had sinned. Therefore, the requirements of the law for man must be met by one who is man. As the incarnate Christ, He was fully man and fully God.

As man, Christ rendered perfect obedience to the law in His life. As man, He suffered the penalty for sin. However, we must recognize that the human nature of Christ in and of itself could not have suffered an infinite penalty. But since the human nature was in union with the Divine nature, infinite suffering could and did take place at the cross. (For a more thorough development of atonement, see comments on 3:25, 26.)

It is true that some who believe the satisfaction view of atonement see this verse referring to deliverance from the power of sin rather than the penalty of sin. It should be remembered that no person who believes in the governmental view of atonement will see this passage referring to the penalty of sin.

This is true because of the simple fact that they do not believe that Christ's death was a payment of the penalty for sin. For a discussion on the governmental view of atonement and justification, see comments on 3:25, 26 and 4:3-5.

B. A Practical Fulfillment of the Righteousness of the Law Has Been Made Possible For Believers (8:4).

4 That the righteousness of the law might be fulfilled in us, who walk not after the flesh, but after the Spirit.

In order **that the righteousness** (Greek *dikaioma*) **of the law might be fulfilled in us.** This word refers to the requirement of the law. The vast majority of commentators understand the reference here to be the practical fulfillment of the law in the life of the believer. Haldane takes exception with those who give this interpretation. He remarks:

> This fulfillment of the law cannot signify, as some commentators erroneously explain it, that obedience which believers are enabled to yield by the Holy Spirit in their regenerate state; for it is obvious that this is not the righteousness of the law. The very best of all their actions and thoughts come short of the perfection which the law demands; besides, its penalty would in this way be unfulfilled (326).

Hodge would be in essential agreement with Haldane. He explains: "If ver. 3 is understood of the sacrificial death of Christ, and of the condemnation of sin in him as the substitute of sinners, then this verse must be understood of justification, and not of sanctification" (254).

While I am in essential agreement with Haldane and Hodge on vv. 2, 3, I do not agree that the righteousness referred to in v. 4 is the righteousness provided for us in the atonement and applied to us in justification. It is not necessary to conclude with Haldane that the reference here is to a perfect or absolute righteousness. Language can be understood as being absolute or as being relative. The only way to tell whether language is relative or absolute is from the context. Rom. 13:8 and 10 refer to love as the fulfillment of the law. It is obvious that the reference is not to an absolute or perfect righteousness.

In vv. 1-4 Paul begins with justification and ends with sanctification. He is showing how justification contributes to sanctification. This has also been done more extensively in 6:2-11.

The "that" which introduces v. 4 is telling us the Divine *purpose* in justification. Justification is a means to an end. In this case, the end is sanctification. In Christ, the requirement of the law is met in the absolute sense. In our sanctification, the law is fulfulled in a relative sense.

Who walk not after the flesh, but after the Spirit. This part of the verse is a description of the way the righteousness of the law is fulfilled in us. In 6:2-11 Paul insisted that if we are justified, we are also sanctified. In these verses he reaffirms that truth.

While justification and sanctification are distinct, they cannot be separated. To imply that a person can be justified and be void of any experience of sanctification is to grossly misunderstand the gospel. As Hodge says: "The benefits of Christ's death are experienced only by those who walk not after the flesh. The gospel is not antinomian. Those only are justified who are sanctified. Holiness is the fruit and evidence of reconciliation" (255).

In the following verses Paul will

amplify the meaning of "walk[ing] not after the flesh, but after the Spirit."

C. There Is Deliverance From the Flesh By the Indwelling Holy Spirit (8:5-9).

5 For they that are after the flesh do mind the things of the flesh; but they that are after the Spirit the things of the Spirit.

For they that are after the flesh do mind the things of the flesh. Paul has clearly established in 6:2-23 and 8:1-4 that sanctification always accompanies justification. In vv. 5-16 he will develop more fully the contrast between the saved and the unsaved.

Concerning "mind" (Greek *phroneo),* Hodge explains:

> The word *phronein* is derived from *phren*, which is used for the seat of all mental affections and faculties, and therefore *phroneo* has a wide meaning. It expresses any form of mental activity, any exercise of the intellect, will, or affections. *They mind (phronousin),* therefore, means, they make the object on which their hearts are set, and to which their lives are devoted (255).

In the light of this meaning, the first part of the verse is saying that those who are after the flesh have their minds set on the things of the flesh. This same Greek word is translated "set your affections on" in Col. 3:2. Another way to express it is to say, "Those who are after the flesh are bent on following the flesh."

But they that are after the Spirit the things of the Spirit. In other words, they have their mind, heart, and will set on the things of the Spirit. It is usually recognized that there are times when it is hard to decide whether spirit (Greek *pneuma*) refers to the human spirit or the Holy Spirit. It would be agreed by most that the reference in vv. 5-9 is to the Holy Spirit.

We have two drastically different mind-sets in these verses: the mind that is set on the things of the flesh, and the mind that is set on the things of the Spirit.

The flesh here is probably the body representing the whole personality in the context of the here-and-now desires. Christian ethics requires the context of eternity, *i.e.* it operates in the context of eternal values. It is only in the context of eternal values that we can see through the emptiness of hedonism which makes pleasure the highest value.

The flesh is trying to enslave those under its sway to the principle of immediacy. The principle of immediacy narrows the time context to the here-and-now without facing the long-range and the eternal. With the narrowed time context of the immediate, illegal drugs and alcohol offer relief. Sexual immorality offers pleasure.

It is only in the context of the long-range and the eternal that the fallacy of illegal drugs, alcohol, and immorality can be seen. Those whose mind is set on the things of the Spirit see things in the light of God's value system. The here-and-now must be lived out in the context of the long-range and the eternal. In this context, living right makes sense. Right is what God calls right. In the light of eternal values, we can see the importance of standing for and even suffering for the Christian way of truth and life.

The flesh, as seen under the domination of the supremacy of the here-and-now, corrupts what would otherwise be legitimate desires. Legitimate desires must be held in check until the approprite time, place, and circumstances. For example, the Bible strongly condemns all forms of sexual immorality, but it also says, "Marriage is honourable in all, and the bed undefiled: but whoremongers and adulterers God will judge" (Heb. 13:4). It is legitimate to have an interest in material things, but it is not legitimate to become obsessed with them, nor to gain them by dishonest means. The Holy Spirit is working in us to help us have proper values and to live by those values.

6 For to be carnally minded *is* death; but to be spiritually minded *is* life and peace.

For to be carnally minded *is* death. "Carnally" is, literally, "of the flesh" (Greek *sarx*). The whole phrase is, "the mind of the flesh."

Concerning the meaning of "minded" (Greek *phronema*), Sanday and Headlam explain, "The content of *phronein* [see *phroneo* in verse 5], the general bent of thought and motive" (195). Vine says, "It signifies that which one has in mind, the thoughts and purposes." (114). Yeager gives as its meaning, "Attitude; way of thinking, philosophy" (520).

The meaning of the first part of the verse would be, "The fleshly way of thinking is death." The "death" here is the same as in 6:21 and 23. Such a person is already spiritually dead. If he continues to reject Christ and go on in his fleshly way of thinking, he will have his "part in the lake which burneth with fire and brimstone: which is the second death" (Rev. 21:8).

But to be spiritually minded (literally, "the mind (or way of thinking) of the Spirit") ***is* life** (Greek *zoe)* **and peace.** Life as it is used here is more than being alive in contrast to being dead. It is life in the qualitative sense. It is life as Jesus spoke of when He said, "I am come that they might have life, and that they might have it more abundantly" (Jn. 10:10). The life under consideration is eternal life. Many take eternal life to refer to the quality of life rather than the duration. It appears to me that quality is found in the word "life," and "eternal" denotes endless duration.

It is not the subjective thinking of the believer that forms the ground of life. This is resting solely on the atoning work of Christ. However, "the way of thinking of the Spirit" leads a person to place his full confidence in the atoning work of Christ for his life and peace.

Peace is a priceless possession. This is especially true of peace of heart and mind as it relates to eternity. This is the experience of all those who allow the Holy Spirit to lead them to place all of their confidence and hope in Jesus Christ.

7 Because the carnal mind *is* enmity against God: for it is not subject to the law of God, neither indeed can be.

Because the carnal mind ["the mind of the flesh"] ***is* enmity against God.** The verse gives the reason that the mind of the flesh ends up in death. Lenski explains, "By his own thought-product the fleshly-minded man cuts himself off from life and peace because all his thought (and thus all his acts) is enmity toward God, the one fount of life and peace. How can anything but death be left? By means of this enmity he who is fleshly-minded wills death to himself" (506).

The way of thinking of the mind of the flesh originated in the fall of man. When man revolted against God, it resulted in alienation from God. Since most who will read this commentary have been brought up in a context of Christian influence, some aspects of this alienation may not be as obvious as they would be in another setting. On the other hand, the strength of this enmity can be seen more clearly when it is reacting against an encounter with God's message.

In his revolt against God, fallen man has been trying desperately to put together a world-view which: (1) either leaves God out of the picture, or relegates Him to a low-keyed, insignificant role, and (2) limits the context of values to the here-and-now. It should be obvious that this cannot but constitute enmity toward God whether it be in the form of humanitarianism or whether it takes the form of active blasphemy.

For it is not subject (Greek *hupotasso*) **to the law of God.** Wuest observes that "be subject" is "a military term meaning 'to arrange in order under' a commanding general, for instance. Such a mind [in this verse] is not marshalled under the command of God, but Satan" (131). The condition of the carnal mind is such that it is not marching in God's army. It cannot march in God's army.

8 So then they that are in the flesh cannot please God.

So then they that are in the flesh cannot please God. The conjunction translated "so then" (Greek *de*) is more frequently translated "and" or "but." Many think it should be translated "and" here rather than "so then." The essential substance of the verse is not altered by the way it is translated. The message of the verse is loud and clear. The person in the flesh (the unsaved person) cannot please God. Any attempt to put life together without God and the eternal values which are grounded in God cannot help but fail to please God.

Cranfield says:

> Fallen man's fierce hostility to God is the response of his egotism (which is the essence of his fallenness) to God's claim to his allegiance. Determined to assert himself, to assert his independence, to be the centre of his own life, to be his own god, he cannot help but hate the real God whose very existence gives the lie to all self-assertion" (386, 387).

9 But ye are not in the flesh, but in the Spirit, if so be that the Spirit of God dwell in you. Now if any man have not the Spirit of Christ, he is none of his.

But ye are not in the flesh, but in the Spirit, if so be that the Spirit of God dwell in you. If there has been any doubt whether vv. 5-9 are describing the saved and the unsaved rather than the struggles of the believer, this verse should solve that problem. The person who is indwelt by the Holy Spirit is not in the flesh. Dwell (Greek *oikeo*) refers to taking up residence. The noun form (*oikos*) means house. The Holy Spirit has taken up residence in the believer. Sanday and Headlam say, "*Oikein en* denotes a settled, permanent penetrative influence" (196).

Let us turn our attention back to 7:14-24. It is hard to see how an interpreter, after going through 8:5-9 could consider the person in 7:14-24 as one who has set his mind on the things of the Spirit (8:5) which must be the case if 7:14-24 is referring to a believer. It seems to me to be a much better description of one who is "in the flesh."

Now if any man have not the Spirit of Christ, he is none of his. The force of "now" (Greek *de*) will be seen more clearly in this verse if we translate "but." *But* if the Spirit of Christ has not taken up residence in a person, he does not belong to Jesus Christ.

It is a necessary inference from this part of the verse that a person receives the Holy Spirit at the moment he becomes a Christian. This is the only way that the statement "If any man have not the Spirit of Christ, he is none of his" can be true. Certainly, no one would argue that the Spirit of Christ and the Spirit of God in the verse are not the same.

In view of the fact that Acts presents cases where the Holy Spirit was received after conversion (Acts 8:14-17), we need to determine how these statements can be harmonized. The answer is found in the fact that Acts records the history of a transitional period. In a transitional period, things do not always happen like they did before the transition began, nor do they always happen like they will after the transition is completed. To give special attention to the new relationship we have to the Holy Spirit since Pentecost, there were some cases in which the Holy Spirit was received after conversion. Since the close of the transitional period, the Holy Spirit has always been received at conversion. The statement here in v. 9 records the permanent doctrine of the Church. If a person has not received the Holy Spirit, he is not a Christian.

D. The Body Will Be Raised From the Dead By the Holy Spirit (8:10,11).

10 And if Christ *be* in you, the body *is* dead because of sin; but the Spirit *is* life because of righteousness.

And if Christ *be* in you, the body *is* dead because of sin. The reference here is to the fact that the body is mortal. Though we are in Christ, that will not exempt us from physical death.

But the Spirit *is* life because of righteousness. The major point to decide in this part of the verse is whether the reference is to the human spirit or to the Holy Spirit. The KJV translators took spirit (Greek *pneuma*) to be the Holy Spirit as is indicated by the capital "S." A number of commentators can be found who support each view. On the side that the reference is to the Holy Spirit are Cranfield (390); Harrison (90); Hendriksen (252, 253); and Murray (289, 290). On the side that the reference is to the human spirit are Hodge (259); Lenski (512); and Sanday and Headlam (198).

In favor of understanding this as the Holy Spirit is the fact that in vv. 1-9 "the Spirit" always means the Holy Spirit. Also, the two references in v. 11 are to the Holy Spirit.

In favor of seeing this as a reference to the human spirit, according to those who accept this view, is that "body" and spirit are in antithesis with one another. Thus the verse would say that because of sin, the physical body is destined to die. But because of justifying righteousness, the spirit is life. Life would be stressing the quality of life as set forth in v. 6.

The problem that we are faced with here is that either view would make sense in the context. However, as Bruce says, "Paul meant one or the other—which?" (164).

Granted, when a word (in this case *pneuma*) occurs several times in a context, if it clearly means one thing in all the other references, that meaning should be seriously considered in the verse under consideration. However, it is also true that unless a meaning is totally foreign to the whole context, in a given case a word may have one of its other meanings.

It is hard to look at v. 10 and not at least think about the possibility that it may refer to the human spirit. In rejecting this view, Harrison says:

> To be sure, the use of 'body' over against 'spirit' might seem to be sufficient ground for assuming that Paul is talking about two contrasting elements of the human constitution. But whereas such a sharp contrast is congenial to Greek thought, it is alien to the Hebraic concept of life that characterizes both Testaments. In fact, it has been recognized that in Paul's usage, 'body' usually means the totality of one's being (90).

I would certainly concur that Paul at times uses the word body as a synechdoche in which the part (body) is given for the whole (the total person). However, it seems to me that regardless of what the last part of v. 10 may mean, the word "body" in the first part is a reference to the physical body. Surely the "mortal body" of v. 11 is the physical body. It seems to me that the body of v. 10 is unquestionably the physical body which is subject to death.

In commenting on this verse, Barrett says, "'Your body' is 'you,' and you are dead; for this see 6:2-11; 7:1-6" (159). In order to support his conclusion that the body is the total person in this verse, Barrett takes the death here to be the same as the death to sin in 6:2-11 and the death to the law in 7:4. I am in agreement with Cranfield in reference to this interpretation of death in this verse when he says, "But an explanation along these lines is unlikely, since these deaths are (according to chapter 6) 'to sin' rather then 'because of sin'" (389).

Another objection to understanding this verse to mean the spirit of man centers around the word "life" (Greek *zoe*). It is said that Paul would have used "alive" rather than "life" if he had meant to refer to the human spirit rather than the Holy Spirit (Barrett 159; and Harrison 90).

My response is that in v. 6 life is attributed to the Christian. It can refer to the spirit of the Christian in this verse as easily as it did in v. 6. The reason for choosing the noun "life" would seem to be because he wanted to stress more than "aliveness." He wanted to stress the *quality* of life.

Regarding v. 10 as referring to the human spirit seems to make the smoothest flow of thought through v. 11.

11 But if the Spirit of him that raised up Jesus from the dead dwell in you, he that raised up Christ from the dead shall also quicken your mortal bodies by his Spirit that dwelleth in you.

But if the Spirit of him that raised up Jesus from the dead dwell (Greek *oikeo*) **in you.** This certainly refers to the Holy Spirit. The indwelling presence of the Holy Spirit in the believer forms the basis of the assurance given in the last part of the verse.

He that raised up Christ from the dead shall also quicken your mortal bodies. The overwhelming majority understand the reference here to be the assurance that, as believers, though our bodies will die, in the eschatological future, God will raise them from the dead. They will be quickened (or made alive). Death will be conquered.

Some, including Barnes (178) and Calvin (166), understand the reference here to be the experience of sanctification rather than resurrection of the body. Calvin says: "We conclude from this that he is not speaking of the last resurrection which will take place in a moment, but of the continual operation of the Spirit, by which He gradually mortifies the remains of the flesh and renews in us the heavenly life" (166).

The words "the body is dead" in v. 10 and "the mortal body," as I see it, make it unquestionably clear that the reference is that the physical body will die and that it will be raised from the dead.

By his Spirit that dwelleth in you. "Dwelleth in" (Greek *enoikeo*) literally means if the Holy Spirit is housed in you or has his residence in you.

If the genitive case is the correct reading, it will be translated "by" or "through" his Spirit. The Holy Spirit is the One who will raise us from the dead. Some versions read "*by* His Spirit that dwells in you," and others read "*because of* His Spirit that dwells in you." This reflects different manuscripts of the Greek text; many have it one way (Greek *dia* with the genitive case) and many have the other (Greek *dia* with accusative case).

If the accusative case is used, the fact that we are indwelt by the Holy Spirit is the reason we will be raised. See Lenski (514) for a support of the accusative. See Cranfield (391, 392) and Sanday and Headlam for treatments that are in favor of the genitive. Sanday and Headlam say, "On the whole the preponderance seems to be slightly on the side of the gen., but neither reading can be ignored" (199). It is difficult to decide which is the correct reading. I lean toward the genitive reading, which supports the translation of the KJV.

E. There Is a Challenge and an Enablement to Mortify the Deeds of the Body (8:12-14).

12 Therefore, brethen, we are debtors, not to the flesh, to live after the flesh.

Therefore. These words connect what precedes with what follows in the verse. Up to now Paul has said: "To be carnally minded is death," v. 6. "The carnal mind is enmity against God" (v. 7). Those in the flesh cannot please God (v. 8). The believer is not in the flesh (v. 9).

It is easy to see how all of this leads Paul to say, now, **We are debtors, not to the flesh, to live after the flesh.** The flesh is contrary to God's way. It is diametrically opposed to what a Christian should be for.

13 For if ye live after the flesh, ye shall die: but if ye through the Spirit do mortify the deeds of the body, ye shall live.

For if ye live after the flesh, ye shall die (Greek *mellete apothneskein)*. Concerning the Greek expression used here Cranfield explains, "The periphrastic future is used to emphasize that the consequence is necessary and certain, since it is God's judgment" (394). Hodge interprets,"Death to you is inevitable" (264).

While I believe that a Christian can commit apostasy, that is not what Paul is addressing in this verse. In the earliest days of the church, there were people whose living was not consistent with their profession. They had a distorted view of grace. They seemed to think that a person could experience justifying grace without experiencing sanctifying grace. This error was alluded to in 3:8. In 6:1-7:6 Paul dealt at length with the fact that a person who has experienced justifying grace has also experienced sanctifying grace. The answer to the question, "Shall we continue in sin, that grace may abound?" (6:1) was an emphatic "No."

Paul is saying, "If your lifestyle is to live after the flesh you will die." I am in essential agreement with Hodge when he says:

> The death here spoken of, as appears from the context, and

> from the nature of the life with which it is contrasted, cannot be the death of the body, either solely or mainly. It is spiritual death, in the comprehensive scriptural sense of the term, which includes all the penal consequences of sin here and hereafter, chap. 6:21; 8:6; Gal. 6:8 (264).

Paul is saying essentially the same thing that he did in 6:16. He was saying that if a person's life-style is to obey sin, he is a servant of sin. If his life-style is to obey righteousness, he is a servant of righteousness. He was saying that a person belongs to the one he is serving.

But if ye through the Spirit do mortify the deeds of the body, ye shall live.

To mortify (Greek *thanatoo*) means to put to death. "The body" is used here in a negative sense. It is essentially the same as flesh. The deeds, of course, are sinful deeds. (See discussion of "flesh" in the comments on v. 5.)

"To put to death the deeds of the body" means to strike a death blow to such practices. Another way of saying it is, "Put an end to such practices." The tense of this verb is present. It refers to linear (continuous) action.

The Christian has declared war on sin. It is his aim to put to death the sinful practices of the body; he may not win every battle, but his declaration of war stands. When he fails, he will get up, dust himself off, and go for another battle.

With Paul, justification has as its ground the death and righteousness of Christ—nothing else. In no way do a person's works play a part in his justification. It is easy to see how a person could misunderstand this and conceive the idea that since Jesus paid it all, the Christian could partake of sin in almost any degree. However, such thinking manifests a failure to be informed by Paul's teaching on sanctification.

Paul makes it unquestionably clear that sanctification always accompanies justification. The nature of sanctification is such that it guarantees a change in the person's life. Sanctification is an essential accompaniment of justification, but in no way the basis of justification.

There is a popular brand of the doctrine of eternal security that grossly misunderstands Paul's teaching. Buswell calls this approach pseudo-Calvinism. He explains:

> I have heard several pseudo-Calvinistic speakers in Christian college chapel exercises say, 'Dear young people, there are two ways to go to heaven: the spiritual way and the carnal way. It is so much better to take the spiritual way!'
>
> I knew a certain young person who believed this false doctrine and said to the Dean, 'I am a Christian, but I do not mind sitting in the bleachers. I choose to go to heaven the carnal way!'

Buswell goes on to say, "No! The carnal way is the way to eternal punishment.'Those who practice things of this kind are not going to inherit the kingdom of God' (Galatians 5:21)" (146).

Buswell is a Calvinist. A Calvinist who has taken time to do his homework will not fall prey to the doctrine of antinomianism (or cheap-easy believism). It takes time and effort to be able to harmonize the doctrines of justification and sanctification without doing violence to either.

In commenting on the first part of this verse Hodge, a staunch Calvinist, says: "The necessity of holiness, therefore, is absolute. No matter what professions we may make, or what we may indulge, justification, or the manifestation of the divine favor, is never separated from sanctification" (264).

14 For as many as are led by the

Spirit of God, they are the sons of God.

For as many as are led by the Spirit of God. "Led" (Greek *ago*) is a passive voice verb. This is indicated by the translation "led by the Spirit of God." That is something which happens to a person.

The active side of this experience is referred to as "walking after the Spirit" (8:4) and "mortifying the deeds of the body (8:13). "Walking after the Spirit" and "mortifying the deeds of the flesh" are something a person does.

It is easy to oversimplify what is meant by the passive voice in "led by the Spirit of God." It is easy for a person to interpret what is being said in terms of simple "cause and effect." In this case the Holy Spirit is the cause, and walking in the Spirit is the effect.

This kind of reasoning calls upon us to submit to the Holy Spirit and let Him *cause us to walk in the Spirit*. This kind of reasoning leads a person to say, "I didn't do anything. God did it."

The problem with this kind of reasoning is that it tries to apply to interpersonal relationships the same principles of cause and effect that apply to mechanical relationships. As long as a person continues to do this, he will remain confused.

If a person hits a nail with a hammer, the nail will be caused to go into the wood. The nail is purely passive. It is impersonal. When it comes to interpersonal relationships, influence and response are more appropriate terms than cause and effect. If we apply the terms cause and effect to interpersonal relationships, they must not be understood as technical terms.

The difference between cause and effect and influence and response is necessitated by the fact that a person is one who thinks, feels, and acts. We think with our minds, feel with our hearts, and act with our wills. The fact that we can distinguish between mind, heart, and will does not mean that we can separate one from the other. The activity of each is involved in the others. The mind, heart, and will are a functional unity.

Theological debates have been fought over whether man has a free will. It is a mistake to single out the will from the mind and heart. The real question is: Is redeemed man (in another context, the same question can be raised about fallen man) a personal being? Can he think, feel, and act? If he can, his actions are at least to some extent his own and represent a response on his part. The person who is walking in the Spirit has allowed himself to be led by the Spirit.

The person who is led by the Spirit mortifies (or puts to death) the deeds of the flesh. The Holy Spirit is working in him to help him. At the same time, his action *represents a true effort on his part. To say less than that is either to deny the personhood of man or to make the term person meaningless.*

Attention should also be given to the scope included in being led by the Holy Spirit. So far as the meaning in this context is concerned, it is not referring to leading a person into that will of God which is unique to him. It is that scope that is covered by "mortifying the deeds of the flesh." Paul assumes that people know what the deeds of the flesh are. In this context the reference is to following the Holy Spirit into what we already know we should do.

In this context, the reference to being led by the Spirit is not referring to making known to us that which had been unknown. We "follow" that leading by depending on the Holy Spirit to *help (not do for us)* us to have victory over sin.

They are the sons (Greek *huios)* **of God.** The word *son* refers, in this context, to one who is considered an adult son. Since this idea is connected with the word for adoption, I will give my reasons for this conclusion in the next verse.

F. The Holy Spirit Contributes to the Assurance of Salvation (8:15,16).

15 For ye have not received the spirit of bondage again to fear; but ye have received the Spirit of adoption, whereby we cry, Abba, Father.

For ye have not received the spirit of bondage (Greek *douleia*) **again to fear.** Cranfield gives three interpretations of "the spirit of bondage":

> (1) The reference denotes a human disposition. It is contrasted with the Spirit of adoption which is understood to refer to the Holy Spirit. (2) The Holy Spirit is meant by both the 'spirit of bondage' and the 'Spirit of adoption.' The 'spirit of bondage' would refer to the Holy Spirit's ministry in the Old Testament. The 'Spirit of adoption' would refer to His ministry in the New Testament. (3) The sentence does not imply the actual existence of *pneuma douleias* [spirit of bondage] but means only that the Holy Spirit whom they have received is not a spirit of bondage but the spirit of adoption (396).

Cranfield subscribes to the third view.

I agree with Murray when he says: "The solution resides in the consideration that the proposition respecting the 'spirit of bondage' is negative and there is no reason why we should not interpret the thought to be, 'Ye did not receive the Holy Spirit as a Spirit of bondage but as the Spirit of adoption'" (296, 297).

The words "again to fear" imply that there was a time in their past when they were in bondage to fear. It would have been before the coming of Christ. We are reminded of the words of Paul in Galatians when he said, "Be not entangled again with the yoke of bondage" (5:1). The yoke of bondage refers to the time when they were under the law. This bondage was made much greater by the Pharisees. They put together a system of laws in which they extended the concept of law to every area of life. It was elaborated to the point that its minute details became extremely burdensome.

But ye have received the Spirit of adoption (Greek *huiothesia*). Paul's concept of adoption is set forth in more detail in Galatians. His presentation there, I think, makes it unquestionably clear that adoption does not refer to the way a person becomes a member of the family of God. Rather, it refers to placing one who is already a member of the family of God into the position of being an adult son.

Gal. 3:24 refers to the time before Christ came. God's people were viewed as being under the schoolmaster (Greek *paidagogos*). The literal meaning is child-leader. It speaks metaphorically of the law. The law was our child-leader. In ordinary usage he (a *paidagogos*) was a trusted slave who was over Greek and Roman boys in wealthy families. He was over the young boy from the ages of about six to sixteen. He went with him wherever he went, protected him, and helped instill the family values in him. When Paul used this word to refer to the law which God's people were under (before Christ came), he was implying by this that they were immature.

In Gal. 3:25 Paul says, "But after that faith [the time after the coming of Christ] is come, we are no longer under a schoolmaster [Greek *paidagogos*]." Paul's implication is that, by delivering us from such, God is dealing with us as mature sons.

The view that as New Covenant believers we are dealt with as adult, mature sons receives further support in Gal. 4:1-5. In 4:1, 2, Paul explained that a child-heir is under tutors and governors until the time appointed by the father. Release from tutors and governors takes place only after the heir reaches maturity.

In applying this illustration, Paul considers the heirs of God having been dealt with like children prior to the coming of Christ (4:3). When the fullness of time was come (4:5), something very important took place: "God sent forth his Son. . .that we might receive the adoption of sons" (4:5, 6). The "fullness of time" was the time when God viewed his people as being mature enough to be delivered from the child-leader (*paidagogos*), the law serving as the child-leader.

While it seems to me unquestionably clear that adoption (Greek *huiothesia*) must be understood with reference to placing the New Covenant believer into the position of an adult son, this is not the way the word *(huiothesia)* was used in extra Biblical liteature. In spite of this, a good number of commentators on Galatians feel that the development of the thought in the passage is compelling. Among those who support the position in their commentary on Galatians are Brown, Burton, Lenski, and Tenney. John Brown's treatment is particularly helpful. Ralph Hampton supports this position in *A Biblical and Historical Study of Paul's Doctrine of* Adoption (an unpublished thesis submitted in partial fulfillment of the requirement for the Master of Arts degree, 1961).

The view that New Covenant believers are viewed as adult sons is also supported by the use of the word "son" (Greek *huios*) in Gal. 4. In 4:1 it is pointed out that "the heir as long as he is a child (Greek *nepios*, literally infant) differeth nothing from a servant, though he be lord of all." He is like a servant because he is not his own boss. He "is under tutors and governors" (4:2) until he reaches legal age.

In v. 7 a son (Greek *huios*) is no longer a servant (or like a servant). The son is one who has reached legal age. He is an adult son.

Ramsay has some interesting observations on the words for heir and son. He explains:

> Here we observe the distinctly Greek touch that the term 'heir' as used by Paul, is almost convertible with 'son.' The same term is often used in the inscriptions of Asia Minor and elsewhere in precisely the same way as here to indicate 'a son after he has succeeded to the inheritance' as the representative of his father, undertaking all the duties and obligations of his father (391).

Ramsay also observes, "The equivalence of sonship and heirship is familiar in Greek literature. The proofs are given in every hand-book and in every dictionary of Greek antiquity" (339).

The position which considers son (Greek *huios*) as synonymous with heir is given some support by Thayer's contrast between "child" (Greek *teknon)* and "son" *(huios)*. He points out that "*teknon* gives prominence to the physical and outward aspect, *huios* to the inward, ethical, legal" (618).

(Some of my comments on adoption were adapted from my article, "Legalism in the Book of Galatians," in *Dimension*, Volume 1, Number 3, Winter Quarter, 1984, 1985. Adoption in the N.T. and its practical consequences are set forth in my book *Biblical Ethics*, Nashville: Randall House Publications,

1973, 68-82.)

We need, now, to turn our attention back to the meaning of "the Spirit of adoption." As a background for this, we need to look at Gal. 4:6. There is a noticeable similarity between Gal. 4:6 and Rom. 8:15. In both verses the end result is that as believers we cry, "Abba, Father." In Gal. 4:6 it is the Spirit of His Son which leads us to say, "Abba, Father." In Rom. 8:15 it is "the Spirit of adoption" which leads us to cry, "Abba, Father." I think it should be obvious that the Spirit of His Son and the Spirit of adoption both refer to the Holy Spirit.

We can get some light from Gal. 4:6 on why this was done. In Gal. 4:6 Paul says, "And because ye are sons (Greek *huios*)." That gives the reason for God's sending the Holy Spirit into our hearts.

I think we can safely say that the son (*huios*) referred to is an heir who is of legal age. That being true, the giving of the Holy Spirit to live within us grows out of the fact that God is dealing with us as being heirs of legal age. This brings to mind the fact that Paul elsewhere refers to the Holy Spirit as the earnest of our inheritance (Eph. 1:14).

Concerning the word for earnest (Greek *arrabon*), Arndt and Gingrich explain: *"First installment, deposit, down payment, pledge* that pays a part of the purchase price in advance, and so secures a legal claim to the article in question and makes the contract valid" (109).

My first observation is that in order to enter a legal contract, a person must be of legal age. The meaning of Gal. 4:6 is: Because as sons, you are of legal age, God has given you His Holy Spirit in a more intimate relationship than He had with the people of God in the O.T. The Holy Spirit is a guarantee that the inheritance promised will be received at the appropriate time.

Some have thought that the fact that we have received the Holy Spirit as the earnest of our inheritance of necessity leads to "once saved always saved." The earnest in this case binds God. He will not break the contract. It does not prohibit the possibility that the believer could cease to be a believer and thus break the contract. It does mean that God will never break the contract with one who is a believer.

It should be clear now why the Holy Spirit is referred to as the Spirit of adoption. Since as believers we have been placed in the position of an heir of legal age by our adoption, the gift of the Holy Spirit as the earnest of our inheritance is a recognition that we are of legal age. This is true since to receive an earnest is a legal transaction.

Whereby we cry. Concerning "we cry," Cranfield says, "Here it is best taken to denote an urgent and sincere crying to God irrespective of whether it is loud or soft (or even unspoken), formal or informal, public or private" (399).

The word *Abba* is an Aramaic word meaning "father." It has come to us by being transliterated from Aramaic into Greek and from Greek into English. "Father," following "Abba" (Greek *pater*) was apparently given so the Greek readers who were not familiar with the word *Abba* would know what it meant.

Concerning *Abba,* Bruce explains:

> *Abba* is an Aramaic word... which came to be used among the Jews (and is used to this day in Hebrew-speaking families) as the familiar term by which children address their father. In Mark 14:36 Jesus is represented as using it in His prayer in Gethsemane. The significance of this lies in the fact that *abba* was not, and is not, the term used by Jews when addressing God as their Father.

> But the fact that this Aramaic word found its way into the worshipping vocabulary of the Gentile churches strongly suggests that it was used in this way by Jesus and Mark 14:36 confirms this. There is strong presumption, too, that when Jesus taught His disciples to begin their prayers with 'Father, Hallowed be thy name' (Lk. 11:2, RV), the word He used for 'Father' was *Abba* (166).

(The reader may want to consult Briscoe 167; Cranfield 399, 400; Harrison 92, 93; Hendriksen 258-260; Hodge 266, 267; Murray 296; and Sanday and Headlam 203.)

16 The Spirit itself beareth witness with our spirit, that we are the children of God.

This verse will explain how the Holy Spirit works in us that assurance which leads us to call God, Father.

We should refer to the Holy Spirit as "He" or "Himself" rather than "itself" as is done in the KJV. In English, gender is determined by the nature of the subject under consideration. In Greek, words have gender according to the word form, not according to the nature of that under consideration. For this reason since "spirit" (Greek *pneuma*) is a neuter word, it calls for a neuter pronoun in the Greek. We can translate the neuter pronoun of the Greek by a neuter pronoun in the English. If so, the result is the translation "The Spirit itself" as is done in the KJV. The other way would be to translate according to the actual gender of the Holy Spirit. If so, it would read, "The Spirit Himself."

It is better to translate, "The Spirit Himself." This will help us avoid the common notion that the Holy Spirit is simply an influence or force. He is a person. We should avoid referring to Him as "It."

The basic question to be decided is whether "beareth witness with" (Greek *summartureo*) refers to one witness or two. The vast majority, among whom are Haldane (362, 363); Harrison (93); Hendriksen (260, 261); Hodge (267); Murray (297); Plumer (395); Shedd (248); and Vine (*Romans* 120) understand the reference to be to two witnesses—our own witness and the witness of the Holy Spirit.

When a person is confronted with the gospel, he is told "But as many as received him, to them gave he power to become the sons of God, *even* to them that believe on his name" (Jn. 1:12). Therefore, when a person has a believing response to the gospel, his own mind recognizes that according to the gospel he is now a member of the family of God. This being true, our own spirits bear witness that we are children of God. The Holy Spirit bears witness with our own inner selves that we are children of God. That joint-witness gives us a compelling assurance that we are children of God. Our own understanding, based on the word of God, is co-witnessed by the Holy Spirit.

Cranfield rejects the majority view. He takes the meaning to be, not a witness of the Holy Spirit with our spirit, but a witness *to* our spirit. The Holy Spirit is the sole witness that gives us assurance of salvation. Cranfield comments, "But what standing has our spirit in *this* matter? Of itself it surely has no right at all to testify to our being sons of God" (403). Cranfield cites for support the Vulgate. The translations given by Beck (*The New Testament In the Language of Today*) and Taylor (*The Living Bible*) will support Cranfield's position.

We are not to suppose that the human mind reached its conclusion apart from the work of the Holy Spirit. In reaching the conclusion "I am a child of God," by all means the Holy Spirit enabled me. At the same time my own thought processes were actively involved. In that way I conclude that I am a child of God and the Holy Spirit confirms that I truly am a child of God.

The Holy Spirit bears witness with our spirit that we are the children of God. "Children," here (Greek *teknon*) is different from "sons" (Greek *huios*) in v. 14. In the discussion related to adoption in v. 15, I supported the position that "son" (*huios*) refers to an adult or one who is of legal age.

As I see it, "child" *teknon* refers to a member of the family without a necessary implication regarding age—whether a young child or an adult. A son is always a child, but a child is not always a son. The child (*teknon*) by virtue of being a member of the family is an heir. By virtue of being a son (*huios*) he is considered to be of legal age.

If we take Ramsay's position in the quotation given above on v. 15, the Greek word for son (*huios*) is essentially synonymous with the word for heir. If this be the case, there are some interesting implications in the light of Gal. 3:26-28. In Gal. 3:26 the word for "children" is "sons" (*huios*). Paul refers to *all* of his readers as being "sons." This includes both Jew and Greek, slave or free, and male and female (3:28). Regardless of race, station in life, or sex, *all believers are sons*. Being sons all are considered heirs of legal age. In the light of the Jewish-Gentile problem and the laws of inheritance of that day, implications would be very significant. If Ramsay's view is true, the reference to women as sons of God would mean that they are heirs of legal age. If this is the case, it would account for the fact that only once in the N.T. are women referred to as daughters of God (2 Cor. 6:18).

Bruce insists that the words children (Greek *teknon*) and sons (Greek *huios*) are used interchangeably in the N.T. He says:

> In Galatians 3:23-4:7 he does indeed make a distinction between the period of infancy, when his readers were under the guardianship of the law, and the attainment of their responsible status of sons (*huioi*) of God, now that the gospel has been introduced. But their previous status is qualified by the term *nepioi* ('infants'), not *tekna* ('children'). Nowhere in the New Testament can a valid distinction be made between being 'children (*tekna*) of God' and 'sons (*huioi*) of God'" (167).

It is quite clear that one who is a son (*huios*) of God is also a child (*teknon*) of God. However, I believe that the distinction I made above is valid. The "child" is an heir (whether an heir under legal age, or an heir of legal age). The "son" is definitely an heir of legal age.

There are two ways the word "heir" can be used: (1) An heir based on the family relationship. In this case the heir may be under legal age (Gal. 4:1,2). As Bruce observed, the heir in this case was an infant. (2) An heir who is of legal age. The heir in the first sense is under tutors and governors. He is like a servant. The heir in the second sense according to Paul is no longer "a servant, but a son (*huios*)" (Gal. 4:7).

In Gal. 4:1, 2 the child-heir is too young to receive his inheritance. The son-heir is of legal age. I believe that the facts will bear out the position that as children (Greek *teknon*) we are heirs of God. As sons (Greek *huios*) we are of legal age. This is what Paul meant when he said, "And if a son (Greek *huios*) then an heir of God" (Gal. 4:7). The heir of 4:7 is of legal age. The heir of 4:1 is under legal age.

In our own culture the word heir may refer to: (1) One who is to receive an inheritance after the testator dies; (2) One who has already inherited following the death of a testator; (3) One who is named in the will of the testator, but is under age at the time of the testator's death and is, therefore, under a guardian. Which one of these meanings applies to a particular case is determined by the facts of the case and the context.

These observations should help us see how the context in Scripture determines whether the heir is under legal age or is of legal age. The present significance of being an heir of legal age in the N.T. is seen in the fact that we have received the Holy Spirit who is the earnest of our inheritance (see comments on v. 15).

G. The Believer Will Have a Glorious Future (8:17-23).

17 And if children, then heirs; heirs of God, and joint-heirs with Christ; if so be that we suffer with *him*, that we may be also glorified together.

And if children (Greek *teknon*) **then heirs; heirs of God**. The difference between the words "son" (Greek *huios*) and "child" (Greek *teknon*) have already been discussed in v. 16. As a child the believer is an heir of God.

As heirs, we will receive an inheritance. The nature of this inheritance has already been discussed in the comments on 4:13. The inheritance will be eternal life on this earth made new. The promise of this inheritance is anchored in the Abrahamic Covenant. God said to Abraham, "For all the land which thou seest, to thee will I give it, and to thy seed after thee" (Gen. 13:14). Again he says,"And I will establish my covenant between me and thee and thy seed after thee, the land wherein thou art a stranger, all the land of Canaan, for an everlasting possession; and I will be their God" (Gen. 17:8).

The fact that this promise was made to Abraham, as well as his seed, means that it could not reach complete fulfillment in this lifetime. It is inferred that the promise would be fulfilled for Abraham by a resurrection from the dead and an inheritance of the land as an everlasting possession in the next life.

The Abrahamic Covenant is the basic redemptive covenant. It is the covenant which speaks about our inheritance. For a discussion of the Abrahamic Covenant see chapter 4. For a more thorough elaboration of the nature of the inheritance see comments on 4:13.

And joint-heirs with Christ. I am in essential agreement with Barrett when he says:

> The explanation of Paul's point here is to be found in his discussion of the same theme in Galatians 3:6-4:7. In the latter passage it is argued (see especially 3:16) that Christ alone is the true 'seed of Abraham'—the heir of the promise. Others may become sons of God *in Christ Jesus* (3:26); this is effected by putting on Christ in baptism (3:27). Thus believers become the seed of Abraham, and heirs according to the promise (3:29) (164).

When it is said that we are joint-heirs with Christ, the meaning is that we share His inheritance with Him. Lenski explains:

> When Paul calls us Christ's co-heirs, we are not placed on the same level with Christ, for he is the Heir irrespective of the fact that we become God's children and thus co-heirs with him, while we can become co-heirs, not by

getting the inheritance independently as he did, but only as sharing in the inheritance which he has obtained. Yet this is true: he obtained the inheritance only in order to make us his co-heirs, only to have us share it with him (527).

If so be that we suffer with *him*, that we may be also glorified together. Suffering is not to be taken as earning the right to be glorified with Christ. Rather, it is that suffering which cannot be totally avoided in a world that is hostile toward Jesus Christ. As Cranfield says, "The reference is. . .to that element of suffering which is inseparable from faithfulness to Christ in a world which does not know Him as Lord" (408).

This verse speaks of joint-heirs, joint-suffering, and joint-glorification. God will give us far more than we could even dream of. Think of how Jesus Christ will be glorified. On no other basis than a revelation from God could we ever dream that we would share with Christ in the glory that will be bestowed upon Him.

18 For I reckon that the sufferings of this present time *are* not worthy *to be compared* with the glory which shall be revealed in us.

Concerning the word **I reckon** (Greek *logizomai*) Cranfield explains, "It denotes here, as in 3:28 and 6:11, a firm conviction reached by rational thought on the basis of the gospel" (408).

This verse is not designed to minimize the fact that we at times do suffer. It is designed to minimize the significance of our suffering in view of the glorious future which will be ours. Picirilli explains:

> The value, significance, importance, and weight of present sufferings are as nothing when compared to the weight of promised glory. So says Paul in 18a, and so he often said. Compare 2 Corinthians 4:17 where our present 'affliction' is seen as 'light,' and 'but for a moment,' in contrast with the 'glory' that is 'weighty' and 'eternal' (157).

19 For the earnest expectation of the creature waiteth for the manifestation of the sons of God.

For the earnest expectation of the creature. Concerning the meaning of "earnest expectation," Earle explains, "It is composed of three parts: *apo*, 'from;' *kara*, 'head;' *dokeo*, 'watch' (in Ionic Greek). So it means 'to watch with outstretched head, watch anxiously" (156).

It is generally agreed that the Greek word for "creature" (*ktisis*) is better translated "creation." This word has been interpreted a number of different ways. Cranfield observes:

> [The creation] in this verse has been variously interpreted in the course of the centuries as signifying the whole creation, including mankind both believing and unbelieving and also angels; all mankind; unbelieving mankind only; believers only; the angels only; sub-human nature together with the angels; sub-human nature together with mankind in general; sub-human nature only (411).

He goes on to say: "The only interpretation of *ktisis* in these verses which is really probable seems to be that which understands the reference to be the sum-total of sub-human nature both animate and inanimate" (411, 412).

There is almost unanimous agreement that the reference here is to the sub-human sphere of nature, both animate and inanimate. The reference could not be to unbelieving men because they are not eagerly awaiting the manifestation of the sons of God. Angels are not involved because redemption does not apply to them. Believers are not involved because they are treated separately in v. 23. (For good discussions on the meaning of "creation" as it is used here see Bruce 168-172; Hodge 269-272; Lange 269, 270; Murray 301, 302; Plumer 403-407; and Shedd 250-252. Those who are interested in the view which interprets the "creature" to refer to the renewed nature of the Christian should read Barnes 182-187. For the view that the reference is to the Gentile world, see Clarke 98 and Gill 63.)

Waiteth for the manifestation of the sons of God. Concerning the word for "waiteth," (Greek *apekdechomai*), Yeager explains, "To wait for assiduously; to look for; to expect; to expect with longing" (539).

The meaning of manifestation (Greek *apokalupsis*) is to unveil or to reveal. The verb of the same Greek root is translated "reveal" in v. 18.

The word for "sons" (Greek *huios*) refers to believers in the fullest sense of what it means to be an heir of God. (See comments on vv. 15, 16.) The creation, animate and inanimate, is viewed as intensely waiting for the time when we as Christians will be unveiled with the full splendor and glory that shall be ours in the eschatological future. Based on the Greek words used in this verse, Picirilli states, "The picture is of intense expectancy, waiting with head and arms outstretched, almost imploringly. The universe is waiting for something" (157).

Lenski makes an interesting observation:

> The tremendous thought being unfolded here is that all God's inferior creation was from the start bound up with man, and not independent but wholly dependent. And now, since the fall, the creative world in its ultimate destiny, is bound up; not with the ungodly who shall perish in hell, but with the godly and with their coming revelation of glory in heaven (532).

Verses 20-23 will explain why the creation is eagerly waiting for the full unveiling of the sons of God.

20 For the creature was made subject to vanity, not willingly, but by reason of him who hath subjected *the same* in hope.

For the creature (creation) **was made subject to vanity.** Concerning the word vanity (Greek *mataiotes),* Cranfield explains:

> But the simplest and most straight forward interpretation would seem to be to take vanity here in the word's basic sense as denoting the ineffectiveness of that which does not attain its goal. . ., and to understand Paul's meaning to be that the sub-human creation has been subjected to the frustration of not being able properly to fulfil the purpose of its existence, God having appointed that without man it shall not be made perfect. We may think of the whole magnificent theatre of the universe together with all of its splendid properties and all the chorus of sub-human life, created to glorify God but unable to do so fully, so long as man the chief actor in the drama of God's praise fails to contribute his rational part (413, 414).

Not willingly. It was not by any choice or fault of its own that the creation was put into this state of frustration of its intended purpose. Rather, it was because of the fall of man that creation was placed under a curse

(Gen. 3:17-19).

But by reason of him who hath subjected *the same* in hope. God pronounced a curse upon the animate and inanimate creation because of Adam's sin. Yet, this curse was not without remedy.

21 Because the creature itself also shall be delivered from the bondage of corruption into the glorious liberty of the children of God.

Because the creature (creation) **itself also shall be delivered from the bondage of corruption.** The word for bondage (Greek *douleia*) refers to being in slavery to a thing or a person. In this case it is slavery to corruption. The word for corruption (Greek *phthora*) is also translated "decay." Murray explains: "The bondage of corruption is the bondage which consists in corruption and, since it is not ethical in character, must be taken in the sense of decay and death apparent in non-rational creation" (304).

Concerning the practical effects of this corruption (or decay) as it relates to creation, Hendriksen observes:

> Though it aspires, it is not able fully to achieve. Though it blossoms, it does not reach the point of adequately bearing fruit. . . .The curse of plant diseases decimates the crops. Plant pathologists direct their efforts toward developing methods of disease *prevention* or at least *reduction* or *control*. And, in a modified sense, what is true with respect to the world of plants holds too for the animal sphere (268).

(For a discussion of the implications of this corruption or decay as it relates to the scientific process known as entropy see Yeager 541, 542.)

Into the glorious liberty of the children (Greek *teknon*) **of God.** For a discussion of the Greek words translated "son" and "child" see notes on v. 16. The liberty from the process of corruption and decay will come to the animate and inanimate creation in connection with the time of our complete deliverance as children or sons of God. Just as creation was subjected to a curse at the time the curse was inflicted upon man, even so when the full effects of the curse are lifted from us, as believers, it will also be lifted from creation.

It is my conviction that the inheritance of believers is eternal life on this earth made new. This inheritance is rooted and grounded in the Abrahamic Covenant (see the discussion on v. 17 and 4:13). It is commonly held by most commentators that Paul is referring in this passage to a renovation rather than an annihilation of this earth to be followed by a creation of a new and totally different earth. Bruce says:

> If words mean anything, these words of Paul denote not the annihilation of the present material universe on the day of revelation, to be replaced by a universe completely new, but the transformation of the present universe so that it will fulfil the purpose for which God created it. . . .But the transformation of the universe depends upon the completion of man's transformation by the working of grace (170).

In another place Bruce makes an interesting observation:

> It is no accident that the redemption of nature is here seen as coinciding with the redemption of man's body—that physical part of his being which links him with the material creation. Man was put in charge of the 'lower' creation and involved it with him when he fell; through the re-

> demptive work of the 'second man' the entail of the fall is broken not only for man himself, but for creation which is dependent on him. Even now, man can by responsible trusteeship make the desert blossom like the rose; what then will be the effect of a completely redeemed mankind on the creation trusted to his care? (169).

It should be quite clear in the passage before us that the language requires us to understand the reference to be redemption of the animate and inanimate creation rather than an annihilation of the present creation.

A word should be said about the animate creation as it relates to the redeemed state of things. While commentators have freely and almost unanimously stated that the redemption would extend both to inanimate and animate creation, they have almost altogether failed to elaborate on animals as they relate to the new earth. In fact, a person could read most commentaries without stopping to realize that the commentators had actually spoken of the existence of animals on the renewed earth.

Among the few comments that are found are those by Bruce and Hodge. Bruce says: "When Isaiah looked forward to the peaceful coexistence of wolf and lamb in the Messianic age, he voiced his hope in the language of poetry, but his poetry enshrines no pathetic fallacy of poetry, but something much more biblical and substantial" (169). He then refers to Isaiah 11:9.

After expressing some possible doubt about the inclusion of animals, Hodge explains: "The prophetic representations of the Messianic period set forth not only inanimate nature, the deserts, mountains, and forest, as rejoicing in the new order of things, but also the beasts of the field; and therefore there is scriptural ground for including them under the comprehensive words of the apostle" (269).

It seems to me that the passage before us teaches that there will be animal inhabitants on the new earth. However, we are not to think that animals will be resurrected.

Commentators have also, for the most part, failed to comment on how the renewed earth fits into their understanding of the order of eschatological events. A check of the list of names referred to above will reveal that amillennialists, premillennialists, and postmillennialists can be found among those who take the passage to refer to the renewed earth. It would be obvious that in the amillennial view the new earth would follow the general judgment. This could also probably be said for the postmillennial view.

By now it should be clear that a person can believe in the renovation of the earth in the eschatological future and not be a premillennialist. In fact, the emphasis on the thousand year reign of Christ among premillennialists tends at times to overshadow the emphasis on the new earth *as an eternal state.*

I am a premillennialist. In my opinion in the fullest sense of the word, the renovated earth refers to the new earth that will follow the Great White Throne Judgment, which follows the thousand year reign of Christ on the earth. In a lesser sense there will be some major changes in the world of nature during the millennium. I think this is indicated by Isaiah 11:1-8. This cannot refer to the eternal state since sin will be present to be judged during this time (vv. 3-5).

22 For we know that the whole creation groaneth and travaileth in pain together until now.

The Greek word for creation is the same word which was translated "creature" in vv. 19-21. The reference in this verse is still to sub-human creation, animate and inanimate. That believers are not involved is made clear by v. 23. The words "ourselves also" make it clear that the "ourselves" was distinguished from "the whole creation" of v. 22.

With reference to this verse, Picirilli explains: "Two verbs are used to describe the anguish of the personified creation as it waits for the final glorification to come. The first is 'groaneth,' a word that describes the kind of agony caused by pressure. The second is 'travaileth in pain,' which literally refers to the pains of childbirth, labor pains" (159).

Just as the travail of a woman in childbirth points to the birth of a child, the travail of creation points to a time of deliverance. Cranfield says regarding the word for travail, "The metaphor is a very natural one to express the thought of severe distress from which a happy and worthwhile issue is to be looked for" (416, note 2).

Harrison's comments are helpful: "The groaning of the creation looks back to its subjection to frustration (v. 20), whereas the pangs of childbirth anticipate the age of renewal. In other words, the same sufferings are at once a result and a prophecy. Christ spoke of the renewing of the world and called it a 'rebirth,' (*palingenesia*, Matt. 19:28)" (94).

"Until now" means that this condition had persisted from the curse until the present moment.

23 And not only *they*, but ourselves also, which have the firstfruits of the Spirit, even we ourselves groan within ourselves, waiting for the adoption, *to wit*, the redemption of our body.

And not only *they*, but ourselves also. Paul now moves from the experience of the animate and inanimate to the inclusion of believers in what he is saying.

Which have the firstfruits of the Spirit. I agree with Bruce when he says:

> The indwelling of the Spirit here and now is the 'firstfruits' (*aparche*), i.e. the 'first installment' or a 'down-payment' of the eternal heritage of glory which awaits believers. In 2 Corinthians 1:22, v. 5 and Ephesians 1:14 the same teaching about the Spirit is conveyed by the use of *arrhabon*, 'pledge' or 'earnest' (the word employed in modern Greek for an engagement ring, as the pledge or earnest of the coming marriage) (173).

This view is held by the majority of the commentators. (See Hendriksen 270; Hodge 275; Lenski 541; and Plumer 410.)

Murray gives another interpretation. He observes, "'The firstfruits of the Spirit'...should preferably be taken as the token of the Spirit given to believers now as the pledge of the plenitude of the Spirit to be bestowed at the resurrection" (306, 307). (Cranfield 418 and Shedd 258 are in essential agreement with Murray.)

Olshausen (295) and Meyer (327) limit the application of "the firstfruits of the Spirit" to the reception of the Holy Spirit in the days of the early church. It appears to me that Paul's words are intended to be universal in time and scope as they relate to believers.

The first view given above is preferred because it seems to be so closely related to "the earnest of the Spirit" in 2 Cor. 1:22 and Eph. 1:14.

Even we ourselves groan within ourselves. Not only does nature groan (v. 22), we who have the Holy Spirit as our firstfruit (the pledge or assurance that in due time God will give us our full inheritance) also groan. This groaning represents our longing to be delivered from the stress and discomforts of this life.

God has provided us with the possibility of having peace, satisfaction, and contentment. This peace and contentment is not ours by having all undesirable factors removed from our experience. If vv. 18-23 tell us anything, they tell us that *we are not living in a utopia.* At best there is a lot to be desired.

In v. 21 Paul speaks about the fact that at the present the creation (subhuman creation) is in the bondage of corruption (Greek *phthora*). This means that creation is experiencing decay and longs to be delivered from it. In 1 Cor. 15:53, 54, Paul refers to our present body as "corruptible" (Greek *phthartos*). See also 2 Cor. 5:2. At the resurrection it will become "incorruptible" (Greek *aphtharsia*).

Living in a world which is cursed by God (Gen. 3:17), and at the same time in a decaying (or corruptible) body, means that there will be at best a lot to be desired. For that reason we groan.

Waiting (Greek *apekdechomai*—on this word, see v. 19) **for the adoption, *to wit,*** (italicized words meaning "namely") **the redemption** (Greek *apolutrosis*, see comment on this word in 3:24) **of our body.** In commenting on adoption (Greek *huiothesia*) in v. 15 I gave reason for believing that it refers to our position as New Covenant believers. We are now treated as adults. We are of legal age.

Adoption as it is used in this verse refers to an eschatological event. At the time of the resurrection of our body, we will experience the full meaning of our adoption (or sonship). At the present in treating us as being of legal age, God has given us the earnest of our inheritance which is the Holy Spirit. Think what it will be like when we receive our full inheritance!

We are eagerly waiting for the time when our "groaning" shall cease and we will be delivered from the experience of decay and the curse will be lifted from the earth. Just as the groaning of the creation anticipates the time of deliverance, so our own groaning anticipates the time of deliverance.

H. The Believer's Hope of the Resurrection Produces Patience (8:24, 25).

24 For we are saved by hope: but hope that is seen is not hope: for what a man seeth, why doth he yet hope for?

For we are saved by hope. (On hope, see comments on 5:2.) Paul is not saying that hope is the condition of salvation. Rather, he is saying, "We are saved *with* hope" (Greek instrumental/dative of association). In other words hope is an ingredient of the salvation which we have already received. The hope to which Paul refers was already evident in v. 23.

Hope refers to more than a simple desire. It refers to a joyful, confident, expectation. As Vine says, "Hope is the joyous anticipation of good, in this passage the redemption of our body" (*Romans*, 126. See also Murray, 308, 309).

But hope that is seen is not hope. The very nature of hope implies that it is not seen. **For what a man seeth, why doth he yet hope for?** Murray makes an interesting observation, "In the first clause, 'hope' refers to *the thing hoped for*, the object of hope; in the second, hope denotes *the state of mind* entertained in reference to the thing hoped for" (Murray 309, italics mine).

25 But if we hope for that we see

not, *then* do we with patience wait for *it*.

The concept of hope is seen beginning with v. 17, though the word hope was not mentioned until v. 24. This hope is tied in with the glorious future which will be ours. The hope also carries with it a present benefit. Since we are confident that the time will come when we will be delivered from the negative factors of the present existence, this confidence (or hope) helps us develop a patient endurance while we wait. It helps us to be able to handle the pain and discomfort of a sickness, when we know it will be cured.

I. The Holy Spirit Helps Us by Making Perfect Intercession for Us (8:26, 27).

26 Likewise the Spirit also helpeth our infirmities: for we know not what we should pray for as we ought: but the Spirit itself maketh intercession for us with groanings which cannot be uttered.

Likewise the Spirit also helpeth our infirmities. "Likewise" connects with the hope mentioned in the preceding verses. The hope of the resurrection helps us bear the unavoidable sufferings of this life. This help contributes to patient endurance. Just as the hope of the resurrection helps us, the Holy Spirit helps us with our infirmities.

The word for infirmities (Greek *astheneia)* means weakness. Moule explains, "It may well indicate (as 5:6) not mere imperfection of strength, but absence of strength; a condition of *helplessness* without Him" (*Cambridge Bible*, 153).

Murray explains: "In the preceding verses the accent falls upon the *sufferings* and the *support* afforded in these; in verses 26, 27 the accent falls upon our *infirmity* and the *help* given for its relief. As hope sustains our suffering, so the Holy Spirit helps our infirmity" (310, 311).

Concerning "helpeth" (Greek *sunantilambanomai*) Picirilli explains: "Literally the Greek word means 'take up together on the other end.' The picture presented is that of one who has a load to carry. Our infirmities do so burden us down. But the Holy Spirit picks up and helps us carry that burden. He helps by sharing the load" (161).

For we know not what we should pray for as we ought. Concerning the Greek word for prayer used here (Greek *proseuchomai*), Vine explains: "*Proseuchomai*, 'to pray,' is always used of requests addressed to God, whereas *deomai*, 'to pray,' may be used of requests addressed to man as well. *Proseuchomai* carries with it the notion of worship which is not present in the word *deomai*" (*Romans* 127).

Concerning the expression, "what we should pray for" in the KJV, most recent translations seem to prefer "how we should pray." Hendriksen translates, "what we ought to pray" (273).

Harrison says concerning the translation:

> The word 'how' could suggest that we do not know the art of prayer—how to phrase our petitions properly. But this is not the Greek word commonly used for 'how.' [The word here is "*tis*." The word most frequently used is "*pos*."] Even the wording 'what we should pray for' is questionable, since 'for' has no equivalent in the original text. So we come by elimination to the more literal wording 'what we should pray,' that is, the content of our prayers rather than simply the topics (95, 96).

Cranfield points out that it is difficult to decide whether the meaning is "what to pray" or "what to pray for." He decides in favor of "what to pray for" (421).

Perhaps the ultimate meaning would be either "what for?" "what?" or "how?" In the finality each of these concepts is inferred if it is not the intended direct meaning. So far as the basic thrust is concerned, we will be on safe ground if we stick with the KJV and translate, "for we know not what we should pray for as we ought."

It is clear that Paul is addressing our inadequacy to pray as we should. We do not always understand what the need really is. We do not always know what the remedy for the need is.

But the Spirit itself [himself—see v. 16] **maketh intercession for us with groanings which cannot be uttered.** Concerning the word for intercession (Greek *huperentugchano*), Robertson explains, "It is a picturesque word of rescue by one who 'happens on' (*eutugchanei*) one who is in trouble and 'in his behalf' (*huper*) pleads 'with unuttered groanings' (instrumental case) or with 'sighs that baffle words' (Denney)" (377).

The word (Greek *alaletos*) which is translated "cannot be uttered" can mean either "unexpressed" or "incapable of expression" i.e., incapable of being expressed in human language. I take the true meaning to be the latter.

It seems that the concern addressed in v. 27 arises out of the idea that human words cannot adequately convey this intercession to God. The purpose of v. 27 is to convey the fact that the inadequacy of human language to communicate the intercession will present no difficulty of understanding on the Father's part.

The big issue in this verse is: (1) Does the Holy Spirit, Himself, actually make the intercession and experience the groaning? (Among those who would say, "yes" are Cranfield 423; Hamilton 126; Harrison 96; Hendriksen 275-278; and Meyer 331, 332.) (2) Is the groaning in intercession that which happens within the believer when he prays with the aid of the Holy Spirit? This is the view set forth in the majority of commentaries. (Among those who take this view are Alford 397; Bruce 175; Denney 651; Godet 321; Haldane 386, 387; Hodge 279; Lenski 547, 548; Moule, *Cambridge Bible* 154; Murray 312; and Shedd 261.)

If we take the most obvious meaning of the verse as the true one, we will understand the meaning to be that the Holy Spirit, Himself, does the interceding and the groaning. However, as can be seen above, the majority have not chosen to take the most obvious meaning. They choose to say that the intercession and groaning take place in the believer when he prays.

The basic reason for rejecting the view that Paul means the Holy Spirit's interceding and groaning is that the experience of groaning cannot be properly attributed to the Holy Spirit as a member of the Trinity. Lenski says, "The dogmaticians are right: The Holy Spirit does not and cannot groan; these groans are ours" (547). Haldane comments: "It is not to be supposed that the Divine Spirit can be subject to such emotions or perturbations of mind; but it is so represented, because he draws forth these groans from our hearts and excites them there" (388).

Hodge explains, "We are not to suppose that the Spirit itself prays, or utters the inarticulate groans of which the apostle here speaks. He is said to do what he causes us to do" (279).

It seems that the most *natural* way to interpret this verse would be to attribute the interceding and groaning to the Holy Spirit. If so, that is the way it *should* be interpreted unless such an interpretation would do violence to some other well-established doctrine.

Genesis 6:6 reads, "And it repented the LORD that he had made man on the earth, and it grieved him at his heart." I understand that the use of the word "repented" with reference to God cannot mean everything for God that it does for us. It was a word that with due consideration for difference of implications could be used to describe a Divine experience. I must say that I have considerably less difficulty seeing how the word "groan" could be used of the Holy Spirit than how the word "repent" can be used of a Divine experience. Yet we know that it was so used.

Hendriksen has gone to greater length to defend the position that the reference is to the Holy Spirit's experience of intercession and groaning (275-278). He explains:

> In verse 26 these groanings are linked inseparably with the Spirit's intercession. This intercession is mentioned again in verse 27. In verse 34 the verb which is used in verse 27 to describe *the Spirit's* intercession, is used in connection with *the Son's* intercession. If, then, verse 34 refers to *Christ's own* intercessory prayer, why should not verse 27 describe *the Spirit's* own intercession, accompanied by groanings (276).

In support of this same position Harrison points out "that when we refer to intercessory prayer, we mean prayer for others rather than for ourselves" (96). When we are involved in "intercessory" prayer, we can rely on the Holy Spirit to help us, but the very fact that we call it intercessory means that it is for someone else other than ourselves.

Verse 26 has been considered by some as dealing with the use of tongues in prayer as mentioned in 1 Cor. 14:2, 14, 16. Kasemann takes this position, but refers it to the congregation rather than an individual (240, 241). Bruce (175) suggests a possible reference to the "tongues" of 1 Cor. 14:2. Cranfield takes issue with this view, but points out that it is "an interpretation with a long history going back to Origen and Chrysostom" (423).

I see no possibility at all that Paul had tongues as a prayer language in mind in this verse. If a person takes the viewpoint that tongues refer to a foreign language, there would be no reason to think that another language would be preferred in prayer to his mother tongue. If the reference is to an ecstatic tongue, the tone of the passage does not fit.

Cranfield's observation, I think, is decisive on this point:

"There seems to be force in the contention that the *stenagnioi* [groaning] mentioned here are not likely to be the utterances of glossolaly [tongues], since they clearly have to do with bringing the needs and longings of Christians before God, whereas glossolaly [tongues] was pre-eminently praise" (423).

It can safely be said that the modern charismatic movement presents tongues as being much closer to euphoria than groaning. Whatever Paul might have meant by groanings, I am quite certain that euphoria would not have been involved in the groanings.

27 And he that searcheth the hearts knoweth what *is* the mind of the Spirit, because he maketh intercession for the saints according to *the will of* God.

And (Greek *de*) **he that searcheth the hearts knoweth what *is* the mind of the Spirit.** I believe that "but" translates the conjunction used in this verse better than "and." In v. 26 Paul has said that the groanings involved in the intercession of the Holy Spirit on our behalf are such that they cannot be expressed in human language. The basic thrust of this verse is, "*But* that does not present a problem to God. The Father, who searches the heart understands the mind of the Spirit." The word for mind (Greek *phronema*) has reference to that which is in the mind (see comments on v. 6). A good way to say it is, "The Father understands the 'thinking' of the Spirit."

Because he maketh intercession for the saints according to *the will of* God. It will be observed that in the KJV the words, "*The will of*" are in italics. This means that they are not translated from Greek words. While the majority favor the use of the words, I am under the impression that the meaning is clearer without them.

The last part of the verse is explaining why there will be no problem on the part of the Father in understanding the intercessory groaning of the Holy Spirit on our behalf. The reason this is true is, "because the Spirit makes intercession according to God." I take the meaning of "according to God" to mean according to the Divine way of doing things (see NEB and Beck).

The intercessory groanings of v. 26 which cannot be expressed in human language present no problem to God. This is true because the intercession is made in the language of Deity. We constantly find ourselves unable to clearly communicate what we mean. God does not have such a problem because perfect understanding and perfect communication are experienced between the members of the Trinity.

We may not understand our need. We may not understand what it takes to meet that need. In fact, what we ask for at times could be harmful to us. We need not fear. The Holy Spirit knows what we need and what it will take to meet that need. His intercession will be perfectly understood by the Father.

J. God Works in All Things Toward Good For the Believer (8:28).

28 And we know that all things work together for good to them that love God, to them who are the called according to *his* purpose.

And we know that all things work together for good to them that love God. Let us first give attention to the meaning of "all things." Most interpreters take the position that "all things" refers to the sufferings and adversities of life.

Cranfield comments:

> The primary reference of *panta* [all things] is, no doubt, to 'the sufferings of the present time' (v. 18), to what Calvin in his comment calls 'adversities' or 'the cross.' That this is so is confirmed by vv. 35-39. Sins committed against believers by other people are clearly included (compare 'persecution' and 'sword' in v. 35). Paul might perhaps, if pressed, have said that even believers' own sins were included in this *panta* [all things] (the question whether they are included, or not, has been discussed from patristic times) (428).

Some make it a point to restrict the meaning to adversities. For example, Calvin says: "We must, however, remember that Paul is speaking only of adversities, as though he had said, 'All that befalls the saints is so controlled by God that the final issue shows that what the world regards as harmful is to their advantage" (179).

Liddon would agree that sufferings are included but goes on to say, "*Panta* [all things] here does not appear to include sinful acts, into which the regenerate may fall." He goes on to say, "S. Chrys. [Chrysostom] limits *panta* [all things] to the sum of hindrances and sufferings which Christians experience in serving God. Yet S. Aug. [Augustine] takes in their *falls* as well" (138).

Godet explains:

> The term *panta, all things*, includes all that comes on us, especially everything painful in consequence of the miseries of the present time and of the sins of our neighbors. But it would be wrong to embrace under it what we may do ourselves in opposition to God's will, since that would contradict the idea: *Them that love God*" (322; see also Yeager 559).

Haldane rejects the attempts to limit "all things" to afflictions. He explains:

> If all things work together for good, there is nothing within the compass of being that is not, in one way or other, advantageous to the children of God. All the attributes of God, all the offices of Christ, all the gifts and graces of the Holy Spirit, are combined for their good. The creation of the world, the fall and the redemption of man, all the dispensations of Providence, whether prosperous or adverse, all occurrences and events—all things, whatsoever they be—work for their good....
>
> Even sins of believers work for their good, not from the nature of sin, but by the goodness and power of Him who brings light out of darkness (392, 393).

I am going to suggest an approach altogether different from the ones quoted above. There is one thing about which there is almost unanimous agreement on in commentaries. That is, that Paul is saying that all *bad* things (some interpreters except the person's sins) work for the believer's good. Another way to say it is that all of the difficulties of life are an advantage for the believer.

Even if the above observations are true in life's experiences, I am going to suggest that Paul is not saying this in the verse before us. *It seems to me that there has been a woeful lack on the part of commentators to develop the thought in the context. Up to this point in chapter 8 Paul has not been talking about suffering being good for us.*

The first occurrence of the word "suffer," as it relates to believers, is in v. 17. The next is in v. 18. The word "groan" occurs in v. 23. In v. 26 we find the word "infirmities" (or weakness).

In v. 17 nothing was said about suffering being good for us. The point of the verse is that in order to be glorified together with Christ in the next life, we must be identified with Christ in this life. This identification with Christ in this life will involve suffering with Him.

Verse 18 does not say that suffering is good for us. What it says is that in comparison "with the glory which shall be revealed in us" the sufferings of the present are reduced to insignificance. In this case it is our confidence that we will have a glorious future that helps us bear the suffering of this life.

In this life we groan as we wait for the resurrection (v. 23). In vv. 24, 25 Paul points out that since we do have the hope of the resurrection of the body, we are able to have patient endurance as we wait. The hope of the resurrection helps us, in this life, as we cope with the groaning of v. 23. He does not say that groaning is good for us or helps us.

In v. 26 Paul does not say that our infirmities are for our advantage. Rather, he says that the Holy Spirit helps us cope with our inadequacies.

Consider also what he says about

animate and inanimate creation. In v. 20 he speaks of creation as being "subject to vanity." In v. 21 he speaks of creation as being in "the bondage of corruption." Another way he describes it is to say that "the whole creation groaneth and travaileth in pain until now."

Paul did not say that these experiences were good for creation. The reason these groanings could be called travailing as in childbirth and thus denote an expectancy for deliverance, is not because of the nature of suffering. It is because God "hath subjected *the same* in hope" (v. 20).

The meaning of what Paul has been saying in vv. 17-27 in regard to suffering is: Yes, we do live in a world of harsh reality. There is suffering on every hand. However, we know that for the believer this will one day come to an end. He will experience the full redemption of his body. He will be glorified together with Christ. Not only will he experience full redemption in the totality of his being; the very creation that surrounds him will also experience full redemption. By anticipating this glorious future the believer will be able to develop patient endurance as he waits for that time to come.

In living in this world of harsh reality, things can be so complicated that we may be totally inadequate to know what our real need is or what it will take to meet that need. We need not be destroyed by our inadequacy. The Holy Spirit comes to our aid and helps us. This He does by making intercession for us in groanings that supercede the adequacy of human language for expression. Far from creating a problem (in that it cannot be expressed in human language), this actually proves to be to our advantage. This is true because it is the perfection of this intercession which lifts it above human language. While it would be beyond our comprehension, it is not beyond the comprehension of the Father. It is perfectly understood because it is done in the language of Deity.

The question now is: How does v. 28 fit in this view of the context? Our first concern is with how the verse is translated. Cranfield gives a rather elaborate discussion on the possible ways to translate the first part of the verse (425-428).

Part of the problem of translating the verse is that some Greek manuscripts have a longer reading, adding "God" (Greek *ho theos*) as the subject of the verb "works together". (Neither the *Textus Receptus*, the *Majority Text* nor the *United Bible Society Text* includes this (*ho theos*). For a discussion of this problem see Earle 161-163, who shows some inclination toward accepting this longer reading.) The commonly accepted reading is referred to as the "shorter reading."

There are basically two ways of translating the longer reading: (1) "God causes all things to work together." (2) "God works in all things." (Actually, such renderings are not dependent on the manuscripts that have the extra "God." By *supplying* the word "God" in the translation, either of the translations given above for the longer reading is also possible with the shorter reading. The addition of "God" is possible if the context should support it.)

We could, of course, stick with the more common translation, "All things work together."

Cranfield, for example, is more inclined toward the shorter reading, and toward the translation, "All things work together." His second choice would be, "God works in all things" (425).

If the context is to be understood as I have outlined it above, the translation which best suits this context is, "God works in all things." (As just indicated, this is possible with either the longer or the shorter reading.)

If we take the meaning to be "God works in all things," we could stick with the absolute interpretation of "all things" as including both the bad and the good. This would mean that God will be with us in all circumstances of life. He will be with us and sustain us in spite of the circumstances.

This would be in keeping with what has already been seen in the context. Paul has been talking about the help that God gives us in times of adversity. Paul would be saying, "We can be sure that at all times and in all difficulties, God will be on our side. His sustaining grace will give us strength for the hard times that come our way."

I am strongly of the opinion that the context supports my view. I am also of the opinion it will fit Scripture and the facts of life better than the view which teaches that "all of the adversities of life are for our good."

Before I show why I think my view fits Scripture and the facts of life better than the other view, let me make one point clear. I am very much aware that God uses adversity to work positive benefits in the life of the saint. My own experience bears testimony of that. The problem arises when we try to make it an absolute to fit every negative experience. The quotations given above show that some of the commentators were struggling with this idea by saying that the "all things" did not include the believer's sins.

Most Christians have two contradictory opinions about negative experiences. When Rom. 8:28 is not on their mind, they speak about the tragedies which have come to people. When looking at Rom. 8:28, it sounds as if God has especially designed these experiences for their good, that tragedies do not exist. When talking about Rom. 8:28, even Arminians sound like five-point Calvinists.

Are we going to tell a woman who has been raped that it was for her good? Such an observation will not be very comforting. In fact, it will create more problems than it will solve. I think she would feel like saying that she would not want any more good if it had to come that way.

I am aware that in the case of a particular woman, she may, as a result of her experience, develop a ministry to women who have been raped. Another woman, as a result of her experience, may become active in rape prevention. However, the number of such cases would be few.

Anyone who has ever counseled the victims of rape and sex abuse knows that such cases are extremely devastating on the personality of the victims. Some with proper help may be able to cope with the problems brought on by this experience. Most will probably suffer from the devastation of this experience for the rest of their lives.

Or consider the problem of divorce. Apart from the question of whether divorce is right or wrong, it is an extremely devastating experience for both the wife and the husband as well as the children of that marriage. In the cases where the victims of divorce are Christians, are we going to say that it was good for them that the divorce occurred? If anyone does not know that divorce is very devastating on those who are its victims, it is because he has not been able to read that which is written in big letters in every segment of our society.

Here again, some may develop a ministry out of that experience. However, most will not. The children of that divorce, if they do not receive help, will run a higher risk of divorce on the whole than the children of marriages that stay together.

How comforting will it be to the mother of a two-year old who dashes out into the front of an automobile and is killed instantly to say, "Remember Romans 8:28. God meant this to be for your good"?

I am not denying that God uses tragic events to further His purposes. I am saying that when we try to make that fit every experience in the absolute sense, it is hard to defend.

Nor am I suggesting that God's purposes are ever thwarted. But God has chosen to work in a context where He does not forbid the possibility of events that are harmful to believers. Even God cannot allow sin to be at work and at the same time make our experience on earth like Heaven. There is something better ahead of us.

What we can be assured of is that God will work for our good "in all things." This does not mean that every event as such was for our good. *In fact some of our experiences are not for our good.* (We certainly tell our children that some things are not for their good.) What the Christian can be assured of is that even though we may suffer harm, God will work on our behalf to help us through these difficulties.

To them who are the called according to *his* purpose. The promise of this verse is to those who love God and are called according to God's purpose or plan. Some take this to be a promise to a special group of Christians rather than all believers. I am in agreement with Picirilli when he says: "You must realize that this phrase is meant to include *all* believers. There is no such thing as a Christian who does not love God. This verse does not mean to limit the truths expressed here to some select group of Christians, special servants of God" (164).

We could also add that there is no such thing as a Christian who is not "called according to God's purpose".

K. The Believer Is Predestined to Be Conformed to the Image of Christ (8:29, 30).

29 For whom he did foreknow, he also did predestinate *to be* conformed to the image of his Son, that he might be the firstborn among many brethren.

For whom he did foreknow. "For" (Greek *hoti*) has the force of "because." What follows gives a reason for believing that God works in all things for the believer's good.

Concerning the word for foreknowledge (Greek *proginosko),* Hodge (283, 284) explains: "The word may express *prescience* simply according to its literal meaning; or, *as to know* is often *to approve* and *love*, it may express the idea of peculiar affection in this case; or it may mean *to select* or *determine upon*."

In discussing these different interpretations, Hodge concludes by saying, "The idea, therefore, obviously is, that those whom *he elected* he predestined, etc." (283, 284). It is obvious that Hodge, in making foreknowledge essentially synonymous with election, is taking the position of unconditional election.

Observations about Election

Unconditional election says that God in eternity past chose to elect certain ones from the fallen race of men for salvation. This election was in no way related to foreknowledge of faith on the part of the individual. Those who were thus elected will in due time be saved. God provides the death and righteousness of Christ for their justification. In the course of time, those who have been chosen will be called. This call is an effectual call (or an irresistible call). It cannot fail to result in saving faith. This salvation is an absolute gift. Man did not in anyway do anything to merit it or receive it. The elect are in no way responsible for having faith. That faith is his as an absolute gift of God.

The place of regeneration in Calvinism is quite different from its place in Arminianism. In Calvinism, regeneration precedes faith. In Arminianism, faith precedes regeneration. With many Calvinists, regeneration is equated with the effectual call. Berkhoff (471) takes a slightly different approach. He views regeneration as taking place "from within, while calling comes from without." With reference to regeneration he explains, "In this act of God the ear is implanted that enables man to hear the call of God to the salvation of his soul. *This is regeneration in the most restricted sense of the word.*" The point is that regeneration makes the person spiritually alive. Then faith follows; then justification occurs.

Calvinists work on the assumption that unconditional election is necessary in order to maintain the doctrines of the sovereignty of God, the total depravity of fallen man, and the fact that salvation is free (or by grace). The theological world owes a debt of gratitude to Calvinism for its insistence that salvation is the free gift of God. I am sure that at times some Arminians have needed this reminder. However, I am in sharp disagreement with those Calvinists who claim that unconditional election is necessary if salvation is to be free. Calvinists have not hesitated in criticizing Arminians. I am sure they will understand some criticism in return.

An examination of commentaries will reveal that about 80 percent of the commentaries on Romans will support the concept of unconditional election. For those who are interested in good treatments on unconditional election, I recommend the comments on Rom. 8:29, 30 in the following commentaries: Haldane, Harrison, Hendriksen, Hodge, Murray, Olshausen, Plumer, and Shedd. For treatments that support the position of conditional election see the following commentaries on Rom. 8:29, 30: Clarke, Godet, Greathouse, Lenski, Meyer, Picirilli, and Sanday and Headlam. It should be pointed out that though Lenski and Meyer in their comments support the *concept* of conditional election as Lutherans they would not use the *term* conditional election.

One may wonder why it is that in the area of scholarly writings Calvinists have produced so much more than Arminians. The tendency among Arminians is to be more inclined to activity than to scholarly pursuits. Also, Arminians are inclined to think that common sense would direct people to take the Arminian approach. My advice to fellow Arminians is that if we expect to be a force to be reckoned with, we must give time and effort to producing some well-thought-out treatments of our doctrine. It does not help our cause when some end up denying the omniscience of God and rejecting the concept of individual election.

Before dealing with the interpretation of the passage, I want to make a few observations about Calvinism. Calvinism has oversimplified the relationship of God to man in the ministry of redemption. As I see it, it is very important to distinguish between cause and effect relationships and influence and response relationships.

In the relationship of the physical to the physical, or the relationship of the parts of a machine to one another, we are dealing with cause and effect relationships. The concepts of active and passive apply in their simple meaning. When a hammer hits a nail, the hammer is active and the nail is passive. The hammer causes the nail to be driven into the wood. The nail had no choice. It was caused to be driven into the wood.

Inter-personal relationships do not submit to such a simple analysis. Influence and response are more appropriate terms. A person is one who thinks (with his mind), feels (with his heart), and acts (with his will). In the simple sense of the terms cause and effect, *one person cannot cause another person to do anything*. This does not depend upon the lack of ability that one person has to influence another. Rather, the inability of one person *to cause* another person to do something grows out of the nature of what it means to be a person. When an appeal is made to a person, it is inherent within the person to consider the appeal and then make a decision. *There is no such thing as a person doing or not doing something without having made a decision*. This is true regardless of how strong the influence upon him was.

Calvinism's approach to the effectual call fails to distinguish between cause and effect and influence and response. When the appropriate time comes with regard to the elect, God regenerates him. As a regenerated person, he is caused by God to have faith in Jesus Christ as Lord and Savior. In such a case, the believer had nothing whatsoever to do with the fact that he is a believer. In such a view, faith is considered to be a gift; it cannot be considered his choice, his act, or his response. All of this is considered necessary if salvation is to be a gift.

In explaining the gift of faith that way, the Calvinist is thinking along the lines of cause and effect. The only problem is that if being a person means anything beyond being a puppet with conscious awareness, it is impossible to describe the experience of a *person* in such a manner. We must keep in mind that a human being is a personal being because God has made him that way. Can anyone really deny that faith is a personal response to the working of God with that individual? At least in some sense, the response of faith is a decision on the part of the person who believes.

In my opinion, it has been a mistake over the centuries to focus the conflict between Calvinists and Arminians on whether fallen or redeemed man has a free will. The real question is: Is fallen man a personal being, or is he subpersonal? (The same question can be asked concerning redeemed man.) Does God deal with fallen man as a person? If He does, He deals with him as one who thinks, feels, and acts. To do otherwise undercuts the personhood of man. This God will not do; not because something is being imposed on God to which He must submit, but because God designed the relationship to be a relationship between personal beings. God will not violate His own plan.

It is fully consistent with being a person to be influenced and assisted. We know from Scripture that it takes more than a presentation of the gospel for a person to believe it. Jesus said, "No man can come to me, except the Father which hath sent me draw him" (Jn. 6:44).

The Word of God must be accompanied by the convicting and drawing power of the Holy Spirit before a positive response to the gospel can be given. If a human being is a person, there must be at least some sense in which he is involved in his experience of saving faith. If a person believes in Jesus Christ he has at least in some way made a decision to believe. At the same time, he could not have made a decision without the drawing power of the Holy Spirit.

It is the drawing power of the Holy Spirit that makes faith a gift. Faith is not some substance or entity that has a separate existence which can be imparted to us as a gift. Saving faith can only exist as a personal experience. The only way in which saving faith can be a gift is in the sense that the Holy Spirit works within us to help us believe.

My treatment of atonement and justification in 3:21—4:8 should make it unquestionably clear that I believe that justification is a gift. It is by grace. Not one thing that I have ever done or ever will do is placed on my account with God as part of the price of my redemption. The only way that God, as the Supreme Judge of the universe, can ever justify a member of the fallen human race is to have Christ's righteousness and Christ's death placed on his account. That and that alone is the ground for justification. That is it and nothing else.

Is anyone really going to insist that for God to require faith in Christ *as a condition for receiving* the death and righteousness of Christ would mean justification by works? Does not Paul insist in Rom. 4 that to be justified by faith (faith as a condition, not ground) is in contradiction to justification by works?

The unconditional election taught in Calvinism seems to rest on *a priori* convictions: (1) That the sovereignty of God precludes conditional election. (2) That total depravity precludes any response from any sinner unless he is first regenerated by the Holy Spirit. (3) That the only way salvation could be free is by unconditional election.

The first conviction works on the assumption that the only way God can work with man is through a cause and effect relationship. If God influenced a person to believe in Christ and that person could fail to believe, the Calvinist thinks this would be incompatible with the sovereignty of God. Such a view works on an *a priori* assumption that God cannot work in an influence and response relationship with man.

Surely we will not say that a sovereign God cannot work in an influence and response relationship! Surely God could create a personal being (one who thinks, feels, and acts) and give him some moral options! If a being is truly personal, there must be (at least in this life) the possibility of obedience or disobedience. Adam and Eve chose to disobey. We certainly do not have to assume that God planned to bring about their disobedience. It is obvious that He did not choose to prevent it. But he certainly did not cause it.

If the sovereignty of God was not forfeited when Adam and Eve disobeyed, it need not be forfeited in the case of the person who refuses to respond to the call of God for salvation. *There is nothing inherent in the sovereignty of God that prohibits God from working to influence a person to exercise faith, without guaranteeing a positive response. The marvel of the sovereignty of God is not in the fact that by bare omnipotence He accomplishes His purposes by cause and effect. The marvel is that God can carry out His purposes and work with man through an influence and response relationship.* Through His wisdom, God will carry out His sovereign purposes in spite of the fact that men so frequently disobey God. Not one plan of God, in which He plans for a particular thing to happen, will ever fail to happen. I do not believe that God has planned to regenerate anyone prior to saving faith.

Now let us give attention to the second *a priori* conviction. I believe very strongly in total depravity. Fallen man is depraved in every part of his being. However, fallen man is still a personal being. Fallen man is in a terrible predicament. He is in revolt not only against God, but also against himself. (See discussion on 1:21 and 7:14-24.) *Depravity is of such a nature that God must initiate any move that would result in saving faith. The Holy Spirit must work with a person before he can respond with saving faith. In no way whatsoever does man do anything that would make salvation in any way by works.* However, in response to the presentation of the gospel and the drawing power of the Holy Spirit, a person can respond with saving faith or, since he is a person, he can also give a negative response.

Calvinism has not only erred in placing regeneration before faith; it has also erred in making the intial act of sanctification precede justification. Calvinists know full well that sanctification is dependent upon justification rather than the other way around. Yet, they violate their own conviction in making regeneration precede faith. By any person's definition, regeneration is designed to change behavior which is exactly the province of sanctification. In saying that depravity requires unconditional election, Calvinism ends up making sanctification precede faith. This cannot be. (See comment on 6:5.) In taking an *a priori* conviction that total depravity necessitates unconditional election and an effectual (irresistible) call, Calvinism is on a collision course with its own theology by making the initial act of sanctification precede justification.

The *a priori* conviction that a free salvation requires unconditional election has been given an answer above. If Calvinism's claim is to be established, it will not be based on an *a priori* assumption's necessity. Once this approach is set aside we can study the Scripture, considering other options.

From the standpoint of conditional election, there are two possible ways to understand foreknowledge as is used in 8:29. Meyer explains: "God has *fore*known those who would not oppose to his gracious calling the resistance of unbelief, but would follow its drawing; thereafter He has *fore-ordained* them to eternal salvation; and when the time had come for the execution of His saving counsel, has called them, etc. (ver.30)" (337).

Godet offers the same view, worded somewhat differently, "There is but one answer: foreknown as sure to fulfill the condition of salvation, viz. *faith*; so: foreknown as His *by faith*" (325).

Lenski takes a somewhat different approach concerning the word *know* (Greek *ginosko*). The meaning is "'to know with affection and with a resultant effect.'" He goes on to say that to add the prefix "fore" (Greek *pro*) "dates this affectionate and effective knowing back into eternity" (557).

If there is any doubt where Lenski stands on election, the following statement from him should settle the issue.

"If it be asked why God did not foreknow, foreordain, call, justify the rest, the Biblical answer is found in Matt. 23:37 and similar passages: God did not exclude them, but despite all that God could do *they* excluded themselves" (562).

Lenski's view is probably the correct view. "Whom he foreknew" speaks of knowing persons rather than simply knowing something about them. God foreknew the elect with affection, or He foreknew them as being His.

What Meyer and Godet say about foreknowledge as referring to foreknowledge of faith is a necessary inference. To know a person implies a time of getting acquainted with that person. If God foreknew the elect as being His, it is necessarily inferred that this foreknowledge presupposes the person's belief in Jesus Christ as his Lord and Savior.

The Calvinist will insist that we cannot know why God chose the elect. In speaking of unconditional election, Strong says, "It represents God, not as arbitrary, but as exercising the free choice of a wise and sovereign will, in ways and for reasons which are inscrutable to us" (787).

Boettner in defense of unconditional election says: "Nor may any one object that this view represents God as acting arbitrarily and without reason. To assert that is to assert more than anyone knows. His reasons for saving particular ones while passing others by have not been revealed to us" (97).

When we try to insist that God, in eternity, chose the elect based on His foreknowledge of their faith in Christ, the Calvinist insists that we cannot know why God chose the elect since God has not told us. If this be the case, on what basis can the Calvinist say that election was unconditional? God has not told us that either!

The only way that we can understand God's eternal decisions, beyond what He has told us, is based on the immutability of God. Precisely the same principles which guide God's operation now were the same that guided His choice in eternity past. If we can discover the condition of being chosen by God in time, we have discovered the condition for election in eternity past.

For Calvinism's unconditional election to stand, it must be maintained that God is now choosing people for salvation apart from any conditions. Do the Calvinists preach an unconditional gospel? Can anyone deny that a person must believe in Christ in order to be saved? Did not Paul argue conclusively that we are saved by (on the condition of) faith in chapter 4? The Calvinist cannot escape by saying faith is a gift. I believe faith is a gift also. It is a gift in that God enables us to believe. Without His enablement, we could not have saving faith. (This point is discussed more fully above.)

Now, let us take a look at what Scripture has told us about our eternal election. Paul says, "According as he hath chosen us in him before the foundation of the world. . ." (Eph. 1:4). The words of Arminius in commenting on this verse are well-chosen.

> God acknowledges, as His own, no sinner, and He chooses no one to eternal life except in Christ, and for the sake of Christ. . . .He who is not in Christ, cannot be loved in Christ. But no one is in Christ, except by faith; for Christ dwells in our hearts by faith [Ephesians 3:17], and we are ingrafted and incorporated in him by faith. It follows then that God acknowledges His own, and chooses to eternal life no sinner, unless He considers him as a believer in Christ, and made one with him by faith (III:314).

Let me now give a further word as it relates to foreknowledge of faith and election. I am not saying that God, as a *bystander*, looked through the corridors of time and saw that certain ones would believe and thus elected or chose them for salvation. *If God were only a bystander, there would be no one believing in Christ. There would be no salvation.*

In eternity past, God foresaw Himself as having the same kind of active involvement in the human race that He is now having. He foresaw the same program of preaching, witnessing, and teaching that is now taking place. God saw Himself working through the redeemed as they would make known the gospel. He saw the work of the Holy Spirit working in the hearts of those who would hear His Word. In that context, He saw those who would believe, and He chose or elected them to be His. These He affectively foreknew as being His own.

There is much more that could be said about foreknowledge and election, but I believe the following conclusions have been established: (1) There are no *a priori* reasons related to the sovereignty of God, the doctrine of depravity, or the fact that salvation is free, which would necessitate unconditional election. (2) Based on the immutability of God, we can conclude that just as God chooses people now for salvation on the condition of faith, in eternity past, based on His foreknowledge of faith, He elected them for salvation.

He also did predestinate *to be* conformed to the image of his Son. The word for "predestine" (Greek *proorizo)* never has saving faith as its object. When predestination comes into the picture, it is always presupposed that the person is already a believer. It is never said that any person was predestinated to believe. In the verse before us, it is predetermined that believers will be conformed to the image of Christ.

Apart from the verses before us, the only verses which require our attention are Eph. 1:5 and 11. In Eph. 1:5, the word which is translated "adoption of children" is the word (Greek *huiothesia*) already discussed in the comments on "adoption" in 8:15. Adoption refers, in the N.T., to placing one who is already a child into the position of being an heir of legal age.

When Paul said, "having predestinated us," it is clear that "us" refers to those who are already believers. God has predestined the believer to be in the position of an heir of legal age.

In Eph. 1:11 there are different opinions on the meaning of "being predestinated," but none would understand this verse to say that faith is the focal point of predestination. Again those under consideration are already considered to be believers.

In the verse before us, the focal point of predestination is "conformity to the image of Christ." To be conformed to the image of Christ refers to the sanctification of the believer. Some are of the opinion that the final sanctification of the believer in connection with the resurrection is what Paul is referring to (Lenski 561 and Murray 319). Others understand the reference to be to the total process of sanctification both during this life and the final and complete sanctification in connection with the resurrection (Cranfield 432 and Hendriksen 283). I take the latter position to be the correct view. It is the entire process of sanctification which is the focal point of predestination.

The word *conformed* (Greek *summorphos)* is an interesting word. Sanday and Headlam explain that this word "denotes inward and thorough and not merely superficial likeness" (218). In sanctification the conformity to the image of Christ is not mere superficial conformity. It is an inward conformity to the image of Christ. The believer's personality (the way he thinks, feels, and acts) is being conformed to the image of Christ and will in the eschatological future be completely conformed to the image of Christ. (For a more thorough discussion of the transformation of the believer's personality to the image of Christ, see my *Systematics*, 182-189.)

It is quite clear that conformity to the image of Christ for the believer, rather than saving faith, is the object of predestination in the verse before us. Briscoe is correct when he says:

> This predestination is not a predestination to faith but a decision on God's part that glory will be the ultimate of salvation. If my wife invites a friend for dinner and determines that roast beef will be the main course, this fact in no way infringes on the friend's freedom to accept or reject the invitation, but it does preclude her from choosing to eat roast lamb or turkey. The call of God to respond in faith and repentance to the gospel brings the human will into center stage, but the divine

will has already determined what the final result [conformity to the image of Christ] will be (177, 178).

That he might be the firstborn. The word "firstborn" (Greek *prototokos*) is not a reference to chronological order, but a refrence to Christ's exalted position. Hodge explains it very well:

> The purpose of God in the salvation of men, was not mainly that men should be holy and happy, but that through their holiness and happiness his glory, in the person of the Son, should be displayed, in the ages to come, to principalities and powers. Christ, therefore, is the central point in the history of the universe. His glory, as the glory of God in the highest form of its manifestation, is the great end of creation and redemption. And this end, the apostle teaches, is accomplished by making him the *first-born among many brethren*, that is, by causing him to stand as the first-born, the head and chief, among and over that countless multitude who through him are made the sons of God (285, 286).

(See also Cranfield 432, and Murray 319, 320.)

30 Moreover whom he did predestinate, them he also called: and whom he called, them he also justified: and whom he justified, them he also glorified.

Moreover whom he did predestinate. "Whom he did predestinate" is a reference to those whom "he also did predestinate to be conformed to the image of his Son" (v. 29). This verse refers to the order of events as they occur in the ministry of redemption. This is generally agreed upon by commentaries. Therefore, we need not give further attention to this fact.

Calvinists make a point of saying that whenever the call is mentioned in the epistles, it only refers to believers. But that is because believers are being addressed. Paul likes to use the word "called," in referring to believers, to stress that our personal redemption owes its existence to the fact that God first took the initiative toward us. We are not intruders into this salvation which is ours through Jesus Christ.

On the Calvinist's limitation of the word "called" to believers I would make two observations: (1) To refer to believers as being "called ones" does not mean that the call has not been extended to anyone else. A speaker at a special occasion may address the audience as invited guests. The only thing that he is affirming is that those who are present have been invited. They are not intruders. It does not mean that no one else was invited. When believers are referred to as called, it is not necessary to conclude that others have not been called.

(2) While the word "called" may not be used in the epistles to refer to those who have not responded, the concept of a call is seen where the word is not used. There is no plainer reference to this than Paul's statement when he says,"And the times of this ignorance God winked at; but now commandeth all men every where to repent" (Acts 17:30). Paul's use of "whosoever" in 10:11-13 implies a call that extends to all men. It makes no difference whether a reference to God's calling sinners to salvation appears in the epistles in connection with the word "call." The concept is undeniably there.

No one is justified who was not first called. There can be no question that Paul is referring to those cases where the call has had its desired effect. That is not the same as saying that the call is irresistible, nor that it has succeeded in every case. This simply cannot be read out of the language. (At the appropriate time in chapters 9 and 10, this will be given more attention.)

When the person responds in faith, God justifies him. In due time the one who is justified will be glorified.

It will be observed that called, justified, and glorified are all in the past tense (the Greek aorist tense). The believing recipients of Paul's epistle had been called and justified, but not glorified. There has been some question about the use of the past tense with reference to "glorified" since glorification is yet future. The explanation commonly given is that it refers to the certainty of this future glorification (Bruce 177; Hendriksen 285; and Meyer 337).

Murray points out that calling, justification, and glorification are solely the acts of God. He explains, "It is contrary to this emphasis to define any of these elements of the application of redemption in any other terms than those of *divine actions*" (320). I find no problem with Murray's statement. The very nature of a call means that it is the activity of the one who extends the call. Justification is a Divine act in which God declares us righteous based on the death and righteousness of Christ. The foundation of our justification is solely the merits of Christ rather than our own. But if Murray wants to insist that there is no involvement of the human personality in meeting the condition of faith as it relates to justification, I must differ with him. However, this verse says nothing about faith. I concur with Godet when he says, "If his intention had been to explain *the order of salvation* in all its elements divine *and human*, he would have put *faith* between calling and justification, and *holiness* between justification and glorification" (327).

I certainly have no quarrel with the statement that future glorification will be bestowed on us by Divine action. It is quite clear that v. 30 speaks only of Divine action. At the same time it is quite clear that it is not an exhaustive treatment of the doctrine of salvation. Paul approached the verse in terms of Divine action because he was still giving reasons for believing that God will be with us under any and all circumstances as set forth in v. 28.

Concerning why Paul moved from justification to glorification without mentioning sanctification, I think Bruce is on the right track when he says:

> The difference between sanctification and glory is one of degree only, not one of kind. Sanctification is progressive conformity to the image of Christ here and now (cf. II Cor. 3:18; Col. 3:10); glory is perfect conformity to the image of Christ there and then. Sanctification is glory begun; glorification is sanctification completed (178).

Calvinists have sometimes thought that this verse guarantees that everyone who is called will respond, everyone who is called will be justified, and everyone who is justified will be glorified. I find myself in essential agreement with John Wesley:

> St. Paul does not affirm, either here or in any other part of his writings that precisely the same number of men are called, justified, and glorified. He does not deny that a believer may fall away and be cut off between his special calling and his glorification, Romans 11:22, neither does he deny that many are called who never are justified. He only affirms that this is the method whereby God leads us step by step toward heaven (*Explanatory Notes Upon the New Testament*).

There is a parallel with the words of Jesus when He said, "For the earth bringeth forth fruit of herself; first the blade, then the ear, after that the full corn in the ear" (Mk. 4:28). The process that is followed from the appearance of the blade until the grain is fully developed is stated, but Jesus does not guarantee that, once the blade appears, in every case all of the other steps follow. In some cases the stalk of grain dies before reaching full development.

While the wording of Rom. 8:30 could fit the idea of an effectual call followed by justification of all the called and glorification without exception of all who are justified, it is not necessary to interpret it so. Such a view would require support from some other source. I do not believe that such is found.

L. God's Being For Us Rules Out the Possibility of Anyone's Being Successfully Against Us (8:31-34).

31 What shall we then say to these things? If God *be* for us, who *can be* against us?

What shall we then say to these things? "These things" refers back to all that God is doing for us and will do for us that has been mentioned in chap. 8 up to this verse.

If God *be* for us, who *can be* against us? It is obvious that there are those who oppose us. The meaning is that with God on our side no one can be *successfully* against us.

Verses 31-39 are used by those who deny the possibility of shipwreck of faith (or apostasy) to support their doctrine. That will be dealt with when comments on these verses are completed.

32 He that spared not his own Son, but delivered him up for us all, how shall he not with him also freely give us all things?

He that spared not his own Son. God's holiness is so strong that it insisted that the penalty of our sin must be paid by Christ if we were to experience forgiveness. God's love for us is so strong that He sent His own Son. If God had spared His Son, He could not spare us from the punishment of an eternal Hell.

But delivered him up for us all. Cranfield observes: "Isaac was rescued by divine intervention (Gen. 22:11-13), but for Jesus there was no such intervention, no other lamb could take the place of the Lamb of God; and the delivering up meant making to drink to the very dregs the cup of wrath (see on 1:18)" (436).

How shall he not with him also freely give us all things? Godet observes:

> There is a marked shade of difference between the verb: *freely give* [*charizesthai*], and the preceding verbs: *not sparing, giving up.* While the latter express something painful, the former denotes an act full of pleasure to the heart of the one who does it. How, after carrying through the sacrifice would He not do the pleasant part of a gracious giver? Thus it is that all possible gifts, however great or small they may be, whether for this life or the next, are virtually comprised in the gift of the Son,...To give *all things* is a small matter after the best is given (330).

Lenski limits the application of "all things" to the things needed for the comforts of this life (567). The basic thrust of "all things" in this context is dealing with help for the here and now. However, there is no reason for denying the inclusion of our eternal inheritance in the "all things."

This verse furnishes us with a clear illustration of the fact that "all things" is not always used with an absolute meaning. For example sin is not given to us by God, nor does God grant our foolish requests. He gives us all things that relate to His purpose in our lives.

33 Who shall lay anything to the charge of God's elect? *It is* God that justifieth.

Who shall lay anything to the charge of God's elect? Let us first give attention to "God's elect." There are two phases of God's elective process: (1) That election which took place in eternity past. (2) That election which takes place when a person becomes a believer. Murray says, "The election can be none other than that specified in different terms in verse 29, and Ephesians 1:4 as election in Christ before the foundation of the world." (327).

While it is certainly to be understood that when God chooses the one who believes in Christ in time, this person was also chosen in eternity past, the focus of "God's elect" in 8:33 is on those who have already become believers, not on those who have not yet believed. All of God's decisions that He makes in time are the implementation of His eternal decisions. However, a person is not justified until he believes. The elect of whom Paul speaks have already been justified. Therefore, they have already believed.

This verse is asking, "Who can successfully bring a charge against one who is justified by faith in Christ?"

The general meaning of vv. 33 and 34 is clear. It is not so clear how the parts fit together. Some, instead of placing a period at the end of v. 33, connect it with the first part of v. 34. It would read, "It is God that justifieth; who is he that condemneth?" (See Cranfield 437, 478 and Murray 327, 328.)

To punctuate this way would remove the awkwardness that appears with v. 33 but it would not remove the awkwardness of v. 34. By awkwardness I mean that the first reading of v. 33 may sound as if Paul is saying that God is the One who will bring a charge against the elect. Verse 34 may sound as if Christ is the One who will condemn us. We know of course that these conclusions are false.

Plumer says: "Augustine, Grotius, Locke, Whitby, Bowyer, Doddridge, Pyle, Griesbach and Clarke continue the interrogatory form of the last clause: Is it God that justifieth? That is, will the same God justify and bring charges against His chosen? The same commentators do the same in the next verse" (439). (See also Vincent 711.)

This rendering states a truth in that it is intended to affirm that God (v. 33) and Christ (v. 34) will not accuse nor condemn the elect. The problem is that there is no reason even to ask such a question.

It seems that the best way to understand the verse is to translate, "Who shall lay anything to the charge of God's elect, [since] it is God that justifieth?" The implication is that if God says we are justified nothing that anyone else can say will alter that fact. Our justification is dependent upon our relationship with God—Him and Him alone—not anyone else.

34 Who *is* he that condemneth? *It is* Christ that died, yea rather, that is risen again, who is even at the right hand of God, who also maketh intercession for us.

As with the previous verse, we may read: **Who *is* he that condemneth [since] *it is* Christ that died, yea rather, that is risen again, who is even at the right hand of God, who also maketh intercession**

for us? With God as Judge who has justified us and Christ who has fully satisifed the law on our behalf pleading for us, we have nothing to fear.

M. A Person Cannot Be a Child of God and at the Same Time Be Separated From the Love of Christ (8:35-39).

35 Who shall separate us from the love of Christ? *shall* tribulation, or distress, or persecution, or famine, or nakedness, or peril, or sword?

Who shall separate us from the love of Christ? It should be obvious that Paul is speaking here of Christ's love for us rather than our love for Him. Harrison gets to the heart of Paul's question when he says:

> Can there conceivably be a contradiction between Christ's love for his own and his allowing suffering to overtake them? Should the saints question whether Christ's love has grown cold? Severance from his love is no more thinkable than that the Father ceased to love his Son when he allowed him to endure the agonies of the cross, apparently forsaken (99).

Lenski correctly says, "The point of the thought is lost when the question of our faith is introduced: 'Can anything sunder the tie of faith that connects us with the love of Christ?' and when the answer is given: 'No, the elect cannot lose their faith'" (573). Without question Paul is intending to convey the idea that the person who is a child of God cannot at the same time be separated from the love of Christ. Difficult times and experiences are not to be taken to mean that God does not love us.

***Shall* tribulation** (Greek *thlipsis*). Godet understands the meaning to be "overwhelming circumstances."

Or distress (Greek *stenochoria*). In Rom. 2:9 this word is translated "anguish." Concerning the meaning, Godet says, "Literally, compression of heart, the inward effect produced by tribulation" (333). See also the comments on Rom. 2:9.

Or persecution, or famine (Greek *limos*). This word is used by Paul in 2 Cor. 11:27 to mean hunger.

Or nakedness (Greek *gumnotes*). Hendriksen observes, "Often the meaning is somewhat more general than *naked* might suggest; hence, *in need of clothes* is at times a better rendering" (290).

Or peril, or sword? Godet explains, "The *sword*: the symbol of capital punishment. When Paul writes this word, he designates, as Bengel observes, his own future mode of death" (333).

36 As it is written, For thy sake we are killed all the day long; we are accounted as sheep for the slaughter.

This quotation from Ps. 44:22 points out that adversity for believers is not new. There is no Scriptural warrant for the idea that if Christians will have enough faith they will have a trouble-free life.

37 Nay, in all these things we are more than conquerors through him that loved us.

Nay (Greek *alla*). In the vast majority of places in the N.T., this word is translated "but." Several prefer this translation in this verse. It appears to me that the way it is translated depends upon whether: (1) v. 37 is considered to be an answer to v. 35, or (2) v. 37 is connected with v. 36.

If v. 37 is connected with v. 36, "but"

would be the better translation. The meaning would be, "We are accounted as sheep for the slaughter, but (in spite of this) we are more than conquerors."

If v. 37 answers v. 35, we would take v. 36 to be a parenthetical reference which would affirm that God's people have the kind of experiences referred to in v. 35. If v. 36 is a parenthetical statement, v. 37 would then be considered an answer to v. 35.

My opinion is that the second view is correct. That would mean that "nay" (no) would be an appropriate answer. Or we could translate as Yeager does, "on the contrary" (572).

We are more than conquerors is translated from only one Greek word, (*hupernikao*). Concerning this word Earle explains: "It is compounded of *huper* (Latin *super*) meaning "above," and *nikao*, from *nike*, 'victory.' So it means literally 'we are super victory.' Paul did not believe in barely getting by, in hardly holding his head above the water. He experienced the more abundant life which Jesus said He came to bring, Jn. 10:10" (174).

In all these things refers back to the things listed in v. 35. Unless God gives a particular individual assurance that he will not experience a particular problem, there is no evidence that can be given for saying that a believer will not partake of the harsh reality mentioned in v. 35. What we can be assured of is that in these experiences God's love is with us. His sustaining grace is with us and is sufficient (2 Cor. 12:9). We can say with Paul, "I have learned in whatsoever state I am, therewith to be content (Phil. 4:10).

38 For I am persuaded, that neither death, nor life, nor angels, nor principalities, nor powers, nor things present, nor things to come.

For I am persuaded that neither death nor life. Paul knew that death by whatever means would not separate him from God's love. In fact, it would usher him into an even greater experience of God's love. Life is filled with problems and difficulties. Many are more afraid of life than death. Negativism, pessimism, depression, frustration, and despair are what many see facing them in this life. Paul knew what harsh reality was (2 Cor. 11:23-27). In view of Paul's knowledge that God's love was with him, he could face the future no matter what it might hold.

Nor angels, nor principalities, nor powers. Picirilli explains,"Angels, principalities, and powers stand for the varius orders and ranks of angelic beings, especially here the wicked ones who are our supernatural enemies (compare Ephesians 6:11, 12)" (171).

Nor things present, nor things to come. There is nothing that is now with us nor anything which may come on the scene in the future which will be able to separate us from God's love.

39 Nor height, nor depth, nor any other creature, shall be able to separate us from the love of God, which is in Christ Jesus our Lord.

Nor height, nor depth. The meaning here is that no matter where we go God will be there to love His own. Vine explains, "This refers to the dimensions of space, just as 'things present,' 'things to come,' referred to matters of time. The words 'height' and 'depth' may here indicate heaven and earth (see also Isa. 7:11)" (*Romans* 135).

Nor any other creature. Paul adds this expression to include anything that he had not already mentioned.

Shall be able to separate us from the love of God, which is in Christ Jesus our Lord. In v. 35 Paul started with the question: "Who shall separate us from the love of Christ?" His answer is that nothing whatever can separate us from the love of God. It is impossible for a person to be a child of God and at the same time be separated from his love. The supreme manifestation of God's love has come to us through the love of Christ.

Notes on Perseverance

Those who deny the possibility that a Christian can make shipwreck of his faith (or commit apostasy) and be lost usually consider that Rom. 8:31-39 supports their doctrine. I want to challenge this assumption.

The main thrust of vv. 31-39, as I see it, is referring to the assurance that God will sustain us as we face the trials of life. Verses 33,34 do have some bearing on the security of the believer. There is security from the possibility that any outside force or person could condemn a believer.

If God declares us justified, no one else can successfully bring a charge against us (v.33). With God as judge on our side and Christ as the one who pleads our case, there is no one else that could possibly condemn us (v. 34).

We must believe in the security of the believer *as a believer*. But these verses in no way contradict the viewpoint that if a believer ceases to be a believer and becomes an unbeliever, he will no longer be justified.

More frequently, vv. 35-39 are used to support the denial that a saved person can commit apostasy and be lost. This comes from a misinterpretation of the question, "Who shall separate us from the love of Christ?" (v. 35). It is interpreted as denying that one who is now a believer could be separated from Christ. In the comments on these verses above, I think it is clear that Paul is not addressing the doctrine of security. Rather, he is saying that there is no such thing as being a child of God and at the same time not being loved by God.

Let us suppose that vv. 35-39 were saying that no one could sever us from Christ so as to end our salvation relationship with Christ. Even so, it still does not say that under no circumstances could one who is now a believer cease to be a believer and be lost. The believer's relationship with God is a personal relationship between him and God. No matter what others say or do they cannot sever another person's relationship with God. That is not the same as saying the believer can never make shipwreck of faith and be lost. The Bible never says that unbelievers are saved. (For a more complete development of the doctrine of the possibility of apostasy, see my *Systematics* 207-30.)

Summary
8:1-39

Based on what he has said before, Paul confidently states, "There is therefore now no condemnation to them which are in Christ" (v. 1). He goes on to say that the resultant union with Christ, effected by the Holy Spirit, frees us from the law which says if we sin we die (v. 2).

Paul's interest is in showing the inseparable relationship between justification and sanctification. The law could not bring justification. Christ did what the law could not do. He accomplished our justification through His death. This was purposely done to enable us, in a practical sense, to live in accord with the righteousness of the law (vv. 3, 4).

Paul makes it quite clear in vv. 5-8 that a sinner neither does nor can live after the Holy Spirit. He cannot please God. On the other hand, Paul makes it clear that the believer does not set his mind on the things of the flesh.

He then proceeds to say that if we have the Holy Spirit living in us we are not in the flesh. He goes on to say that if a person does not have the Holy Spirit dwelling in him he does not belong to Christ (v. 9).

There are some definite advantages in being in Christ. Though the body is mortal and will thus die, yet because we have the righteousness of Christ, the "Spirit is life." By "life" he means life that has quality to it (v. 10). Another advantage of having the Holy Spirit live in us is that it assures us that in the eschatological future our bodies will be raised from the dead (v. 11).

In view of all the negative factors involved in living after the flesh and the positive factors in living after the Spirit, Paul reminds us that we have no obligation to the flesh (v. 12). Furthermore, he reminds us of the negative consequences of living after the flesh (death) and the positive consequences of living after the Spirit (life) (v. 13). He goes on to say that if we are led by the Spirit of God we can know that we belong to God (v. 15).

In a further elaboration of the benefits he reminds us that the Holy Spirit who is in us helps us to be aware that we are sons of God. One of the great benefits of being children of God is that we are joint-heirs with Christ. In this life we suffer at times because we belong to God. In the next life we will share Christ's inheritance with Him (vv. 16, 17).

Once we look at the glorious future that will be ours, it minimizes the sufferings. They lose their significance (v. 18).

Paul points out that the animate and inanimate creation is eagerly waiting for the full redemption of the saints. When we are resurrected and enter the eternal state, the whole creation will be renovated or will become new. It will experience redemption along with us. At this time we will experience the resurrection of our bodies (vv. 19-23).

We live in a world that is decaying. It is under the curse. We face difficulty. However, we can develop patient endurance because we know that full redemption awaits us in the future. We will then enter a problem-free life (vv. 24, 25).

Just as the confidence of the resurrection helps us develop patient endurance, the Holy Spirit helps us as we pray. Even though we do not know what our real needs are sometimes, we need not worry. The Holy Spirit is interceding on our behalf with an intercession that is so perfect that human language cannot convey it. However, we need not be concerned because it is done in the language of deity. God will fully understand (vv. 26, 27).

Paul has not tried to gloss over the fact that Christians partake of harsh reality. He has pointed out the way God helps us. In v. 28, with an emotion filled outburst, Paul reminds us that no matter what the circumstances are God will work with us and help us overcome.

To show why we should have confidence of God's help in trials, Paul tells us what God's plan is. His plan, predetermined in eternity past, is that believers will be conformed to the image of Christ. In time God works in calling people and justifying them. In the future God will glorify us. If He will do all that for us, does it not stand to reason that He will help us face the trials of life now? If God spared not His own Son when it came to providing for our redemption, surely He will give us what we need (vv. 29-32).

God is the One who justifies us and Christ is pleading our case. Since that is true, no one else can condemn us (vv. 33-34).

Paul raises the question: "Who shall

separate us from the love of Christ?" Another way of saying it is: Is it possible to be a believer and at the same time be separate from God's love? The answer is no. Christians do have painful experiences as they live in this troubled world. This does not mean that God does not love them. Rather, He gives us grace to handle what we face. By His grace we are super victors. It is Paul's conviction that nothing whatever can sever us from God's love.

Application: Teaching and Preaching the Passage

1. The law could not deliver, but it could prepare the way for the gospel. The message of the gospel is that "There is therefore now no condemnation to them which are in Christ Jesus" (v. 1). It is in union with Christ that there is no condemnation (see notes on 6:3-5 on the union of Christ and the believer).

2. In Jesus Christ we are under grace and have been delivered from the law which says, "If you sin, you die." He was our only hope. Our justification rests on the death and sinlessness of Jesus Christ, not our own sinlessness.

3. Justification is designed to contribute to sanctification. (See comments on 6:5-8 along with the comments on 8:1-4.)

4. The church has always been plagued by the problem of false professions, i.e. those who profess to be saved but are not. Paul made it clear in vv. 5-9 that an unsaved person is carnally minded, i.e., he has a mind-set or pattern of thinking that follows the flesh. The saved person is spiritually minded: that is, he has a mind-set or pattern of thinking that is sensitive to the leading of the Holy Spirit. Paul does not give assurance of eternal life to those who have a carnal mind-set.

5. Paul makes it clear that if a person does not have the Holy Spirit, he is not saved. In v. 9 "the Spirit of God" and "the Spirit of Christ" are the same. They refer to the Holy Spirit.

6. When Paul said in v. 10 "the Spirit is life because of righteousness," the word "life" means more than alive. It refers to the quality of life involved in "abundant life" (Jn. 10:10).

7. The presence of the Holy Spirit within us assures us that our bodies will one day experience resurrection (v. 11).

8. Paul makes an appeal to the readers to realize that they have no obligation at all to live after the flesh. The flesh has nothing worthwhile to offer (v. 12).

9. Paul, in v. 13, shows again that sanctification cannot be separated from justification. While it is unquestionably clear in Romans that we are saved by grace and not by works, it is equally clear that those who are saved will show the evidence of a change of life-style. It does violence to Scripture and the gospel to say that a person can be saved without being changed.

10. The leading that Paul talks about in v. 14 is not a leading into some unknown area. It refers to following the Holy Spirit in mortifying the deeds of the flesh mentioned in v. 13.

11. Adoption is a very important doctrine in the N.T. It refers to the privileged position that N.T. believers have as adult sons (see comments on v. 15).

12. When v. 16 says, "The Spirit bears witness with our spirit" it means that based on Scripture we already believe that we are children of God. The Holy Spirit bears witness that this assurance is true.

13. As children of God we are heirs of God. We are joint-heirs with Christ. This means that we will share Jesus Christ's inheritance with Him. Most of us will probably never recieve a great inheritance in this life. In one way or

another all of us will partake of suffering and difficulty in this life. However, as believers we know that a glorious eschatological future awaits us. When we receive those blessings which God has in store for us, all of the problems of this life will fade into insignificance (vv. 17, 18).

14. Along with the full manifestation of our redemption in the eschatological future will be the redemption of creation, both animate and inanimate (vv. 19-24).

15. In this life through Christ we receive peace, joy, and happiness. But this is not the only side of the picture. "We groan within ourselves." Our bodies have not been redeemed. Everything is not all that it should be. We are waiting and yearning for something better. That something better is the resurrection of the body. At the resurrection we will experience all that it means to be privileged, adult sons of God. On the one hand we are rejoicing in what we have. On the other hand we are longing for something better. We know that one day we will experience the resurrection of our bodies. Then things will be better beyond comparison. Because we know that the day of full redemption is coming, we wait for it with steadfast endurance (vv. 23-25).

16. If we stop to think about it, many times we do not know exactly what our need is. We do not know exactly what it would take to meet that need. Even when we think we know, we may be wrong. Verses 26, 27 offer us encouragement. The Holy Spirit takes every sincere prayer and desire and makes a perfect intercession to the Father for us. This intercession is perfectly understood by the Father (see notes on these verses).

17. The notes on v. 28 should be studied thoroughly. There is great comfort in this verse, but it takes more than a mere quoting of the verse for people to get its message. Whatever happens to us as believers, we can rest assured that God will bring things to bear upon our case that will help us through it.

18. We need not be afraid of the word "predestinate." In fact, we should be encouraged by it. What it tells us is that God has before determined that believers will be conformed to the image of Christ (v. 29).

19. God's plan is eternal, but our salvation in time begins with a call. When we respond to this call we are justified. In the eschatological future we will be glorified (see notes on v. 30).

20. As Christians, we have a lot going for us. With God on our side no one can be successfully against us (v. 31). If God spared not, but gave His Son for us, it follows that He will care for us and stand by us (v. 32). Since God has said we are justified, no one else can make a charge against us stick (v. 33). Since Christ is our intercessor, no one can condemn us (v. 34).

21. In vv. 35-39 two important truths are established:

(1) The Bible does not promise a trouble-free life to Christians.

(2) We are not to interpret difficulty, when it comes, to mean that God does not love us. As believers we will never be separated from God's love. It is God's love and presence with us that makes us "more than conquerors through him that loved us" (v. 37).

Part Two

Israel and the Gentiles in God's Plan of Redemption (9:1—11:36).

I. GOD'S SOVEREIGN RIGHT IN REJECTING THE UNBELIEVING ISRAELITES (9:1-29).

A. Paul Expresses His Deep Concern for His Kinsmen According to the Flesh (9:1-5).

1 I say the truth in Christ, I lie not, my conscience also bearing me witness in the Holy Ghost.

Chapter 8 ended on a triumphant note. While in this emotion-filled state, Paul suddenly thought of his kinsmen—the Jews. When he did that, deep compassion and concern which he had for his kinsmen was activated within him. It is out of this deep concern that he speaks.

I say the truth in Christ, I lie not. The words which Paul was going to utter in v. 3 are words which very few people could in truth utter. It is for this reason that Paul prefaces those words with the most solemn commitment to truth possible. To speak in Christ is to speak truth; as Cranfield observes,"One who speaks in a way that is worthy of his union with Christ cannot but speak truth" (II:452).

My conscience also bearing me witness in the Holy Ghost. Lenski explains, "Paul's own statements are one witness, Paul's conscience is another. The idea is that two witnesses are sufficient to settle any point. Conscience is another voice, one that cannot be bribed, one that speaks independently and unhesitatingly contradicts us if we are wrong or false" (582).

Our conscience judges our actions by the standard of right that we subscribe to. Our conscience is as accurate as our convictions are. Our convictions may not always be right. Concerning the witness of Paul's conscience, Murray explains,"It is most significant that he regards this witness as borne 'in the Holy Spirit.' Just as the certification of the earlier assertion [I lie not] is derived from union with Christ, so the veracity of the witness of his conscience is certified by the Holy Spirit" (II:2). When the witness of the conscience can truthfully be said to be borne in the Holy Spirit, its witness is true.

2 That I have great heaviness and continual sorrow in my heart.

Concerning this verse Picirilli explains, "'Great heaviness' means great grief. 'Continual sorrow' refers to uninterrupted pain. The pangs of grief Paul feels for Israel weigh heavily on him. He is never free from that burden. Weiss calls attention to the triple intensity indicated here: from 'heaviness' to 'sorrow,' from 'great' to 'continual,' from 'I' to 'my heart'" (174).

Moule remarks, "Very wonderful and profoundly true, is this expression of intense grief just after the 'joy unspeakable' of ch. 8" (162).

Joy is a positive value reaction. Sorrow is a negative value reaction. Value reactions are experienced in the heart. These reactions are felt in the heart which is the seat of the emotions. (See comments on heart in the notes on 1:21.)

Paul's view of grace was the occasion for some to misunderstand his attitude toward the law. For that reason in 7:7-25 Paul defended the fact that the law is good and that it has served a useful purpose. Just as some misunderstood his view of law, some might have felt that Paul had turned against the Jews (Acts 21:28 and 24:5). In order to deny the veracity of such a claim, Paul comes forth with the strongest possible show of compassion and concern for his fellow Israelites whose eyes were still blinded to the truth.

3 For I could wish that myself were accursed from Christ for my brethren, my kinsmen according

to the flesh.

For. "For" indicates that Paul is going to give a reason for the deep concern mentioned in v. 2.

I could wish that myself were accursed from Christ. Concerning the word for accursed (Greek *anathema*), Sanday and Headlam explain that it originally meant, "'That which is offered or consecrated to God.' But the translators of the Old Testament required an expression to denote that which is devoted to God for destruction, and adopted *anathema* as a translation of the Hebrew *cherem*" (228).

Concerning the word for "I could wish" (Greek *euchomai*), the vast majority take the meaning to be "I could wish." Those who are interested in a discussion of the different ways it might be understood should consult Cranfield (II:454-457). His own translation is, "For I would pray" (II:456).

Paul is saying that if it were possible, in so doing, for him to bring about the salvation of the Jews, he would be willing to be separated from Christ and accept the eternal consequences of such a separation. As Cranfield says, "Nothing less than the eschatological sentence of exclusion from Christ's presence (cf. Mt. 7:23; 25:41) is involved" (II:458). Picirilli comments, "Paul's feelings are deep and self-sacrificing. He *could* go to Hell for his racial brethren were that possible!" (174).

Many call attention to Moses' prayer as being similar in nature to the deep concern that Paul expresses in this verse. Moses said, "Yet now, if thou wilt forgive their sin—; and if not, blot me, I pray thee, out of thy book which thou hast written" (Ex. 32:32).

My brethren, my kinsmen according to the flesh. Paul knew what it meant to be a Jew. He knew that they were the Covenant People of God. He knew that Jesus Christ was the Jewish Messiah. It hurt him deeply to know that so many among the Covenant People of God were abiding in unbelief. Any study of Romans that fails to comprehend the significance of Israel in the history of redemption fails to grasp a major contribution of this great book.

4 Who are Israelites; to whom *pertaineth* the adoption, and the glory, and the covenants, and the giving of the law, and the service *of God,* and the promises.

Who are Israelites. Cranfield gives us a good summary of the meaning of Israel. He explains:

> In early times (e.g. Judg. 5:2,7) the name of the sacred confederacy, 'Israel' was from the first a sacred term, denoting the whole community of those chosen by, and united in the worship of Yahweh. From the division of the kingdom until the fall of Samaria it was limited to the northern kingdom; but from 722 B.C. it was applied to the southern kingdom of Judah (e.g. Isa. 5:7; 8:18; Mic. 3:1), though the hope of a restored whole Israel was still cherished. In later Palestinian Judaism the name 'Israel' was the regular self-designation of the Jews expressing their consciousness of being the people of God; the name 'Jew' was used by foreigners and by the Jews themselves in their dealings with foreigners. . . .In the NT the names 'Israel' and 'Israelite' continue to have a salvation-historical significance (cf. for example, the occurrences in the Fourth Gospel: 1:31, 47, 49; 3:10; 12:13). So here Paul, by saying that his fellow-

Jews are Israelites, is asserting that they are the chosen people of God (II:460, 461).

To whom *pertaineth* the adoption. The meaning of adoption (Greek *huiothesia*) here is different from the meaning in 8:15. In that reference, adoption refers to the position New Covenant saints enjoy as being mature sons, sons of legal age. That is in distinction from the position of immaturity of the Old Covenant saints (see notes on 8:15).

Adoption, as it is used here, refers to that distinct privilege enjoyed by Israel as being the Covenant People of God. Collectively, they were called "God's son" (see Ex. 4:22 and Hos. 11:1). In Hos. 1:10 the reference is to the individuals as the "sons of the living God." They were called sons because they were members of the Covenant People of God. (See Murray II:4,5 for a good discussion on the difference between adoption here and adoption as referred to in 8:15 and Gal. 4:5.)

And the glory. The reference here is to what the Jews called the *Shekinah* which was the visible expression of the Divine presence. Murray gives a good summary of what is involved:

> 'The glory' should be regarded as referring to the glory that abode upon and appeared on Mount Sinai (Exod. 24:16, 17), the glory that covered and filled the tabernacle (Exod. 40:34-38); the glory that appeared upon the mercy-seat in the holy of holies (Lev. 16:2), the glory of the Lord that filled the temple (I Kings 8:10, 11; II Chron. 7:1,2; cf. Ezek. 1:28). This glory was the sign of God's presence with Israel and certified that God dwelt among them and met with them (cf. Exod. 29:42-46)" (II:5).

And the covenants. Piper explains:

> There is no consensus among commentators concerning which covenants are referred to. Murray (*Romans,* II, 5) suggests the covenants with Abraham, Moses and David. Munck (*Christ and Israel,* 31), Alford (II, 404), Schlatter (*Gerechtigkeit*, 294), and Sanday and Headlam (*Romans,* 230) refer to the covenants 'from Abraham to Moses.' Schlier (*Roemerbrief*, 287), includes the Covenant with Noah. Barrett (*Romans,* 177f) follows a rare rabbinic reference (Strack-Billerbeck, III, 262) to 'three covenants within the great covenant of the Exodus—a covenant at Horeb, a second in the plains of Moab, and a third at Mount Gerizim and Ebal.' What we learn from this assortment of guesses is that Paul's term 'covenants' in Rom. 9:4b is open-ended (19).

Concerning the meaning of "covenant" (Greek *diatheke*), Archer explains:

> Since the ordinary Greek word for 'contract' or 'compact' (*syntheke)* implied quality on the part of the contracting parties, the Greek-speaking Jews prefered *diatheke* (coming from *diatithemai,* (to make a disposition of one's property') in the sense of a unilateral enactment. In secular Greek this word usually meant 'will' or 'testament,' but even classical authors like Aristophanes (*Birds* 439) occasionally used it of a covenant wherein one of the two parties had an overwhelming superiority over the other and could dictate his own terms. Hence the biblical *diatheke* signified (in a way much more specific than did *berit* [Hebrew for covenant]) an arrangement made by one party with plenary power,

> which the other party may accept or reject but cannot alter ("Covenant" in *Evangelical Dictionary of Theology* 278; see Galatians 3:15-18).

Vine points out that "The word *diatheke* does not involve the idea of joint obligation, but signifies that which is undertaken by one person only. Hence it is frequently interchangeable with the word 'promise,' as in Gal. 3:16, 18" (138, 139).

It would be hard to overestimate the importance of covenants in the development of the program of redemption. The major development of such is seen in the covenants that God made with Israel.

In my opinion the covenants that Paul had in mind in this verse began with Abraham and include all the redemptive covenants since that time. The basic redemptive covenant is the Abrahamic. All others are either made or promised to Israel. Later covenants serve to broaden the understanding of the Abrahamic Covenant by enlarging our understanding of what was already inherent in it. Or they help in the implementation of it.

The fact that redemption is promised only to the seed of Abraham makes it important that we understand what Paul means when he says in Romans 4 and Galatians 3 that believing Gentiles are the seed of Abraham. God has never made a redemptive covenant with the Gentiles (Eph. 2:11, 12). As Mills rightly observes, "Every covenant that God made with the sons of Jacob, from the one with Abraham on, is the possession of Israel, whether it be the Abrahamic, Mosaic, Davidic, Palestinian, Messianic, and even the New Covenant. These are all the *eternal* possessions of the nation Israel" (293). Wuest comments, "God never makes any covenants with the Gentiles. He made these covenants with Israel because that nation was to be used as a channel to bring salvation to the human race" (155).

Any attempt to understand the history of redemption that does not come to grips with the covenant relationship between God and Israel is greatly lacking. A grasp of the significance of the covenant relationship between God and Israel will help us to understand: (1) why not all who are the natural seed of Abraham are saved; (2) why the Jews seemed to think that merely being the natural seed of Abraham guaranteed their standing before God; (3) why Gentiles must become the seed of Abraham to be saved. If we are to understand chapters 2, 4, 9 and 11 of Romans, we must understand the covenant relationship between God and Israel, and we must see how the unbelieving Jews misunderstood this relationship.

And the giving of the law. Kasemann (259) and Murray (II:6) understand the reference here to be to the act of *giving* the law rather than the possession of the law. Bruce (185), Cranfield (II:462, 463), Harrison (102), Hodge (259), and Piper (20-22) understand the meaning to be the *possession* of the law. It appears to me that Godet may be correct in combining both of these ideas. He explains, "This term embraces along with the gift of the law itself, the solemn promulgation of it on Mount Sinai; comp. the saying of the psalmist 147:20: 'He hath not dealt so with any nation'" (341). This would stress the fact that Israel had the law as a deposit of Divine revelation.

The Pharisees placed tremendous value on the Torah (Hebrew for law). The Torah was as central to Pharisees as Jesus Christ is to Christianity. While Paul did not accept some aspects of the Pharisees' idea of law, he did place great value on the law. This he had made clear in 7:7-25. (See the comments there for how Paul defended the fact that the law is good.)

And the service *of* God. "The service of God" is from the Greek word *latreia*. Picirilli says, "This looks back to the priestly ministry and tabernacle-temple worship system, including all the rituals, cermonies, and sacrifices involved" (175). (See also Hodge 299; Murray II:6; Piper 22, 23; and Sanday and Headlam 231.) Those interested in a more thorough development of the meaning and significance of *latreia* should see Piper.

Cranfield suggests that the meaning goes beyond the temple service. He explains, "But it does not seem altogether unlikely that, as used by Paul here, the term embraced also the faithful non-sacrificial worship of synagogue and pious Jews at home, including such things as prayer, the reading of the Scriptures, the observation of the Sabbath, the reciting of the Shema, and, indeed, all that is meant by the phrase of Mic. 6:8, 'to walk humbly with thy God'" (II:463. See also Hendriksen 312, 313.)

It seems to me that to limit the service (Greek *latreia*) to the tabernacle-temple worship would be the more probable interpretation. This is based on the idea that what Paul is referring to is that which was Israel's as a direct gift of God. Synagogue worship was a later development rather than the result of a direct revelation from God.

Mills, a Hebrew Christian, remarks:

> The beauty, the majesty, and the glory that were portrayed in this 'service to God,' laid the foundation for the preaching of the Gospel of the Grace of God. Only God knows how many countless thousands of souls have been saved through the preaching of the tabernacle and its sacrifices as a picture of the work of the Savior and the accomplishments of the cross. My fellow Christians, do not minimize 'the service of God' for this service made it not only possible but also easier for you and me to preach the Gospel of salvation through faith in Jesus Christ, and to see the atoning sacrifice on the cross as the grand foundation stone upon which the Gospel rests (294).

And the promises. Most commentaries do not give a developed discussion on what is meant by the "promises." It is usually concluded that the reference would be to the Messianic promises. Some suggest that it embraces all promises made to Jews in the O.T.

We miss the point that Paul had in mind if we do not take a more careful look at what is meant by the promises. The promise of eternal life to the seed of Abraham is at the root of what Paul had in mind. This is a necessary implication from Gen. 13:15 and 17:18. (See discussion about the Abrahamic Covenant in the comments on 4:13.)

Abraham and his seed will possess the land for eternity. This is a reference to the eschatological future of the redeemed. The redeemed are the seed of Abraham. It is for this reason that Gentiles must become the seed of Abraham as presented in Rom. 4 and Gal. 3.

The promise of the Messiah is involved also. The Messiah, by His redemptive work, provides the basis for the fulfillment of the eschatological promise of Gen. 13:15 and 17:8. A number of other promises were made to Israel, but these promises are involved in the outworking and the implementation of the promise of the eschatological future and the Messianic promises.

Piper is on the right track when he observes with regard to the Gentiles, "They become fellow beneficiaries of the promises which already belong to the 'saints,' the 'household of God' (Eph. 2:19). Only by being grafted into the cultivated olive tree do the Gentiles become heirs of the promise (Rom. 11:17). Therefore the salvation which Gentile believers enjoy as beneficiaries of the promise of God is a salvation which belongs to Israel because 'theirs are the promises' (Rom. 9:4b)" (24, 25).

5 Whose *are* the fathers, and of whom as concerning the flesh Christ *came,* who is over all, God blessed for ever. Amen.

Whose *are* the fathers. Everyone agrees that Abraham, Isaac, and Jacob are included. Piper states that the reference is limited to these patriarchs. He explains, "The reference in Rom. 9:5a is probably to Abraham, Isaac and Jacob since the privilege would lose its point if 'fathers' meant all the ancestors, and since these patriarchs are alluded to in 9:6-13" (25). (See also Hodge 299; Lenski 585; Shedd 277; and Wuest 155.)

While agreeing that Abraham, Isaac, and Jacob were referred to by Paul, Murray remarks, "It would not appear reasonable to exclude the father expressly mentioned in 1:3 [David]. Thus we should have to extend the line beyond Jacob and conclude that the fathers of distinction in redemptive history from Abraham onwards are in view" (II:6). (See also John Brown 304; Cranfield II:464; Hendriksen 314, 315; and Plumer 458.)

I agree with those who restrict the reference to Abraham, Isaac, and Jacob. It seems to me that it suits Paul's purpose to use the restricted reference to fathers since stress would be on the fact that they were highly esteemed. They were a great treasure. The fathers of the nation seem to be in view rather than a more general reference to the Jew's forefathers.

And of whom as concerning the flesh Christ *came.* As it relates to the fathers, Paul says, "whose are the fathers." The fathers were the possession of Israel. As it relates to Christ, he was "from Israel," but not their exclusive possession. As it relates to His human nature, He was a Jew. But He belongs to all who believe in Him, both Jew and Gentile.

Who is over all, God blessed for ever. Amen. Opinions differ over whether these words refer to Christ or to God the Father. If these words refer to Christ, they constitute an acknowledgment of the deity of Christ on the part of Paul. If they refer to God the Father, they would neither affirm nor deny the deity of Christ although in that case these words could not be used to argue for the deity of Christ.

There are several good treatments of these words which take them to refer to Christ. Harrison gives a concise treatment in favor of referring them to Christ. He explains:

> Several considerations favor the traditional wording, which refers 'God' to Christ: (1) Christ's relationship to Israel on the human side has been stated in such a way as to call for a complementary statement on the divine side. This is provided by the usual translation, but not the other rendering. (2) 'Who' can properly be coupled only with the foregoing subject (Christ). If another subject (God [the Father]) is being introduced, there is no reason at all for the 'who.' (3) A doxology to God [the Father] can hardly be intended since in doxologies the word 'blessed' is regularly placed before the one who is praised. Here it comes after. (4) A doxology to God [the Father] would be singularly out of place in a passage marked by sorrow over Israel's failure to recognize in Christ her

crowning spiritual blessing. (5) The definite article, 'the,' is not linked in the text with 'God,' but with the foregoing words (literally, 'the one being over all'), so Paul is not trying to displace God with Christ, but is doing what John does in saying that the word was God (John 1:1), that is, has the rank of God. In any case, this is really implied in recognizing him as 'over all' (it is very awkward, with NEB, to refer this to God in distinction from Christ) (103).

(For other treatments supporting this position, see Bruce 186, 187; Earle 180-185; Godet 342-345; Hodge 300-302; Lenski 586-589; Murray II:6, 7, and Appendix A, 245-248; and Sanday and Headlam 233-238.)

Denny (658, 659), Kasemann (259, 260), and Meyer (360-364) reject the view that applies the closing words of v. 5 to Christ. Rather, they understand them to refer to the Father. These words are taken to be a doxology and would read,"'God who is over all be blessed forever'" (Denny 658).

There are two main reasons given for taking the last part of the verse to refer to the Father rather than Christ: (1) It is said that Paul does not refer to Christ as God. (2) To use Meyer's words, "Besides the insuperable difficulty would be introduced, that here Christ would be called not merely and simply *theos* [God], but even *God over all*, and consequently would be designated as *theos pantokrator* [the Almighty, the Ruler over all], which is absolutely incompatible with the entire view of the N.T. as to the dependence of the Son on the Father. . ., I Cor. 3:23; 8:6; 11:3; Eph. 4:5, 6; and notably I Cor. 15:28" (362).

With regard to the question of whether Paul elsewhere refers to Christ as God, I would call attention to Tit. 2:13 where Paul says, "The great God and Saviour Jesus Christ." Some may insist that even this reference is to two persons rather than one. Dana and Mantey quote Granville Sharp, who explains, "When the copulative *kai* [and] connects two nouns of the same case, if the article *ho* [the] or any of its cases precedes the first of the said nouns, or participles, and is not repeated before the second noun or participle, i.e., it denotes a farther description of the first-named person" (140). The application of this rule to Titus 2:13 tells us that "the great God" and "our Saviour Jesus Christ" refer to the same person, thus affirming that Paul calls Christ "God." When this rule is applied to Eph. 5:5 the words "Christ" and "God" at the end of the verse refer to the same person again affirming that Paul calls Christ "God."

With regard to Meyer's problem in applying the words "over all" to Christ, it may not be easy to explain all that is said in the N.T. about the relationship between the Son and the Father. However, there should be no problem in applying the words "over all" to Christ. Jesus' words, "All power [Greek *exousia,* authority] is given unto me in heaven and earth" (Mt. 28:18) are saying essentially the same thing. First Cor. 15:27, 28 may not be easy to explain in every respect, but the verses clearly state that at the present all things are now under Christ. Earle comments, "But Meyer seems to miss the point. Of course Paul would not assert that Christ was over the Father. The word 'all' means 'all things,' as elsewhere. That Christ is over all things is based on His creatorship of all things (Col. 1:16)" (182, 183).

B. God's Rejection of the Unbelieving Israelites Is Not to Be Taken to Mean That God Is Not True to His Promise (9:6).

6 Not as though the word of God hath taken none effect. For they *are* not all Israel, which are of Israel.

Not as though the word of God hath taken none effect. Paul had made it quite clear that he did not believe that the Jews who failed to believe in Jesus as the Messiah were saved. The Jews were not prepared for such an observation because they were (for the most part) of the opinion that since they were Abraham's seed, that within itself guaranteed their relationship to God. This they felt was involved in the promise of the eternal possession of the land to Abraham and his seed (Gen. 13:14, 15 and 17:8). As Hodge explains, "It was a common opinion among the Jews, that the promise of God being made to Abraham and to his seed, all his natural descendants, sealed, as such, by the rite of circumcision, would certainly inherit the blessings of the Messiah's reign. It was enough for them, therefore, to be able to say, 'We have Abraham to our father'" (304).

It sounded to the unbelieving Jew as if Paul were saying that God had failed in His covenant promise to Abraham and his seed. Of course, Paul could not entertain such a thought. In the light of prevailing Jewish thought, it was necessary for Paul to explain why the fact that many Jews were lost was not in conflict with the Abrahamic Covenant.

It is absolutely essential at this point that we understand both prevailing Jewish thought and the true meaning of the promise made to Abraham and to his seed in the Abrahamic Covenant. The reader may want to read the introductory comments on chap. 2; the comments on 2:25; and the notes on "The Abrahamic Covenant and the Inheritance of Abraham and His Seed" in connection with 4:13.

For they *are* not all Israel, which are of Israel. In this part of the verse Paul is giving his explanation for saying that the covenant promise that God made to Abraham and his seed had not failed. This passage as it is developed through the chapter has been called "The Justification of God." It is Paul's defense of the fact that God is completely justified in not saving unbelieving Jews. This fact is in no way in contradiction to the promise God made to Abraham and his seed. As Piper explains, "If Paul can show that God's ultimate 'purpose according to election' never included the salvation of every Israelite, then the situation described in Rom. 9:1-5 would not so easily jeopardize God's reliability" (33).

Paul's words make it clear that there are at least two uses of the word "Israel." (1) It refers to all who have descended from Abraham through Jacob. (2) There is an Israel within Israel which consists of those who will actually inherit the promise of the Abrahamic Covenant. This promise is the everlasting possession of the land of Canaan in the eschatological future. The following diagram will illustrate what Paul is talking about.

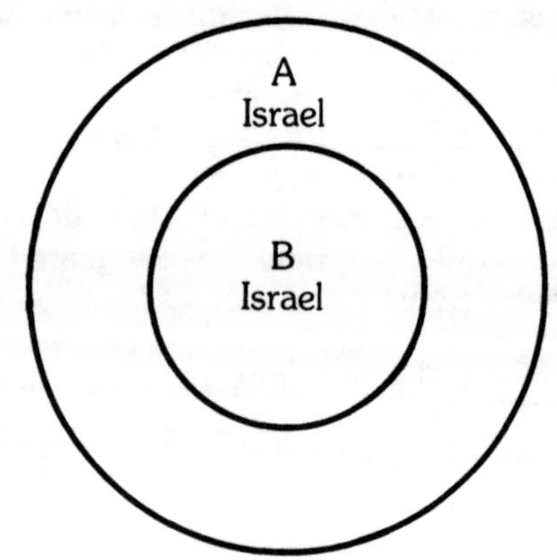

All who are descendants of Abraham through Jacob would be "A," but not all would be "B." All "A" would be the

Covenant People of God, *i.e.*, they are the Covenant Seed of Abraham. However, when it comes to the individual, those who actually receive the promise are those who respond in faith. This group would be "B." Those who are A, but not B, will not receive the promise of eternal life on the new earth.

The Covenant promise is made to all of the descendants of Abraham. But it is made on the condition of faith. It is no violation of the Covenant promise made to the seed of Abraham if unbelievers do not inherit the promise. Abraham "believed in the LORD; and he counted it to him for righteousness" (Gen. 15:6).

C. God's Choice of The Patriarchs Is Discussed (9:7-13).

What follows in these verses will serve as an illustratrion that the way God dealt with Abraham, Isaac, and Jacob illustrates the fact that the concept of Abraham's seed does not include all who descended from Abraham. For that reason it should be understandable that the further limitation of the saved to those who believe need not mean that God's promise to the seed of Abraham has failed.

7 Neither, because they are the seed of Abraham, *are they* all children: but, In Isaac shall thy seed be called.

Neither because they are the seed of Abraham, *are they* all children. The "seed of Abraham" in this part of the verse is equivalent to the descendants of Abraham. The "children" refers to those who were to be the "Covenant Seed."

But, In Isaac shall thy seed be called. Ishmael and his descendants were, from a purely physical viewpoint, as much the seed of Abraham as Isaac and his descendants. However, they were not a part of the Covenant Seed to whom the promise was made in Gen. 13:14, 15 and 17:8. The Covenant Seed were to be called through Isaac.

8 That is, They which are the children of the flesh, these *are* not the children of God: but the children of the promise are counted for the seed.

That is, They which are the children of the flesh, these *are* not the children of God. This explains the first part of v. 7. Those who merely descended from Abraham, as was the case with Ishmael and his descendants, are not the children of God, *i.e.*, they are not the Covenant Seed.

But the children of the promise are counted for the seed. This points to the narrowing down of the Covenant Seed to Isaac by the exclusion of Ishmael as is explained in the next verse. Hodge (306, 307) sees this passage as analogous to Gal. 4:22-31. It seems to me better to stick to the simpler interpretation.

9 For this *is* the word of promise, At this time will I come, and Sarah shall have a son.

The words, "but, In Isaac shall thy seed be called" (v. 7, from Gen. 21:12) and the words here in v. 9 (from Gen. 18:10 and 14) make it clear that only Isaac's descendants are the Covenant Seed. In other words, not all of the seed of Abraham are the Covenant Seed.

10 And not only *this;* but when Rebecca also had conceived by one, *even* by our father Isaac.

And not only *this*. The choice of Isaac and the rejection of Ishmael clearly illustrates that natural descent from Abraham does not guarantee that a person is considered to be the Covenant Seed of Abraham. However, Paul will give even more evidence that this is true.

But when Rebecca also had conceived by one, *even* by our father Isaac. While it is true that Isaac and Ishmael were both sons of Abraham, they did not have the same mother. Some might have wanted to make a point of that. They might have said that Ishmael was rejected because his mother was Abraham's handmaid. Isaac, they might have said, was accepted because his mother, Sarah, was Abraham's wife. If such an argument was developing in the mind of the Jew, Paul quickly silenced it. Jacob and Esau had the same father and mother. In fact, they were twins. Yet by Divine choice Jacob was chosen and Esau was rejected.

11 (For *the children* being not yet born, neither having done any good or evil, that the purpose of God according to election might stand, not of works, but of him that calleth).

(For *the children* being not yet born, neither having done any good or evil. This points out the time of the statement about to be quoted in v. 12 from Gen. 25:23. The timing is mentioned to support what follows in the last part of the verse.

That the purpose of God according to election might stand, not of works. The fact that God's choice of Jacob was made before he was born does not within itself prove that God's choice was not by works. God in His foreknowledge could have chosen Jacob on the basis of works if He had desired to do so. He can foresee works as well as He can other things. However, to make the choice before he was born helps accent the fact that the choice was made without any consideration of works. If the choice had been announced after Jacob had proved himself more worthy than Esau, it would not have been convincing to say that the choice in no way took their works into account.

But of him that calleth. When it is said that the choice was "not of works," that rules out any consideration that human merit was the basis of God's choice of Jacob. When it is said, "but of him that calleth" the stress is on the fact that it was God's free choice as distinguished from a choice being imposed on God.

The important observation in this verse is: What is "the purpose of God according to election"? No one needs to be informed of the fact that Calvinists insist that their view of unconditional election is the only consistent and adequate interpretation of this verse. I think it is time that they faced a challenge.

It seems that there have been basically three interpretations given to vv. 6-13. (1) The passage has nothing to do with election or rejection for individual salvation. Rather, it refers to the election of Jacob as the third of the partriarchal ancestors (the other two being Abraham and Isaac) of the nation of Israel. Thus, the Covenant Seed of Abraham were chosen through Jacob rather than Esau. Jacob was elected. Esau was rejected (Clarke 111, 112; Godet 350, 351; and Sanday and Headlam 245). Lenski's view is a modification of this view. He denies that Paul is dealing here with eternal salvation and damnation. At the same time, he denies that Paul is including the two nations that would descend from Jacob and Esau. He thinks Paul's concern is to deal only with the fact that Jacob was chosen for the third patriarch while Esau was not chosen (603, 604).

(2) This view in agreement with the first recognizes that the passage deals with the election of Jacob as the third patriarchal head of the Covenant Seed of Abraham and that Esau was rejected. However, it goes on to say that:

> Jacob and Esau, like Isaac and Ishmael, are *types* of two classes that have been spoken of: viz: the 'children of the promise,' and the 'children of the flesh' (ver. 8). The theocratic election of Isaac and Jacob illustrates the spiritual election of individuals; and the theocratic reprobation of Ishmael and Esau illustrates the spiritual reprobation of individuals (Shedd 285).

This view goes on to develop the doctrine of unconditional election of individuals for salvation from this passage. Hodge would also support this line of thinking (306, 307, and 312).

(3) The more common view (among those who see unconditional election as being taught in the passage) seems to take the passage to be directly concerned with unconditional election rather than to support it by analogy (Hendriksen 323, 324; Murray II:15-19; and Piper 48-52).

After taking a look at vv. 12, 13, I will deal with the question of what vv. 6-13 teach and how it relates to the subject of election.

12 It was said unto her, The elder shall serve the younger.

Cranfield explains:

> The interest of this Genesis verse as a whole is clearly in Jacob and Esau not just as individuals but also, and particularly, as the ancestors of two nations; for the part quoted is preceded by 'Two nations are in thy womb, and two peoples shall be separated even from thy bowels: and the one people shall be stronger than the other people.' It is important to stress that neither as they occur in Genesis nor as they are used by Paul do these words refer to the eternal destinies either of two persons or the individual members of the nations sprung from them; the reference is rather to the mutual relations of the two nations in history. What is here in question is not eschatological salvation or damnation, but the historical function of those concerned and their relations to the development of the salvation-history (II:479).

Lenski would agree with Cranfield that this verse does not deal with the eternal destinies of Jacob and Esau. However, he does not believe that Paul is intending to include a reference to the two nations which descended from Jacob and Esau: Israel and Edom. He thinks the reference is limited to the fact that God chose Jacob to be "the third patriarch. As 'in Isaac' seed was to be called for Abraham so also in Jacob. Esau had the covenant in his twin brother, and not that brother in Esau. Jesus also said: 'Salvation is of the Jews,' John 4:22" (603, 604).

Lenski calls attention to the fact that Paul, in quoting from Gen. 25:23, omits the reference to two nations in Rebecca's womb. He thinks the reference to the nations was purposely omitted by Paul because he did not want to include a reference to the nations.

I am sure that Paul's concern was with the fact that Jacob, and not Esau, was chosen as the one through whom the Covenant Seed would be called. However, it seems that it would be impossible in this verse to think of Jacob as the last chosen partriarch without thinking also of the nation that descended from him. However, no matter what other things may be involved in the relationships and differences between these two nations, the central thought of Paul was that the Covenant Seed was called through Jacob.

While seeing a reference to the nations as well as the individuals, Shedd says, "The theocratic election of Isaac and Jacob illustrates the spiritual election of individuals; and the theocratic reprobation of Ishmael and Esau illustrates the spiritual reprobation of individuals" (285. See also Hodge 311, 312).

I will reserve my own comments on how all this relates to the subject of election after completing comments on the next verse.

13 As it is written, Jacob have I loved, but Esau have I hated.

Lenski, as in his comment on v. 12, does not think the reference here includes the nations which descended from Jacob and Esau. He thinks the reference is "to the individual acts when God took Jacob and did not take Esau" (604).

It is important to remember that the choice of Jacob as the third patriarch is at the heart of what Paul has in mind. However, that choice cannot be restricted in meaning to Jacob as an individual. Jacob, as patriarch, has meaning only as it is understood that he, not Esau, is the one through whom Israel as the Covenant Seed was called. Once this is understood, there is no way to eliminate the nation of Israel from the mention by Malachi (from 1:2, 3) referred to by Paul. Of course it is the nation as the Covenant Seed that descended from Jacob that would be in focus—not simply the nation as a nation. It should be obvious that if Jacob includes the nation of Israel, Esau includes the nation of Edom.

The purpose of v. 13 in Paul's thought is to show that the quotation from Gen. 25:23, "The elder shall serve the younger," was actually fulfilled. That is what is implied by the words, "As it is written." In addition to the fact that Esau was not a part of the Covenant Seed, there would be other advantages that Jacob would have over Esau. The quotation from Mal. 1:2, 3 support this prediction from Gen. 25:23.

We should avoid over-interpreting Paul's quotation from Malachi. The only purpose in the reference to the fact that God loved Jacob and hated Esau is to confirm the fact that the advantage spoken of in Gen. 25:23 actually came to pass. The hating of Esau is illustrated by the fact that God "laid his mountains and his heritage waste for the dragons of the wilderness" (Mal. 1:3). It is not said that this destruction was wrought upon the nation simply because God did not include Esau and his descendants among the Covenant Seed. For the basis for judgment being brought on Edom, see Am. 1:11, 12, and Ob. 1-14. When we see that the "hating" of Esau refers to God's judgment on the nation of Edom for their sins, we do not need to get involved in whether "hating" as used refers to loving less.

Verses 6-13 and Election.

In commenting on v. 11 above, I pointed out that some do not see individual election for salvation in this passage. Rather, they see it as dealing only with the choice of Jacob as the one through whom the Covenant Seed of Abraham were chosen. Thus Israel as the Covenant Seed descended from Jacob. Esau and his descendants were not a part of the Covenant Seed.

Others are not content in leaving

individual election out of the passage. Murray explains:

> The thesis that Paul is dealing merely with the election of Israel collectively. . .would not meet the precise situation. The question posed for the apostle is: how can the covenant promise of God be regarded as inviolate when the mass of those who belong to Israel, who are comprised in the elect nation. . .have remained in unbelief and come short of the covenant promises? His answer would fail if it were simply on appeal to the collective, inclusive, theocratic election of Israel. . . . Paul's answer is not the collective election of Israel but rather 'they are not all Israel, who are of Israel.' And this means, in terms of the stage of discussion at which we have now arrived, 'They are not all elect, who are of Israel. . .' the conclusion, therefore, is that when Paul says 'The purpose of God according to election' he is speaking of the electing purpose of God in a discriminating, differentiating sense that cannot apply to all who were embraced in theocratic election (II,18).

Murray develops from this passage the doctrine of unconditional election. He says, "It does not proceed from nor is it conditioned by the human will but by the determinate will of God (cf. Eph. 1:5, 11)" (II:20).

I agree that Paul does not stop with the election of the nation of Israel in vv. 6-13. It is clear that this passage is intended to deal with the problem expressed in vv. 1-3 concerning the fact that large numbers of Jews were not saved.

It is important to understand why Paul's contention that large numbers of Jews were not saved would present such a serious problem to Jewish thought. The problem goes beyond the question of why they are not saved or how to reach them.

To the vast majority of Jews, it was unthinkable that any Jew would be denied his part in the eternal inheritance. This is true because they believed in the unconditional election of the Covenant Seed of Abraham. (See quotation in notes on v. 6 from Hodge along with other comments in the notes on v. 6 that deal with the Jewish attitude about what was theirs as Abraham's seed.) All of their thinking had not been fully harmonized, and for that reason some of their comments on works may not seem to fit the concept of unconditional election. However, there can be no doubt that the unconditional election of the seed of Abraham permeated Jewish thought. For this reason, the possibility that large numbers of the Jews might be unsaved was to them absolutely unthinkable.

To think that large numbers of Jews would not be saved meant to them either one of two things: (1) God had broken His covenant with Israel as the seed of Abraham, or (2) since Christianity did not concur with the idea that all Jews were saved, it could not possibly be true.

More was involved than merely clarifying whether some or all Jews would be saved. Paul had to show that being the Covenant Seed of Abraham did not guarantee that everyone who descended from Abraham through Jacob would be saved. The gospel would not be received by the Jew unless this point was cleared up. It was this point of clarification that Paul sought to make in vv. 6-13.

The following will clarify what is meant by the Covenant Seed of Abraham. God entered into a covenant with Abraham in which He promised the eternal possession of the land of Palestine to the seed of Abraham (Gen.

13:14, 15, and 17:8). The Covenant Seed of Abraham are those to whom the promise was made. This promise was not made to all who could be considered in the literal sense the seed of Abraham. Ishmael's descendants, those who descended from Abraham through the children of Keturah, and those who descended from Esau could all be considered as being the seed of Abraham in the literal sense. However, none of these were the Seed of Abraham to whom the promises were made. Those to whom the promises were made were those who descended from Abraham through Jacob. These were the Covenant Seed of Abraham.

Paul's point was that not even all Israel, who made up the Covenant Seed of Abraham, would be saved and receive the eternal inheritance of the land of Palestine. Further, he was saying that the fact that not all of the Covenant Seed of Abraham would actually be saved and receive the land as an everlasting possession did not mean that the promise which God made to the Covenant Seed of Abraham had proved to be ineffective.

The question that needs to be answered is: Why is it that not all of the Covenant Seed are saved? Those who advocate the doctrine of unconditional election say that it is because not every member of the elect nation (Israel) was elected for individual salvation by God. Since this was the case, the fact that many in Israel were not saved does not mean that the Word of God "hath taken none effect" (v. 6). It simply means that God's unconditional election for salvation did not embrace everyone who made up the Covenant Seed of Abraham.

Piper takes the position that in vv. 6-13 Paul is talking about unconditional election all the way through. As he sees it, the only way God's Word could always be effective would be for God always to work on the principle of unconditional election (38-52). He explains, "The principle established is that God's promised blessings are never enjoyed on the basis of what a person is by birth or by works, but only on the basis of God's sovereign, free predestination (Rom. 9:11, 12). The ultimate decision of who will experience God's grace or mercy is never based on a person's 'willing or running' (Rom. 9:16)" (46).

Piper is not simply saying that the exegetical evidence supports the conclusion that God operates on the principle of unconditional election. He is also saying that, theologically and logically, the only way God's Word could be effective is to operate on the principle of unconditional election. Unconditional election makes the work depend on nothing other than God. Since the program of redemption depends altogether on God, it must succeed. If God did not unconditionally elect *every* individual Jew, that is all that is needed to explain how many were not saved and yet God's Word was not without effect.

Is the case sewed up for unconditional election? Is that the only possible way for us to understand why all of the Covenant Seed (Israel) are not saved? I think not.

I do agree with those who insist that vv. 6-13 are not to be restricted to helping us understand that Jacob and his descendants made up the covenant Seed of Abraham while Esau and his descendants were not included in the Covenant Seed of Abraham. *These verses must deal with the Jewish concern that not all who descended from Abraham through Jacob are saved.* The fact that Jacob's and not Esau's descendants make up the Covenant Seed of Abraham, within itself, does not explain why some Jews are not saved. Apparently, Paul's discussion of who made up the Covenant Seed of Abraham must have some value in dealing with the fact that not all of the Covenant Seed of Abraham are saved. However, the simple fact within itself is not the answer. Yet, it is obvious that in vv. 6-13, Paul intended to address the Jewish concern about the fact that not all Jews are saved.

Let me restate the problem that Paul is dealing with in v. 6. Then I will show how the rest of the passage (vv. 7-13) throws light on this problem.

It is quite clear that for Paul to indicate that large numbers of Jews were unsaved (vv. 1-3) presented a serious problem to Jewish thought. Such an idea was intolerable because they thought that God had unconditionally elected all of the seed of Abraham that descended from Abraham through Jacob. As they saw it, Paul's approach would mean that the unconditional election of all of the Covenant Seed of Abraham had not come to pass. God's Word in this case would have failed.

Obviously Paul did not work on the assumption that God had unconditionally elected all of the Covenant Seed of Abraham (Israel). This he acknowledges in the last part of v. 6: "For they *are* not all Israel, which are of Israel." This implies that the name of "Israel" is used in two different ways.

The first way of using the name Israel is the all-inclusive use. It refers to all who descended from Abraham through Jacob. These can be rightly called the Covenant Seed of Abraham or the Covenant People of God.

The second way of using the name Israel is to refer to those in Israel who are saved and will thus inherit the promises of God made to the seed of Abraham that will be experienced in the eschatological future (Gen. 13:14, 15, and 17:8).

Jewish thought did not recognize this distinction made by Paul. The only thing that Paul had to do to prove his point was to prove that it was possible for the name Israel to be so used in a broad and in a narrow use.

To prove his point, Paul illustrates that the expression "seed of Abraham" can indisputably be used in a broad and in a narrow sense. In the broad sense, the seed of Abraham (the descendants of Abraham) include Ishmael and his descendants, those who descended from Abraham through the sons he had by Keturah, and Esau and his descendants as well as those who descended through Jacob.

While it is obvious that in the literal sense the seed of Abraham could be understood in such a broad way, it is equally obvious that when the seed of Abraham is used in a theological sense it is not used in this broad sense. Every Jew would have known that.

Paul's point is simply this. If there can be a broad and a narrow use of the expression "the seed of Abraham," there is no reason to reject the idea that in a similar way there can be a broad and a narrow sense of the name Israel.

It must be remembered that the Jewish problem grew out of the significance that they gave to the fact that they were the seed of Abraham rather than that they were the descendants of Jacob (Mt. 3:9 and Jn. 8:33-40). Why? Because it was to the seed of Abraham that the promises were made (Gen. 3:14, 15, and 17:8).

The Jewish case, if it were to stand, would have to mean that "the seed of Abraham" in Gen. 13:14, 15, and 17:8 was all-inclusive. The problem with this is that it would include what Jewish thought would not include, i.e., it would include *all* of the descendants of Abraham, not just those who descended through Jacob.

Once it is conceded that not all the seed of Abraham are the Covenant

Seed of Abraham, it should not be too hard to realize that not all the Covenant Seed of Abraham (those who descended from Abraham through Jacob) are the heirs of the promises made to the seed of Abraham. Or to say it another way, "They are not all Israel, which are of Israel" (9:6). Once this position is taken, the Jew should not have a theological difficulty in realizing that some Jews would be lost.

The question of whether election is conditional or unconditional is not decided by this passage. What is decided by this passage is that not all Jews were saved and that this is consistent with Biblical thought.

So far as Paul's thought is concerned, as it is set forth in Romans, it is quite obvious why not all Jews are saved. It is because they have failed to believe in Jesus as the Messiah (see 9:30-33, especially v. 32).

I will reserve further thoughts on election and how all this fits into the sovereignty of God until it fits appropriately into the following verses.

D. The Matter of Having Mercy on Some and Hardening Others Is Based on God's Choice (9:14-18).

14 What shall we say then? *Is there* unrighteousness with God? God forbid.

What shall we say then? In the light of Paul's comments in vv. 1-13, it is reasonable to assume that certain questions would arise in the mind of those Jews who were still under the power of unbelief. Following Paul's use of rhetorical questions in Rom. (3:1, 9, 31; 6:1, 15; and 7:7), it is time again for Paul to pose a question which an objector would likely be raising in his own mind.

***Is there* unrighteousness with God?** The negative (Greek *me*) means that Paul expected a negative answer. It is not simply *implied* that the answer is to be negative. Paul *emphatically negates* such an assumption by saying **God forbid.** (For comments on the Greek construction used here, see notes on 3:4.) It was unthinkable both to Paul and the Jew that God could be unrighteous.

It is important to get a true picture of who it is among the objectors that would raise such a question and why. Without doubt, the person who would think that Paul's statements (in vv. 1-13) would reflect on the righteousness of God would be a Jew who was abiding still in unbelief.

Why would the Jew think that Paul's statements in vv. 1-13 would reflect on the righteousness of God? As a means of answering that question, it helps to raise another. What is the Jew's chief concern as it relates to what Paul said in vv. 1-13?

It is obvious where the Jew's chief concern lay. He worked on the assumption that God unconditionally elected *all* of the seed of Abraham that descended through Jacob. For that reason, the Jew found Paul's view that not all Jews would be saved highly objectionable and very puzzling. In fact, since he thought that all Jews, as the Covenant Seed of Abraham, were unconditionally elected to receive the eternal inheritance (Gen. 13:14, 15, and 17:8), for him to think otherwise would be casting reflection on the righteousness of God. God would be considered unrighteous in that He would not, in the eye of the Jew, be following through with a promise, and that a covenant promise!

If a person does not keep his word, he is unrighteous. To the Jew still abiding in unbelief, it would appear that according to Paul's view God had failed to keep His word. The idea that God would not keep His word was as abhorrent to Paul as it was to his Jewish objector.

Let me say at this point that whether there actually was a Jewish objector is beside the point. In all likelihood Paul had encountered some Jews who raised such a question. Whether that be the case or not, the question which Paul raises is one that an unbelieving Jew would have had in his mind after reading or hearing what Paul had to say in vv. 1-13. Paul was wise to raise this question and deal with it.

The view which I have presented concerning why Paul raised the question, "Is there unrighteousness with God?" is not the view given in the commentaries. Haldane explains, "The Apostle anticipated the objection of the carnal mind in this doctrine. Does not loving Jacob and hating Esau before they had done any good or evil, imply that there is injustice with God?" (467). Harrison observes, "God's dealings with Jacob and Esau might be challenged as arbitrary, on the ground that Esau was the object of injustice" (106). Plumer says, "The meaning is this: Does God's treatment of Isaac and Jacob display injustice to Ishmael and Esau?" (473). Shedd explains, "The objection is raised that in such discrimination as that between Jacob and Esau, God acts unjustly" (288).

I believe it is quite obvious that these commentators (there is almost a consensus among the commentators with this viewpoint) have misunderstood why Paul raised this question. Any careful reading of vv. 1-13 should make it clear that in this passage Paul is dealing with an objection or a concern that would have been raised in the mind of a Jew who was still abiding in unbelief. If this is the case, let it be said that the Jews had no difficulty with the rejection of Ishmael and Esau. This is true whether the concern was with individual salvation or with the exclusion of Ishmael, Esau, and their descendants from the Covenant Seed of Abraham.

The only trouble that the Jews had with unconditional election was that, *according to Paul*, God had not unconditionally elected *all* Jews as they had thought. The concern that the unbelieving Jew would have had about God's righteousness was that for God not to follow through with the unconditional election of *all* Jews meant that God had not kept His word. For God to fail to keep His word would mean that He would be unrighteous. Such a conclusion was unthinkable. *The only hope of getting them to acknowledge Jesus as the Messiah must be connected with evidence that God had never said that all Jews were unconditionally elected. If they could see this, then they could look at the question of their own salvation in the light of the fact that not all Jews are saved. If in fact God never said that all Jews would be saved, Christ and Christianity would not have to be written off without a hearing. However, if God did unconditionally elect all Jews and Christianity denied that this was the case, Christ and Christianity would be written off without further investigation.*

The problem with those who have taken the view that the real difficulty, as it relates to the righteousness of God, was with the rejection of Ishmael and Esau is that they have interrupted vv. 1-13 in the light of their own theological encounters rather than the encounters that Paul had with the Jews.

15 For he saith to Moses, I will have mercy on whom I will have mercy, and I will have compassion on whom I will have compassion.

How do vv. 15-18 relate to v. 14?

Since v. 15 is connected with v. 14 by the conjunction "for" (Greek *gar*), we need to take a look at how the conjunction is used here. We naturally expect a reason or proof to follow "for." However, such is not the case here. It is obvious that what follows does not take on the form of an argument defending the righteousness (or justice of God) in not saving all Jews. As Lenski explains, "The *gar* is not to prove the statement that there is no justice on the part of God in these promises; for what follows is not proof . . . *Gar* is at times used simply to confirm; it does so here: 'yea'" (607).

The question of whether God could be unrighteous (or unjust) was not debatable between Paul and the Jew. One would reject such an implication as quickly as the other. The difference came in applying the truth of the righteousness of God to the question of whether all Jews were saved.

The Jews took the position that God had unconditionally elected all Jews since they were the Covenant Seed of Abraham. To them the thought that large numbers of Jews were not saved would be a denial of the righteousness of God. The righteousness of God would require Him to keep the Covenant promise made to Abraham and his seed.

Paul's position was that God had never promised that every member of the Covenant Seed of Abraham would be saved. The fact that eternal life on this earth in the land of Palestine was promised to the seed of Abraham in Gen. 13:14, 15, and 17:8 is not to be taken to mean that everybody who descended from Abraham would be saved. In vv. 7-13 Paul clearly showed that even though Ishmael and Esau were descendants of Abraham, they were not a part of the Covenant Seed of Abraham.

When the Jew recognized that Ishmael and Esau were not a part of the Covenant Seed of Abraham, they were already recognizing the principle that Paul wanted to make. The mere fact of being the seed of Abraham could not guarantee the salvation of anybody. The Jew was already recognizing this when he did not hold the same hope for the descendants of Ishmael and Esau that he did for those who descended from Jacob.

Whenever a person will apply the principle that eliminates Ishmael's and Esau's descendants from the Covenant People of God, though being the seed of Abraham, he can see that the salvation of every Jew is not guaranteed by the fact that they are the seed of Abraham. In principle the possibility exists that some Jews are not saved. Paul's position that a large number of Jews are not saved cannot be ruled out as being in contradiction to the covenant promise made to the seed of Abraham in Gen. 13:14, 15, and 17:8. Such a position is not to be rejected on the grounds that it violates the righteousness of God since God has never promised salvation to all Jews.

In v. 14 Paul emphatically denied that God was unrighteous. What follows in v. 15 is not evidence that God is not unrighteous. That was settled by an emphatic denial. What does follow is an illustration from Scripture of how the action of God, who can do no wrong, supports the principle that some, but not all, from among Israel are chosen for salvation.

That Paul is appealing to the authority of Scripture rather than building an argument in v. 15 finds broad agreement. Liddon explains,

> For the disputant with whom the Apostle conceives himself to be arguing, who takes his stand on the Jewish Scriptures, and accuses God of being unjust to the majority of Israel in the Apostolic

> age, the reply is sufficient. It lies in the fact that the citation is from Hebrew Scriptures; that is an authority which the objector must own to have a binding force...no good Jew, or Jewish Christian, can doubt that what God says about Himself in his own Law, must be in harmony with this absolute Righteousness (162, 163).

Shedd, after pointing out the appeal to the authority of Scripture, observes, "The argument runs back, ultimately, into the idea and definition of God. The absolutely perfect Being can do no wrong" (288).

Both Paul and the unbelieving Jew were in agreement that in no way could unrighteousness be attributed to the God of the O.T. If Paul could show O.T. support for the idea that God had not promised that every Jew had been chosen for salvation, that should settle the issue.

For he saith to Moses, I will have mercy on whom I will have mercy, and I will have compassion on whom I will have compassion. See notes on "for" in the introductory notes on v. 15. This verse is taken from the Septuagint translation of Ex. 33:19.

These words of God to Moses make it clear that God is in charge of dispensing grace. He will give grace to whom He chooses. Whom (Greek *hon an*) is singular. The meaning of the Greek is "whomever." The stress is on the individual person. Williams translates it, "For He says to Moses, 'I will have mercy on any that I choose to have mercy on, and take pity on any man that I choose to take pity on.'"

Picirilli explains, "Even in the wilderness, when we might think all the nation was automatically entitled to His favor, he said: 'I will show mercy on whom I will show mercy.' In other words, He wanted it clearly established that neither Moses nor Israel had any special claims on Him that took away His sovereign right to act as He chose. Nor will He show mercy to all of them, just because they were Israelites in the flesh" (183).

Since this verse tells us that God shows mercy and compassion to whomever He chooses, the Calvinist thinks that this gives conclusive proof of the doctrine of unconditional election. It seems to me to be involved in the very concept of God that He would be the one who decides who is saved and who is not saved. However, I do not believe that such an observation automatically decides on the side of unconditional election.

In Jer. 18:1-4 Jeremiah observed the work of the potter. The potter had control over the clay to make it into a vessel as it seemed good to the potter to do so. After he made this observation, God said, "O house of Israel, cannot I do with you as this potter? saith the LORD. Behold, as the clay *is* in the potter's hand, so *are* ye in mine hand, O house of Israel" (18:6).

God was saying to Israel, "You are in my hands. I can do with you what I choose." Or to put it another way, "I will do with you as I choose." The exercise of this right on the part of God did not mean that He would not take into consideration anything done by Israel in deciding what He would do with Israel. That he would take Israel's action into account in deciding what to do with Israel is clear in the context of Jer. 18:6; see vv. 7-10.

The essence of what God said to Jeremiah in these verses is as follows. "If a nation obeys me I will build it up. If it disobeys me I will destroy it."

It should be obvious from Jer. 18:1-10 that the Divine prerogative to exercise His right to do as He chooses with people does not mean that His decisions must always be unconditional choices. When we read that God will do as He chooses, it will help if we will ask a simple question: What does God choose to do? When God told Jeremiah that He could do with Israel what He chose just as the potter could with the clay, He followed that observation by telling them what He wanted to do.

When we read in Rom. 9:15 that God will have mercy and compassion on whomever He wills, it behooves us to ask: On whom does God will to show mercy and compassion? Once it is decided that the mercy and compassion under consideration is that shown in salvation, the answer is easy.

God told Isaiah whom He wanted to have mercy on when He said, "Let the wicked forsake his way, and the unrighteous man his thoughts: and let him return unto the LORD, and he will have *mercy* [italics mine] upon him; and to our God, for he will abundantly pardon" (55:7).

We certainly do not have to list an array of references from the N.T. in order to identify those to whom God wishes to give the mercy of salvation. Let's take the answer given by Paul and Silas to the question, "What must I do to be saved?" "And they said, Believe on the Lord Jesus Christ, and thou shalt be saved, and thy house" (Acts 16:30,31).

When God chooses the one who believes in Jesus Christ as his Lord and Savior to show His mercy in salvation, *He is choosing whom He wills.* Such a decision can in no way be viewed as a decision that God is forced to make. The whole idea of salvation was God's idea from the outset. He could have chosen to have left the whole human race in sin without offering salvation had He chosen to do so. He planned to provide and offer salvation to lost mankind long before (in eternity past) man felt the pangs of being lost. It was not even in response to man's pleading (much less demanding) that God chose to offer redemption.

The provision of salvation through the death and righteousness of Christ was totally God's idea and totally God's provision. It came about as a result of His own free acts. The decision to offer salvation on the condition of faith in Jesus Christ as Lord and Savior originated with God and no one else. The decision to commission believers to take the gospel into the world was God's decision, not man's. The decision for the Holy Spirit to work in men's hearts in connection with the preached Word was God's decision.

The whole plan of salvation from beginning to end is the work and plan of God. God is in charge. When salvation is offered on the condition of faith in Christ, that in no way weakens the words, "I will have mercy on whom I will have mercy, and I will have compassion on whom I will have compassion." God's sovereignty is fully in control in this view.

The problem arises in that the Calvinist wants to view the relationship with God and man as if it were a cause and effect relationship rather than an influence and response relationship. (See discussion in connection with comments on election in notes on 8:29.)

The word "condition" creates a problem for the Calvinist because a condition represents a response on the part of man. On the one hand according to the Calvinist, election is viewed as being unconditional. On the other hand, faith is recognized as the condition of justification.

It seems to me that if we think of conditional justification, we should also be able to think of conditional election. The Calvinist tries to get around this problem by saying that faith is a gift and, in effect, not really a condition. As a means of trying to give the appearance that faith is the work of God and not in any true sense the response of man, Calvinism introduces the concept of the effectual call. The effectual call is regeneration. Regeneration precedes faith and gives birth to faith. Regeneration is designed to change behavior. That is what sanctification does. This puts Calvinism in conflict with its own theology by putting sanctification prior to justification. (See more development of this thought in notes on 8:29 that deal with election.)

I agree that faith is a gift, but it is a human experience. "Faith is not some substance that exists outside of us that is to be given to us. It is an experience that must take place within us. That is the only way we can have faith. Faith is a gift in the sense that God gives to us the aid that is necessary, without which we could not exercise faith. It is not a gift in the sense that it is not an exercise of our own personality" (Forlines, *Systematics*, 204).

To try to drain the word "condition" of its meaning, or to try to deny that faith is the "condition" of salvation, is fruitless. The only way for a human being to experience faith is to exercise faith. It is impossible for a person to be totally passive (to have faith as something done to him or for him by God) in the experience of saving faith. *Man is not only acted upon; he is active in the experience of faith.* It cannot be otherwise.

To think so is to rob man of his personhood. He would be a deceived machine. He is consciously aware that he has faith. He would be deceived because he thinks he responded in faith. *Saving faith is a response of a personal being to Divine influence and enablement.*

When God justifies a person who exercises faith in Jesus Christ as Lord and Savior, He is showing mercy to whom He wills. He wills to show mercy to those who respond to the gospel by exercising faith in Jesus Christ. This is not a plan being imposed on God by man. It is a plan provided by God, and offered by God on God's terms to fallen man. *Surely the sovereignty of God does not hem God into a system whereby He can only operate through unconditional election!*

The Calvinistic claim that for God to require the response of faith is to place salvation on the basis of works will not stand. The contrast between works and faith by Paul in Rom. 4:1-5 should lay that argument to rest.

Some seem to fear, if faith is required for salvation, that such a requirement undercuts the idea that salvation is free. Such fear is unfounded. When we say that salvation is free (without cost), we are saying that the grounds of our justification is altogether God's provision. The righteousness of Christ to satisfy the demand of God's law for absolute righteousness, and the death of Christ to satisfy the demand of God's law that the full penalty of sin be paid, is the *only* thing that gives us justification. We participate in no way in that provision. Nothing that I ever do will ever make up the slightest bit of the debt owed to God for my justification. Justification is free to us. It was not free to Jesus Christ. He paid for it dearly. He *earned* the right to offer us *free* salvation. He paid the only price that was or will ever be paid for my salvation. That is what makes it free.

16 So then *it is* not of him that willeth, nor of him that runneth, but of God that sheweth mercy.

So then. These words show that what follows is the logical consequence of what is said in v. 15.

***It is* not of him that willeth, nor of him that runneth.** Piper takes the position that

> Not the physical effort of the

> Greek games, but the moral resolve to keep the law may well be the background of Paul's metaphor. . . .
>
> The allusion to 'running the way of the commandments' would cohere very closely with Rom. 9:30f where the similar word *dioko* [pursue] appears: 'The Gentiles who did not *pursue* righteousness attained righteousness, the righteousness from faith; but Israel, though *pursuing a law* of righteousness did not reach the law' (cf. also Phil. 3:14-15) (132).

Piper also cites sources from Jewish writings for support for his interpretation (132).

But of God that sheweth mercy. In order to see the meaning of this verse, we must see what the converse would be. What would it mean if it were of him that wills and runs rather than of God who shows mercy? It would mean that a person would merit or earn salvation. It would mean that his merit would obligate God to save him.

Such a concept is foreign to all that Christianity stands for. Man was shut off from God by his own sin. God was under no obligation to save him or even provide a way of salvation. It was out of God's mercy that He provided the death and righteousness of Christ for our salvation. It was out of God's love that He sent the Holy Spirit to woo us to Christ. It was out of God's love that He has commissioned believers to tell unbelievers about Christ.

God has offered salvation on the condition of faith. We must distinguish between the "condition" and the "ground" of salvation. Salvation is grounded solely in the death and righteousness of Christ provided through atonement. It is conditioned on the response of faith in Christ.

God has taken the initiative in providing what man needs for salvation. He has met the condition for salvation. He sends the messenger with the gospel. He woos through the Holy Spirit. The personal response of faith as the condition for salvation can in no way be considered in conflict with or in violation of "So then *it is* not of him that willeth, nor of him that runneth, but of God that sheweth mercy."

The Calvinist seems to be quite certain that this verse strikes a death blow to conditional election. Piper sees a parallel between the "willing" and the "running" of this verse to embrace the "willing" and "working" of Phil. 2:13. He explains,

> God's mercy determines man's willing and working (Phil. 2:13). And since the 'willing and working' referred to in Phil. 2:13 is not evil 'works' but the obedience of faith, it follows that the assertion of Rom. 9:16 cannot be limited to only some kinds of willing and running. For these reasons Rom. 9:16 should be construed so as to sweep away forever the thought that over against God there is any such thing as human self-determination in Pauline theology (133, 134).

I think the real question that Piper needs to face is: How is he using the expression "self-determination"? If he means that man's action is not the *cause* or *ground* of his salvation, I could not agree more. On the other hand, if he means that man's action in believing cannot be a determining factor in God's bestowal of salvation on the one who believes and withholding salvation from the one who does not believe, I cannot agree. Such a view is in conflict with the obvious and direct teaching of Scripture (Jn. 3:16, 18, 36; Acts 16:31, etc.).

Faith as a condition (as distinguished from a cause or a ground) does determine on whom God bestows salvation. God is the one, not man, who has decreed that faith is the condition of salvation. *When a person responds in faith, it is not he who is obligating God to save him. Rather, it is God who has obligated himself by His very righteous commitment to His promises, to save the person who believes. When properly understood, there is not the remotest possibility that such a view can rightly be understood as salvation by works.*

Piper is aware of the place of faith in salvation, but attempts to make it fit with his concept of unconditional election. He observes, "Faith is indeed a *sine qua non* [the necessary condition] of salvation; Rom. 9:16, therefore, necessarily implies that the act of faith is ultimately owing to the prevenient grace of God" (137).

I have no quarrel with his statement, "The act of faith is ultimately owing to the prevenient grace of God." The problem is how it is interpreted. If we would say that without the work of the Holy Spirit (Jn. 6:44) no man will ever believe in Christ, I would agree. However, such a statement still leaves room for obedience or disobedience.

As I perceive it, this is not Piper's interpretation of the statement. The work of the Holy Spirit "guarantees" or "causes" the response of faith. For a person to be *caused* to believe violates what it means to be a person. Faith is a response of the person. It is a personal experience. It is a choice. Divine assistance and influence, yes. Divine cause, no.

Experiences of the personality where personal action is involved can never be passive only. There is an active involvement. The active response of faith is genuine. It can in no way be said to be totally the work of God with no human involvement. The person made a choice. It did not pay for his salvation.

A word needs to be said about why Paul is giving attention to a denial that a person can establish his own righteousness before God. It seems that we see two apparently contradictory lines of thought in Jewish thinking: (1) The Jews were unconditionally elected when God made the Covenant with Abraham (Gen. 13:14, 15, and 17:8). (2) The Jews were seeking to establish their righteousness by works (9:31, 32, and 10:3). See the introduction to chap. 2 as well as the comments on 9:6-14.

It appears that those two observations are mutually exclusive. However, from all that I can gather, Jews were not as concerned with harmonization as some of us are. They were more content to let some loose ends dangle in their thought.

Their concept of corporate, unconditional election of all Jews through Abraham was by far the most basic of the two thoughts. All the rest of their thoughts must be weighed in the light of that foundational thought. (This is an area where research needs to be done so as to help us better understand the seeming contradictions concerning the Jewish attitude about salvation in the N.T.)

17 For the scripture saith unto Pharaoh, Even for this same purpose have I raised thee up, that I might shew my power in thee, and that my name might be declared throughout all the earth.

Just as vv. 15 and 16 show the concept of God's sovereignty as it relates to the showing of compassion, vv. 17 and 18 show the relationship of God's sovereignty as it relates to hardening.

Even for this same purpose have I raised thee up. Bruce explains, "The Hebrew uses the causative conjugation of the verb *amad,* 'stand,' which Paul renders by Greek *exegeiro* (raise up).

(He translates here direct from the Hebrew. LXX says 'thou hast preserved.') The reference may be not merely to God's raising up Pharaoh to be king, but to His patience in preserving him alive, in spite of his disobedience" (194). (For further discussion on whether the reference is to raising up Pharaoh to be king or whether it was the preservation of his life, or yet other views, see Cranfield II:485, 486; Earle 191; Godet 353, 354; Harrison 106; Lenski 613, 614; Sanday and Headlam 255, 256; and Shedd 290, 291. Shedd has a clear listing of different views.) It is not easy to decide which interpretation is correct. Probably, the preference should be given to the view which takes it to be raising up Pharaoh to be king.

That I might shew my power in thee, and that my name might be declared throughout all the earth. God had a world-wide purpose in mind for Pharaoh. Nothing that Pharaoh would do could thwart God's purpose. Pharaoh's response could affect the detailed manner in which God would accomplish His purpose, but it could not keep God's purpose from being fulfilled. Neither obedience nor disobedience could have interfered with God's purpose to show His power or to declare His name throughout the whole earth.

As it was, Pharaoh resisted God and hardened his heart. God responded by the miracles of the ten plagues and the parting of the waters of the Red Sea. Delivering Israel through this means brought glory to God's name and caused His name to be declared throughout the whole earth. If Pharaoh had, without the pressure of the plagues, let Israel go, that, too, would have shown His power. It would have been quite unusual if Pharaoh had freely allowed this mass of slave labor to go free!

18 Therefore hath he mercy on whom he will *have mercy,* and whom he will he hardeneth.

This verse in addition to restating v. 15 adds, *"and whom he will he hardeneth." "Mercy" and "hardening" are not exact opposites.* It is important that this observation be made. "Mercy" in this context refers to the bestowal of salvation. "Hardening" in this context *does not* refer to the infliction of penal wrath.

In my opinion, the word "harden" is carefully chosen in this context. Those who were saved among the Jews were already experiencing the saving mercy of God. Those who were lost were hardened, but they were not already experiencing the penal wrath of God. That is reserved for the eschatological future.

I think there would be general agreement that "blinded" in 11:7 would mean the same as "harden" in 9:18. At the moment of Paul's writing the Jews who had already received the saving mercy of God, would be considered the "elect" of 11:5 and 7. The rest of the Jews who had not experienced the saving mercy of God would be considered the "hardened" or the "blinded."

It is important to observe that Paul did not consider all Jews who were at that time hardened or blinded to be hopelessly locked by God in that state. The burden of Paul's heart was for their salvation (9:1-3; 10:1; 11:11-14, 28-32). There was no hope that all would come to Christ and be saved in the near future, but saving work was taking place among the Jews. Paul was using the words "to have mercy on" and "to harden" to refer to the distinction at that time between believers and unbelievers among the Jews. He was not saying that all those who were hardened at the time he wrote Romans were predestined by God without hope to be damned in the eschatological future. Once this observation is made, this passage offers no help to Calvinism.

Some Calvinists show an awareness that the word "harden" is not well suited to their purposes. The following quotation from Hendriksen shows how he is struggling to make "harden" suit his purpose. He explains, "There is no reason to doubt that the hardening of which Pharaoh was the object was final. It was a link in the chain: reprobation—wicked life—hardening—everlasting punishment. This does not mean, however, that divine hardening is always final. See on 11:7b,11" (326).

Piper is dealing with the same difficulty when he says, "Must we not conclude, therefore, that the hardening in 9:18 has reference, just as the hardening in 11:7, to the action of God whereby a person is left in a condition outside salvation and thus 'prepared for destruction' (9:22)?" (159).

John Brown, in defense of the Calvinistic position, shows the problem even more clearly. He explains:

> The introduction of the idea of judicial hardening seems to destroy the antithesis. *Hardening* is not the natural antithesis of showing mercy. Had it been, 'whom He wills He melts into penitence, and whom He wills He hardens into impenitence,' the antithesis would have been complete; but the one term in the antithesis, being showing mercy, the other must correspond to it—He does not show mercy; He relents in reference to one, He does not relent in reference to another.
>
> I am therefore disposed to concur with those interpreters (and they are distinguished both for learning and judgment) who consider the word rendered 'harden,' as equivalent to 'treat with severity' in withholding favors and inflicting deserved punishments (338).

I think it is quite evident that the word "harden" does not play into the hands of the Calvinist. But I would hasten to say that even if the passage had read "whom He wills He saves and whom He wills He condemns," the case would still not be won for Calvinism.

To clear the matter up, all we have to do is to ask two simple questions: (1) Whom does He choose to save? (2) Whom does He choose to condemn? The answer to the first according to Scripture is those who believe in Christ (Jn. 3:16, 18, 36; Acts 16:31; Rom. 3:28 and others). The answer to the second question is those who do not believe in Christ (Jn.3:18 and 36). The sovereign choice of God of those who will be saved and those who will be condemned does not require the doctrine of unconditional election and reprobation.

The problem of hardening is admittedly not a simple one. However, the use of the word in this context does not play into the hands of the Calvinist. The Calvinist is quite aware that hardening is not in all cases without remedy. The quotation from Hendriksen above acknowledges this fact. Piper acknowledges in end note 31 of chap. 9, "This does not imply that the condition sometimes called hardness of heart (Eph. 4:18) or mind (2 Cor. 3:14) cannot be altered by the merciful revivifying act of God (Eph. 2:1-4)." In defense of his Calvinism, he goes on to say, "But it does imply that God is the one who sovereignly decides who will be shown such mercy and who will be decisively and finally hardened. It is hardening in this decisive sense that meets the demands of the argument in 9:1-18" (275).

I have already shown above in the earlier comments on this verse that the Jews who were saved were called the elect. Those who did not believe and thus were not saved were hardened or as 11:7 says, "they were blinded." It is quite obvious that Paul is considering all the unbelieving Jews as hardened or blinded. It is equally obvious that he does not consider all hardened Jews as chosen for reprobation without hope.

The Hardness of Pharaoh's Heart

In Ex. 4:21; 7:3, 13; 9:12; 10:1, 20, 27; 11:10; and 14:4 and 8, the reference is to hardening of Pharaoh's heart by God. In Ex. 8:15,32, and 9:34, the reference is to Pharaoh's hardening of his own heart. In Ex. 7:14, 22; 8:19; and 9:7 and 35, reference is made to the fact that Pharaoh's heart is hardened.

Since we do not have a developed explanation in Scripture of all that was involved in the hardening of Pharaoh's heart by God, we can only make a conjecture which would seem to be consistent with what we know about God and man from the Bible. We can attempt to come up with an explanation that would fit with what we know about God and man from a study of Systematic Theology.

As a minister of the gospel, I preach the gospel. Not all who hear the Word preached respond favorably. Some resist. Resistance over a period of time hardens the heart. When a person resists my preaching, it can be said that he hardens his heart. Or it could be said that my preaching hardens his heart. It is not my desire that my preaching should harden a person's heart, but I will not fail to preach because it may harden someone's heart. We are reminded of the old saying, "The same sun that melts the butter hardens the clay."

God raised Pharaoh to show His power and that His name might be declared through all the earth. When God moved upon Pharaoh, it would not have hindered God's purpose if Pharaoh had complied rather than hardened his heart. However, Pharaoh responded negatively. He hardened his heart. Since he hardened his heart against God's request through Moses that he let the people go, it can be said that God hardened his heart. This would parallel preaching, which is designed to bring compliance with the gospel but contributes instead to the hardening of a sinner's heart.

If my reasoning is valid, God could have said to Moses:

> While I desire a positive response from Pharaoh, I know that Pharaoh will harden his heart at my request. However, that will not keep me from making the request, neither will it keep me from accomplishing my purpose through Pharaoh. Since he will harden his heart, I will bring judgment upon him through miraculous plagues until he lets my people go. That will be the means I will use in showing my power and causing my name to be declared through all the earth.

Instead of giving a theological explanation, God just said, "I will harden Pharaoh's heart." Moses did not need a theological explanation. He needed confirmation that God was sovereign. He got it!

The Hardening of the Jews

As pointed out earlier in the comments on this verse, I take those who are hardened in the passage to be those Jews who were not saved at the time. This is based on the view that in 11:7 the saved are the elect. "The rest" are "blinded." I take the blinded and the hardened to be the same.

In 11:7-10 it is obvious that the blinding is judicial. Some light is shed on this from Jesus' statement on why He spoke in parables (Mk. 4:11, 12). It is a blessing to know the truth. The blessing of knowing the truth is reserved for those whose heart is right (Jn.7:17). A part of the judgment of those whose heart is not right is that, in the nature of things, they will not properly understand the truth. They will be blinded.

The Jewish attitude toward unconditional, corporate election of all the seed of Abraham through Jacob caused them to be blinded to Paul's gospel which denied such unconditional, corporate election of all Jews. God could be said to be the one who blinded or hardened them because it was His truth which denied that all Jews were automatically saved. There are other aspects of the truth that could be mentioned that could have contributed to this blindness. (See comments on 11:8, 9.)

Piper's View of Unconditional Election and Reprobation

Piper explains,

> The point then of 18a ('On whom he wills, he has mercy') is, according to 9:16, that God is wholly free in determining the beneficiaries of his mercy: his decisions are not ultimately conditioned by man's will or actions. It follows, therefore, from the identical form of 18b ('Whom he wills, he hardens'), that God asserts the same sovereign freedom in determining whom he will harden: his decisions are not ultimately conditioned by man's will or acts (153).

In another place he says, "God evidently always acts this way and thus chooses to harden not simply those who have met the condition 'but whom he wills'" (155).

It seems to me that what comes through in Piper's treatment is that God, as Sovereign, is absolutely free to choose apart from conditions (and it would appear without ground or cause) to save or damn any human being. If this be the case, his thinking has some serious flaws, and not all Calvinists would concur with his thinking.

Apparently Piper is saying that grace is a prerogative of sovereignty. If that be the case, God could have shown grace apart from the atoning work of Christ. This I take to be a serious error. I doubt that Piper would really want to say that grace could operate apart from atonement, but that seems to be logically implied at times.

Grace is not a Divine right inherent in God's nature. It is a Divinely purchased right. It was absolutely necessary that sin be punished. Sovereignty could not ignore this necessity. Divine justice would not tolerate such. Jesus Christ purchased the right to bestow grace when He paid the penalty for our sin and lived an absolutely righteous life.

It is also a mistake to think about unconditional reprobation. Sin is the cause of condemnation. A holy God cannot condemn without a cause. This is not a matter of rights; it is a matter of God's responsibility to be consistent with His own attributes.

E. God's Sovereign Right Is Analogous to The Potter's Right Over The Clay (9:19-24).

19 Thou wilt say then unto me, Why doth he yet find fault? For who hath resisted his will?

If God chooses whom He wills for salvation and if He hardens whom He wills, and if Pharaoh was unable to interfere with God's purpose, the question arises, "Why doth he yet find fault [or charge with blame]? For who hath resisted his will?" The word for "will" (Greek *boulema*) means purpose (see Earle 194).

The verse does not suggest that a person cannot resist in the sense of *opposing* God's purpose. Rather, no one can *defeat* God's purposes. A person can disobey God and will be held responsible for his disobedience. However, God has purposes that are carried out in spite of disobedience (Gen. 50:19, 20).

20 Nay but, O man, who art thou that repliest against God? Shall the thing formed say to him that formed *it,* Why hast thou made me thus?

The maker has rights over that which he has made (see Isa. 29:16 and 45:9). This does not mean that Divine rights include arbitrary rights or rights that ignore right and wrong. Rather, the very nature of God is such that He cannot do otherwise than right. Thiessen has well said, "In God we have purity of being before purity of willing. God does not will the good because it is good, nor is the good good because God wills it; else there would be a good above God or the good would be arbitrary and changeable. Instead, God's will is the expression of his nature, which is holy" (129).

God is absolute Sovereign. For that reason, we need to find out what He has said and submit to it rather than argue with Him.

21 Hath not the potter power over the clay, of the same lump to make one vessel unto honour, and another unto dishonour?

There can be no doubt that Paul has in mind the account of the potter in Jer. 18:1-10. (See also Wisdom of Solomon 15:7.) I have already alluded to Jer. 18:1-10 in commenting on 9:15. This passage is very instructive in interpreting the passage before us. After having Jeremiah observe the work of the potter, God said, "O house of Israel, cannot I do with you as this potter? saith the LORD. Behold, as the clay *is* in the potter's hand, so *are* ye in mine hand, O house of Israel" (18:6).

God was declaring His sovereign right to do with Israel as He chose to do. In vv. 7-10 He told them what He wanted to do. In essence He said, "I can do with a nation whatever I choose to do. I choose to build up the nation that obeys me and tear down the one that disobeys me." There is no arbitrary sovereignty here.

God is also the Sovereign who chooses whom He wills for salvation and damnation. The arbitrariness is removed when we simply ask the question and let Scripture answer. "Whom does God choose to save and whom does He choose to damn?" He chooses to save those who believe in Christ (Jn.1:12; 3:16, 18, 36; and Acts 16:31). He chooses to damn those who fail to believe in Christ (Jn.3:18 and 36).

Cranfield is right when he observes, "And it cannot be emphasized too strongly that there is naturally not the slightest suggestion that the potter's freedom is the freedom of caprice, and that it is, therefore, perverse to suppose that what Paul wanted to assert was a freedom of the Creator to deal with His creatures according to some indeterminate, capricious, absolute will" (II:492).

22 *What* if God, willing to shew *his* wrath, and to make his power known, endured with much longsuffering the vessels of wrath fitted to destruction:
23 And that he might make known the riches of his glory on

the vessels of mercy, which he had afore prepared unto glory.

***What* if God, willing.** We have two points of concern: (1) How is Paul using the word "willing" (Greek *thelo*)? (2) What is the significance of the *form* of the verb he uses (a Greek participle)?

Concerning the meaning of "willing," Shedd is on the right track when he says:

> The mere permission of God is not meant; nor the purpose of God: which would require *Bouleuon*; but the deep and strong desire: a will that was so profound and intense as to require that self-restraint which is denominated the patience and long-suffering of God (2:4). The phrase [willing to shew his wrath] denotes the spontaneity of the divine holiness, 'the fierceness and wrath of Almighty God' against sin (Rev. 19:15), which is held back by the divine compassion, upon the ground of *hilasterion* [3:25] (298).

The participle "willing" or "desiring" might be rendered either "because desiring" (Greek: causal participle) or "*although* desiring" (Greek: concessive participle). "Although desiring" seems to be preferred. (For discussion on which is meant, see Cranfield 494; Denney 664; Earle 195, 196; Godet 359, 360; Murray II:33, 34; and Sanday and Headlam 261.)

Although God was strongly desiring to show His wrath toward those who were "vessels of wrath fitted to destruction," He "endured with much longsuffering" these "vessels of wrath" (objects of wrath, not instruments of wrath) "that he might make known the riches of his glory." If God had released His wrath immediately, the human race would have been taken immediately into eternal punishment. In this case, there would have been no vessels of mercy (those who are saved by God's grace). However, instead of immediately releasing His wrath, God through longsuffering withheld His wrath to give people time to repent (Rom. 2:4). This was done so that there would be those who would respond to the gospel; thus God can "*make known the riches of his glory on the vessels of mercy, which he had afore prepared unto glory.*"

It is generally agreed that the language of the expression "vessels of wrath fitted to destruction" does not imply unconditional reprobation (see Harrison 107; Hodge 321; Murray II:36; and Shedd 299).

Piper, however, would interpret the reference to an unconditional *fitting* for destruction of the vessels of wrath by God. He develops his argument from the point of view that Paul has been dealing with double predestination in chap. 9. He explains:

> It seems to me that, after the clear and powerful statements of double predestination [unconditional election or predestination of who was to be saved and unconditional predestination to reprobation of who was to be lost] in Rom. 9, it is grasping at a straw to argue that the passive voice of *katertismena* proves that Paul denied divine agency in fitting men for destruction . . . . And since Paul's inference from the Pharaoh story is that 'God hardens whom he wills' (9:18), the most natural suggestion from the context is that 'fitted for destruction' (9:22) refers precisely to this divine hardening (194).

I think it has been conclusively shown, in commenting on chap. 9 up to this point, that it is misconstruing what Paul is saying to interpret it to support either unconditional election or unconditional reprobation. So far as vv. 22 and 23 are concerned, I am not acquainted with anyone who would insist that these two verses apart from the rest of the chapter must be interpreted in the Calvinistic framework.

I might say with reference to Piper's double predestination, I am not averse to double predestination as such. What I reject is *unconditional* double predestination. I believe in conditional double predestination. On the condition of foreknown faith in Christ, God has predestined believers to eternal life. He has on the condition of foreknown sin and unbelief predestined unbelievers to eternal damnation. Apart from such predestination, we cannot assure the believer of eternal life or the unbeliever of eternal damnation. I do not reject predestination. I reject the Calvinistic interpretation of predestination.

The words "afore prepared" (Greek *proetoimazo*) mean to prepare beforehand. In one sense all of God's decisions are eternal. Based on His foreknowledge He knows who will believe in Christ and has chosen them in Christ (Eph. 1:4). Those who were foreknown have been prepared in eternity past for glory. For them, things have been prearranged. As Picirilli says, "They are headed for Heaven, 'prepared for glory'" (187).

24 Even us, whom he hath called, not of the Jews only, but also of the Gentiles?

While God is through longsuffering withholding His wrath from the vessels of wrath, He is withholding it to give an opportunity for salvation for both Jews and Gentiles. It is important to keep in mind that while Paul is deeply concerned that there were so many of his fellow Jews who were unsaved, he was keenly aware and wanted others to know that Jews were being saved.

F. The Fact That Many of the Jews Were Unsaved Is in Full Accord With the Old Testament (9:25-29).

25 As he saith also in O'see, I will call them my people, which were not my people; and her beloved, which was not beloved.
26 And it shall come to pass, *that* in the place where it was said unto them, Ye *are* not my people; there shall they be called the children of the living God.

These two verses are taken from Hosea. Murray explains, "Verse 26 is a verbatim quotation of the LXX and with the exception of *ekei* [there], which nevertheless is implied, is a literal rendering of the Hebrew (Hosea 2:1 in both Hebrew and LXX). But verse 25 does not exactly correspond to the Hebrew.... Paul has retained the thought but has adapted the actual terms" (II:38, note 46).

There is an almost unanimous agreement that while in Hosea the "not my people" who are called "the children of the living God" refers to Israel (directed by Hosea to the ten northern tribes), Paul is using it to refer to Gentiles. If this were demanded by the context, I could accept it, but it appears that such is not the case.

It is very clear that vv. 27-29 refer to Israel and call attention to the fact that Scripture should prepare the Jews to understand that not all of them are saved. To Paul, the position that not all Jews were saved was not a merely academic preservation of theological accuracy. It tore at his heart. He wanted the Jews to know that their belief in the unconditional election of all Jews in connection with Abraham was false. That was the only way they would entertain the idea of being saved through faith in Jesus Christ.

It is true, of course, that Paul, as the apostle to the Gentiles, was deeply concerned about the conversion of Gentiles. It is also true that he had just indicated that there were Gentiles as well as Jews among the vessels "afore prepared unto glory" (vv. 23, 24). However, that is not the burden of chap. 9.

The burden of chap. 9 is that Israel had misunderstood God's promise to Abraham. They were not unconditionally saved. Salvation was conditioned on faith in Jesus as the Messiah.

Out of this burden, Paul calls attention to the words of Hosea. These references clearly show that Hosea emphasized that there were Israelites who would come from an unsaved state into a saving relationship with God. This reference should put away once and for all the idea of unconditional election to salvation of all Israelites.

Barrett takes the reference to be mainly to Gentiles, but says that it is "possible that he is also thinking (as Hosea did) of the temporary lapse of Israel and their subsequent return" (191). Black (135) concurs with Barrett. See also Harrison (107).

Lenski's position is the nearest to my own that I have found. He applies the fulfillment to the ten tribes rather than to Gentiles (627).

27 Esaias also crieth concerning Israel, Though the number of the children of Israel be as the sand of the sea, a remnant shall be saved:
28 For he will finish the work, and cut *it* short in righteousness: because a short work will the Lord make upon the earth.

(For a discussion on the way vv. 27, 28 correspond to the Hebrew and the LXX of Is. 10:22, 23, see Cranfield II:501, 502 and Sanday and Headlam 265.) Lenski observes, "Those who refer v. 25, 26 to Gentiles naturally make *de* ["also"] adversative ["but"] and say that Paul now turns to the Jews; but since both Hosea and Isaiah speak of the Jews, and the latter adds a vital point as to numbers, *de* = 'moreover'" (630).

It is evident that Isaiah would not be surprised (disappointed, but not surprised) that large numbers of Jews were not saved. It is clear that he was stressing that *only* a remnant among Israel would be saved (v. 27).

Verse 28 sheds light on why only a remnant will be saved. The longsuffering that Paul mentioned in v. 22 will not be extended forever. The Lord will finish His work. He will "cut it short in righteousness." This means that many will have waited too late.

29 And as Esaias said before, Except the Lord of Sabaoth had left us a seed, we had been as Sodoma, and been made like unto Gomorrha.

Again, Paul refers to Isaiah. Paul quotes the LXX on Is. 1:9. "Lord of Sabaoth" means the "Lord of Hosts" or the "Lord of Armies." ("Sabaoth" is actually a Hebrew word, transliterated into Greek and, in the KJV, into English letters.)

The Scripture is saying that only by the mercy of God was a remnant of Israel even surviving. Certainly, the O.T. is opposed to the concept of the unconditional election of all who descended from Abraham through Jacob!

Summary
9:1-29

When Paul completed chap. 8, he was in a state of ecstasy. He was rejoicing over all of the things that God had done and was doing for him through the glorious salvation which we have with God through Jesus the Messiah. In this state of elation, he was suddenly and painfully reminded of the fact that the majority of his people, the Jews, were not saved.

The thought that so many Jews were unsaved produced great heaviness of heart on the part of Paul. Paul was so deeply burdened for their salvation that, if it would have accomplished their salvation, he would have been willing to have paid the price of being cut off from Christ to have accomplished their salvation.

Paul recounted the special blessings that were the Jews' as the Covenant People of God. It was tragic for a people who had been so blessed of God as to have been the recipients of the covenants, the law, and the promises, to miss salvation. To have had the patriarchs Abraham, Isaac, and Jacob as their fathers magnified the tragedy. Worse yet, the Messiah, who brought salvation to the world, had come to and through them and in spite of this they were strangers to the very salvation he brought.

When Paul took the position that large numbers of Jews were unsaved, this was diametrically opposed to prevailing Jewish thought. It was their opinion that they had been unconditionally and corporately elected for salvation by the promise made to Abraham in Gen. 13:14, 15, and 17:8. They thought that such a view as Paul's would suggest that God had been unfaithful to the promises He made to Abraham. If that was what Paul was saying, they did not want to have anything to do with it.

Paul took on the responsibility of trying to convince the Jews that they had misunderstood God's promise to Abraham. God had never promised unconditional salvation to all who would descend from Abraham through Jacob. Only those seed who were believers like Abraham could be called Israel in the truest and fullest sense of the word.

It should not be unthinkable to the Jew that a limitation would be placed on the descendants of Abraham who would be saved. As the Jews themselves knew well, there were a lot of people who could in one sense be called the seed of Abraham who were not a part of the Covenant Seed. Ishmael's and Esau's descendants were the seed of Abraham too, but they were not the Covenant Seed of Abraham. The Covenant Seed refers only to those who descended from Abraham through Jacob. God had made this clear in the choice of Isaac, not Ishmael, and of Jacob, not Esau. If the Jews could see that the limitation of the natural seed to those that descended through Jacob did not contradict Gen. 13:14, 15, and 17:8, surely they could see that a distinction among those who descended from Jacob would not contradict these verses. If that be the case, they should be able to see that a distinction between believers and unbelievers among those who descended from Abraham through Jacob need not destroy the Abrahamic Covenant.

Paul raises the question: "Can God be charged with unrighteousness?" Both Paul and the unbelieving Jews abhorred such an idea. To say that some Jews were unsaved in no way meant that God had shown Himself to be unrighteous. Both Paul and the Jew respected the authority of the O.T. so Paul made his appeal to the O.T.

God told Moses that He would have mercy on whomever He chose for mercy. That applied to Israel. God's righteousness had not obligated Him to show saving mercy to every Jew. If it had, God would not have talked that way to Moses.

If it seemed to bother the Jews to think that God did not melt the heart of every Jew to be a believer if Christianity was true, Paul pointed out that God had reserved to Himself the right to harden whom He willed according to the O.T. That was an adequate explanation that, in spite of being the Covenant People of God, many Jews were hardened in unbelief against Jesus Christ.

Instead of arguing with God, it would be better if the Jew recognized that God has the same rights over them that a potter has over the clay. God will save those whom He chooses and will damn those whom He chooses. That means that we should listen to Him. He has chosen to save those who believe in Jesus Christ and will damn those who do not.

While God will most definitely show His wrath on those who reject Christ, through much longsuffering He is delaying His wrath. This delay is so that He can give time for those who are still unsaved to come to the point of believing in Christ. During this time of patient longsuffering God is calling people from among Jews and Gentiles for this glorious salvation.

The Jews should have never been caught up with this idea of their unconditional election by God through Abraham anyway. Hosea had made it plain that there was such a thing as Jews "not being God's people" and later getting saved out of that condition. Isaiah had certainly made it clear that not all Israelites were saved. By taking what Paul told them, the Jews should have been able to set aside the idea that they were all unconditionally saved. This for them would be such a drastic change of thought that they should be able to consider believing in Jesus Christ for salvation.

Application: Teaching and Preaching the Passage

1. The greatest example of human compassion ever expressed is stated by the Apostle Paul in vv. 1, 2. His heaviness and sorrow were so strong for the salvation of the Jews that he was willing to be separated from Christ and suffer eternal damnation for it.

2. Part of what bothered Paul was that Israel was a privileged group in God's program of redemption. It hurt to see so many from this background who were lost. (See comments on vv. 4, 5 on the privileged position of Israel.)

3. The very idea that Paul would suggest that large numbers of Jews were lost raised serious questions in the minds of Jews. This is true because they thought God unconditionally elected all of the descendents of Abraham through Jacob when He called Abraham. Paul's point was that such was not the case.

He explains, "For they are not all Israel (the true and saved Israel), which are of Israel (the descendants of Jacob)" (v. 6). He then points out that though Ishmael and Esau were descendants of Abraham as much as Isaac and Jacob, they were not a part of the Covenant Seed. The Jews would agree on this.

Paul's aim in all of this was to get them to see that if not all who descended from Abraham became a part of the Covenant Seed, it is not necessary to believe that all who descended from Jacob would automatically be saved (vv. 6-13).

4. This passage (vv. 6-24) is very important to the doctrine of election. The Calvinist has felt that this passage is unquestionably on the side of unconditional election. I believe my comments on this passage make it clear that Paul did not propound the doctrine of unconditional election. In fact what

he was doing was challenging the Jewish form of the doctrine of unconditional election. I can point out a few of the highlights here, but to really understand the passage from my viewpoint a person will need to make a careful study of my comments on the passage.

Some of my main observations are:

(1) When Paul in v. 14 raised the question of whether "there is unrighteousness in God?" it was not: Is God unrighteous to unconditionally choose Jacob and reject Esau? A study of the passage will reveal that the significance of the question is: Is God unrighteous if He does not save all unconditionally who descended from Abraham through Jacob?

(2) For God to say, "I will have compassion on whom I will have compassion" (v. 15) does not put the matter on the side of unconditional election. All we have to do is ask the question: On whom does God will to have compassion? The answer is: on those who believe in Christ. Believing is a condition.

(3) When Paul said "whom he will he hardeneth" (v. 18), that is not the same as saying "whom he will he condemns to eternal death." The hardened may still be led to Christ out of their hardness.

(4) Paul's aim was to get the Jews to see that not all of them would be saved. Some will be (those who believe) and some will not be saved (those who do not believe). A comparison of the work of the potter in vv. 21-23 with Jer. 18:1-10 will show that we need not interpret the work of the potter as being unconditional and arbitrary.

(5) The aim of Paul in the quotation from the O.T. in vv. 25-29 is to get the Jews to see that the message of the O.T. should be quite clear in saying that not all Jews were to be considered as being saved.

(6) These ideas, when studied well, should be of benefit today in helping us reach Jews for Christ.

II. HUMAN RESPONSIBILITY IN ACCEPTANCE AND REJECTION BY GOD (9:30—10:21).

A. Paul Explains Why Some Gentiles Were Righteous Before God While Some Israelites Were Not (9:30—10:3).

30 What shall we say then? That the Gentiles, which followed not after righteousness, have attained to righteousness, even the righteousness which is of faith.

What shall we say then? Paul raises this question to call attention to the fact that what follows is the last thing that people would have expected.

That the Gentiles. Cranfield notes that in the Greek there is no article before Gentiles. He goes on to say, "The reference is not to Gentiles generally, but just to some Gentiles, namely, those who have believed" (II:506).

Which followed not after righteousness. Murray explains:

> When Gentiles are said to follow righteousness, there is allusion to the fact that they were outside the pale of special revelation and had been abandoned to their own ways (cf. 1:18-32; Acts 14:16; 17:30). But thought is focused on what is central to the theme of the epistle in the earlier chapters and again in Chapter 10, namely, that they did *not seek after the righteousness of justification*. It is not that they were destitute of all moral interests (cf. 2:12-15) but that the matter of

justification and of the righteousness securing it was not their pursuit (II:42, 43).

The time period in which they "followed not after righteousness" was from the call of Abraham until the gospel began to be preached to Gentiles. During this time the Gentiles were pagan. Except for a few rare exceptions, they were outside the reach of God's redemptive revelation. They were not in pursuit of a means of that which would give them right standing with Yahweh.

Have attained to righteousness. They had received the God-provided righteousness made available by the atoning work of Christ.

Even the righteousness which is of faith. The God-provided righteousness has been received by the Gentiles by faith in Jesus Christ.

31 But Israel, which followed after the law of righteousness, hath not attained to the law of righteousness.

Though Israel, from the time of the call of Abraham on, was the recipient of God's redemptive revelation as it was unfolded, and many, in a way, followed after righteousness they (many) missed it. While Paul has clearly brought the Gentiles into the picture, the main burden of this passage is still for the salvation of the Jews.

32 Wherefore? Because *they sought it* not by faith, but as it were by the works of the law. For they stumbled at that stumblingstone.

The reason so many missed justification was simple. They sought it by works rather than faith. (For a discussion of the tension between the Jewish concept of unconditional election and salvation by works, see the introduction to chap. 2 and the comments on 9:16.)

For they stumbled at that stumblingstone. This is a reference to Is. 8:14. Jesus Christ was a stumblingstone to most among the Jews. This was particularly true of the Pharisees. Jesus was in direct conflict with their constituted authority because He did not recognize it (Lk. 20:1-8), and with their concept of oral tradition which is referred to by Jesus as "the tradition of the elders" (Mt. 15:1-9). Jesus could not accept their constituted authority or their oral tradition. Therefore, they could not accept Jesus as the Jewish Messiah.

33 As it is written, Behold, I lay in Sion a stumblingstone and rock of offence: and whosoever believeth on him shall not be ashamed.

This verse combines Is. 8:14 and 28:16. Murray explains:

> Paul takes parts of both passages, weaves these parts together into a unit, and by this abridgement and combination obtains the diverse thought of both passages. This twofold aspect he applies to the subject with which he is dealing, the failure of Israel and the attainment of the Gentiles. He thus shows that the Scripture had foretold in effect the twofold outcome. The main interest, however, is confirmation of the stumbling of Israel. It is this tragedy that looms high in the apostle's concern, as is apparent from the preceding and succeeding contexts (II:44).

Paul's interest in confirming the stumbling of Israel is not an end within itself, but is a means of helping Israelites see that the facts of Scripture do not accord with the unconditional election or salvation of every Jew. The Scripture supports the opposite. Jews are pictured as being lost and in need of being saved. When they see that they need to be saved, then they will be in a position to see Christ as the true way of salvation.

And whosoever believeth on him shall not be ashamed. Instead of stumbling over Christ, the Jews should have believed in Him. In commenting on the difference in the Hebrew and the Greek for "shall not be ashamed," Murray explains, "The idea expressed by the Greek is that the believer will not be confounded, he will not have occasion to be ashamed of his confidence. And the Hebrew may express the closely related thought that he will not flee in disappointment" (II:45). Another way of expressing the Hebrew thought is that he will not feel like making a fast getaway.

1 Brethren, my heart's desire and prayer to God for Israel is, that they might be saved.

The word for desire (Greek *eudokia*) occurs 9 times in the N.T. It is translated desire only in this verse. It is translated "good" in Mt. 11:26 and Lk. 10:21; "good will" in Lk. 2:14 and Phil. 1:15; and "good pleasure" in Eph. 1:5, 9; Phil. 2:13; and 2 Th. 1:11. Earle gives a good summary of the different views of how it should be translated here and settles for "good will" (199, 200). It is evident that Paul means to say that his whole being goes out to the unbelieving Jews. His attitude is totally favorable toward the idea of their salvation. He is their friend. He is on their side when it comes to wanting them to have this salvation.

The unbelieving Jews were on Paul's prayer list. He was praying that they might be saved.

It is important to keep in mind that, as in chap. 9, so in chap. 10 Paul's main burden is for the salvation of unbelieving Jews. This burden permeates everything that he says.

2 For I bear them record that they have a zeal of God, but not according to knowledge.

To bear record (Greek *martureo*) is to bear witness or to testify on their behalf. Having once been where they were, Paul was well qualified to be a witness of their zeal for God. The tragedy was that their "zeal of God" was "not according to knowledge." Cranfield observes, "There is a perverse and obstinate ignorance at the very heart of their knowledge of God, and in the centre of their dedication and meticulous obedience an obstinate disobedience" (II:514).

3 For they being ignorant of God's righteousness, and going about to establish their own righteousness, have not submitted themselves unto the righteousness of God.

For they being ignorant of God's righteousness. This tells why they had a zeal of God which was not according to knowledge. It was because they were ignorant of the God-provided righteousness through Jesus Christ. Once they were confronted with the gospel, this ignorance was the ignorance of a hardened heart, not any longer the ignorance of one who was uninformed.

And going about to establish their own righteousness. They were trying to prepare their own righteousness so that it would stand before God. See 9:31, 32, and the comments on 9:16 regarding the tension in Jewish thought between the concept of unconditional salvation and salvation by works.

Have not submitted themselves unto the righteousness of God. The righteousness which forms the basis for our justification is a righteousness that we submit to receive rather than one we establish. The unbelieving Jews had gone at this the wrong way. They had sought to establish their own righteousness rather than submit to the righteousness provided by God through Jesus Christ.

B. Paul Describes the Righteousness of Faith (10:4-13).

The righteousness provided by God differs from the righteousness of the law (vv. 4,5). It is easily accessible (vv. 6-9). It is offered on the condition of faith (vv. 4, 6, 9, 10, and 11). It is offered to all (vv. 4, 11-13).

4 For Christ *is* the end of the law for righteousness to every one that believeth.

The differences of opinion on this verse mainly center around the meaning of the word "end" (Greek *telos*). There are basically three different views given by commentators concerning what it means here: (1) termination, (2) goal, and (3) fulfillment. Sometimes there seems to be a mixing of these views.

It appears to me that "termination" is the most likely meaning. Christ is a termination of the law way or the law-keeping way of producing a righteousness that would make one acceptable before God. This is not to suggest that there ever was a time when law-keeping made one righteous before God. It did not. As "a way" it had failed for every human being. When Christ came and provided righteousness for us, He brought an end to a way that had failed for every human being (Harrison 110, 111, and Murray II:49-51 would support this view).

The second view would be that the law leads to Christ as the goal (Cranfield II: 515-520; Moule, *Cambridge Bible* 179, and Vine, *Romans* 154). Murray shows the weakness of this view when he says, "But this would give an awkward if not impossible construction as will appear from the translation that would be required: 'the end of the law is Christ for righteousness to every one that believeth'" (II:49, 50). Paul is saying that Christ is the termination of the way which the Jews had tried to follow which had been a total failure. It had not produced a righteousness that would stand before God in even one person.

The third view which sees Christ as the *fulfillment* of the law would mean that Christ would fulfill the typology of the law and the requirements of the law for a penalty and righteousness (Hodge 335-337 and Shedd 313). This view is certainly stating something that is true as such, but something that does not seem to fit the context here. In objecting to this view, Murray explains, "If Paul were speaking of the purpose of the law as fulfilled in Christ, we would expect the absolute statement: 'Christ is the end [fulfillment] of the law for righteousness,' and no addition would be necessary or in place" (II:50).

To every one that believeth. The reference to everyone is, of course, to include both Jew and Gentile. However, Paul's main burden in the context is for the Jew who is blinded to that for which his heritage should have especially prepared him.

In 2:1—3:7 Paul had made it unquestionably clear that the unbelieving Jew had failed before God because he did not have absolute righteousness. God's principles of judgment are universal. Since God required absolute righteousness of the Gentile, He must also require it of the Jew. Neither Jew nor Gentile by his own efforts could produce absolute righteousness. Yet God would accept nothing less.

Out of the dark picture of helplessness, Paul sounded the note of hope in 3:21-31. What God required, that man could not produce, He provided through Jesus Christ. Paul did not paint a dark picture for the Jew and leave him without hope. He pointed out that through the death and righteousness of Christ, God had provided and made available for man that which He required. Paul's burden had advanced from very forcefully pointing out the need of the Jew to pointing out the remedy God had provided.

In chap. 9 Paul came at the Jewish need from a different angle. He expressed his burden for their salvation in the strongest terms in 9:1-3. The biggest problem the Jew had was that he did not recognize he was lost. This was because he thought that Gen. 13:14, 15, and 17:8 gave an unconditional promise of eternal life to all Jews.

Paul's contention was that God had never promised salvation to all Jews. In chap. 9 Paul called attention to several things that should have struck a death blow to the Jewish concept of unconditional election.

Just as in chap. 2 and 3 Paul moved from a forceful attempt of making the Jew aware of his need to making him aware that God had made provision for that need: unconditional election was a false hope for the Jew. The attempt to produce a righteousness that would stand before God had been a miserable failure. But that was not the end of the story. Jesus Christ is the end of this failure of the law way. To everyone who believes, He gives this God-provided righteousness that meets every demand that God, as the Supreme Judge of the universe, has made on man whether he be Jew or Gentile.

The mistake of the Jew was believing in unconditional election or unconditional salvation. Paul's point was that Jesus Christ had made the provision of the righteousness that was required for man's salvation whether he be Jew or Gentile. The only condition required for this was faith in Jesus Christ as Lord and Savior. This condition was required. It was possible, and it would work. God would honor this condition of faith by giving the Divinely provided gift of righteousness.

Calvinism has erred in replacing the Jewish view of the unconditional election of all Jews for the unconditional election of some Jews and some Gentiles. Paul's answer to the Jewish unconditional election or unconditional salvation is that salvation is given to all who meet the condition of faith. It is a salvation "to everyone that believeth" whether he be Jew or Gentile.

The only doctrine of election that is consistent with conditional salvation is conditional election. The Calvinists insist that God has not told us why He chose people for salvation in eternity past. Since God is the same yesterday, today, and forever, we do know why God chose people in eternity past. He chooses for salvation now those who believe in Christ. That is exactly what He did in eternity past based on His foreknowledge. (See discussion in comments on 8:29, 30, and "Verses 6-13 on Election" at the end of the comments on 9:13, the comments on 9:14-16 and "Summary Observations About Election in Chapters 9 and 10" at the end of this chapter.)

5 For Moses describeth the righteousness which is of the law, That the man which doeth those things shall live by them.

For Moses describeth the righteousness which is of the law. Paul is not suggesting that such righteousness exists. As Picirilli explains, "'the righteousness which is sought by observing the law'" (202). What follows is the way righteousness would be obtained if it could be obtained by law-keeping.

That the man which doeth those things shall live by them. This is quoted from Lev. 18:5. These words are capable of being understood as either absolute law-keeping or relative law-keeping. The context in which it is used determines which is the case.

If law-keeping is referred to as a basis of being blessed as the people of God, it is relative (or less than absolute). It would be useless for God to promise us a blessing based on absolute obedience. It seems apparent that Lev. 18:5 was in a context of promising blessings to the people of God based on law-observance. Therefore, in its original context, it would be capable of being obeyed with less than absolute obedience.

If law-keeping (or law-doing) is placed in a context dealing with justification, the only kind of obedience that could bring justification is absolute obedience. Paul uses the words "the man which doeth those things" in a context dealing with justification. Therefore, the obedience referred to would be absolute. It is the kind of obedience that no one can render. Therefore, justification cannot be by the law. (For a somewhat similar discussion, see Murray, Appendix B, "Leviticus 18:5" II:249, 250.)

We could sum it up by saying that in a "justification context" law-keeping refers to absolute obedience. In a "sanctification context," law-keeping refers to relative obedience.

6 But the righteousness which is of faith speaketh on this wise, Say not in thine heart, Who shall ascend into heaven? (that is, to bring Christ down *from above*:) 7 Or, Who shall descend into the deep? (that is, to bring up Christ again from the dead.)

While these words are applicable to both Jews and Gentiles, it must be remembered that in this context, Paul's special burden is for the Jew. In chap. 2:1—3:7 and in chap. 9 Paul had labored long and hard to get the Jew to see that he was not saved unconditionally. God did not corporately elect all Jews because they are the seed of Abraham. Salvation is conditional. If the Jew does not meet the condition, he will be lost. But he need not be lost because the condition of salvation is faith in Jesus Christ as the Messiah.

The stress that Paul is now giving is how easily accessible and possible this salvation is. The Jew need not worry about his plight in view of the fact that salvation is not unconditional. He can easily become a believer and be saved.

Picirilli explains:

> Verses 6, 7 (after 'wise') are quoted freely from Deuteronomy 30:12, 13 where Moses stressed the fact that the poeple should not regard their obligations to God as impossible; they should not say that to fulfil God's expectations they would have to climb up to Heaven or swim the ocean and back; they should not blaspheme God by claiming that He expected more of them than they could reasonably accomplish.
>
> Here in Romans Paul borrows that same language, adjusts and expands it to refer to Christ's redemptive work. He says, in effect, that now the ancient words of Moses are genuinely true in Christ. God does *not* expect an impossible achievement of us; in fact he expects *no achievement at*

> *all!* Christ has done it for us.... The righteousness which comes by faith calls on no one to climb to Heaven or descend to Hell: Christ has done both for us. Nor did anyone have to bring Christ from Heaven to earth or bring Him back from death: Those were accomplished by Christ's own work, in the free and gracious provision of God (202, 203).

The spirit of the Deuteronomy passage is fulfilled in this passage, but it is not necessary to think that those verses directly predicted such a fulfillment in Christ. Paul chose to use the passage because of its spirit, and because the words so nearly suited his purpose. (For a discussion which seeks to establish the position that Paul uses the verses from Dt. 30:12-14 as being more directly fulfilled, see Cranfield 524-526.)

8 But what saith it? The word is nigh thee, *even* in thy mouth, and in thy heart: that is, the word of faith, which we preach;
9 That if thou shalt confess with thy mouth the Lord Jesus, and shalt believe in thine heart that God hath raised him from the dead, thou shalt be saved.

Verse 8 continues Paul's use of Deuteronomy. It comes from 30:14. This verse stresses the accessibility and the availability of this righteousness. The condition of salvation is so readily available that it simply depends on something that can be exercised with the mouth and the heart.

The word of faith, which we preach. "Word" (Greek *hrema*) both here and in the first part of the verse means that which is spoken or written. In the Greek the article appears before "faith." In Paul's writings when the article appears before faith, in the vast majority of times, it refers to "the gospel," "the New Covenant teachings," or "the faith way." It is usually synonymous with "The New Covenant" (see comments on this in connection with 3:30). Barrett says, "The 'word of faith' means the Gospel, as preached by Paul" (199, 200).

That if thou shalt confess with thy mouth the Lord Jesus. Paul is no longer quoting from Deuteronomy, but the reference to "mouth" and "heart" in vv. 9 and 10 hearkens back to the reference to "mouth" and "heart" in Dt. 30:14.

Salvation is so near that in response to the gospel, the sinner only has to respond by letting faith happen. A part of this process is vocalizing that Jesus is Lord. Cranfield explains:

> We take it that, for Paul, the confession that Jesus is Lord meant the acknowledgment that Jesus shares the name and the nature, the holiness, the authority, power, majesty and eternity of the one and only true God. And, when, as is often the case, there is joined with the title *kurios* a personal pronoun in the genitive, there is expressed in addition the sense of His ownership of those who acknowledge Him and of their consciousness of being His property, the sense of personal commitment and allegiance, of trust and confidence (II:529).

The inclusion of the recognition of Jesus as Lord as part of the meaning of saving faith should put to rest once-and-for-all the claim that a person can in saving faith receive Christ as Savior without receiving Him as Lord. See also Acts 16:31.

And shalt believe in thine heart that God hath raised him from the dead. Just as the first part of this verse eliminates the possibility of exercising saving faith without receiving

Christ as Lord, the last part eliminates the possibility of saving faith without believing in the resurrection of Christ. To believe in the resurrection of Christ is also to believe the rest of what Scripture says concerning Jesus Christ. The resurrection stamps God's approval on all the claims which Jesus Christ made for Himself.

To believe in the heart is to believe with the total personality, not just the rational mind as distinguished from the rest of the personality (the heart and the will). To believe in the heart means that that which is grasped by the mind also takes on feelings and attitudes in the heart. (See comments on "heart" in connection with 1:21.)

Thou shalt be saved. Salvation refers both to the present and the eschatological future.

10 For with the heart man believeth unto righteousness; and with the mouth confession is made unto salvation.

This verse reverses the order of confessing and believing from the order used in v. 9. The order of heart belief which leads to confession with the mouth is the way the actual process works.

When a person exercises saving faith, it is natural and to be expected that he will confess his faith to others. However, it is fruitless to claim that if a person dies before he gets the chance to tell someone about his faith in Christ that he is not saved. Confession is an essential *result* of being saved rather than the last step before being saved. It is assumed that there may be some brief period of time before salvation works itself out in confession in a few cases. If quibbling were important, the Scripture would have been more detailed in its explanation.

11 For the scripture saith, Whosoever believeth on him shall not be ashamed.

This verse is quoted from the Septuagint version of Is. 28:16. See quote from Murray in comments on 9:33 concerning the difference between the Hebrew and Greek concepts of "shall not be ashamed."

While Paul was interested in driving home the idea that this salvation is available for both Jew and Gentile, he had another point in mind. He wanted to drive home, particularly to the Jews, the ease with which this salvation can be received. The only requirement is to believe in Jesus Christ as Lord and Savior.

12 For there is no difference between the Jew and the Greek: for the same Lord over all is rich unto all that call upon him.

For there is no difference between the Jew and the Greek. See comments on "For there is no difference" in the notes on 3:22. When it comes to offering salvation, God sees no distinction that could justify offering salvation to either Jews or Gentiles without offering it also to the other. The Jew is not to perceive his situation as being such that his hardness (9:18; 11:7) has shut him off from the gospel offer.

13 For whosoever shall call upon the name of the Lord shall be saved.

The verse is from Jl. 2:32 (LXX). Paul has multiplied his proof from the O.T. that anyone (Jew or Gentile) who will call upon God through faith in Jesus Christ will be saved. The converse of this is also true. Those who do not believe will not be saved whether they be Jew or Gentile.

Harrison explains concerning the use of "Lord" in this verse, "When v. 13 is compared with v. 9, it becomes evident that the Lord of Joel 2:32 is being identified with the Lord Jesus Christ. This poses a problem for those who refuse to ascribe full deity to the Savior" (113).

C. The Universality of the Gospel Offer Is of No Avail If There Is Not An Aggressive Program of Evangelism (10:14, 15).

14 How then shall they call on him in whom they have not believed? and how shall they believe in him of whom they have not heard? and how shall they hear without a preacher?
15 And how shall they preach, except they be sent? as it is written, How beautiful are the feet of them that preach the gospel of peace, and bring glad tidings of good things!

It is natural, based on the context, to ask first if Paul's special attention in these verses is upon Israel. It appears to me that Paul's attention in these verses is on what it takes for people to be able to believe whether they be Jew or Gentile. They cannot call on Jesus as Lord if they do not believe in Him. Believing in Him necessarily infers that they have heard of Him. Hearing implies that there has been a preacher who has proclaimed the gospel. An authorized preacher necessarily implies that someone has officially commissioned the preacher to preach the gospel. This kind of program is necessary if there is going to be a harvest of souls among either Jews or Gentiles. Instead of these verses being restricted in their application, it appears to me that they set the stage for a particular discussion of the Jewish problem in the following verses. (For a discussion on who these verses apply to, see Bruce 205, 206; Cranfield II:533; Haldane 512; Hendriksen 349; and Picirilli 203, 204.)

Some observations need to be made: (1) about the "preacher" and (2) about being "sent." It should be readily obvious to us that the preacher that Paul speaks about in this passage is not restricted to those among the ordained ministry. There should be no confusion over whether a person can preach the gospel without being ordained. Any Christian can proclaim the gospel. I recognize the place of the ordained ministry, but any Christian can tell somebody about Jesus. That is the kind of preaching spoken of here. The word for preaching (Greek *kerusso*) means to proclaim as a herald. According to Paul, people cannot be saved without a preacher. We all know that people can be saved without hearing the gospel from an ordained minister or without the presence of an ordained minister.

The word "send" (Greek *apostello*) is referring to sending with a commission rather than sending with financial support. Though we know that sending in many cases requires financial support, that is not what is in view here. Concerning the word *send,* Picirilli explains, "The verb in Greek is built on the same root as the noun 'apostle,' which Paul uses of himself in Romans 1:1. . . .This means to send on a mission, to send as an emissary or official representative. Before anything else can happen toward a man's salvation, someone must be commissioned to go, sent from the Lord" (210).

With reference to the words for preaching and sending, Picirilli observes,

> We pause here to take note that there is absolutely nothing about these first two verbs that limits their performance to *or-*

dained persons! Every Christian ought to recognize himself as commissioned by Christ, sent as an official representative with the gospel to lost men. Likewise the 'preaching' is not limited to pulpit oratory. Nothing more than telling someone else the gospel is required, and that is something all God's children ought to be doing (210).

As it is written, How beautiful are the feet of them that preach the gospel of peace, and bring glad tidings of good things! The quotation is from Is. 52:7. Bruce explains, "Paul here gives his own Greek rendering of the gist of the Hebrew instead of reproducing the LXX, which obscures the sense of the verse" (208).

The picture here is that of a runner who had been sent out to herald good news. Feet under normal circumstances are not necessarily viewed as being beautiful. However, they would be considered beautiful when belonging to one who is bearing good news. Lenski explains:

> The prophet voices the jubilation of the Israelites still faithful in the Babylonian captivity at the thought and the sight of the herald runners speeding over the mountains to make the great announcement to them that they are now free. . . .Do not miss the touch regarding the feet of these bearers of glad tidings. Covered with dust because of the long running, they are simply 'beautiful' to the eyes of these longing captives because of the message they are bringing. No more beautiful sight to them than these feet! So comes the gospel word. 'Go,' cried Jesus, 'disciple all nations!' and with that commission speeded the feet of his heralds: 'teaching them all things that I have commanded you,' as true heralds of mine. Such were the feet of Paul when he wrote this quotation; such are the feet of all true missionaries to this day (663, 664).

D. The Situation Which Included the Salvation of Some Gentiles and the Rejection of Some of the Israelites Should Not Have Caught Israel Off Guard (10:16-21).

16 But they have not all obeyed the gospel. For Esaias saith, Lord, who hath believed our report?

While the gospel has been preached by those who have been duly commissioned by God, both among Jews and Gentiles, not all who have heard have obeyed (believed) the gospel. Paul gives Biblical support for this assertion. The quotation is from Is. 53:1 (LXX). This reference is to unbelief on the part of at least some of the Jews.

In vv. 14, 15, Paul explained what was necessary to have a program of evangelism appropriate to a "whosoever will" gospel. In this verse, Paul takes up the discussion of how the Jews fit into all of this. In spite of the fact that they had heard, many did not believe.

17 So then faith *cometh* by hearing, and hearing by the word of God.

So then faith *cometh* by hearing. "So then" seems to connect this verse with v. 15 rather than v. 16. This verse gives the essence of what is involved in vv. 14, 15. Picirilli observes, "The verse is basically a shortened summary repetition of the five steps of salvation outlined above in verses 14,

15" (212).

It is the common practice among commentators to pay little attention to the absence or presence of the article before faith. I am personally convinced that it is important to observe this distinction in Paul's writings. In this verse the article occurs before faith in the Greek. Without the article the reference is to the experience of believing. With the article, the reference is to that which is believed, as in the statement "contend for the faith" (Jude 3). I am of the opinion that faith with the article is essentially synonymous with the New Covenant or the gospel. (See comments on v. 9 and a more thorough treatment in the notes on 3:30.)

The word "report" in v. 16 and the word "hearing" in v. 17 are the same (Greek *akoe)*. "Hearing" refers to the experience of hearing. "Report" refers to that which is heard—message, or report. It may be that the word "message" would be better suited than "hearing" in v. 17.

I would suggest for the verse the meaning, "So then the New Covenant (which is the faith way) comes to us as a message." The message of the New Covenant comes from God (or according to the *United Bible Society Text*, "Christ"). We participate in the New Covenant by hearing about it and by responding with faith when we do hear.

18 But I say, Have they not heard? Yes verily, their sound went into all the earth, and their words unto the ends of the world.

This verse is from Ps. 19:4 (LXX). In Ps. 19 these words refer to the fact God is known throughout the whole earth through general revelation. We are not to understand that Paul actually took this verse to refer to the spread of the gospel. Paul is taking the words of Ps. 19:4 and putting them in a different context. Bruce explains, "It is unnecessary to suppose that Paul regarded Psalm 19:4 as a *prediction* of the world-wide dissemination of the gospel; he means that the gospel is becoming as world-wide as the light of the heavenly bodies" (209).

Paul introduced the verse by "But I say, Have they not heard?" The question was asking if Israel had not heard the gospel. Paul's answer was, "yes." This means that in quoting Ps. 19:4 Paul was using the words, in his own context, to point out that the Jews had heard the gospel. Bruce comments, "The language of the quotation as thus used here often seemed to be an exageration; after all, the gospel had not been carried throughout all the earth, not even to all the lands that were then known to inhabitants of the Graeco-Roman world. Paul was well aware of that; at this very time he was planning the evangelization of Spain, a province where the name of Christ was not yet known. All he means is that, wherever there were Jews, there the gospel had been preached" (206, 207).

19 But I say, Did not Israel know? First Moses saith, I will provoke you to jealousy by *them that are* no people, *and* by a foolish nation I will anger you.

But I say, Did not Israel know? I do not take Paul to be asking a question here about whether Israel understood the gospel. What he is asking is, "Did not Israel know that there would be a time when God would be using the Gentiles to help bring them into a right relationship with God?" The answer is, "yes." As evidence for this affirmative answer, Paul quotes Dt. 32:21 (LXX).

Murray catches the spirit of Paul's use of the quotation from Moses. He explains:

> The meaning of the quotation, particularly as interpreted and applied by the apostle, is that Israel would be provoked to jealousy and anger because another nation which had not enjoyed God's covenant favour as Israel had would become the recipient of the favour which Israel had despised. This implies the extension of the gospel privilege to all peoples, the particular truth emphasized in verse 18. But the distinctive feature of verse 19 is not the universal diffusion of the gospel; it is the provocation of Israel as the by-product of this diffusion. Strangers and aliens will become partakers of covenant favour and blessing. This, therefore, is what Israel *knew*; they had been apprized and forewarned of the outcome, that the kingdom of God would be taken from them and given to a nation bringing forth its fruit. All the more forceful as proof of this knowledge is the appeal to the word of Moses (II:62).

20 But Esaias is very bold, and saith, I was found of them that sought me not; I was made manifest unto them that asked not after me.

This verse is taken from Is. 65:1 (LXX). There is not full agreement that this verse referred to Gentiles as it was originally given by Isaiah (Bruce 211 and Cranfield II:540 take the position that the original reference was to Israel. Godet 389 defends the position that the original reference was to Gentiles).

There seems to be no doubt that from the way Paul introduces v. 21 with the words, "But to Israel he saith," we are to understand that Paul uses Is. 65:1 in v. 20 to refer to the salvation of Gentiles. That would make v. 20 add support to what had been said in v. 19. Israel should not have been caught off guard by this great ingathering of Gentiles since it was clearly supported by the O.T.

21 But to Israel he saith, All day long I have stretched forth my hands unto a disobedient and gainsaying people.

This verse comes from Is. 65:2 (LXX). With words like this in their own prophetic writings, which they revered, there was no excuse for Israel to be misled into the false security of the position that all Israelites were unconditionally saved through Abraham.

Summary Observations About Election in Chapters 9 and 10

In introducing chap. 9, Paul expressed the deepest possible concern over so many Jews being unsaved. This view that many among Israel were unsaved ran counter to Jewish thought. Their thinking was that when God made the covenant with Abraham, He unconditionally promised salvation to all the seed of Abraham (Gen. 13:14, 15; 17:8) which, of course, meant Israel. In other words, in their thinking, "all Israel" was unconditionally elected in the covenant God made with Abraham.

Paul's rejection of the unconditional election of all Israel in the Abrahamic Covenant, to the Jewish mind, would mean that God would be unfaithful to His promise and would make the Word of God ineffectual. It would be ineffectual because, as the Jews understood it, what was promised by God would not be coming to pass.

Paul insists that the Word of God is not ineffectual. The problem is that the Jews have misunderstood it. It is true that God had promised eternal life to the seed of Abraham in Gen. 13:14, 15, and 17:8. However, that did not mean that, apart from any condition, every Jew would be saved. Righteousness according to the Abrahamic Covenant was conditional on faith (Gen. 15:6).

The evidence is quite clear that, when God promised salvation to the seed of Abraham in Gen. 13:14, 15, and 17:8, it is not to be taken to mean that every person who descended from Abraham would be saved. The Jews recognized well that the descendants of Abraham through Ishmael and Esau were the seed of Abraham too. Yet at the same time they did not consider them to be a part of the Covenant Seed of Abraham. The Covenant Seed of Abraham embraced only those who descended from Abraham through Jacob.

Once it is conceded that not all of the seed of Abraham are the Covenant Seed of Abraham, there is no contradiction involved in saying that God did not promise salvation to all the seed of Abraham. The Jew certainly understood that, as it related to the descendants of Ishmael and Esau. If we say that not all of the descendants of Jacob are saved, there is certainly not any conflict between that statement and Gen. 13:14, 15, and 17:8.

In 9:14 Paul says, "What shall we say then? *Is there* unrighteousness with God? God forbid." Why does Paul raise this question? The Calvinist says the question is raised with regard to the rejection of Esau. Was God unrighteous to reject Esau while choosing Jacob? It is understandable that a person might think that is why Paul raised the question. However, the context will not support such a position. It must be remembered that Paul's burden in this chapter is to deal with problems raised by the Jews. The Jews had no problem with God's rejection of Esau while choosing Jacob.

The problem with unrighteousness which bothered the Jews was that as they perceived it, according to Paul, God was not faithful to the promise that He made to Israel as the seed of Abraham in Gen. 13:14, 15, and 17:8. They perceived God as promising salvation to all the Covenant Seed of Abraham (Israel). They understood Paul to say that God was not saving all Israelites. Their response would be to say: If that is the case, then, God is unrighteous because He is not faithful to His promise to Israel.

Paul had already shown that the facts do not justify the idea that God promised salvation to all Israel. There is the Israel that descended from Abraham through Jacob. Then, there is the Israel that is the true Israel (9:6). These are not coextensive. This in no way contradicts the Abrahamic Covenant.

Paul, in dealing with the question whether God was unrighteous in not saving all Jews, develops another line of thought. First, he rejects altogether any thought that God could be considered unrighteous. The idea that God could be unrighteous was as abhorrent to Paul as it was to the Jew. Since both Paul and the Jew abhorred the thought of God being unrighteous, and since both held to the Divine authority of the O.T., Paul chose to make his appeal to Scripture.

His first reference was to Ex. 33:19. In this verse in its context, God was telling Moses that He could choose whom he willed to save from among Israel. That was consistent with what Paul was saying, but it was not consistent with what the Jews were saying.

To say that God saves whom He wills does not settle the case for unconditional election. We simply need to ask, Whom does God will to save? The answer according to 9:30—10:21 is those who exercise faith in Christ.

When Paul says in 9:18, "whom he will he hardeneth," the case is not won for Calvinism. The Calvinistic commentators recognize that "harden" is not the exact opposite of "have mercy on." They seek to give it a meaning like "prepare for destruction" or "treat with severity" (see comments on 9:18).

It is quite evident that Paul deliberately chose "harden" as distinguished from "condemn." There were two groups of Jews: (1) those who were saved and (2) those who were hardened. Those who were hardened are the same as the blinded of 11:7 while those who were saved were the elect of 11:7.

Paul chose the word "harden" because he wanted a word that did not represent a hopeless state. It was a serious state, but not a hopeless one. In a sense it could be said that God hardened the unbelieving Jew. (See comments on hardening in the notes on 9:18.) However, everything that Paul says indicates that it is possible for the Jew to be saved out of this hardness. Yet if they continue to resist God's gospel, they will continue in a state of hardness.

In 9:25-29 Paul quotes from the O.T. to show the Jew that the concept of some Jews being unsaved is well-supported in the O.T. Such passages should have exploded the Jewish concept of unconditional election of all Jews long ago.

When Paul shows, beginning in 9:30, why Jews had not attained righteousness, he does not say that it is because they had the wrong view of unconditional election. He does not say that the proper view of unconditional election is one where God chose some from among the Gentiles and only some from among the Jews. Rather, he says that it is, "Because *they sought it* not by faith, but as it were by the works of the law" (9:32).

The answer to why all Jews were not saved was that instead of their view of unconditional election (or unconditional salvation), salvation is conditional. It is conditioned on faith in Jesus Christ. Paul's burden was not in wishing that God had unconditionally elected more Jews. Rather, it was that more Jews would respond to the whosoever will gospel.

If Paul could ever get the Jews to part with their view of the unconditional election of all Jews, then it would be incumbent upon them to decide what the condition of salvation is. Maybe they could see that it is by faith in Christ. He had bared his soul to them to get them to see this.

The difficulty in chap. 9 and 10 is not for those who believe in conditional election. Rather, the difficulty is for those who feel that these chapters support unconditional election.

Summary 9:30—10:21

Up to this point in chap. 9, Paul had been trying to get the Jews to see that not all Jews were saved by unconditional election through Abraham. Now, he turns to what the real problem was. The real problem was that they had sought righteousness by works of the law rather than by faith.

Paul was deeply burdened for the salvation of the Jews. He wanted them to see that it was not a dark picture for them if they gave up their view of unconditional election. A right standing with God was easily available to them through faith in Christ. It was as simple as believing with the heart and confessing with the mouth the Lord Jesus. This also involved believing in the resurrection of Christ.

The gospel of Christ is a gospel for all. It is for whosoever will—including Jew or Gentile. If people are to call on

Christ, they must believe in Him. If they are to believe in Him, they must hear about Him. If they are to hear about Him, there must be a duly commissioned preacher to herald forth the message. The feet of the herald are beautiful when he brings the good news of peace.

The problem with the Jews was not that they had *not* heard. Rather, it was because they had not believed the gospel they *had* heard. The gospel, by the time of Paul, had gone to all the areas where there were Jews. Paul uses the words of Ps. 19:4 to illustrate this.

The New Covenant (or the faith way) comes to people as a message. The message of the New Covenant comes from Christ.

Israel certainly knew that there would be such a time when there was a great ingathering of Gentiles and Jews would be a mission field for the Gentiles. Their own Scriptures, which they revered, had already pointed this out. The O.T. had clearly shown Israel to be a "disobedient and gainsaying people." Certainly, the Jews from their own Scripture should be able to see the fallacy of the universal salvation of all Jews.

Application: Teaching and Preaching the Passage

1. In this passage Paul gets to the heart of why some Jews were not saved. As was pointed out in the earlier part of chapter 9, the Jews were alarmed at Paul's teaching because he did not agree that God had unconditionally elected all Jews when He called Abraham. Paul did not say, "You are wrong in saying that God unconditionally elected all Jews. The true answer is that He unconditionally elected only some of the Jews." No, that is not what he said. He said that those who had not received the God-provided righteousness had not received it "because they sought it not by faith" (9:31, 32). Salvation is clearly conditional, not unconditional. If salvation is conditional, election is conditional.

2. Paul restates his deep concern for the salvation of the Jews (vv. 1-3). The strongest burden that Paul has in the Book of Romans is his burden for the salvation of the Jews.

3. The righteousness which forms the basis of our justification is not a righteousness which we establish, but a righteousness to which we submit (v. 3). It is given to us.

4. Dependence upon the law way, which was a totally unworkable way to receive righteousness, came to an end with Jesus Christ. The law way could not provide righteousness. Jesus Christ does (vv. 4, 5).

5. Several things are pointed out about this righteousness:

(1) It is readily available (vv. 6-9).

(2) It is on the condition of faith (vv. 4 and 6-11).

(3) It involves a belief in the resurrection (v. 9).

(4) It is offered to whosoever will including both Jews and Gentiles (vv. 11-13).

(5) An aggressive program of worldwide evangelism is needed to proclaim it (vv. 14, 15).

6. Paul's special concern is still with the Jews. As Isaiah said, they have not all believed the report (or the gospel) (v. 16).

7. Verse 17 basically sums up what is said in vv. 14, 15. The faith way (or the New Covenant) comes to people as a message. This message is from God (see notes on this verse).

8. The basic thrust of what Paul is saying in vv. 18-21 is:

(1) The gospel had gone out to the Jewish world at that time (v. 18).

(2) Israel had been well warned in

the O.T. that there would be a time when Gentiles would be used by God to help bring the Jews into a right relationship with God (v. 19).

(3) Israel was clearly told in the O.T. that there would be a time when many Gentiles would come to God (v. 20).

(4) In the light of the quotation from Isaiah in v. 21, it should not surprise the Jews to find out that not all of them were saved.

9. The comments after v. 21 entitled "Summary Observations About Election in Chapters 9 and 10" give a perspective on Paul's contribution to the doctrine of election. It does not take the place of a thorough study of these two chapters.

III. THE PRESENT AND FUTURE OF ISRAEL AND THE GENTILES IN THE PROGRAM OF GOD (11:1-36).

A. Paul Affirms That God Has Not Cast Israel Away (11:1-6).

1 I say then, Hath God cast away his people? God forbid. For I also am an Israelite, of the seed of Abraham, *of* the tribe of Benjamin.

I say then, Hath God cast away his people? God forbid. Then (Greek *oun*) connects with the idea in the previous context about the fact that so many among Israel have not believed the gospel. In light of this Paul raises the question about whether God has cast away His people. This he does so he can emphatically deny it. (See comments on the Greek words for "God forbid" in the notes on 3:4.) The promises made by God in 1 Sam. 12:22; Ps. 94:14; and Jer. 31:37 would be violated if God should cast away His people.

The vast majority of the commentators take the reference here to be to Israel (the seed of Abraham that descended through Jacob). Paul's own personal experience, as an Israelite, is given as the first proof that God has not cast away His people. This appears to be the obvious meaning of Paul's reference to himself. (This view is accepted by Godet 391; Haldane 523; Hamilton 183; Hodge 353; Lenski 678; Moule, *Cambridge Bible* 187; Phillips 166; Plumer 527, 528; and Shedd 329.)

Meyer takes another view. He thinks rather that it is an emotional response. He explains, "For Paul, as a true Israelite of patriotic feeling, cannot in virtue of his theocratic self-esteem, admit that *aposato* [cast off], but can only repel the suggestion with abhorrence" (426).

Alford takes yet another view. Paul's reason for referring to himself in denying that God had cast away Israel was: "that if such a hypothesis were to be conceded, it would exclude from God's kingdom the *writer himself, as an Israelite*" (424).

I take the position that views Paul's case as a proof that God had not cast away Israel. His own salvation was clear evidence that God was still at work among Israelites bringing them into a saving relationship with Himself.

Now the question: What does all of this mean? The most common interpretation is that the casting away of Israel is neither total nor final. It is not total because there is a remnant of saved Jews, and it is not final because God will once again save the mass of Jews, then living, in connection with the second coming of Christ (Alford 424; John Brown 381; Godet 391; Hodge 353; Johnson 154; Phillips 166; and Griffith Thomas 293). Those who hold this view would accept the idea that Israel as a nation is cast away at the present time. However, not all members of the nation have been cast away; thus the casting away is not total. Though the nation has been cast away, that will be remedied in the eschatological future; thus the casting away is not final.

Hamilton has a different view. The essence of his view is as follows: God has not cast away His people [Israel] in the sense of all of them being cast away. However, Israel as a nation has been cast away (183, 184). His comments on 11:26 show that, while believing in the salvation of the mass of Jews in connection with the second coming of Christ, he rejects any concept of a national restoration of Israel (196).

I will give my own view in comments on v. 5.

2 God hath not cast away his people which he foreknew. Wot ye not what the scripture saith of Elias? how he maketh intercession to God against Israel, saying.

God hath not cast away his people which he foreknew. The majority of commentators take "his people which he foreknew" to be the same as "his people" in v. 1 and take the reference to be to the Israel that descended from Abraham through Jacob.

Others give a different interpretation for v. 2. Concerning this interpretation, Hodge explains that it "requires more stress to be laid upon the words *which he foreknew*, as qualifying and distinguishing the preceding phrase, *his people*. 'God has indeed rejected his external people, the Jewish nation as such, but he has not cast away his people whom he foreknew.' According to this view, *his people* means the elect, his spiritual people, or the true Israel" (354). (See also Barnes 237, 238; Calvin 239; and Moule, *Cambridge Bible* 187. For answers to this view, see Cranfield II:545; Murray II:67, 68; and Shedd 329.)

Part of the problem with Hodge's view is that while sticking with the clear message that "God hath not cast away his people which he foreknew" in v. 2, he clouds the issue of v. 1. He says that God has cast away the nation of Israel. This is explained above by the first view as being cast away, but not totally, nor finally. This approach confuses the issue. It is better in both verses to stick with simple negation and say that *God has not cast Israel away.* This thought will be developed more in the comments at the end of v. 5.

God had foreknown Israel as His people. It is unthinkable that He would cast them away.

Wot (know) **ye not what the scripture saith of Elias** (Elijah)**? how he maketh intercession to God against Israel, saying.** The reference here is to the accusation Elijah makes to God against Israel.

3 Lord, they have killed thy prophets, and digged down thine altars; and I am left alone, and they seek my life.

This verse is taken from 1 Kg. 19:10, 14. In v. 14 Elijah repeats again what he had said in v. 10. Murray explains, "Apart from the inversion of order and some abridgement the quotation in verse 3 follows the Hebrew and Greek of the passage concerned" (II:68).

4 But what saith the answer of God unto him? I have reserved to myself seven thousand men, who have not bowed the knee to *the image of* Baal.

But what saith the answer of God unto him? The answer is taken from 1 Kg. 19:18. Murray explains, "The reproduction, though conveying the thought, is modified from both the Hebrew and the Greek in accord with the freedom the apostle applies in other cases" (II:69).

While the picture was dark in Israel, God had preserved a remnant. The picture was brighter than Elijah had supposed.

5 Even so then at this present time also there is a remnant according to the election of grace.

Paul affirms that, just as in the days of Elijah, there is a remnant that was saved. The word for remnant (Greek *leimma*) according to Yeager means, "A small number salvaged from destruction out of a larger number" (76). Lenski explains, "'a portion left,' but the main bulk gone" (683).

The "election of grace" means those who have been chosen by grace, rather than works. The gospel which Paul preached was being effective among the Jews, but it was not saving all Jews.

The fact that Paul would consider valid a gospel that saved only part of the Jews had proved to be of great concern to the Jews. This concern was based on the false assumption on their part that every Jew was unconditionally elected in connection with the covenant God made with Abraham. This is the concern that Paul dealt with in chap. 9 and to some extent in chap. 10.

According to Paul, salvation is conditional rather than unconditional. Salvation was offered to those who descended from Abraham through Jacob on the condition of faith (Gen. 15:6).

The Meaning of Israel Not Being Cast Away

I believe that Paul made a simple and plain denial in vv. 1 and 2, "God has not cast Israel away." If he had meant to say that they had been cast away but not totally and finally, he would have phrased his questions and denials differently.

It is understandable that people have sought to use such qualifications as "not totally" and "not finally." "Their fall" (v. 11), "the fall of them" (v. 12), and "the casting away of them" (v. 15) have no doubt added a touch of confusion. However, in all of these verses Paul is clearly dealing with a "part"—the unbelieving Israelite. In vv. 1 and 2 Paul is dealing with Israel *as Israel*, or to state it more clearly Israel as the Covenant People of God.

What Paul is saying is that *God has not broken His covenant with Israel.* They are still, and will remain, the Covenant People of God. The question of whether they will remain the Covenant People of God is *unconditional.* However, so far as individual participation in the eternal life offered to the Covenant People of God (Gen. 13:14, 15, and 17:8) that is conditioned on faith (Gen. 15:6). This being true, the fact that only a remnant was saved did not in any way violate the covenant that God had made with Abraham. All of the promises that God made to Israel that have not yet been fulfilled will yet be fulfilled.

This approach has a number of important implications which will be developed in the allegory of the olive tree in vv. 17-24.

6 And if by grace, then *is it* no more of works: otherwise grace is no more grace. But if *it be* of works, then is it no more grace: otherwise work is no more work.

And if by grace, then *is it* no more of works: otherwise grace is no more grace. Salvation by works and salvation by grace are two mutually exclusive ideas. If one is true, the other is not true. A choice must be made. For Scripture, the choice is grace.

But if it be of works, then is it no more grace: otherwise work is no more work. While the majority of the Greek manuscripts includes this part of the verse, it is omitted in many. The thought is implied by the first part of the verse. The substance will not be changed whether it is included or excluded.

B. Paul Discusses The Blindness of The Unbelieving Israelites (11:7-10).

7 What then? Israel hath not obtained that which he seeketh for; but the election hath obtained it, and the rest were blinded.

What then? Israel hath not obtained that which he seeketh for. It is obvious that the thought here is essentially the same as that in 9:31 and 10:3. The reference is to those among Israel who sought to establish their own righteousness by works. They were not successful.

But the election hath obtained it. These are the chosen of God. They are those among the Jews who have come to God through faith in Jesus Christ. They have obtained or received that righteousness which is provided by God through Jesus Christ.

And the rest were blinded. The blindness here and the hardness in 9:18 are the same experience. See comments on hardening in connection with that verse. As will be shown in vv. 9, 10, this refers to a judicial hardening by God. The result of the Divine encounter with their resistance was the hardening of their hearts.

8 (According as it is written, God hath given them the spirit of slumber, eyes that they should not see, and ears that they should not hear;) unto this day.

Hodge explains:

> This passage, as is the case in 9:33, is composed of several passages found in the Old Testament. In Isa. 6:9, it is said, 'Hear ye indeed, but understand not; see ye indeed, but perceive not;' ver. 10, 'Lest they see with their eyes, and hear with their ears.' Deut. 29:4, 'Yet the Lord hath not given you an heart to perceive, and eyes to see, and ears to hear, unto this day.' Isa. 29:10, 'For the Lord hath poured upon you the spirit of deep sleep, and hath closed your eyes.' The spirit, and to some extent the language of these passages, Paul cites in support of his argument (357, 358).

That God does work in such a way that spiritual blindness results is clear. That this is a judicial work is clear. What we do not know is how to explain this, to our fullest satisfaction, in keeping with human responsibility. Yet, we know that from God's perspective these concepts are consistent with one another.

The Jews in Paul's day, like those in the times referred to in the O.T., were blinded or hardened. When they were encountered by the message of God's grace, the majority resisted and were hardened. God could not reward this attitude. In a sense it can be said that God hardened them. In a sense it can be said that they hardened themselves. The same can be said by anyone today who resists the gospel. This makes resistance to the gospel dangerous.

9 And David saith, Let their table be made a snare, and a trap, and a stumblingblock, and a recompence unto them:

10 Let their eyes be darkened, that they may not see, and bow down their back alway.

These verses are taken from Ps. 69:22, 23 (LXX). Hodge explains, "The enemies of the Psalmist were the enemies of God; the evils imprecated upon them were imprecated on them as such, and not as enemies of the writer. These denunciations are not the expression of the desire of private revenge, but of the just and certain judgments of God" (358).

Moule comments, "The whole Psalm [69] is full of Messiah—the point of the quotation is that the Psalm indicates a judicial turning of blessings into curses, and a judicial blindness and impotence of the soul, as the way in which retribution would come on Messiah's enemies" (*Cambridge Bible* 190).

A few observations need to be made: (1) God does not take a person who is submissive to Him and decide to harden his heart. (2) God hardens the hearts of those who resist Him. (3) Hardness is a Divine judgment. (4) Hardness, while not to be taken lightly, does not necessarily imply that a person is in a hopeless condition. Paul himself was hardened before his conversion. Many other Jews were saved out of hardness. (5) As a practical observation, many reach the peak of their hardness just before they are brought down by conviction.

C. Paul Discusses God's Purpose in the Fall of the Unbelieving Israelites (11:11).

11 I say then, Have they stumbled that they should fall? God forbid: but *rather* through their fall salvation *is come* unto the Gentiles, for to provoke them to jealousy.

I say then, Have they stumbled that they should fall? God forbid. See comments on 3:4 on "God forbid."

The first point of consideration is the force of "that" (Greek *hina*). There are two views: (1) design or purpose which would mean "in order that" (Hodge 361; and Murray II:26); (2) what Sanday and Headlam refer to as "contemplated result" and would translate "so as to" (320). (See also Cranfield II:554.)

It appears to me that in the context, Divine *purpose* is what Paul is discussing. While v. 11 is based on a broader preceding context, it is particularly raising a question growing out of vv. 8-10. The resistance of the unbelieving Jews to the gospel of grace brought the verdict of judicial hardening from God. This hardness or blindness brought the result of stumbling. In light of this, one might conclude that in Divine purpose the stumbling was an end within itself. That would suggest that God delighted in their fall. Paul abhorred such an idea.

It is usually thought that whether Paul is meaning purpose or design, or contemplated result, that he is dealing with whether the fall of Israel is irrevocable or final (Barrett 212; Cranfield II:555; Hodge 361; and Sanday and Headlam 320). The vast majority who have written commentaries on Romans do not believe that the fall of Israel is final. This is true regardless of what millennial view they may hold. Those of the amillennial persuasion would not accept a national restoration at the second coming of Christ, but many do believe in a mass conversion of Jews in connection with the second coming of Christ. So the issue with most would not be whether the rejection of Israel would be final, as such, but whether that is what Paul is stressing in this verse.

The fact that in the eschatological future there will be a mass conversion of Jews out from the unbelieving ones, I think is made clear in the verses following. However, it does not seem to me that Paul is dealing in this verse with that idea.

As was pointed out above, a person could get the idea that God had designed the hardness or blindness of Israel just so they would fall. It would be as if God wanted them to fall for the sake of their falling. Paul denies such an interpretation. God had other purposes in mind which, as developed in the following verses, show that all of this was ultimately intended to reach unbelieving Jews for Christ.

But *rather* through their fall salvation *is come* unto the Gentiles, for to provoke them to jealousy. The word for fall (Greek-*paraptoma*) is translated only here and in v. 12 as "fall." The other places where it occurs, it is translated "trespass," "offence," "sin," and "fault." Based on the kinship of this (*paraptoma*) with the word fall (Greek *ptaio*) Sanday and Headlam comment, "'by their false step' continuing the metaphor of *eptaisan*" (321). Cranfield says, "The metaphorical uses of *paraptoma* [trespass] were so well established that it seems doubtful whether the literal sense [fall, or false step] would spring at all readily to mind,..It seems preferable, therefore, to translate *paraptoma* 'trespass' rather than to adopt such a rendering as 'false step'" (II:555, 556). In the light of the other uses of *paraptoma* in the N.T. "trespass" is the better translation.

If we take the translation to be "trespass," the trespass is the unbelief on the part of the Jews regarding the gospel. The unbelief of the Jews was the occasion for a more rapid spread of the gospel to the Gentiles (Acts 13:46; 18:6; and 28:28). We are not, however, to suppose that if the Jews had more readily accepted the gospel that the gospel would not have gone to the Gentiles. It did, however, in the early days of the church spread more quickly to the Gentiles as a result of Jewish rejection.

Concerning, "for to provoke them to jealousy," Cranfield explains,

> The coming of salvation to the Gentiles as a result of Israel's rejection of its Messiah is to make Israel jealous in accordance with the words of Deut. 32:21 already quoted in 10:19. When Israel, the people whom God has made peculiarly His own, His special possession, see others the recipients of the mercy and goodness of their God, they will begin to understand what they are missing and to desire that salvation which they have rejected (II:556).

We are not to understand jealousy to have the negative connotations which we attribute to jealousy. Rather, we are to think of it as provoking a desire in the heart of the Jews to want the salvation which they see in the Gentile believers.

Sanford C. Mills, a believing Jew, comments:

> By blinding Jewish eyes and hardening Jewish hearts God has opened the door of heaven to the Gentiles, and has not shut the door to the Jews. The life of the saved Gentile should be so changed, so different, so revolutionized, so diverse from the unregenerate Gentile that even a spiritually-blinded Jew should be able to see the difference. This is what the Gospel will do and must do for every born-again child of God. In this way the blindness and hardness can be removed from the eyes and heart of the unsaved Jew and he, too, will be converted. God is grieved because Israel is dying in her sin. He has extended His invitation, "Say unto

them, as I live, saith the Lord Jehovah, I have no pleasure of the death of the wicked; but that the wicked turn from his way and live; turn ye, turn ye from your evil ways; for why will ye die, O house of Israel?" (Ezekiel 33:11; see also 18:23, 32) (367, 368).

D. Paul Raises the Question of What Influences the Conversion of the Unbelieving Israelites Would Have on the World (11:12-15).

12 Now if the fall of them *be* the riches of the world, and the diminishing of them the riches of the Gentiles; how much more their fulness?

Now if the fall (trespass: see comments on v. 11) **of them *be* the riches of the world.** The meaning here is that the Jewish unbelief of the gospel contributed to a quicker spread of the gospel to the Gentiles. (See comments on v. 11.)

And the diminishing of them the riches of the Gentiles. The Greek word for diminishing (*hettema*) according to Harrison "seems to involve the idea of defeat, both here and in 1 Corinthians 6:7. It is basically a military figure. An army loses the battle because of heavy casualties" (120). This part of the verse restates the essence of the first part of the verse. It is a slightly different way of saying the same thing.

How much more their fulness? Harrison explains,

> The logic of the verse compels us to take it in this sense, that as surely as Israel's defeat (identified with her stumbling) has brought the riches of God's grace to the Gentiles on a large scale, the conversion of Israel to her Messiah (v. 26) will bring even greater blessing to the world. The word 'fulness' refers to the conversion, meaning the full complement in contrast to the remnant. It will mark the end of hardening that now characterizes the nation (120). (In essential agreement are Barrett 214; Hodge 363, 364; Moule, *Cambridge Bible* 195; Murray II:79; and Shedd 366.)

Lenski takes a considerably different view. He applies the "fulness" to that which was already taking place then, and would later, in the Jewish remnant. He explains,

> What he writes is that already *then* and, of course, even after also the Jewish fall and loss must be considered the world's, the Gentiles' riches, then and there and ever after salvation is being broadcast to the whole world, to all Gentiles; and he asks, if this is true, 'by how much more' must not the fulness of salvation attained by the Jewish remnant already then and to be attained after likewise be considered the world's, the Gentiles' riches, this fulness now being devoid of the least trace of Jewish exclusiveness, this fulness sharing the salvation of the Gentiles? (695, 696).

Lenski is an amillennialist. However, not all amillennialists would agree. For example, Hamilton interprets the verse to mean, "if the rejection of the Jews brought good, their full restoration will bring more good" (189).

I take the reference to "their fulness" to be to the conversion of the mass of Jews in the eschatological future. How we interpret it will depend to a large extent on how we interpret vv. 25 and 26. That is where the strongest defense of the position will be. If there will be a mass conversion of Jews in connection with the second coming of

Christ, it stands to reason that this verse has reference to that.

13 For I speak to you Gentiles, inasmuch as I am the apostle of the Gentiles, I magnify mine office:
14 If by any means I may provoke to emulation *them which are* my flesh, and might save some of them.

Paul's burden for the Jews had come across so strongly that he felt he needed to remind his Gentile readers that he had not forgotten he was the apostle to the Gentiles. However, his burden for the Jews is seen even in this reminder to the Gentiles. Even his ministry to the Gentiles was with a hope that the salvation of the Gentiles might make that kind of impact on the Jews which would make them want to be saved. The word for "provoke to emulation" (Greek *parazeloo*) is the same that is translated "provoke to jealousy" in v. 11.

The word for "magnify" (Greek *doxazo*) is usually translated "glorify." The word for "office" (Greek *diakonia*) is understood more frequently to mean "ministry." Cranfield explains, "What he actually says in this sentence is surely most naturally explained as meaning that he honours and reverences his ministry to the Gentiles, and so fulfils it with all his might and devotion, in the hope—though we are not to infer that this is the only motive of his labours—that its success may provoke the Jews to jealousy and so bring about the conversion of some of them" (II:560).

15 For if the casting away of them *be* the reconciling of the world, what *shall* the receiving *of them be,* but life from the dead?

For if the casting away of them *be* the reconciling of the world. This casting away is not of Israel *as Israel*, but of the unbelieving Israelites. This is made clear by the broken off branches in v. 17.

These words are a restatement of what Paul said in the first part of v. 12. "The reconciling of the world" is "the riches of the Gentiles" (see comments on v. 12).

What shall the receiving of them be, but life from the dead? See comments on "their fulness" on v. 12.

Different interpretations have been given for "life from the dead." (1) Some understand this as a reference to the resurrection from the dead. Barrett explains, "Paul means that the final return of Israel (v. 26) will be the signal for the resurrection, the last stage of the eschatological process initiated by the death and resurrection of Jesus. The full conversion of Israel therefore stands on the boundary of history" (215). (See also Black 144; Bruce 216; Cranfield II:562, 563; Liddon 207; Meyer 437, 438; and Sanday and Headlam 325, 326. See Cranfield for a developed argument.)

(2) Others take "life from the dead" to refer to a world-wide spiritual awakening. The thought is that if there was a great ingathering of Gentiles, as believers, that followed the unbelief of the Jews, something far greater must follow the mass conversion of the Jews in the eschatological future (Barnes 248; David Brown 259; Denney 679; Godet 404; Harrison 121; Hodge 365, 366; Johnson 158; Mills 371; Moule 193; Murray II:81-84; Plumer 542; Shedd 337; and Thomas 295).

(3) Lenski gives yet another view. He explains, "Every Jew whom Paul converts he regards as 'life from the dead' (see 6:13 on this phrase). To be rescued from a nation that is so obdurate, so hardened (v. 7), again to be received by

God through the gospel is like 'life from the dead' (Ezek. 37:1-10)" (701). Hamilton's view seems to be similar (191). This view would have an ongoing fulfillment of this part of v. 15 rather than have it await fulfillment in the eschatological future.

The first view, which interprets "life from the dead" to refer to the resurrection, would be favored by most amillennialists. The third view, of course, is also an amillennial view. The second view is favored by both pre- and postmillennialists. They would, of course, interpret the details differently. I see this view as the correct view. It fits the thrust of the passage better. It seems that Paul is saying, "If the fall of the unbelieving Jews was the occasion of the conversion of many Gentiles, how much greater will be the effect when the mass of unbelieving Jews are converted in the eschatological future!" The resurrection of the body cannot be considered the effect of the conversion of the Jews. World-wide revival could be considered the effect of their conversion. This would parallel "through their fall salvation is come unto the Gentiles" (v. 11). We should also keep in mind Murray's words against the interpretation that refers to the resurrection. He explains, "Nowhere else does 'life from the dead' refer to the resurrection and its closest parallel 'alive from the dead' (6:13) refers to spiritual life" (II:83).

E. Paul Discusses the Nature of Israel and the Relationship Between Israel and the Gentiles Through the Allegory of the Olive Tree (11:16-24).

16 For if the firstfruit *be* holy, the lump *is* also *holy:* and if the root *be* holy, so *are* the branches.

For if the firstfruit *be* holy, the lump is also holy. Bruce explains, "The allusion is probably to Numbers 15:17-21, where the Israelites are commanded to offer to God a cake from the dough of the first-ground flour, newly come from the threshing-floor. The presentation of this cake to God hallows the whole baking" (216).

And if the root be holy, so are the branches. This introduces the allegory of the olive tree. An allegory is an extended metaphor as distinguished from a parable which is an extended simile.

The big question in this verse is, Who is intended by the "firstfruit" and the "root"? Some take the position that the firstfruit and the root are not to be applied to the same thing. Those who take this approach usually take the "firstfruit" to be to the believing Jewish remnant and the "root" to refer to the patriarchs (Bruce 217; Cranfield II:564, 565; and Harrison 121).

Others understand the figurative reference of both the "firstfruit" and the "root" to be the same. They take the reference to be to the patriarchs Abraham, Isaac, and Jacob (Godet 404, 405; Hodge 366, 367; Lenski 703; Murray II:85; Sanday and Headlam 326; Shedd 337, 338; Stifler 151; and Thomas 295).

As I see it, the second view is correct. There is no reason to think that the remnant would be able to convey any spiritual quality to the mass of Jews. However, there is reason to believe that such could be conveyed from the patriarchs. This is not because of them as individuals, but their place in the establishment of the covenant. Those who are properly related to them through the covenant that God made with Abraham will experience the salvation promised in the Abrahamic Covenant (Gen. 13:14, 15, and 17:8).

17 And if some of the branches

be broken off, and thou, being a wild olive tree, wert graffed in among them, and with them partakest of the root and fatness of the olive tree.

And if some of the branches be broken off. The broken off branches are the unbelieving Jews.

And thou, being a wild olive tree, wert graffed in among them. The wild olive tree refers to the Gentiles. However, we are not to think of the wild olive tree itself being grafted into the tree. Rather, they were grafted in as individual branches.

And with them partakest of the root and fatness of the olive tree. This is, in my opinion, one of the most important statements in the book. This is especially true with regard to the relationship of Gentile believers to Israel. In commenting on the comparisons in v. 16 Godet explains, "It follows from these two comparisons, that to obtain salvation the Jewish people had only to remain on the soil where they were naturally rooted, while the salvation of the Gentile demands a complete transplantation" (405).

Godet further explains:

> As there mounts up from the root into the whole tree a fruitful and unctuous sap which pervades all its branches, so the blessing assured to Abraham (*he eulogia tou Abraam,* Gal. 3:14) remains inherent in the national life of Israel, and is even communicated by believing Jews to those of the Gentiles who become children of the patriarch by faith; comp. Gal. 3:5-9. . . .The fact is, that in the view of Paul, as in that of the Twelve, the believers of Israel are the nucleus round which are grouped the converts from among the Gentiles, and God's ancient people, consequently, the flock with which the Gentiles are incorporated. 'I have yet other sheep, said Jesus (John 10:16), who are not of this fold; them also I must bring, and there shall be one flock, one Shepherd.' Excepting the figure, the thought is identical with our passage (406).

The Allegory of the Olive Tree

The Olive Tree As Israel

I take the position that the olive tree is Israel (cf. Jer. 11:16, 17; and Hos. 14:6). This is based on the Gentiles being called "a wild olive tree" which is apparently in contrast to Israel as the domesticated olive tree (v. 17). Also, v. 24 raises the possibility of the unbelieving branches (Jews) being grafted back into "their own olive tree." (Among those who take the position that the olive tree is Israel are Bruce 218; Harrison 121; Mills 374; and Murray II:85.) Those who take Israel to be the olive tree will probably not agree with all of my thoughts related to the olive tree though some interesting common ground may be seen.

In the discussion on v. 5 concerning whether Israel has been cast away, the position was taken that Israel has not been cast away. In addition to that being the necessary conclusion based on vv. 1, 2, I believe that it is also established by the illustration of the olive tree. The olive tree (Israel) has been severely pruned, but it has not been either cut down or dug up. *The pruning and grafting is done to a tree of prior existence which continues to exist. Israel continues to exist and is the tree into which Gentile branches have been grafted and "with them partakest of the root and fatness of the olive tree"* (v. 17).

It should be observed that this

describes a *conjunctive* relationship between the N.T. Church and O.T. Israel as distinguished from a *disjunctive* relationship. There are two views which take a disjunctive view: (1) Some amillennialists take the position that Israel was totally and finally rejected. The Church, while not a continuation of Israel, takes the place of Israel and may be called Israel. (2) Dispensationalists take the position that, at the present time, Israel has been cast off. The Church cannot be called Israel. There is no continuity between the O.T. Israel and the N.T. Church.

The conjunctive relationship between the O.T. Israel and the N.T. Church is evident in Eph. 2:11-19:

The Past (Prior to The Coming of Christ) Condition of Gentiles

1. "Aliens from the commonwealth of Israel" (Eph. 2:12).
2. "Strangers from the covenants of promise" (Eph. 2:12).
3. "Sometimes were afar off" (Eph. 2:13).

The Present Condition of Gentiles

1. "Made nigh by the blood of Christ" (Eph. 2:13).
2. One with Israel in the body (Eph. 2:14,15).
3. "Ye are no more strangers and foreigners" (Eph. 2:19).
4. "Fellowcitizens with the saints, and of the household of God" (Eph. 2:19).

In Eph. 2:11-22 Paul is contrasting the Gentiles' relationship with Israel now with what it had been in the past. In the past they were alienated from Israel. They were not partakers with Israel of the promises. Now, by the blood of Christ, this condition has been changed. They are no more strangers and foreigners, but fellowcitizens with the household of God (Israel) and partakers of the same body. Harrison is observing the same truth when he says, "Here we may consider with profit what the apostle says in Ephesians 2:11-22. The Gentiles, once aliens and foreigners, are now fellow citizens with God's people and members of God's household. The two are made one in Christ" (121).

Mills, a believing Jew, makes some interesting comments. He remarks:

> Notice that the branches of the wild olive tree were grafted in *among* them, not *instead* of them. This is a further elaboration of Romans 11:5, 7. The faithful remnant was bearing fruit. If there had not been a remnant, the Gentiles would never have heard the Gospel. It was the Jewish Christians who preached the Gospel to the Gentiles. They (the Gentiles) were 'grafted in among them,' and they (Gentiles) became a 'partaker with them.' In other words, the Gentile at his conversion was spiritually grafted into the good olive tree and became a *part*-taker, not an *all*-taker, with the Jewish believers. Jewish and Gentile believers became one. They partook of the root, Abraham (Romans 4), and of the fatness (of the righteousness which is by faith, Romans 4:3) of the good olive tree (373, 374).

Murray's comments are instructive. He explains, "Gentiles are reminded that they draw all the grace they enjoy from the tree whose root is Israel's patriarchs. Gentiles and Jews partake together of the privilege that stems from the same root. This same lesson is pressed home forcibly in verse 18: 'it is not thou that bearest the root, but the root thee'" (II:86).

Bruce's comment is also helpful at this point. He explains, "The new life which enables them to produce fruit for God is the life of the old stock Israel on which they have been grafted. Israel owes no debt to them; they are indebted to Israel" (218).

Munck's comments support the conjunctive relationship between the O.T. Israel and the N.T. Church when he says, "The image of the olive tree shows, as is pointed out by *Sanday and Headlam, Lietzmann,* and *Nygren,* that God's people are one and the same throughout the ages. Branches may be broken off and new branches grafted onto the trunk, but the tree remains to draw up sap from its holy root. The new Israel of the church is thus a continuation of the original Israel" (128).

This is the sum of the matter. God made a covenant with Abraham promising eternal life to Abraham and his seed (Gen. 13:14, 15, and 17:8). (See comments on "The Abrahamic Covenant and the Inheritance of Abraham and His Seed" in notes on 4:13.) The Mosaic Covenant and the Davidic Covenant served to help amplify and bring to pass the promises made in the Abrahamic Covenant. The New Covenant is and will be the fulfillment of that which is promised to Israel in the Abrahamic Covenant.

It should be observed that none of these covenants were made with Gentiles. Paul points out in 9:5 that the covenants belong to Israel. Also, in Eph. 2:12 Paul in speaking of the past times of the Gentiles referred to them as "strangers from the covenants of promise."

What we see unfolding before us in Romans is that though no covenants of promise were made with the Gentiles, yet there is an arrangement whereby they can partake of the salvation promise made in the Abrahamic Covenant. By being grafted into the olive tree, Gentile believers partake of the salvation that God promised to the seed of Abraham; in fact, they become the seed of Abraham. Since the olive tree is Israel, Gentile believers become members of Israel. It is better to say that the Gentiles are saved the same way the Jews are than to say the Jews are saved the same way Gentiles are. As Jesus said, "Salvation is of the Jews" (Jn. 4:22).

I am aware that many strongly disagree with any identification of the Church with Israel. They say that the Church is never called Israel. It is debatable whether the "Israel of God" in Gal. 6:16 refers to the Church.

Let me say, first of all, that in identifying the Church with Israel, I am not robbing Israel of its identification as the seed of Abraham that descended through Jacob. If we take that identification away from Israel, we have destroyed it. There is no redemptive covenant with an Israel that did not descend from Abraham through Jacob.

That is why we cannot tolerate any such idea that God has cast away Israel (the seed of Abraham through Jacob). *If God had cast away Israel, it would be the termination of redemption. There is no redemptive covenant with anyone else.* The only people who are saved are believing descendants of Abraham through Jacob, and those who have been grafted in with them into the olive tree.

Gentiles who have been grafted into the olive tree are Jews in the same way that adopted members of a family are members of a family. While they cannot trace their ancestry through the family, they are real members of the family. (I am not saying that this is the meaning of adoption in the N.T. I am simply referring to adoption to illustrate my point.)

The line of thought which I have

developed gives the reason Paul labored so hard in Gal. 3 and Rom. 4 to point out that Gentile believers are the seed of Abraham. *We are not called seed simply because we have imitated Abraham's faith. We are called seed because we are members of Abraham's family.*

Now, let's deal with the point that unless Gal. 6:16 calls the Church Israel, the Church is not called Israel in the N.T. *Gentile believers are called the seed of Abraham in Rom. 4 and Gal. 3. That is the more basic term. Israel is the Covenant People of God because they are the Covenant Seed of Abraham. Being the seed of Abraham in its deepest and truest sense is what counts. That is why Paul spent his time on that. The Covenant Seed of Abraham is Israel. When it is clear that Gentile believers are a part of the Covenant Seed of Abraham, then it follows that they are a part of Israel. All believers make up the Church. All believers are Israel. It follows that the Church is Israel. Remember, it is not that the Church takes the place of Israel. Israel in its deepest and truest sense is the Church.* It is probably better to say that Israel is the Church than to say that the Church is Israel.

A word now needs to be said about how the "casting away" of v. 15 fits in all of this. Based on what is said above, I must reject the idea that Israel, as Israel, has been cast away. It is the unbelieving branches that have been cast away. The pruning off of most of the branches is far different from cutting the tree down.

The olive tree was unpruned until the pruning took place in regard to the unbelief toward Jesus as the Messiah. We are not to suppose that these were believers who had become unbelievers. All of this raises the question: What exactly is this pruning off of the unbelieving branches?

Before the time of Christ, there was not a clearcut outward division between the believing and unbelieving in Israel. In connection with the rejection of Jesus as the Messiah on the part of most Jews a cleavage took place between the believing and the unbelieving Jews. The unbelieving Jews stayed with the synagogues. The believing Jews went with the Church.

The unbelieving Jews are cast off in that they are outside the avenue of God's redemptive ministry which is the Church. God has not broken His covenant with them, but they have not met the condition required for personal salvation. It is still their covenant. All they have to do is believe.

The believing Jews have met the condition of the covenant for salvation. They are in the Church, which is the instrument of God's redemptive ministry. The time will come in the eschatological future when unbelieving Jews who will be living at that time will in mass turn to Jesus as their Messiah and will be grafted back into the olive tree.

It is a mistake, as some do, to consider the unbelieving Jews as the real Israel and the believing Jews as if they have become Gentiles. That reverses what Paul said in 9:6. The unbelievers are those who are "Israel" and "not Israel." The believing Jews are those who are "of Israel" and "are Israel." Believing Jews are clearly "true Israel."

If we follow through with my position that Israel has not been cast off, the situation about the New Covenant is cleared up. The New Covenant has been established with Israel (Heb. 8:6-13). It is a conditional covenant. Only those who believe have experienced the salvation offered in the New Covenant. Gentiles, by faith in Christ, can come in with the Jewish believers and partake of the blessings of their covenant. The inclusion of the masses, into the Covenant implied in Heb. 8:11, awaits the eschatological future.

The Olive Tree As The Church

Among those who take the olive tree to be the Church rather than Israel are Hamilton (192); Hodge (368); Moule, *Romans* (194, 195); and Sanday and Headlam (327). Sometimes what the holders of this view say sounds a lot like what I say. However, it is a different view. A major difference seems to be that the distinction of Israel as Israel is more pronounced in my view, while in this view Israel is overshadowed by the Church. Perhaps that is what Hamilton is saying when he says, "The Gentile Christians were not made a part of the Jewish nation but with the church of God" (192).

My view and the view of many who take the olive tree to be the Church is that there is a *conjunctive* relationship between the O.T. Israel and the N.T. Church. Some who take the olive tree to be the Church see a *disjunctive* relationship between the O.T. Israel and the N.T. Church. It appears that Moule, *Romans* (184) would fit this category.

The Olive Tree As The Place of Blessing

Others, especially dispensationalists, believe "the olive tree" is the place of blessing. They are particularly strong on denying any identification between Israel and the Church. There would be a disjunctive relationship between the O.T. Israel and the N.T. Church. It should be obvious why they would reject my view of Israel as the olive tree, and the view that makes the olive tree the Church. Among those who hold this view are Newell (421) and Ryrie (*The Basis of Premillennial Faith* 66).

McQuilkin refers to an illustration used by G. Allen Fleece which illustrates the disjunctive relationship between the O.T. Israel and the N.T. Church. He explains:

> Many who have been zealous to maintain rights of Israel in obtaining the blessing promised in the Old Testament have taught that the church had nothing to do with Israel. They illustrated by saying that Israel was like the train on the track of redemption which was switched to a side track. A new train called the Church, a mystery never mentioned in the Old Testament, is now on the track. When the Church is raptured, and Christ returns, this train Israel, on the side track, will be switched back on the main track (131).

McQuilkin goes on to say, "Dr. Fleece has now changed his illustration, and says that the same train is on the same track, but many passengers, namely, the Gentiles, have boarded the train" (132). This illustrates the conjunctive relationship between the O.T. Israel and the N.T. Church.

The only verse that has presented any problem to me concerning a conjunctive relationship between the O.T. Israel and the N.T. Church is Mt. 21:43 where Jesus in speaking to the chief priests and Pharisees said, "The kingdom of God shall be taken from you, and given to a nation bringing forth the fruits thereof." The answer seems to be found in the fact that Jesus was addressing the Jewish *leaders*, not the nation *as such.* The leadership in the N.T. Church (Israel) has been largely from Gentile believers. Or, Jesus might have meant that the kingdom of God was to be taken away from them as *unbelieving* Jews, distinguished from believing Jews.

18 Boast not against the

branches. But if thou boast, thou bearest not the root, but the root thee.

This verse is addressed to the Gentile believers. Since there were more Gentile Christians than Jewish Christians, it would be easy for the Gentile believers to develop the wrong attitude.

In the event there was still a misunderstanding on the part of the Gentile believer, Paul says, "thou bearest not the root, but the root thee." The Gentile believer owes his salvation to the Jews, not vice versa. (See comments on v. 17 including the notes on "Israel As The Olive Tree.")

Mills, a believing Jew, makes some interesting comments:

> The Jewish Christian is not grafted into a Gentile Church. To a Jewish Christian the Church has become a Gentile Christian Church in its thinking and concept. It is a Church with the Jews left out. The Gentile who becomes a believer in the Jewish Messiah and accepts Christ as his Saviour, is grafted into the Church, the Body of Christ. If there could be boasting it would have to be on the part of the Jewish Christian since, "Salvation is from the Jews" (John 4:22). We must not forget that the Jewish nation, collectively and individually, is what Paul calls the natural good branches of the tree! Only some of the natural branches have been broken off. The stock is not sterile. It is still drawing the living sap and distributing it among the branches (374).

19 Thou wilt say then, The branches were broken off, that I might be graffed in.

As Cranfield points out, this verse "exposes the logic behind such Gentile boasting. 'Branches were broken off in order that I may be grafted in'—that is how a self-complacent egotism sees the matter. And to such an egotist this half-truth seems conclusive proof of his own superior importance and a sufficient justification for his contemptuous attitude" (II:568).

20 Well; because of unbelief they were broken off, and thou standest by faith. Be not highminded, but fear.

The pruned out branches were not broken off so the Gentile branches could be grafted into the olive tree. The reason they were broken off was unbelief. It was a by-product (not end-product) of their being broken off which led to the gospel being taken to the Gentiles. The Gentile believers were saved by faith; this did not indicate any personal superiority to the branches that were broken off. There was no personal ground for boasting. It behooved the Gentiles to fear instead of give way to an inflated estimate of their importance.

21 For if God spared not the natural branches, *take heed* lest he also spare not thee.

Paul warned the Gentile believers lest calamity befall them as it had befallen the Jewish unbelievers. If they would cease to believe they would not be spared. Their continued salvation depends on continued believing.

22 Behold therefore the goodness and severity of God: on them which fell, severity; but toward thee, goodness, if thou continue in *his* goodness: otherwise thou also shalt be cut off.

Paul reminds the Gentiles that God is capable of both goodness and severity. Holiness requires that God judge sin and unbelief. Therefore, He judged the unbelieving Jews. The Gentiles were beneficiaries of God's goodness (kindness) because they had believed in Jesus Christ. They will continue to benefit from God's goodness if they continue to believe. Otherwise, they will be cut off.

23 And they also, if they abide not still in unbelief, shall be graffed in: for God is able to graff them in again.

It was important for Gentile believers to be reminded that the Jewish situation was not non-reversible. If they would become believers, God would graft them back into the olive tree.

24 For if thou wert cut out of the olive tree which is wild by nature, and wert graffed contrary to nature into a good olive tree: how much more shall these, which be the natural *branches*, be graffed into their own olive tree?

It should be far easier for the Gentiles to believe that the broken off branches could be grafted back into their own olive tree than that the Gentiles were grafted into the tree. The Gentile graft was contrary to nature by grafting a wild olive branch into the domesticated olive tree.

F. Paul Discusses The Eschatological Future of Israel (11:25-27).

25 For I would not, brethren, that ye should be ignorant of this mystery, lest ye should be wise in your own conceits; that blindness in part is happened to Israel, until the fulness of the Gentiles be come in.

For I would not, brethren, that ye should be ignorant of this mystery. Concerning the word mystery (Greek *musterion*), Shedd explains, "not in the pagan sense of an esoteric doctrine known only to the initiated, but in the Christian sense of a doctrine that requires a divine revelation in order to be known" (346). The content of the mystery which is revealed is the fact that the blindness of Israel, which is now in part, will in the eschatological future be removed.

Lest ye should be wise in your own conceits. Paul is speaking out against wisdom that would have developed from within themselves. Such wisdom is really not wisdom. Their knowledge needed to be that which was given by Divine revelation. The knowledge of the truth about Israel's blindness in part and the removal of that blindness would help the Gentile believers have a proper perspective on their relationship to Israel. This would in turn help with their attitude.

That blindness in part is happened to Israel, until the fulness of the Gentiles be come in. The expression, "the fulness of the Gentiles" is not easy to interpret. It has been interpreted in different ways. Most have interpreted it to mean "the full number of Gentiles." It is not clear always what a commentator means by this. Some take it to mean the complete number of Gentiles that God has planned to be saved (at least in this age). Others take it to mean the number of Gentiles to be saved required to make up for the void left by the Jews who were pruned out of the olive tree. (For those who take the meaning to be "the full number of Gentiles" see Briscoe 211; Cranfield II:575; Gifford 198; Hamilton 196;

Hendriksen 378; Lenski 720; Plumer 552; and Sanday and Headlam 335. Not all would agree with Sanday and Headlam in making the "full completed number" mean "the Gentile world as a whole.")

A second view removes the emphasis from the *number* of individuals and takes the emphasis to be on nations—when the gospel has been preached in and perhaps successful in all nations (Alford 435; Barnes 253; Godet 410; Lange 369, 370; and Moule, *Cambridge Bible* 199).

A third view (which may be a modification of the second view) does not stress nations as such, but lays stress on extensive success among Gentiles so far as gospel outreach is concerned (Denney 683; Hodge 374; Munck 135; Murray II:95, 96; and Shedd 347). Johnson, whose view would be with this group, says, "It seems better to understand 'fulness of the Gentiles' to indicate some sort of sweeping revival in the future resulting in the conversion of most of the Gentiles just prior to the great harvest of the Jews" (162).

It is hard to be dogmatic on the meaning of "the fulness of the Gentiles," but it seems to me that a fourth view is the correct one. "The fulness of the Gentiles" seems to refer to the completion of the time of Gentile dominance. Gentiles have been on the center stage in the program of redemption rather than the descendants of Abraham through Jacob. The end of the present age will mark the end of this dominance, and Israel will again be given the position of dominance in God's program of redemption. There is some agreement between my position and that of David Brown (261) and Phillips (176).

This verse sets the stage for interpreting the next verse. The blindness in part of Israel will be removed when the fullness of the Gentiles has come to pass.

26 And so all Israel shall be saved: as it is written, There shall come out of Sion the Deliverer, and shall turn away ungodliness from Jacob:
27 For this *is* my covenant unto them, when I shall take away their sins.

And so all Israel shall be saved. The vast majority who have written commentaries understand the reference here to be to the Israel that descended from Jacob. They understand that at a time in the eschatological future the mass of Jews will be converted. This is true regardless of what millennial view the author holds. Out of 36 commentaries investigated, which made a position clear, 31 took this position. (Among those are Alford 435; Barnes 254; Barrett 223, 224; David Brown 261; Bruce 221, 222; Cranfield II:576, 577; Denney 683; Gifford 199; Godet 411; Hamilton 196; Harrison 123; Hodge 374; Johnson 163; Lange 370; Liddon 217; Mills 386; Munck 136; Murray II:96-98; Philipps 177; Plumer 553; Sanday and Headlam 335; Shedd 348; and Wuest 199, 200.) The vast majority do not understand "all" in "all Israel" to refer to every individual Jew living at the time. However, Haldane (541) and Meyer (448) do not allow for limitation. A clear example of an "all" that is less than absolute is found in Mt. 3:5. I do not think we are to understand that every Jew living then will be saved. Rather, the mass of them will be saved.

This view seems to be the true view. What it says has already been necessarily implied in the preceding verses. Verses 23 and 24 had already talked about the possibility of unbelieving Jews becoming believers and being grafted back into their own olive tree. Verse 25 had already necessarily implied that an end was coming for the blindness in part that had happened to Israel. There is no doubt about it. The Israel in view in v. 25 is the Israel that descended from Jacob. The stage is too clearly set to deny that Israel in v. 26 is that Israel which descended from Jacob; Paul certainly means that the time will come when the mass of them will be saved. (For those who are interested in reading some helpful treatments of this view I recommend Bruce 221, 222; Cranfield II:576, 577; Gifford 199; Mills 386, 387; Murray II:96-98; and Sanday and Headlam 335.)

Another view takes the reference to be to the Israel that descended from Jacob, but rejects the concept of a mass conversion of Jews in the eschatological future. The reference is to the *elect* Jews. Just as v. 25, according to the holders of this view, refers to the end of God's saving work among the Gentiles, so v. 26 marks the end of God's saving work among the Jews. "All Israel" refers to all the elect of all ages. (For supporters of this view, see Hendriksen 381, 382; Lenski 725-727; and Olshausen 375.) The previous context (discussed above) is contrary to this view. The truth that the mass of Israel will one day be saved would be taught by vv. 23-25 even if this verse were not given. Also as Murray says, "While it is true that all the elect of Israel, the true Israel, will be saved, this is so necessary and patent a truth that to assert the same here would have no particular relevance to what is the apostle's governing interest in this section of the epistle" (II:97).

Calvin takes the position that the word *Israel* extends to all the people of God (both Jewish and Gentile believers). This verse would mark the end of God's redemptive ministry among both Gentiles and Jews, thus all Israel (Jews and Gentiles) *will have been saved,* (255). To say that all Israel is not restricted to those who descended from Jacob, I take to be in obvious contradiction to the preceding context, especially v. 25.

As it is written, There shall come out of Sion (Zion) **the Deliverer, and shall turn *away* ungodliness from Jacob.** Certainly, the "Jacob" in this part of the verse is the "Israel" in the first part of the verse. Concerning the quotation in vv. 26, 27, Shedd explains: "The citation [in v. 26] is given freely from the Septuagint of Isa. 59:20"; "V. 27 is cited freely from the Septuagint of Isa. 59:21, in combination with a clause from Isa. 27:9" (348, 349).

For those who take the position that "all Israel" is the elect Jews of all ages, and those who take the reference to be to all the people of God, the coming of Christ referred to here would be the first coming since the salvation referred to is going on now (Hendriksen 383 and Lenski 729). Those who look for a mass conversion of Jews in connection with the second coming of Christ will take the reference to be primarily (or altogether) to the second coming of Christ.

For this *is* my covenant unto them, when I shall take away their sins. In the light of Jer. 31:31-34, we know that this is the New Covenant. The first phase, which deals with the initial establishment of the New Covenant at Christ's first coming, has already been established with Israel. (See comments on v. 17 on "The Olive Tree As Israel.") The second phase depends upon the first phase but relates to its numerical extension to include all Israel. This will take place in the eschatological future (Jer. 31:34).

G. Paul Discusses God's Attitude Toward Israel (Including the Unbelieving Branches) (11:28, 29).

28 As concerning the gospel, *they are* enemies for your sakes: but as touching the election, *they are* beloved for the fathers' sakes.

As concerning the gospel, they are enemies for your sakes. It was not *designed* so that they would be enemies for the sake of the Gentiles. Rather, it *worked out* that way. Their unbelief was the occasion of a more rapid spread of the gospel to the Gentiles (see comments on v. 11).

But as touching the election, *they are* beloved for the fathers' sakes. The "election" referred to here is not the elect among Israel. Rather, it refers to the nation of Israel as the elect or chosen nation. Through the call and covenant of Abraham, Israel became God's chosen people or the Covenant People of God. Regardless of what they have done, they still remain loved as the Covenant People of God. God is still working among them. The Abrahamic Covenant is still valid and forever will be.

The reference to the "fathers" is to the patriarchs Abraham, Isaac, and Jacob. God still remembers His covenant which He made with them.

29 For the gifts and calling of God *are* without repentance.

God breaks no covenants. If a covenant is unconditional, it remains unconditional. If it is conditional, it remains conditional. Israel is and forever will remain the Covenant People of God.

H. Paul Shows How the Conversion of Gentiles Is Designed to Bring About the Conversion of the Jews (11:30-32).

30 For as ye in times past have not believed God, yet have now obtained mercy through their unbelief.

For as ye in times past have not believed God. The reference here is the time from the call of Abraham to the preaching of the gospel to the Gentiles. During this time Gentiles were outside the sphere of God's redemptive ministry. With few exceptions, growing out of encounters with Israel, they did not believe in Yahweh.

Yet have now obtained mercy through their unbelief. The unbelief of the bulk of the Jews caused the gospel to be taken more quickly to the Gentiles.

31 Even so have these also now not believed, that through your mercy they also may obtain mercy.

This verse repeats again what Paul had said in vv. 11-14. As the unbelieving Jews saw what God was doing through saving Gentiles, that would make the Jews want what the Gentiles have (see comments on vv. 11-14).

32 For God hath concluded them all in unbelief, that he might have mercy upon all.

For God hath concluded them all in unbelief (or disobedience). In 1:18—3:20 Paul established this point. God judges the whole world as guilty before Him. This includes both Jews and Gentiles.

That he might have mercy upon all. God's desire with fallen man has always been that he might be saved. This includes both Jews and Gentiles. God will judge and condemn to eternal punishment if people do not come to

Christ by faith. However, He declares guilt and judgment now with the hope that men will repent; He is not gleefully waiting to send people to Hell. On the word "all," Bruce explains, "That is, upon all without distinction rather than all without exception" (224).

I. Paul Glories in the Wisdom of God (11:33-36).

33 O the depth of the riches both of the wisdom and knowledge of God! how unsearchable *are* his judgments, and his ways past finding out!

Paul reached this point in the epistle bursting with emotion. He was in high praise of God's wisdom, knowledge, judgments, and ways. God's glory is so great that we cannot fully grasp it. It was amazing to Paul how the heart of God is so set on turning events and circumstances into bringing about the salvation of people from among both Jews and Gentiles.

34 For who hath known the mind of the Lord? or who hath been his counselor?

Bruce calls this verse, "An echo of Isa. 40:13" (224). Paul is still in a high state of elation. No one has known the mind of God except as God has made such knowledge possible. Even that which is revealed to us is not always fully grasped by us.

In our vain moments, we may wish we could counsel God. That may be what we sometimes mistakenly call praying. God is the Counselor. He is counseled by no one.

35 Or who hath first given to him, and it shall be recompensed unto him again?

Bruce calls this verse, "An echo of Job 41:11" (224). God is in debt to no man. All men are in debt to God. That which obligates God to man is not something that man does that makes God owe him something. Rather, it is the faithfulness of God to His promises. God has promised to save those who believe in Christ. To believe in Christ does not make God in debt to us, but He is obligated to save us because His holiness obligates Him to fulfill His promises.

36 For of him, and through him, and to him, *are* all things: to whom *be* glory for ever. Amen.

God is the ultimate source of all things either directly or indirectly. He is the Creator and the Sustainer of the universe and its inhabitants. He is the Originator and the One who implements the plan of redemption. He is the giver of "every good and perfect gift" (Js. 1:17). He is worthy of all glory and praise.

Summary 11:1-36

From what had been said in chapters 9 and 10, it was possible for a misunderstanding to develop. In order to clear up this misunderstanding, Paul raised a question about whether God had cast Israel away. His answer was an emphatic, "No!" For God to cast Israel away would mean, not simply that He was chastising them, but that He had broken His covenant with them. That He would not do.

Paul's own salvation was living proof that God was in a covenant relationship with Israel. So was the presence of a remnant that had been saved by trusting in Jesus Christ. God had entered into a covenant with Israel promising them eternal life (Gen. 13:14,

15, and 17:8) on the condition of faith (Gen. 15:6). Paul and the remnant were living proof of the fact that God was still honoring that covenant.

The facts are that a large part of Israel had sought righteousness the wrong way and were blinded. The remnant (the election of grace) had responded with faith in Jesus Christ and were saved.

The blindness on the part of most in Israel was in a sense a Divine judgment (or judicial hardening). When God's work with them was encountered by resistance, hardening took place. This was all in accord with what David had said in the Psalms.

Israel has not been cast away. That would have been the end of redemption. All redemptive Covenants were made with Israel. While it is true that Israel has not been cast away, it is also true that the unbelieving ones have "fallen" or have "been cast away." They have been pruned out of the Olive Tree.

All of this about Israel's falling could have been misunderstood, so Paul talks about it to clear matters up. He raised the question, "Have they stumbled just so they might fall?" Or was their fall an end within itself? Paul denies this. Their fall had furnished the occasion for a more rapid spread of the gospel to the Gentiles. The spread of the gospel to the Gentiles had another purpose. It was designed to make the Jews want what the Gentiles have and thus would help bring about their salvation.

Paul raises a question: "If their fall has been the riches of the world (or the salvation of the Gentiles) how much greater will be the result when the mass of the Jews get saved?"

Paul again reminds the Gentiles how he is hoping that the salvation of Gentiles will be the occasion of the salvation of Jews. He again points out that if such a great blessing came when they were cast away, how much greater will it be when the mass of the Jews get saved in the eschatological future.

Paul now resorts to the allegory of the Olive Tree to show the Gentiles their indebtedness to Jews. The root of the Olive Tree refers to the patriarchs Abraham, Isaac, and Jacob and the covenant that God made with them. This is the basic redemptive covenant, and is important both to Jews and Gentiles. That is why Paul labored so hard in chap. 4 to show that Gentile believers are the seed of Abraham.

Paul goes on to point out that the Gentiles have been brought into the Olive Tree, which is Israel. That makes Gentile believers partakers "of the root and fatness" of the Olive Tree. That means that Gentiles partake of the salvation promises made in the Abrahamic Covenant (Gen. 13:14, 15, and 17:8). As Jesus said, "Salvation is of the Jews" (Jn. 4:22).

Paul warns Gentiles that "thou bearest not the root, but the root thee." They owed a debt of gratitude to Israel in this regard, rather than Israel being in debt to them. He warns the Gentiles against highmindedness. They could suffer the same fate suffered by the unbelieving Jews. Also, things can turn around for the Jews. If they continue not in unbelief, they will be grafted back into their own olive tree.

Paul goes on to point out that the "blindness in part which has happened to Israel" will come to an end in the eschatological future. This blindness in part will be removed when the time of Gentile dominance comes to an end. Israel will be put back on center stage in the drama of redemption. The result will be that all Israel (the mass, not every individual) will be saved. This will take place when Jesus returns.

As it relates to the unbelieving Israelites, they are enemies for the sake of Gentiles. It turned out to be for our benefit because the gospel spread more rapidly to the Gentiles because the unbelieving Jews were "enemies" to the gospel. However, they are still the Elect or Chosen Nation of God. God still loves them. They are beloved for the sake of Abraham, Isaac, and Jacob. God will not go back on His Covenant with Israel.

Whatever has taken place has been used by God to help bring about the salvation of both Jews and Gentiles.

Paul was absolutely overwhelmed about the wisdom, judgments, and ways of God. No one has ever counseled God. No one can. God is the counselor of others. No man has done that which makes God his debtor. No one can. God is the ultimate source of all. We owe all to Him.

Application: Teaching and Preaching the Passage

1. Paul raises a most important question. "Has God cast Israel away?" The answer to that question is no. Paul develops his case for the negative answer in vv. 1-5. There is a difference of opinion on what Paul is saying (see the comments on these verses). As I see it, Israel is the Covenant People of God. The basic redemptive Covenant (the Abrahamic Covenant) along with the Mosaic Covenant, the Davidic Covenant, and the New Covenant were all made with Israel. To cast Israel away would mean to break His redemptive covenants with them. If we are going to get a picture of how God through history brought about the plan of redemption, it is imperative for us to develop an insight into the covenants, especially the Abrahamic Covenant.

2. In v. 6 Paul makes it unquestionably clear that salvation cannot be by both works and grace at the same time.

3. Paul divides the Israel of his day into two groups: the elect and the blinded (v. 7). It is clear from what follows in vv. 8-10 that this was a judicial blinding or hardening. It is hard for us to understand God's role in hardening. However, in some way hardening is a Divine punishment for those who resist and rebel against God. Hardening does not produce a hopeless state, but it does produce a dangerous state.

4. Even in the fall of the unbelieving Jews, God was working to bring about their salvation. God used their fall to hasten the spread of the gospel to the Gentiles. God was working through the Gentiles in such a way that it would make the Jews want the salvation that the Gentiles had received (vv. 11, 13, 14 and 30-32).

5. Paul looks to a time in the future when there will be a mass conversion of Jews and talks about what a great time it will be (vv. 12, 15). Not all are agreed that there will be a mass conversion of Jews in the eschatological future. However, among those who have written commentaries on Romans, the vast majority do believe in a mass conversion of Jews in the eschatological future. This is true regardless of their views on eschatology.

6. Paul writes about the Olive Tree in vv. 16-24. For the different points of view on the Olive Tree see "The Allegory of the Olive Tree" in connection with the comments on v. 17.

I take the Olive Tree to be Israel. This means that there is a continuity between the O.T. Israel and the N.T. church. The church is a continuation of O.T. Israel.

The Olive Tree as Israel is the Covenant People of God. The unbelieving branches (the unbelieving Jews) are pruned out. Believing Gentiles are grafted into the Olive Tree. This means that Gentiles who believe have been brought into the redemptive Covenant promises that God made with Israel (see vv. 17, 18).

In the eschatological future there will

be a mass conversion of Jews. They will be grafted back into the Olive Tree (vv. 23-26).

7. Israel is the Covenant people of God and will remain so. God cannot break His Covenant promises with them. Some promises are conditional such as salvation. For that reason each Jew must believe in order to be saved. However, we should keep in mind that there will always be a Covenant People of God who have descended from Abraham through Jacob (vv. 28, 29).

8. Paul is overwhelmed at the wisdom of God and how He works to bring about the salvation of both Jews and Gentiles. He stands in awe before God (vv. 33-36).

Part Three

Practical Instructions and Personal Remarks (12:1—15:13).

I. INSTRUCTIONS IN THE PRACTICAL ASPECTS OF THE CHRISTIAN LIFE (12:1—15:13).

A. The Believer is Challenged to Dedicate Himself to God (12:1,2).

1 I beseech you therefore, brethren, by the mercies of God, that ye present your bodies a living sacrifice, holy, acceptable unto God, *which is* your reasonable service.

I beseech you therefore, brethren, by the mercies of God. "Therefore" (Greek *oun*) connects with the entire previous context insofar as it has been a development of the "mercies" of God. We would be repeating the essence of what Paul says if we made it read, "I beseech you therefore, brethren, in the light of the cross."

The word for beseech (Greek *parakaleo)* is translated in the KJV as beseech, comfort, exhort, desire, pray, and entreat. It occurs over 100 times. Of these occurrences about 60 are used where one Christian is seeking to influence the action or behavior of another Christian. In most contexts our word "encourage" would be a good translation. This term is used more than all other terms combined such as "command," "charge," reprove," "rebuke," "enjoin," and "admonish." It is a mild term as opposed to a harsh or strong term. It appeals to a person's sensitivities and better judgment rather than trying to control through a decree. The thrust of this word is made clear when Paul said to Philemon, "Wherefore, though I might be much bold in Christ to enjoin thee...yet for love's sake I rather beseech *thee*, being such an one as Paul the aged, and now also a prisoner of Jesus Christ" (Phil. 8, 9).

That ye present your bodies a living sacrifice. "Bodies" here is a synechdoche where the part is given for the whole—the whole being, or person. For the most part, in the O.T. sacrificial system a sacrifice was made by slaying an animal. Paul is referring not to sacrificing that which is dead, but that which is alive. It is living for Christ, not dying for Christ that Paul has in mind.

Sacrifice (Greek *thusia*) means an offering to God. It does not necessarily imply that it is hard or costly. Even thanksgiving to God is considered to be a sacrifice (Heb. 13:15). All that we offer to God is a sacrifice whether it be easy or hard. An experience does not have to be painful to be a sacrifice.

Sacrifice in this verse seems to reflect: (l) the principle of full dedication as taught by the burnt offering (Lev. l), and (2) the principle of thanksgiving as taught by the peace offering which is referred to as the thank-offering as distinguished from the vow-offering and the voluntary offering (Lev. 7:11-17).

Holy. The primary reference in holiness is dedication to God. It also includes separation from sin and conformity to righteousness.

Acceptable unto God. The meaning of the word acceptable (Greek *euareston*) is well-pleasing. Check this word in 12:2; 14:18; 2 Cor. 5:9; Eph. 5:10; Phil. 4:18; Col. 3:20; Tit. 2:9; and Heb. 13:21. Those of us who were once in revolt against God and under the wrath of God can now through Jesus Christ do that which God finds well-pleasing!

Which is your reasonable service. The word "reasonable" (Greek *logikos*) is understood by some to mean "spiritual" (perhaps in the sense of the inner being). It seems that sometimes those who take it to mean "rational" and those who take it to mean "spiritual" tend to overlap in meaning. Hodge gives a helpful summary:

> The word (*logiken*) rendered *reasonable*, is indeed variously explained. The simplest interpretation is that which takes the word in its natural sense, viz. *pertaining to the mind;* it is a mental or spiritual service, in opposition to ceremonial and external observations. Compare the phrase (*logikon gala*), 'milk suited, or pertaining to the mind,' I Peter 2:2. [The only other place this word is used in the N.T.] Others understand these words as expressing the difference between the sacrifices under the Christian dispensation and those under the Old. Formerly animals destitute of reason (*alogios dzoa*) were offered unto God, but now men possessed of a rational soul. But this interpretation is neither so well suited to the meaning of the word, nor does it give a sense so consistent with the context; compare I Peter 2:5 (384).

(For other treatments of this word, see Barrett 231, 232; Black 151; Bruce 226; Cranfield II:604, 605; Murray II:112; Picirilli 241; and Sanday and Headlam 353.)

I take the word rational (or reasonable) to be the best translation. It seems that the commentaries take the reference here to be stressing that it is rational or spiritual in nature. We need to draw more from the context. In the context, Paul is stressing that it is reasonable for us to present ourselves fully to God. It is reasonable (or rational) in the light of the mercies of God. In view of our need and God's provision for our need, it makes sense to serve God.

On the word "service," Barclay gives an interesting development of the history. He explains,

> It is *latreia*, the noun of the verb *latreuein*. Originally *latreuein* meant *to work for hire or pay.* It was used of the labouring man who gave his strength to an employer in return for the pay the employer would give him. It denotes, not slavery, but the voluntary undertaking of work. It then came to mean quite generally *to serve;* but it also came to mean *that to which a man gives his whole life.* For instance, a man could be said *latreuein kallei,* which means *to give one's life to the service of beauty.* In that sense, it came very near meaning *to dedicate one's life to.* Finally, it came to be the word distinctively used of *the service of the gods.* In the Bible it never means human service; it is always used of service

to and worship of God (156, 157).

2 And be not conformed to this world: but be ye transformed by the renewing of your mind, that ye may prove what *is* that good, and acceptable, and perfect, will of God.

And be not conformed to this world. The word conformed (Greek *suschematizo*) refers to an outward, superficial change. The fashions of this world which are based on the values of secular humanism are to be avoided by the Christian. Probably, a good way to say it is, "Be not fashioned after the changing values of this world (or age)."

But be ye transformed. Transformed (Greek *metamorphoo*) refers to an internal change rather than a mere external change. Our outward behavior is to be the expression of a deep inner reality.

By the renewing of your mind. The word for mind in the Greek is *nous*.

> I believe the Greek word *nous* as Paul is using it embraces mind, heart, and will. Concerning the meaning of *nous*, J. H. Thayer gives as one of its meanings: 'The *mind, comprising* alike *the faculties of perceiving and understanding* and those of *feeling, judging, determining*....' This use of the word mind is closely related to person or personality. We would be correct in saying that in Romans 12:2 when Paul speaks of a change in our basic inner nature by the renewing of our mind that he was referring to a basic change in our personalities (Forlines, *Systematics* 185).

Most commentaries agree with the difference noted between "conformed" (Greek *suschematizo*) and "transformed" (Greek *metamorphoo*). (For discussions which agree see Barclay 157, 158; Hendriksen 405, note 338; and Sanday and Headlam 353. For discussions that deny this distinction, see Barrett 232, 233; and Cranfield II:605, 608.)

That ye may prove what is that good, and acceptable, and perfect, will of God. Concerning the word for prove (Greek *dokimazo*) Earle explains, "It means 'test,' 'prove' by testing, or 'approve' as the result of testing. But it may also mean 'discover' or 'discern'" (216). Earle supports the meaning "discover" or "discern." This seems to be the correct view. By presenting ourselves as a living sacrifice to God, by avoiding conformity to the age, and by being transformed by the renewing of our personality, we develop that kind of experience that will help us discern the will of God for our lives.

The knowledge of the will of God can be discerned by every Christian. There is no special group that discerns the will of God for those who are not so gifted. Concerning the last clause of this verse, Cranfield observes, "It indicates the dignity of the individual Christian called on as he is to exercise a responsible freedom, and is the decisive refutation of every impudent sacerdotalism that would reduce the Christian layman to a kind of second class citizenship in the church" (II:609, 610).

The words "good, acceptable well-pleasing, and perfect" may either modify the will of God, or they may actually be defining what the will of God is. If they modify the will of God, the meaning would be that the will of God is good, well-pleasing, and perfect to the believer. If they tell what the will of God is, they mean that God wills for us to do that which is good, well-pleasing (to Him), and perfect. This is the opinion held by the majority (see Cranfield II: 610; Denney 688; Hodge 385; and Murray II:115, 116).

Picirilli takes the meaning to be that

God's will is modified as being "good, acceptable, and perfect" (242). I am inclined to agree because of the way the verse is connected with the following verses. The will of God in the following verses would be related to spiritual gifts rather than the ethical nature of the will of God as would be implied by equating what is good, acceptable, and perfect with the will of God.

B. The Believer Is Challenged to Serve God According to His Gifts (12:3-8).

3 For I say, through the grace given unto me, to every man that is among you, not to think *of himself* more highly than he ought to think; but to think soberly, according as God hath dealt to every man the measure of faith.

For I say, through the grace given unto me. For (Greek *gar*) connects with vv. 1 and 2. The thought seems to be: Give proper diligence to knowing the will of God (vv. 1, 2), *for* it is important that we know and practice the will of God as it relates to spiritual gifts. The grace referred to here is the grace of God in bestowing the office of apostleship.

Not to think of himself more highly than he ought to think. Paul is not simply dealing with the question of humility. What he is dealing with is the idea that we should not seek positions in the church for which our gifts have not prepared us. Calvin caught the spirit of the passage when he said, "Paul forbids anyone to take upon himself more than his calling and capacity may bear" (266).

But to think soberly. The word for "think soberly" (Greek *sophroneo*) occurs six times in the N.T. In Mk. 5:15 and Lk. 8:35 it is translated "right mind"; 2 Cor. 5:13 and 1 Pet. 4:7 "sober"; and Tit. 2:6 "to be sober minded." Its meaning is to be sane and sensible.

Many take Paul's admonition in this verse to mean that we are to have a low opinion of ourselves. That is not what Paul is saying. He is saying that we are to have an accurate or proper opinion of ourselves. Moule's comments are helpful. He explains, "The special direction to be taken by this 'sober-thinking' was the recognition by each Christian of the limits of his own gifts, the reality of the gifts of others, and the position of the individual as only part of the great community; as well as the ever-important fact that 'gifts,' whether many or few are the sovereign bounty of God" (*Cambridge Bible* 207).

Shedd gets to the heart of the matter when he says, "Some are called to a more distinguished service in the church than others; and the personal estimate which the believer should have concerning himself should be exactly proportioned to the gifts which he has received. To think neither too much nor too little of the grace of God within the soul, is one of the most difficult of all duties" (360, 361).

According as God hath dealt to every man the measure of faith. Harrison is on the right track when he says regarding the use of "faith" here, "faith in the sense of grasping the nature of one's spiritual gift and having confidence to exercise it rightly" (129). As he grows in the use of his gifts, the believer should have a God-given confidence what his gifts are.

4 For as we have many members in one body, and all members have not the same office:
5 So we, *being* many, are one body in Christ, and every one members one of another.

The observation in these verses is very simple, yet extremely important. Just as the human body is one, but has many parts of differing use, so the body of Christ is one with many members who belong to one another.

6 Having then gifts differing according to the grace that is given to us, whether prophecy, *let us prophesy* according to the proportion of faith.

Having then gifts differing according to the grace that is given to us. Nothing should be any clearer than that God has bestowed different gifts upon different believers. Paul is not simply passing this on as information. It is very important. When the significance of the difference in gifts is not recognized, it can lead to confusion (see 1 Cor. 12-14) in the church and frustration on the part of the individual believer. When it is properly recognized, it can result in harmony in the church, increased effectiveness, and deep personal satisfaction.

Whether prophecy, let us prophesy according to the proportion of faith. The gift of prophecy (Greek *propheteia*) was exercised by a prophet (Greek *prophetes*). A prophet was one who spoke at times from Divine revelation (Acts 11:27, 28; 21:10, 11). These utterances appear to have been related to the immediate needs or circumstances. Their utterances were practical in nature. (For good discussions on the meaning of this gift, see Cranfield II:620; Hendriksen 410; Hodge 388, 390; and Shedd 362, 363.)

With regard to "according to the proportion" (Greek *analogia,* from which our word "analogy" is derived) Shedd gives two views:

> 1. Subjective faith is meant. The clause is equivalent to *kata metron pisteos* [according to the measure of faith, verse 3]. The prophet must be true and sincere, communicating only what God has revealed to him (Origen, Chrysost., Ambrose, Bengel, DeWette, Tholuck, Meyer). 2. The objective rule of faith is meant. The individual prophecy must harmonize with the body of doctrine which has come down from the beginning (Aquinas, Luther, Calvin, Pareus, Flatt, Klee, Umbreit, Philippi, Hodge) (363).

Shedd goes on to give his reasons for choosing the second view as his own. (See also Cranfield II:620, 621. For support for the first view, see Harrison 130.)

Denney takes the subjective view but explains it differently. He says that to prophesy according to the proportion of faith "...implies that the more faith one has—the more completely Christian he is—the greater the prophetic endowment will be" (690). It can be seen that Denney takes the reference to be to the degree of faith.

In the expression "according to the proportion of faith," the article occurs before faith in the Greek. It was pointed out earlier (see comments on 1:5) that when Paul omits the article before faith he is referring to the subjective experience of faith. When he uses the article before faith (except in constructions denoting possession and an occasional use of the article of previous reference), objective faith is intended. It is that which is believed—New Covenant doctrine. It is essentially synonymous with "The New Covenant" just as "The Law" is essentially synonymous with "The Old Covenant."

It was the responsibility of the prophet, in the exercise of his gift, to be sure that what he said was consistent with the teachings of the New Covenant (New Testament). If it were not consistent, it was false and should not be expressed.

What Paul is getting at by "according to the analogy [used here with the sense of a 'rule' or 'standard'] of the faith" is in sharp conflict with contemporary theology's claim that knowledge of God is irrational. The basic test of whether anything is rational is whether the law of non-contradiction applies. According to the law of non-contradiction, two statements cannot be contradictory and both be true. Both could be false, but only one can be true.

The full exercise of the gift of prophecy does not exist today. No one speaks from a personally received revelation from God. We may have impressions from God, but not revelation. All of our impressions should be subjected to the authority of Scripture. It is imperative that we let Scripture be the authority that stands in a corrective relationship to all else.

We may in a loose use of the word *prophet* refer to a person as a prophet who speaks with penetrating insight and authority. However, *we should deny the validity of all claims of direct revelation from God.* A careful look at such a person's preaching and teaching will likely indicate that he has not always been faithful in checking his teachings by the Word of God. Some of the saddest and most tragic moments in the history of the church have been associated with claims of revelation from God. For illustrations, check the founders of many modern cults.

7 Or ministry, *let us wait* on *our* ministering: or he that teacheth, on teaching.

Or ministry, let us wait on our ministering. Concerning the word for ministry (Greek *diakonia*) Earle explains,

> It occurs three times in Romans and is translated three different ways (cf. 11:13, 'office'; 15:31, 'service'). It is used in Luke 10:40 of preparing a meal. But almost always in the N.T. it refers to service in the Christian Church, whether of a common sort in the local congregation or of the apostolic office and its administration. It is not clear just what type of service is intended here (217, 218).

The Greek word for "deacon" is *diakonos*. Many are of the opinion that Paul has deacons in mind when he refers to the gift of "ministry" (see Cranfield II:622; Harrison 131; Hendriksen 410; and Murray 124).

In view of the broad use of the word for ministry (Greek *diakonia*) and deacon (Greek *diakonos*), it is hard to decide whether ministry is used here in a more general sense or whether it refers to deacons. In the absence of compelling evidence to restrict it to the work of deacons, I am inclined to give it a more general meaning, i.e., ministering to the needs of others. Surely deacons should be gifted in ministering to the needs of others, but there are opportunities for this service for those who have not been elected as deacons. Also, there are those who show themselves gifted in ministering to the needs of others who have not been elected as deacons.

Or he that teacheth, on teaching. Teaching differs from prophesying in that the prophet received his message by direct revelation from God while the teacher studies, interprets, and communicates God's message as given in Scripture. The teaching referred to here would in all likelihood refer to all the gifted teaching in the church whether by pastor or layman.

On the importance of the gift of teaching, it is important to observe that the pastor is to be a teacher. It is usually agreed, based on the Greek construction in Eph. 4:11, which deals with gifts, that "pastors and teachers" refers not to two different people, but one person who is both pastor and teacher.

What we refer to as the pulpit ministry, we call preaching. However, if we take our terminology from Scripture, there is more teaching than preaching in most of what we call preaching. The following excerpt will compare the two words. It is taken from my series of articles, "The Pastor and His People" (*Contact*, Vol. XXVII, No. 5 [May, 1980], 26, 27).

The Scope Of Preaching

The New Testament scope of material covered in preaching and teaching is not the same.

Two Greek words account for the vast majority of words translated *preach* in the New Testament. The word which occurs more than any other is *kerusso*. This word occurs 61 times. It is translated 'preach' 53 times, 'publish' five times, 'proclaim' twice, and 'preacher' once.

We will focus on these verses in Acts and the epistles which deal with the scope of preaching. The content of preaching in Acts 8:5; 9:20; 10:42; I Corinthians 1:23; 9:20; 10:42; II Corinthians 1:19; 4:15; and Philippians 1:15 is Christ and doctrinal truth about Him.

In Acts 20:25 and 28:31, the content of the preaching is the kingdom of God. In Galatians 2:2; Colossians 1:23; and I Thessalonians 2:9, it is the gospel that is preached.

In Romans 2:21 Paul mentions that the Jews preached that a man should not steal. In II Timothy 4:2 Paul charged Timothy to preach the Word.

It is clear that the word *kerusso* (preach) has as its scope Christ, the gospel and matters that are indisputably true so far as Christian truth is concerned. It does not include the entire scope of Christian truth.

The second most frequently used Greek word that is translated 'preach' is *euaggelizo*. This word occurs 51 times. It is translated 'preach' 24 times, 'preach the gospel' 23 times, 'bring good tidings' twice, 'show glad tidings' twice, 'bring glad tidings,' 'declare,' 'declare good tidings,' and 'by the gospel is preached' all one time each.

The word for gospel which means good news is *euaggelion*. The word *euaggelizo* is the verb form while *euaggelion* is the noun form. *Euaggelizo* by its meaning is restricted to good news. It is limited to Christ and the gospel.

Kerusso involves a proclamation which may involve 'thou shalt nots,' judgment and the gospel. In either case when these words are used for preaching, the scope is limited to foundational, indisputable facts of Christian truth, not the whole scope of Christian truth.

Scope Of Teaching

The New Testament Greek word accounting for most occurrences of teach is *didasko*. It occurs 97 times and is always translated teach, teaching, or taught.

The scope of teaching is the whole of Christian truth. This is obvious from its use in several places. A few instances will demonstrate this fact.

The Sermon on the Mount

(Matthew 5-7) is considered teaching. 'And he opened his mouth and taught them' (Matthew 5:2). In Luke 11:1 the disciples said to Jesus 'teach us to pray.' In Matthew 28:20 Jesus said, 'Teaching them to observe all things whatsoever I have commanded you....'

In Acts 20:20 Paul explained, 'And how I kept back nothing that was profitable unto you, and have taught you publicly from house to house.'

Another factor which points out the importance of teaching is that of the 56 times that Jesus is called "Master" in the KJV, 40 of these times is a translation of the word for teacher (Greek *didaskalos).*

8 Or he that exhorteth, on exhortation: he that giveth, *let him do it* with simplicity; he that ruleth, with diligence; he that sheweth mercy, with cheerfulness.

Or he that exhorteth on exhortation. Concerning the word for "exhort" (Greek *parakaleo*), Thayer says, "It combines the ideas of *exhorting,* and *comforting* and encouraging in Romans 12:8; I Cor.14:31; I Th. 3:2" (483). I take this to be the correct meaning. The word encourage is a good translation. We encourage people to do right. We encourage people to persevere. We encourage people during times of grief and loss.

This gift is sorely needed in our day. Every church needs several people with this gift.

He that giveth, let him do it with simplicity. The word for simplicity (Greek *haplotes*) can mean either simplicity, denoting sincerity or pureness of motive, or it may mean generous or giving with liberality. (See 2 Cor. 1:12 and 11:3 where it is translated "simplicity," Eph. 6:5 and Col. 3:22 where it is translated "singleness" of heart; 2 Cor. 8:2 where it is translated "liberality"; 9:11 where it is translated "bountifulness"; and 11:3 where it is translated "liberal.")

Translations frequently render it as liberality or the equivalent. Most commentators tend toward an interpretation in keeping with the translation "simplicity" (see Cranfield II:625; Harrison 131; and Murray II:125, 126).

Arndt and Gingrich (85) take the translation "generosity, liberality" to be the appropriate one for Rom. 12:8; 2 Cor. 8:2; and 9:11,13. Earle (218, 219) tends to favor this view also.

Either "simplicity" or "generosity" would make good sense in Rom. 12:8. However, since Paul uses "generosity" or "liberality" as the meaning in 2 Cor. when he deals with giving, it seems to me to be the most likely one here.

The gift of giving should be exercised with generosity. Every Christian should give, but some have the gift of giving. It appears that God has blessed some people with the ability to make money so they can give generously to support His work.

He that ruleth, with diligence. The word for "ruleth" (Greek *proistemi*) literally means to stand before. According to *Kittels Theological Dictionary of the New Testament,* it means to lead with a strong emphasis on caring (Vol. II:701). This meaning is supported by 1 Tim. 3:5,"For if a man know not how to rule his own house, how shall he take care of the church of God?" To rule and to take care of have essentially the same meaning in this verse.

The gift of leadership in this verse applies both to pastors and to lay leaders. There is no place in the church for harsh authoritarianism that rules by decree. The leadership taught in

Scripture is a strong, caring type leadership. The leader is to go about his work with diligence, zeal, and earnestness.

He that sheweth mercy, with cheerfulness. This gift would overlap with some of the above. The special emphasis in this gift is help toward the sick and needy. All can do something along this line, but there are some who are especially gifted. They know just the thing to say and how to say it. They do what they do cheerfully, not with a "well if I must" attitude (see 2 Cor. 9:7).

C. The Believer Is Challenged to Have a Proper Attitude Toward and to Be in a Proper Relationship With Others (12:9-21).

9 *Let* love be without dissimulation. Abhor that which is evil; cleave to that which is good.

Let love be without dissimulation. Love is an affectionate concern that leads to appropriate action. When we love others, we have a genuine concern for their welfare. We want to do something about it. The word "dissimulation" (Greek *anupokritos*) means without hypocrisy. Paul admonishes us not to act and talk like we love as just an act. Our love is to be genuine, not staged. Paul gives this same admonition in 2 Cor. 6:6 where the same Greek word is translated "unfeigned."

Abhor that which is evil. Concerning the word "abhor" (Greek *apostugeo*), Sanday and Headlam say, "The word expresses a strong sense of horror" (360). Cranfield says, "What is required is not just a refraining from doing what is evil, but an intense inward rejection of it" (II:631, footnote 5). The right relationship to evil starts with the attitude of abhorrence. If we abhor evil, we will automatically stay away from it. We will not indulge in taking pleasure in the trash that the world produces.

Cleave to that which is good. On the word "cleave" Earle explains, "The Greek word for 'cleave' is the verb *kollao* which means 'glue.' It may be represented in English by either *cleave* or *cling*. It suggests that we are to be cemented securely to what is right" (221). The Christian is to form a permanent bond with that which is good. We are not simply to refrain from evil. We are to seek out the good and experience it.

10 *Be* kindly affectioned one to another with brotherly love; in honour preferring one another.

Be kindly affectioned one to another in brotherly love. Earle explains,"'Be kindly affectioned' is an adjective *philostorgos* found only here in N.T. The first part, *philos,* means 'beloved.' The second is from the noun *storge,* meaning family affection" (221). As Christians our love for one another is to be like the affection that family members are to have for one another. This concept is strengthened by the word for brotherly love (Greek *philadelphia*). We are to love each other as natural brothers in a family would.

In honour preferring one another. The word "preferring" (Greek *proegeomai*) literally means "to lead before." We are to take the lead in bestowing honor and respect on the other person. It is not necessary for us to get hung up on our worth or the lack of it in comparison to other Christians. What we are to be sure to do is to pay them proper respect. They should also pay us proper respect, but we should not wait for it. It should be a mutual bestowal of respect.

11 Not slothful in business;

fervent in spirit; serving the Lord;

Not slothful in business. The word for "business" (Greek *spoude*) is the same that is translated "diligence" in v. 8. We are not to be slothful, sluggish, or reluctant in our diligence in serving the Lord.

Fervent in spirit. The word fervent (Greek *zeo*) means to boil or be hot. "Not slothful in diligence" states our responsibility negatively."Fervent in spirit" states our responsibility positively. Probably most are of the opinion that the reference in this expression is to the Holy Spirit (see Bruce 229 and Cranfield II:633, 644).

I take the "spirit" to be to our human spirit. The only other place where this expression is found is in Acts 18:25 where it refers to Apollos when he was "knowing only the baptism of John." At this stage of his experience, it is unlikely that he would have been considered fervent in the Holy Spirit. It seems that fervency in spirit is the meaning both in Acts 18:25 and the present reference. I concur with Godet when he says, "The word *spirit* undoubtedly refers here to the spiritual element in man himself, but that as penetrated and quickened by the Divine Spirit" (435; see also Sanday and Headlam 361). We would know that the human spirit is energized by the Holy Spirit not from the word itself, but from the theology of Christian experience.

On the words "serving the Lord" Picirilli explains:

> The word for service is the usual one referring to bondservice. This means full and unquestioned submission and obedience, recognizing Him as Lord with absolute authority over us. Probably this third phrase is intended to add more specific content to the ideas suggested in the two previous phrases. By themselves, those two phrases might remain somewhat vague. We must have an eager zeal, but zeal for what? And for what should our spirits burn with the Spirit of fire? The answer is the service of the Lord. All together, then, verse 10 refers to our devotion to the Lord Jesus that results in fervent service to Him (251).

12 Rejoicing in hope; patient in tribulation; continuing instant in prayer.

Rejoicing in hope. Hope refers to the joyful, confident expectation of "the glory of God" (5:2) as it relates to the eschatological future. It is the confidence that we have that "if so be that we suffer with *him,* that we may be also glorified together" (8:7).

Patient in tribulation. The first observation to be made is that Christians do suffer tribulation. There is no warrant whatever for telling someone that if he loves God enough or if he has enough faith that he will have a trouble-free life. Romans 8:35-39 and Paul's own experience in 2 Cor. 11:23-27 attest to this fact. What God has promised us is sustaining grace (2 Cor. 12:9). By God's grace we are to bear up under tribulations with patient endurance and steadfastness (see 5:3). When we handle tribulation this way, we fare better ourselves, and we have an effective testimony.

Continuing instant in prayer. "Continuing instant in" (Greek *proskartereo*) means to continue steadfastly, to be persistent, or to persevere. Picirilli explains, "'Continuing instant in' means 'to give constant attention to.' Compare I Thessalonians 5:17, 'Pray without ceasing,' which has the same meaning. In both places Paul does not mean around-the-clock vigil of conscious prayer but a consistent, regular, habitual prayer life. He knows we must be faithful in prayer if our spiritual temperature is to remain hot, if we are to burn always with spiritual fervor for the service of God" (252).

13 Distributing to the necessity of saints; given to hospitality.

Distributing to the necessity of saints. With reference to "distributing" (Greek *koinoneo*), Picirilli explains,

> Literally, this word means 'being partners with' or 'being in fellowship with' or 'sharing with' or 'having in common with.' At least two things must be involved for this kind of response to a brother's needs. First, is identification. We must see ourselves as one with our brethren. Then comes sharing. We act to meet the need by sharing what we have because we hold that what we have is theirs, too (cf. Acts 2:44b). This is Christian service to others in its most blessed form. Such selfless, sacrificial giving in response to the needs of fellow believers is everywhere commended in the Word (as in 2 Corinthians 8 and 9) and is one of the most significant expressions and experiences of Christian fellowship (253).

We are to be concerned about the needs of all people. However, we are to be particularly concerned about the needs of fellow believers (Gal. 6:10).

Given to hospitality. The word for "given" (Greek *dioko*) means "to pursue." The word for hospitality (Greek *philoxenia*) means "love for strangers." This word is used only here and in Heb. 13:2 in the N.T. The Christian is to pursue a love for strangers. This would have special reference to how we treat those who are new in our neighborhoods and churches.

14 Bless them which persecute you: bless, and curse not.

Bless them which persecute you. We may not meet persecution in its severest forms, but most of us who take our Christian experience seriously will encounter some form of mistreatment. What Paul is asking us to do was expressed well by Jesus when He said, "Bless them that curse you, do good to them that hate you, and pray for them which despitefully use you, and persecute you" (Mt. 5:44).

Bless, and curse not. Murray comments,

> When Paul adds, 'bless and curse not,' he underlies the fact that our attitude is not to be a mixture of blessing and cursing but one of unadulterated blessing. The demand points up two considerations: (1) that nothing less than the pattern of God's own lovingkindness and beneficence is the norm for us (cf. Matt. 5:45-48) and (2) that only the resources of omnipotent grace in Christ Jesus are equal to the demands of the believer's vocation (II:134, 135).

15 Rejoice with them that do rejoice, and weep with them that weep.

Rejoice with them that rejoice. This, for some, may be harder than the second admonition in the verse. It is easy for the spirit of envy and jealousy to arise within us when it seems that others experience good fortune more than we do. We must train ourselves to rise above this kind of littleness. We will be better off, and it will help bring out the best both in us and in others.

And weep with them that weep. While it may be easier, so far as attitude is concerned, to do this than to rejoice with those who rejoice, to weep with those who weep makes more demands upon us. Rejoicing with those who rejoice does not make great time demands upon us. However, to weep with those who weep may so identify us with their problems that we will become involved in the solution to their problems. We live in a hurting world. This is true both in the church and outside the church. If people attend our churches and find their hurts ministered to, there is a good likelihood that they will return.

16 *Be* of the same mind one toward another. Mind not high things, but condescend to men of low estate. Be not wise in your own conceits.

Be of the same mind one toward another. Picirilli explains,

> The expression 'be of the same mind' (literally: 'think the same') is a frequent one of Paul's. Note Philippians 2:2 and 4:2, and 2 Corinthians 13:11, for examples. In all these, Paul emphasizes the fact that the Christians in a congregation ought to be of 'one accord' (Acts 2:1). This means they have the same philosophy and purposes. It also means they regard each other with mutual love and respect; no one thinking himself an exception to the rules that apply to all, or better than the others; each eager to serve the others as his brethren in Christ (258).

Mind not high things, but condescend to men of low estate. The words translated "men of low estate" (Greek *tois tapeinois)* are taken by some to be neuter, meaning "lowly" or "humble" *things.* Others take them to be masculine and understand the reference to be to "humble" or "lowly" *people.* (For treatments supporting the reference to be to people see Cranfield II:644 and Harrison 134. For a treatment supporting the reference to be neuter, see Sanday and Headlam 364. For a good survey of treatments which seeks to hang on to both views, see Earle 225, 227).

It is difficult to make a dogmatic choice. However, since the other references to *tapeinos* in the N.T. are masculine, it may be better to take the masculine as the proper gender of the word and take the reference to be to persons of low estate. Either way Paul is speaking against highmindedness. We should avoid a haughty spirit whether with reference to people or things.

On the word "condescend" (Greek *sunapagomai*), Earle makes a good case for translating it "associate" rather than "condescend" (227, 228). If we accept this translation, the bad connotations that may go with the word "condescend" are removed. We are to associate with people of low estate.

Be not wise in your own conceits. The admonition here is against a wisdom (so called) that a person thinks he has developed within himself all on his own. This kind of "wisdom" would give a person a sense of superiority and would make him hard to get along with. Paul is not intending to shatter a person's confidence in his wisdom which he has developed with full recognition to God, the authority of the Word of God, and appreciation for the contribution others have made to his life.

17 Recompense to no man evil for evil. Provide things honest in the sight of all men.

Recompense to no man evil for evil. We are not to pay back evil with evil. We are not to take the attitude of, "I will get even with him if it is the last thing I ever do."

Provide things honest in the sight of all men. The word for "honest" (Greek *kalos*) is broader than honesty. It refers to moral excellence, which of course includes honesty.

The word for "provide" (Greek *pronoeomai*) means "to think before" or to "plan ahead." What Paul is telling us is to plan ahead to so conduct our lives that they will exemplify moral excellence in the sight of all men. This is the kind of life that will be of value in winning people to Jesus Christ.

In 2 Cor. 8:18-21 Paul demonstrates this kind of planning ahead. The churches had chosen a representative to travel with Paul as he went to Jerusalem to deliver the offering that the churches were sending to help the poor saints in Jerusalem. By having this chosen and trusted brother to travel with him, Paul was avoiding the possibility that a tale could get out that he had mishandled these funds. This precaution he called, "Providing for honest things, not only in the sight of the Lord, but also in the sight of men" (2 Cor. 8:21). Paul planned ahead. It is our responsibility not only to *do* right, but also to go about it in such a way that it will *look* right.

18 If it be possible, as much as lieth in you, live peaceably with all men.

On the part which is translated "as much as lieth in you," Vincent says that it means, "Lit., *as to that which proceeds from you,* or *depends on you*" (745). What Paul is saying is, "If it is possible, so far as your part is concerned, live peaceably with all men." Or, "If you cannot succeed in living peaceably with all men, don't let it be your fault." (See Earle 228.)

There are issues over which division is justified if they cannot be resolved. However, much of the division in the church world today is a result of a failure of one or more parties to be willing to abide by the admonition of this verse.

19 Dearly beloved, avenge not yourselves, but *rather* give place unto wrath: for it is written, Vengeance *is* mine; I will repay, saith the Lord.

Dearly beloved, avenge not yourselves, but rather give place unto wrath. Paul admonishes us against taking matters into our own hands. Rather, we are to "give place unto wrath." We are to leave it in God's hands who will in due time administer wrath in accord with His justice if repentance does not take place in the meantime.

For it is written, Vengeance is mine; I will repay, saith the Lord. This part of the verse is from Dt. 32:35. God has reserved the administration of vengeance for Himself. We need to leave it up to Him.

20 Therefore if thine enemy hunger, feed him; if he thirst, give him drink: for in so doing thou shalt heap coals of fire on his head.

This verse is taken from Pr. 25:21, 22. **Therefore, if thine enemy hunger, feed him; if he thirst, give him drink.** In vv. 9-21 no theme receives as much stress from Paul as how we should relate to those who mistreat us. This is the theme of vv. 14, 17, 18, 19, 20, and 21. Our aim must be to live, around and toward those who mistreat us, that we may be able to help bring about the change needed in their lives.

For in so doing thou shalt heap coals of fire on his head. Cranfield observes,

> Chrysostom and a number of other Greek Fathers following his lead (e.g. Theodoret, Oecumenius, Theophylact) see in *anthrakes puros* [coals of fire] of the latter part of the quotation a reference to future divine punishment and understand the thought to be that one's doing good to one's enemy will cause his punishment, in the event of his not repenting, to be greater (though it is only fair to add—something which those who refer to this interpretation sometimes omit to add—that the same Fathers also say that one is not to do good to one's enemy with this intention) (II:648, 649).

Cranfield goes on to reject this view. (See also Murray II:142, 143.) This view is foreign to the spirit of the context.

It is generally agreed that doing good to one's enemy would be heaping coals of fire on his head so as to bring about repentance either by making him develop a feeling of guilt or a feeling of shame over his deed. The aim is by good treatment to turn an enemy into a friend.

21 Be not overcome of evil, but overcome evil with good.

Be not overcome of evil. If we take the matter of vengeance into our own hands, we will have been overcome. To fight sin with sin is to sin.

But overcome evil with good. When our enemy is brought to repentance by our good treatment of him, good will have triumphed over evil.

Summary
12:1-21

Paul had said a great deal about God's mercy in providing a God-provided righteousness for fallen man through Jesus Christ. He had labored to point out how God was working to bring both Jews and Greeks into a saving relationship with Jesus Christ. In chapter 12 he appeals to believers, in the light of the mercies of God, to present themselves totally to God. This was to be a living sacrifice in contrast to the sacrifice of dead animals in the O.T. In light of all that God has done for us, it is reasonable to make such a sacrifice to Him.

Paul admonishes believers not to be conformed to the passing fashions of this age, but instead to experience a deep inner transformation of personality. This inner transformation will manifest itself in behavior which is truly expressive of the inner person.

When we pursue our relationship with God in the way described, we will be able to discern the will of God, particularly as it relates to our gifts. We will find the will of God to be good, well-pleasing, and perfect.

Through the grace of apostleship that God had given to Paul, he admonishes believers not to seek out positions in the church for which their gifts have not prepared them. We are to think accurately about our gifts and abilities in accord with the confidence that God has given to us.

Just as the physical body is one body, but has many members to serve the different needs of the body, so believers are one body in Christ. We have different gifts to enable us to serve the needs of the church.

Since we have gifts that differ in accord with God's plan, it behooves us to serve according to our gifts. Those who had the gift of prophecy (to receive and communicate direct revelation from God about immediate concerns) were to serve in keeping with their gift. Whatever the prophet thought was a message revealed from God was to be put to the test whether it conformed to the teaching of the New Covenant. If it did not pass this test, it was not to be communicated.

Those who have received the gift of ministering to the needs of others are to serve in that capacity. Those who have the gift of teaching are to devote their time to teaching. Those who have the gift of encouragement are to encourage fellow believers to do right, and to persevere; they are also to encourage those who are experiencing problems. Those who have the gift of giving are to be generous in their giving. Those who have the gift of leadership are to lead with sincere diligence. Those who have the gift of ministering to the sick and the needy are to perform this ministry with cheerfulness.

In regard to their relationship to others, they are to have genuine affectionate concern for one another. They are to truly love one another, not merely act like they do.

It is important for us to have the right attitude about the right and the evil. We are to abhor that which is evil. We are to form a permanent bond between believers and what is right and good.

It is the responsibility of those in the church to have that affectionate feeling for one another that is to characterize family members in their relation to one another. They are to love as brothers. When it comes to bestowing honor and respect, we are each to take the lead in bestowing it upon the other.

Reluctance and slothfulness are to be avoided in the Lord's service. They should be replaced by diligence. Such service is to be characterized by a fervent spirit.

We are to rejoice that God has prepared for us such a wonderful future in the life to come. We are to develop patient endurance in times of tribulation. We are to continue steadfastly in prayer.

We are to be alert to the needs of others and so identify with those needs that we would share with them so as to relieve their needs. We are to love strangers and show that love by being alert to their needs and concerns.

When it comes to those who mistreat us, we are to pray for them and wish them well. We are not to mix curses in with our prayers.

When something good happens to another person, we should rejoice with him. We are to weep with those who are hurting. We are to identify with their need and minister to that need.

We are so to relate to one another in the church that a spirit of harmony prevails. We are to avoid a haughty spirit and should be willing to associate with those less fortunate than we are. We are to avoid the idea that we are solely responsible for the wisdom we have developed. Such an idea will give us an inflated ego and will make us hard to get along with.

We are to avoid the spirit of, "I will get even with you." We are to plan ahead so that we will not only do that which is morally excellent, but so we will appear to others as doing that which is morally excellent.

It is our responsibility to be sure and do our part to live peaceably with others. If we cannot be at peace with another, let it be clear that it is not because we have not done our part.

When it comes to vengeance, we are to leave that up to God. We are not to take matters into our own hands. God has promised to take care of such matters.

If our enemy has a need we are to minister to that need. In so doing, there is a good possibility that he will either feel guilty or ashamed and will repent. He may even become our friend. In this way we will avoid being overcome by evil. Rather, we will overcome evil with good.

Application: Teaching and Preaching the Passage

1. Having completed the most thorough theological treatment in Scripture, Paul now turns his attention to the realm of the practical. By appealing to the mercy of God in the plan of redemption, Paul appeals to his readers to come forth with a complete dedication of their lives to God (vv. 1, 2).

I think it is significant that Paul sounds this note of complete surrender at the very beginning of this presentation of practical Christian truth. There is no way that readers then or now could come to grips with the practical truth that Paul presents apart from being committed to and loving God. That is the only way we can have twenty-twenty moral and spiritual vision. I think Paul is getting at this very point when he says that the aim of the surrender, transformation, and renewing of your mind is that "ye may prove what is that good, and acceptable, and perfect will of God" (see notes on the Greek word for "prove" which here means to discern or know). Paul is telling us that discerning or knowing the will of God requires real commitment and a deep burning desire on our part.

2. Paul's major concern in this context is the will of God as it relates to the use of our gifts in the service of God (vv. 3-8).

3. Paul warns against seeking out high positions in the church apart from having received gifts which prepared us for these positions (v. 3).

4. Paul illustrates with the fact that we have many members which work together as one body. Together we make up one body in Christ. God has designed us to work together in harmony and for what each does to complement the other (vv. 4, 5).

5. In vv. 6-8 Paul lists several gifts that God has bestowed for service in the church. It is quite clear that we have different gifts and that each person should serve according to his gifts.

Just as it is incumbent upon the members to serve according to their gifts, it is also incumbent upon the church to help each member find avenues of service where he can make use of his gifts for the glory of God. This will require some creativity on the part of church leadership.

The responsibility of helping people find avenues of service is not over when the elected positions of the church have been filled. Many times capable people sit around not knowing how to fit in. This is especially true of capable women. Can we blame these people when they look elsewhere for a church home? We cannot expect capable people to stay with us when we do not help them find a place to use their gifts and talents. They have a responsibility to God to use them.

6. In vv. 9-21 Paul gives a great deal of attention to how we should get along with one another. (For an examination of the specifics see the comments on the verses.) It is exceedingly important that we learn to get along with one another. Probably, no other area of Christian responsibility gives more trouble in our churches than our failure to learn to apply the truth of Scripture to interpersonal relationships.

7. The principle of "abhorring that which is evil and cleaving to that which is good" (v. 9) is one which deserves serious attention. It is especially true concerning what we read, listen to, and set before our eyes.

8. In v. 17 Paul said, "Provide things honest in the sight of all men." The word for "provide" means to "think before" or "to plan ahead." This verse establishes the principle that if we are to live right we must *plan* to live right.

We must work at it ahead of time.

9. Paul must have been especially burdened that we learn to get along with those who mistreat us (note vv. 14, 17, 18, 19, and 20).

D. The Believer Is Challenged to Be in Subjection to Civil Government (13:1-7).

Some have felt that this passage is not properly related to the context. Here are four observations: (1) In dealing with practical matters, it is not necessary that there be a logical tie-in with the context beyond the fact that it is in a context dealing with practical concerns. (2) There is a good likelihood that there were serious questions about a Christian's responsibility to a government that was administered by pagans. (3) Paul had challenged the believers at Rome to totally surrender themselves to God (12:1, 2). The believer's relationship to civil authority is involved in that surrender. (4) In 12:19 the believer is told to leave vengeance in the hands of God. He will take vengeance. It appears that one of the ways God takes vengeance is by using civil authorities to punish evildoers. These reasons give adequate justification for considering this passage to be properly fitted into the context (For a good discussion of this problem see Hendriksen 429-432.)

1 Let every soul be subject unto the higher powers. For there is no power but of God: the powers that be are ordained of God.

Let every soul be subject unto the higher powers. The word "soul" (Greek *psuche*) in this context means "person."

The word for "powers" (Greek *exousia*) means "authority." Joined with the word "higher" the meaning is "higher authorities." It is generally agreed that the reference here is to "governing authorities," those in civil government. Another view has been set forth; Hendriksen explains, "Oscar Cullman, in his book *Christ and Time* (tr. of *Christus und die Zeit,* Zurich, 1948), London 1962 (see especially pp. 192-196), proceeds from the supposition that the late Jewish teaching concerning angels belongs to the content of New Testament doctrine. According to him evil angels, having been overcome by Christ, lost their sinister character, and were recommissioned to render favorable service for Christ" (430, note 354).

This view does not merit our consideration. It is unthinkable that evil angels would have experienced this kind of sanctification. (For developments and evaluations of this view, see Cranfield II:656-659; Hendricksen 430, 431, note 354; and Murray, Appendix C, "The Authorities of Romans 13:1," II:252-256).

For there is no power (authority) **but of God: the powers** (authorities) **that be are ordained of God.** This part of the verse tells why we are to be subject unto the governing authorities. God has ordained human government. In spite of all the weaknesses of human governments, the world is a much better place to live than it would be without government.

On the word "subject" (Greek *hupotasso*) Murray explains, "The term for 'subjection' is one more inclusive than that for obedience. It implies obedience when ordinances to be obeyed are in view, but there is more involved. Subjection indicates the recognition of our subordination in the whole realm of the magistrates' jurisdiction and willing subservience to their authority" (II:148).

There can be no doubt about it. Paul takes a very serious view of the Christian's responsibility toward government. The matter is complicated because at times, in the history of the church, some civil authorities have issued decrees which conflict with the commands of God. It has been generally agreed that under such circumstances we are to obey God rather than the civil authorities (Acts 4:19, 20).

Paul does not raise the question of how to deal with such conflicting situations. This does not mean that Paul had no appreciation for this problem. As Hendriksen explains: "We should not forget that Paul was a Jew, well-versed in the Old Testament, as he proves again and again in his epistles. Therefore he also knew about, and heartily approved of, the courage shown by Daniel and/or his three friends when they disobeyed royal edicts and ordinances that were manifestly contrary to God's will as revealed in his law. See chapters 1, 3 and 6 of the book of Daniel" (433).

There may be a reason that Paul chose not to deal with exceptional cases. It is very difficult to deal with exceptions without weakening the rule. Paul wanted to leave us with the conviction that it is very important to have proper respect for civil government.

In cases where there is a clear, obvious, direct conflict with a command of God, it may not be so hard for a Christian to know what to do. However, when it is not so obvious, we should probably accept some mistreatment from government before we defy the laws. As nearly as possible, we should follow proper channels in trying to change laws and the interpretation of them. We, as believers, should never be comfortable about defying the government even if we think it is necessary.

2 Whosoever therefore resisteth the power, resisteth the ordinance of God: and they that resist shall receive to themselves damnation.

Whosoever therefore resisteth the power, resisteth the ordinance of God. Picirilli explains,

> This truth is a logical application of the principle laid down in the previous verse: All existing civil authorities have been arranged by God. Consequently, when we resist civil authority, we are resisting 'the ordinance of God.'
>
> The word 'resist' means to set or place oneself against. The 'ordinance' is the same basic word as the 'ordained' in verse 1: arranged, placed in order. Since God has arranged the powers that be, then God's own authority is behind them. And so we are rebelling against God himself when we rebel against properly constituted authority (265, 266).

And they that resist shall receive to themselves damnation. Concerning the word "damnation" (Greek *krima*), Picirilli explains, "Actually, the Greek word used can refer to any kind of judgment or chastisement, whether temporal or eternal, civil or spiritual. 'Condemnation' would be an accurate translation, as would 'judgment'" (266).

I take the "judgment" referred to in this verse to be the penalty inflicted by civil authorities. It could also be said to be inflicted by God since God has ordained civil authority (Cranfield II:664; and Murray II:149). Hodge (407) and Shedd (377) take the reference to be to Divine judgment as distinguished from judgment by civil authority.

3 For rulers are not a terror to good works, but to the evil. Wilt thou then not be afraid of the power? do that which is good,

and thou shalt have praise of the same.

For rulers are not a terror to good works, but to the evil. Murray points out that "The 'terror' which rulers are to the evil work is the fear of punishment evoked in the hearts of men by reason of the authority vested in rulers to execute this punishment. The fear can be of two kinds, the fear that inhibits wrongdoing and the fear that results when wrongdoing is committed" (II:150).

Governments do not do a perfect job of being a terror to evil and not to good works. However, when we consider the different philosophies of unbelievers in various governments of the world, it is amazing to what extent this is true in spite of the unbelief and depravity of man. As Moule says, "Civil authority, even in its worst form never systematically favours wrong *as wrong* and punishes right *as right*" (216).

Wilt thou not be afraid of the power? do that which is good, and thou wilt have praise of the same. While fear can be overdone for motivational value, most of us will admit that we have behaved better on many occasions because of fear. As said above, government is not always on the side of right, but in most cases those who do "good" will be protected and appreciated as law-abiding citizens.

4 For he is the minister of God to thee for good. But if thou do that which is evil, be afraid; for he beareth not the sword in vain: for he is the minister of God, a revenger to *execute* wrath upon him that doeth evil.

For he is a minister of God to thee for good. This statement harks back to "the powers that be are ordained of God" (v. 1). The ruler is performing a Divine service when he carries out his duties.

Concerning the "good" referred to, Murray comments, "Paul provides us with a virtual definition of the good we derive from the service of the civil authority when he requires that we pray for kings and all who are in authority 'That we may lead a tranquil and quiet life in all godliness and gravity' (I Tim. 2:2). The good the magistrate promotes is that which subserves the interests of piety" (II:152).

But if thou do that which is evil, be afraid; for he beareth not the sword in vain. It is often said that while the O.T. prescribes the death penalty, the N.T. does not. This verse proves the contrary to be true. The sword is the symbol of the right to kill. Hodge explains, "As the common method of inflicting capital punishment was by decapitation with a sword, that instrument is mentioned as the symbol of the right of punishment, and as many infer from this passage, of the right of capital punishment" (408; see also Gifford 212; Godet 441, 442; Hendriksen 435; Lenski 792; and Shedd 378). Denny (697) and Harrison (138) question whether this passage supports capital punishment.

Some are of the opinion that the sword symbolizes the right of the emperor to use military force to quell rebellion. Cranfield shows an interest in this view (II:667). Hendriksen says, "The opinion according to which Paul simply means that the emperor and those who represent him wield military power merely to enable them to quell the forces of rebellion, hardly does justice to the present context, which refers to wrong-doers in general, not only to rebels. By means of the sword wrong-doing is punished. In fact, the vicious, dangerous criminal may even be put to death" (435).

For he is the minister of God,

a revenger to execute wrath upon him that doeth evil. The "wrath" appears to be the wrath of God rather than the government official. Murray observes, "Thus the magistrate is the avenger in executing the judgment that accrues to the evil-doer from the wrath of God. Again we discover the sanction belonging to the ruler's function; he is the agent in executing God's wrath" (II:153).

5 Wherefore *ye* must needs be subject, not only for wrath, but also for conscience sake.

The believer is not to be subject to government only to avoid punishment. His own conscience obligates him because Scripture obligates him to be subject to the civil government (see 1 Pet. 2:13-15).

6 For for this cause pay ye tribute also: for they are God's ministers, attending continually upon this very thing.

For for this cause pay ye tribute also. Tribute (Greek *phoros*) according to Vine "was especially the yearly tax levied on persons or real property. It was frequently used of the tribute laid upon a subject nation (Neh. 5:4, Luke 20:22). Here it is used in a general way, of any kind of tax levied by a government for the exercise of its power" *(Romans* 188).

The Christian is required by conscience to pay taxes. It is good that God saw fit to have this placed in Scripture because otherwise, in the light of some of the ways tax money is spent, some with a more conscientious bent might feel that it would be wrong to pay taxes. They might feel that to pay taxes would support some wrong way the money might be used. Paul's admonition should clear that matter up for all of us. Not only is it all right to pay taxes, we are bound by Scripture to pay taxes.

For they are God's ministers, attending continually upon this very thing. The word for "ministers" (Greek *leitourgos*) is used in the N.T. in other places of one who ministered in religious matters (Rom. 15:16; Phil. 2:25; Heb. 1:7; 8:2). According to Arndt and Gingrich it was also used in extra-biblical literature to refer to government officials (472). In a sense, public officials are carrying out a religious service because government is particularly ordained of God to perform functions that are necessary for the good of mankind and the cause of Christ. Since they do perform these all important functions, it is our responsibility to pay taxes.

7 Render therefore to all their dues: tribute to whom tribute *is due;* custom to whom custom; fear to whom fear; honour to whom honour.

Render therefore to all their dues. Since government is ordained of God and government officials are ministers or servants of God, it behooves us to render to them what is due them. The rest of the verse tells what is due them.

Tribute to whom tribute. This means taxes. See on v. 6.

Custom to whom custom. Concerning the word for custom (Greek *telos*), Moody explains, "There was also the local *revenue* (*telos*) for use of roads, bridges, markets, harbors, animals, carts, and wagons. The first of these [referring back to 'tribute'] was a direct tax, and the second was indirect; but Paul instructs Christians to pay both" (259).

Fear to whom fear. It is generally agreed that the reference here is the respect owed to government officials. However, Cranfield is inclined toward a different view. The word for fear (Greek *phobos*) he says "is not characteristically used of what is due to an earthly ruler" (II:671). He thinks the reference is to fear toward God (II:670-673; see also Harrison 140). It seems to me that since all of the other terms relate to attitudes toward government officials this one would also. The translation "respect" seems to convey the meaning better.

Honour to whom honour. Murray observes,

> It is possible that difference of rank among officers of state is indicated by the terms 'fear' and 'honor,' that the former has in view the respect paid to those of the highest level of authority and the latter paid to those of lower rank. But there is not sufficient evidence to insist on this distinction. Both terms could be used for the purpose of emphasizing the obligation to exercise not only the subjection due rulers but also the veneration that belongs to them as ministers of God (II:156,157).

E. The Believer Is Challenged to Love His Neighbor As Himself (13:8-10).

8 Owe no man any thing, but to love one another: for he that loveth another hath fulfilled the law.

Owe no man any thing, but to love one another. The word "dues" in "Render therefore to all their dues" is a noun (Greek *opheile*) which means "that which is owed." The word "owe" (Greek *opheilo*) in v. 8 is the verb form of the same word and means "to owe" or "to be under obligation to." In talking about civil authorities, Paul had said, "Give them what is owed to them, which includes tribute, custom, respect, and honor." In v. 8 Paul is continuing with our obligations to others, extending it to what we owe to *all* people.

On the expression "owe no man any thing," some have thought that it means that it is wrong to owe money. However, as Harrison says, "If incurring any indebtedness whatever is contrary to God's will, the Lord would not have said, 'Do not turn away from the one who wants to borrow from you' (Mt. 5:42). On the other hand, to be perpetually in debt is not a good testimony for a believer, and to refuse to make good one's obligations is outrageous" (141).

What Paul is talking about is being caught up on our obligations to other people. As we can tell from v. 7, the obligation to others is to be understood on a much broader scale than money. A person who is always on the receiving end of accommodations instead of the giving end would also be in violation of "owe no man any thing." We "owe" it to people to take our turn.

Love itself is not an obligation that we can catch up with because by its very nature, love is a perpetual obligation. It is a basic Christian value and should always characterize our lives.

For he that loveth another hath fulfilled the law. When we love another person that motivation will lead us to treat a person in accord with the moral teachings of the Ten Commandments.

9 For this, Thou shalt not commit adultery, Thou shalt not kill, Thou shalt not steal, Thou shalt not bear false witness, Thou shalt not covet; and if *there be* any other commandment, it is briefly comprehended in this saying,

namely, Thou shalt love thy neighbour as thyself.

For this, Thou shalt not commit adultery. To either abuse or seduce a person sexually is very degrading. No other sin that is practiced widely is so devastating to a person's personality as sexual sin. Anyone who understands the nature of love will have more respect for other people than to mistreat them sexually.

Thou shalt not kill. It should go without saying that if we love another person, we will have the highest regard for their lives and safety.

Thou shalt not steal. What is said above certainly applies here.

Thou shalt not bear false witness. To love another obviously means that we would not give a false witness in court that could lead to a conviction of the innocent. It should be just as obvious that if we love another person, we will not spread lies and half-truths so as to damage his reputation and influence.

Thou shalt not covet. When we covet that which is another's, whatever else it says about us, it means that we do not have a proper regard for the person. If we did, we would rejoice with him (12:15) rather than let our greed lead us into an unholy desire to have it for ourselves.

And if there be any other commandment. Paul is saying that he did not give a complete listing of moral laws.

It is briefly comprehended in this saying, namely, Thou shalt love thy neighbour as thyself. Paul, in dealing with love, did not feel it necessary to list every law that love motivates us to fulfill. If love is genuine, it can find out some things for itself. It will tend to arrive at, on its own, what the law has said without always being informed by law. However, love is willing to be informed by law.

It should also be observed that "Love thy neighbour as thyself" suggests that it is appropriate for a person to have a healthy regard for himself. It is a poor basis for loving our neighbor if we love them as ourselves and cannot love ourselves. There is a proper love and respect that we can have for ourselves (Eph. 5:28). We are God's by both creation and redemption. We dare not downgrade the handiwork of God.

10 Love worketh no ill to his neighbour: therefore love *is* the fulfilling of the law.

Love worketh no ill to his neighbour. A reading of the comments on v. 9 will show that to violate the moral teachings of the Ten Commandments does work ill or do injury to another.

The common ground between love and holiness embraces the morality of the Ten Commandments. However, when it comes to retributive justice, love and holiness do not share a common ground. It is retributive justice, not love, that metes out penalties for law violation. This justice does, of course, need to be tempered by love.

Therefore love is the fulfilling of the law. Love is the fulfilling of the law for the simple reason that it motivates a person to do the same as the law has prescribed. Picirilli explains:

> Paul summarizes his reason for teaching that love for one's neighbor will fulfil the law. That 'love worketh no ill to his neighbour' means that love always operates in such a way as to seek the neighbor's good, not his hurt. Love desires others' happiness, not misery; others' advancement, not hindrance; others' welfare, not poverty. Consequently, we desire to help others, to see them

prosper when we love them. We will not hold back that which they need, whether material or spiritual need is involved (274).

F. The Believer Is Challenged to Moral Purity in View of the Meaning of the Completion of His Salvation in the Eschatological Future (13:11-14).

11 And that, knowing the time, that now *it is* high time to awake out of sleep: for now *is* our salvation nearer than when we believed.

And that, knowing the time, that now it is high time to awake out of sleep. The word for "time" (Greek *kairos*) in the first part of the verse means "season." The period of time is viewed from the standpoint of the nature of the time. It is a time for concern. (See Earle 238, 239 for a discussion on the meaning of the Greek word.) The second use of the word "time" (Greek *hora*) is different and means "hour." The meaning is, "The hour (or time) has come for you to awaken out of moral sleepiness or lethargy. It is a time for moral and spiritual vigilance."

For now is our salvation nearer than when we believed. The time referred to is the completion of our salvation in the eschatological future. It is the time of the second coming of Christ. We do not know when Jesus Christ will return. But we do know that the time is closer than it has ever been. Realizing that He could come at any time, we are motivated toward moral earnestness.

12 The night is far spent, the day is at hand: let us therefore cast off the works of darkness, and let us put on the armour of light.

The night is far spent, the day is at hand. "The night" characterizes the age in which we live. "The day" refers to the time of Christ's return. Picirilli explains, "The time we live in is called 'night' because Christ is not here. The spiritual darkness of our age, and its ignorance of God, means that our times are more like night than day. When Jesus comes, and only then, it will be day. Compare 2 Peter 1:19, where we are told to take heed, now, to the Scripture as a light shining in a dark place, awaiting the dawning of the true day" (276). (See Murray II:167-169 for a good discussion on "the night" and "the day.")

Let us therefore cast off the works of darkness, and let us put on the armour of light. Though we live in the night, we are to cast off the works of darkness. Though "the day" is to come only in the eschatological future, we already know the Christ who will make that day the time of light that it will be. As the writer of Hebrews tells us, we "have tasted...the powers of the world [age] to come" (6:5). Having partaken of the age to come, we are able "to put on the armour of light" and walk in light. We need the "armour of light" because we face opposition while still living in the night.

Harrison explains, "Even though the day as an eschatological point has not yet arrived, the believer belongs to the day (I Thess. 5:8), anticipating by the very atmosphere of his transformed life the glory that will then be revealed (2 Cor. 3:18: 4:4)" (143).

13 Let us walk honestly, as in the day; not in rioting and drunkenness, not in chambering and wantonness, not in strife and envying.

Let us walk honestly, as in the day. The word "honestly" (Greek *euschemonos*) occurs in two other places in the N.T.: (1) 1 Cor. 14:40 where it is translated "decently," and (2) 1 Th. 4:12 where it is translated "honestly." It means to walk in a "becoming" way. (See Earle 239, 240 for a discussion on the meaning of this word.)

"Walking as in the day" means that as one who already partakes of the power of Christ in his life, the believer should be walking so as to demonstrate the powers which will be shown on a larger scale in the eschatological day.

Not in rioting and drunkenness. This is the first of three pairs of words that deal with evils to be avoided. Picirilli explains:

> The first pair, 'rioting and drunkenness,' refers to excessive indulgence on the stomach's side of the flesh. The rioting (Greek *komos*) is reveling, carousal. Originally this was the practice of drunken celebrants who paraded through the Greek city with torches and music in honor of the god of wine, Bacchus. Thus, rioting can refer to any feast and drinking-party characterized by unrestrained celebration and revelry. The 'drunkenness' refers to any intoxication, whether at a party or alone, what Trench calls a 'drinking-bout': a binge, a drunken spree. These two are together again in Galatians 5:21 (277).

Not in chambering and wantonness. Picirilli explains:

> The second pair, 'chambering and wantonness,' refers to excessive indulgence on the sexual side of the flesh. 'Chambering' is the Greek word *coitus* [sic] and thus refers to illicit sexual relations. 'Wantonness' (Greek *aselgeia* literally means without restraint and refers to any lack of self-control: lust or any of the fruits of lust. Especially does the word carry with it an idea of shameless abandon (277).

Barclay's comments are helpful on "wantonness." He explains,

> *Aselgeia* is one of the ugliest words in the Greek language. It does not describe only immorality; it describes the man who is lost to shame. Most people seek to conceal their evil deeds, but the man in whose heart there is *aselgeia* is long past that. He does not care who sees him; he does not care what people think of him. *Aselgeia* is the quality of the man who dares publicly to do the things which are unbecoming for any man to do (179).

Not in strife and envying. Of these words, Picirilli explains: "The third pair of words, 'strife and envying,' refers to sins of attitude and emotion, especially in relationship to others (thus bringing us back to our duty to love others). Strife is contention or wrangling. Envying is jealousy or hatred. Real love for others will not tolerate such emotions or the actions that grow from them. These two are together again in Galatians 5:20 and 1 Cor. 3:3" (277).

We greatly underestimate the significance of these sins. Their presence here with the other two pairs should tell us something about the seriousness of strife and envy.

14 But put ye on the Lord Jesus Christ, and make not provision for the flesh, to *fulfil* the lusts *thereof*.

But put ye on the Lord Jesus Christ. The reference here is not to putting on the righteousness of Christ in justification. The "putting on of Christ" in this reference has to do with sanctification. We are to put on the attitude and ways of Christ.

And make not provision for (the ways of) **the flesh.** The word for "provision" (Greek *pronoia*) is a noun. We have seen the verb form (Greek *pronoeo*) in 12:17 (see discussion there). This noun means "forethought." We are to give no forethought (make no plans) for the fulfillment of the desires of the flesh. All forms of sin should be left out of our plans.

Summary 13:1-14

In discussing the practical concerns Paul had for the believers at Rome, he felt it necessary to deal with the Christian view of civil government. Every person is to be subject to civil authorities. The reason is that civil authority is ordained of God. To resist civil authority is to resist the ordinance of God, and the authorities have a Divine right to inflict punishment.

Paul did not get involved in the cases where it would be justified to disobey a directive of government. This does not mean that he did not recognize that such a case could occur. However, since he did not mention possible exceptions, it probably means that we should take our responsibility to government with such seriousness that we would fail to submit to government only with extreme caution.

Government serves a necessary purpose both for mankind and the church. The Divine design for government is to produce that fear that would help curb wrongdoing, and to encourage right doing. In spite of the weakness of human government, it is amazing to what extent things are better with government than they would be without it.

Paul not only points out that government, itself, is ordained of God, but he also refers to its officials as being ministers and servants of God. All of this adds up to a very high respect for government.

The government in the carrying out of its Divine responsibility has the authority to fix penalties for law violation. These penalties may go so far as to inflict capital punishment as is borne out by the words, "He beareth not the sword in vain" (v. 4).

The Christian is obligated to submit to government and be a law-abiding citizen not only to avoid the penalty of the law, but also for conscience sake. Since government is ordained of God and the officials are servants of God, it follows that a Christian's conscience binds him to being a law-abiding citizen.

In addition to obeying the law, we are to pay tribute and custom and to render respect and honor to whom such is due.

With regard to people in general, we are to avoid getting behind in our obligations to them. We are to let the only unfulfilled obligation be to love one another. When we love one another, it will lead us to fulfill the moral teachings of the Ten Commandments. That is true because love does not want to inflict harm and injury on its object. To violate the morality of the Ten Commandments necessarily involves inflicting harm and hurt on others.

By considering the nature of the time, Christians must awaken out of moral and spiritual lethargy. The time of the completion of salvation in the eschatological future is getting nearer. We do not know how near. The time we are living in is night. It is a time of moral darkness. When Christ comes back the day will come. It will be a time of moral and spiritual prosperity. In view of all this, believers are to cast off the works of darkness and put on the armor of light. Since we already partake of the power of Christ, we are to walk now as though we were in the day (the time after Christ returns).

Believers are to walk in a becoming way. We are to avoid reckless revelry, drunkenness, sexual immorality, strife, and envyings. We are to put on the attitudes and ways of Christ. We are to leave out plans for fulfilling the lust of the flesh.

Application: Teaching and Preaching the Passage

1. This passage (vv. 1-7) is the single most important passage in the Bible on the Christian view of government.

2. Civil government, according to vv. 1-7 is a Divine provision:

(1) Civil authority is ordained of God (v. 1).

(2) Law officials are the ministers of God to us for good (v. 4).

(3) A civil official is "the minister of God, a revenger to execute wrath upon him that doeth evil" (v. 4).

(4) To resist civil authority is to resist the ordinance of God (v. 2).

3. Stated positively, the Christian's responsibility to government is as follows:

(1) He is to be subject to it (v. 5).

(2) He is to pay taxes to support the government (vv. 6, 7).

(3) He is to have respect for government officials (v. 7).

4. Stated negatively, the Christian's responsibility to government is:

(1) He is not to resist its authority (v. 2).

(2) Failure to obey government can result in suffering a penalty for violation (vv. 2, 4, and 5) and a bad conscience (v. 5).

5. Many are of the opinion that v. 4 is N.T. support for capital punishment. (See comments on "He beareth not the sword in vain.")

6. The thought of civil disobedience is a very serious matter. It should not be entered into lightly (see comments on the last part of v. 1).

7. As Christians we are to keep up with our obligations to other people. These obligations include far more than monetary obligations. They include treating people with proper respect. Love is a continuing obligation. We never get caught up with this obligation (v. 8).

8. An examination of the moral teachings of the Ten Commandments tells us that if we love our neighbors as ourselves we will not violate the moral teachings of the Ten Commandments (see comments on vv. 9, 10).

9. Paul encourages us by the nearness of the second coming to awake out of moral and spiritual lethargy (v. 11).

10. The age we live in is called night in comparison to the age that will follow the return of Christ. Though we live in the night, we are to put on the armor of light. We are to cast off the works of darkness and live as those who are partaking of the light and the power of the coming age (see comments on v. 12).

11. Though this age is called night, we are to live "as in the day." This calls for casting off the sins named in the verse. (See comments on these sins in the notes on v. 13.)

12. Putting on the Lord Jesus Christ in this verse does not refer to putting on the righteousness of Christ in justification. Rather, it refers to putting on the likeness of Christ in *sanctification* (v. 14).

13. Our plans for our lives should include none for fulfilling the lust of the flesh. They should be to resist the lust of the flesh (v. 14).

G. Believers Are Challenged to Manifest an Understanding Attitude Toward Each Other With Regard to Differences Over Questionable Matters (14:1-12).

Paul dealt with things in 13:13 which were unquestionably wrong. In this chapter, Paul deals with matters where the decisions are not so easy. He deals with matters not specifically condemned in Scripture as being inherently sinful.

These matters rightfully belong to the subject of Christian liberty, which has as its scope things not directly condemned in Scripture as being wrong. This is the liberty of each individual to consider the facts and principles involved and arrive at his own conclusion about what he should do. This by no means is to be understood to mean that each Christian can do as he pleases about such matters. *That is obviously not what Paul is teaching in this chapter.* One of the greatest tests of a person's love for God, fellow believers, and sinners is the attitude with which he approaches the type of things dealt with here.

Paul is concerned basically with two things: (1) diet and (2) special religious days. Those who are designated "weak" are vegetarians and have a problem regarding special days. Those designated "strong" are those who do not concur with those who have problems about religious diet and days. Paul admonishes both groups to have respect, appreciation, thoughtfulness, and consideration for one another.

Barrett says that the problem of the weak "attests a failure to grasp the fundamental principle, which page after page of this epistle emphasizes, that men are justified and reconciled to God not by vegetarianism, sabbatarianism, or teetotalism, but by faith alone—or, better, by God's own free electing grace, faith being man's recognition that all is dependent not upon himself but God" (256, 257).

I reject Barrett's view as does Cranfield. He explains, "But what is surely a conclusive objection to this view of the matter has quite often been stated, namely, that to seek to be justified on the ground of one's works would have been, for Paul, a matter of having ceased to have, or of never having had, true faith, and, had the people referred to really failed to grasp the truth that justification is by faith alone, Paul would not have regarded them as genuine believers" (II:691).

A great deal of confusion exists by failing to distinguish between soteriological legalism and ethical legalism. Soteriological legalism is a wrong dependence upon law which in some measure depends on works for salvation. Ethical legalism is a wrong dependence on law which seeks to use law as the only means of ethical responsibility.

In Galatians Paul dealt with both kinds of legalism. In 1:1—3:18 he dealt with soteriological legalism. In 3:19—4:31 he dealt with ethical legalism. (See my *Biblical Ethics* 115-117, as well as my "Legalism in Galatians" in *Dimension*, Winter quarter 1984-85.)

Paul showed no tolerance for soteriological legalism because it threatened the very existence of the gospel. When ethical legalism is separated from soteriological legalism, it is quite possible that a person can be an ethical legalist, to some extent, without jeopardizing his view of grace. This leads to hang-ups and may make the person unnecessarily hard to get along with, but it does not necessarily corrupt the doctrine of grace. It is quite evident that to whatever extent the "weak" showed any influence of legalism in chap. 14, it is ethical rather than soteriological.

There is no sure explanation of why the "weak" were vegetarians. The most likely interpretation seems to be that there were some among the Jewish converts who were: (1) not able to shake off concern for the O.T. dietary laws, and (2) were afraid that meat offered to idols, sold freely, would find its way to their table. Since their consciences were not trained so as to give them freedom in these areas, they became vegetarians rather than run the risk. (For a defense of this view as the most likely view and other helpful introductory information on this chapter, see Cranfield II:690-698. For other helpful introductions, see Bruce 243, 244 and Hendriksen 452-455.)

1 Him that is weak in the faith receive ye, *but* not to doubtful disputations.

Him that is weak in the faith receive ye. In the Greek the article occurs before faith. In my opinion faith without the article refers to the experience of believing. Faith with the article, except in cases denoting possession and a few cases of the article of previous reference, refers to that which is believed. Just as "the Law" was a synonym for the Mosaic Law, "the Faith" seems to be a synonym for the New Covenant (see comments on 3:30). I would take the meaning to be him that is weak in the "New Covenant" or "the faith way."

But not to doubtful disputations. Picirilli explains,

> This means that the acceptance of the weaker brother must be wholehearted and unselfish. The stronger brother might be tempted to take the brother he disagrees with into fellowship just to argue with him. But that is not the proper spirit. The word translated 'disputations' (Greek *diakrisis*) literally means judgments, discernments, or opinion passing. The 'doubtful' (Greek *dialogismos*) refers to uncertain debate over foods, the questions the two sides disagree about. In other words, then, the so-called stronger brother is not to receive the other in a conceited spirit and with the purpose of passing judgment on the weaker brother's doubts (281, 282).

(For good discussions on this expression see Cranfield II:700, 701 and Earle 241, 242.)

In this chapter, it is obvious that Paul considers the "strong" to be correct in believing that it was alright for the Christian to eat meat as well as vegetables. He considered the decision of the "weak"—that it was inappropriate to eat meat—to be incorrect. He considered both the weak and the strong to be wrong in their attitudes toward one another.

We must keep in mind that this position is given by an inspired apostle. That makes his decision right. However, in the application of the principles of this chapter, we cannot assume that those we may call "weak" are always incorrect and that the "strong" are always right. We must, of course, conclude that in matters where the principles of this chapter apply, we should be able to respect one another. That message is clear.

2 For one believeth that he may eat all things: another, who is weak, eateth herbs.

Some of the believers had no problems with the matter of diet so far as religious conviction is concerned. There were others who were not, for whatever reason, able to accept that position. They would eat only herbs (or vegetables).

It is not certain who the vegetarians were, nor why they refused to eat meat. It is thought by many that they were overscrupulous Jewish Christians who because of complicating circumstances took that approach as the safe way. (See discussion in the introductory comments above.)

3 Let not him that eateth despise him that eateth not; and let not him which eateth not judge him that eateth: for God hath received him.

Let not him that eateth despise him that eateth not. This part of the verse is addressed to the strong. Wuest explains the word for "despise" (Greek *exoutheneo*) means, "'to throw out as nothing,' thus, 'to treat as nothing and so with contempt'" (231). The problem of the strong ones is that they look down their noses at the weak. Paul admonishes them to refrain from such an attitude.

And let not him which eateth not judge him that eateth: for God hath received him. This part of the verse is addressed to the weak. The danger of the weak brother is that he will manifest a condemning attitude toward the person who violates his scruples. He may even question whether the person has evidence of salvation. Paul admonishes the weak against such an attitude because God has received the person who "eats meat."

4 Who art thou that judgest another man's servant? to his own master he standeth or falleth. Yea, he shall be holden up: for God is able to make him stand.

Paul continues to address the weak with regard to their condemning attitude. He refers to an illustration from life. We would not judge another man's servant. That judgment belongs to the master of the servant. God is the Master of the one who eats meat. God will take care of him.

5 One man esteemeth one day above another: another esteemeth every day *alike*. Let every man be fully persuaded in his own mind.

One man esteemeth one day above another: another esteemeth every day *alike*. Paul gives another illustration of conflict where difference of opinion was to be allowed. In all likelihood the reference is again to Jewish believers who were not ready to loose themselves from the instructions of the O.T. with regard to special days (see Lev. 23). That there was such a problem in the early church is evidenced by Gal. 4:10, 11 and Col. 2:16, 17.

Harrison takes another view. He explains, "The close contextual association with eating suggests that Paul has in mind a special day set apart for feasting or a time for fasting" (146).

Since Paul says such a little bit about the matter of days, we cannot have absolute assurance what he had in mind. However, we can know that the principles he laid down could apply to any situation where they fitted. It is possible that part of what Paul was asking for was patient understanding during this period of transition from the seventh day to the first day of the week as the special day of worship. It is not necessary to take the words "another esteemeth every day *alike*" to mean that such a person gave no value to having a special day for worship. It may mean that, with regard to the special days laid out in the O.T. (Lev. 23) as special feast days, he saw no difference in those days and other days. (For discussion on the problem of the days in this verse, see Cranfield II:705, Murray II:178, and Appendix D, "Romans 14:5 and the Weekly Sabbath," 257-259.)

Let every man be fully persuaded in his own mind. This does not mean that whatever a person decides will be right, but it does tell us that every man should live by his own integrity. Paul is by no means encouraging a light approach to dealing with such matters. The Christian is to take such matters seriously. He is to look at the evidence and weigh the facts. He is duty bound to abide by that which the evidence supports, not what he wishes it supported.

What Paul is saying in this verse and in this chapter does not mean that we have no right to approach another believer about matters that may seem to be, in principle, covered in this chapter. It does mean that we should respect them. We should not seek to intimidate them, nor to rule by decree. In a respectful way we can appeal to their hearts and minds. We must respect their rights in deciding the issue.

6 He that regardeth the day, regardeth *it* unto the Lord; and he that regardeth not the day, to the Lord he doth not regard *it*. He that eateth, eateth to the Lord, for he giveth God thanks; and he that eateth not, to the Lord he eateth not, and giveth God thanks.

It is obvious that in this verse Paul is dealing with differences among those who are sincere in their commitment to God. Whether the person keeps the day as a special day or does not, he is doing what he thinks God wants him to do. He is abiding in his own integrity. The same goes for the person who eats meat and the one who eats only vegetables. Each in his own way gives thanks.

It is important to observe that Paul is talking about differences of opinion among those who take their relationship to God seriously. There is no formula for finding how to serve God acceptably apart from loving God.

**7 For none of us liveth to himself, and no man dieth to himself.
8 For whether we live, we live unto the Lord; and whether we die, we die unto the Lord: whether we live therefore, or die, we are the Lord's.**

Human beings are "relationship creatures." We cannot be explained apart from relationships. Absolute isolationism is impossible. The most important relationship that we have is that which we have to God through Jesus Christ. We belong to Him. All of our ethical, moral, and spiritual decisions must be made with that in mind. We must also allow other people to do the same. Our obligation to Christ remains unchanged even by death.

9 For to this end Christ both died, and rose, and revived, that he might be Lord both of the dead and living.

Christ by His Divine nature partakes in the sovereignty of God over creation. However, His Lordship over the redeemed is not His by His nature, but is His by achievement. There could be no redemption apart from His death and resurrection. By His death He made atonement. By His resurrection, He conquered death and lives to administer the salvation which He purchased for us by His death. He is the Lord of both those who are now living and those who are now dead. He will demonstrate His Lordship over the dead by restoring them to life in the resurrection. It is ours to live with an awareness that His Lordship applies not only to this life but also to the next one.

10 But why dost thou judge thy brother? or why dost thou set at nought thy brother? for we shall

all stand before the judgment seat of Christ.

But why dost thou judge thy brother? Paul again addresses the weak. He had already in v. 3 admonished the weak not to have a judgmental or a condemning attitude toward those who felt at liberty to eat meat.

Or why dost thou set at nought thy brother? The strong are addressed here as in v. 3. The same word (Greek *exoutheneo*) which is translated "despise" is translated "set at nought" in this verse. Paul is saying, "Why do you look with such contempt on your brother?"

For we shall all stand before the judgment seat of Christ. There are three reasons that an awareness of the coming judgment seat of Christ should temper our attitude toward others in matters affected by the principles taught in this chapter: (1) The fellow believer about whom we are concerned will stand before Him who will have a perfect understanding of His action. If in fact it is inappropriate, he will be held accountable. (2) We should be careful in our attitude toward others because we ourselves will stand before Him who will not be affected by our blind spots. Our faults will be seen in the clear light of day. (3) We will not be responsible for his actions, but our own.

The Christian's judgment is also referred to in 1 Cor. 3:12-15 and 2 Cor. 5:10. A healthy awareness of the judgment seat of Christ will help us in our relationship to others.

11 For it is written, *As* I live, saith the Lord, every knee shall bow to me, and every tongue shall confess to God.

This verse is taken from Is. 45:23. The concept of a time of judgment is supported in both Testaments. Picirilli observes, "The 'bowing' and 'confessing' do not necessarily represent true heart-felt submission, but the enforced submission of all before the Lord as Judge" (286).

12 So then every one of us shall give account of himself to God.

Paul drives home this most sobering thought. We will each have our turn before God to give our own account. Picirilli explains, "We will not answer for others, nor will others answer for us. Thus the 'weaker' brother will not have to answer for the carefree brother, or vice versa. Nor will either be judged by the other's standards—a comforting thought! But each will be judged by God's standards—a not-so-comforting thought!" (287).

H. Believers Are to Be Guided by Certain Principles With Regard to Questionable Matters (14:13-23).

13 Let us not therefore judge one another any more: but judge this rather, that no man put a stumblingblock or an occasion to fall in *his* brother's way.

Let us not therefore judge one another any more. This is the conclusion of what Paul has said in vv. 10-12.

But judge this rather, that no man put a stumblingblock or an occasion to fall in *his* brother's way. These words are addressed to the strong. It should be observed that all was not well with those whom we refer to as "strong". They needed to know what it meant to love a brother whom they considered weak. They were to conduct themselves with the deepest interest in the spiritual welfare of the brother who seemed to be guided by a more sensitive conscience.

On the words for "stumblingblock" and "occasion to fall" Harrison explains, "A stumbling block (*proskomma*) is literally something against which one may strike his foot, causing him to stumble or even fall. The second term (*skandalon* rendered 'obstacle' here ['an occasion to fall,' KJV]) presents a different picture, that of a trap designed to ensnare a victim" (148).

Most do not see any difference intended by the metaphorical significance of these two words. Those who do think the last one represents that which is more serious (see Godet 460 and Lenski 832, 833).

It is important that we understand Paul's meaning in this verse. We should not assume that we are to refrain from doing something simply because another believer may not like what we do. What we are to refrain from is that which may do serious spiritual detriment to another. As Picirilli says, "Paul is not referring to something that one's brethren will merely dislike but something that threatens the brother's spiritual progress, that may make him stumble into sin" (290).

Paul showed himself to be quite willing to live by the admonition of this verse when he said, "Wherefore, if meat make my brother to offend, I will eat no flesh while the world standeth, lest I make my brother to offend" (1 Cor. 8:13). See also 1 Cor. 8:19-23.

14 I know, and am persuaded by the Lord Jesus, that *there is* nothing unclean of itself: but to him that esteemeth any thing to be unclean, to him *it is* unclean.

I know, and am persuaded by the Lord Jesus, that *there* is nothing unclean of itself. It is possible that Paul is limiting the impact of his statement to foods. He may simply mean that no food is unclean of itself (1 Tim. 4:4). He could simply mean that under the New Covenant the distinctions made under the Old Covenant between clean and unclean are no longer binding. However, it seems to me that he means more than that by "there is nothing unclean of itself." It seems that he is saying that in its created state, nothing is immoral. It has a legitimate use. That does not mean of course that there is a legitimate use of all manufactured products.

This does not mean that there are not some things which are sinful within themselves. As Cranfield explains, "He is not thinking of men's actions, attitudes, desires, thoughts, etc. but only of the resources of the created world which are available for men's use" (II:713).

But to him that esteemeth any thing to be unclean, to him *it* is unclean. Matters such as adultery, murder, covetousness, etc., are inherently (or intrinsically) sinful. They are sinful whether a person thinks they are or not. It is intrinsically evil to rejoice in iniquity. However, there are many things, such as various kinds of foods, as Paul observed in the first part of the verse, which are not within themselves sinful. But if a person based on a misunderstanding of the case, thinks that it is sinful to eat a particular food (or some other matter to which these principles would apply), it is wrong for him to go contrary to his own sense of obligation. In this sense, it can be a sin for one person and not another. But in cases where an action is intrinsically evil, that action will be a sin for anyone whether he thinks it is or not.

15 But if thy brother be grieved with *thy* meat, now walkest thou not charitably. Destroy not him with thy meat, for whom Christ died.

But if thy brother be grieved with *thy* meat, now walkest thou not charitably (not according to love). The word for "meat" (Greek *broma*) is a general term for food. In this case it would be meat-eating because that is what was questioned by the vegetarians.

The "grief" in view in this verse would be more than just a mild concern. It would refer to a deep hurt. If we love a person, we do not want to hurt him. The Christian with the right attitude does not flaunt his rights at the expense of hurting another brother.

Destroy not him with thy meat (food), **for whom Christ died.** What Paul is talking about here is a matter of extreme seriousness. It could even lead to a shipwreck of faith. Earle explains:

> No less than ten Greek verbs are translated 'destroy' in the KJV. The one used here, *apollymi,* means to 'destroy utterly.'
>
> But the thing that concerns us is that this word is used frequently in the NT of sinners *perishing* without salvation. So here the idea is not of the weak brother having his reputation ruined or his life wasted in this world. The peril is that in causing him to stumble by our selfish liberties we may be responsible for his soul perishing forever. That danger should always act as a deterrent to any thoughtlessness toward others on our part. We may say that it is nobody's business what we do. But no one can hide behind that deceptive alibi. How we live *does* affect others, whether we want it to or not. In a very real sense every one of us is his brother's keeper (248).

In addition to the damage that can be brought to a brother by our careless actions, we also need to keep in mind that Christ died for him. Jesus Christ has a tremendous investment in the weak brother. We dare not treat with contempt the person in whom Jesus Christ has made the investment of His life to save him.

16 Let not then your good be evil spoken of.

When we parade our liberties before those who do not agree with these liberties, they will take our actions to be wrong. It is not enough to do right. We must do right in such a way that it will not be misunderstood.

We must always be mindful of the way our actions are perceived by others. To have an effective ministry, we must have a good influence. To have a good influence, we must have a good testimony. To have a good testimony, we must keep in mind the way other people think about issues.

17 For the kingdom of God is not meat and drink; but righteousness, and peace, and joy in the Holy Ghost.

For the kingdom of God is not meat and drink. The real issue is not whether we eat certain things or whether we do not. There are far more important issues. Cranfield observes, "It is not one's insistence on expressing one's freedom to eat a particular food which attests the presence of God's kingdom (nor is one in the slightest degree worse off in relation to it for having foregone the expression of one's freedom for one's brother's sake)" (II:718).

Murray's comments are in order here: "When questions of food and drink have become our chief concern, then it is apparent how far removed from the interests of God's kingdom our thinking and conduct have strayed (cf.

Mt. 6:31-33)" (II:193).

But righteousness, and peace, and joy in the Holy Ghost. The righteousness referred to here is the righteousness of sanctification, not justification. The hassle about dietary matters was not dealing with righteousness.

The hassle between the weak and the strong over dietary matters was affecting the unity of believers. They were not at peace with one another. They were allowing themselves to fall short in an area where it really counts—peace, and that over matters that were at very best minor. The church was hurting because of this.

Joy is greatly dampened whenever Christians get involved in squabbles over matters where the principles of this chapter are involved. The things that really count suffer. Under such circumstances, the Holy Spirit cannot produce the joy which is His work to produce.

Barnes makes the observation:

> A contentious, quarrelsome spirit; a disposition to magnify trifles; to make the Shibboleth of party an occasion of alienation, and heart-burning, and discord; to sow dissensions on account of unimportant points of doctrine or discipline, is full proof that there is no attachment to Him who is the Prince of Peace. Such a disposition does infinite dishonour to the cause of religion, and perhaps has done more to retard its progress than all other causes put together. Contentions commonly arise from some small matter of doctrine, in dress, in ceremonies; and often the smaller the matter the more fierce the controversy, till the spirit of religion disappears, and desolation comes over the face of Zion (308).

18 For he that in these things serveth Christ *is* acceptable to God, and approved of men.

"These things" refers back to "righteousness, and peace, and joy" in v. 17. These are the things which really count. These are things that are acceptable to God and are the things that will help us have a good testimony with others.

19 Let us therefore follow after the things which make for peace, and things wherewith one may edify another.

Since peace with one another is one of the things that really counts, since it is one of the things that is acceptable with God, and since it helps us have a good testimony before others, it behooves us to labor for a spirit of unity. It is a Christian obligation. We will never clear up all differences. Certainly, there are some things that are worth dividing over if necessary. However, much of the strife that afflicts the conservative church world reflects a failure to follow the principles laid down in this chapter.

The hassle over diet and days in the Roman church was not serving to build up one another. Rather, it was detrimental. It is our responsibility to build up one another in the faith rather than tear one another down.

20 For meat destroy not the work of God. All things indeed *are* pure; but *it is* evil for that man who eateth with offence.

For meat destroy not the work of God. It seems that this problem weighed heavily on the heart of Paul. He keeps coming back and saying what he had said before from a different angle. He did not spare any effort to get both the strong and the weak to see the error of their way. He again appeals to them not to destroy the work of God over the question of what foods to eat and not to eat.

Vine explains, "The word for 'destroy' (Greek *kataluo*) means, 'To overthrow,' literally 'to loosen down.' Here it is used of the marring of spiritual well-being, the pulling down of the work of God in a brother's life, and is set in contrast to building up (2:19)" (203).

All things indeed are pure; but *it* is evil for that man who eateth with offence. This verse is similar in meaning to v. 14. See comments there.

On the words "It is evil for that man who eateth with offence," Sanday and Headlam explain,

> It is a nice question to decide to whom these words refer. (1) Are they addressed to the strong, those who by eating are likely to give offence to others (so Va. Oltr., and the majority of commentaries)? or (2) Are they addressed to the weak, those who by eating what they think is wrong to eat injure their own consciences (So Gif. Mey. W. and others)? In the former case *dia proskommatos* [KJV 'with offence']... means, 'so as to cause offence,' in the latter 'so as to take offence' (Tyndale, 'who eateth with hurt to his conscience'). Perhaps the transition to ver. 21 is slightly better if we take (1) (392, 393).

Cranfield agrees with Sanday and Headlam in taking the position that it is evil for the strong to eat meat and so doing cause the weak to stumble by eating that which violates his conscience (II:723, 724).

Vine takes the other approach. He explains, "It is true that the strong are here addressed, but that is not a sufficient indication to guide us, for the evil is not necessarily predicated of the action of the party addressed" (*Romans* 203).

I take a little different approach. The words "evil for that man who eats with offence" are "about" the weak person. When he violates his conscience by eating, he sins. The words are "addressed" to the strong. Paul is reminding them of the fact that when a weak person violates his conscience by eating meat he sins. This reminder is to keep them from putting a stumblingblock in the path of the weak person. They are to consider the serious consequences that their action can have on a fellow believer.

21 *It is* good neither to eat flesh, nor to drink wine, nor *any thing* whereby thy brother stumbleth, or is offended, or is made weak.

This verse calls for us to live our lives with the deepest consideration for our fellow believers. Regardless of our own opinion about the rightness or wrongness of a matter, there may still be good reasons not to do a particular thing. If we adhere to the most literal application of the principles set forth in this chapter, it would have very little to say to us in our day. However, if we get to the heart of the principles, this chapter has much to say to us. Without doubt, it teaches me that I should have the deepest concerns about how my actions have a bearing on the moral and spiritual life of another person.

It is not always easy to know how to interpret some passages in the Bible on the subject of wine. However, to anyone who has caught the spirit of this chapter, this verse leads us to total abstinence. Partaking of alcoholic beverages is destructive to a person's testimony and puts a stumblingblock into the pathway of others. The moderate drinker is a stumblingblock to the one who cannot control his intake of alcohol. The alcoholic beverage industry has nothing to commend itself to us. We do not need to give it our endorsement. Whatever needs that might have existed in ancient society with its limited availability of medicine, absence of refrigeration, bottled drinks, and canned juices, that need does not exist among us.

We must always be alert to the sensitivities and the weaknesses of others. If we really love other people, and if we want to see the cause of Christ move forward, we will not find it so difficult to understand and apply the principles of this chapter. However, if we do not truly love others, and if we do not have a deep desire to see the cause of Christ go forward, we will resent the teachings of this chapter.

22 Hast thou faith? have *it* to thyself before God. Happy *is* he that condemneth not himself in that thing which he alloweth.

Hast thou faith? have it to thyself before God. Bruce explains,"'Faith' in this sense is a firm and intelligent conviction before God that one is doing right, the antithesis of feeling self-condemned in what one permits oneself to do" (253). Paul does not ask the "strong" to give up his conviction. He does ask him to maintain his conviction that "meat eating" is all right alongside a proper recognition of and a right relationship with God. It is not enough just to be technically right.

Happy *is* he that condemneth not himself in that thing which he alloweth. It is a good state to be in when a person's actions and conscience concur. One of the foundation blocks of happiness is for a person to practice that which his deep inner self is convinced of as being right. To violate our ethical values cuts away at our self-respect.

23 And he that doubteth is damned if he eat, because *he eateth* not of faith: for whatsoever *is* not of faith is sin.

And he that doubteth is damned if he eat. The word for doubt (Greek *diakrino*) is translated in Js. 1:6 as "wavering" and "wavereth." Such a person is considered to be double-minded (Js. 1:8): that is, he has two minds about the same thing—one mind agreeing and the other disagreeing.

By his own experience, the weak person thought it was wrong to eat meat. By observing the strong, another "mind" might arise within him telling him that it was alright. The problem was that he was not fully convinced that it was alright to eat. The "mind" that felt that it was wrong was the stronger mind. Thus, for him to eat under such circumstances was a sin. Such action would be condemned by God because he had violated his own conscience.

Because he eateth not of faith. He failed to have a conviction that his action was alright.

For whatsoever is not of faith is sin. Whatever is not of "conviction" is sin. It is wrong to violate our own conviction even when it is a misguided conviction. Our conviction must be properly informed before we have the freedom to perform the act.

Some have taken this part of the verse to mean that anything done by a person without saving faith is sin. The view given above has much more to commend itself. It fits the context better. I see no value in trying to tell an unsaved person that everything he does is a sin. There is plenty to convict him of his sins without taking such an approach.

This verse reminds the weak that he will have to get his thinking straight on the matter of eating meat before he can partake. This verse reminds the strong that by flaunting his liberty before the weak, he may cause the weak to sin by violating his own conscience.

I. THE STRONG ARE ADMONISHED TO BEAR THE INFIRMITIES OF THE WEAK (15:1-3).

1 We then that are strong ought to bear the infirmities of the weak, and not to please ourselves.

We then that are strong ought to bear the infirmities of the weak. Paul, at least in a measure, identifies himself with the strong. He identifies himself with their position but not their attitude. The strong were technically right, but they were not right in their lack of consideration and their attitude of contempt. They needed to be reminded that there are some responsibilities that go with being "strong."

In applying the principles of 14:1—15:13, it is natural that we consider those who have fewer convictions as being "strong" and those who tend to have more as being "weak." However, we need to be cautious. In the cases about the meat eating and the question of days, the strong were technically correct. In choosing between those who have fewer convictions and those who have more convictions today, this passage has no message for us concerning who is technically correct. However, what this passage says about attitudes and about loving one another is as applicable to us now as it was to the people in Rome when Paul wrote the epistle.

And not to please ourselves. This message cuts across the grain of self-centeredness. Only when we have the deepest love for others will we regulate our lives by the teaching of this verse.

2 Let every one of us please *his* neighbour for *his* good to edification.

Our aim should be so to conduct ourselves that we will help in the building up of others. This is the opposite of behaving in such a way that we put a stumblingblock into the pathway of another.

3 For even Christ pleased not himself: but, as it is written, The reproaches of them that reproached thee fell on me.

Paul appeals to the example of Christ who sought not to please Himself. The illustration of how He did not please Himself is taken from Ps. 69:9. Murray explains, "It is not our reproaches that are in view but the reproaches of dishonour levelled against God. These reproaches vented against God by the ungodly fell upon Christ. This is to say that all the enmity of men against God was directed to Christ; he was the victim of this assault. It is to this Paul appeals as exemplifying the assertion that Christ 'pleased not himself'" (II:199). (See also Cranfield II:733. For a view that it is man rather than God that is addressed and that Christ bore the reproaches of men, see Sanday and Hedlam 395.)

I take it that God is addressed and that the reproaches that were hurled against God were also hurled against Christ. This, of course, was not Christ's greatest suffering. That came from the wrath of God. However, for Christ to bear the reproaches that were hurled against God illustrates well the fact that He did not please Himself. If He could handle all of that, it should be a small matter for the strong Christian to direct his life with the best interest of the weak in mind.

J. Jewish and Gentile Believers Are Challenged to Receive One Another (15:4-13).

4 For whatsoever things were written aforetime were written for our learning, that we through patience and comfort of the scriptures might have hope.

Concerning this verse Picirilli explains:

> In essence, then, verse 4 is a defense, a justification for Paul's free use of the Old Testament both here and elsewhere in the epistle and that defense is simple: Whatever things were written before (the Old Testament Scriptures) were written for our learning (that is, to instruct us), with the purpose that we may have (that is, keep a hold on) hope, by means of the patience and comfort which these Scriptures produce in us (300).

Even for a person who is not well informed in the O.T., it is a great source of comfort and a strength for hope. Once we see, even on an elementary level, that the O.T. prepared the way for the coming of Christ, it helps us to believe in Him. It helps us to develop that kind of hope that we need to keep going.

5 Now the God of patience and consolation grant you to be likeminded one toward another according to Christ Jesus.

God as the God of "patience" (Greek *hupomone*) is the God who enables us to develop "steadfast endurance." The God of "consolation" (Greek *paraklesis*) is the God of "comfort" or the God of "encouragement."

Admonishing the people to be "likeminded one toward another" is not an admonition that the weak come to agree with the strong. It is toward a harmony that transcends the kind of differences in view in this passage. If harmony (or oneness of mind) never occurs until there is agreement on detail, it will never happen.

6 That ye may with one mind *and* one mouth glorify God, even the Father of our Lord Jesus Christ.

The harmony desired in v. 5 would make it possible for them to "with one mind *and* one mouth glorify God." We must not let petty differences cause us to fail to render to God the glory that is due Him.

7 Wherefore receive ye one another, as Christ also received us to the glory of God.

This verse is addressed both to the strong (the meat eaters) and the weak (the vegetarians). In spite of the difficulties involved, they should receive one another. When we consider that Christ has received us, it should be a small matter for us to receive one another in matters that involve the principles of this passage.

8 Now I say that Jesus Christ was a minister of the circumcision for the truth of God, to confirm the promises *made* unto the fathers.

As "a minister of circumcision," Jesus Christ was a minister to the Jews to confirm the promises made to the patriarchs Abraham, Isaac, and Jacob. Jesus Christ confirms and fulfills the promises made in the Abrahamic Covenant.

9 And that the Gentiles might glorify God for *his* mercy; as it is written, For this cause I will confess to thee among the Gentiles, and sing unto thy name.

And that the Gentiles might glorify God for his mercy. There is difficulty in deciding how the first part of this verse connects with v. 8. (For a presentation of possible explanations, see Cranfield II:742-744.) It seems to me that the first part of this verse is dependent upon "to confirm the promises made to the fathers [the patriarchs]." Jesus Christ was a minister to the Jews to confirm the promises made to the patriarchs "that the Gentiles might glorify God for his mercy."

The Abrahamic Covenant is the basic redemptive Covenant. Its fulfillment is necessary for the salvation of either Jew or Gentile. The covenant promises were made to Israel, but a way has been provided for Gentiles to come in with believing Jews and partake with them of these salvation promises. (See notes on "Israel as The Olive Tree" in comments on 11:17.)

9 And that the Gentiles might glorify God for *his* mercy; as it is written, For this cause I will confess to thee among the Gentiles, and sing unto thy name.
10 And again he saith, Rejoice, ye Gentiles, with his people.
11 And again, Praise the Lord, all ye Gentiles; and laud him, all ye people.
12 And again, Esaias saith, There shall be a root of Jesse, and he that shall rise to reign over the Gentiles; in him shall the Gentiles trust.

These verses consist of quotations from the O.T. to support the inclusion of Gentiles into a saving relationship with God. Picirilli explains:

> Paul uses four Scriptures to back up his claim that we are to glorify God for His mercy on all, especially on us Gentiles. The first (9b) is Psalm 18:49, which speaks of the Jew who praises God out among the heathen nations, rejoicing in his own and in their salvation. The second quotation (verse 10) is Deuteronomy 32:43 and speaks of the Jew and Gentile rejoicing together over God's mercy. The third (verse 11) is Psalm 117:1 and speaks directly of all heathen nations praising and glorifying God. The fourth (verse 12) reflects Isaiah 11:1,10 and refers clearly to Gentile salvation by Christ, the root of Jesse (father of David: note the connection between the *royal* family and the *reigning* of Christ over the Gentiles). All four of these citations do two things. First they speak clearly of God's mercy to Gentiles and of the glorification of God that results. Second, they cleverly link together the salvation of the Gentiles with that of the Jews, reminding us (and Paul's original readers) that Christ received *both*, and thus that both must receive each other (303).

It is important to observe that Paul is not talking abut two families of God—one Jewish and one Gentile. He is talking about only one family of God to which both Jews and Gentiles belong. The roots of this family of God go back to the Abrahamic Covenant. The Covenant Seed of Abraham is Israel. God has made it so that through Christ the Gentiles come in with the Covenant seed of Abraham (see notes on 11:17, "Israel as The Olive Tree").

Since Jews and Gentiles, as believers, both belong to the same family of

God, it behooves them to receive one another and get along well together. The stress on Jews and Gentiles receiving one another suggests the possibility that most of those who were concerned about meat eating were Jews and those who enjoyed the greater freedom were mostly Gentiles. It would certainly be understandable if this should be the case.

13 Now the God of hope fill you with all joy and peace in believing, that you may abound in hope, through the power of the Holy Ghost.

Now the God of hope fill you with all joy and peace in believing. The God of hope is the God who inspires hope. Hope is inspired by His promises and His faithfulness to His promises.

The reference to "joy and peace" reminds us of 14:17. It seems that Paul is particularly making a prayer wish that they would experience the peace that goes along with harmony. This peace would be accompanied by joy. The words "in believing" seem to imply the desire that they would have the joy and peace which appropriately go along with believing.

That ye may abound in hope, through the power of the Holy Ghost. Paul seems to have a very strong concern about their hope. The word "hope" occurs twice in this verse and once in v. 4. During the difficulties of life it is important to have hope. Hope gives the strength and motivation to keep on keeping on. This hope is theirs through the "patience and comfort of the scriptures" (v. 4) and "through the power of the Holy Spirit."

Summary
14:1—15:13

A problem was threatening the peace in the church at Rome. One group whom Paul called the "weak" were vegetarians. They, for some reason, had scruples against eating meat. This same group also had problems with regard to Holy days, perhaps the special feast days of the O.T. The other group whom Paul called the "strong" had no scruples about eating meat, and they felt no obligation with regard to the problem of Holy days that was bothering the weak.

In this passage, Paul repeatedly addresses both the strong and the weak. He pleaded with the strong not to look with contempt on the weak. He pleaded with the weak not to have a judgmental attitude toward the strong. In the sincerity of his own relationship with God, each was to make up his mind what to do about these matters.

Both the strong and the weak belong to God. Both the strong and the weak will be judged by God. The ultimate responsibility of judgment belongs neither to the strong nor the weak. God will take care of that. On this basis Paul appeals to them not to judge one another.

Paul urges the strong not to put a stumblingblock in the way of the weak brother. He says that while there is nothing wrong with the eating of meat, it is wrong if when doing so the weak violates his own conscience.

If the strong brother disregards this and becomes the occasion of influencing the weak brother to violate his conscience and eat meat, he is not showing proper love for his brother. The careless attitude of the strong could bring serious detriment to the spiritual life of the weak brother.

Paul reminds them that what really counts is not meat and drink. Rather, what really counts is righteousness, peace, and joy in the Holy Spirit. These are matters that bring approval from both God and man. Paul appeals to them to do those things which make for peace and things which build up another. It is good to avoid anything that could bring spiritual detriment to another.

The position of the strong about his conviction to eat meat is one to be maintained, but in a way that pleases God. The strong one, however, should keep in mind that it is wrong for the weak to violate his own conscience by eating the meat.

It is the obligation of both the strong and the weak to learn to live together in peace and harmony. However, the strong have the greater responsibility (14:1 and 15:1).

Paul appeals to the people on both sides to keep in mind that Christ pleased not Himself. He suffered all the reproaches that were vented against God. If He could do all of that, surely the strong and the weak could receive one another.

Paul reminds them that the things written in the O.T. were written to help them develop hope and steadfast endurance. He states a prayer wish that God would help them live in harmony with one another so they could with one mind and one mouth glorify God.

Paul develops support from the O.T. for the idea that there is one family of God. That family is now made up of both Jews and Gentiles. He closes this section with a prayer wish that God would fill them with all joy, peace, and that they would abound in hope through the power of the Holy Spirit.

Application: Teaching and Preaching the Passage

1. This passage is addressed to those Paul calls the "weak" and the "strong." The word "weak" is used in 14:1,2, and 15:1. The word "strong" is used only one time (15:1). While these are the only occurrences of the words referring to these two classes, it is always clear whether Paul is referring to the weak or to the strong.

2. The weak are those who have oversensitive consciences. They tended to think that some things were wrong which were not. The main example that Paul used was the omission of meat from their diet. Paul insisted that there was no Divine ordinance against eating meat. Those who were weak wanted to pass judgment on those who did not draw the line where they did.

The strong were those who made right decisions. They did not draw the line closer than Scripture required. However, they were not without fault. They tended to take a condescending view of the weak.

3. Paul reminds the weak:

(1) To refrain from judging the brother who felt at liberty to eat meat (vv. 3,4).

(2) That eating meat does not destroy the kingdom of God (v. 20).

(3) That there was nothing inherently wrong about eating meat (vv. 14, 20).

(4) That in judging a fellow brother who ate meat, he was passing judgment upon God's servant. He should let God do the judging of the brother who eats meat (v. 4).

(5) All, both the strong and the weak, will stand before God in judgment (vv. 10-12).

4. Paul reminds the strong:

(1) To receive the weak, but not just to criticize or argue with him about his scruples (v. 1).

(2) To bear the infirmities of the weak (15:1). Paul places the greater responsibility on the strong when it comes to learning to get along and accept one another.

(3) That the strong are not to look down on the weak (vv. 3, 10).

(4) That both the strong and the weak will stand in judgment before God (vv. 10-12).

(5) That no man should put a

stumblingblock or an occasion to fall in his brother's way (vv. 13, 15, 21).

(6) That when the weak think something is wrong, the strong contribute to his sinning when they influence him to violate his own thinking (vv. 14, 20, and 23).

(7) To give attention to things that make for peace and that will build up one another.

5. It is a mistake in our day to conclude that the person with fewer convictions is always the strong one and that the person with more convictions is always the weak person. Some people may have fewer convictions than others because they are not hungering and thirsting after righteousness.

6. It is incumbent upon both the weak and the strong to contribute to the peace and harmony of the church. We must learn to promote our convictions and concerns in such a way that unnecessary strife and division are not brought into the church (14:19; 15:2, 5-7).

7. As a part of Paul's call for unity he uses quotations from the O.T. to support the idea that Jews and Gentiles make up one family of God, not two. For that reason they should live in harmony with one another (15:6-13).

8. This passage should be carefully studied so as to establish its principles. We need to give our best spiritual effort to putting these principles to work. It would help do away with unnecessary strife. The spirit of unity achieved would help the spiritual growth of the members of our churches. It would also give us the kind of testimony before the lost that would greatly increase the effectiveness of our evangelistic efforts (Jn. 17:21).

II. PERSONAL REMARKS (15:14—16:27).

A. Paul Relates His Concern Over the Christians at Rome to the Fact That He Is the Apostle to the Gentiles (15:14-19).

14 And I myself also am persuaded of you, my brethren, that ye also are full of goodness, filled with all knowledge, able also to admonish one another.

Having pointed out a need that existed among the people, in this verse Paul sounds a positive note. This was to encourage the positive side of their experience. The people had faults, but Paul's opinion of them was not based simply on an analysis of their faults. His opinion also took into account their strong points. This produces a much healthier situation than simply dwelling on negatives would have.

Concerning the word for "goodness" (Greek *agathosune*) Vine explains that it "signifies, not moral excellence of itself, but a disposition to do good, to show a kindly activity toward others" (*Romans* 210). Picirilli says, "The goodness referred to is the practical manifestation of inner character. Thus the word often refers to kindness, benevolence, generosity, and similar demonstrations of inner goodness" (306).

By "filled with knowledge" is meant that they had an adequate knowledge of doctrinal, moral, and spiritual matters. They had grown in their spiritual experience.

Being "full of goodness" and "filled with all knowledge" made them "able to admonish one another." The word "admonish" (Greek *noutheteo*) combines the meanings "to warn" and "to encourage." To admonish means that you let a person know the seriousness of a situation, but you also go about it in a way that encourages. The warning helps people see the value or the importance of a matter. The encouragement helps the person to build hope and confidence that he can take the action necessary.

While the problem between the strong and the weak (dealt with in 14:1—15:13) presented a concern to Paul, he had hope that the situation could be cleared up. His remarks about the strong and the weak did not mean that they were to take a hands-off policy toward one another. They were to admonish one another. But they were to go about it in such a way that it would add to the solution of the problem rather than add to the problem.

15 Nevertheless, brethren, I have written the more boldly unto you in some sort, as putting you in mind, because of the grace that is given to me of God.

Though he had confidence in the people, he had written to them rather boldly about some matters which needed correction. There is no contradiction between having confidence in people and feeling that they need to be reminded. If there is not some degree of confidence in people, it is doubtful that reminding will be of any value. Most people need reminders and encouragement to bring out the best that is in them.

Paul reminded them of these matters because of the grace that God had given him. Grace is used here the same way it is in 12:3. Grace here is not the unmerited favor of saving grace, but the grace of God in the bestowal of gifts. In Paul's case it was the gift of apostleship.

16 That I should be the minister of Jesus Christ to the Gentiles, ministering the gospel of God, that the offering up of the Gentiles might be acceptable, being sanctified by the Holy Ghost.

The purpose of Paul's apostleship was that he might be the minister of Jesus Christ to the Gentiles. The word for minister (Greek *leitourgos*) refers here to rendering religious service.

Ministering the gospel of God. The word for ministering (Greek *hierourgeo)* is made up of temple (Greek *hieron)*, and to work (Greek *ergo)*. The meaning here is to do priestly service. In this priestly service, the offering is not the gospel, but as the next part of the verse will show, it is the converts.

That the offering up of the Gentiles might be acceptable. In performing his priestly ministry, Paul offered his Gentile converts as a sacrifice to God. Concerning the word "acceptable" (Greek *euprosdektos*), Vine states that it "signifies a very favourable acceptance" (*Dictionary* 22). When we win another person to Christ, we have performed a priestly service. We have offered that to God which He finds very acceptable.

The thought of Paul is similar in thought to the words of Isaiah when he said, "And they shall bring all your brethren *for* an offering unto the LORD out of all nations" (Is. 66:20).

Being sanctified by the Holy Ghost. An offering to God must be sanctified. The offering of the Gentiles had not followed the ceremonial procedures of the Mosaic law. However, they had been made holy in a far more significant and acceptable way by the Holy Spirit. Bruce explains: "There were some, no doubt, who maintained that Paul's Gentile converts were 'unclean' because they were not circumcised. To such cavillers Paul's reply is that his converts were 'clean' because they were sanctified by the Holy Spirit who had come to dwell in them (cf. verse 19, 'by the power of the Spirit of

God')" (260).

17 I have therefore whereof I may glory through Jesus Christ in those things which pertain to God.

Paul gloried, rejoiced, or was proud of what God had done through him. It was not a self-centered type of being proud or rejoicing. It was a rejoicing in Jesus Christ for the ministry that He had given him as the apostle to the Gentiles and for making that ministry fruitful.

18 For I will not dare to speak of any of those things which Christ hath not wrought by me, to make the Gentiles obedient, by word and deed.

Paul restricts his glorying to that which Christ had wrought through him in his ministry to the Gentiles. He had a right to be proud of this ministry. He was not claiming that his success was due to his own endeavors apart from God. He gave due credit, honor, and glory to Jesus Christ.

In giving proper credit to Christ, he did not deny the genuineness of his own involvement. Concerning "by word and deed," Picirilli explains, "The 'word' is the preaching Paul has done, the verbalization of the gospel (whether in person or in letter). The 'deed' refers to the effort of Paul, the work he has done, the energy he has expended, even the suffering he has experienced—all to get the gospel out to the Gentiles" (309).

19 Through mighty signs and wonders, by the power of the Spirit of God; so that from Jerusalem, and round about unto Illyricum, I have fully preached the gospel of Christ.

Through mighty signs and wonders, by the power of the Spirit of God. Paul is dealing here with the fact that miraculous signs accompanied his ministry. To see the significance of what he is saying we need to comment on the place and significance of the miraculous in the N.T.

There are three Greek words which are used in the N.T. to describe those supernatural works which we designate as miracles. They are translated "mighty works" (Greek *dunamis*), "signs" (Greek *semeion*), and "wonders" (Greek *teras*). These three words occur in this verse. "Mighty" refers to the miracle as a manifestation of supernatural power. "Signs" refers to the event as having theological significance. It is designed to reveal the presence of God and to authenticate the one performing the miracle as having the approval of God. "Wonders" describes the event as evoking amazement because the event is extraordinary.

To show the force of these words, we could translate the first one (*dunamis)* as "miraculous power" in this verse. It would read "through the miraculous power of signs and wonders."

There were four reasons for the miraculous in the N.T. (1) The miracles performed by Jesus were designed to show God's approval on Him and to aid in believing His claims and His message (Jn. 20:30, 31 and Acts 2:22). (2) They were designed, in the early church, to help people believe that the N.T. gospel was true (Heb. 2:3, 4). (3) They were designed to help the disciples believe in the new relationship entered into with the Holy Spirit on the day of Pentecost (Acts 2:4-11, 19). (4) They were designed to authenticate the apostleship of a true apostle (2 Cor. 12:12). If a man claimed to be an apostle and miracles at no time accompanied his ministry, his claim was to be dismissed.

In this verse, Paul is telling us that God had stamped His approval on his apostleship by having miracles to accompany his ministry. These miracles had also aided people in believing the gospel which he preached. Paul was especially indebted to God for the way He had blessed his ministry.

So that from Jerusalem, and round about unto Illyricum, I have fully preached the gospel of Christ. Picirilli explains:

> From Jerusalem, and round about unto 'Illyricum' stresses the breadth; 'fully preached' stresses the thoroughness. Illyricum was a country adjoining Macedonia on the far northwest. Paul considered that territory his, reaching out from Jerusalem in a semicircle through Antioch (in Syria), through Asia Minor, and across the Aegean into Greece. All three missionary journeys had been in that territory. He had covered that area with the gospel (309).

B. Paul Explains Why He Has Not Been to See Them Before This Time (15:20-22).

20 Yea, so have I strived to preach the gospel, not where Christ was named, lest I should build upon another man's foundation.

Paul considered his calling to be a church planter. He wanted to blaze new trails. It was his desire to plant churches in major cities so that these churches could serve as places from which the gospel could go out into the surrounding areas. Since he was a church planter, he avoided building on another man's foundation. He preferred to extend the gospel into areas where it had not yet reached.

21 But as it is written, To whom he was not spoken of, they shall see: and they that have not heard shall understand.

This verse is taken from Is. 52:15. Paul considered his ministry to be part of the fulfillment of this verse. Murray observes, "This text is derived from a context in which the world-wide effects of Messiah's sacrifice are in view and the appropriateness of the application to the apostle's Gentile ministry is apparent. He conceives of his own work as the minister of Christ to be conducted in pursuance of this prophecy and, therefore, as not only in accord with God's design but as specifically demanded by Scripture" (II:215).

22 For which cause also I have been much hindered from coming to you.

The reason Paul had been hindered from going to Rome earlier was that of an unfinished task. There had been places in the areas covered by his missionary journeys that he felt obliged to plant new churches.

C. Paul Speaks of Plans to Come to See Them Soon (15:23-29).

23 But now having no more place in these parts, and having a great desire these many years to come unto you.

Paul had desired for many years to go to Rome and visit the church. This probably indicates that Paul's converts had had a strong enough hand in the church at Rome that it would not violate his principle of not building on another man's foundation to visit and minister to the people at Rome.

Paul was now free to go to Rome because the unfinished task had been finished. He had planted enough churches in the area from Jerusalem to Illyricum to feel that his plan had been fulfilled. The churches which had been planted in this area could asume the responsibility for evangelizing the surrounding areas now.

24 Whensoever I take my journey into Spain, I will come to you: for I trust to see you in my journey, and to be brought on my way thitherward by you, if first I be somewhat filled with your *company.*

Whensoever I take my journey into Spain, I will come to you. There is no way of being sure whether Paul ever made this trip into Spain. While acknowledging that we cannot be certain, Cranfield observes,

> I Clement 5:7 would seem to be fairly strong evidence in favor of the view that he did get there, since *to terma tes duseos* [the extreme west] can scarcely refer to anywhere other than Spain in a document written in Rome and it is difficult to believe that firm information about the end of Paul's life was not readily available in the Roman church in the last decade of the first century, when people who had known him must surely still have been alive (II:768).

(See also Lightfoot, *Apostolic Fathers*, Part I, Vol. II:30.)

For I trust to see you in my journey, and to be brought on my way thitherward by you. Gifford observes, "St. Paul hoped to receive from Rome the same kindness and respect as from other churches, which sent companions to escort him on his further journeys: Acts 15:3; 1 Cor. 16:6; and 2 Cor. 1:16" (228).

It would appear to be obvious that a part of what would be involved in "brought on my way" was that the church at Rome would assist him with money and material goods for his journey.

If first I may be somewhat filled with your company. Paul was looking forward to a time of fellowship with the believers at Rome. He was not interested in a quick stop. He wanted to spend some time with them.

25 But now I go unto Jerusalem to minister unto the saints.

While Paul had finished his church planting in the area of his missionary journeys, there was still an important ministry which he had to fulfill before going to Rome. He had to minister to the saints at Jerusalem.

26 For it hath pleased them of Macedonia and Achaia to make a certain contribution for the poor saints which are at Jerusalem.

Paul was in Corinth at the time he wrote Romans. So he had an up-to-date picture of the money that had been raised by those of Macedonia and Achaia. This offering is referred to in 1 Cor. 16:1-3 and 2 Cor. 8:1—9:15. Observe that Paul had a deep concern for the needs of the poor and that he taught believers to share this concern.

27 It hath pleased them verily; and their debtors they are. For if the Gentiles have been made partakers of their spiritual things, their duty is also to minister unto them in carnal things.

Paul, while commending the Gentiles for giving to the needs of the poor saints at Jerusalem, also calls attention to the fact that they are in debt to these Jewish Christians. Murray explains, "It is not in the same category as a commercial debt incurred which we are under contractual obligation to pay. It is indebtedness arising from benefits received as when we acknowledge our indebtedness to a great benefactor" (II:219).

There were two reasons for this indebtedness. (1) The gospel had come out from Jerusalem. (2) The people in need were Jews, and the Gentiles were greatly indebted to the Jews. Paul had brought this last reason out in 11:17, 18. All of the covenants were made with Israel. Gentiles were brought in with them to partake of their covenant promises. As Jesus said, "Salvation is of the Jews" (Jn. 4:22). It is for this reason that Paul said, "For if the Gentiles have been made partakers of their spiritual things, their duty is also to minister unto them in carnal [material] things."

28 When therefore I have performed this, and have sealed to them this fruit, I will come by you into Spain.

When Paul has completed the delivery of the offering to the saints in Jerusalem, then he plans to go by Rome on his way to Spain. There seems to be no real certainty concerning the meaning of the words "sealed to them this fruit." I am inclined to take Vincent's explanation, "Secured to them the product of the contribution" (752) as the correct view. The delivery of the offering will at that time be made official and complete. (For different ideas on the meaning, see Cranfield II:774, 775.)

29 And I am sure that, when I come unto you, I shall come in the fulness of the blessing of the gospel of Christ.

Paul was convinced that when the time came that he would be with them in Rome that the full blessing of the gospel of Christ would be upon him. This, of course, would mean that they would be blessed by his coming.

D. Paul Requests Prayer That He Will Be Protected and Blessed to Come Unto Them (15:30-33).

30 Now I beseech you, brethren, for the Lord Jesus Christ's sake, and for the love of the Spirit, that ye strive together with me in *your* prayers to God for me.

Paul felt a deep need for the Roman believers to join him in prayer. His request appeals to them to give full consideration to who the Lord Jesus Christ is. He also urges them to keep in mind the love which the Holy Spirit had for them. Some take the reference to be the love the Holy Spirit works out in our hearts for one another (see Hodge 443). However, it seems to me that the parallel is better with the appeal to the Lord Jesus Christ if we take it to mean the love which the Holy Spirit has for us (see Murray II:221).

Paul implores the believers at Rome to enter into deep, earnest prayer for him. Hendricksen observes: "There is nothing superficial about genuine prayer. Isaiah describes it as a *taking* hold of God (64:7). For Jacob—that is, 'Israel'—it was a *wrestling* with God (Gen. 32:24-30). And Paul here similarly calls it a *struggle*. Cf. Col. 2:1; 4:12. The apostle desires that the Roman believers join him in an intensely earnest and yearning petition" (496).

On the word for strive (Greek *sunagonizomai*) Wuest explains:

> This word was used in classical Greek as an athletic term, describing the concerted action of

a team of athletes in the Greek games. It meant 'to contend along with, to share in a contest.' Paul asks the Roman saints to contend with him in prayer against the opposition of the hosts of wickedness, contending with him as athletes would do with one another, with intensity of purpose and in perfect cooperation (255).

31 That I may be delivered from them that do not believe in Judaea; and that my service which *I have* for Jerusalem may be accepted of the saints.

That I may be delivered from them that do not believe in Judaea. There was every good reason for Paul to be concerned about how he might be treated by the unbelieving Jews in and around Jerusalem. It had been his frequent experience to encounter difficulty from the unbelieving Jews (Acts 9:29; 13:45, 50; 14:19; 17:5-8; 18:12; and 19:9). The encounter with Jewish unbelievers, once he got to Jerusalem, shows that his concern was fully justified (Acts 21:27-36). But we see that Paul's prayer and the prayers of others that he might be "delivered from them that do not believe in Judaea" were ultimately answered (Acts 21:31-33 and 23:12-35).

And that my service which *I have* for Jerusalem may be accepted of the saints. Paul's teaching presented a problem for Jews who did not have a good grasp of how the New Covenant delivered them from Mosaic ceremonialism. There were Jews in Jerusalem who were not ready to accept all of Paul's teachings. We see Jewish believers in Rome (Acts 21:20, 21) who were somewhat sensitive about Paul's approach. In Acts 21:17 Paul was well received by the Jewish believers in Jerusalem. Thus this prayer was answered.

Paul was also interested in improving relationships between Jewish and Gentile believers. For Jewish believers at Jerusalem to receive gladly an offering coming largely from Gentile believers, meant a step in the right direction.

32 That I may come unto you with joy by the will of God, and may with you be refreshed.

Another part of Paul's prayer request is that it may be God's will for him to go to Rome. While there he desired to be refreshed by the people. Paul had already been praying that it would be God's will for him to go to Rome (1:9,10). Now, he asks the believers at Rome to join him in this request.

33 Now the God of peace *be* with you all. Amen.

For the God of peace to be with them would mean that they would experience the blessing of peace from Him.

E. Paul Commends Phebe to the Church at Rome (16:1, 2).

1 I commend unto you Phebe our sister, which is a servant of the church which is at Cenchrea.

Phebe was the bearer of the epistle to the church at Rome. Cenchrea was a seaport about eight miles from Corinth. She was probably involved in a business trip to Rome which would account for the fact that she took the epistle to Rome.

The word for "servant" is the feminine form of the word for "deacon" (Greek *diakonos*). This has led some to take the position that Phebe held the office of deaconess. The word itself does not require us to believe that it refers to the office of deaconess. The Greek word for deacon in its masculine form is used frequently for one who is a minister or servant in a very general sense. For that reason, the feminine form could be used here to indicate that Phebe was a servant of the church in a general sense rather than being a deaconess. Bruce (270) and Cranfield (II:781) take the position that Phebe held the office of deaconess. Murray does not think we are justified in considering Phebe to be a deaconess (II:276). Barrett doubts that at the time of the writing of the epistle the word had come to refer to the office of deaconess (282).

The time did come when the office of deaconess was established. Whether it had when Paul wrote Romans is open to question. Once the office of deaconess was established, it appears that their duties were with the women of the church (see Barnes 326).

Whatever the truth may be about whether women held the office of deaconess in the N.T., it is clear that they were active, worthwhile members of the churches. The fact that Phebe was the bearer of the epistle of Romans plus what is said about her in v. 2 tells us that she had an active and significant role in the work of the church.

Concerning the commendation of Phebe, Harrison explains, "It was customary for believers who traveled from place to place to carry with them letters of commendation (2 Cor. 3:1) roughly similar in function to letters of transfer used today when Christians move from one church to another" (160).

2 That ye receive her in the Lord, as becometh saints, and that ye assist her in whatsoever business she hath need of you: for she hath been a succourer of many, and of myself also.

The church at Rome was requested to receive Phebe as a fellow believer and to give her whatever assistance she might need.

The reason the church at Rome is asked to give assistance is "for she hath been a succourer of many, and of myself also." Concerning the word for "succourer" (Greek *prostatis*), Picirilli observes,

> The Greek word 'succorer' means, literally, 'one stationed in front' and refers originally to a guardian or protector. But then one who protects can do so in the milder sense of a patron, provider, or sponsor, and that is probably the sense the word has here. The guess is that she had filled this office in a monetary way, underwriting the needs of many Christians on various occasions and on at least one occasion for Paul. Or she may have 'ministered' in a more personal way, as in nursing sick ones back to health. It is even possible she—if she were a businesswoman of position—used her influence to rescue Christians who (as Paul often was) would be falsely accused and in trouble with authorities (315, 316).

F. Paul Greets His Acquaintances in Rome (16:3-16).

3 Greet Priscilla and Aquila my helpers in Christ Jesus.

We first see Priscilla and Aquila in Acts 18:2. Paul found them in Corinth on his second missionary journey. They had come to Corinth because Claudius had commanded all Jews to leave Rome. They spent some time travelling with Paul (Acts 18:18). They had helped Apollos, who when they first met him in Ephesus, knew only John's baptism, to understand what it meant to believe in Christ (Acts 18:24-26). They had had a church meet in their house while in Corinth (1 Cor. 16:19). Paul placed great value on them as fellow workers.

4 Who have for my life laid down their own necks: unto whom not only I give thanks, but also all the churches of the Gentiles.

We do not know when or under what circumstances Priscilla and Aquila risked their lives for Paul. Cranfield explains, "It is possible that it was during the serious disturbance at Ephesus, which is related in Acts 19:23-40, that Prisca and Aquila risked their lives to save Paul's life; but we cannot be certain" (II:285).

While we do not know anything about their risking ther lives to save Paul's life, except what is written here, it was a well-known fact in those days because Paul says, "not only I give thanks, but also all the churches of the Gentiles."

5 Likewise *greet* the church that is in their house. Salute my well beloved Epaenetus, who is the first fruits of Achaia unto Christ.

Likewise *greet* the church that is in their house. They must have made a good livelihood because we also saw in 1 Cor. 16:19 that while in Corinth a church met in their house. This also shows the great love they had for the work of the Lord.

Salute my well beloved Epaenetus, who is the first fruits of Achaia unto Christ. The word for "salute" (Greek *aspazomai*) is the same as the word for "greet" in vv. 3-16. Today we would use the word "greet."

While the numerical majority of manuscripts read "Achaia," many read "Asia." A problem arises with the "Achaia" reading. In 1 Cor. 16:5, "the house of Stephanas" is said to be the firstfruits of Achaia. If we take "Asia" to be the correct reading there is no problem. "The house of Stephanas" would be the firstfruits of Achaia. Epaenatus would be the firstfruits of Asia. If we keep the Achaia reading in the verse before us, we would understand Epaenetus to be of the household of Stephanas.

All we know about Epaenetus comes from this verse. Since Paul refers to him as "well-beloved," we know that he was the kind of person who had endeared himself to Paul.

6 Greet Mary, who bestowed much labour on us.

Again there is a textual variation here, with the majority of the manuscripts having "us" (Greek *hemas*), and many others having "you" (Greek *humas*). If we take the reading to be "us," Mary bestowed much labor on Paul and his associates. If we take the reading to be "you," Mary bestowed much labor on the Christians at Rome. Most would probably take the correct reading to be "you." Either way it makes sense. Murray says, "The 'much labor' suggests that Mary was one of the earliest members of the church at Rome" (II:229).

7 Salute Andronicus and Junia, my kinsmen, and my fellowprisoners, who are of note among the apostles, who also were in Christ before me.

Several observations are made about Adronicus and Junia who were most likely a husband and wife team. (1) They were Paul's kinsmen. (2) They are referred to as Paul's fellowprisoners. (3) They were of note among the apostles. (4) They were saved before Paul was.

Some take the position that to be Paul's kinsmen only meant that they were Jews (Godet 491; Harrison 104; and Picirilli 318). Others are of the opinion that they were relatives (Barnes 328; Hodge 449; and Shedd 426). It seems to me that we should settle in favor of relatives since there are Jews in the list who are not designated as "kinsmen."

They, too, had been imprisoned because of the gospel. We do not know when or where this was.

"Of note among the apostles" most likely means that they had a good reputation among the apostles (Hodge 449). The word apostle is taken by some to refer not to apostle in the most limited sense like Paul and Peter, but "apostles" in the sense of being itinerate missionaries. Taking this position Adronicus and Junia would be notable apostles (Cranfield II:789).

"Who were also in Christ before me" means that they were saved before Paul was.

8 Greet Amplias my beloved in the Lord.

Only a little is said about Amplias, but we sense a deep, warm love that Paul has for him.

9 Salute Urbane, our helper in Christ, and Stachys my beloved.

Urbane is referred to as "our helper." The word for helper (Greek *sunergos*) refers to a co-worker.

With Stachys we see a warm personal attachment signified by "my beloved."

10 Salute Apelles approved in Christ. Salute them which are of Aristobulus' ***household*****.**

Salute Apelles approved in Christ. Harrison observes, "Apelles (v. 10) was a fairly common name, but this man has an uncommon pedigree, for he is one who is 'tested and approved in Christ.' That was Paul's desire for Timothy (2 Tim. 2:15) and for himself (1 Cor. 9:27)" (164).

Salute them which are of Aristobulus' household. Harrison explains:

> Something of an enigma confronts us in trying to identify those who belong to the household of Aristobulus (v. 10). Lightfoot identified Aristobulus as the grandson of Herod the Great, who lived in Rome and apparently died there (*Philippians*, pp. 174, 175). If this is correct, Aristobulus was either not a believer or had died before Paul wrote, since he is not personally greeted. Those addressed would then be his slaves and employees who had become Christians. On the other hand, if this identification is incorrect, we must think of an otherwise unknown figure whose family is mentioned here. The former alternative is somewhat favored by the fact that the next person to be greeted (v. 11) is Herodian, a name suggestive of association with, or admiration for, the family of Herod (164).

11 Salute Herodion my kinsman. Greet them that be of the ***household*** **of Narcissus, which are in the Lord.**

Salute Herodion my kinsman. "My kinsman" either meant a fellow Jew, or a relative. I tend to think the meaning here is relative (see comments on "kinsmen" in v. 7). Herodion was probably associated with the family of Herod, either as a slave or a freedman.

Greet them that be of the household of Narcissus, which are in the Lord. Bruce explains,

> Calvin and others have identified this Narcissus with Tiberius Claudius Narcissus, a wealthy freedman of the Emperor Tiberius, who exercised great influence under Claudius, but was executed by order of Nero's mother Agrippina soon after Nero's accession in A.D. 54. His goods being confiscated his slaves would become imperial property and would be distinguished from other groups in the imperial household by the designation *Narcissiani.* If the identification is sustained, then this greeting would be addressed to Christians among those *Narcissiani* (273).

12 Salute Tryphena and Tryphosa, who labour in the Lord. Salute the beloved Persis, which laboured much in the Lord.

Salute Tryphena and Tryphosa, who labour in the Lord. Harrison explains: "Similar in name, Tryphena and Tryphosa (v. 12) were likely sisters. It was not uncommon then, as now, to give daughters names with a certain resemblance (cf. Jean and Joan). Possibly they belonged to an aristocratic family, since 'dainty' and 'delicate' (or 'luxuriating'), as their names mean would seem to fit this category. If so, their Christian convictions led them to put aside any tendency to live a life of ease. They are given an accolade for being hard workers in the Lord's cause" (165).

While we cannot be certain that they were sisters, they most likely were. Some have suggested that they might have been twins (Bruce 273 and Cranfield II:793).

Salute the beloved Persis, which laboured much in the Lord. Stifler in comparing what Paul said about Tryphena and Tryphosa with what he said about Persis, explains: "These two women with 'the beloved Persis' are hailed for their labor 'in the Lord.' The first two were still engaged in it; Persis for some reason—she may have been disabled in some way—had ceased, for note the tenses. Persis 'labored much,' which may indicate length of service. Observe that while Paul in speaking of men says 'my beloved,' he now delicately omits the pronoun before this woman's name" (197).

On the name "Persis" Bruce explains, "This name (meaning 'Persian woman') appears on Greek and Latin inscriptions at Rome and elsewhere as that of a slave or a freedwoman, but not in connection with the imperial household" (274).

13 Salute Rufus chosen in the Lord, and his mother and mine.

There is a good possibility that the Rufus mentioned here is the same as the one mentioned in Mk. 15:21. If that be the case he would be the son of Simon the Cyrenian who was compelled to bear the cross on the way to Golgotha.

Cranfield explains,

> Lightfoot's considered opinion that, since the fact that Mark alone of the Evangelists describes Simon of Cyrene as 'the father of Alexander and Rufus' (Mk. 15:21) implies that someone called Rufus must have held a prominent place among the Christians at Rome [based on the idea that Mark was written from Rome], there is, in spite of the commonness of the name 'Rufus,' at least fair ground

for identifying the Rufus of St. Paul with the Rufus of St. Mark still stands as a balanced scholarly judgment. We should not wish to rank the probability that the Rufus of this verse is the son of Simon of Cyrene more highly than this: at the same time, to rank it less highly seems to us (*pace* Kasemann) unreasonable (II:793, 794; see also Harrison 165).

"Chosen in the Lord" probably means that he is one of the elect, or he is a Christian. Some take the expression "chosen in the Lord" to mean that Rufus was an outstanding Christian. I am in agreement with Cranfield (II:794) in considering this interpretation to be unlikely.

We do not know when nor where Rufus' mother was like a mother to Paul. When we consider the numerous difficulties that Paul faced in life, we know that such help would have been a great source of encouragement to him.

14 Salute Asyncritus, Phlegon, Hermas, Patrobas, Hermes, and the brethren which are with them.

All of the names in this verse are masculine. On the words, "and the brethren which are with them," it is usually thought that this has reference to a house-church which was attended by these five and others.

15 Salute Philologus, and Julia, Nereus, and his sister, and Olympas, and all the saints which are with them.

The names are all masculine except Julia. It is usually thought that Philologus and Julia were husband and wife. The words "and all the saints which are with them" seem to imply that reference is made to a house-church where these attended.

16 Salute one another with an holy kiss. The churches of Christ salute you.

Salute one another with an holy kiss. Concerning saluting one another with a holy kiss, Moody explains, "The custom among Rabbis was practiced by the disciples of Jesus (Luke 7:45; 22:48), and it became a part of early Christian worship (1 Thess. 5:26; 1 Cor. 16:20; 2 Cor. 13:12; 1 Peter 5:14). It was a part of the eucharistic liturgy in Rome in the second century (Justin Martyr, *First Apology*, 65), but the form has been greatly modified or completely eliminated in most of Western Christianity" (282).

It seems to concern some people that we practice the church ordinances, but do not practice the holy kiss in our churches. I find the distinctions between "form" and "substance" helpful in this case. The substance is the basic principle or bottom line truth involved. The form is the means of conveying or expressing the bottom line truth. For example, in Communion the bottom line truth is that we remember the broken body of Christ on the cross and His blood which was shed. The form is the eating of the bread and the drinking of the cup. Beyond doubt, in communion we are to obey both in substance and in form.

In the "holy kiss" the bottom line principle is that we convey our love one to another. In those days one of the forms for doing this was the holy kiss. We do not have the same clear message from Scripture that both substance and form are Divinely instituted in the case of the "holy kiss" that we do with the church ordinances.

With changing customs, we do not change the form of the church ordinances because the form has been Divinely instituted. With changing customs, we do change the form in matters like the holy kiss while maintaining the substance. We are to love one another and convey the same, but we are not obliged to do so with a holy kiss.

The churches of Christ salute you. This indicates the concern that the churches had one for another. The churches that Paul founded would have had a special interest in the church at Rome because Rome was the capital city of the Roman Empire.

G. Paul Admonishes Them to Stand For Right and to Be on Guard Against False Doctrine (16:17-20).

17 Now I beseech you, brethren, mark them which cause divisions and offences contrary to the doctrine which ye have learned; and avoid them.

In this verse Paul is dealing with those kinds of problems which may undermine the very gospel itself. Some are surprised that Paul uses such strong language here in light of the fact that up to this point his tone has been milder. That should be no surprise. False teachers had followed Paul everywhere he went and had tried to lead his converts away from the truth. Whether such teachers had made their way to Rome or not, a warning such as this could be in order since they might appear at any time.

Murray explains,

> We need not suppose that these agitators and false teachers had actually invaded the Roman scene. Probably they had not. If they had we would expect direct encounter with them in the body of the epistle, as, for example, in the epistles to the Galatians and Colossians. But, Paul was well aware of the existence of these heretics and, if their propaganda had not reached Rome, there was good ground for fear that the danger was impending. The similarity of the warnings to those of Philippians 3:2,18,19 is apparent and Colossians 2:16-23 deals with the same or at least closely allied evil (II:234, 235).

The Christian's responsibility toward such false teachers is to "mark" them and "avoid" them. Concerning this twofold responsibility, Hodge observes that Christians are "first, *to mark (skopein)* i.e., to notice carefully, and not allow them to pursue their corrupting course unheeded; and, secondly, *to avoid*, i.e., to break off connection with them" (450). Hendriksen explains:

> Paul does not say, '*Oppose* them'; for, though some of those whom he addresses might have been able to do this successfully, others could easily have been led astray if they had entered into debate. Therefore Paul urges the *brothers...to avoid* these dissenters altogether. He knew that the possibiity that some of the members might otherwise have lost their bearings was real, especially in view of the clever methods employed by the propagandizers (510).

Harrison's comments are helpful on this point. He observes, "As a practical measure, it is necessary to 'keep away from them,' giving no opportunity for inroads into the congregation. Religious errorists covet opportunities for 'friendly discussion'" (167).

18 For they that are such serve not our Lord Jesus Christ, but their own belly; and by good

words and fair speeches deceive the hearts of the simple.

This verse gives additional information about the teachers mentioned in verse 17. These false teachers were serving their own selfish desires. They were not serving Jesus Christ. They had a way with words so they could sweep the simple off their feet.

Picirilli explains concerning these false teachers,

> We must not be fooled by them. Paul uses 'belly' to emphasize the base, selfish, fleshly nature of anything that perverts true Christianity. These teachers' 'fair speeches' serve to aid them in deceiving the naive ('simple') believers. We do not need, in the church, naive piety that believes everything and everyone is good. We need courageous, intelligent exposure of hurtful heresy (319).

19 For your obedience is come abroad unto all *men.* I am glad therefore on your behalf: but yet I would have you wise unto that which is good, and simple concerning evil.

For your obedience is come abroad unto all men. This part of the verse reminds us of "your faith is spoken of throughout the whole world" (1:8). Word of the Christians at Rome and their devotion to God had been heard throughout the church world.

For this, Paul says, **I am glad therefore on your behalf.** Then he adds a concern, **but yet I would have you wise unto that which is good, and simple concerning evil.** To be "wise unto that which is good" means to recognize the value of that which is good and to understand ways of achieving and maintaining that which is good. In this context the "good" probably refers to sound doctrinal truth.

Concerning the word for simple (Greek *akeraios*) Moule, *Romans* explains, "The original idea (freedom from *alloy,*) passes into that of freedom from ill motives, or (as here) from defiling knowledge" (253). The meaning seems to be, an unmixed commitment against evil. It may mean, "not double-minded as it relates to evil." The evil in focus here is probably the bad doctrine propounded by the false teachers.

20 And the God of peace shall bruise Satan under your feet shortly. The grace of our Lord Jesus Christ *be* with you. Amen.

And the God of peace shall bruise Satan under your feet shortly. We are reminded here of Gen. 3:15. The questions concerning this verse are: (1) Does the bruising of Satan refer to a final defeat of Satan in the eschatological future (Cranfield 803)? or (2) Does the bruising of Satan refer to resolving internal problems among believers at Rome (Harrison 68)? It is hard to be sure which is right, but I tend to agree with Harrison. The bruising of Satan "under your feet" would seem to make the application to a problem in the church. The problem, as we see it, in the Book of Romans, that seemed to threaten the peace of the church more than any other was between the weak and the strong (see 14:12-19).

The grace of our Lord Jesus Christ *be* with you. Amen. This was much like it would be if we said, "May God's richest blessings be with you."

H. Paul Sends Greetings From Those Who Were With Him (16:21-23).

21 Timotheus my workfellow, and Lucius, and Jason, and Sosipater, my kinsmen, salute you.

Timothy is well known and clearly deserves to be called "my workfellow." He first joined Paul in Acts 16:1-3 and had travelled with Paul since that time.

It is possible that Lucius is the same as the Lucius in Acts 13:1, but we cannot be certain of this. It is not considered likely that he was Luke. It is not certain whether the Jason of Acts 17:5-9 is the Jason in this verse. It is possible that "Sosipater" is the same as "Sopater of Berea" (Acts 20:4). Cranfield says, "Sosipater is very likely to be identified with the 'Sopater of Berea, *the son* of Pyrrhus,' mentioned in Acts 20:4. 'Sopater' would be a quite likely abbreviated form of 'Sosipater'" (II:806).

"My kinsmen" probably means that they were related to Paul. (See discussions about kinsmen in comments on v. 7.)

22 I Tertius, who wrote *this* epistle, salute you in the Lord.

We know nothing about Tertius except that he served as Paul's scribe in writing down the Book of Romans as Paul dictated it.

23 Gaius mine host, and of the whole church, saluteth you. Erastus the chamberlain of the city saluteth you, and Quartus a brother.

Gaius mine host, and of the whole church saluteth you. Gaius is probably the one mentioned in 1 Cor. 1:14. It appears that a house-church was meeting in his home in Corinth.

Erastus the chamberlain of the city saluteth you. Bruce explains:

> This Erastus has been identified with the civic official of that name mentioned in a Latin inscription on a marble paving-block discovered at Corinth in 1929 by members of the American School of Classical Studies at Athens: 'ERASTVS PRO: AED: S: P: STRAVIT' ('Erastus, commissioner for public works, laid this pavement at his own expense'). The pavement belongs to the first century AD, and may well have been laid by Paul's friend. The public offices, however are not the same: in Greek the commissioner for public works, or 'aedile,' is called *agoranomos*, whereas the city treasurer (as here) is *oikonomos tes poleos* [KJV, chamberlain of the city]. If we have to do with the same Erastus, he had presumably been promoted to the city treasurer from the lower office of 'aedile' by the time Paul wrote this epistle. There is no good reason to identify Erastus with the Erastus of Acts 19:22 or 2 Tim. 4:20; the name was common enough (280, 281.)

(See also Cranfield (II:807, 808). He is not as certain as Bruce that the Erastus of Acts 19:22 and 2 Tim. 4:20 are not the same.)

And Quartus a brother. This is all that we know about Quartus. By the use of "brother" Paul probably means "a Christian brother" rather than a brother to Erastus or someone else in the list of names.

I. He Closes With a Benediction (16:24-27).

24 The grace of our Lord Jesus Christ *be* with you all. Amen.

The verse is included in the majority of the Greek manuscripts but is omitted in many. The same words (except for "all" and "Amen") are found in v. 20.

Paul's basic thrust is not altered whether this verse is included here or omitted.

25 Now to him that is of power to stablish you according to my gospel, and the preaching of Jesus Christ, according to the revelation of the mystery, which was kept secret since the world began.

Now to him that is of power to stablish you according to my gospel. According to Paul's gospel God is fully able to establish not only the saints at Rome, but all other saints.

And the preaching of Jesus Christ. The preaching of Jesus Christ is the gospel. We would get the connection better if we would translate, "according to my gospel, even the preaching of Jesus Christ." Some understand the reference to be to the preaching done by Jesus Christ. It seems to me to be more likely that the "preaching of Jesus Christ" is synonymous with the gospel in this verse.

According to the revelation of the mystery, which was kept secret since the world began. The word "mystery" is not intended to refer to that which is difficult to understand or that which only the initiated can understand. Rather, it refers to that which was not known until it was made known by Divine revelation.

There are two views concerning the meaning of "the mystery" as it is used in this verse. (1) The mystery was that Gentiles would come in with the Jews and be a part of one family of the redeemed, as in Eph. 3:5, 6 (Bruce 283; Hendriksen 517; and Shedd 437). (2) The mystery is the gospel as in Eph. 6:19 and Col. 1:25-27 (Cranfield II:810, 811 and Hodge 452). If we think of the context of Romans as a whole, it would be easy to take the reference to be to the inclusion of the Gentiles in with the Jewish believers. However, the immediate context seems to favor the view that the mystery is the gospel.

26 But now is made manifest, and by the scriptures of the prophets, according to the commandment of the everlasting God, made known to all nations for the obedience of faith.

But now is made manifest. That which was a mystery has now been clearly revealed.

And by the scriptures of the prophets. This means the O.T. Scriptures.

According to the commandment of the everlasting God. This refers to the Great Commission.

Made known. This mystery of the Gentiles being "fellowheirs" (Eph. 3:6) with the Jews has been seen to be in accord with the O.T. Paul had given a great deal of attention to this subject in the Book of Romans.

To all nations (Gentiles) **for the obedience of faith.** The gospel had been preached to the Gentiles. Murray observes, "The prophetical scriptures were not the property of all the nations until the gospel went into all the world in accordance with Christ's command and in the power of Pentecost (cf. Matt. 28:18-20; Acts 1:4-8). With this worldwide proclamation these scriptures became the property of all without distinction and so *through their medium* the mystery is made known to all nations" (II:242).

"For the obedience of faith" means for the purpose of getting the response of obedience which is faith (see comments on 1:5 where the same wording appears in the Greek).

27 To God only wise, *be* glory through Jesus Christ for ever. Amen.

Paul had been profoundly impressed with the wisdom of God as it had been manifested through Jesus Christ, through Israel as the Covenant Seed, through the covenants, through the inclusion of the Gentiles, and the effects of the practical outworking of the gospel in the lives of believers. And so have I.

Summary 15:14—16:27

Paul had spent a great deal of time admonishing the strong not to look with contempt on the weak and the weak not to have a judgmental attitude toward the strong. On a positive note, he reminds them that they are able to admonish one another. Yet he had written the way he had because he was the apostle to the Gentiles. Paul viewed his ministry among the Gentiles as a priestly ministry in which Gentile converts were his offering to God. He felt very good about his ministry. It had extended from Jerusalem to Illyricum.

Paul had long desired to go to Rome, but had been hindered by an unfinished task in the area of his missionary journeys. He had completed the establishment of churches in the key cities and was now ready to go to Rome. This he planned to do on his way to Spain. He hoped to stop by Rome and be refreshed and sent on his way to Spain by them.

He had one more responsibility to discharge before going to Rome. That was to deliver an offering for the saints at Jerusalem which had been received by the Gentile Christians of Macedonia and Achaia. When this was done, he planned to go to Rome on his way to Spain.

Paul was aware that he had many enemies among the unbelieving Jews in the area of Jerusalem. Therefore he entreated the believers at Rome to be in earnest prayer for his personal safety. He also requested prayer that the offering would be accepted by the saints at Jerusalem. He further requested prayer that it would be the will of God for him to go to Rome after delivering the offering.

Paul then speaks words of commendation for Phebe who was the bearer of the epistle. He asked the church to accommodate her in the ways she might need help. She was worthy of all this because she had been a helper to many.

Paul then calls attention to a long list of the names of acquaintances that were among the Christians at Rome. He greets them and says kind words about them.

Paul was very much aware that false teachers had followed his work trying to subvert the believers. He knew that it was possible for them to go to Rome so he advised the people what to do if they encountered false teachers.

Some of those who were with Paul sent greetings to those in Rome. The place given to names in this chapter shows that Paul was a people-oriented person.

Paul commends the people to God who was able to establish them. The gospel which Paul preached was well supported by the O.T. Scriptures. It was also a well supported fact in the O.T. that the Gentiles would be received into the family of God with the Jews. They would not be second class citizens, but fellow-heirs. The time had come for the gospel to be preached to Gentiles everywhere to win them to faith in Christ.

Paul ended on a note of praise to the wisdom of God as it had been manifested in the various subjects dealt with in this epistle.

Application: Teaching and Preaching the Passage

1. We learn a good lesson from Paul in vv. 14, 15. He had confidence that the

people could work out their problems, yet he reminded them what their problems were and the need for working on them. We need to work at reminding people of their shortcomings without leaving the impression that we do not trust them.

2. The offering up to God of Gentile converts was a priestly service for Paul. When we lead people to Christ, they are our priestly offering to God (v. 16).

3. Paul was very careful not to build on another man's foundation. He was a pioneer missionary. He blazed the trail. His responsibility in the areas of his missionary journeys had kept him occupied in those areas until the time of the writing of Romans. Having finished his missionary work in these areas he was nearing the time he could go to Rome and Spain (vv. 18-24). It behooves us to be faithful to the responsibility that God has given to us and stick with it until the job is done.

4. It is important for us to recognize that the miracles in the N.T. did not happen just to make people feel better. Nor did they happen simply because of the spirituality of the person performing the miracle. Rather, they happened to help people believe certain things. (See the comments on v. 19 which discuss the sign value of miracles.)

5. The N.T. demonstrates to us a sincere interest in the physical needs of fellow believers (vv. 25-28). We need to follow this N.T. example and be sensitive to the needs of others, especially other believers (Gal. 6:10).

6. Paul realizes that he will face difficulty when he goes to Jerusalem so he requests prayer that he will be delivered from unbelievers in Judea. He wanted to go to Rome and be a blessing and be blessed by the believers who were at Rome (vv. 29-32). Paul illustrates for us both a person who was strong and a person who had needs. The prayers of others were very important to him. He was not so self sufficient that he did not need others.

7. Paul was people oriented; they were very important to him. His mention of a long list of names in 16:1-15, 21-23, illustrates this point very well. These people had been a blessing to Paul and the cause of Christ. The names included women as well as men. People are important. We need to follow Paul in being more people oriented.

8. The church is never free from difficulty. We must always be alert to those who cause trouble. In extreme cases we must separate from these people (vv. 17, 18).

9. Paul gives us a good illustration of mixing commendation and admonition in v. 19.

10. Paul had a deep interest that the Christians at Rome experience peace with one another. The problem he had in mind was probably the tension between the "weak" and the "strong" in 14:1—15:13 which was mainly over whether to eat meat or not (v. 20). It is imperative that we have a renewed interest in peace and unity among believers.

11. Paul ended the epistle on a note of victory and praise (vv. 25-27). There are always problems. Paul was aware of problems too, but he did not let his whole outlook become colored by the problem side of life.

ROMANS

BIBLIOGRAPHY

Alford, Henry, *Alford's Greek Testament,* vol. II, Acts, I, II Corinthians (Guardian Press, reprinted 1976).

The Apocrypha of the Old Testament, Revised Standard Version (Thomas Nelson, 1957).

Archer, G. L., "Covenant" in *Evangelical Dictionary of Theology* (Baker Book House [1984], 276-278), ed. Walter A. Elwell.

Arminius, James, *The Writings of James Arminius,* vols. II and III (Baker Book House, 1956), vol. II tr. James Nichols, vol. III tr. W. R. Bagnal.

Arndt, William F. and Gingrich, F. Wilbur, *A Greek English Lexicon of the New Testament,* a translation and adaptation of Walter Bauer's *Griesch-Deutsches Worterbuch zer den Schriften des Neuen Testaments und der Ubrigen Urchristlichen Literatur* (The University of Chicago Press, 1957), Fourth Revised and Augmented Edition, 1952.

Barclay, William, *The Letter To The Romans, Revised Edition* (The Daily Study Bible Series, The Westminster Press, 1975).

Barnes, Albert, *Romans Barnes' Notes on The New Testament,* ed. Robert Frew (Baker Book House, reprinted 1983).

Barrett, C. K., *A Commentary On The Epistle To The Romans (Harper's New Testament Commentaries,* General Editor: Henry Chadwick, Harper and Row, 1957).

Berkhof, Louis, *Systematic Theology,* Revised and Enlarged Edition, (Eerdmans, 1953).

Birnbaum, Philip, *A Book of Jewish Concepts* (Hebrew Publishing Co., 1964).

Black, Matthew, *Romans (The New Century Bible Commentary,* General Editors: Ronald E. Clements (Old Testament) and Matthew Black (New Testament), Eerdmans and Marshall, Morgan, and Scott, England, softback edition, 1981), Copyright held by Marshall, Morgan, and Scott (1973).

Briscoe, D. Stuart, *Romans (The Communicator's Commentary,* vol. 6. General Editor, Lloyd J. Ogilvie, Word Books, 1982).

Brown, David, *Acts-Romans in A Commentary Critical, Experimental, and Practical on the Old and New Testaments,* vol. III (Eerdmans, n.d.).

Brown, John, *An Exposition of The Epistle of Paul The Apostle to the Galatians* (The Sovereign Grace Book Club. Evansville, Indiana, reprinted 1957).

Brown, John, *Analytical Exposition of The Epistle of Paul The Apostle To The Romans* (Baker Book House, reprinted 1981).

Bruce, F. F., *The Epistle of Paul To The Romans,* Tyndale New Testament Commentaries (Eerdmans, 1963).

Buswell, James Oliver, Jr., *A Systematic Theology of The Christian Religion,* vol. II, (two vols., Zondervan, 1962).

Calvin, John, *The Epistle of Paul to the Romans and to the Thessalonians* tr. Ron Mackenzie (Eerdmans, reprinted 1980), *Calvin's Commentaries.*

Chalmers, Thomas, *Lectures on The Epistle of Paul To The Romans* (Robert Carter, 1843).

Clarke, Adam, *The New Testament of Our Lord and Savior Jesus Christ,* vol. VI, *Romans-Revelation* (Abingdon-Cokesbury Press, n.d.).

Coltman, William G., *An Exposition of Romans* (Designed Products, Inc., 1950).

Conybeare, W. J. and Howson, J. S., *The Life and Epistles of St. Paul* (Eerdmans,

reprinted 1978).
Cranfield, C.E.B., *A Critical And Exegetical Commentary on The Epistle To The Romans* (two vols, ICC, T. & T. Clark Limited, vol. I, 1975, vol. II, 1979).
Dana, H. E. and Mantey, Julius R., *A Manual Grammar of the Greek New Testament* (MacMillan Co., 1957).
Denny, James, *Romans* in *The Expositor's Greek Testament,* vol. II (Eerdmans, reprinted 1983), ed. W. Robertson Nicoll.
Dodd, C. H., *The Epistle of Paul To The Romans Moffatt New Testament Commentary* (Harper and Brothers, 1932).
Earle, Ralph, *Word Meanings In The New Testament,* vol. III, *Romans* (Beacon Hill Press, 1974).
Erdman, Charles R., *The Epistle of Paul To The Romans* (The Westminster Press, 1925).
Forlines, F. Leroy, "Legalism in the Book of Galatians" in *Dimension* Winter Quarter, 1984, 85.
Forlines, F. Leroy, "The Pastor and His People," vol. XXVII, No. 5, May 1980, 26,27.
Forlines, F. Leroy, *A Study of Paul's Teaching on The Believer's Death to Sin and its Relationship To a New Life* (an unpublished thesis, submitted in partial fulfillment of the requirements for the Master of Arts degree, Winona Lake School of Theology, 1959).
Forlines, F. Leroy, *Systematics* (Randall House Publications, 1975).
Gifford, E. H., *The Epistle of St. Paul to The Romans* (The James Family, reprinted 1977).
Gill, John, *Gill's Commentary,* vol. VI (Baker Book House, reprinted 1980).
Godet, F. L., *Commentary on The Epistle To The Romans* (Zondervan, reprinted 1956).
Greathouse, William M., *Romans* in *Beacon Bible Commentary* vol. VIII (Beacon Hill Press, 1968).
Guthrie, Donald, *The Pauline Epistles.* New Testament Introduction (Inter-Varsity Press, reprinted 1964).
Haldane, Robert, *An Exposition of The Epistle to The Romans* (MacDonald Publishing Co., reprinted, n.d.).
Hamilton, Floyd E., *The Epistle To The Romans* (Baker Book House, 1958).
Harrison, Everett F., *Romans* in *The Expositor's Bible Commentary,* vol. X *Romans-Galatians* (Zondervan, 1976).
Hendriksen, William, *Exposition of Paul's Epistle To The Romans* (Baker Book House, 1980).
Hills, A. M., *Holiness in The Book of Romans* (Beacon Hill Press, 1951).
Hodge, Charles, *Commentary on The Epistle to The Romans* (Eerdmans, reprinted 1983).
Holy Bible, New International Version c. 1973,1978 by the International Bible Society. Used by permission.
Ironside, H. A., *Lectures on Romans* (Loizeaux Brothers, Inc., 1972).
Johnson, Alan F., *The Freedom Letter* (Moody Press, 1974).
Kasemann, Ernst, *Commentary on Romans* (Eerdmans, 1980), tr. Geoffrey W. Bromiley.
Knox, John, *Romans* in *The Interpreter's Bible* vol. IX (Abingdon Press, 1954), ed. George Arthur Buttrick.

ROMANS

Lange, John Peter, *Commentary on The Holy Scriptures* (Zondervan, reprinted n.d.), tr. Philip Schaff.

Lenski, R. C. H., *The Interpretation of St. Paul's Epistle To The Romans* (Augsburg Publishing House, 1961).

Leupold, H. C., *Exposition of Genesis,* vol. I (Baker Book House, 1950).

Liddon, H. P., *Explanatory Analysis of St. Paul's Epistle to The Romans* Zondervan Publishing House, reprinted 1961).

Lightfoot, J. B., *The Epistle of Paul to The Galatians* (Zondervan Publishing House, reprinted n.d.).

Lightfoot, J. B., *Notes on The Epistles of St. Paul* (Zondervan Publishing House, reprinted 1957).

Lloyd-Jones, D. M., *Romans, An Exposition of Chapters 7:1-8:4* (Zondervan Publishing House, 1975).

Luther, Martin, *Commentary on The Epistle to The Romans,* a New Translation by J. Theodore Mueller (Kregel Publications, 1976).

McQuilkin, Robert C., *The Message of Romans* (Zondervan Publishing House, 1947).

Meyer, August Wilhelm, *Critical And Exegetical Handbook To The Epistle To The Romans* (Alpha Publications, reprinted 1980).

Mills, Sanford C., *A Hebrew Christian Looks at Romans* (Dunham Publishing Co., 1968).

Moody, Dale, *Romans* in *The Broadman Commentary* vol. 10, *Acts-I Corinthians* (Broadman Press, 1970), gen. ed. Clifton J. Allen.

Morris, Leon, "Atonement" in *The New International Dictionary of the Christian Church* (Zondervan Publishing House, 1978), gen. ed. J. D. Douglas.

Morris, Leon, "Propitiation" in *Evangelical Dictionary of Theology* (Baker Book House, 1984, 888), ed. Walter L. Elwell.

Morrison, James, *St. Paul's Teaching on Sanctification,* A Practical Exposition of Romans VI (Hodder and Stoughton, 1886).

Moule, Handley C. G., *The Epistle of Paul The Apostle To The Romans* in *The Cambridge Bible For Schools and Colleges* (Cambridge University Press, reprinted 1952).

Moule, Handley C. G., *The Epistle To The Romans* (Klock & Klock Christian Publishers, reprinted 1980).

Munck, Johannes, *Christ and Israel, An Interpretation of Romans 9-11* (Fortress Press, 1967).

Murray, John, *The Epistle of Paul To The Romans* (two vols., Eerdmans, 1982).

The New Century Dictionary (Appleton-Century-Crofts, Inc., 1959).

Newell, William R., *Romans Verse by Verse* (Moody Press, 1948).

Nygren, Anders, *Commentary on Romans* (Fortress Press, 1949), tr. Carl S. Rasmussen.

Olshausen, Hermann, *Studies In The Epistle To The Romans* (Klock & Klock Christian Publishers, Inc., reprinted 1983).

Packer, J. I. "Regeneration" in *Evangelical Dictionary of Theology* (Baker Book House, 1984, 924-26), ed. Walter L. Elwell.

Phillips, John, *Exploring Romans* (Moody Monthly, 1969).

Picirilli, Robert, *The Book of Romans* (Randall House Publications, 1975).

Piper, John, *The Justification of God, An Exegetical and Theological Study of Romans 9:1-23* (Baker Book House, 1983).

ROMANS

Plumer, William S., *Commentary on Romans* (Kregel Publications, reprinted 1979).

Quebedeaux, Richard, *The Worldly Evangelicals* (Harper and Row Publishers, 1978).

Ramsay, William M., *A Historical Commentary on St. Paul's Epistle To The Galatians* (Baker Book House, reprinted 1965).

Robertson, Archibald Thomas, *Word Pictures In The New Testament,* vol. IV (Broadman Press, 1931).

Sanday, William, *The Epistle To The Romans* (Zondervan, reprint 1957) ed. Charles John Ellicott.

Sanday, William and Headlam, Arthur C., *A Critical and Exegetical Commentary on The Epistle To The Romans* (fifth edition, T. & T. Clark, reprinted 1960).

Shedd, William G. T., *A Critical and Doctrinal Commentary on the Epistle of St. Paul To The Romans* (Zondervan, reprinted 1967).

Shedd, William G. T., *Dogmatic Theology* (vol. II, Zondervan, reprinted n.d.).

Stifler, James, *The Epistle To The Romans* (Moody Press, reprinted 1983).

Steele, David N. and Thomas, Curtis C. *Romans An Interpretive Outline* (Presbyterian and Reformed Publishing Co., 1984).

Stuart, Moses, *A Commentary on The Epistle To The Romans* (Andover, N.H., 1832).

Thayer, John Henry, *Thayer's Greek-English Lexicon of The New Testament* (Associated Publishers and Authors, Inc., reprinted n.d.).

Thiessen, Henry Clarence, *Introductory Lectures In Systematic Theology* (Eerdmans, 1968).

Tholuck, Fred. Aug. Gottreu, *Exposition of St. Paul's Epistle to The Romans* (Sorin and Ball, 1844) tr. Robert Menzies.

Thomas, W. H. Griffith, *St. Paul's Epistle to The Romans* (Eerdmans, 1984).

Trench, Richard Chenevix, *Synonyms of The New Testament* (Associated Publishers and Authors, Inc., reprinted, n.d.).

Vincent, M. R., *Word Studies In The New Testament* in one volume (Associated Publishers and Authors, reprinted 1972).

Vine, W. E., *The Epistle To The Romans* (Zondervan, reprinted 1965).

Vine, W. E., *Vine's Expository Dictionary of New Testament Words* (MacDonald Publishing Co., n.d.).

Wesley, John, *Explanatory Notes Upon The New Testament* vol. II (Baker Book House, reprinted, 1981).

Williams, Charles B., *A Commentary on Pauline Epistles* (Moody Press, 1953).

Williams, Charles B., *The New Testament in The Language of The People* (Moody Press, 1963).

Wuest, Kenneth S., *Romans In The Greek New Testament* (Eerdmans, 1984).

Wuest, Kenneth S., "Victory over Indwelling Sin" in *Bibliotheca Sacra, A Theological Quarterly,* CXVI (January, 1959).

Yeager, Randolph O., *The Renaissance New Testament,* vols. XI and XII (Pelican Publishing Co., 1983).

CPSIA information can be obtained at www.ICGtesting.com
Printed in the USA
LVOW061527170113

316148LV00004B/127/A